Human Relations
in Organizations

Human Relations in Organizations

Applications and Skill-Building

Robert N. Lussier
Springfield College

Fifth Edition

Boston   Burr Ridge, IL   Dubuque, IA   Madison, WI   New York   San Francisco   St. Louis
Bangkok   Bogotá   Caracas   Lisbon   London   Madrid
Mexico City   Milan   New Delhi   Seoul   Singapore   Sydney   Taipei   Toronto

McGraw-Hill Higher Education

*A Division of The **McGraw-Hill** Companies*

*A Division of The **McGraw-Hill** Companies*

HUMAN RELATIONS IN ORGANIZATIONS: APPLICATIONS AND SKILL BUILDING

Published by McGraw-Hill/Irwin, an imprint of The McGraw-Hill Companies, Inc. 1221 Avenue of the Americas, New York, NY, 10020. Copyright © 2002, 1999, by The McGraw-Hill companies, Inc. All rights reserved. Previous editions © 1990, 1993, 1996 by Richard D. Irwin, a Times Mirror Higher Education Group, Inc. company. No part of this publication may be reproduced or distributed in any form or by any means, or stored in a data base or retrieval system, without the prior written consent of The McGraw-Hill Companies, Inc., including, but not limited to, in any network or other electronic storage or transmission, or broadcast for distance learning. Some ancillaries, including electronic and print components, may not be available to customers outside the United States.

This book is printed on acid-free paper.

1 2 3 4 5 6 7 8 9 0 VNH/VNH 0 9 8 7 6 5 4 3 2 1

ISBN 007243645X

Publisher: *John E. Biernat*
Senior editor: *John Weimeister*
Developmental editor: *Trina Hauger*
Marketing manager: *Lisa Nicks*
Project manager: *Ruth Smith*
Production supervisor: *Gina Hangos*
Designer: *Pam Verros*
Cover illustration: *©Warren Gebert/SIS*
Supplement coordinator: *Joyce Chappetto*
New media: *Jenny Williams*
Compositor: *Carlisle Communications, Inc.*
Typeface: *10/12 New Baskerville*
Printer: *Von Hoffmann Press, Inc.*

www.mhhe.com

Library of Congress Cataloging-in-Publication Data
McGraw-Hill Higher Education
Lussier, Robert N.
    Human relations in organizations : applications and skill building /Robert
    N. Lussier.–5th ed.
        p. cm.
Includes bibliographical references and index.
    ISBN 0-07-24365-X
    1. Organizational behavior. 2. Interpersonal relations. I. Title.
HD58.7.L86 2001
658.—dc.21   2001030762
Use the Internet and eliminate mail time and postage costs. http://cip.loc.gov/cip

I would like to dedicate this book to my wife, Marie, and our children, Jesse, Justin, Danielle, Nicole, Brian, and Renee, for their loving support.

Preface

In his book *Power Tools,* John Nirenberg asks: "Why are so many well-intended students learning so much and yet able to apply so little in their personal and professional lives?" He gives two possible answers: the educational environment is inhospitable or students do not have the skill to apply what they learn. I believe it's the latter. Is it surprising that students cannot apply what they read and develop skills when most textbooks and many professors continue to focus on concepts and reading about them with examples, rather than take the next step to develop ability to apply what students read and to develop skills using the concepts? I wrote the first edition of this book back in 1988, prior to AACSB and SCANS calling for skill development and outcomes assessment, to help professors develop their students' ability to apply the concepts and develop skills in human relations and organizational behavior courses.

The fact that competitor human relations books are now offering exercises is a tribute to the success of *Human Relations in Organizations: Applications and Skill Building.* However, according to reviewers, none of the competitors offer the quality and quantity of application and skill development material. As with prior editions, new innovative features continue to be added. To date, no competitor is using my integration approach.

Integration with Flexibility

This book continues to have a balanced three-pronged approach:

- A clear, concise understanding of human relations/organizational behavior (HR/OB) concepts (second to none);
- The application of HR/OB concepts for critical thinking in the business world (there are eight types of applications, including video); and
- The development of HR/OB skills (there are five types of skill building exercises including video).

In addition to writing this text and its supporting ancillary package to support these distinct but integrated parts, this new edition also includes tests to assess student performance in all three areas. I wrote almost every application and skill exercise in this text and IM to ensure complete integration and a seamless course experience.

The concepts, applications, and skill-building material is clearly identified and delineated in this preface, text, and IM/test bank. Our package offers more quality and quantity of application and skill-building material to allow professors to create their own unique course using only the features that will achieve their objectives. Thus, it is the most flexible package on the market. Next is an explanation of features to choose from for concepts, applications, and skill building.

Concepts

- *Research-based and current.* The book is based on research, not opinion. There are over 1,050 references for an average of 70 references per chapter. All but classic references prior to 1994 have been cut and replaced with current references. See pages 593-616 for a list of notes by chapter.

- *Comprehensive coverage.* The text includes more comprehensive coverage than most competitor texts.
- *Systems Orientation.*

1. Throughout the text, this poster appears in the margin, identifying the level of behavior as individual, group, or organizational. The level of discussion is highlighted in blue. Chapters 1 through 3 and 15 focus primarily on individual behavior, Chapters 4 through 8 on skills influencing all three levels of behavior, Chapters 9 through 11 on group behavior, and Chapters 12 through 14 on organizational behavior.

2. Throughout the text, this poster appears in the margin, identifying the scope of study coverage of behavior, human relations, or performance. The level of discussion is highlighted in blue. All chapters discuss how the various concepts affect behavior, human relations, and performance.

3. The goal of human relations is stressed throughout the text. This poster (in the margin) signifies when the goal is discussed in the chapter.

- *Pedagogy.* Each chapter contains: (1) Learning objectives at the beginning and in the body of the chapter where the objective can be met. (2) Key terms at the beginning of each chapter and again at the end of the Chapter Review and Glossary. The key terms appear in color yellow and *are defined within the chapter in italic* so they are easy to find. (3) The chapter outline. (4) Exhibits, some of which contain multiple concepts/theories. See Exhibits 6–7, 6–8, 7–8, and 11–7, for example. (5) A Chapter Review and Glossary. The unique feature of the Chapter Review and Glossary is that it is active. Students must identify the key terms in one of three ways: fill in the blank, matching from a list of key terms, and/or by filling in the key terms from the beginning of the chapter.

REVIEW

Select one or more mehtods: (1) fill in the missing key terms from memory; (2) match the key terms, from the end of the review, with their definitions below; and/or (3) copy the key terms in order fromt hekey terms at the beginning of the chapter.

As was clearly stated, human relations skills are very important for success in organizations for the individual, group, and organization as a whole. _____ are interactions among people, while the _____ is to create a win-win situation by satisfying employee

---

- *Test Bank Assessment of Concepts.* The test bank includes true-false and multiple-choice questions, including the key terms, for the concepts presented in each chapter. Each chapter also has a key term matching test with 10 key terms. The test bank also includes the learning objectives from each chapter, which can be used as short answer questions to test concept understanding. The answers to the learning objectives appear in the Instructor's Manual and test bank.

Applications

1. *Opening Case.* Each chapter opens with a case. Throughout the chapter, how the text concepts apply to the case are presented so that students can understand the application of the concepts to actual people in organizations.

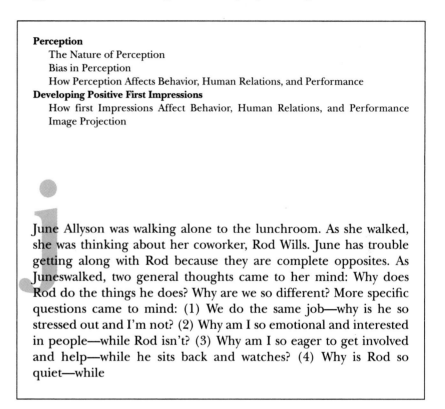

Perception
  The Nature of Perception
  Bias in Perception
  How Perception Affects Behavior, Human Relations, and Performance
Developing Positive First Impressions
  How first Impressions Affect Behavior, Human Relations, and Performance
  Image Projection

June Allyson was walking alone to the lunchroom. As she walked, she was thinking about her coworker, Rod Wills. June has trouble getting along with Rod because they are complete opposites. As June walked, two general thoughts came to her mind: Why does Rod do the things he does? Why are we so different? More specific questions came to mind: (1) We do the same job—why is he so stressed out and I'm not? (2) Why am I so emotional and interested in people—while Rod isn't? (3) Why am I so eager to get involved and help—while he sits back and watches? (4) Why is Rod so quiet—while

2. *Work Applications.* Throughout each chapter there are approximately 11 questions that require the students to apply the concepts to their own work experience. Work experience can be present or past, and part-time, summer, or full-time employment. Work applications require the students to think critically and bridge the gap between the concepts and their world.

> **WORK APPLICATIONS**
>
> 2. Give two examples of when your atitudes affected your performance. One should be a positive effect and the other a negative one. Be sure to fully explain how the attitude affected performace.
> 3. Give an example of when you lived up to or won to someone else's expectations of your performance (the Pygmalion effect). It could be a parent's, teacher's, coach's, or boss's expectation. Be specific.

3. *Application Situations.* Each chapter contains three or four boxes with 5 to 10 questions (20 total) within the chapter that require students to apply the concept illustrated in a specific short example. The questions develop critical-thinking skills through the application process.

APPLICATION SITUATIONS

Media Selection

AS 4–1

Select the most appropriate media for each message.

A. One-on-one   C. Meeting   E. Memo   G. Report

B. Telephone   D. Presentation   F. Letter   H. Poster

_____ 1. The supervisor has to assign a new customer order to Karen and Ralph.

_____ 2. The supervisor is expecting needed material for production this afternoon. She wants to know if it will arrive on time.

---

4. *CASE-Internet with cumulative questions.* Each chapter has a case study from a real world organization. At the end of the case, the organization's Website address is given so that students can visit the web to get updated information on the case. There is also Appendix C, "How to Research Case Material Using the Internet," to help students. Chapters 2-15 include cumulative questions. Cumulative questions include concepts from prior chapters. For example, the case for Chapter 11 has five questions related to Chapter 11, which is followed by four questions relating concepts from Chapters 4, 5, 6, 7, and 10. Thus, students continually review concepts from prior chapters.

5. *Objective Cases.* At the end of each chapter there is a short case. The unique feature is the "objective" part with 10 multiple-choice questions. There are also open-ended questions. The cases require students to apply the concepts to actual people and organizations.

OBJECTIVE CASE

Friedman's Business Technique

The following conversation takes place between Art Friedman and Bob Lussier. In 1970, Art Friedman implemented a new business technique. At that time the business was called Friedman's Appliances. It employed 15 workers in Oakland, California. Friedman's is an actual business that uses the technique you will read about.

Bob: What is the reason for your success in business?

Art: My business technique.

Bob: What is it? How did you implement it?

---

6. *Video Cases.* At the end of 8 of the 15 chapters (over 50 percent), there is an introduction to a video case, which the instructor shows in class. There are open-ended critical thinking discussion questions in the textbook, with possible answers in the Instructor's Manual. The cases require students to think critically as they apply the specific text concepts to an actual organization shown in the video.

7. *MG Webzine—Fiscal Fairy Tales.* Twelve of the 15 chapters include a *Fiscal Fairy Tale* (FFT). FFTs are cases based on traditional folk tales re-written by Tom

---

VIDEO CASE 9

◆ **Ethics: Arthur Anderson**

Critical Thinking Questions:

This video presents separate short cases.

Vignette 1: The High-Bid Dilemma

A purchasing agent and his assistant are reviewing bids from seven companies. They disagree on who to give the contract to. Place yourself in the role of the assistant.

1. Is there a conflict of interest in this case?

2. From the purchasing manager's view, is this Type I or II ethical behavior.

3. Should you, as the assistant, agree with the purchasing agent and give the business to Spin Cast or disagree and object to giving the business to Spin Cast?

Brown, Editor of the Management General (MG) Webzine, with a humorous spin to stimulate your thinking and discussion about today's real work world. Students go to the MG Webzine (*www.mgeneral.com*) outside of class time, read the case/tale, and answer general questions and questions relating the chapter concepts to the tale. Appendix B, "Internet Exercises," provides help using the Internet; it is particularly helpful for the novice Internet user.

8. *Internet Exercises.* At the end of each chapter, there are three or four Internet Exercises (IE). Students are instructed to go to the Internet for a variety of exercise experiences that enhances the concepts in the textbook. For example, IE 1–2 and 1–2 provide tutorials on how to use search engines and to conduct Internet research; IE 2–1 (Personality), IE 4–2 (Presentations), IE 7–2 (Leadership Style), IE 9–1 (Influencing Quotient), and IE 11–1 (Teams) provide self-assessment instruments (and are labeled); IE 3–2 provides plans to develop your self-concept through the use of Self-Talk; IE 7–3 is a Leadership Challenge Simulation. There is a total of 63 MG Webzine and Internet Exercises to chose from.

No Special In-Class Equipment Needed. As with *Fiscal Fairy Tales*, the Online Internet exercise to get information is done out of class, and no class time is required. No special equipment (Internet access from the classroom) is required. However, there is an in-class discussion part of all exercises for those who want to share the Internet applications.

9. *Test Bank Assessment of Applications and IM.* The test bank includes the work applications from the text and multiple-choice questions, similar to the Application Situations and case questions, to evaluate critical thinking skills. The Instructor's Manual includes the recommended answers for all of the application features above, except the opening case which is illustrated in the text.

Skill-Building

1. *Self-Assessment Exercises.* Each chapter has between one and three (27 total) self-assessment exercises to enable students to gain personal knowledge. Some of the exercises are tied to skill-building exercises to enhance the impact of the self-assessment. All information for completing and scoring, and self-assessment, is contained within each exercise.

2. *Group Skill-Building Exercises.* Fourteen (30 percent) of the skill-building exercises primarily focus on small-group (2–6 members) activities. Thus, breaking into small groups is required. All group exercises are labeled **iii** as illustrated below.

SKILL-BUILDING EXERCISE 11–1

**In–Class
Team Dymanics**

iii

Note: This exercise is designed for groups that have met for some time. (Five or more hours are recommended.)

Objectives: To gain a better understanding of the gropup structure components and how they affect group performance, and to improve group structure.

SCANS: The SCANS competencies of resource, interpersonal skills, information, and especially systems and the foundations of basic, thinking in the area of problem solving and decision making, and personal qualities are developed through this exercise.

---

3. *Role-Play Skill-Building Exercises.* Six (13 percent) of the skill-building exercises primarily focus on developing skills through behavior modeling, as discussed next. Thus, breaking into groups of three and role playing is required.

4. *Models, Behavior-Model Videos and Icons, and Skill-Building Exercises.* Throughout the book are 25 models with step-by-step instructions for handling day-to-day human relations situations. How to use several of the models is illustrated in the behavior-modeling videos. For example, students read the model in the book and watch people send messages, give praise, resolve conflicts, handle complaints, and coach an employee following the steps in the model. Following viewing the video, students role-play how they would handle these human relations situations. Students may also give each other feedback on the effectiveness of their role plays. However, videos can be used as stand-alone activities. The icon combination in the margin illustrates when the video serves as a behavior model to a Skill-Building (SB) exercise. The SB icon also appears in the text when the concepts have been presented that enable the skill-building exercise to be completed. The lecture may stop and skill-building begin in class to break up the lecture.

 Video

 Skill-Building

5. *Behavior Model Videos and Icon.* There are one or more behavior model videos (19 total) for each chapter. Behavior model videos 2 through 19 show people successfully handling day-to-day human relations situations. Videos can be followed by class discussion. Also, many videos are used in conjunction with skill-building exercises. The video icon appears in the margin of the text, with the video behavior module number 1 through 19, to indicate when the concepts illustrated in the video have been covered. Thus, instructors may stop lecturing and show the video to break up the lecture.

 Video

6. *Video Exercise and Icon.* The video exercises are designed to illustrate specific text concepts/styles that the students identify. Each exercise has a place for the students to write their answers. The video icon indicates that a specific video module serves as a video exercise. The first number represents the chapter and the second is the number of the video exercise within the chapter. Some of the video exercises can be used as part of a skill-building exercise or separately, and some are self-contained. Chapters 2, 4, 5, 7, 9, and 10 have video exercises.

Video

7. *Test Bank Assessment of Skill-Building and IM.* The test bank includes skill-building questions to assess skill-building. The Instructor's Manual gives detailed instructions on using all skill-building exercises, answers, etc., and states how students can be tested on the exercises and instructions to give to students.

**Self-Assessment
Exercise 9-2**

Political Behavior

Select the response that best describes your actual or planned use of the following behavior on the job. Place the number 1–5 on the line before each statement.

(5) Usually   (4) Frequently   (3) Occasionally   (2) Seldom   (1) Rarely

_____ 1. I get along with everyone, even those recognized as difficult. I avoid or delay giving my opinion on controversial issues.

---

8. *Skill-Building Objectives and SCANS.* Each skill-building exercise begins by listing its objective. The objective is followed by listing the Secretary's Commission on Achieving Necessary Skills (SCANS) competencies developed through the exercise.

SKILL-BUILDING EXERCISE 6–2

● **In-Class
Giving Praise**

Objective: To develop your skill at giving praise.

SCANS: The SCANS competencies of information and especially interpersonal skills and the foundations of basic, thinking, and especially personal qualities are developed through this exercise.

Preparation: You will need your prepared praise.

Experience: You will give and receive praise.

*Procedure
(12–17 minutes)*

Break into groups of five or six. One at a time, give the praise.

1. Explain the situation.

2. Select a group member to receive the praise.

---

9. *Individual and Group Skill-Building Exercises.* Twenty-seven (57 percent) of the skill-building exercises primarily focus on individual skill building, most of which are out of class as preparation for the exercise. However, in-class work in groups using the concepts and sharing answers can enhance skill building. Thus, the instructor has the flexibility to: (1) simply have students complete the preparations out of class and during class and go over the answers with concluding remarks, and/or lead a class discussion without using any small-group time, or (2) spend group class time as directed in the exercise. All individual and group exercises are labeled ▮ ▮▮▮ as illustrated below.

SKILL-BUILDING EXERCISE 12–2

● **In–Class Your
College Climate**

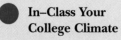

*Procedure 1
Tabulate the Class's
Survey Responses*

Objectives: To better understand organizational climate and the climate at your college.

SCANS: The SCANS competencies of interpersonal skills, information, and especially systems and the foundations of basic, especially thinking in the area of problem solving, and personal qualities are developed through this exercise.

Preparation: You should have completed the preparation questionnaire.

Experience: Your class will calculate its climate and discuss it.

Option A: Break up into teams of five or six and tabulate team members' responses to each of the questions selected by your instructor. Each group reports its responses to the instructor, who tabulates the total responses for the entire class. He or she summarizes the results on the board.

Summary of Unique Innovations

- The three-pronged approach to the text: concepts, applications, skills.
- The three-pronged test bank: concepts, applications, skills.
- Eight types of applications that are clearly marked in the text for developing critical thinking skills, including 61 Internet exercises.
- Six types of skill-building exercises clearly marked in the text that truly develop skills that can be used in ones' personal and professional life.
- An unsurpassed video package: 19 Behavior Models and 8 Video Cases.
- Flexibility—use all or only some of the features that work for you.

Changes to the Fifth Edition

- *Case-Internet-Cumulative Questions.* A new longer case from a real world organization has been added to each chapter. The case includes the organization's Web-site and cumulative questions from prior chapters. Appendix C, "How to Research Case Material Using the Internet," has been added to help students use the Internet with cases.
- *MG Webzine and Internet Exercises.* Four exercises have been added to each chapter. Appendix B, "Internet Exercises," has been added to provide help using the Internet.
- *PowerPoint.* PowerPoint is available for a more flexible and professional presentation in the classroom.
- *Research-based and current.* There are over 1,050 references for an average of 70 references per chapter. All but classic references prior to 1994 have been cut and replaced with current references. See pages 593-616 for a list of notes by chapter.
- *Chapter Updates.*

   Chapter 1. The reasons why human relations/OB skills are important has been updated and a new section added to more effectively state the objectives of the course/book and benefits to students.

   Chapter 2. The chapter subtitle "Intelligence" has been changed to "Learning" to better reflect the learning organization; coverage of the learning organization has been increased. The Big Five Personality has been added with a self-assessment exercise. In the first impression section, there is a new short discussion of impression management and a new subsection presenting tips on apparel and grooming.

Chapter 3. Spirituality in the workplace is a new subsection of Values.

Chapter 4. Emotional intelligence and emotional quotient and 360-degree feedback have been added.

Chapter 5. A new section on organizational structure has been added as the first section.

Chapter 7. The Managerial Grid has been updated to the revised Leadership Grid. Charismatic and transactional leadership have been added.

Chapter 9. Etiquette tips for job interviewing, table manners, telephone, e-mail, meetings, and hoteling have been added.

Chapter 12. Quality is now a separate section with TQM, ISO 9000, and Six Sigma. Material on quality from Chapter 14 has been moved to this chapter.

Chapter 13. "Equal Employment Opportunity and Affirmative Action," has been changed to "EEO for All." And "Affirmative Action Programs" has been changed to "From AA to Valuing Diversity" to emphasize this shift. "Sexism in Organizations" has been changed to "Sexism and Work and Family Balance," as sexism has been cut back some and work family increased.

Chapter 14. The chapter title has been changed slightly replacing "Quality" with "Technology." The prior material on quality has been moved to Chapter 12, and new material on technology has been added. Appendix A, "Unions," has been moved to the Instructor's Manual.

Acknowledgments

I would like to dedicate my first acknowledgment for this book to Judi Neal, University of New Haven, because of her influence on my work. Judi indirectly influenced my use of the three-prong approach by making me aware of an article in the *Journal of Management Education* (Vol. 17, No. 3, 1993, 399-415) comparing my *Human Relations in Organizations* (Irwin/McGraw-Hill) to other skills books. Author John Bigelow gave it a top rating for a general OB course in "Managerial Skills Texts: How Do They Stack Up?" I got the three-prong idea by reading John's article suggestions for improving skills training books (thanks, John). The three-pronged approach has been used successfully in the fourth edition and in my current *Management Fundamentals: Concepts, Applications, Skill Development,* and *Leadership: Theory, Application, Skill Development* books (Southwestern, 2000 and 2001). Judi introduced me to using the MG Webzine as a supplement to the book, and I thank her for introducing me to Tom Brown, its editor (who gets his own thanks). I'm deeply honored that she wrote the "Spirituality" section of Chapter 3.

I thank Tom Brown for reviewing and giving his input into using the MG Webzine in the MG and Internet exercises, creating a seamless integration between the book and Website. My students use the MG Webzine and also thank him.

Justin Lussier also deserves credit for reviewing Appendix B "Basic Information about the Internet and its Software."

I also want to thank my mentor and co-author of many publications, Joel Corman, for his advice and encouragement during and after my graduate education at Suffolk University.

Special thanks to the reviewers of the fifth edition of my manuscript for their excellent recommendations:

Lee Higgins, Southeast Community College—Beatrice Campus

Janet Weber, McCook Community College

Thanks also to reviewers of past editions:

William Weisgerber, Saddleback College

Andy C. Saucedo, Dona Ana Community College

Charleen Jaeb, Cuyahoga Community College

John J. Heinsius, Modesto Junior College

Roger E. Besst, Muskingum Area Technical College

Rebecca S. Ross, Shenango Valley School of Business

Thomas E. Schillar, University of Puget Sound

Rosemary Birkel Wilson, Washtenaw Community College

Thomas J. Shaughnessy, Illinois Central College

Edward J. LeMay, Massasoit Community College

Julie Campbell, Adams State College

John Gubbay, Moraine Valley Community College

Ruth Dixon, Diablo Valley College

John J. Harrington, New Hampshire College

Robert Wall Edge, Commonwealth College

Abbas Nadim, University of New Haven

Steve Kober, Pierce College

Dee Dunn, Commonwealth College

Marlene Frederick, New Mexico State University at Carlsbad

Linda Saarela, Pierce College

David Backstrom, Allan Hancock College

Rob Taylor, Indiana Vocational Technical College

Warren Sargent, College of the Sequoias

Jane Binns, Washtenaw Community College

Charles W. Beem, Bucks County Community College

Robert Nixon, Prairie State College

Leo Kiesewetter, Illinois Central College

Stephen C. Branz, Triton College

William T. Price, Jr., Virginia Polytechnic Institute and State University

Jerry F. Gooddard, Aims Community College

Rex L. Bishop, Charles Community College

Bill Anton, DeVard Community College

Stew Rosencran, University of Central Florida

John Magnuson, Spokane Community College

Doug Richardson, Eastfield College

Thanks to students for suggesting improvements:

Richard Gardner, New Hampshire College

Peter Blunt, New Hampshire College

Christianne Erwin, Truckee Meadows Community College

Robert Neal Chase, New Hampshire College

Contact Me with Feedback

I wrote this book for you. Let me know what you think of it. Write to me and tell me what you did and/or didn't like about it. More specifically, how could it be improved? I will be responsive to your feedback. If I use your suggestion for improvement, your name and college will be listed in the acknowledgment section of the next edition. I sincerely hope that you will develop your human relations skills through this book.

Robert N. Lussier, Professor of Management and Director of Israel Programs
Management Department
Springfield College
Springfield, MA 01109
413-748-3202
rlussier@spfldcol.edu

About the Author

Robert N. Lussier, is a professor of management at Springfield College and has taught for more than 25 years. He has also developed some innovative and widely copied methods for developing and applying human relations skills that can be used in one's personal and professional life.

Dr. Lussier is also a prolific writer, with more than 160 publications to his credit. These include four other textbooks and a myriad of textbook supplements. His great interest in empirical research is demonstrated by the fact that his articles have been published in the *Academy of Entrepreneurship Journal, Business Horizons, Business Journal, Entrepreneurial Executive, Entrepreneurship Theory and Practice, Journal of Business & Entrepreneurship, Journal of Business Strategies, Journal of Small Business Management, Journal of Small Business Strategy,* and *SAM Advanced Management Journal.*

Dr. Lussier has consulted a wide array of commercial and nonprofit organizations. In fact, some of the material in this book was developed for such clients as Baystate Medical Center, Coca-Cola, Friendly Ice Cream, Institute of Financial Education, Mead, Monsanto, Smith & Wesson, the Social Security Administration, the Visiting Nurses Association, and YMCA's.

Presently, he is the director of Springfield College's program in Israel, and negotiated a joint venture contract with an Israeli college to offer Springfield degrees in that country. Dr. Lussier visits Israel twice yearly, and teaches courses there. His other international experiences include work in Namibia and South Africa.

Dr. Lussier holds a bachelor of science in business administration from Salem State College, two Master's degrees in business and education from Suffolk University, and a doctorate in management from the University of New Haven.

Contents in Brief

Contents

Human Relations
in Organizations

Behavior,
Human Relations,
and Performance
Begin with You

Understanding Behavior, Human Relations, and Performance

1

Learning Objectives

After completing this chapter, you should be able to:

1. Explain why human relations skills are important.
2. Discuss the goal of human relations.
3. Describe the relationship between performance at the individual and group levels and organizational performance.
4. Describe the relationship among behavior, human relations, and organizational performance.
5. Identify your personal low and high human relations ability/skill levels.
6. Identify five personal human relations goals for the course.
7. Explain nine guidelines for effective human relations.
8. Briefly describe the history of the study of human relations.
9. State some of the trends and challenges in the field of human relations.
10. Define the following 14 key terms (in order of appearance in the chapter):

human relations	**levels of behavior**	**systems affect**
goal of human relations	**group behavior**	**Elton Mayo**
win-win situation	**organization**	**Hawthorne effect**
total person approach	**organizational behavior**	**Theory Z**
behavior	**performance**	

Chapter Outline

When Olin Ready graduated from college, he accepted his first full-time job with IBM. As he drove to work on his first day, he thought: How will I fit in? Will my peers and new boss Nancy Westwood like me? Will I be challenged by my job? Will I be able to get raises and promotions? At about the same time, Nancy was also driving to work thinking about Olin, with thoughts like: Will Olin fit in with his peers? Will he be open to my suggestions and leadership? Will Olin work hard and be a high performer?

What would you do to ensure success if you were Olin? What would you do to ensure Olin's success if you were Nancy? Meeting employees' needs while achieving the organization's objectives is the goal of positive human relations in any organization.

Why Human Relations Skills Are Important

Some advice and reasons human relations skills are so important to you as an individual and to organizations include:

- Advice from the richest man in the world Bill Gates, cofounder and CEO of Microsoft Corporation, is to learn to work with people in school.[1]

- Leslie Wexner, founder and CEO of Limited Inc., says that the most important asset of every organization is its people; the organization needs to take care of them.[2] Organizations are made of people, not technology or structure; it's the process of human interactions that is important.[3] Corporate America has concluded that investing in people is the way to stay ahead competitively.[4] Global companies are investing heavily in developing their intellectual capital, promoting individual growth.[5] A consulting firm evaluates human capital and states that the highest-performing companies have the highest human-resources scores. Human capital is as powerful as research and development as a link to performance.[6]

- However, although it is commonly stated that people are our most important asset, it is frequently ignored.[7] According to Hammer, coauthor of the book that coined the term reengineering, "The biggest lie told by most corporations, and they tell it proudly, is that people are our most important assets. Total fabrication. They treat people like raw materials."[8] Poor human relations are common in the workplace, and they need to be improved.

- Fred Smith, founder and CEO of FedEx, developed the "People, Service, Profit," or P-S-P slogan, which is take care of people and they in turn will deliver service, which will result in profits.[9]

- CEOs of 29 leading global companies agree that human relationships with customers and suppliers are becoming as important as the product itself.[10]

- Entrepreneur Donna Hope, of The Gift Basket Emporium in Merrick, New York, credits her business success to her human relations training.[11]

- Human relations skills represent the single biggest reason for career success and failure. Personal qualities account for 85 percent of the factors contributing to job success, while technical knowledge accounts for only 15 percent, according to the Carnegie Foundation. Of the people fired from their jobs, 66 percent were fired because they failed to get along with people and only 34 percent lost their job due to lack of technical knowledge, according to The Harvard Bureau of Vocational Guidance. For example, AT&T President John Walter was told he would not be promoted to chief executive officer (CEO) as planned because his relations with the CEO had grown increasingly strained.[12] In other words, John did not get promoted because he did not have good human relations with his boss.

- As global competition increases, so does the need to increase productivity to be competitive. Poor human relations can be detrimental to productivity. It can decrease employee morale, reduce work satisfaction, and result in stress.[13] Collaborative employee-management relationships have the potential for increasing productivity equal to or greater than that of technology, according to a congressional hearing of Human Factors in Technological Innovation and Productivity Improvement.

- Since managers work with people, they should study human relations as intensely as they study their field of technical expertise. Many organizations offer human relations training. For example, IBM gives the average employee 40 hours of training per year, with about 32 of these hours related to human relations training.

Learning Objective

1. Explain why human relations skills are important

Throughout this book we will be using many important, or key, terms. To ensure that you have a clear understanding of these terms, when a key term first appears it is presented in **bold letters** with its definition *italicized*.

Goal of Human Relations

The term **human relations** *means interactions among people.* When Olin Ready arrives at IBM on his first day of work, he will interact with his new boss, Nancy. Next, a variety of people will help orient and train Olin. Later, as he performs his daily tasks, Olin will interact with Nancy and his coworkers, as well as with people from other departments and customers. Olin's success at IBM will be based on human relations.

Learning Objective

2. Discuss the goal of human relations

The **goal of human relations** *is to create a win-win situation by satisfying employee needs while achieving organizational objectives.* A **win-win situation** *occurs when the organization and the employees get what they want.* When an employee asks "What's in it for me?" that employee is expressing his or her needs. When a manager expects high levels of performance from his or her employees, that manager is identifying organizational objectives. Many employees and union representatives have argued that company owners don't share their profits or that management exploits employees, creating an organization-wins–employees-lose situation. When employees feel as though they are being taken advantage of by management, they often hold back performance to create an employees-win–management-loses situation. Actually, unmet employee needs often result in a lose-lose situation. For example, Carla has a college degree in education. However, since she cannot find a teaching job, she takes a job as a computer data-entry typist, which she finds boring. Carla makes many careless errors and her performance level is low. She has been caught using the company telephone during work hours to call several schools about jobs. Because Carla's needs for job satisfaction are not being met, she is not helping the organization meet its objectives. In her current job, Carla is not working to her full capability. However, as a teacher, Carla's performance level might be higher and she might help the school meet its objectives. Have you ever had a job in which your needs were not being satisfied? Was your performance level low or high in this situation?

Creating a win-win situation applies to human relations at all levels, not just management-employee relations. For example, members of a department often must share the work. If Olin does not do his share of the work at IBM, he creates problems within the department. (This would be an I-win–coworkers-lose situation.) Coworker Mary may decide it is not fair that she has to do more work than Olin. Consequently, Mary may argue with Olin, slow down her performance, or complain to their boss, Nancy. Or, if Olin and coworker Ray do not like each other, their dislike may affect their behavior, the human relations in the department, and the department/organization's performance. Nancy's job is to make sure the human relations within her department have a positive effect on her department's performance. Conflicts usually arise because of a lack of a win-win situation. You will learn to create win-win situations when facing conflicts in Chapter 8.

WORK APPLICATIONS

1. Give an example, personal if possible, of a situation when the goal of human relations was met. Explain how the individual's needs were met and the organizational objectives achieved.

Goal of
Human Relations

This book discusses the goal of human relations as it applies to various topics. One goal of this book is to develop your ability to create win-win situations in a variety of settings, including your professional and personal life. To help you know when the text focus is on the goal of human relations, a poster box will appear in the margin, as shown here.

The Total Person Approach

The **total person approach** *realizes that an organization employs the whole person, not just his or her job skills.* People play many roles throughout their lives, indeed, throughout each day. Olin, therefore, is more than just an employee; he is also a father, a member of the PTA, a scout leader, a jogger, a student, and a fisherman. At work, Olin will not completely discard all other roles to be a worker only. His off-the-job life will affect his job performance at IBM. Thus, if Olin has a bad day at work, it may not be related to his job, but to another of his life's roles.

Goal of
Human Relations

Organizations such as 3M, Analog Services, Marriott, Hewlett-Packard, IBM, and numerous others view employees as total people. Such organizations are trying to give employees a better quality of work life. One example is Federal Express Corporation, the nation's leading provider of overnight, door-to-door delivery of packages and letters. Federal Express has a no-layoff policy, pays good wages, offers a profit-sharing program, and maintains excellent communications with employees. Fred Smith, founder and chairman of Federal Express, states that management is interested in making this a good place to work where people are dealt with as human beings rather than as numbers.

Many organizations are turning problems into win-win situations. Hoffman-La Roche is one example. At Hoffman-La Roche, employees with young children were often tardy or absent due to problems of finding reliable day care. Rather than get tough and discipline these people, Hoffman-La Roche created a win-win situation by instituting an extensive child care program.

Also, many organizations realize that employees' physical fitness and nutrition affect their job performance. The Shawmut-Merchants Bank places bottles of vitamins on cafeteria tables for employees to take. Friendly Ice Cream and Kimberly-Clark Corporation offer free aerobic exercise classes. Adolph Coors Company spent $600,000 on a "wellness" center offering group exercise and clinics devoted to nutrition, stress management, and control of drinking, smoking, and weight. These are only a few examples of the thousands of organizations creating win-win situations all over the world; other examples appear throughout the text.

WORK APPLICATIONS

2. Give a specific example, personal if possible, that supports the total person approach. Explain how an individual's job performance was affected by off-the-job problems.

What's in It for Me? and the Objectives of the Book

In this section, we'll discuss what you can get from this book and how the benefits to you tie in with the objectives of the book.

What's in It for Me?

It's natural to be thinking, what can I get from this book, or what's in it for me? This is a common question in all human relations, although, it is seldom directly asked and answered. My overall goal is to meet the goal of human relations. In writing this book, I strive to create a win-win situation by developing your human relations skills, while meeting the needs of your professor and college to provide a valuable learning experience. Generally, the better you can work with people, and this is what the course is all about, the more successful you will be.

In a survey of college graduates, human relations is rated among the most valuable course taken.[14] Many students state that their human relations course is their most interesting course because it is about them. In fact, human relations is about you and how you get along with your family, friends, coworkers and everyone you interact with. Students also state that they like the course because they can use it in their day-to-day human relations immediately in both their personal and professional lives. Do you like to get your own way or to get what you want? Human relations skills will help you ethically achieve your personal and professional goals, as well as organizational goals. By studying human relations, you will learn skills that will help you in situations like Nancy's and Olin's. In the fourth and fifth sections of this chapter, Assessing Your Human Relations Abilities and Skills and Developing Human Relations Skills, you will learn the important skills that you can develop through this course.

Objectives of the Book

As indicated in the title of the book, it has three-pronged approach objectives:

- To teach you the concepts and theories of human relations.
- To develop your ability to apply the human relations concepts through critical thinking.
- To develop your human relations skills in your personal and professional life.

This book offers some unique features related to each of the three objectives; features are listed in Exhibit 1–1. You may be tested relating to each objective. To get the most from this book, turn back to the preface and read the descriptions of the features.

EXHIBIT 1–1   **THE THREE-PRONGED APPROACH: FEATURES OF THE BOOK**

Concepts	Applications	Skill Building
Research-based and current	Opening cases	Self-assessment exercises
Comprehensive coverage	Work applications	Skill-building objectives and SCANS
Systems oriented	Application situations	Skill-building exercises (three types)
Learning objectives	Cases	Behavior models
Key terms	Objective cases	Behavior model videos
Exhibits	Video cases	Video exercises
Chapter review and glossary	MG Internet exercises	

Flexibility

There are so many features that your professor will most likely not use every feature with every chapter. Students have different learning style preferences. Most students who use this book like to read about a concept and to apply it right away. Many professors like the application material within the chapter to break up the lecture. Thus, the learning objectives, work applications, application situations, and self-assessment material are placed within the chapter with their concepts. However, some students find that applying the concepts as they read through the chapter breaks the continuity of reading. These students prefer to complete the self-assessments then read the entire chapter, skipping over the applications and then to go back and do them after reading the chapter. There is no one best learning style; you have the flexibility to use either approach, some combination, or your own method.

3. In your own words, why are human relations skills important? How will they help you in your career?

Behavior, Human Relations, and Organizational Performance

Levels of Behavior

The study of human relations looks closely at the way people behave. **Behavior** *is what people do and say.* Human relations fuel behavior.[15] The three **levels of behavior** *include individual, group, and organizational.* Human relations take place at the group and organizational level.

Individual and Group Level Behavior

As Olin types a letter on the computer or fills out requisition forms by hand, he is engaged in individual behavior. **Group behavior** *consists of the things two or more people do and say as they interact.* Individual behavior influences group behavior.[16] For example, as Olin and Mary work on a project together or attend department meetings, their actions are considered group behavior. Studying the chapters in this book, particularly Chapters 1 through 3, should help you understand and predict your own behavior, and that of others, in an organizational setting. In addition, Chapters 10 and 11 will help you gain a better understanding of how your behavior affects others, and how their behavior affects you.

Organizational Level Behavior

An **organization** *is a group of people working to achieve an objective(s).* This book focuses on human relations in both profit and nonprofit organizations in which people work to make a living. Organizations are created to produce goods and services for the larger society. If you have ever worked, you have been a part of an organization. You also come into contact with organizations on a regular basis, such as when you go into a store, school, church, post office, or health club.

As individuals and groups interact, their collective behavior constitutes the organization's behavior. Thus **organizational behavior** *is the collective behavior of an organization's individuals and groups.* IBM is an organization, and its collective behavior is based on Olin's behavior, the behavior of Nancy's department, and the behavior of all other departments combined.

This book explores all three levels of behavior. Chapters 2–3 focus primarily on individual behavior, Chapters 4–8 on the skills influencing all three levels of behavior, Chapters 9–11 on group behavior, and Chapters 12–14 on organizational behavior. Throughout Chapters 2–15 you will see an icon in the margin, highlighting the level of behavior being discussed for easy identification.

Exhibit 1–2 illustrates the three levels of behavior. The focus of level three is on the organization as a whole. At this level, the responsibility of the board of directors and president is to focus on the entire organization. The focus of level two is on the behavior and human relations within and between groups. Some of the organization's groups include the president and vice presidents, the managers and their supervisors, and the supervisors and their employees. This level also takes into consideration the behavior and human relations between groups such as the marketing, production, and finance departments. The focus of level one is on the behavior of any one person in the organization.

Organization
Group
Individual

EXHIBIT 1-2   **LEVEL OF BEHAVIOR**

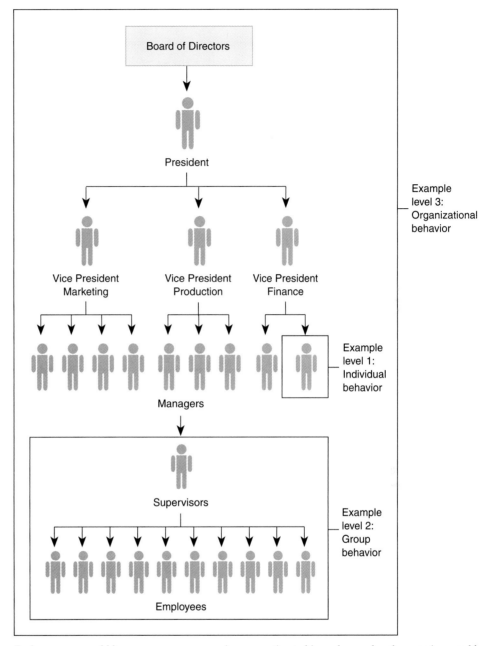

Each manager would have one or more supervisors reporting to him or her, and each supervisor would have several employees reporting to him or her.

The president, vice president, managers, and supervisors are responsible for the behavior of the individuals and groups reporting to them. As a manager, at any level, you are responsible for the behavior and human relations skills of your employees. Your success depends upon your employees' behavior and human relations.

Exhibit 1–3 is a formal organization structure showing authority and reporting relationships. However, it does not show the multiple possible human relations that exist outside the formal structure. For example, the president could interact with any employee, an employee could interact with a manager, a supervisor could interact with a vice president's secretary who is not even shown on the organization chart, and so on. A common term used for this informal communication is the *grapevine*.

EXHIBIT 1–3   THE RELATIONSHIP AMONG INDIVIDUAL, GROUP, AND ORGANIZATIONAL PERFORMANCE

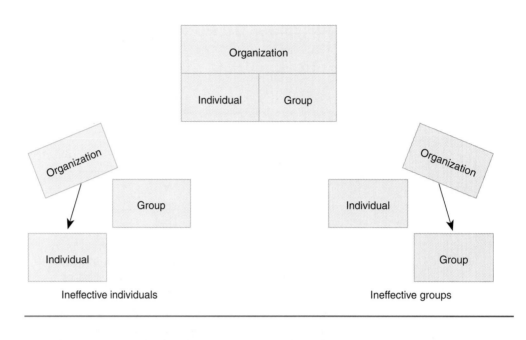

WORK APPLICATIONS

4. Give two specific examples of when you are involved in human relations—one a positive example, the other a negative one. Also identify the level of behavior for each example.

The Relationship between Individual and Group Behavior and Organizational Performance

Human relations has an effect on performance.[17] Throughout this course you will learn how human relations affects individual and group behavior, and the resulting effects on organizational performance. **Performance** *is the extent to which expectations or objectives have been met.* Performance is absolute when objectives are set. For example, if the objective of a production worker is to produce 100 widgets per day and the employee produces 100 widgets, performance is at the expected level. However, some workers may produce less than 100 widgets, while others may produce more than 100 widgets. Performance is usually measured on a continuum contrasted by high and low levels of performance, or ranked on a scale of 1–10. The same concept holds true for the entire organization. An organization may have an objective to make a $100,000 profit, for a set period of time such as one quarter, one half, or one year. If the organization makes the $100,000 profit, how do you classify the level of performance? It depends on prior periods. For example, if the last period's profits were $90,000, you may say that $100,000 this period is a high level of performance; however, if the profits in the past have consistently been $125,000, the level of performance may be considered low, even though the objective was met. Performance is a relative term. Performance levels are more meaningful when compared to past performance or the performance of others within and/or outside the organization.

**Understanding
Important Terms**

AS 1–1

Identify each statement by its key term.

A. Behavior   C. Human relations   E. Performance

B. Goal of human relations   D. Organization   F. Total person approach

_____ 1. Bill and Sara are discussing how to complete a project they are working on together.

_____ 2. Julio just delivered his report to the outgoing mailbox.

_____ 3. It's 4:50 and Cindy typed the last bill to be sent out today with the 5:00 PM mail.

_____ 4. All of the people listed above are members of an _____.

_____ 5. Because I've been doing a good job, I got a raise, and now I can buy that new car I want so badly.

The Systems Affect

A system is a set of two or more interactive elements. The systems approach, developed by Russell Ackoff, focuses on the whole system with an emphasis on the relationships between its parts. The whole cannot be decomposed into independent subsets.[18] For our purposes, under the **systems affect** *all people in the organization are affected by at least one other person, and each person affects the whole group/organization.* The organization's performance is based on the combined performance of each individual and group. To have high levels of performance, the organization must have high-performing individuals and groups. Groups are the building blocks of the organization. Due to the systems affect, the destructive behavior of one individual hurts that group and other departments as well. In addition, the destructive behavior of one department affects other departments and the organization's performance. Systems thinking is needed to understand performance.

The challenge to management is to develop high-performing individuals and groups. According to Ackoff, management's responsibility is to increase employee ability and desire to satisfy their own needs and legitimate desires, and those of others.[19] And this is accomplished through exchange relationships.[20]

In a sense, individuals and groups are the foundation of an organization. If either is ineffective, the organization will fall. See Exhibit 1–3, The Relationship among Individual, Group, and Organizational Performance, for a graphic illustration.

Goal of Human Relations

Learning Objective

3. Describe the relationship between performance at the individual and group levels and organizational performance

The Relationship among Behavior, Human Relations, and Organizational Performance

The focus of this book is behavior, human relations, and performance from a systems affect perspective. The United States fell behind other countries in performance. If the United States is to retain world leadership, we must continually develop our people into higher-level performers or our standard of living will decrease.[21] The late Edwards Deming, world-renowned quality and performance consultant, often credited with helping Japan become a world leader in business, has repeatedly stated that people, not simply technology, are the key to increased levels of performance.

5. Give two specific examples of how human relations affected your performance—one a positive example, the other a negative one. Be specific in explaining the effects of human relations.

Video

Focus of Study

AS 1–2

Identify the focus of study by selecting two answers. First select the level of behavior:

A. Individual   B. Group   C. Organizational

Then select the scope of study:

A. Behavior   B. Human relations   C. Performance

_____ 6. Bill and Sara are discussing how to complete a project they are working on together.

_____ 7. The management hierarchy from president down to the employee level.

_____ 8. Carl is writing a letter to a supplier to correct an error in billing.

_____ 9. The marketing department has just exceeded its sales quota for the quarter.

_____ 10. IBM has just completed its income statement for the quarter.

Performance
Human Relations
Behavior

Just as people are the foundation of the organization, behavior and human relations are the foundation supporting performance. If either is ineffective, performance will fall. Exhibit 1–4, The Relationship among Behavior, Human Relations, and Performance, gives a graphic illustration. Throughout Chapters 2–15 you will see the icon in the margin with the scope of study highlighted for easy identification.

EXHIBIT 1–4   THE RELATIONSHIP AMONG BEHAVIOR, HUMAN RELATIONS, AND PERFORMANCE

Learning Objective

4. Describe the relationship among behavior, human relations, and organizational performance

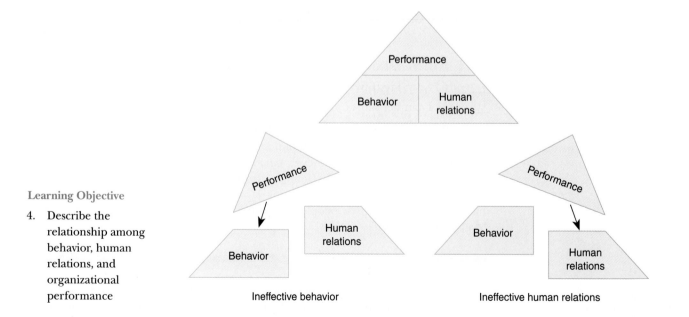

Assessing Your Human Relations Abilities and Skills

You will now assess your human relations abilities and skills. For each of the 43 statements below, record in the blank the number from 1 to 7 that best describes your level of ability or skill. You are not expected to have all high numbers. This assessment will give you an overview of what you will learn in this course. Appendix A contains the same assessment to enable you to compare your skills at the beginning and end of the course.

Low ability/skill						High ability/skill
1	2	3	4	5	6	7

_____ 1. I understand how personality and perception affect people's behavior, human relations, and performance.

_____ 2. I can describe several ways to handle stress effectively.

_____ 3. I know my preferred learning style (accommodator, diverger, converger, assimilator) and how it affects my behavior, human relations, and performance.

_____ 4. I understand how people acquire attitudes and how attitudes affect behavior, human relations, and performance.

_____ 5. I can describe self-concept and self-efficacy and how they affect behavior, human relations, and performance.

_____ 6. I can list several areas of personal values and state how values affect behavior, human relations, and performance.

_____ 7. I can describe the communication process.

_____ 8. I can list several transmission media and when to use each.

_____ 9. I can identify and use various message response styles.

_____ 10. I understand organizational communications and networks.

_____ 11. I can list barriers to communications and how to overcome them.

_____ 12. I know my preferred communication style and how to use other communication styles to meet the needs of the situation.

_____ 13. I understand the process people go through to meet their needs.

_____ 14. I know several content and process motivation theories and can use them to motivate people.

_____ 15. I can list and use motivation techniques.

_____ 16. I can identify behavioral leadership theories.

_____ 17. I can identify contingency leadership theories.

_____ 18. I know my preferred leadership style and how to change it to meet the needs of the situations.

_____ 19. I can describe transactional analysis.

_____ 20. I can identify the difference among aggressive, passive, and assertive behavior. I am assertive.

_____ 21. I can identify different conflict resolution styles. I understand how to resolve conflicts in a way that does not hurt relationships.

_____ 22. I can identify bases and sources of power. I know how to gain power in an organization.

_____ 23. I can list political techniques to increase success.

_____ 24. I can state the difference between Type I and Type II ethics.

_____ 25. I understand the roles and various types of groups in organizations.

_____ 26. I can help groups make better decisions through consensus.

_____ 27. I know when, and when not, to use employee participation in decision making.

_____ 28. I understand how to plan and conduct effective meetings.

_____ 29. I can identify components of group dynamics and how they affect behavior, human relations, and performance.

_____ 30. I know the stages groups go through as they develop.

_____ 31. I understand why people resist change and know how to overcome that resistance.

_____ 32. I can identify and use organizational development techniques.

_____ 33. I understand how to develop a positive organizational culture and climate.

_____ 34. I understand equal employment opportunity (EEO) and the rights of legally protected groups like minorities, handicapped, alcohol and drug addicts, and people with AIDS.

_____ 35. I can define sexism and sexual harassment in organizations.

_____ 36. I can handle a complaint using the complaint model.

_____ 37. I know how to increase performance.

_____ 38. I can list and describe various participation programs.

_____ 39. I understand total quality management (TQM).

_____ 40. I understand how to use a time management system.

_____ 41. I understand how to use time management techniques in order to get more done in less time with better results.

_____ 42. I know how to develop a career plan and manage my career successfully.

_____ 43. I understand how to plan for improved human relations.

To use the profile form, place an X in the box whose number corresponds to the score you gave each statement above.

Review your profile form. Your lower score numbers indicate areas where behavior changes are most warranted. Select the top five areas, abilities/skills, you want to develop through this course. Write them out below. In Chapter 6, we will discuss how to set objectives. At that time you may want to return to write what you wish to learn as objectives.

Learning Objective

5. Identify your personal low and high human relations ability/skill levels

1.

2.

3.

Learning Objective

6. Identify five personal human relations goals for the course

4.

5.

Skill-Building

1 – 1

As the course progresses, be sure to review your course goals, and work toward attaining them.

Profile Form

	Your Score							Parts and Chapters in Which the Information Will Be Covered in the Book
	1	2	3	4	5	6	7	
								Part I. Behavior, Human Relations, and Performance Begin with You
1.								2. Diversity in Personality, Learning, and Perception
2.								
3.								
4.								3. Diversity in Attitudes, Self-Concept, and Values
5.								
6.								
								Part II. Communication Skills: The Foundation of Human Relations
7.								4. Interpersonal Communication
8.								
9.								
10.								5. Organizational Structure and Communication
11.								
12.								
								Part III. Other Skills Influencing Behavior, Human Relations, and Performance
13.								6. Motivation
14.								
15.								
16.								7. Leadership
17.								
18.								
19.								8. Transactional Analysis, Assertiveness, and Conflict Resolution
20.								
21.								
								Part IV. Team Behavior, Human Relations, and Performance
22.								9. Power, Politics, and Ethics
23.								
24.								
25.								10. Teams and Creative Problem Solving and Decision Making
26.								
27.								
28.								11. Team Dynamics and Leadership
29.								
30.								

Profile Form (*concluded*)

	Your Score							Parts and Chapters in Which the Information Will Be Covered in the Book
	1	2	3	4	5	6	7	
								Part V. Organizational Changes
31.								12. Change: Managing Culture, Diversity, and Climate
32.								
33.								
34.								13. Valuing Diversity Globally
35.								
36.								
37.								14. Productivity, Technology, and Participative Management
38.								
39.								
								Part VI. Personal Development
40.								15. Time and Career Management
41.								
42.								
43.								Appendix A. Applying Human Relations Skills

Developing Human Relations Skills

Organizations recruit workers with good human relations skills.[22] Many people view human relations as just good common sense. If human relations is nothing more than common sense, why do organizations have so many human relations problems? Obviously, human relations is much more. Through gaining a better understanding of your behavior and that of others in organizations, you will be more skilled at interacting with people and better prepared to anticipate and eliminate human relations problems before they occur. As you develop your human relations skills, you will be better prepared to deal effectively with specific human relations problems. This skill is not a gimmick to give you power to manipulate people, and it will not offer simple solutions to the human relations problems you will face in organizations. People are complex and different, and the approach you use to solve a human relations problem with one person may not work with a different person.

This book gives you suggestions, guidelines, and models to follow. Although these guidelines do not guarantee success, they will increase your probability of successful human relations in organizations.

Human relations is one of the few courses you can use immediately. Most of the material you will learn can and should be used in your daily personal life with your family, friends, and other people with whom you interact. If you presently work, use the material on the job to develop your human relations skills.

WORK APPLICATIONS

6. Do you believe that you can and will develop your human relations abilities and skills through this course? Explain your answer.

Human Relations Guidelines

Are you the kind of person others enjoy being around? Find out by completing Self-Assessment Exercise 1–1 on page 13. Then read on.

Self-Learning
Exercise 1–1

Likability

Select the number 1 to 5 that best describes your use of the following behavior and write it on the line before each statement.

(5) Usually   (4) Frequently   (3) Occasionally   (2) Seldom   (1) Rarely

_____ 1. I'm an optimist. I look for the good in people and situations, rather than the negative.

_____ 2. I avoid complaining about people, things, and situations.

_____ 3. I show a genuine interest in other people. I compliment them on their success.

_____ 4. I smile.

_____ 5. I have a sense of humor. I can laugh at myself.

_____ 6. I make an effort to learn people's names and address them by name during conversations.

_____ 7. I truly listen to others.

_____ 8. I help other people cheerfully.

_____ 9. I think before I act and avoid hurting others with my behavior.

_____ 10. If I were to ask all the people I work/worked with to answer these nine questions for me, they would select the same responses that I did.

To determine your likability, add the 10 numbers you selected as your answers. The number will range from 10 to 50. Place it here _____ and on the continuum below.

Unlikable   10 -------- 20 -------- 30 -------- 40 -------- 50   Likable

If you want to get ahead in an organization, it is important to do a good job. But it is also important that people like you. If people like you, they will forgive just about anything you do wrong. If they don't like you, you can do everything right and it will not matter. Many hardworking, talented people have been bypassed for promotion and fired simply because their boss or some other high-level manager didn't like them. In fact, when Henry Ford fired Lee Iacocca, he used only four words to explain his decision: "I don't like you."

No one can tell you exactly how to be likable. People who try too hard are usually not well liked. However, in this section you will learn guidelines for being likable through successful human relations. The guidelines are based on the behavior of successful, likable people who possess human relations skills. They are general in nature and apply to most situations.

The nine human relations guidelines are: (1) be optimistic, (2) be positive, (3) be genuinely interested in other people, (4) smile and develop a sense of humor, (5) call people by name, (6) listen to people, (7) help others, (8) think before you act, and (9) create win-win situations.

Be Optimistic

We usually find what we're looking for. If you look for, and emphasize, the positive, you will find it. Optimists see opportunity in difficulty. If you catch yourself thinking or behaving like a pessimist, stop, and change to an optimistic thought or action. With time you will need to catch yourself less frequently. Most successful people are optimistic.

Be Positive

Praise and encourage people. People generally don't like to listen to others complain. Have you ever noticed that people ask each other "How is it going?" but if the other person starts complaining about something, they find an excuse for not listening. People often avoid complainers, and you should too. Associating with complainers will only depress you.

Don't go around criticizing (putting people down), condemning, or spreading rumors. Do you like people to criticize you even when it is called constructive criticism? Do you like people who go around complaining and criticizing? As a manager, you will be responsible for changing behavior, but it can be done in a positive way, rather than with negative criticism. You will learn how throughout the book.

Be Genuinely Interested in Other People

Think about the bosses you have had. Who was your favorite? Why? There is a good chance that this boss was genuinely interested in you as a person, not simply as a means of getting the job done. Think about your friends. One of the reasons you like them is that they show a genuine interest in you. One of the five main reasons managers fail is the "me only" syndrome. Managers who are preoccupied with themselves and too concerned with how much credit they get are insensitive to others. If people feel as though you don't care about them, they will not come through for you. Do you like self-centered people? Develop a network of people who support you.[23]

Smile and Develop a Sense of Humor

A smile shows interest and caring. It takes fewer muscles to smile than it does to frown. The old adage, "Smile and the world smiles with you; weep and you weep alone," has a lot of truth to it. You have probably noticed that frowners are usually unhappy and pessimistic.

Develop a sense of humor. Relax, laugh, and enjoy yourself. Be willing to laugh at yourself. Likable people do not take their job or themselves too seriously. Do you like people who always frown and never laugh?

Call People by Name

A person's name is the most important sound in any language. Calling people by the name they prefer shows an interest in them and makes them feel important. Bob, a recent college graduate, met an executive and about one month later met him again. The executive greeted him by saying, "Hello, Bob." Bob replied, "Hi, Jim," and kept walking, but he surely felt important; Bob would have done anything for Jim. If you're not good at remembering names, work at it. Like any skill, it takes a conscious effort and some practice to develop. One simple technique you can use to help you remember people's names when you are introduced is to call them by name two or three times while talking to them. Then call them by name the next time you greet them. If you forget a person's name, whenever possible, ask someone else what it is before contacting the person. Do you like to be called "Hey, you"? However, in some cultures it is not polite to call a person by their first name. In such a culture, use last names, titles, or positions as expected.

Listen to People

We learn more by listening than we do by talking. To truly listen we must honestly try to see things from the other person's point of view. Show respect for the other person's opinions. Don't say, "You're wrong," even when the other person is wrong. Such statements only make people defensive and cause arguments, which you should avoid. Saying you disagree has less of an emotional connotation to it. However, when you are wrong, admit it quickly and emphatically. Admitting you're wrong is not a sign of weakness and is often interpreted as a strength. However, not admitting you are wrong is often interpreted as a weakness.

Encourage others to talk about themselves. Ask them questions about themselves, rather than telling them about yourself. This gives you the opportunity to listen and learn while making people feel important. Listening also shows your interest in people. Do you like people who don't listen to you?

Help Others

If you want to help yourself, you can only do so by helping others. It's a basic law of success.[24] People who use people (by not helping them), may be somewhat successful in the short run, but those being used usually catch on. People who use other people are usually not successful in the long run. Open and honest relationships in which people help each other meet their needs are usually the best ones. Help others, but don't pry when it is not welcomed. Do you like people who don't help you when you need help?

Think before You Act

Learning Objective

7. Explain nine guidelines for effective human relations

Use good manners. Good manners are those personal qualities that make life at work more enjoyable. Be polite and say please and thank you.

Feel your emotions but control your behavior. Try not to do and say things you will regret later. Watch your language; don't offend people. It is not always what you say but how you say it that can have a negative impact on human relations. Before you say and do things, think about the possible consequences. Being right is not good enough if it hurts human relations. Conduct your human relations in a positive way.

Create Win-Win Situations

Goal of Human Relations

The goal of human relations is to create win-win situations. The best way to get what you want is to help other people get what they want and vice versa. Throughout the book you will be given specific examples of how to create win-win situations.

If Olin follows these nine human relations guidelines at IBM, he will increase his chances of success. If you follow these general guidelines, you too will increase your chances of success in all walks of life. These nine guidelines are just the starting point of what you will learn in this course. For a review of the nine guidelines to effective human relations, see Exhibit 1–5.

EXHIBIT 1–5   **NINE GUIDELINES TO EFFECTIVE HUMAN RELATIONS**

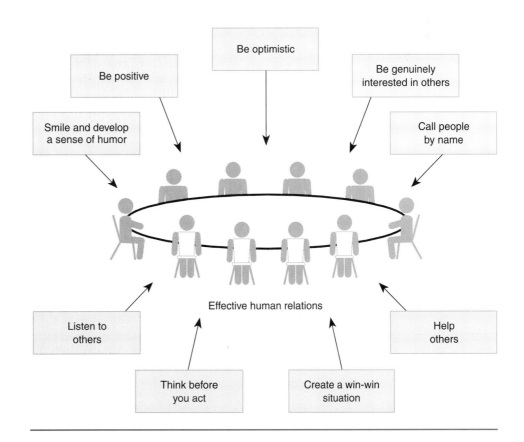

WORK APPLICATIONS

7. Which two of the nine human relations guidelines need the most effort on your part? The least? Explain your answers.

Handling Human Relations Problems

Even though you follow the human relations guidelines, in any organization there are bound to be times when you disagree with other employees.

Human relations problems often occur when the psychological contract is not met. The *psychological contract* is the shared expectations between people. At work you have expectations of the things your boss and coworkers should and should not do, and they in turn have expectations of you. As long as expectations are met, things go well. However, if expectations are not met, human relations problems exist. Thus, when people share information and negotiate expectations, have clear roles, and are committed to meeting others expectations, things go well. We'll focus on sharing information negotiating expectations throughout this book.

When you encounter any human relations problems, you have to decide whether to avoid the problem or to solve it. In most cases, it is advisable to solve human relations problems rather than ignore them. Problems usually get worse rather than solve themselves. When you decide to resolve a human relations problem, you have at least three alternatives:

1. Change the other person. Whenever there is a human relations problem, it is easy to blame the other party and expect them to make the necessary changes in their behavior to meet our expectations. In reality, few human relations problems can be blamed entirely on one party. Both parties usually contribute to the human relations problem. Blaming the other party without taking some responsibility usually results in resentment and defensive behavior. The more we force people to change to meet our expectations, the more difficult it is to maintain effective human relations.

2. Change the situation. If you have a problem getting along with the person or people you work with, you can try to change the situation by working with another person or other people. You may tell your boss you cannot work with so and so because of a personality conflict, and ask for a change in jobs. There are cases where this is the only solution; however, when you complain to the boss, the boss often figures that you, not the other party, are the problem. Blaming the other party and trying to change the situation enables us to ignore our behavior, which may be the actual cause of the problem.

3. Change yourself. Throughout this book, particularly Part I, you will be examining your own behavior. Knowing oneself is important to good human relations.[25] In many situations, your own behavior is the only thing you can control. In most human relations problems, the best alternative is to examine the other party's behavior and try to understand why they are doing and saying the things they are; then examine your own behavior to determine why you are behaving the way you are. In most cases, the logical choice is to change your own behavior. That does not mean doing whatever other people request. In fact, you should be assertive. We are not being forced to change; rather, we are changing our behavior because we elect to do so. When we change our behavior, the other party may also change.

In each chapter, there are one or more self-assessment instruments to help you better understand your behavior and that of others. It is helpful to examine behavior and to change it, when appropriate, not only throughout this course but throughout life.

8. Give a specific example of a human relations problem in which you elected to change yourself, rather than the other person or situation. Be sure to identify your changed behavior.

Human Relations: Past, Present, and Future

Human Relations Is a Multidisciplined Science

Human relations, more popularly called *organizational behavior*, is rooted in the behavioral sciences and was developed in the late 1940s. It is based primarily on psychology (which attempts to determine why individuals behave the way they do) and sociology (which attempts to determine how group dynamics affect organizational performance); social psychology, economics, and political science have also contributed to organizational behavior.

During the 1950s, research in human behavior was being conducted in large organizations. By the late 1970s, organizational behavior was being recognized as a discipline in its own right, with teachers, researchers, and practitioners being trained in organizational behavior itself. Organizational behavior is a social science that has built its knowledge base on a sound foundation of scientific theory and research. Human relations takes a practical applied approach. It attempts to anticipate and prevent problems before they occur and to solve existing problems of interpersonal relations in organizations.

The Early Years: Frederick Taylor and Robert Owen

In early America, most people worked on farms or were self-employed tailors, carpenters, shoemakers, or blacksmiths. Then, during the Industrial Revolution people left the farms to work in factories that were all privately owned. The corporation form of business did not become prominent until much later. These early family-run businesses were concerned with profits, not employees, and managers viewed people as only a source of production. They did not realize how workers' needs affected production. Since the labor supply was plentiful and the cost of labor low, they could easily replace employees who had complaints. In this situation, most of the early owner/managers gave little thought to the working conditions, health, or safety of their employees. Working conditions were very poor—people worked from dawn until dusk under intolerable conditions of disease, filth, danger, and scarcity of resources. They had to work this way just to survive; there was no welfare system—you worked or you starved.

Frederick Taylor   Frederick Taylor, an engineer known as the Father of Scientific Management, focused on analyzing and redesigning jobs more efficiently in the late 1800s and early 1900s, which led to the idea of mass production. Scientific managers focused on production, not people. They were not in touch with human behavior, assuming that workers always acted rationally and were motivated simply by money, which were later found to be false assumptions. Also, Taylor failed to recognize the social needs of employees and would place them in isolated jobs.

Robert Owen

Robert Owen, a young Welsh industrialist and social theorist, in 1800 was considered the first manager-entrepreneur to understand the need to improve the work environment and the employee's overall situation. In 1920, Owen was called "the real father" of personnel administration.[26] He believed that profit would be increased if the employees worked shorter hours, were paid adequately, and were provided with sufficient food and housing. He refused to employ children under the age of 11. (In the early 1800s, children went to work full-time at the age of nine.) Owen taught his employees cleanliness and temperance and improved their working conditions. Other entrepreneurs of this time period did not follow his ideas. Compared to today's conditions, Owen's were primitive—but it was a beginning.

Elton Mayo and the Hawthorne Studies

From the mid-1920s to the early 1930s, Elton Mayo and his associates from Harvard University conducted research at the Western Electric Hawthorne Plant near Chicago. The research conducted through the Hawthorne Studies has become a landmark in the human relations field. In fact, **Elton Mayo** *is called the "father of human relations."* As a consequence of these studies, several unexpected discoveries were made in regard to the human relations in organizations including:[27]

1. The Hawthorne effect. The **Hawthorne effect** *refers to an increase in performance caused by the special attention given to employees, rather than tangible changes in the work.* During the research, Mayo changed the lighting and ventilation. To his surprise, performance went up regardless of the working conditions. Through interviews, Mayo realized that the control group during the research felt important because of all the attention it got; therefore performance increased due to the special attention given to employees. It wasn't until Mayo discovered the Hawthorne effect that he extended his study. What was to last only a few months lasted six years. With the knowledge of the results of the Hawthorne Studies, some managers used human relations as a means of manipulating employees, while others took the attitude that a happy worker is a productive worker. Studies have shown that happy workers are not always more productive than unhappy workers. In this context, both approaches were unsuccessful at improving performance.

WORK APPLICATIONS

9. Give a specific example, personal if possible, of the Hawthorne effect. It could be when a teacher, coach, or boss gave you special attention that resulted in your increased performance.

---

2. Employees have many needs beyond those satisfied by money.

3. Informal work groups have a powerful influence within the organization. For example, work group members can band together and decide the level of production, regardless of management's standards, and influence the group to produce at that level. The group will pressure members who produce more or less than the group's established production rate.

4. Supervisor-employee human relations affects the quality and quantity of employee output. Employees who enjoy their relations with their boss are more productive than employees who do not like their boss. Having good human relations does not mean that a manager has to be popular. No relationship exists between popularity and the speed at which people are promoted to the top of the management ladder.

5. Many employee needs are satisfied off the job. Managers do not always control motivating factors of employees.

6. Employee relations affect employee performance. Employees meet social needs through their interactions with fellow employees. More recent research studies have shown that breaking up groups of interdependent members to form independent jobs actually caused a decrease in production, rather than the expected increase.

The 1930s to the 1970s

During the depression of the 1930s, unions gained strength and in many cases literally forced management to look more closely at the human side of the organization and meet employees' needs for better working conditions, higher pay, and shorter hours.

During the 1940s and 1950s, other major research projects were conducted in a number of organizations. Some of the research was conducted by the Research Center for Group Dynamics, University of Michigan, which conducted studies in leadership and motivation; the Personnel Research Board, Ohio State University, which also studied leadership and motivation; Tavistock Institute of Human Relations in London, which studied various subjects; and the National Training Laboratories in Bethel, Maine, which studied group dynamics.

During the 1960s, Douglas McGregor published Theory X, Theory Y.[28] A discussion of his theory, which contrasts the way managers view employees, appears in Chapter 3. In the same time period, Eric Berne introduced transactional analysis (TA).[29] (See Chapter 8 for a detailed discussion of TA.)

During the 1970s, the interest in human relations probably peaked. Books on self-improvement hit all-time highs in sales volume. Considerable research provided a better understanding of how to improve organizations and management. By the late 1970s, the term *human relations* was primarily replaced with the more commonly used term *organizational behavior*. Through the 1970s, as international competition increased, Americans looked to the competition for ways to increase performance.

The 1980s

In the 1980s, the U.S. rate of productivity was much lower than that of Japan. William Ouchi, who conducted research to determine why Japan was more productive than the United States, discovered that Japanese organizations were managed differently than U.S. organizations. Because of sociocultural, economic, and technological differences between the two countries, it was not feasible to implement the Japanese management style in the United States without modification. After studying several U.S. organizations, Ouchi discovered that a few particularly successful firms (including IBM, Hewlett-Packard, Eastman Kodak, and Procter & Gamble) did not follow the typical U.S. model. After years of research and investigation, Ouchi developed Theory Z.[30] **Theory Z** *integrates common business practices in the United States and Japan into one middle-ground framework appropriate for use in the United States.* Theory Z has been criticized for lack of scientific research. However, many organizations are implementing his suggestions, particularly collective decision making as a means of increasing employee participation in management.

In search of excellence, Peters and Waterman conducted research to determine the characteristics of successful organizations. Research identified the following:[31] (1) They have a bias for action; (2) they are close to the customer; (3) they use autonomy and entrepreneurship; (4) they attain high productivity through people; (5) they are hands-on and value-driven; (6) they stick to the knitting and do not diversify greatly; (7) they use a simple organization form with a lean staff; (8) they have simultaneous loose-tight properties. During the 1980s, Peters and Waterman's work was criticized as companies identified as excellent began to have problems. However, many organizations are implementing their suggestions, particularly techniques for increasing performance through people.

The 1990s

Learning Objective

8. Briefly describe the history of the study of human relations

In the 1990s, the trend toward increased participation of employees as a means of improving human relations and organizational performance continued. However, Edward Lawler suggested that the United States move from the participative management programs toward the use of high-involvement management, which includes greater levels of participation at the lowest level of the organization.[32] Employees will have more input into management decisions and how they perform their jobs. Employee participation will be discussed in Chapter 14.

APPLICATION SITUATIONS

Human Relations History

AS 1–3

Identify the following people with their contribution to human relations:

A. Eric Berne   C. William Ouchi   E. Tom Peters

B. Elton Mayo   D. Robert Owen   F. Frederick Taylor

_____ 11. Excellence in American corporations.

_____ 12. Theory Z.

_____ 13. Transactional analysis.

_____ 14. The father of personnel administration.

_____ 15. The Hawthorne Studies.

Trends and Challenges in the Field of Human Relations in the 21st Century

The rate of change has been increasing with each new decade.[33] Changes in the work environment have a direct impact on behavior, human relations, and organizational performance. In this section, we will discuss the challenges of the external environment, the changing work force, and technology.

External Environmental Forces

Organizations do not operate in a vacuum. What happens outside the organization affects employees' behavior, human relations, and organizational performance. Thus, the changing environment is of major concern to managers.[34] Some of the external trends, which we will talk about in more detail in later chapters, are as follows:

- **Globalization.** CEOs of 29 companies rated globalization as the number one challenge to business leadership in the 21st century.[35] Increasing international competition is changing the way we do business and industries consolidate.[36] The trend toward global competition will continue to increase.[37] As stated, customer and supplier human relations become increasing important.

- **Productivity, quality, and teams.** To compete globally, organizations have to increase productivity and the quality of their products and services.[38] To do so, organizations are reengineering, reorganizing, and downsizing.[39] Teams are being used to increase productivity and quality.[40] However, as teams increase productivity and quality, employees tend to get laid-off. There has been a large-scale reduction of managerial and professional jobs.[41] As the organization goes through these changes, human relations are strained.

- **Innovation and speed.** Through globalization, the need to develop innovative products and services and processes at a faster rate becomes more important to stay ahead of the competition.[42] Thus, risk taking becomes critical to success.[43] A firm that follows cannot be a leader. Human relations directly impact innovation and speed, as people who work well together as a team increase innovation and speed.

The Changing Workforce: Diversity

Diversity continues to be a major factor in the 21st century.[44] As the workforce continues to diversify, management can no longer expect employees to fit into the white male mold. How will working with a diverse work group affect your behavior and human relations? Below are just some of the diversity issues.

- **Minorities.** The percentage of minorities in the U.S. population and workforce has continued to grow. By the year 2030, it has been predicted that less than 50% of the U.S. population will be white. Working with a diversity of races/ethnicities is a human relations challenge for most people.

- **Aging.** The average age of the U.S. population continues to increase. The fastest-growing age group is age 50 and up baby boomers.[45] People are living longer and many also work longer.

- **Gender and work-family issues.** Women continue to want the same equal employment opportunities as men. The two-income marriage is now the norm. Male and female human relations are different.[46] However, both genders are very concerned about a balance of work and family.[47] In today's reengineered, reorganized, and downsized companies, the employees who remain are being asked to work longer hours, to work more days each week, and to maintain this pace for longer uninterrupted periods.[48] Thus, creating human relations problems at work and home as work-family conflicts continue to be a problem.[49]

Technology

Keeping up with technology as it changes the way we live and do business will become an even greater challenge in the 21st century.[50] Two important technology challenges include:

- **Internet revolution and e-business.** We have gone from the age of the personal computer (PC) to the Internet revolution. As technology goes wireless, PC networking is being replaced. People can now get on the Internet and get unlimited information and check their e-mail from their wireless cellular phones from anywhere in the world. Organizations are connected through the Internet in business-to-business (B2B) e(electronic)-business.[51] People and machines in different organizations order from one another and pay electronically. The Internet is changing the way we communicate, which affects our human relations.

- **The virtual office.** With the Internet, it is no longer necessary to have all employees in one facility. With the virtual office people in remote locations almost anywhere in the world, often at home or on the road, work as though they were in one place.

Learning Objective

9. State some of the trends and challenges in the field of human relations

Automation changes without regard to how these changes will affect human behavior and relations in organizations have caused increased human relations problems and have not resulted in the expected productivity gains. Balancing technology and human relations is necessary for maximum performance, and thus creates a real challenge for organizations. As stated, we will talk more about all these challenges in later chapters.

WORK APPLICATIONS

10. Explain how one of the trends or challenges does, or will, personally affect your human relations.

APPLICATION SITUATIONS

Trends and Challenges of Human Relations

AS 1–4

Identify the factor in each statement as:
A. External forces   B. Changing workforce   C. Technology

_____ 16. First we had to contend with the Japanese; now the Koreans and Chinese are serious competitors as well.

_____ 17. The number of immigrants employed is increasing because they are the only ones applying for the jobs.

_____ 18. Every time I look in the business section of the paper, it seems as though someone is coming out with a new or improved computer. How does one know which one to choose?

_____ 19. We had better do some training to help prevent getting charged with sexual harassment.

_____ 20. These kids today don't have the dedication to come to work, and on time, like we did when we were their age.

REVIEW

Select one or more methods: (1) fill in the missing key terms from memory; (2) match the key terms, from the end of the review, with their definitions below; and/or (3) copy the key terms in order from the key terms at the beginning of the chapter.

As was clearly stated, human relations skills are very important for success in organizations for the individual, group, and organization as a whole. _____ are interactions among people, while the _____ is to create a win-win situation by satisfying employee needs while achieving organizational objectives. A _____ occurs when the organization and employees get what they want. The _____ realizes that an organization employs the whole person, not just his or her job skills.

_____ is what people do and say. The three _____ include individual, group, and organizational. _____ are the things two or more people do and say as they interact (human relations). A(n) _____ is a group of people working to achieve an objective(s). _____ is the collective behavior of its individuals and groups. _____ is the extent to which expectations or objectives have been met. The _____, all people in the organization are affected by at least one other person, and each person affects the whole group/organization. This helps to explain the relationship among individual, group, and organizational performance.

You have assessed your human relations abilities and skills and have set some goals for the course. This book provides you with suggestions, guidelines, and models to help you develop your human relations skills. This course should help you develop your human relations abilities and skills through a better understanding of your behavior and that of others in organizations. You will be more skilled at interacting with people, better prepared to anticipate and eliminate human relations problems before they occur, and better prepared to deal effectively with specific human relations problems.

The nine human relations guidelines include: (1) be optimistic, (2) be positive, (3) be genuinely interested in other people, (4) smile and develop a sense of humor, (5) call people by name, (6) listen to people, (7) help others, (8) think before you act, and (9) create win-win situations. When faced with human relations problems, you can attempt to change the other person, change the situation, or preferably change yourself.

Human relations is a multidisciplined science based primarily on psychology and sociology, with social psychology, economics, and political science contributions as well. Robert Owen was considered the first manager-entrepreneur to understand the need to improve the human conditions at work. _____ is called the father of human relations, and conducted the Hawthorne Studies in the mid-1920s to the early 1930s, considered to be the first true human relations research. One of the outcomes of the studies was the understanding of the _____, which refers to an increase in performance due to the special attention given to employees, rather than tangible changes in the work. From the 1930s to the 1980s, several researchers conducted studies and offered theories. A few include McGregor—Theory X, Theory Y; Berne—Transactional Analysis; Ouchi— _____, which integrates common business practices in the United States and Japan into one middle-ground framework appropriate for use in the United States; and Peters and Waterman—excellence. Worker involvement will dominate the agenda of human resource issues for the 1990s as participative management increases.

Some of the many trends and challenges of human relations include a global economy, workforce diversity, and technology.

KEY TERMS

behavior 08	human relations 05	systems affect 11
Elton Mayo 22	levels of behavior 08	Theory Z 23
goal of human relations 05	organization 08	total person approach 06
group behavior 08	organizational behavior 08	win-win situation 05
Hawthorne effect 22	performance 10	

CASE

Al Scott—Wilson Sporting Goods

The Wilson Sporting Goods Humboldt, Tennessee facility was considered to be one of the least efficient plants within the corporation. The facility consistently lost money producing golf balls. Humboldt's lack of profitability was caused by major problems in the following areas: productivity, quality, cost, safety, morale, and housekeeping. The management employee attitude towards each other was its "us against them" mentality.

Al Scott, the plant manager, wanted to change the situation by solving these problems. He wanted Humboldt to make the best golf balls and have the most efficient production facilities in the world. To achieve the mission, Al developed the following five guiding philosophies, or what he wanted to become shared values: (1) employee involvement, (2) total quality management, (3) continuous improvement, (4) lowest total-cost manufacturing, and (5) just-in-time manufacturing.

Al held a meeting with groups of employees to tell them about the vision, mission, and values he wanted them to share. Everyone was asked to radically change the way of doing business. Al stressed the need to change from the old dictate management style to the new employee involvement style. Employees were called associates and empowered to find new solutions to old problems. Managers were trained in employee involvement management and through training developed skills to include employees in decision making, to develop teams, to develop better human relations, to coach employees, to better manage time, and to manage total quality. The old attitude of "we cannot do it or cannot afford to do it" was changed to "we can do it and we cannot afford NOT to do it."

To solve Humboldt's problems, Al instituted a voluntary employee participation program called Team Wilson. Teams of associates were developed to participate in problem solving. Teams focus on reducing operating expenses, increasing cash flow, reducing inventory, and improving safety and housekeeping. To ensure team success, all associates on teams were given similar training given to managers at the beginning of the change in process.

Within a few years, 66% of associates had formed voluntary teams. Each team represented a specific area of the plant. The teams created their own unique logo, T-shirt, and posters, which hang in the plant. Wilson holds several cookouts, picnics, and parties each year to show its appreciation to all associates. To recognize team accomplishments, three Team Wilson teams are chosen each quarter for awards that are presented by Al before the entire plant. The Humboldt facility dramatically increased performance in all five areas and productivity increased by over 100%. As a result, Humboldt was named one of the "Best Plants in America" by *Industry Week* magazine.

Go to the Internet: For more information on Al Scott and Wilson Sporting Goods and to update the information provided in this case, do a name search on the Internet and visit Wilson's web site at www.wilsonsports.com. For ideas on using the Internet with cases, see Appendix C.

Support your answers to the following questions with specific information from the case and text, or other information you get from the web or other source.

1. How important were Al Scott's human relations skills to changing Humboldt's performance from poor to excellent?

2. What role did effective human relations play throughout Wilson? Explain.

3. What level of behavior had the greatest impact on performance at Wilson?

4. Which two human relations guidelines did Al Scott primarily use to change behavior and human relations?

5. Which trends and challenges were the major concerns for Wilson?

6. What new information about Wilson Sporting Goods did you find on the Internet

Supervisor Susan's Human Relations

Peter has been working for York Bakery for about three months now. He has been doing an acceptable job until this week. Peter's supervisor Susan has called him in to discuss the drop in performance. (*Note:* Susan's meeting with Pete and/or a meeting held by Tim with Susan and Pete can be role-played in class.)

SUSAN: "Peter, I called you in here to talk to you about the drop in the amount of work you completed this week. What do you have to say?"

Peter: "Well, I've been having a personal problem at home."

Susan: "That's no excuse. You have to keep your personal life separate from your job. Get back to work and shape up or ship out."

Peter: (Says nothing, just leaves.)

Susan goes to her boss, Tim.

Susan: "Tim, I want you to know that I've warned Peter to increase his performance or he will be fired."

Tim: "Have you tried to resolve this without resorting to firing him?"

Susan: "Of course I have."

Tim: "This isn't the first problem you have had with employees. You have fired more employees than any other supervisor at York."

Susan: "It's not my fault if Peter and others do not want to do a good job. I'm a supervisor, not a baby-sitter."

Tim: "I'm not very comfortable with this situation. I'll get back to you later this afternoon."

Susan: "See you later. I'm going to lunch."

Answer the following questions. Then in the space between questions, state why you selected that answer.

_____ 1. There _____ a human relations problem between Susan and Pete.

a. is   *b.* is not

_____ 2. Susan has attempted to create a _____ situation.

a. lose-lose   *b.* win-lose   *c.* win-win

_____ 3. Susan _____ an advocate of the total person approach.

a. is   *b.* is not

_____ 4. Through the systems affect, Peter's decrease in output affects which level of behavior?

a. individual   *c.* organizational

b. group   *d.* all three levels

_____ 5. The scope of study illustrated in this case covers

a. behavior   *c.* performance

b. human relations   *d.* all three

_____ 6. The focus of study by Susan is

a. individual/behavior   *c.* group/human relations
b. individual/performance   *d.* organizational/performance

_____ 7. The focus of study by Tim should be

a. individual/behavior   *c.* group/human relations
b. group/behavior   *d.* organizational/performance

_____ 8. Later that afternoon Tim should

a. reprimand Pete
b. talk to Pete and tell him not to worry about it
c. bring Susan and Pete together to resolve the problem
d. do nothing, let Susan handle the problem herself
e. fire Susan

_____ 9. The major human relations skill lacking in Susan is

a. be optimistic
b. smile and develop a sense of humor
c. think before you act
d. be genuinely interested in other people

_____ 10. Tim _____ work with Susan to develop her human relations skills.

a. should   *b.* should not

11. Will Pete's performance increase? If you were Pete, would you increase your performance?

12. Have you ever had a supervisor with Susan's attitude? Assume you are in Susan's position. How would you handle Pete's decrease in performance?

13. Assume you are in Tim's position. How would you handle this situation?

The Evolution of Management

Critical Thinking Questions:

This video presents the evolution of management by dividing it into two major groups: classical approaches and contemporary approaches and then presents modern management theories.

1. What is the major similarity and difference between scientific management and human relations?

2. What is the difference between the contemporary quantitative approaches and organizational behavior?

3. What does systems theory thinking offer an organization as an approach to managing?

4. In general, how do classical approaches differ from contemporary approaches to management?

5. Why should managers today be concerned about globalization?

6. Why are managers more concerned about quality today than in the past?

7. Which management approaches will be the focus of this course?

INTERNET EXERCISES

The MG Webzine (IE 1–1)

Online Internet Exercise 1–1

The objective of this Internet exercise is to get you on the Net by visiting one website. Read Appendix B, Internet Exercises, at the back of this book. Remember to read Appendix B while using the computer so you can see what you are reading about. Use the information in Appendix B as you do the following:

1. *Go to the Management General (MG) website homepage.* All you need to do to get to the MG home page is to get on the web and type in *www.mgeneral.com* Click the full-screen icon for better viewing, and every time you visit. (Your instructor may ask you to print a copy of the home page and bring it to class.)

2. *Take the MG Tour.* Click "About Us" and scroll down to the maroon/brown box that says "Tour All MG—Just Like That!" Quickly read the tour. Write the one thing from the tour that is of most interest to you. (Your instructor may ask you type out the answer and bring it to class.) Press the back icon on the tool bar to return to About.

3. *About Us—Contact Information.* Read the about MG subsite. Write down the one thing from "About" that most impresses you. (Your instructor may ask you type out the answer and bring it to class.)

4. *Optional Favorites.* Set up a favorite from the homepage so that you can quickly get to it every time you do an MG exercise, or just to visit on your own. If you will be doing many of the *Fiscal Fairy Tales,* you may want to set up a favorite from its table of contents/chaplets for quick return.

5. *Surf the MG Subsites.* From the MG homepage, click the subsites and surf around to see the wealth of information available on the MG website.

In-Class Internet Exercise 1–1

The instructor simply asks the class if they found the MG website and answers any questions. The class may discuss the answers to Questions 2 and 3 using one of the six options in Appendix B page 589. The instructor states which Internet exercises students will be doing during the semester. The instructor may also discuss if students will be graded in any way for Internet exercises.

Search Engines (IE 1–2)

Online Internet Exercise 1–2

The objective of this Internet exercise is to get tips on using search engines to develop your search skills. Read Appendix B, Internet Exercises, at the back of this book. Remember to read Appendix B while using the computer so you can see what you are reading about. Use the information in Appendix B as you do the following:

1. Go to the homepage of the Search Engine Watch website— *www.searchenginewatch.com*

2. Click "first time visit."

3. Click "Web searching tips" and read the web search engine tips (your instructor may ask you to copy them).

4. Question: (1) What two–four tips for searching did you learn that you did not know or that can improve your searching skills? (Your instructor may ask you to type and print out your tips.)

In-Class Internet Exercise 1–2 and IE 1–3

The instructor simply asks the class if they found the Search Engine website and/or Internet tutorial and answers any questions. The class may discuss their tips using one of the six options in Appendix B page 589. The instructor states which Internet exercises students will be doing during the semester. The instructor may also discuss if students will be graded in any way for Internet exercises.

Internet Research Tutorial (IE 1–3)

The objective of this Internet exercise is to improve your Internet research skills. You can also find lots of free business information and company profiles. Using Appendix B information do as follows:

Online Internet Exercise 1–3

1. Go to the homepage of the Intellifact International website—*www.intellifact.com*

2. Click "Research" and find the "business research tutorial" through using search, or

3. Click Free Net Guides "select" and from the pop-down menu double-click "business research tutorial."

4. Question: (1) What two–four tips for researching did you learn that you did not know or that can improve your searching skills? (Your instructor may ask you to type and print out your tips.)

E-books—Fiscal Fairy Tales

An E-book is an electronic book on the Internet. Some E-books you have to pay for. The one we will be using, *Fiscal Fairy Tales,* is free.

Fiscal Fairy Tales.   *Fiscal Fairy Tales* (FFT) contains 12 traditional folk tales rewritten by Tom Brown with a humorous spin to stimulate your thinking and discussion about today's real work world. The second Internet Exercise in all but Chapters 4 and 11 is a FFT. You can read the original tale by clicking the option to do so. The tales are called chaplets, as they are short chapters of around four textbook pages for the actual tale. They are independent tales, so they can be read in any sequence and/or some can be skipped. Average readers can finish most of them in 10 minutes or so. All the other FFT exercises ask you read a tale and to write your response to the tale, and other questions that relate the concepts in the chaplet to the textbook chapter.

Online MG Webzine Exercise 1

Steps to Getting to Read a Fiscal Fairy Tale Online. MG Internet Exercises at the end of the chapters will tell you to go to a specific "chaplet" tale. Follow the steps below to get to the tale for each chapter.

1. Go to the MG homepage (you may want to set/use Favorites)— *www.mgeneral.com*

2. Click "E-Books" at the bottom of the homepage.

3. Click *"Fiscal Fairy Tales."*

4. Click "Go to Table of Contents."

5. Click the "chaplet title" you want to read, two places.

6. Scroll down for the overview of the tale and read it. It is not necessary to read any of the tales; you will read them as preparation for other chapters. For now, make sure you can find them and understand what they are. You can also copy a tale from within it using the print function, or you can download and print the entire book free of charge rather than continue to go back to the website.

In-Class MG Webzine Exercise 1

The instructor simply asks the class if they found the FFTs and answers any questions. The instructor states which tales, possibly all of them, students will be reading during the semester. The instructor may also discuss if students will be graded in any way for FFT.

SKILL-BUILDING EXERCISE 1–1

● **In-Class
Course Objectives**

Objective: To share your course objectives.

SCANS: The SCANS competencies of interpersonal skills and information and the foundations of basic, thinking, and personal qualities are developed through this exercise.

Experience: You will share your course objectives in small groups or with the entire class.

Preparation: You should have completed the self-assessment section of this chapter, including five written objectives.

*Procedure 1
(5–30 minutes)*

Option A: Volunteers state one or more of their course objectives to the class. The instructor may make comments.

Option B: Break into groups of three to six members and share your course objectives.

Option C1:   Same procedure as Option B with the addition of the group selecting a member to share five of the group's objectives.

Option C2:   Each group's spokesperson reports its five objectives.

Conclusion: The instructor leads a class discussion and/or makes concluding remarks.

Application (2–4 minutes):   Should I change any of my objectives? If yes, rewrite it/them below.

Sharing: Volunteers give their answers to the application section.

SKILL-BUILDING EXERCISE 1–2

● **In-Class
Human Relations**

Objectives:
1.   A. To get acquainted with the members of your permanent group and to name the group.

   B. To get acquainted with some of your classmates.

SCANS: The SCANS competencies of interpersonal skills and information and the foundations of basic, thinking, and personal qualities are developed through this exercise.

2.   To get to know more about your instructor.

   Preparation: None needed for this exercise.

   Experience: You will be involved in a small group discussion, and one person from each group will ask the instructor questions.

Procedure 1
(2–5 minutes)

A. Your instructor will assign you to your permanent group.

B. Break into groups of three to six, preferably with people you do not know, or do not know well.

Procedure 2
(8–12 minutes)

Each group member tells the others his or her name and two or three significant things about himself or herself. After all members have finished, ask each other questions to get to know each other better.

Procedure 3
(2–4 minutes)
Permanent groups only

Everyone writes down the names of all group members. Addresses and telephone numbers are also recommended.

Procedure 4
(2–3 minutes) All groups

Each person calls all members by name, without looking at written names. Continue until all members call the others by name.

Procedure 5
(5–10 minutes)
Permanent groups only

Members decide on a name for the group; a logo is optional.

Procedure 6
(5–12 minutes)

Elect a spokesperson to record and ask your group's questions. The members select specific questions to ask the instructor under the three categories below. The spokesperson should not identify who asked what questions.

1. Questions about course expectations. (What do you hope to learn or gain from this course?)

2. Questions about doubts or concerns about this course. (Is there anything about the course that you don't understand?)

3. Questions about the instructor. (What would you like to know about the instructor to get to know him or her?)

Procedure 7
(10–20 minutes)

Each spokesperson asks the group's question under one category at a time. When all questions from category 1 are asked and answered, proceed to category 2, then 3. Spokespersons should not repeat questions asked by other groups.

Questions (2–10 minutes): For the groups or class.

1. Is it important to know and call people by name? Why or why not?

2. What can you do to improve your ability to remember people's names when you first meet them, and at later times?

Conclusion: The instructor may make concluding remarks.

Application (2–4 minutes): What have I learned through this exercise? How will I use this knowledge in the future?

Sharing: Volunteers give their answers to the application section.

Diversity in Personality, Learning, and Perception

Learning Objectives

After completing this chapter, you should be able to:

1. Describe the Big Five personality dimensions.
2. Explain the benefits of understanding and identifying personality profiles.
3. Describe your stress personality type.
4. List causes of stress, and describe how to be more effective at controlling stress.
5. Describe the four learning styles and know which is your preferred learning style.
6. Explain how intelligence and learning styles affect behavior, human relations, and performance.
7. Describe five biases to perception.
8. Explain the importance of first impressions and how to project a positive image.
9. Define the following 19 key terms (in order of appearance in the chapter):

personality	**controlling**	**perception**
Type A personality	**stress plan**	**stereotyping**
Big Five model	**intelligence**	**perceptual**
of personality	**accommodators**	**congruence**
locus of control	**divergers**	**primacy effect**
stress	**convergers**	**four-minute barrier**
stressors	**assimilators**	**image**
burnout		

June Allyson was walking alone to the lunchroom. As she walked, she was thinking about her coworker, Rod Wills. June has trouble getting along with Rod because they are complete opposites. As June walked, two general thoughts came to her mind: Why does Rod do the things he does? Why are we so different? More specific questions came to mind: (1) We do the same job—why is he so stressed out and I'm not? (2) Why am I so emotional and interested in people—while Rod isn't? (3) Why am I so eager to get involved and help—while he sits back and watches? (4) Why is Rod so quiet—while I'm so outgoing? (5) Why do I dislike routine and detail so much—while Rod enjoys it so much? (6) Why does he believe that everything that happens is because of fate—while I don't? (7) When we have to agree on a decision, why is he so slow and analytical while I'm not? (8) Why is it that we see our jobs differently when they are the same? (9) When I first met Rod, I thought we would hit it off fine. Why was I so wrong?

Although June's questions have no simple answers, this chapter will give you a better understanding of behavioral differences. As the workplace becomes more diverse, it becomes increasingly important to understand what makes people different in order to work productively as a team. Personality, or personal style, makes people different yet similar in many ways. The amount of stress you experience depends, in part, on your personality type. Your intelligence affects your personality, and your learning style is based on personality traits. Your personality and intelligence influence your

perception, which, in turn, affects your first impressions of others. The better you understand how diverse people are, the more effective will be your human relations.

Personality

● Organization
● Group
● Individual

As June Allyson's dilemma illustrates, different people behave differently in their everyday lives. Personality, or personal style, is a very complex subject, yet in our daily lives we use trait adjectives like *warm, aggressive, easygoing,* and so forth, to describe people's behavior. Personality is the word commonly used to describe an individual's collection (total person) of such behavioral traits or characteristics. Personal style or **personality** *is a relatively stable set of traits that aids in explaining and predicting individual behavior.* Individuals are all different, yet similar, in many ways.

Substantial progress in the development of personality theory and traits has been made since the early 1980s.[1] In this section you will learn about traits and personality and the Big Five Model of personality. But first, complete Self-Assessment Exercise 2–1 to determine your personality profile. Throughout this chapter, you will gain a better understanding of your personality traits, which helps explain why you and others do the things you/others do (behavior).

**Self-Assessment
Exercise 2–1**

Personality Profile

There are no right or wrong answers, so be honest so that you will really increase your self-awareness. We suggest doing this exercise in pencil or making a copy before you write on it. We will explain why later.

Identify each of the 25 statements according to how accurately it describes you. Place the number 1–7 on the line before each statement.

Like me		Somewhat like me			Not like me	
7	6	5	4	3	2	1

_____ 1. I step forward and take charge in leaderless situations.

_____ 2. I am concerned about getting along well with others.

_____ 3. I have good self-control; I don't get emotional and get angry and yell.

_____ 4. I'm dependable; when I say I will do something, it's done well and on time.

_____ 5. I try to do things differently to improve my performance.

_____ 6. I enjoy competing and winning; losing bothers me.

_____ 7. I enjoy having lots of friends and going to parties.

_____ 8. I perform well under pressure.

_____ 9. I work hard to be successful.

_____ 10. I go to new places and enjoy traveling.

_____ 11. I am outgoing and willing to confront people when in conflict.

_____ 12. I try to see things from other people's point of view.

_____ 13. I am an optimistic person who sees the positive side of situations (the cup is half-full).

_____ 14. I am a well-organized person.

_____ 15. When I go to a new restaurant, I order foods I haven't tried.

_____ 16. I want to climb the corporate ladder to as high a level of management as I can.

_____ 17. I want other people to like me and to be viewed as very friendly.

_____ 18. I give people lots of praise and encouragement; I don't put people down and criticize.

_____ 19. I conform by following the rules of an organization.

_____ 20. I volunteer to be the first to learn/do new tasks at work.

_____ 21. I try to influence other people to get my way.

_____ 22. I enjoy working with others more than working alone.

_____ 23. I view myself as being relaxed and secure, rather than nervous and insecure.

_____ 24. I am considered to be credible because I do a good job and come through for people.

_____ 25. When people suggest doing things differently, I support them and help bring it about; I don't make statements like: it will not work, we never did it before, who else did it, or we can't do it.

To determine *your personality profile,* below (1) place the number 1–7 that represents your score for each statement. (2) Total each column—7–35. (3) Make a bar chart by placing the total score on the vertical bar. Each statement/column represents a specific personality dimension.

Surgency		Agreeableness		Adjustment		Conscientiousness		Openness to experience	
	35		35		35		35		35
_____ 1.	25	_____ 2.	25	_____ 3.	25	_____ 4.	25	_____ 5.	25
_____ 6.	20	_____ 7.	20	_____ 8.	20	_____ 9.	20	_____ 10.	20
_____ 11.	15	_____ 12.	15	_____ 13.	15	_____ 14.	15	_____ 15.	15
_____ 16.	10	_____ 17.	10	_____ 18.	10	_____ 19.	10	_____ 20.	10
_____ 21.	5	_____ 22.	5	_____ 23.	5	_____ 24.	5	_____ 25.	5
_____ Total Bar		_____ Total Bar		_____ Total Bar		_____ Total Bar		_____ Total Bar	

The higher the total number, the stronger is the personality dimension that describes your personality. What is your strongest and weakest dimension? Continue reading the chapter to find out the specifics of your personality in each of the five dimensions.

Personality Development

Why are some people outgoing and others shy, loud and quiet, warm and cold, aggressive and passive? This list of behaviors is made up of individual traits. *Traits* are distinguishing personal characteristics. Personality is developed based on genetics and environmental factors. The genes you received before you were born influence your personality traits.[2] Your family, friends, school, and work also influence your personality. In short, personality is the sum of genetics and a lifetime of learning. Personality, however, can be changed, with work. For example, people who are shy have become more outgoing.

There are many personality classification methods. One developed for leadership identifies 16 leadership personality types.[3] However, the Big Five Personality trait is the most widely accepted way to classify personalities because of its strong research support.[4]

Type A, Type B Personality

Before we discuss the Big Five, let's discuss one other popular classification that cuts across the Big Five—Type A and B. *The* **Type A personality** *is characterized as fast moving, hard driving, time conscious, competitive, impatient, and preoccupied with work.* The Type B personality is the opposite of Type A. The Type A personality is commonly associated with a high level of stress; thus it will be discussed more with stress in Part 2.

The Big Five Model of Personality

The purpose of the Big Five is to reliably categorize most, if not all, of the traits that you would use to describe someone else into one of five dimensions. Thus, each dimension includes multiple traits. **The Big Five Model of Personality** *categorizes traits into the dimensions of surgency, agreeableness, adjustment, conscientiousness, and openness to experience.* The dimensions are listed in Exhibit 2–1 and described below. However, the five dimensions have been published with slightly different descriptor names.[5]

EXHIBIT 2-1   **BIG FIVE DIMENSIONS OF TRAITS**

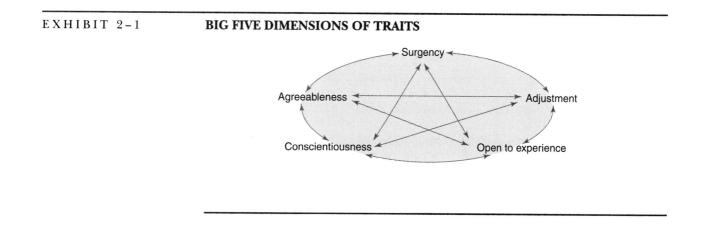

Surgency

The *surgency personality dimension* includes leadership and extraversion traits. (1) People strong in surgency, more commonly called dominance, personality traits want to be in charge. Their dominance behavior includes interest in getting ahead and leading through competing and influencing. People weak in surgency want to be followers, and they don't want to compete or influence. (2) Extraversion is on a continuum between extrovert and introvert. Extraverts are outgoing and like to meet new people and are willing to confront others, whereas introverts are shy. Review Self-Assessment statements 1, 6, 11, 16, and 21 for examples of surgency traits. How strong is your desire to be a leader?

Agreeableness

Unlike surgency behavior to get ahead of others, the *agreeableness personality dimension* includes traits related to getting along with people. Agreeable personality behavior is strong when called warm, easygoing, compassionate, friendly, and sociable or weak when called cold, difficult, uncompassionate, unfriendly, and unsociable. Strong agreeable personality types are sociable, spend most of their time with people, and have lots of friends. Review Self-Assessment statements 2, 7, 12, 17, and 22 for examples of agreeableness traits. How important is having good relationships to you?

Adjustment

The *adjustment personality dimension* includes traits related to emotional stability. Adjustment is on a continuum between being emotional stable and unstable. Stable refers to self-control, being calm—good under pressure, relaxed, secure, and positive—praise others; whereas unstable is out of control—poor under pressure, nervous, insecure, and negative—criticize others. Review Self-Assessment statements 3, 8, 13, 18, and 23 for examples of adjustment traits. How emotionally stable are you?

Conscientiousness

The *conscientiousness personality dimension* includes traits related to achievement. Conscientiousness is also on a continuum between responsible/dependable to irresponsible/undependable. Other traits of high conscientiousness include credibility, conformity, and organized. This trait is characterized as willing to work hard and put in extra time and effort to accomplish goals to achieve success. Review Self-Assessment statements 4, 9, 14, 19, and 24 for examples of conscientiousness. How strong is your desire to be successful?

Openness to experience

Learning Objective

1. Describe the Big Five personality dimensions.

The *openness to experience personality dimension* includes traits related to being willing to change and try new things. People strong in openness to experience seek change and try new things, while weak openness persons avoid change and new things. Review Self-Assessment statements 5, 10, 15, 20, and 25 for examples of openness to experience traits. How willing are you to try change and new things?

Another classification of personality types that fits under openness to experience is locus of control. **Locus of control** *is a continuum between an external and internal belief over who has control over one's destiny.* People with an external locus of control believe that they have little control over their performance and are closed to new experiences. Internalizers believe they are in control and are open to new experiences to improve performance.[6]

Personality Profiles

IE 2-1

Personality profiles identify individual stronger and weaker traits. Students completing Self-Assessment Exercise 2–1 tend to have a range of scores for the five dimensions. Review your personality profile. Do you have higher scores (stronger traits) and lower scores (weaker traits) on some dimensions?

WORK APPLICATIONS

1. Describe your Big Five personality profile.

APPLICATION SITUATIONS

Personality Dimensions

AS 2–1

Identify each of the five traits/behaviors by its personality dimension.

a. surgency   b. agreeableness   c. adjustment   d. conscientiousness   e. openness to experience

_____ 1. The manager is influencing the follower to do the job the way the leader wants it done.

_____ 2. The sales rep passed in the monthly expense report on time as usual.

_____ 3. The leader is saying a warm friendly good morning to followers as they arrive at work.

_____ 4. The leader is seeking ideas from followers on how to speed up the flow of work.

_____ 5. As a follower is yelling a complaint, the leader calmly explains what went wrong.

How Personality Affects Behavior, Human Relations, and Performance

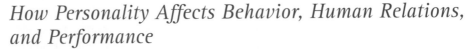

Performance
Human Relations
Behavior

Understanding people's personalities is important because personality affects behavior, as well as perceptions and attitudes.[7] Personality types also affect human relations[8] and retaliation.[9] People with similar personality types tend to get along well at work, while opposites don't, however, there are many exceptions. Think about the people you enjoy being with the most at school and work.

Are their personalities similar to or different from yours? Knowing personalities can also help you to explain and predict others job performance.[10] So-called personality conflicts can have negative effects on behavior, human relations, and performance.[11]

Recall June's six question about why she and Rod are so different. A major reason is they have different personalities that affect their behavior, human relations, and performance. June has a Type B personality while Rod has Type A. June is a surgency extrovert while Rod is an introvert. Not surprisingly, June has a higher agreeableness personality dimension than Rod. They may both be similar on the adjustment and conscientiousness personality dimension. June is an internalizer and more open to experience than Rod who is an externalizer.

Personality profiles are used to categorize people as a means of predicting job success. Some personality characteristics are more productive than others.[12] Conscientiousness is a good predictor of performance, but it's not the only dimension. Many organizations (including Sears and the National Football League teams the Giants, 49ers, and Dolphins)[13] give personality tests to ensure a proper match between the worker and the job.[14] For example, a study revealed that engineers' and accountants' personality profiles tended to be lower in the trait of surgency but higher in the trait of conscientiousness. Marketing and salespeople were lower in conscientiousness but higher on surgency.[15]

As you know, people are complex, and identifying a person's personality type is not always easy. Many people are in the middle of the continuum, rather than clearly at the ends. However, understanding personality can help you to understand and predict behavior, human relations, and performance in a given situation.

Improving Behavior, Human Relations, and Performance

Before you interact with another person, ask yourself questions like:

- What type of personality does the other person (or people) have?
- How are they likely to behave in this situation during our interaction?
- How can I create a win-win situation?
- Is there anything I should or should not do to make this interaction successful? (You may want to behave differently with different people. For example, with a formal personality type, it may be best to be formal as well, even if your personal style is informal.)

After such encounters, ask yourself questions like these:

- Was my assessment of the other person's personality correct?
- Did the other person behave as I predicted? If not, how was my assessment incorrect?
- Did I create a win-win situation?
- Did my behavior help the relations and should I continue it with this person?
- Did my behavior hurt the relations and should I discontinue it with this person?

Learning Objective

2. Explain the benefits of understanding and identifying personality profiles.

WORK APPLICATION

2. Select a present or past boss and describe how his or her personality profile affected behavior, human relations, and performance in your department.

The Big Five Has Universal Application across Cultures

Studies have shown that people from Asian, Western European, Middle Eastern, Eastern European, and North and South American cultures seem to use the same five personality dimensions. However, some cultures do place varying importance on different personality dimensions. Overall, the best predictor of job success on a global basis is the conscientiousness dimension.[16]

● Organization
● Group
● Individual

Stress

Stress-related claims are the fastest-growing segment of the Workers' Compensation System.[17] People are almost as likely to skip work because of stress as they are because of physical illness.[18] Today white-collar occupations have a higher stress rate than blue-collar jobs.[19] This is partly because of technology changes that cause stress. Technology stress is called techno stress, and we discuss it in Chapter 14 with technology. In this section, we will discuss what stress is, problems associated with stress, causes of stress, stress as it relates to Type A and Type B personalities, signs of stress, and how to control stress.

What Is Stress?

People react to external stimuli internally. **Stress** *is an emotional and/or physical reaction to environmental activities and events.*

The Positive Side (eustress)

Some stress helps improve performance by challenging and motivating us. Many people perform best under some pressure. When deadlines are approaching, their adrenaline flows and they rise to the occasion with top-level performance. In order to meet deadlines, managers often have to apply pressure to themselves and their employees. However, too much stress is often harmful to the individual and to the organization.

Situations in which too much pressure exists are known as stressors. **Stressors** *are situations in which people feel anxiety, tension, and pressure.* Stressors are events and situations to which people must adjust, and the impact of the stressor and how people react depend on the circumstances and on each person's physical and psychological characteristics. Stress is an individual matter. In a given situation one person may be very comfortable while another feels stress. For example, riding on a bus or plane is a stressor for some, but not for everyone. Too much stress over an extended period of time can have negative consequences, which will be discussed next.

Problems Associated with Too Much Stress

Stress was labeled the illness of the eighties, and it is still a major problem as corporate downsizing requires employees to increase their job responsibilities. Too much stress affects personal health, morale, productivity, organizational efficiency, absenteeism, medical costs, and profitability.[20]

Stress also causes physical illness. It has been linked to heart problems, ulcers, asthma, diabetes, multiple sclerosis, cancer, and other maladies. Three-fourths of the visits to family doctors are because of stress. Stress may lead to alcohol and drug problems and even suicide. Mental stress is increasingly a reason for calling in sick,[20] and stress can be blamed for about 21 percent of all headaches.[21]

Causes of Stress

Employees with little control over their work environment are more stressed.[22] There are four common stressors related to work: personality type, organizational climate, management behavior, and the degree of job satisfaction. Complete the questionnaire in Self-Assessment Exercise 2–2 to determine your personality type as it relates to stress.

**Self-Assessment
Exercise 2–2**

Stress Personality Types

Below are 20 statements. Identify how frequently each item applies to you:

(5) Usually   (4) Often   (3) Occasionally   (2) Seldom   (1) Rarely

Place the number 1, 2, 3, 4, or 5 on the line before each statement.

_____ 1. I work at a fast pace.

_____ 2. I work on days off.

_____ 3. I set short deadlines for myself.

_____ 4. I enjoy work/school more than other activities.

_____ 5. I talk and walk fast.

_____ 6. I set high standards for myself and work hard to meet them.

_____ 7. I enjoy competition, I work/play to win; I do not like to lose.

_____ 8. I skip lunch or eat it fast when there is work to do.

_____ 9. I'm in a hurry.

_____ 10. I do more than one thing at a time.

_____ 11. I'm angry and upset.

_____ 12. I get nervous or anxious when I have to wait.

_____ 13. I measure progress in terms of time and performance.

_____ 14. I push myself to the point of getting tired.

_____ 15. I take on more work when I already have plenty to do.

_____ 16. I take criticism as a personal put-down of my ability.

_____ 17. I try to outperform my coworkers/classmates.

_____ 18. I get upset when my routine has to be changed.

_____ 19. I consistently try to get more done in less time.

_____ 20. I compare my accomplishments with others who are highly productive.

_____ Total. Add up the numbers (1–5) you have for all 20 items. Your score will range from 20 to 100. Below place an X on the continuum that represents your score.

Type A 100 _____ 80 _____ 60 _____ 40 _____ 20 Type B
                  A   A–   B+   B

The higher your score the more characteristic you are of the Type A stress personality. The lower your score the more characteristic you are of the Type B stress personality. An explanation of these two stress personality types follows.

Personality Types

Learning Objective

3. Describe your stress personality type

The degree to which stressors affect us is caused, in part, by our personality type. Since stress comes from within, the things we do can cause us stress. The Type A personality is characterized as fast moving, hard driving, time conscious, competitive, impatient, and preoccupied with work. The Type B personality is the opposite of Type A. The 20 statements of Self-Assessment Exercise 2–2 relate to the personality types. People with Type A personalities have more cardiovascular disorders over time than people with Type B personalities.[23] If you score 60 or above, you have a Type A personality and could end up with some of the problems associated with stress. Also, external personality types are more stressful than internal ones.

WORK APPLICATIONS

3. What was your stress personality type score and letter? Should you work at changing your personality type? Explain why or why not. Will you change?

Organizational Climate

The amount of cooperation, motivation, and morale affects stress levels. The more positive the organizational climate, the less stress there is.

Management Behavior

Calm, participative management styles produce less stress. Tight control through autocratic management tends to create more stress. About 70 percent of workers said bosses are the cause of stress.[24] Some bosses use awful behavior,[25] some are even abusive,[26] and have caused stress to the point of driving employees to quit their jobs.[27]

Degree of Job Satisfaction

People who enjoy their jobs and derive satisfaction from them handle stress better than those who do not. In some cases, a change of jobs is a wise move that can lower or rid one of stressors.

Signs of Stress

Some of the mild signs of stress are an increase in the rate of breathing and increased amounts of perspiration.

When you continually look at the clock and/or calendar and feel pressured and fear that you will not meet a deadline, you are experiencing stress.

When stress continues for a period of time, it tends to lead to disillusionment, irritableness, headaches and other body tension, the feeling of exhaustion, and stomach problems. Drinking, taking drugs, eating, or sleeping more than usual, is often a means of escaping stress.

People often lose interest in and motivation to do their work because of stress. Stress that is constant, chronic, and severe can lead to burnout over a period of time. **Burnout** *is the constant lack of interest and motivation to perform one's job because of stress.* People sometimes experience temporary burnout during busy periods, as is the case with students studying for exams and retailers trying to cope with Christmas. However, when things slow down again, the interest and motivation come back. When the interest and motivation do not return, permanent burnout has occurred.

The use of stress-controlling techniques can often prevent stress and burnout.

Controlling Stress

Controlling stress is the process of adjusting to circumstances that disrupt or threaten to disrupt a person's equilibrium. Ideally, we should identify what causes stress in our lives and eliminate or decrease it. We can better control stress by following a three-stage plan. The **controlling stress plan** *includes step 1, identify stressors; step 2, determine their causes and consequences; and step 3, plan to eliminate or decrease the stress.* Employees often require coaxing to watch their stress/health.[28] Below are five ways in which you can help eliminate or decrease stress.

Exercise

Physical exercise is an excellent way to release tension. Many people find that exercising helps increase their ability to handle their jobs. Unfortunately, the popularity of exercising decreased in the 1990s.

Aerobic exercise, which increases the heart rate and maintains it for 20 to 30 minutes, three or more days per week is generally considered the best type of exercise. Exercises like fast walking or jogging, biking, swimming, and aerobic dance also fall in this category. Other exercises that require you to increase your heart rate, but not maintain it for 20 or more minutes, include sports like racquetball, tennis, and basketball, which are also beneficial.

Before starting an exercise program, however, check with a doctor to make sure you are able to do so safely. Start gradually and slowly work your way up to 20 to 30 minutes.

Nutrition

Good health is essential to everyone, and nutrition is a major factor in one's health. Since being overweight is stressful, you should watch how you eat and what you eat.[29]

Breakfast is considered the most important meal of the day. A good breakfast gets you off to a good start. When you eat, take your time because rushing is stressful and can cause stomach upset.

Try to minimize your intake of junk food containing high levels of salt and sugar. Consume less fat, salt, caffeine (coffee, tea, cola), alcohol, and drugs. Eat and drink more natural foods like fruits and vegetables and drink plenty of water.

Relaxation

Get enough rest and sleep. Slow down and enjoy yourself. Have some off-the-job interests that are relaxing. Have some fun, and laugh. Some of the things you can do to relax include prayer, meditation, music, reading, TV, movies, hobbies, and so forth.

When you feel stress, you can perform some simple relaxation exercises.[17] One of the most popular and simplest is deep breathing. You simply take a deep breath, hold it for a few seconds (you may count to five), then let it out slowly. If you feel tension in one muscle, you may do a specific relaxation exercise; or you may relax your entire body going from head to toe, or vice versa. For a list of relaxation exercises that can be done almost anywhere, see Exhibit 2–2.

EXHIBIT 2–2

RELAXATION EXERCISES

Muscles	Tensing Method
Forehead	Wrinkle forehead. Try to make your eyebrows touch your hairline for 5 seconds. Relax.
Eyes and nose	Close your eyes as tightly as you can for 5 seconds. Relax.
Lips, cheeks, jaw	Draw corners of your mouth back and grimace for 5 seconds. Relax.
Neck	Drop your chin to your chest, then slowly rotate your head in a complete circle in one direction and then in the other. Relax.
Hands	Extend arms in front of you; clench fists tightly for 5 seconds. Relax.
Forearms	Extend arms out against an invisible wall and push forward with hands for 5 seconds. Relax.
Upper arms	Bend elbows. Tense biceps for 5 seconds. Relax.
Shoulders	Shrug shoulders up to your ears for 5 seconds. Relax.
Back	Arch your back off the floor or bed for 5 seconds. Relax.
Stomach	Tighten your stomach muscles for 5 seconds. Relax.
Hips, buttocks	Tighten buttocks for 5 seconds. Relax.
Thighs	Tighten thigh muscles by pressing legs together as tightly as you can for 5 seconds. Relax.
Feet	Flex your feet up toward your body as far as you can for 5 seconds. Relax.
Toes	Curl toes under as tightly as you can for 5 seconds. Relax.

Positive Thinking

Be optimistic and think positively.[30] Make statements to yourself in the affirmative,[31] such as "I will do it." Be patient, honest, and realistic. No one is perfect. Admit your mistakes and learn from them; don't let them get you down. Have self-confidence; develop your time management skills (as discussed in Chapter 15). Don't procrastinate or be a perfectionist.

Support System

Learning Objective

4. List causes of stress, and describe how to be more effective at controlling stress

We all need people we can depend upon. Have family and friends you can go to for help with your problems.[32] Having someone to talk to can be very helpful but don't take advantage of others and use stress to get attention.

For an illustration of the causes of stress and how to control it, see Exhibit 2–3.

If you try all of the stress-controlling techniques and none of them work, you should seriously consider getting out of the situation. If you are experiencing permanent burnout, you should ask yourself two questions: Am I worth it? and Is it worth dying for? If you answered yes and no to these two questions, a change of situation/job is advisable.

EXHIBIT 2–3   **CAUSES OF STRESS AND HOW TO CONTROL STRESS**

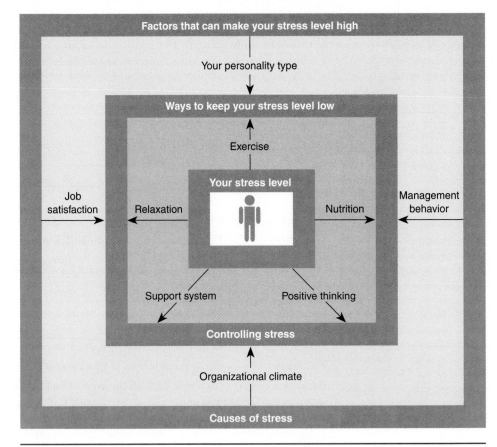

WORK APPLICATIONS

4. Following the controlling stress plan, (1) identify your major stressor, (2) determine its cause and consequences, and (3) develop a plan to eliminate or decrease the stress. Identify each step in your answer.

5. Of the five ways to eliminate or decrease stress, which do you do best? Which needs the most improvement and why? What will you do, if anything, to improve in this area?

■ Performance
■ Human Relations
■ Behavior

How Stress Affects Behavior, Human Relations, and Performance

Some stress helps performance. However, when people are under too much stress, they tend to be emotional, causing changes in their behavior, like being irritable, impatient, aggressive, and hostile. When a normally calm person begins to yell at others, human relations often suffer. Stress often affects people's thinking and decreases their ability to perform.

APPLICATION SITUATIONS

Stressors

AS 2–2

Identify each stressor as:

A. Personality type   C. Management effectiveness

B. Organization climate   D. Job satisfaction

_____ 6. The morale in our department is poor.

_____ 7. This job is OK, I guess.

_____ 8. I'm always racing against the clock.

_____ 9. Our priorities keep changing from week to week. It is very confusing when you're not sure what's expected of you.

_____ 10. I work at a comfortable pace.

● Organization
● Group
● Individual

Intelligence and Learning

Many organizations view intellectual excellence as the key to their success.[20] However, nearly two-thirds of managers and workers surveyed said their companies do not use more than half their employees' brainpower.[21] This section discusses the development of intelligence, learning styles, how intelligence affects behavior, human relations, organizational performance, and about learning organizations.

Intelligence

There are numerous theories of intelligence, many of which view intelligence as the ability to learn and involve cognitive processes. For our purposes we will say that **intelligence** *is the level of one's capacity for new learning, problem solving, and decision making.* Today it is generally agreed that intelligence is a product of both genetics and the environment. Most scientists today believe there are at least two and perhaps as many as seven or more different components or kinds of intelligence.[33]

People often perform at different levels for different tasks. As you know, you are good at doing some things (math, tennis, etc.) and not as good at doing others (biology, writing, etc.). For example, a person with a low IQ of 80 may be able to tune an engine while a person with a high IQ of 130 may not. Therefore, people have multiple intelligences, two of which (interpersonal and intrapersonal) involve working with people.[34]

Intelligence is a strong predictor of many important outcomes in life, such as educational and occupational attainment.[35] Microsoft values intelligence over all other qualifications for all jobs.[36] Cofounder and CEO Bill Gates advice to you is to take advantage in college to learn how to learn.[37] The more independent you are, the greater is your chance of success. Managers today are so busy that they often don't spend much time training employees. They expect you to be able to catch on quickly and learn on your own. Although learning new things can cause anxiety,[38] in this fast-changing global environment, if you don't keep up you will be left behind.

Learning Styles

Our capacity to learn new things is an important aspect of our intelligence. However, we do not all learn things in exactly the same way. We will examine four styles people use when learning.[39] Before we describe the four styles, determine your preferred learning style. Complete Self-Assessment Exercise 2–3 before reading on.

Self-Assessment
Exercise 2–3

Learning Styles

Below are 10 statements. For each statement distribute 5 points between the A and B alternatives. If the A statement is very characteristic of you, and the B statement is not characteristic of you, place a 5 on the _____ A. line and a 0 on the _____ B. line. If the A statement is characteristic of you and the B statement is occasionally or somewhat characteristic of you place a 4 on the _____ A. line and a 1 on the _____ B. line. If both statements are characteristic of you place a 3 on the line which is most characteristic of you and a 2 on the line which is less characteristic of you. Be sure to distribute 5 points between each A and B alternative for each of the 10 statements. When distributing the five points, try to recall recent situations on the job or in school.

1. When learning:

    _____ A. I watch and listen.

    _____ B. I get involved and participate.

2. When learning:

    _____ A. I rely on my hunches and feelings.

    _____ B. I rely on logical and rational thinking.

3. When making decisions:

    _____ A. I take my time.

    _____ B. I make them quickly.

4. When making decisions:

    _____ A. I make them based on my "gut feelings" about the best alternative course of action.

    _____ B. I make them based on a logical analysis of the situation.

5. When doing things:

    _____ A. I am careful.

    _____ B. I am practical.

6. When doing things:

    _____ A. I have strong feelings and reactions.

    _____ B. I reason things out.

7. I would describe myself in the following way:

    _____ A. I am a reflective person.

    _____ B. I am an active person.

8. I would describe myself in the following way:

    _____ A. I am influenced by my emotions.

    _____ B. I am influenced by my thoughts.

9. When interacting in small groups:

    _____ A. I listen, watch, and get involved slowly.

    _____ B. I am quick to get involved.

10. When interacting in small groups:

    _____ A. I express what I am "feeling."

    _____ B. I say what I am "thinking."

**Self-Assessment
Exercise 2–3** *continued*

Scoring: Place your answer numbers (0–5) on the lines below. Then add the numbers in each column vertically. Each of the four columns should have a number between 0 and 25. The total of the two A and B columns should equal 25.

1. _____ A. _____ B.   (5)   2. _____ A. _____ B.   (5)

3. _____ A. _____ B.   (5)   4. _____ A. _____ B.   (5)

5. _____ A. _____ B.   (5)   6. _____ A. _____ B.   (5)

7. _____ A. _____ B.   (5)   8. _____ A. _____ B.   (5)

9. _____ A. _____ B.   (5)   10. _____ A. _____ B.   (5)

Totals   _____ A. _____ B.   (25)   _____ A. _____ B.   (25)

Style   Observing Doing   Feeling Thinking

There is no best or right learning style; each of the four learning styles has its pros and cons. The more evenly distributed your scores were between the As and Bs, the more flexible you are at changing styles. Understanding your preferred learning style can help you get the most from your learning experiences.

Determining your preferred learning style. The five odd-numbered statement As refer to your self-description as being "observing," and the Bs refer to your self-description as "doing." The column with the highest number is your preferred style of learning. Write it below:

I described myself as preferring to learn by _____.

The five even-numbered statement As refer to your self-description as being a "feeling" person, and the Bs refer to your self-description as being a "thinking" person. The column with the highest number is your preferred style. Write it below:

I described myself as preferring to learn by _____ .

Putting the two preferences together gives you your preferred dimension of learning. Check it off below:

_____ Accommodator (combines doing and feeling)

_____ Diverger (combines observing and feeling)

_____ Converger (combines doing and thinking)

_____ Assimilator (combines observing and thinking)

Exhibit 2–4 illustrates the four learning styles.

EXHIBIT 2–4   **THE FOUR LEARNING STYLES**

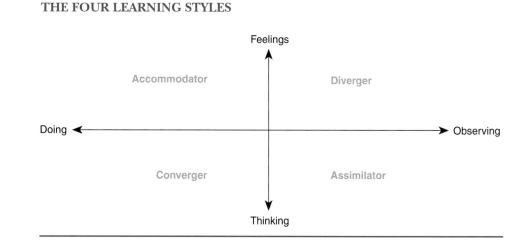

As stated above, people learn based on two personality dimensions or types—feeling versus thinking and doing versus observing. Even though people have a preferred learning style, they cannot always use it. For example, the accommodator and converger prefer to learn by active involvement rather than by observing, while the diverger and assimilator prefer to observe rather than to be actively involved. In this course, you probably don't determine how the instructor will teach it. If the instructor spends more time in class discussion and skill-building exercises, the accommodators and convergers will be enjoying their preferred learning style and using their feelings or thoughts when being actively involved. On the other hand, if the instructor spends more class time lecturing on the material and showing films, the diverger and assimilator will be using their preferred learning style, while emphasizing feelings or thinking. Your instructor's preferred learning style will most likely influence the way he or she teaches this course. For example, the author of this book is a converger, which influenced his writing the book with a skill-building approach that includes more emphasis on thinking than on feelings and on doing more than observing.

Below, you will learn the basic characteristics of each style and the pros and cons associated with each style.

Accommodator

People who are **accommodators** *prefer learning by doing and feeling*.

Characteristics: Accommodators tend to learn primarily from hands-on experience. They tend to act on gut feelings rather than on logical analysis. When making decisions, they tend to rely more heavily on people for information than on their own technical analysis. Accommodators enjoy carrying out plans and enjoy involvement in new and challenging experiences. They often seek action-oriented careers such as marketing, sales, politics, public relations, and management.

Pros: Accommodators are usually good leaders, they are willing to take necessary risks, and they get things done.

Cons: Accommodators do not always set clear goals and develop practical plans. They often waste time on unimportant activities.

Diverger

People who are **divergers** *prefer learning by observing and feeling*.

Characteristics: Divergers have the ability to view concrete situations from many different points of view. When solving problems, they enjoy brainstorming. They take their time and analyze many alternatives. They tend to have broad cultural interests and like to gather information. Divergers are imaginative and sensitive to the needs of other people. They often seek careers in the arts, entertainment, and the service sector, and jobs in design, social work, nursing, consulting, and personnel management.

Pros: Divergers tend to be imaginative and are able to recognize problems. They brainstorm and understand and work well with people.

Cons: Divergers tend to overanalyze problems and are slow to act. They often miss opportunities.

Converger

The **convergers** *prefer learning by doing and thinking*.

Characteristics: Convergers seek practical uses for information. When presented with problems and making decisions, they tend to focus on solutions. Convergers tend to prefer dealing with technical tasks and problems rather than with social and interpersonal issues. They often seek technical careers in various science fields and work at engineering, production supervision, computer, and management jobs.

Pros: Convergers are usually very good at deductive reasoning, solving problems, and decision making.

Cons: Convergers tend to make hasty decisions without reviewing all the possible alternatives, and they have been known to solve the wrong problems. They often use their ideas without testing them first.

Assimilator

Assimilators *prefer learning by observing and thinking.*

Characteristics: Assimilators are effective at understanding a wide range of information and putting it into concise, logical form. It is more important to them that an idea or theory is logical than practical. They tend to be more concerned with abstract ideas and concepts than with people. Assimilators tend to seek careers in education, information, and science and jobs as teachers, writers, researchers, and planners.

Pros: Assimilators are skilled at creating models and theories and developing plans.

Cons: Assimilators tend to be too idealistic and not practical enough. They often repeat mistakes and have no sound basis for their work.

Learning objective

5. Describe the four learning styles and know which is your preferred learning style

After reading about the four learning styles, you should realize that there is no best learning style; each has its own pros and cons. You probably realize that you have one preferred learning style, but you also have characteristics of other styles as well. To verify your preferred learning style, you may have people who know you well fill out the self-assessment exercise as it relates to you, or have them read the four learning styles and select the one they believe is most characteristic of you.

In the next part of this section, you will learn how learning styles affect behavior, human relations, and organizational performance.

WORK APPLICATIONS

6. What is your preferred learning style? Are the characteristics of the style a good description of you? Explain. Can you change your learning style?

APPLICATION SITUATIONS

Learning Styles

AS 2–3

Identify the learning style of the people by the statement made about them.

A. Accommodator   C. Converger

B. Diverger   D. Assimilator

_____ 11. The reason I don't like to work with Wendy is that she is slow to make decisions, and she keeps analyzing the problem to death.

_____ 12. Auto repair is a good job for Lou Ann because she enjoys fixing things and solving problems.

_____ 13. I don't want Ted on the committee because he is a daydreamer. We can't use his ideas on the job.

_____ 14. Ken doesn't use any standard approach like I do when selling. Ken says he "feels" the customer out, then decides his approach.

_____ 15. Identify which style would be most likely to have made the comment about Ted in situation number 13.

The Learning Organization

Recall from Chapter 1 the organization's need for innovation and speed to be competitive in a global environment. There is a relationship between learning/intelligence and innovation.[41] When employees work together, learning and innovation are optimized.[42] Employees learn by working together to foster some of the most important innovations.[43] To be innovative, organizations are recruiting people with the ability to continuously learn new things.[44] Probably the most important skill that college provides is the ability to continuously learn. You should not view your education as being over when you get your degree, but only beginning, as much of what college graduates do on the job was learned at work because it did not exist when the person was going to school. Organizations can also learn since they are based on individual learning. Thus, organizations also need continual[45] *Learning organizations* cultivate the capacity to learn, adapt, and change with the environment to be innovative with speed.

The learning organization focuses on improving learning and how knowledge is circulated throughout the organization. The learning organization questions old beliefs and ways of doing things, yet it makes the learning process as painless as possible.[46] Many researchers have demonstrated the importance of knowledge to management.[47] In fact, knowledge management was ranked among the top-10 challenges to business leaders in the 21st century.[48]

What a Learning Organization Does

IE 2-2

The learning organization learns to:

- Operate using the systems effect (Chapter 1).
- Avoid making the same mistakes.[49] Employees learn from their mistakes and don't repeat them throughout the organization, as they share the knowledge of what went right and wrong.
- Make continuous performance improvements. Though learning, constant improvements are made. Improvements are shared with others throughout the organization to further continue improvement.
- Share information. The habit of knowledge hoarding is broken.[50] Employees are rewarded for sharing their best practices that help others improve performance throughout the organization.[51]

How Intelligence and Learning Affect Behavior, Human Relations, and Performance

■ Performance
■ Human Relations
■ Behavior

People's intellectual ability directly affects their behavior. You may have observed that people with high levels of intelligence behave differently than people with low levels of intelligence.

Learning styles are not determined by intelligence. People with high or low intelligence can feel comfortable with the same learning style and therefore use it. People have different characteristics that lead them to behave differently. An understanding of the four learning styles helps one to realize why people behave differently. If a decision needs to be made and you know the person's preferred learning style, you can anticipate the behavior that will lead to the decision. For example, when convergers have to make a decision, they do so quickly, while divergers are slow to make a decision and analyze more alternatives.

People with similar learning styles tend to behave in the same way, while people with different learning styles tend to act differently. When working with a person who has the same learning style as yourself, you will tend to get along well with him or her. However, when working with a person with a different learning style, you may have human relations problems.

◆ Video
2-1
BM-2

● Skill-Building
2-1

Learning Objective

6. Explain how intelligence and learning styles affect behavior, human relations, and performance

WORK APPLICATIONS

7. Think about the person you work/worked with whom you enjoy/enjoyed working with the most. Identify that person's learning style. Is it the same as yours? What is it that you enjoy about the person?
8. Think about the person you work/worked with whom you dislike/disliked working with the most. Identify that person's learning style. Is it the same as yours? What is it that you dislike about the person?

Performance lies more in the organization's intellectual capabilities than in its hard assets.[52] Slow-learning managers and organizations behavior differently, have different human relations, and lower levels of performance than fast-learning managers and organizations.[53] Intelligence is a strong predictor of job performance.[54] This is why Microsoft values intelligence over all else.[55] However, intelligence is not enough to be successful. In some cases, motivation to learn is more important. So don't think that if you don't have a high IQ that you cannot be highly successful. Lots of overachievers are willing to work hard and continue to learn to excel, and I'm one of them.

Organizational learning is not new, as it has been discussed as a topic over 30 years ago. However, today a major challenge to learning organizations is linking the learning of individual, group, and organizational levels behavior and human relations to maximize performance.[56] The key link is the group. Teams that are effective at learning attain better performance than those that do not.[57] We'll talk more about teams and learning in Chapters 10 and 11.

● Organization
● Group
● Individual

Perception

In this section we discuss the nature of perception, bias in perception, and how perception affects behavior, human relations, and performance.

The Nature of Perception

People with different personalities perceive things differently,[58] especially in the area of locus of control.[59] The term **perception** *refers to a person's interpretation of reality.* In the perception process, you select, organize, and interpret all environmental stimuli through your senses. No two people experience anything exactly the same through this perception process. Your perception is influenced by heredity, environment, and more specifically by your personality,[60] intelligence, needs, self-concept, attitudes, and values. Notice that the definition of perception states "interpretation of reality." In human relations, perception is just as important as reality. People often encounter the same thing and perceive it differently. For example, June and Rod have the same job, but they see their job differently. In such situations, who is right?

What is the reality of any situation? We tend to believe that our perception is reality, and the other party's perception is not reality. With an increasing global and diverse work environment, perception differences will continue to increase. Remember, people will behave according to their perception, not yours. Perception also affects stress.[61] So use your understanding of personality, intelligence, and perception to improve your ability to work with a diversity of people.

Bias in Perception

Some of the biases affecting perception include stereotypes, frame of reference, expectations, selective exposure, interest, and projection.

Stereotypes

Consider the bias of **stereotyping,** *which is the process of generalizing behavior of all members of a group.* Stereotypes are drawn along all kinds of lines, including race, religion, nationality, sex, and so forth. Most, if not all, of us stereotype people as a way of quickly perceiving a person's behavior. Women and minorities are often stereotyped in organizations. Women managers have been stereotyped as being too emotional to be effective leaders. Research has shown this stereotype to be incorrect. The stereotype of women managers is beginning to fade and should continue to do so.

Goal of
Human Relations

Much of what passes for humor (jokes) in the workplace is based on stereotypes and may be considered discriminatory and harassment. Such jokes usually have negative effects on human relations. We should consciously attempt to get to know people as individuals, rather than to stereotype.

Frame of Reference

Our frame of reference is our tendency to see things from a narrow focus that directly affects us. It is common for unions and management to perceive the same situation from a different frame of reference. For example, if managers want to make a change to increase productivity, they perceive the change as positive (ignoring the union's perception), while employees may perceive the change as negative (ignoring management's perception). Employees may view the change as a way to get more work out of them for less money when, in the broader scope, both groups may benefit from the change. Parents and their children often have frame of reference perception differences.

To be effective in our human relations, we should try to perceive things from the other person's frame of reference and be willing to work together for the benefit of all people to create a win-win situation.

Expectations

Read the phrase in the triangle below.

Did you read the word *the* twice? Or, like most people, did you read what you expected, only one *the*. We perceive, select, organize, and interpret information as we expect it to appear.

Over the years, a writer developed many experiential exercises that had been typed by different secretaries. However, it was common for secretaries to change the word *experiential* to *experimental* because it was the word they expected to type. Even after telling one secretary about it a few times, the writer still received it as the secretary expected, rather than as it was written.

Often people, especially those who know each other well, do not really listen to each other. They simply hear what they expect to hear.

To improve our human relations, we must be careful to listen to reality, rather than what we expect reality to be.

Selective Exposure

We tend to see and hear what we want to. For example, you may be in a room reading while other people are talking and a radio is on, yet you select to ignore the people and radio and concentrate on reading.

People sometimes selectively pick information they want to hear and ignore information they don't want to hear.[62] For example, when a manager uses the sandwich technique of telling an employee something about performance, then switching to something negative and then back to something good, the employee may selectively perceive the conversation as praise and ignore the negative information.[63] Or sometimes when a manager delegates a task with a specific deadline, the employee selectively does not hear, and therefore misses, the deadline.

To ensure effective human relations, we should listen to the entire message, rather than use selective exposure.

Interest

What interests you also affects how you perceive things.[64] Have you ever taken a course and not liked it, while others in the class thought it was great? This difference in perception may be due to different levels of interest in the subject. Interest influences job selection.

Projection

To avoid psychological threat, people use a defense mechanism known as *projection*. Projection means attributing one's attitudes or shortcomings to others. A person may say, "Ted is prejudiced against blacks." This statement about Ted may be accurate, or it may instead be a projection reflecting the speaker's own prejudice. People who steal and cheat may make statements like "Everyone steals from the company" and "All students cheat in college." Projection may be an effective defense mechanism, but it generally does not help human relations.

WORK APPLICATIONS

9. Give an example of when you and someone else experienced the same situation but perceived it differently. Which of the six biases to perception seems to be the major reason for the difference in perceptions? Explain your answer.

APPLICATION SITUATIONS

Bias in Perception

AS 2–4

Identify the people's perception bias by the statements made about them.

A. Stereotyping   C. Expectations   E. Projection

B. Frame of reference   D. Selective exposure   F. Interest

_____ 16. Wayne gets on his employees' nerves because he doesn't really listen to their opinions, he thinks he knows what they want, and he makes decisions without their input all the time.

_____ 17. Lily is always accusing others of taking longer breaks, when in reality she is the violator.

_____ 18. Ben keeps asking me about basketball. Just because I'm a tall black doesn't mean I like the game or the L.A. Lakers.

_____ 19. A major problem between the Arabs and Israelis is their . . .

_____ 20. Val has communication problems because she only hears what she wants to.

■ Performance
■ Human Relations
■ Behavior

Skill-Building
2-2

How Perception Affects Behavior, Human Relations, and Performance

Needs and perceptions are the starting point of our behavior. Through the perception process we select, organize, and interpret information as the basis of our behavior. Our perception can lead to different behavior. For example, if an employee perceives the manager is giving a legitimate order, he or she will carry it out. However, if the order is not perceived as legitimate, the employee may refuse to carry out the order. Students who perceive grades as a valued reward for studying hard tend to be motivated to study harder than students who do not.

How we perceive people affects how we treat them. If we stereotype people in negative ways, we may not take an interest in them and have friendly chats. If we only see things from our frame of reference, we may be in constant conflict with others. If we only see and hear what we expect, we may turn people off. Selective exposure can cause people to get angry at us for not listening to them. People generally do not like to hear people making projective statements about others. People who continually have different perceptions of reality than others tend to be ignored or avoided.

Learning Objective

7. Describe five biases to perception

The term **perceptual congruence** *refers to the degree to which people see things the same way.* When people perceive things the same way, it generally has positive consequences in the organization. We do realize that perception biases can result in lower performance. However, the exact relationship between perceptual congruence and performance is not known. Employees who perceive management as supportive are generally happier with their jobs[65] and perceive management's performance more favorably.[66]

For a review of the biases affecting perception, see Exhibit 2–5.

EXHIBIT 2–5   **BIASES AFFECTING PERCEPTION**

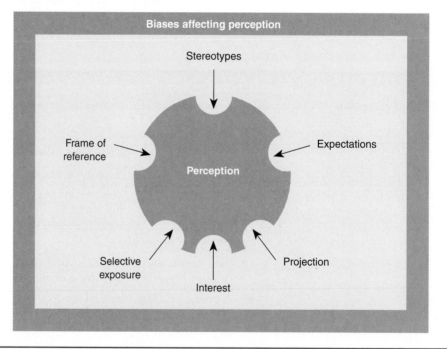

● Organization
● Group
● Individual

Developing Positive First Impressions

In this section we discuss how first impressions affect behavior, human relations, and performance. We also examine image projection and apparel and grooming.

How First Impressions Affect Behavior, Human Relations, and Performance

When we meet people, we form quick impressions of them. Social psychologists call this process the primacy effect. The **primacy effect** *is the way people perceive one another during their first impressions.* Our perceptions are open to biases (stereotyping, frame of reference, expectations, selective exposure, interest, and projection).

Performance
Human Relations
Behavior

These first impressions establish the mental framework within which people view one another, and they are based on personality.[67]

The **four-minute barrier** *is the time we have to make a good impression.* We have up to four minutes to make a good first impression.[68] It is also called the *four-minute sell*[69] because it is the average time during which people make up their minds to continue the contact or separate during social situations. However, in business and social situations, the time could be less; some first impressions are developed in seconds.

Our first impressions can affect our behavior in a positive or negative way. During this short period of time, human relations will be established, denied, or reconfirmed. If our first impressions are favorable, we will tend to be nice to the person and continue the contact; if not, we end the contact. In ongoing work situations, first impressions of our fellow employees set the tone for our human relations. The old adage "first impressions are lasting impressions" is true for many people.

First impressions usually linger, but they can be changed. Have you ever disliked someone as a result of first impressions that linger to the present time? On the other hand, can you recall meeting someone you disliked at first, but once you got to know the person you changed your impression?

During the four-minute barrier, people's attention spans are at their greatest and powers of retention at their highest.[70] If you register negative first impressions in other people, you will have to "prove" yourself to change them. It is easier to begin by projecting an image people will like. We will discuss how to project a positive image.

But first, here is an example from an organizational setting of how first impressions have an effect on the organization's performance.

Mary was brought in from another organization to manage the accounting department at Waynright. During her initial meeting with her employees, Mary began by telling them that she graduated from Harvard with honors and how well she did in her previous management position. Then Mary told them about the changes they were going to make to increase productivity. After the meeting the employees generally agreed that Mary had a "big head." As time went on, Mary found that her suggestions for improving productivity were not implemented.

Image Projection

Our **image** *is other people's attitudes toward us.* Image can be thought of as being on a continuum from positive to negative. To a large extent we can control the image we project. People's attitudes toward us, our image, are developed by our appearance, nonverbal communications, and behavior. Each of these three areas is discussed separately below. Later in this chapter we will provide tips on apparel and grooming. In Chapter 4, we will talk more about nonverbal communications, and in Chapter 9, you will learn about behavioral etiquette.

Before we begin talking about image, you should realize that image from your perspective is called *impression management.*[71] You can bolster your image of competence.[72] Impression management is associated with job offer.[73] In other words, if you project a positive image during a job interview, you greatly increase your chances of getting the job offer, and visa versa. One last thing before we get into how to project a positive image, organizations are also concerned with impressions management and work to project a positive image.[74] Each of the organization's employees image send a message to customers who judge the organization by its people. As an employee, your image impacts the organizational image.

Appearance

When people first see you, before you can do or say anything, they begin to develop their first impressions. If a person doesn't like the way you look, your clothes, hairstyle, or grooming, he or she may not give you the opportunity to show who you really are. If you want to be successful, you should dress appropriately for the situation. For example, if you went to a job interview for a sales representative position at IBM wearing jeans and a T-shirt, the interviewer would probably decide not to hire you before asking you one question. At IBM employees wear dark suits and white shirts or blouses, so if you wear these clothes you will start the interview on a positive note. There are various dress-for-success books on the market, containing advice that can help your career progress. A simple rule to follow is to establish the dress and grooming standards of the organization and, specifically, of the job you want. Dress like the successful people in the organization.

Nonverbal Communication

Our facial expressions, eye contact, and handshake all project our image, as well as our tone/volume of voice.

After noticing someone's appearance, we tend to look at a person's face. Facial expressions convey feelings more accurately than words. A smile tends to say things are OK, while a frown tends to say something is wrong. One of the eight guidelines to human relations is to smile. It is especially important when we first meet someone; we want to project a positive, caring image.

When meeting someone, eye contact is very important.[75] If you don't look a person directly in the eye, he or she may assume that you do not like him or her, that you are not listening, or that you are not a trusting individual. Maintaining eye contact is important, but don't make others uncomfortable by staring at them. Look in one eye, then the other, then briefly look away. However, in some cultures eye contact is considered rude behavior.

In many introductions the handshake is used. Your handshake can convey that you are a warm, yet strong person. Your handshake is judged on five factors: (1) firmness—people tend to think that a firm handshake communicates a caring attitude, while a weak grip conveys indifference; (2) dryness—people don't like to hold a clammy hand; it sends a message of being nervous; (3) duration—an extended handshake can convey interest; (4) interlock—a full, deep grip conveys friendship and strength; shallow grips are often interpreted as a weakness; and (5) eye contact—you should maintain eye contact throughout the handshake.

Behavior

Skill-Building
2-3

Learning Objective

8. Explain the importance of first impressions and how to project a positive image

After the other person notices our appearance and nonverbal expressions, they observe our behavior. As stated earlier in the guidelines to effective human relations, while talking to the person, be upbeat and optimistic, don't complain, show a genuine interest in the person, smile, laugh if appropriate, call the person by name, listen, be helpful, and think before you act. Do not do or say anything that is offensive to the person. Watch your manners and be polite. During the four-minute barrier, avoid discussing controversial topics and expressing personal views about them.

Following the above guidelines should help you develop positive first impressions.

WORK APPLICATIONS

10. Give an example of when others formed a positive and negative first impression of you. Explain the causes (appearance, nonverbal communication, behavior) of these impressions.

11. Which area of projecting a positive image (appearance, nonverbal communication, behavior) is your strongest? Which is your weakest? Explain your answers. What will you do to project a positive image in the future?

Apparel and Grooming

Apparel and grooming play a major role in making a good first impression. However, they are also important to keep your image to help you get raises and promotions. Your clothes should be proper business apparel that is well coordinated, well tailored, and well maintained. Your hair should be neat, trimmed, organized, clean, and away from your face. Clean teeth and fingernails and fresh breath are expected. Avoid tattoos, body piercing jewelry, and loud jewelry that shows at work.

Over 23 million American employees wear uniforms to work, from the professional level of judge to the more technical level of bank teller. Many professionals don't wear an actual uniform, but a suit or other accepted dress for specific types of jobs are a type of uniform. John Molloy coined the term *wardrobe engineering* to describe how clothing and accessories can be used to create a certain image.[76] There are hundreds of image consultants, and they don't agree on everything. However, here are some generally agreed-on suggestions if you want a successful career in most organizations.

Dress for the Organization and Job

Again, dress and groom like the people in the organization and specific job that you want. If you are not sure of the dress style, visit the organization before the job interview and find out, or at least possibly over dress as suggested for job interviews. Once you are on the job, at least dress like your peers. If you are serious about climbing the corporate ladder, however, you should consider dressing like the managers. Dressing like the managers can help in your career advancement.[77]

Job Interview

As a general guide, during a job interview never underdress (such as jeans and t-shirts) and possibly overdress. As a college graduate seeking a professional job, wear a suit if managers do (tie for men), even if you will not need to wear one for the job. You may be thinking, "Why bother? No one else does." That's exactly the point. You will look more professional, like the managers, and stand out in the crowd and may have the edge on getting the job. In an actual job situation, a young applicant was asked by the interviewer why he was not dressed in a jacket and tie. The applicant responded that he was dressed like the others in the organization. The interviewer said there is one major difference between you and them. They already have a job here, you don't.

Wear Quality Clothes

Quality clothes project a quality image, and visa versa. Start with a quality suit for job interviews and important days at work, such as your first day, to develop a good first impression. Look for *sales* when buying apparel, but don't buy a suit, or anything you will wear to work, unless you really like it. If you feel good about the way you look, you will generally project a more positive self-image of confidence, which will help your career. So never buy anything you don't really like, even if it is on sale, because it is not a good deal if you don't feel good about yourself wearing it.

Dress and Groom Conservatively

The latest dress fad is often inappropriate in the professional business setting. You may not be taken seriously if you exhibit faddish or flashy apparel and grooming.

Casual Dress

What is considered casual business dress does vary. In most situations, don't go to the job interview casual unless you know that is the expected apparel for the interview. In most cases, casual doesn't include jeans and t-shirts for professional employees. Dress similar to others in the firm.

Suggestions for Men

You may want to follow these guidelines.

- **Grooming.** If other men in the organization do not have facial hair, long hair, or wear earrings, you may consider shaving, getting a haircut, and leaving the earrings at home, at least for the job interview, if you want to increase your odds at getting a job with that organization.
- **Suit.** The suit is still the most appropriate apparel in most organizations. Your business suit is blue or gray, commonly dark and stripes are acceptable. The fabric

is wool, or at least 45% wool-blend; in warmer climates, cotton or linen suits may be acceptable, but be careful as they wrinkle easily. It is conservatively cut, and the width of the lapels and the pants are in conservative style.

- **Shirt.** The business shirt is a solid color white or light blue and may have thin strips, not loud. The shirt has long-sleeves and they show about 1/2-inch from the suit sleeves when the arms are by your side. The collar is conservative and looks good with your tie.
- **Tie.** The wrong tie can hurt the quality image of your suit. The business tie is silk and usually has some conservative design, no animals, sayings, or cartoon characters. A tie tack is not needed; a small conservative one is acceptable.
- **Shoes.** Conservative dark leather business shoes, not sneakers, are worn with a suit. If in doubt about whether your shoes, or any part of your business attire is conservative for business, ask a qualified sales rep.
- **Matching.** The suit, shirt, and tie all match. Be careful not to mix three sets of stripes. Generally, with a striped suit wear a solid-color shirt. Match the color of the design in the tie to the suit and shirt. The color of the conservative belt (small simple buckle) is the same color as your shoes. The color of the thin socks match the color of the pants (no heavy wool or white socks), and the socks are long enough so that your legs never show.

Suggestions for Women

You may want to follow these guidelines.

- **Grooming and jewelry.** Wearing heavy makeup, such as very obvious eye shadow, dark outlined lips, and excessive-smelling perfumes, is not appropriate for business; don't wear it, at least for the job interview. Makeup should be subtle to the point that people don't think you are wearing any, and if worn, perfume should be light. Jewelry is simple and tasteful, never overdone.
- **Skirted Suit.** The professional skirted wool or wool-blend suit is most appropriate, however, the conservative business dress with coordinated jacket is also acceptable. The skirt matches the blazer-cut jacket, and it reaches just to below the knee. With proper business apparel, you are not trying to make a fashion statement, or show off your legs or body, with low-cut shirts and dresses, nor long cut. Women have more color choice, but blue and gray are good for the first suit. Solids, tweeds, and plaids are acceptable, but pinstripes may make you appear as though you are trying to imitate male apparel.
- **Blouse.** The business blouse is silk or cotton and free of frills, patterns, or unusual collars; it is not low-cut. Solid colors are preferred, with a greater range of collars acceptable so long as they contrast and coordinate with the color of the suit. The collar should be equivalent to that of a man's shirt, and the top button should be open.
- **No tie, scarf optional.** It is generally agreed that a women wearing a tie may appear as though she is trying to imitate male apparel. However, a conservative scarf is acceptable if you want to wear one.
- **Shoes.** Leather shoes match the suit and are conservative. Shoes are not a fashion statement—they are comfortable with a moderate heel; plain pumps are a good choice.
- **Matching and Attaché Case.** All apparel matches. Neutral or skin-tone pantyhose are worn with your business suit. Businesswoman carry an attaché case, which replaces a purse or handbag, whenever feasible.

If you are thinking that it is unfair to be judged by your appearance, rather than for who you really are and what you can do, you are correct. However, if you haven't found out yet, life is not always fair. Fair or not, in most organizations, your appearance will affect your career success and you have control.

REVIEW

Select one or more methods: (1) fill in the missing key terms from memory; (2) match the key terms, from the end of the review, with their definitions below; and/or (3) copy the key terms in order from the key terms at the beginning of the chapter.

Personality or personal style makes us different, yet similar, in many ways. The amount of stress you have is based, in part, on your personality type. Intelligence affects personality, and learning styles are based on personality traits. Our perception is influenced by our personality and intelligence. And first impressions are based on our perceptions.

_____ is a relatively stable set of traits that aids in explaining and predicting individual behavior. Our personalities are the product of both genetics and environmental factors. Our personality traits are the basis for our behavior and human relations. The _____ is characterized as fast moving, hard driving, time conscious, competitive, impatient, and preoccupied with work; _____ categorizes traits into the dimensions of surgency, agreeableness, adjustment, conscientiousness, and openness to experience.

_____ is a continuum between an external and internal belief over who has control over one's destiny. When organizations are hiring people, they often look for a certain personality type that they feel will be successful for the job. Personality types are often successful in one situation, but not in another.

_____ is an emotional and/or physical reaction to environmental activities and events. _____ are situations in which people feel anxiety, tension, and pressure. Stress leads to lower levels of performance, and is caused by the Type A personality, organizational climate, management behavior, and degree of job satisfaction. An increased rate of breathing and perspiration, clock watching, and the feeling of pressure are common signs of stress. Too much stress can lead to _____ , the constant lack of interest and motivation to perform one's job due to stress. The _____ includes step 1, identify stressors; step 2, determine their causes and consequences; and step 3, plan to eliminate or decrease the stress. Some of the methods of reducing stress include exercise, nutrition, relaxation, positive thinking, and support systems.

_____ is the level of one's capacity for new learning, problem solving, and decision making. Our intelligence is a consequence of genetics and environmental factors. We have multiple intelligences, which helps explain why some people are good at one thing but not another. The four learning styles are: _____ , who prefer learning by doing and feeling; _____ , who prefer learning by observing and feeling; _____ , who prefer learning by doing and thinking; and _____ , who prefer learning by observing and thinking. Our learning styles lead us to behave and relate to others differently. Generally, the more flexible your learning style, the easier it is to work with different styles. Different jobs require different learning styles to be effective. Understanding your preferred learning style and selecting an appropriate career can contribute to career success. There is a direct relationship between verbal ability and occupational level. Improving one's verbal skills can lead to promotions. Continue to be interested in continuously learning new things to be a valuable asset to the learning organization.

_____ is a person's interpretation of reality. Through the perception process, we select, organize, and interpret information through our senses. Our perception is influenced by heredity and our environment and more specifically by our personality, intelligence, needs, self-concept, attitudes, and values. Some of the biases in perception include _____ , the process of generalizing behavior of all members of a group; frame of reference; expectations; selective exposure; interest; and projection. Perception is the starting point of our behavior, and our perception influences how we interact with people. _____ refers to the degree to which people see things the same way. Performance is generally higher when people have perceptual congruence.

The _____ is the way people perceive one another during their first impressions. The _____ is the time we have to make a good impression. First impressions affect behavior, human relations, and performance. Our _____ is other people's attitudes toward us. The three major image projectors are our appearance, nonverbal communication, and behavior.

KEY TERMS

accommodators 52

assimilators 53

Big Five Model
  of Personality 41

burnout 46

controlling stress plan 46

convergers 52

divergers 52

four-minute barrier 59

image 59

intelligence 49

locus of control 42

perception 55

perceptual congruence 58

personality 39

primacy effect 58

stereotyping 55

stress 44

stressors 44

Type A personality 40

CASE

Wayne Huizenga: Entrepreneur

Wayne Huizenga was called the leading American entrepreneur by *Success* Magazine.[78] Wayne started his business career working for a waste removal company. Before long, he started his own company and later merged with another waste disposal company to form WMX Technologies, which grew to become the largest waste-hauling business in the world.

Wayne Huizenga is best known for building companies and making deals. In addition to WMX, he started Blockbuster Entertainment with the idea of developing a McDonald's of videos with the policy of not renting or selling pornographic videos. He later sold Blockbuster to Viacom in a stock swap valued at $8.4 billion. Speaking bluntly, as usual, he told shareholders he would leave the company because he cannot tolerate working for anyone else; he leads or leaves.

Wayne Huizenga also acquired Republic Services and is a dominant player in three industries: electronic security, superstore chains of used-cars dealerships, and waste disposal. He also owns the Miami Dolphins, Florida Panthers, and Florida Marlins professional sports teams.

Huizenga is highly disciplined, hard driving, and hard working; his workday usually begins at 4:00 A.M. He enjoys giving advice and solving problems. His basic approach to growing the business is to gather his key people and discuss ideas for expansion and possible deals. Wayne presents his ideas to the key people so they can point out weaknesses and give him ideas for improving his proposals. When making deals, he talks in a relaxed, calm, chummy manner relating to the other party, and he makes an effort to be clearly understood. At age 58, Huizega's net worth had grown to over $1 billion, and he had no intentions of slowing down. Nova Southeastern University honors him with its Wayne Huizenga Graduate School of Business and Entrepreneurship in Davie, Florida.

Go to the Internet: For more information on Wayne Huizenga and one or more of his companies or sports teams and to update the information provided in this case, do a name search on the Internet to get a web address for that business. You may find out that he has bought or sold some businesses since this case was written. For ideas on using the Internet with cases, see Appendix C.

Support your answer to the following questions with specific information from the case and text, or other information you get from the web or other source.

1. Explain Wayne Huizenga's personality traits for each of the Big Five dimensions.

2. Would you say Huizenga has a Type A or Type B personality?

3. Do you believe it would be stressful to work for Huizenga?

4. Which learning style do you think Huizenga prefers?

5. Which biases in perception do you think Huizenga had to overcome during his early business years?

OBJECTIVE CASE

Personality Conflict

Carol is the branch manager of a bank. Two of her employees, Rich and Wonda, came to her and said that they cannot work together. Carol asked them why, and they both said, "We have a personality conflict." She asked them to be more specific, and this is what they told her:

RICH: Well, Wonda is very pushy; she tells me what to do all the time, and I let her get away with it because I'm a peace-loving man.

WONDA: That's because Rich is so gullible; he believes anything he is told. I have to look out for him.

RICH: We have different outlooks on life. Wonda believes that if we work hard, we can get ahead in this bank, but I don't agree. I believe you have to be political, and I'm not.

WONDA: That's because I'm motivated and enjoy working.

RICH: Motivated—is that what you call it? She's preoccupied with work. Wonda is rushing all the time, she is impatient, and she always wants to make a contest out of everything.

WONDA: If you were more cooperative, and morale was better, I would not feel stressed the way I do.

RICH: We cannot make decisions together because I am very logical and like to get lots of information, while Wonda wants to make decisions based on what she calls "intuition."

WONDA: I thought working here was going to be different. I didn't know I was going to be stuck working with a person who is uncooperative.

RICH: Me, I feel the same way about you.

At this point Carol stopped the discussion.

Answer the following questions. Then in the space between questions, state why you selected that answer.

_____ 1. In Rich's first statement it appears that Wonda has a(n) _____ , while he has a(n) _____ personality trait.

   a. outgoing, reserved   *c.* conscientious, expedient

   b. aggressive, passive   *d.* imaginative, practical

_____ 2. In statement 2, it appears that Wonda is _____ and Rich is _____ .

   a. shrewd, forthright   *c.* stable, emotional

   b. high, low intelligence   *d.* suspicious, trusting

_____ 3. In statement 3, it appears that Rich has an _____ locus of control while Wonda has an _____ locus of control.

   a. internal, external   *b.* external, internal

_____ 4. In statement 4, Wonda appears to be an:

   a. internalizer   *b.* externalizer

_____ 5. In statement 5, Wonda appears to have a Type _____ personality.

        a. A   *b.* B

_____ 6. In statement 6, Wonda states that _____ is the cause of her stress.

        a. personality   *c.* management effectiveness

        b. organizational climate   *d.* job satisfaction

_____ 7. In statement 7, Rich has described himself as having a(n) _____ learning style.

        a. accommodator   *c.* converger

        b. diverger   *d.* assimilator

_____ 8. In statement 7, Rich has described Wonda as having a(n) _____ learning style.

        a. accommodator   *c.* converger

        b. diverger   *d.* assimilator

_____ 9. In statement 8, the perception problem appears to be due to:

        a. stereotyping   *d.* selective exposure

        b. frame of reference   *e.* projection

        c. expectations   *f.* interest

_____ 10. Who needs to change their behavior?

        a. Rich   *b.* Wonda   *c.* both

11. Overall, is your personality, locus of control, stress type, and learning style more like Rich or Wonda? If you were Rich or Wonda, what would you do?

12. If you were Carol, what would you do? Note: Carol's meeting can be role-played in class.

VIDEO CASE 2

Stress Management

In this video several stress professionals presents how stress affects workers and the importance of stress management. Cummins Engine Company employees explain what the organization is doing to help its employees manage their stress.

Critical Thinking Questions:

1. What does personality have to do with stress?

2. What does perception have to do with stress?

3. What is the relationship between stress and performance?

4. What are some of the causes of stress?

5. What are some of the signs that a person is experiencing stress?

6. What are some of the things people can do to help control stress?

7. Do you think that the high cost of Cummins Engine's health/recreation facilities outweigh the costs?

8. Work application number 4 may be used in conjunction with this video.

Fiscal Fairy Tale #11: Gingerman

Following the steps to getting to read a fiscal fairy tale in MG Webzine Exercise 1 in Chapter 1 page 34, go to the MG website (*www.mgeneral.com*) and read *Fiscal Fairy Tale #11: Gingerman* (your instructor may ask you to print a copy and bring it to class). Answer these questions (your instructor may ask you to type them and bring them to class):

Online MG Webzine Exercise 2

Questions Relating to the Tale Only

1. As stated at the end of the tale, in 50 words or so, what is your response to this tale? You may send it to MG.

2. Have you, or anyone you know, worked for an organization that had an attractive male or female and/or charming personality like Gingerman? Was the charmer highly capable and productive?

3. Did the charmer get any special treatment? Give some examples of things the organizational managers do/did for the charmer that it doesn't do for others who may be more qualified and productive.

4. What is the role of traits in business? Should organizations give special treatment to attractive people and/or people with charming personalities (assuming they are not a job requirement)? Is it ethical to give them preferences?

Questions Relating the Tale to the Chapter Concepts

5. Which of the Big Five personality styles is dominant in Gingerman?

6. Does Gingerman have a Type A or Type B personality? Is he stressed?

7. Is Gingerman intelligent?

8. Which learning style does Gingerman prefer?

9. Is the kingdom a learning organization?

10. What perception bias is a problem in this tale?

11. What type of image does Gingerman project?

In-Class MG Webzine Exercise 2

The instructor selects one of the six options from Appendix B page 589.

Personality—Optimistic or Pessimistic (IE 2–1)

Online Internet Exercise 2–1 (Self-Assessment)

In-Class Internet Exercise 2–1, IE 2–2, and IE 2–3

The objective of this Internet exercise is to learn if you have a more optimistic or pessimistic personality. Use the information from Appendix B and IE 1–2 and 1–3 as you do the following:

1. Go to the Body-Mind QueenDom website homepage—*www.queendom.com*

2. Click "Tests" and scroll down to the personality tests section and Click "Optimism/Pessimism Inventory" and take the test by clicking your selections then click score to get your score and interpretation (your instructor may ask you to make a copy of it to bring to class).

3. Questions: (1) What was your score? (2) Are you more optimistic or pessimistic? (3) What can you do to be more optimistic? (Your instructor may ask you to type and print your answer and bring them to class.)

The instructor selects one of the six options from Appendix B page 589.

The objective of this Internet exercise is to learn more about the Society for Organizational Learning (SOL). Use the information from Appendix B and IE 1–2 and 1–3 as you do the following:

Society for Organizational Learning (IE 2–2)

Online Internet Exercise 2–2

1. Go to the SOL homepage—*www.solonline.org*

2. Clock and read "About" SOL then return to the homepage, click back.

3. Clock any of the subsites and read the information (your instructor may require a copy).

4. Questions: (1) What is SOL? (2) Which subsite did you visit? (3) What did you learn at the subsite? (Your instructor may ask you to type and print out your answer.)

Search Engines (IE 2–3)

Online Internet Exercise 2–3

The objective of this Internet exercise is to try three different search engines to develop your search skills. It is a continuation of IE 1–2. Read Appendix B, Internet Exercises, and use the information as you do the following:

1. Go to the Search Engine Watch website at—*www.searchenginewatch.com* homepage.

2. Clock "Search engine listings."

3. Read about the different search engines (your instructor may ask you to copy them).

4. Select a concept from Chapters 1 or 2, such as a key term, that you want to learn more about.

5. Using at least three different search engines, type in your concept and review the resources available to you (your instructor may ask you to print the resources.)

6. Write a comparison of the three different search engines; be sure to state which ones you used and what you did and did not like about each. Search the best search engine, and state why it was the best for your search (your instructor may ask you to type out your report).

VIDEO EXERCISE

◆ **Learning Styles**

VE 2–1

Objectives: To better understand the four learning styles.

Preparation: You should understand the four learning styles.

The instructor shows Video Module 2, Learning Styles. As you view the meeting, identify the four learning styles being used by each of the group members.

Procedure 1
(10–20 minutes)
BM–2

_____ Chris   _____ A. Accomodator

_____ Bob   _____ B. Diverger

_____ Sandy   _____ C. Converger

_____ Jesse   _____ D. Assimilator

After viewing each scene, identify/match each group member's style by placing the appropriate letter on the line next to the person's name. After viewing the meeting the class discusses the styles used by each person. The instructor states the correct answers.

Procedure 2
(2–5 minutes)

Discussion: Option A: In groups of six, answer the questions below. Option B: As a class, answer the questions below.

1. Which two people have opposite learning styles? (You should have two sets of two people.)

2. How do the two sets of opposites want to work on selecting a computer?

3. Is it beneficial or harmful to have diversity of learning styles in this group? Explain your answer.

4. What positive contribution can each member make to the group based on their learning style?

Conclusion: The instructor may make concluding remarks. If the class had trouble identifying the correct learning styles and/or answering the questions, the video may be shown again to reinforce understanding of the learning styles.

Application (2–4 minutes):   What did I learn from this exercise? How will I use this knowledge in the future?

Sharing: Volunteers give their answers to the application section.

This video exercise serves as a good preparation for doing Skill-Building Exercise 2–1.

SKILL-BUILDING EXERCISE 2-1

● **In-Class
Learning Styles**

Objectives: To better understand your learning style and how to work more effectively with people with different learning styles.

SCANS: The SCANS competencies of resources, interpersonal, informational, and systems; and basic, thinking, and personal qualities are developed through this exercise.

Preparation: You should have read the chapter and determined your preferred learning style in Self-Assessment Exercise 2–3.

Experience: The entire class breaks into four groups: The accommodators, divergers, convergers, and assimilators meet in different groups.

*Procedure 1
(2–3 minutes)*

Each of the four groups elects a spokesperson-recorder. Assume the class was shipwrecked on a deserted island and had to develop an economic system with a division of labor. During this process, what strengths would your group offer each of the other three groups if you were working one on one with them? For example, the accommodators state how they would help the divergers if they were the only two styles on the island. Then they assume the convergers and then the assimilators are the only other learning style of the island. Each group does the same. Feel free to refer to the book at any time.

*Procedure 2
(5–10 minutes)*

*Procedure 3
(5–15 minutes)*

The spokesperson for the accommodators tells the other three groups how they would be helpful to that group if they were the only two styles on the island. The divergers go next, followed by the convergers, then assimilators.

*Procedure 4
(3–7 minutes)*

Break into as many discussion groups as there are members of the smallest of the four learning style groups. Each discussion group must have at least one person from all four learning styles; some will have more. For example, if the smallest group is the assimilators with five members, establish five discussion groups. If there are nine convergers, send two members to four groups and one to the remaining group. If there are six divergers, send one to four of the groups and two to one of the groups. Try to make the number of students in each discussion group as even as possible.

*Procedure 5
(3–7 minutes)*

Elect a spokesperson-recorder. Each group decides which learning style(s) to include in establishing the economic system. During the discussion, the instructor writes the four styles on the board for voting in procedure 6.

*Procedure 6
(2–3 minutes)*

The instructor records the votes from each group to be included in establishing the economic system.

Conclusion: The instructor leads a class discussion and/or makes concluding remarks.

Application (2–4 minutes): What have I learned from this exercise? What will I do to be more open to working with people of different learning styles?

Sharing: Volunteers give their answers to the application section.

● **Preparation**
Personality
Perceptions

You should read the sections on personality traits and complete Self-Assessment Exercise 2–1. From this exercise, below rank yourself from highest 1 to lowest score 5 for each of the Big Five. Do not tell anyone your ranking until told to do so.

_____ surgency   _____ agreeableness   _____ adjustment
_____ conscientiousness   _____ openness

● **In-Class**
Personality
Perceptions

iii

Objective: To develop your skill at perceiving others' personality traits. With this skill, you can better understand and predict people's behavior, which is helpful to leaders in influencing followers.

SCANS: The SCANS competencies of resources, interpersonal skills, and information and foundations of basic, especially thinking in the areas of decision making and personal qualities are developed through this exercise.

Procedure 1 (2–4 minutes)

Break into groups of three with people you know the best in the class. You may need some groups of two. If you don't know people in the class, and you did Exercise 1–1 Getting to Know You by Name, get in a group with these people.

Procedure 2 (4–6 minutes)

Each person in the group writes down his or her perception of each of the other two group members. Simply rank which trait you believe to be the highest and lowest (put the Big Five dimension name on the line) for each person. Write a short reason for your perception, which should include some behavior you observed that leads you to your perception.

Name _____ Highest personality score _____ Lowest score _____

Reason for ranking _____

Name _____ Highest personality score _____ Lowest score _____

Reason for ranking _____

Procedure 3 (4–6 minutes)

One of the group members volunteers to go first to hear the other group members' perceptions.

(1) One person tells the volunteer which Big Five dimension he or she selected as the person's highest and lowest score, and why they were selected. Do not discuss it yet.

(2) The other person also tells the volunteer the same information.

(3) The volunteer tells the two others what their actual highest and lowest scores are. The three group members discuss the accuracy of the perceptions.

Procedure 4 (4–6 minutes)

A second group member volunteers to go next to receive perceptions. Follow the same procedure as above.

Procedure 5 (4–6 minutes)

The third group member goes last. Follow the same procedure as above.

Conclusion: The instructor may lead a class discussion and/or make concluding remarks.

Application (2–4 minutes):   What did I learn from this exercise? How will I use this knowledge in the future?

Sharing: Volunteers give their answers to the application section.

**In-Class
First Impressions**

Objectives: To practice projecting a positive first impression. To receive feedback on the image you project. To develop your ability to project a positive first impression.

SCANS: The SCANS competencies of interpersonal and informational and the foundations of basic, thinking, and especially personal qualities are developed through this exercise.

Preparation: You should have read and understand how to project a positive first impression.

Procedure 1
(2–4 minutes)

Pair off with someone you do not know. If you know everyone, select a partner you don't know well. Make one group of three if necessary. Do not begin your discussion until asked to do so.

Procedure 2
(Exactly 4 minutes)

Assume you are meeting for the first time. A mutual friend brought you together but was called to the telephone before introducing you. The mutual friend has asked you to introduce yourselves and get acquainted until he returns. When told to begin, introduce yourselves and get acquainted. Be sure to shake hands.

Procedure 3
(7–12 minutes)

Using the Image Feedback sheet below, give each other feedback on the image you projected. To be useful, the feedback must be an honest assessment of the image you received of your partner.

Image Feedback

Human Relations Guidelines

1. I was optimistic _____ , neutral _____ , pessimistic _____ .

2. I did _____ did not _____ complain and criticize.

3. I did _____ did not _____ show genuine interest in the other person.

4. I did _____ did not _____ smile, and laugh when appropriate.

5. I did _____ did not _____ call the person by name two or three times.

6. I was a good _____ , fair _____ , poor listener.

7. I was/tried to be _____ wasn't _____ helpful to the other person.

8. I did _____ did not _____ do or say anything that offended the other person.

Image Projection

Appearance:

9. My appearance projected a positive _____ , neutral _____ , negative _____ image to the other person.

Nonverbal communication:

10. My facial expressions projected a caring _____ , neutral _____ , uncaring _____ attitude toward the other person.

Image Feedback (concluded)

11. My eye contact was too little _____ , about right _____ , too much.

12. My handshake was firm _____ weak _____ ; dry _____ wet _____ ; long _____ short _____ ; full grip _____ shallow grip _____ ; with eye contact _____ without eye contact _____ .

13. The behavior the other person liked most was

14. The behavior the other person liked least was

Overall
By receiving this feedback, I realize that I could improve my image projection by

Perception
It is important to understand both our first impression of others and theirs' of us (image). After discussing your images, do you think you made any perception errors? If yes, which one(s)?

_____

Conclusion: The instructor leads a class discussion and/or makes concluding remarks.

Application (2–4 minutes):   What did I learn from this exercise? How will I use this knowledge in the future?

Sharing: Volunteers give their answers to the application section.

Diversity in Attitudes, Self-Concept, and Values

3

Learning Objectives

After completing this chapter, you should be able to:

1. Define attitudes and explain how they affect behavior, human relations, and performance.
2. Describe how to change your attitudes.
3. List six job satisfaction determinants.
4. Explain how job satisfaction is measured and how it affects performance.
5. Determine whether you have a positive self-concept and how it affects your behavior, human relations, and performance.
6. Understand how your manager's and your own expectations affect your performance.
7. Demonstrate how to develop a more positive self-concept.
8. Identify your personal values.
9. Define the following 12 key terms (in order of appearance in the chapter):

attitude	**job satisfaction survey**	**self-fulfilling**
Theory X	**self-concept**	**prophecy**
Theory Y	**self-efficacy**	**value**
Pygmalion effect	**attribution**	**value system**
job satisfaction		

Rayanne was walking back to work after a meeting with her supervisor, Kent. Rayanne recalled that Kent said she had a negative attitude, and that it was affecting her performance, which was below standard. Kent had asked Rayanne if she was satisfied with her job. She had said, "No, I really don't like working, and I've messed up on all the jobs I've had. I guess I'm a failure." Kent tried to explain how her poor attitude and negative self-concept were the cause of her poor performance. But Rayanne didn't really listen. Work is not important to her, and she doesn't believe Kent knows what he's talking about. Is Kent's analysis correct? Can Rayanne change her attitudes?

Employees need human relations to realize their potential. In today's workplace, these relationships demand an interdependence that can most effectively be achieved through better quality interpersonal communication. Among the skills to be taught and learned are: perception, attitudes, self-concept, and values development.[1]

Your attitudes and others' attitudes toward you affect your behavior, human relations, and performance. Your job satisfaction is based on your attitudes, which in turn are shaped by your values. Your self-concept is your attitude about yourself, and your self-concept affects your behavior, human relations, and performance. The better you understand how and why people are different, the more effective will be your human relations.

● Organization
● Group
● Individual

Attitudes

In this section, we examine what an attitude is, the importance of attitudes, how you acquire attitudes, how attitudes affect behavior, types of supervisory attitudes and how they affect performance, and how to change attitudes.

What Is an Attitude?

An **attitude** *is a strong belief or feeling toward people, things, and situations.* We all have favorable or positive attitudes, and unfavorable or negative attitudes about life, human relations, work, school, and everything else. Attitudes are not quick judgments we change easily. Our friends and acquaintances usually know how we feel about things. People interpret our attitudes by our behavior. For example, if you make a face behind your boss's or instructor's back, peers will assume you have a negative attitude toward him or her. Rayanne appears to have a negative attitude toward many things.

WORK APPLICATION

1. Describe your attitude about college in general and the specific college you are attending.

Are Attitudes Important?

Attitudes are definitely important.[2] Employers generally place more emphasis on attitude than on academic grades.[3] J. W. Marriott, Jr., president of Marriott Corporation, stated, "We have found that our success depends more upon employee attitudes than any other single factor."

A Xerox executive stated that organizations want to affect not only employee behavior, but their attitudes. Attitudes must change as the workplace becomes more diverse and as self-directed work teams increase. Studies have shown that corporate diversity programs that expose employees to diversity issues affect workplace attitudes by helping to eliminate negative stereotypes.

How We Acquire Attitudes

Attitudes are primarily developed through experiences. As people develop from childhood to adulthood, they interact with parents, family, teachers, and friends. From all of these people, they learn what is right and wrong and how to behave.

When encountering new people or situations, you are the most open and impressionable because you usually haven't had time to form an attitude toward them. Before entering new situations, people often ask others with experience about it. This begins the development of attitudes before the encounter. For example, before you signed up for this class, you may have asked others who completed the course questions about it. If they had positive attitudes, you too may develop a positive attitude; if they were negative, you may have started the course with a negative attitude as well. Getting information from others is fine, but you should develop your own attitudes. Managers' attitudes[4] and work group[5] also affect employee attitudes.

■ Performance
■ Human Relations
■ Behavior

How Attitudes Affect Behavior and Human Relations

Attitudes have an important influence on behavior. A person's attitudes generally cause that person to behave in certain ways. However, attitudes are not the sole determinant of behaviors, nor are they always a reliable predictor of behavior. For example, your attitude toward a class or job will influence your behavior. Generally, if you like a class or job, you will attend more often and work harder, but not necessarily.

Attitudes are complex. Even if you have a negative attitude toward a class or job, you may still attend and work hard because of other attitudes such as a positive attitude toward the teacher or boss, or your peers, or your attitude toward grades or promotions, and so forth.

Strong attitudes directly affect your human relations.[6] When you have strong positive attitudes toward people, you generally try to develop positive relations with them. On the other hand, if you have negative attitudes toward people, you generally try to avoid them or do not make an effort to be nice to them. Some people even consciously develop poor relations by insulting others they do not like.

Management's Attitudes and How They Affect Performance

Before reading on, answer the 10 questions in Self-Assessment Exercise 3–1 to determine if you have Theory X or Theory Y attitudes.

Management Attitudes

Douglas McGregor classified attitudes, which he called *assumptions*, as Theory X and Theory Y. Managers with **Theory X** *attitudes hold that employees dislike work and must be closely supervised to get them to do their work.* **Theory Y** *attitudes hold that employees like to work and do not need to be closely supervised to get them to do their work.* In the global environment, American workers are among the world's most closely watched. Managers with dominant personalities often do not trust employees; thus, they have Theory X attitudes.[7] Employee attitudes also affect managers' attitudes. When managers perceive, correctly or not, negative employee attitudes, managers are quick to adopt Theory X attitudes.

Over the years research has shown that managers with Theory Y attitudes tend to have employees with higher levels of job satisfaction than the employees of Theory X managers. However, managers with Theory Y assumptions do not always have higher levels of productivity in their departments.

APPLICATION SITUATIONS

Theory X, Theory Y

AS 3–1

Identify each manager's comments about employees as being:

A. Theory X   B. Theory Y

_____ 1. "Be careful with it now. I don't want you to mess it up like you did the last time."

_____ 2. "Thanks, I'm confident you will do a good job."

_____ 3. "Select the format you want to use and get it to me when you finish it."

_____ 4. "I'll be checking up on you to make sure the job gets done on time."

_____ 5. "I know you probably think it's a lousy job, but someone has to do it."

Management Attitudes

Circle the letter that best describes what you would actually do as a supervisor. There are no right or wrong answers.

Usually (U)   Frequently (F)   Occasionally (O)   Seldom (S)

U   F   O   S   1. I would set the objectives for my department alone (rather than include employee input).

U   F   O   S   2. I would allow employees to develop their own plans (rather than develop them for them).

U   F   O   S   3. I would delegate several tasks I enjoy doing (rather than doing them myself).

U   F   O   S   4. I would allow employees to make decisions (rather than make them for employees).

U   F   O   S   5. I would recruit and select new employees alone (rather than include employees' input).

U   F   O   S   6. I would train new employees myself (rather than have employees do it).

U   F   O   S   7. I would tell employees what they need to know (rather than everything I know).

U   F   O   S   8. I would spend time praising and recognizing my employees' work efforts (rather than not do it).

U   F   O   S   9. I would set several (rather than few) controls to ensure that objectives are met.

U   F   O   S   10. I would closely supervise my employees (rather than leave them on their own) to ensure that they are working.

To better understand your own attitude toward human nature, score your answers. For items 1, 5, 6, 7, 9, and 10, give yourself one point for each usually (U) answer; two points for each frequently (F) answer; three points for each occasionally (O) answer; and four points for each seldom (S) answer. For items 2, 3, 4, and 8, give yourself one point for each seldom (S) answer; two points for each occasionally (O) answer; three points for each frequently (F) answer; and four points for each usually (U) answer. Total all points. Your score should be between 10 and 40. Place your score here ____. Theory X and Theory Y are on opposite ends of a continuum. Most people's attitudes fall somewhere between the two extremes. Place an X on the continuum below that represents your score.

Theory X 10 ------------ 20 ------------ 30 ----------- 40 Theory Y

The lower your score, the stronger the Theory X attitude, and the higher your score, the stronger the Theory Y attitude. A score of 10–19 could be considered a Theory X attitude. A score of 31–40 could be considered a Theory Y attitude. A score of 20–30 could be considered balanced between the two theories. Your score may not accurately measure how you would behave in an actual job; however, it should help you to understand your own attitudes toward people at work.

How Management's Attitudes Affect Employees' Performance

Managers' attitudes and the way they treat employees affect employees' job behavior and performance.[8] If managers have a positive attitude and expect employees to be highly productive, they will be highly productive. Research by J. Sterling Livingston and others has supported this theory.[9] It is called the *Pygmalion effect*. The **Pygmalion effect** *states that supervisors' attitudes and expectations of employees and how they treat them largely determine their performance.* In a study of welding students, the foreman who was training the group was given the names of students who were quite intelligent and would do well. Actually, the students were selected at random.

■ Performance
■ Human Relations
■ Behavior

Learning Objective

1. Define attitudes and explain how they affect behavior, human relations, and performance

▲ Goal of Human Relations

◆ Video
BM-3

IE 3–1

The only difference was the foreman's expectations. The so-called intelligent students significantly outperformed the other group members. Why this happened is what this theory is all about. The foreman's expectations became the foreman's self-fulfilling prophecy. Thus, managers' behavior and attitudes affect employees' performance.[10]

In a sense, the Hawthorne effect is related to the Pygmalion effect because both affect performance. In the Hawthorne studies, the special attention and treatment given the workers by the management resulted in increased performance.

Through the positive expectations of others, people increase their level of performance. Unfortunately, many managers tend to stereotype and see what they expect to see: low performance. And their employees see and do as the managers expect. We all need to expect and treat people as though they are high achievers to get the best from them. Marva Collins, recognized as one of the nation's most determined and successful teachers, opened her own inner-city school where very high standards are demanded from students of all abilities. In grade school these students read Shakespeare and do hours of homework each night while many of the public school children cannot read and do not do any homework. Many of her students have gone on to successful careers, rather than being recipients of welfare, because of the Pygmalion effect of Collins's attitude.

Although others' attitudes can affect your behavior, human relations and performance, you are responsible for your own actions. Try to ignore negative comments and stay away from people with negative attitudes.

As a manager, create a win-win situation. Expect high performance and treat employees as being capable and special, and you can get the best performance from them.

WORK APPLICATIONS

2. Give two examples of when your attitudes affected your performance. One should be a positive effect and the other a negative one. Be sure to fully explain how the attitude affected performance.
3. Give an example of when you lived up to or down to someone else's expectations of your performance (the Pygmalion effect). It could be a parent's, teacher's, coach's, or boss's expectations. Be specific.

Changing Attitudes

Complete Self-Assessment Exercise 3–2. Determine your own job attitude.

Self-Assessment
Exercise 3–2

Job Attitude

For each of the 10 statements below, identify how often each describes your behavior at work. Place a number from 1 to 5 next to each of the 10 numbers.

(5) Always   (4) Usually   (3) Frequently   (2) Occasionally   (1) Seldom

_____ 1. I smile and am friendly and courteous to everyone at work.

_____ 2. I make positive, rather than negative, comments at work.

_____ 3. When my boss asks me to do extra work I accept it cheerfully.

_____ 4. I avoid making excuses, passing the buck, or blaming others when things go wrong.

_____ 5. I am an active self-starter at getting work done.

_____ 6. I avoid spreading rumors and gossip among employees.

_____ 7. I am a team player willing to make personal sacrifices for the good of the work group.

_____ 8. I accept criticism gracefully and make the necessary changes.

_____ 9. I lift coworkers' spirits and bring them up emotionally.

_____ 10. If I were to ask my boss and coworkers to answer the nine questions and to answer them for me, they would put the same answers/numbers that I did.

_____ Total. Add up the 10 numbers.

Interpreting your score. We can think of our job attitude as being on a continuum from positive to negative. Place an X on the continuum below that represents your score.

Negative attitude   10 - - - - - 20 - - - - - 30 - - - - - 40 - - - - - 50   Positive attitude

Generally, the higher your score the more positive is your job attitude. You may want to have your boss and trusted coworkers answer these nine questions, as suggested in question 10, to determine if their perception of your job attitude is the same as your perception.

WORK APPLICATIONS

4. Based on Self-Assessment Exercise 3–2, what will you do to improve your job attitude? Be specific.

A positive job attitude is vital to career success. Your superiors and coworkers will "read" your attitudes to determine whether they can count on you to be a hardworking, quality-conscious, upbeat team player. You need to have, and communicate, a good job attitude.

Would you rather work with people who have good, moderate, or poor job attitudes? We may not be able to change our coworkers' job attitudes and behavior, but we can change our own. Review the first nine questions and think about ways you can improve your job attitude. To help you, here are some suggestions for changing attitudes.

Changing Your Attitudes

The environment around us influences our attitudes. Usually we cannot control our environment, but we can control our attitudes. You can choose to be optimistic or pessimistic. You can look for the positive and be happier and get more out of life. The following hints can help you change your attitudes:

1. Be aware of your attitudes. People who are optimistic have higher levels of job satisfaction.[11] Consciously try to have and maintain a positive attitude. If a situation gives you lemons—make lemonade.

If you catch yourself complaining or being negative in any way, stop and change to a positive attitude. With time you can become more positive.

2. Think for yourself. Develop your own attitudes based on others' input; don't simply copy others' attitudes.

3. Realize that there are few, if any, benefits to harboring negative attitudes. Negative attitudes, like holding a grudge, can only hurt your human relations, and hurt yourself in the end, and it's stressful.

4. Keep an open mind. Listen to other people's input. Use it to develop your positive attitudes.

Learning Objective

2. Describe how to change your attitudes

In the 19th century, researchers discovered that changing the inner attitudes of your mind can change the outer aspects of your life. You can gain control of your attitudes and change the direction of your life. Start today. Think and act like a winner, and you will become one. For example, Rayanne, in the opening case, does not seem to be interested in changing her attitude.

Shaping and Changing Employee Attitudes

It is difficult to change your own attitudes; it is even more difficult to change other people's attitudes. But it can be done. The following hints can help you (and Kent) as a manager to change employee attitudes.

1. Give employees feedback. Employees must be made aware of their negative attitudes if they are to change. The manager must talk to the employee about the negative attitude. The employee must understand that the attitude has negative consequences for the individual and the department. The manager should offer an alternative attitude. In the opening case, Kent has done this.

2. Accentuate positive conditions. Employees tend to have positive attitudes toward the things they do well. Make working conditions as pleasant as possible; make sure employees have all the necessary resources and training to do a good job.[12]

3. Provide consequences. Employees tend to repeat activities or events followed by positive consequences. On the other hand, they tend to avoid things followed by negative consequences. Encourage and reward employees with positive attitudes. Try to keep negative attitudes from developing and spreading.

4. Be a positive role model. If the manager has a positive attitude, employees may too.[13]

See Exhibit 3–1 for a review of changing attitudes.

EXHIBIT 3–1   **CHANGING ATTITUDES**

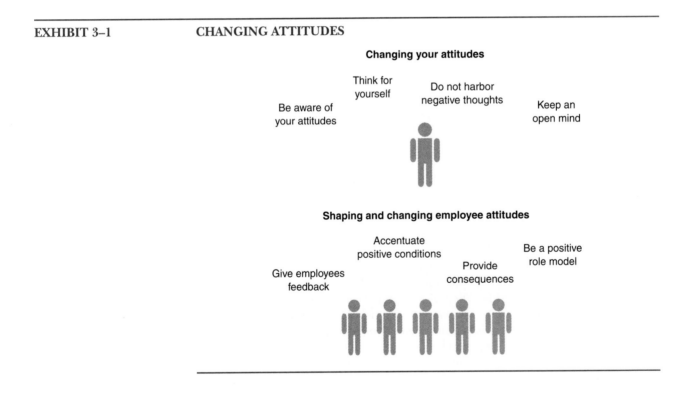

● Organization
● Group
● Individual

Job Satisfaction

In this section, we discuss the importance of job satisfaction; the nature and determinants of job satisfaction; facts about job satisfaction in the United States; measuring job satisfaction; and how job satisfaction affects performance.

APPLICATION SITUATIONS

Job Attitudes

AS 3–2

Identify each employee's attitude statement as being:

A. Positive   B. Negative

_____ 6. "Why do I have to do it?"

_____ 7. "I'd be happy to go pick up the mail for you."

_____ 8. "Get out of the way. Can't you see I'm trying to get through here?"

_____ 9. "It's not my fault. The guy didn't give me enough time."

_____ 10. "I heard you missed your sales quota this month. Don't worry. You'll make it up next month."

The Importance of Job Satisfaction

A person's **job satisfaction** *is a set of attitudes toward work.* Job satisfaction is what most employees want from their jobs, even more than they want job security or higher pay.[14] High job satisfaction is a hallmark of a well-managed organization. Low job satisfaction is often the cause of wildcat strikes, work slowdowns, absenteeism, and high employee turnover.[15] It may also result in grievances, low performance, poor product quality, employee theft and sabotage, disciplinary problems, and a variety of other organizational problems.

Goal of Human Relations

Today, managers see less interest in extra hours, job dedication, attendance, and punctuality. Improving job satisfaction may lead to better human relations and organizational performance by creating a win-win situation.

Absenteeism

Job satisfaction tends to be associated with lower absenteeism, especially when employees have some control over absences, that is, when they are not really sick or injured.[16] Satisfaction with a course also affects class attendance.

Absenteeism is very expensive. For example, at General Motors (GM) absenteeism is 5 percent. This means 25,000 employees are absent each day. This results in 50 million lost hours each year at an annual cost of $1 billion. GM is not the only organization with absenteeism problems. Wells Fargo, Johnson & Johnson, and DWG Corp. have all taken action to combat this problem.

WORK APPLICATIONS

5. Has job or school satisfaction affected your absenteeism? Explain your answer. For example, do you attend a class or job more if you are satisfied with it or if you are dissatisfied with it?

Employee Turnover

Turnover is the rate at which employees leave an organization. Although many other factors are involved in the decision to leave an organization, dissatisfaction is the central one. Recruiting, selecting, and training new employees often cost thousands of dollars. The higher the turnover rate, the larger the expense will be. For example, the electronics industry has a 35 percent annual turnover rate, which means that 35 out of every 100 employees leave each year and must be replaced.

Job satisfaction can contribute substantially to the effectiveness of an organization. It can contribute to productive output in the form of high quantity and quality of products and services,[17] as well as to maintenance objectives of low absenteeism and turnover.[18] Rayanne stated in the opening case that she lacks job satisfaction.

The Nature and Determinants of Job Satisfaction

Job satisfaction is on a continuum from low to high. It can refer to a single employee, a group or department, or an entire organization. Notice that the definition of job satisfaction identifies an overall attitude toward work. It does so because people usually have some aspects of work they have positive attitudes about, like the work itself, and other aspects of work they have negative attitudes about, like pay. Job satisfaction is our overall attitude to our jobs. Organizational climate, discussed in Chapter 12, is a main factor of job satisfaction.[19]

The Nature of Job Satisfaction

When employees are hired, they come to the organization with a set of desires, needs, and past experiences that combine to form job expectations about work. If their expectations are met, they generally have high levels of job satisfaction. If expectations are not met, their level of job satisfaction may be low.[20]

Job satisfaction is a part of life satisfaction.[21] As Chapter 1 stated, the total person comes to work. Your off-the-job life also affects your job satisfaction and, in turn, your job satisfaction affects your life satisfaction. For example, Rayanne brought a negative attitude to work, which in turn affected her job satisfaction.

Determinants of Job Satisfaction

There are a variety of determinants of job satisfaction. Each of these determinants is of great importance to some people, and of little importance to others. We now discuss satisfaction with:

1. The work itself. Whether a person enjoys performing the work itself has a major effect on overall job satisfaction. People who view their jobs as boring, dull, or unchallenging tend to have low levels of job satisfaction.[22]

2. Pay. A person's satisfaction with the pay received affects overall job satisfaction. Employees who are not satisfied with their pay may not perform to their full potential. Some employees who are dissatisfied with their pay may steal organizational resources; they see such theft as a morally justifiable supplement to their wages. In reality, a dissatisfied employee may be overpaid for the job compared to employees in other jobs and organizations, but the employee's perception of equitable pay is what counts. With downsizing influences, worker satisfaction was found to be higher in small companies since employees were happier with the pay and their job responsibilities.[23]

3. Growth and upward mobility. Whether a person is satisfied with the personal or company growth and potential for upward mobility may affect job satisfaction. Many, but not all, people want to be challenged and to learn new things.[24] Some people want to be promoted to higher-level jobs, whether in technical or managerial fields. The view that job mobility is limited has an effect on job satisfaction.[25]

4. Supervision. Whether a person is satisfied with the supervision received affects overall job satisfaction. Employees who feel their boss does not provide the needed direction get frustrated and dissatisfied with work. Employees who feel their boss provides too much control over their jobs also feel dissatisfied.[26] The personal relationship between the boss and employee also affects job satisfaction.[27]

5. Coworkers. Whether a person is satisfied with the human relations with coworkers affects overall job satisfaction. People who like their coworkers often have higher levels of job satisfaction than employees who dislike their coworkers.[28]

6. Attitude toward work. Some people view work as fun and interesting, while others do not. Some people have been satisfied with many different jobs, while others have remained dissatisfied in numerous work situations. People with a positive attitude toward work tend to have higher levels of job satisfaction,[29] and intelligence is not related to job satisfaction.[30]

Learning Objective

3. List six job satisfaction determinants

People differ in the way they prioritize these different determinants of job satisfaction. A person can be highly satisfied in some areas and dissatisfied in others, yet have overall job satisfaction. For a review of determinants of job satisfaction, see Exhibit 3–2.

APPLICATION SITUATIONS

Job Satisfaction

AS 3–3

Identify each statement by its determinant of job satisfaction:

A. Work itself   D. Supervision

B. Pay   E. Coworkers

C. Growth and mobility   F. General work attitude

_____ 11. "The boss is always on my back about something."

_____ 12. "I'd like to buy a VCR, but my bills are piling up. I certainly deserve more than I make."

_____ 13. "I enjoy working with my hands and fixing the machines."

_____ 14. "I'm applying for a promotion, and I think I'll get it."

_____ 15. "Pete and Ann are real jerks. I don't get along well with either of them. They think they know it all."

EXHIBIT 3–2   DETERMINANTS OF JOB SATISFACTION

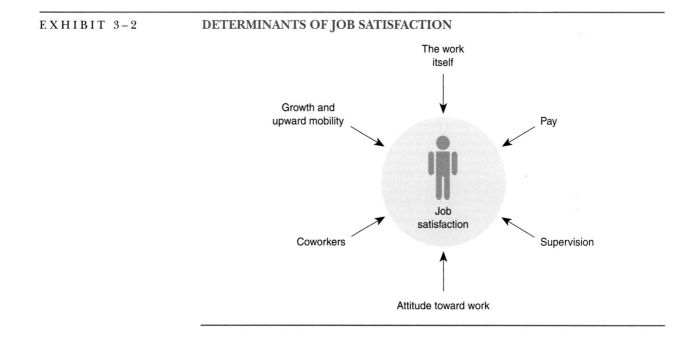

Job Satisfaction in the United States

Overall, U.S. employees have a favorable attitude toward work. College graduates may initially experience high job satisfaction, but this is usually not long lasting. Actually, most people begin interesting new jobs with high expectations and satisfaction. However, overall there is no relationship between how long a person has a job and job satisfaction.[31] And the average number of years employees stay at their jobs continues to decrease.[32]

● Organization
● Group
● Individual

Measuring Job Satisfaction

Because job satisfaction is based on employee attitudes, it is inferred and personal. Job satisfaction is influenced by our perception.[33] People in the same job may perceive their jobs differently. A **job satisfaction survey** *is a process of determining employee* *attitudes about the job and work environment.* The three major ways to measure job satisfaction are observation, interview, and questionnaire. In companies with large numbers of employees, the questionnaire is the most practical. Many organizations use consultants to come in and work with management to design the questionnaire, administer it, tabulate the results, and recommend changes to improve job satisfaction.

The job satisfaction survey enables the organization to measure its employees' attitudes, and serves as a means of comparison for future surveys.[34] Is job satisfaction increasing or decreasing? In which areas are employees dissatisfied? Finding the answers to these questions will help managers make organizational changes that improve job satisfaction.

WORK APPLICATIONS

6. Recall a specific job you have or have held. Measure your job satisfaction for the job by rating each of the six determinants of job satisfaction using a scale from 1 to 5; then add up the total points and divide by 6 to get your average, or overall, job satisfaction level. Be sure to write down the six determinants and your rating from 1 not satisfied to 5 satisfied.

■ Performance
■ Human Relations
■ Behavior

How Job Satisfaction Affects Performance

Until the early 1950s, it was generally assumed that "a happy worker is a productive worker." Therefore, many organizations tried to increase job satisfaction to increase organizational performance. However, by the mid-1950s a number of studies had failed to establish a clear link between satisfaction and performance.

Generally, based on recent studies of the relationship between job satisfaction and performance, we find that a positive correlation does exist.[35] However, the relationship is not very strong, and there are numerous exceptions to the relationship—some low performers are very satisfied with their jobs; some high performers are dissatisfied with their jobs. Nevertheless, an overall positive association exists.[36] When there is a lack of job satisfaction, there is often a lack of motivation and thus lower performance.

As stated in Chapter 2, internals have higher levels of job satisfaction than externals. One could contend that personality or locus of control affects satisfaction and performance. Kent, in the opening case, tried to get Rayanne to understand how her negative attitude is affecting her performance.

Learning Objective

4. Explain how job satisfaction is measured and how it affects performance

WORK APPLICATIONS

7. Has job or school satisfaction affected your performance? Explain your answer. For example, do you work as hard and produce as much for classes or jobs that you are satisfied with as you do for ones you are dissatisfied with?

● Organization
● Group
● Individual

Self-Concept

In this section, we explain self-concept and how it is formed; self-efficacy; how self-concept and self-efficacy affect behavior, human relations, and performance; and how to build a positive self-concept.

IE 3-2

Self-Concept and How It Is Formed

This section focuses on attitudes about oneself. Your **self-concept** *is your overall attitude about yourself.* Self-concept is also called *self-esteem* and *self-image.* Self-concept can be thought of on a continuum from positive to negative, or high to low. Do you like yourself? Are you a valuable person? Are you satisfied with the way you live your life? When faced with a challenge, are your thoughts positive or negative? Do you believe you can meet the challenge or that you're not very good at doing things? If your beliefs and feelings about yourself are positive, you tend to have a high self-concept. Your personality is based, in part, on your self-concept. Self-concept is important.[37] The state of California has a commission involved in developing the self-concept of both children and adults.

Self-concept is your perception of yourself, which may not be the way others perceive you. Your thoughts and feelings about yourself have greater influence in determining your self-concept than your behavior. Even if individuals don't consider themselves likable, others probably do like them.

You develop your self-concept over the years through the messages you receive about yourself from others. Your present self-concept was strongly influenced by the way others treated you—the attitudes and expectations others had of you (Pygmalion effect). Your parents were the first to contribute to your self-concept. Did your parents build you up with statements like "you're smart—you can do it," or destroy you with "you're dumb—you cannot do it"? If you have siblings, were they positive or negative? Your early self-concept still affects your self-concept today. As you grew through adolescence, your teachers and peers also had a profound impact on your self-concept. Were you popular? Did you have friends who encouraged you? By the time you reach adulthood in your early 20s, your self-concept is fairly well developed. However, when you take on more responsibilities such as a full-time job, marriage, and children, your human relations influence your self-concept.[38] Your boss, for example, does or will affect your success (Pygmalion effect) and self-concept.

Apparently, Rayanne came to work for Kent with a negative self-concept. Rayanne stated that she messed up on all her previous jobs, and she called herself a failure. Her self-concept, like yours, however, is dynamic and capable of changing. Kent is trying to develop a win-win situation by trying to get Rayanne to develop a more positive attitude and self-concept so that she can be happier and more productive. Rayanne can change her attitude and self-concept if she really wants to and is willing to work at it. Are you willing to develop a more positive self-concept so that you can be happier and more productive?

In addition to receiving messages from others, we also make social comparisons. We compare ourselves to others all the time. You might think to yourself—am I smarter, better looking, more successful than the people I associate with? Such comparisons can have positive or negative influences on your self-concept. Focusing on negative comparisons can cause you to have a negative self-concept and to be unhappy.

▲ **Goal of Human Relations**

WORK APPLICATIONS

8. Describe your self-concept.

Self-Efficacy

Recall that self-concept is an overall attitude about yourself. You can have a positive self-concept and still want to change some things about yourself. Your self-concept includes perceptions about several aspects of yourself. **Self-efficacy** *is your belief in* *your capability to perform in a specific situation.* Self-efficacy affects your effort, persistence, expressed interest, and the difficulty of goals you select.[39] For example, if your major is business, your self-efficacy may be high for a management course, but low for a language or biology course that you may be required to take.

APPLICATION SITUATIONS

Self-Concept	Identify each statement as:
AS 3–4	A. Positive B. Negative

_____ 16. "Darn, that's the fifth mistake I've made today."

_____ 17. "Sure, I can do that. No problem."

_____ 18. "It's been three weeks, and I still cannot understand why I did not get the promotion I wanted so badly."

_____ 19. "I enjoy going on sales calls and meeting new people."

_____ 20. "I cannot do math."

How Self-Concept and Self-Efficacy Affect Behavior, Human Relations, and Performance

Your self-concept has a major influence on your behavior. It affects your personality, needs, perception, attitudes, and learning. In fact, some behavioral scientists believe that virtually all of one's behavior supports one's self-concept.

How Self-Concept Affects Behavior

Self-concept doesn't just reflect ongoing behavior but instead mediates and regulates behavior. The self-regulation process begins with a goal, conscious or subconscious, and usually a plan to achieve success in different situations. As you strive to achieve your goals, you evaluate your behavioral results against your standards and continually regulate ongoing behavior.

Your self-concept also has a bearing on future behavior through your attribution. **Attribution** *is your perception of the causes of successes and failures.* To protect their self-concept, people tend to blame external causes for failures, but take credit for successes. For example, you might think, "I did not get the promotion because I don't have enough seniority," or "I got the promotion because I worked hard for it." You may know someone who will never admit making a mistake, or always blames someone else. People tend to view behavior this way to protect their self-concept. Continual failure, and blaming external causes, can lead to a feeling of greater external locus of control. Externals are more apt to blame failure on external causes, while internals are more apt to blame their behavior for failure.

How Self-Concept Affects Human Relations

Your attitude toward yourself directly influences the way you interact with others. Employees with a positive self-concept tend to be more receptive to new experiences and meeting new people. Employees who accept themselves are more willing to accept others. They can get along well with a variety of people because they are willing to tolerate differences in others. Generally, people with positive self-concepts have more friends than people with negative self-concepts. They are more willing to share their ideas and feelings with others.

A positive self-concept does not imply egotism, which results in self-superior attitudes and behavior. If you know any egotist, you probably realize that their human relations could be improved by a change in attitude and behavior. People don't like others to flaunt imagined, or real, superiority over them.

How Self-Concept and Self-Efficacy Affect Performance

- Performance
- Human Relations
- Behavior

Video
BM-3

Learning Objectives

5. Determine whether you have a positive self-concept and how it affects your behavior, human relations, and performance

6. Understand how your manager's and your own expectations affect your performance

Workers' self-concept is the key to their performance, which in turn affects the organization's performance through the systems effect.[40]

One of the competency characteristics of people who perform well include self-concept. Self-concept affects individuals' performance and productivity in a variety of ways in the workplace on a daily basis.[41]

In many respects, people with negative self-concepts perform less well than people with positive self-concepts. Low performance contributes to low self-concept, which in turn reinforces low self-esteem. Employees with a positive self-concept are more willing to take on new responsibility and make decisions on their own, and they contribute to the performance of the group, and to group efficacy.[42]

Your expectations affect your performance. If you think you will be successful, you will be. If you think you will fail, you will, because you will fulfill your expectations. You will live up to or down to your expectations. This expectation phenomenon is often referred to as the *self-fulfilling prophecy*. The **self-fulfilling prophecy** *occurs when your expectations affect your success or failure.* Rayanne stated that she had messed up on all the jobs she had, and she called herself a failure. Is there any surprise to find that Rayanne is having problems in her new job working for Kent?

As you can see, self-efficacy and the self-fulfilling prophecy go hand in hand. Your self-efficacy becomes your self-fulfilling prophecy.

WORK APPLICATIONS

9. Give an example of when you lived up to or down to your own expectations (self-efficacy leading to self-fulfilling prophecy).

Building a Positive Self-Concept

Although influenced as discussed, you are the ultimate creator of your self-concept.[43] You can always improve your self-concept, even though it is not easy to evaluate yourself and it is even more difficult to change. Once you recognize the importance of a positive self-concept, you will see that it is worth the time and effort to improve your self-concept. You can change; you don't have to be who you were in the past or are in the present. The general guidelines below are followed by an action plan that will help you to develop a more positive self-concept. As a manager, you can work with employees using these ideas to help them develop a more positive self-concept. Kent could teach them to Rayanne.

General Guidelines

The following are general guidelines you can implement in your daily life to improve your self-concept.

1. View mistakes as learning experiences. Realize that we all make mistakes. Talk to any successful businessperson with a positive self-concept and he or she will admit making mistakes on the way to success. The key to success is examining your mistakes and learning from them. Try to be future oriented. Don't worry about past mistakes. Dwelling on past mistakes will only have a negative effect on your self-concept.

2. Accept failure and bounce back. Since most careers tend to zigzag upward, the ability to handle failures well can make or break a climb on the corporate ladder. Inability to rebound from disappointments is one of the main reasons why managers fail. When the name Lee Iaccoca comes up, most people think of his success at turning Chrysler around. Few people recall Lee being fired from Ford prior to going to Chrysler. In his autobiography, Iaccoca recalls many disappointments during his career. Linda Gottlieb lost her television film job, but went on to become a feature film producer. Dwelling on failure and disappointment will only have a negative

effect on your self-concept. Realize that you will have disappointments but go on to bigger and better things like Iaccoca and Gottlieb.

3. Control negative behavior and thoughts. Emotions, like anger, are a part of life. You cannot control other people's behavior, nor can you completely control your emotional responses. If someone says something negative to you, you cannot be emotionless inside; however, you can control your behavior. You don't have to say something negative back to the person, yell at the person, or hit the person. Become aware of your emotions and work to control your behavior.

Your thoughts are also very important. If your thoughts are full of failure, you will fail. If you catch yourself thinking negative thoughts, be aware of what is happening and replace the negative thoughts with positive ones, such as "I can do this. It's easy." With time you will have fewer and fewer negative thoughts. Always accept a compliment with a thank you. Don't minimize the compliment with the statement, "Anyone could have done it," or "It was not a big deal." Never put yourself down in your thoughts, words, or actions. If you catch yourself doing this, stop and replace the thoughts or behavior in a positive way.

4. Use any religious or spiritual beliefs you have that can help you develop a more positive self-concept: for example, "I am made in the image and likeness of God." "Buddha doesn't make junk."

Action Plan for Building a Positive Self-Concept

The three-part action plan for building a positive self-concept includes:

Step 1. *Identify Your Strengths and Areas That Need Improvement:* What are the things about yourself that you like? What can you do well? What do you have to offer other people and organizations?

What are the things about yourself or behavior that could be improved? Be aware of your limitations. No one is good at everything. Focus on your strengths, not weaknesses. In areas where you are weak, get help and help others in their weak areas.

IE 3-3

Step 2. *Set Goals and Visualize Them:* Before you can get anywhere or get anything out of life, you must first determine where you want to go or what you want. Based on step 1, set some goals for the things about yourself or your behavior that you want to change for the better. Write them down in positive affirmative language. For example, write and tell yourself

- "I am calm when talking to others" (not "I don't yell at people").
- "I am a slim 110 pounds" (not "I must lose weight").
- "I am outgoing and enjoy meeting new people" (not "I must stop being shy").
- "I am smart and get good grades." or "I am good at my job."

Place your goals where you can review them several times each day. Put copies on your mirror, refrigerator, car visor, or your desk, or record them on a cassette and play them several times each day. Start and end each day thinking positive thoughts about yourself.

People often procrastinate because the whole goal or project seems overwhelming. When you don't know where to start, you don't do anything. Remember, success comes one step at a time. Reaching one goal helps motivate you to continue, and each success helps develop a more positive self-concept. Therefore, set short-term goals you can reach. For example, if you presently weigh 150 pounds, start with the goal "I am a slim 110 pounds," but break it up into double parts, "I will weigh 145 pounds by XXX date," and "I will weigh 140 pounds by XXX date." Compliment and reward yourself regularly as you achieve your short-term goals. Rewards do not have to be big. When you hit the new weight, treat yourself to a small ice cream cone or a movie. Rewards will help motivate you to continue until you reach the final 110 pounds. You will learn about goal-setting and motivation in Chapter 6.

Olympic stars and successful businesspeople have increased their performance through mentally imagining their success. Divers mentally see themselves successfully perform the dive. Salespeople often mentally rehearse their sales calls and the closing of the sale. Each day visualize yourself as you want to be in your goals. For example, picture yourself calm when talking to a person you usually yell at. Mentally see yourself at a slim 110 pounds. Picture yourself meeting new people or being successful on the job, and so forth.

Step 3.   *Develop a Plan and Implement It:* What specific action will you take to improve your self-concept through changing your thoughts or behavior? Some goals take much planning while others do not. For example, if you want to lose weight to get down to 110 pounds, you will have to do more than just imagine yourself being 110 pounds. What will be your plan to lose the weight? Exercise? Diet? What are the specifics? With other goals, like not yelling at people, making detailed plans is not so easy. However, you can determine what it is that gets you mad and try to eliminate it. What will you do differently?

Remember, you need to have positive self-efficacy if you want to be successful, and plans are useless if you don't implement them.

Stop comparing yourself to others and downgrading yourself because this hurts your self-concept. We can all find someone who is better than we are. Even the best are eventually topped. Set your goals, develop plans, and achieve them. Compare yourself to *you*. Be the best that you can be. Continue to improve yourself by setting goals, developing plans, and achieving them. Through this process, you will develop your self-concept. If you continually improve yourself, there is less chance of a midlife crisis. You are less likely to look back at your life and ask what have I accomplished? You will know and be proud of yourself. See Exhibit 3–3 for a review of how to develop a positive self-concept.

Skill-Building
3-2
3-3

Learning Objective

7. Demonstrate how to develop a more positive self-concept

EXHIBIT 3–3   **DEVELOPING A POSITIVE SELF-CONCEPT**

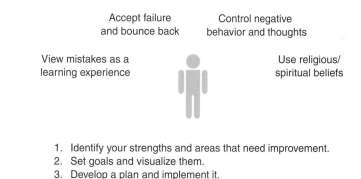

1. Identify your strengths and areas that need improvement.
2. Set goals and visualize them.
3. Develop a plan and implement it.

WORK APPLICATIONS

10. Which of the three general guidelines to building a positive self-concept needs the least work? The most work? Explain your answer.

Values

● Organization
● Group
● Individual

In this section, we cover individual values and how they are related to, yet different from, attitudes. A person's **values** *are the things that have worth for or are important to the individual,* and a **value system** *is the set of standards by which the individual lives.* Values concern what "should be"; they influence the choices we make among alternative behaviors. Values direct the form that motivated behavior will take. For example, if you have three job offers, you will select the one that is of the highest value to you.

Values help shape your attitudes. When something is of value to you, you tend to have positive attitudes toward it. If something is not of value to you, you tend to have negative attitudes toward it. Since work is not important to Rayanne, it is not surprising that she has a negative attitude toward work. What is of value to you? Complete Self-Assessment Exercise 3–3 and identify your personal values in eight broad areas of life.

Self-Assessment
Exercise 3–3

Personal Values

Below are 16 items. Rate how important each one is to you on a scale of 0 (not important) to 100 (very important). Write the number 0–100 on the line to the left of each item.

Not important				Somewhat important				Very important		
0	10	20	30	40	50	60	70	80	90	100

_____ 1. An enjoyable, satisfying job.

_____ 2. A high-paying job.

_____ 3. A good marriage.

_____ 4. Meeting new people, social events.

_____ 5. Involvement in community activities.

_____ 6. My relationship with God/my religion.

_____ 7. Exercising, playing sports.

_____ 8. Intellectual development.

_____ 9. A career with challenging opportunities.

_____ 10. Nice cars, clothes, home, etc.

_____ 11. Spending time with family.

_____ 12. Having several close friends.

_____ 13. Volunteer work for not-for-profit organizations like the cancer society.

_____ 14. Meditation, quiet time to think, pray, etc.

_____ 15. A healthy, balanced diet.

_____ 16. Educational reading, TV, self-improvement programs, etc.

Below, transfer the numbers for each of the 16 items to the appropriate column, then add the two numbers in each column.

	Professional	Financial	Family	Social
	1. _____	2. _____	3. _____	4. _____
	9. _____	10. _____	11. _____	12. _____
Totals	_____	_____	_____	_____

	Community	Spiritual	Physical	Intellectual
	5. _____	6. _____	7. _____	8. _____
	13. _____	14. _____	15. _____	16. _____
Totals	_____	_____	_____	_____

The higher the total in any area, the higher the value you place on that particular area. The closer the numbers are in all eight areas, the more well-rounded you are.

Think about the time and effort you put forth in your top three values. Is it sufficient to allow you to achieve the level of success you want in each area? If not, what can you do to change? Is there any area in which you feel you should have a higher value total? If yes, which, and what can you do to change?

Skill-Building

3-1

11. What is your attitude toward your personal values total in the eight areas of Self-Assessment Exercise 3–3? Do you plan to work at changing any of your values? Why or why not?

Learning Objective

8. Identify your personal values

Values do not necessarily affect behavior, but values do have an influence on attitudes.[44] For example, some people rate the value of physical activity high in Self-Assessment Exercise 3–3, but they rarely get any exercise. Yet, they do have a positive attitude about exercise. In other words, some people talk a good game, or their words speak louder than their actions.

Values are developed in much the same way as attitudes. However, values are more stable than attitudes. Attitudes reflect multiple, often changing opinions. Values about some things do change, but the process is usually slower than a change in attitude. Society influences our value system. What was considered unacceptable in the past may become commonplace in the future, or vice versa. For example, the percentage of smokers and the social acceptance of smoking have decreased over the years. Similarly, your parents may have told you that some of your behavior would not have been tolerated in their parents' home. Value changes over the years are often a major part of what is referred to as the *generation gap*.

 **Goal of Human Relations**

It is not only within the home, but also within the workplace that a general decline of values may be perceived.[45] Business managers state that the work ethic has declined.[46] The number of people who are not honest and do not play fair (lie, cheat, steal, etc.) has led to companies increasingly being judged not only by their products but also by their values. Thus, business success depends on achieving a balance among interest,[47] or what we call the *goal of human relations*. In response, companies are conducting values audits that encourage honesty and strong values.[48] However, audits do not always work, and those who are truly successful know that in all transactions, what matters most is people.[49] Besides, in a study, entrepreneurs with strong personal values had higher levels of performance than entrepreneurs with weaker personal values.[50] Or in other words, honesty and fair play do pay. We will talk more about this issue and ethics in Chapter 9.

Getting to know people and understanding their values can improve human relations. For example, if Juan knows that Carla has great respect for the president, he can avoid making negative comments about the president in front of her. Likewise, if Carla knows that Juan is a big baseball fan, she can ask him how his favorite team is doing.

Discussions over value issues, like abortion, rarely lead to changes in others' values. They usually just end in arguments. We should try to be open-minded about others' values and avoid arguments that will only hurt human relations.

Spirituality in the Workplace

People want to be happy, and the level of happiness has not changed since 1964 even though the average per capita income, controlled for 1964 dollars, has more than doubled in the United States.[51] People are searching for fulfillment at work and at home.[52] Many people are seeking spirituality or soul as a means of fulfillment in their lives. Dr. Edward Wilson, Harvard University professor and two-time Pulitzer Prize–winning expert on human nature says, "I believe the search for spirituality is going to be one of the major historical episodes of the 21st Century."[53] Professor Judith Neal, University of New Haven, now defines spirituality in the workplace followed by guidelines for leading from a spiritual perspective.[54]

Defining Spirituality in the Workplace

Spirituality is difficult to define, and many of the people writing on spirituality in the workplace don't even attempt to try. However, here are some definitions. The Latin origin of the word spirit is *spirare,* meaning, "to breathe." At its most basic, then, spirit is what inhabits us when we are alive and breathing, it is the life force. Spirituality has been defined as, "That which is traditionally believed to be the vital principle or animating force within living beings; that which constitutes one's unseen intangible being; the real sense or significance of something."[55] A fairly comprehensive definition, part of which is provided here, is as follows:

> *One's spirituality is the essence of who he or she is. It defines the inner self, separate from the body, but including the physical and intellectual self. . . . Spirituality also is the quality of being spiritual, of recognizing the intangible, life-affirming force in self and all human beings. It is a state of intimate relationship with the inner self of higher values and morality. It is a recognition of the truth of the inner nature of people. . . . Spirituality does not apply to particular religions, although the values of some religions may be a part of a person's spiritual focus. Said another way, spirituality is the song we all sing. Each religion has its own singer.*[56]

Perhaps the difficulty people have had in defining spirituality is that they are trying to objectify and categorize an experience and way of being that is at its core very subjective and beyond categorizing. Spirituality in the workplace is about people seeing their work as a spiritual path, as an opportunity to grow personally and to contribute to society in a meaningful way. It is about learning to be more caring and compassionate with fellow employees, with bosses, with subordinates and customers. It is about integrity, being true to oneself, and telling the truth to others. Spirituality in the workplace can refer to an individual's attempts to live his or her values more fully in the workplace. Or it can refer to the ways in which organizations structure themselves to support the spiritual growth of employees. In the final analysis, the understanding of spirit and of spirituality in the workplace is a very individual and personal matter.

Guidelines for Leading from a Spiritual Perspective

Here are five spiritual principles that have been useful to many leaders in their personal and professional development.

1. Know thyself. All spiritual growth processes incorporate the principle of self-awareness. Leading provides a great opportunity to become more self-aware. Examine why you respond to situations the way you do. Take a moment in the morning to reflect on the kind of leader you would like to be today. At the end of the day, take quiet time to assess how well you did, and to what extent you were able to live in alignment with your deepest held core values.

2. Act with authenticity and congruency. Followers learn a lot more from who we are and how we behave than from what we say. Authenticity means being oneself, being fully congruent, and not playing a role. Many managers really get into the role "leader" and see managing as a place to assert their superiority and control. They would never want employees to see the more human, softer parts of them. Yet we are finding that managers who are more authentic and congruent tend to be more effective.

It is a real challenge to be authentic and congruent in the workplace. Most people feel that if they are truly themselves and if they say what they are really thinking, it will be the end of their careers. But if we don't do this, we sell a little bit of our souls every time we are inauthentic, and that saps our creative energy and our emotional intelligence. It also reduces our sense of commitment to the work we do, and we cannot perform at our highest level. Experiment with greater authenticity and with showing more of your humanness. You will be surprised at how positively people will respond.

It is also important to create a climate where employees are encouraged to behave authentically and congruently. This means that they should be comfortable expressing feelings as well as thoughts and ideas.

3. Respect and honor the beliefs of others. It can be very risky and maybe even inappropriate to talk about your own spirituality in the workplace. Yet if spirituality is a guiding force in your life and your leading, and if you follow the guideline of authenticity and congruency, you cannot hide that part of yourself. It is a fine line to walk. What seems to work best is to build a climate of trust and openness first and to model an acceptance of opinions and ideas that are different from yours. Then, if an appropriate opportunity comes up where you can mention something about your spiritual beliefs, you should emphasize that they are yours alone. Explain that many people have different beliefs and that you respect those differences. It is extremely important that employees do not feel that you are imposing your belief system (spiritual, religious, or otherwise) on them.

4. Be as trusting as you can be. This guideline operates on many levels. On the personal level, this guideline of "being as trusting as you can be" applies to trusting oneself, one's inner voice, or one's source of spiritual guidance. This means trusting that there is a Higher Power in your life and that if you ask you will receive guidance on important issues.

5. Maintain a spiritual practice. In a research study on people who integrate their spirituality and their work, the most frequently mentioned spiritual practice is spending time in nature. Examples of other practices are meditation, prayer, reading inspirational literature, hatha yoga, shamanistic practices, writing in a journal, and walking a labyrinth. These people report that it is very important for them to consistently commit to whatever individual spiritual practice they have chosen. The regular involvement in a chosen practice appears to be the best way to deepen one's spirituality.[57] When leaders faithfully commit to a particular spiritual practice they are calmer, more creative, more in tune with employees and customers, and more compassionate.[58]

Spirit at Work Website http://www. spiritatwork.com

IE 3-4

Judith Neal created a comprehensive website on spirituality in the workplace that is a free resource to people interested in this field. It consists of an online journal called "The Spirit at Work Newsletter," which features articles written by leaders, academics, consultants, and every day working people. There are also editorials, poetry, and book reviews. An extensive bibliography of hundreds of references on the topic can be found on the site. There is also information on all the conferences worldwide that are being held on spirituality and business. One of the most useful tools is a "Supersite" of websites that allows the visitor to connect to the websites of consultants, authors, conference websites, websites of similar organizations, online newsletters and discussion groups, and online articles. New features are being added constantly.

By implementing the ideas presented in this chapter, you can develop positive attitudes, a more positive self-concept, and clarify your values. Begin today.

REVIEW

Select one or more methods: (1) Fill in the missing key terms from memory, (2) match the key terms, from the end of the review, with their definitions below, and/or (3) copy the key terms in order, from the key terms at the beginning of the chapter.

Your attitudes and others' attitudes toward you affect your behavior, human relations, and performance. Your job satisfaction is based on your attitudes. Your self-concept is your attitude about yourself, and your self-concept affects your behavior, human relations, and performance. Your attitudes are shaped by your values.

A(n) _____ is a strong belief or feeling toward people,

things, and situations, which tends to be positive or negative. We acquire our

attitudes through the people and situations we encounter throughout our lives.

Attitudes affect behavior, but they are only one variable affecting our behavior; they are not always a good predictor of behavior. A supervisor's attitudes toward employees affect their performance. _____ attitudes hold that employees dislike work and must be closely supervised to get them to do their work, while _____ attitudes hold that employees like to work and do not need to be closely supervised to get them to do their work. The _____ states that management's attitudes and expectations of employees and how they treat them largely determine their performance. Attitudes can be changed with time and effort.

_____ is a set of attitudes toward work. Job satisfaction has an effect on absenteeism and employee turnover. Some of the determinants of job satisfaction include the work itself, pay, growth and upward mobility, supervision, coworkers, and attitude toward work in general. Overall, in the United States employees have a favorable attitude toward work. To measure job satisfaction, many organizations conduct a _____, which is a process of determining employee attitudes about the job and work environment. Surveys enable the organization to determine areas in which changes should be made to improve job satisfaction. There is a relationship between job satisfaction and performance, but it is not a strong one because there are numerous exceptions to the relationship. It is also difficult to determine which variable affects the other.

Our _____ is our overall attitude about ourselves. It is on a continuum from positive to negative, or high to low. Our self-concept is our perception of ourselves and may not be the same as others perceive us. Over the years our experiences and comparisons to others have formed our self-concept. Generally, people with positive self-concepts outperform people with low self-concepts. _____ is our belief in our capability to perform in a specific situation. Our self-concept affects our personality, needs, perception, attitudes, and learning. It mediates and regulates behavior.

_____ is our perception of the causes of successes and failures. We tend to take credit for success and blame external factors for failure. People with positive self-concepts tend to be more outgoing and skilled in human relations than people with negative self-concepts. Self-efficacy is a good predictor of performance. If we think we can be successful, we can; if we don't think we can succeed, we will fail. We tend to live up to or down to our expectations. This phenomenon is often referred to as the _____, which occurs when our expectations affect our success or failure. To build a positive self-concept, one should view mistakes as a learning experience, accept failure and bounce back, and control negative behavior and thoughts. Specific action can include: step 1, identify your strengths and areas for improvement; step 2, set goals and visualize them; and step 3, develop a plan and implement it.

_____ are the things that have worth or are important to the individual, and a _____ is the set of standards by which the individual lives. Values influence the choices we make among alternative behaviors. Values are more stable than attitudes, which include multiple opinions that may change often. Values can change, but this change usually requires a long period of time. The search for spirituality in one's personal and professional life is on the increase.

KEY TERMS

attitude 79	Pygmalion effect 81	Theory X 80
attribution 90	self-concept 89	Theory Y 80
job satisfaction 85	self-efficacy 89	values 93
job satisfaction survey 87	self-fulfilling prophecy 91	value system 93

CASE

Frederick Smith:
Federal Express

Frederick W. Smith thought of the idea of an overnight delivery system by airfreight to accommodate time-sensitive shipments such as medicines, computer parts, and electronics. Smith presented the idea in a term paper to a professor in college and received a grade of "C." Despite the criticism, on March 12, 1973, Smith tested his service by delivering six packages. FedEx began operations officially on April 17 with a total of 186 packages shipped. FedEx lost a million dollars a month for the first 27 months. Fred Smith, developed the "People, Service, Profit," or P-S-P slogan which is—take care of people and they in turn will deliver service, which will result in profits. FedEx made a profit in its 28th month.

FedEx developed the hub-and-spokes systems now widely imitated in the airline industry. Using this system, all shipments are flown to a centralized hub, sorted, loaded onto planes, and dispatched. By November 1988, Federal Express delivered 1 million packages in one night. Over the years, FedEx has been the first in its industry to offer innovative ideas and services including: overnight package delivery, the Overnight Letter (1981), 10:30 A.M. next-day delivery (Fall 1982), package tracking in vans, real-time package tracking over-the-phone (1981), time-definite service for freight, Saturday delivery, and pickup service. FedEx now delivers an average of 2 million pieces per night to 186 countries.[59]

Go to the Internet: For more information on Frederick Smith and FedEx and to update the information provided in this case, do a name search on the Internet and visit the FedEx website at *http://www.fedex.com.* For ideas on using the Internet with cases, see Appendix C.

Support your answers to the following questions with specific information from the case and text, or other information you get from the web or other source.

1. What type of attitude does Fred Smith have towards FedEx?

2. Do the Pygmalion effect and self-fulfilling prophecy apply to this case?

3. Do FedEx employees have a high level of job satisfaction?

4. Did the professor's comment and grade and losing 1 million dollars a month for over two years seem to affect Fred Smith's self-concept? Would it have affected yours?

5. What does self-efficacy have to do with this case?

6. Are there any values illustrated in this case?

Job Satisfaction   Kathy Barns was the first woman hired by the Kelly Construction Co. to perform a "man's job." When Kathy was interviewed for the job by Jean Rossi, the personnel director, Kathy was excited to get the opportunity to prove a woman could do a man's job. During the first month, Kathy never missed a day. However, in the second month she missed four days of work, and by the end of the month she came to tell Ms. Rossi she was quitting. Jean was surprised and wanted to find out what happened, so she asked Kathy some questions. (*Note:* Jean's meeting with Kathy can be role-played in class.)

JEAN: How did your orientation to the job go?

KATHY: Well, the foreman, Jack, started things off by telling me that he was against my being hired. He told me that a woman couldn't do the job and that I would not last very long.

JEAN: Did Jack teach you the job?

KATHY: He taught me the different parts of the job by beginning with a statement about how difficult it was. Jack made comments like "I'm watching you—don't mess up." He was constantly looking over my shoulder waiting for me to make a mistake, and when I did he would give me the old "I told you so" speech. A couple of the guys gave me some help, but for the most part they ignored me.

JEAN: Is your job performance satisfactory?

KATHY: It's not as good as it could be, but it cannot be too bad because Jack hasn't fired me. I enjoy the work when Jack leaves me alone, and I do better work, too. But it seems he's always around.

JEAN: Are you really sure you want to quit?

KATHY: *Pauses and thinks.*

Answer the following questions. Then in the space between questions, state why you selected that answer.

_____ 1. Jack had Theory _____ attitudes toward Kathy.

   a. X   *b.* Y

_____ 2. Kathy started at Kelly with a _____ job attitude.

   a. positive   *b.* negative

_____ 3. Most likely there _____ a relationship between job satisfaction and Kathy's absenteeism.

   a. is   *b.* is not

_____ 4. The major determinant of Kathy's job dissatisfaction is:

   a. the work itself   *c.* growth and mobility   *e.* coworkers
   b. pay   *d.* supervision   *f.* general work attitude

_____ 5. Job satisfaction _____ the major reason for Kathy's performance being below her potential.

   a. is   *b.* is not

_____ 6. Jack's behavior contributed to the _____ of Kathy's self-efficacy.

   a. development   *b.* deterioration

_____ 7. The attribution cause for Kathy's lack of success at Kelly is:

        a. internal   *b.* external

_____ 8. There _____ a relationship between Kathy's job satisfaction and her quitting (turnover).

        a. is   *b.* is not

_____ 9. Kathy's _____ changed over the two months at Kelly Construction.

        a. attitude   *b.* job satisfaction   *c.* values

_____ 10. This case best illustrates:

        a. Theory X   *c.* Pygmalion effect   *e.* self-fulfilling
        b. value system   *d.* self-efficacy   prophecy

11. How could Jean have prevented this situation?

12. What would you do if you were in Kathy's situation?

Fiscal Fairy Tale #12: Piety Piper

Following the steps to getting to read a fiscal fairy tale in MG Webzine Exercise 1 in Chapter 1 page 34, go to the MG website and read *Fiscal Fairy Tale #12: Piety Piper* (your instructor may ask you to print a copy and bring it to class). Answer these questions (your instructor may ask you to type them and bring them to class):

Online MG Webzine Exercise 3

Questions Relating to the Tale Only

1. As stated at the end of the tale, in 50 words or so, what is your response to this tale? You may send it to MG.

2. Have you, or anyone you know, worked for an organization something like this one that lays off people? Give some examples of things the organizational managers do/did.

3. Can organizations like the kingdom keep the loyalty of its workers?

4. Does worker loyalty really matter? Does it affect performance?

Questions Relating the Tale to the Chapter Concepts

5. How did Piety's attitude affect his and his coworkers' behavior, human relations, and performance?

6. Is the kingdom management more Theory X or Theory Y?

7. Rate the level of job satisfaction for each of the six determinants for the kingdom workers.

8. What affect do the events of the case have on worker self-concepts?

9. Does the kingdom management value its workers as assets?

In-Class MG Webzine Exercise 3

The instructor selects one of the six options from Appendix B page 589.

INTERNET EXERCISES

Attitudes: MG Ezzays (IE 3–1)

The objective of this exercise is to identify strong attitudes. Use the information in Appendix B and IE 1–2 and 1–3 as you do the following:

1. Go to the homepage of MG website—*www.mgeneral.com*

Online Internet Exercise 3–1

2. Click "Leaders.Now" (opinion Ezzays) at the bottom of the screen. Search around and find an Ezzay of interest to you and read it (your instructor may ask you to print it). Just about all of them are based on strong attitudes.

3. Questions: (1) Who is the author and what is the title of the Ezzay? (2) What are the strong attitudes of the author—do's and don'ts—about leadership? (3) How can you use this information in your personal or professional life? (Your instructor may require you to type and print out your answers.)

In-Class Internet Exercise 3–1, IE 3–2, IE 3–3, and IE 3–4

The instructor selects one of the six options from Appendix B page 589.

Self-Esteem (IE 3–2)

The objective of this Internet exercise is to assess if you have a low or high self-esteem. Use the information from Appendix B and IE 1–2 and 1–3 as you do the following:

Online Internet Exercise 3–2 (Self-Assessment)

1. Go to the Body-Mind QueenDom website homepage—*www.queendom.com*

2. Click "Tests" and scroll down to the Career/Jobs tests section and Click "Assertiveness" and take the test by clicking your selections then click score to get your score and interpretation (your instructor may ask you to make a copy of it to bring to class).

3. Questions: (1) What was your score? (2) Do you have a low, moderate, or high self-esteem? (3) What can you do to improve your self-esteem? (Your instructor may ask you to type and print your answer and bring them to class.)

Self-Talk to Improve Self-Concept (IE 3–3)

The objective of this exercise is to learn how to use self-talk as a means to improve your self-concept and self-efficacy. Use the information in Appendix B and IE 1–2 and 1–3 as you do the following:

Online Internet Exercise 3–3

1. Go to Dr. Helmstetter's Internet homepage—*www.selftalk.com*

2. Click "What is self-talk" and read the overview of self-talk. From this subsite . . .

3. Click "The HOT 100" and read the examples of negative and positive self-talk. Print a copy and highlight the examples that are most relevant to you). Return to the homepage.

4. Click "How to use self-talk" and read the material.

5. Assignment (your instructor may require you to type your plan): Based on the examples of self-talk and how to use self-talk, develop a plan to improve your self-concept and self-efficacy. Be sure to have written self-talk that you will use. Identify your planned behavior and situations for using self-talk.

Spirit At Work (IE 3–4)

The objective of this exercise is to learn more about spirituality in the workplace. Using the information in Appendix B and IE 1–2 and 1–3 as you do the following:

Online Internet Exercise 3–4

1. Go to the Spirit at Work homepage—*www.spiritatwork.com*

2. Scroll down to WELCOME PAGE and click it to enter this subsite. Read the welcome and overview of the website. At the bottom of the welcome page, sign up for the Spirit at Work list as directed to receive e-mails about the latest information on spirituality in the work place. Click the "back" icon on the toolbar to return to the home page.

3. From the home page, scroll to the Newsletter section and click NEW ARTICLES. Review the new articles and then click PAST ISSUES and review prior articles. Select one article of interest to you. After reading the article, answer these questions. (Your instructor may ask you to print the article and/or type the answers to the article questions below.)

4. Questions: (1) Who is the author and what is the title? (2) What is the primary message of the article in 50 words or less? (3) Why did you select this specific article; why and how is it of interest to you? (4) How can you use the information in the article in your personal or professional life?

5. Explore the other Spirit at Work subsites of interest to you.

**In-Class
Self-Learning**

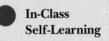

Objective: To better understand human behavior.

Preparation: You should have completed Self-Assessment Exercises 3–1, 3–2, and 3–3 in Chapter 3.

SCANS: The SCANS competencies of interpersonal skills and information and the foundations of basic and thinking qualities, and especially the personal quality of self-esteem, are developed through this exercise.

Experience: You will share your self-learning in small groups to better understand your behavior and that of others.

*Procedure 1
(5–15 minutes)*

Break into groups of two or three members and share the answers you feel comfortable sharing in Self-Assessment Exercises 3–1, 3–2, and/or 3–3. Do not pressure anyone to share anything that makes them uncomfortable. Focus on your similarities and differences and the reasons for them. Your instructor will tell you if you will be doing the sharing in the next section of this exercise.

Sharing: Volunteers state the similarities and differences within their group.

Conclusion: The instructor leads a class discussion and/or makes concluding remarks.

Application: What have I learned from this exercise? How will I use this knowledge in the future?

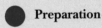

Preparation

**Building a More Positive
Self-Concept**

This may not be an easy exercise for you, but it could result in improving your self-concept, which has a major impact on your success in life. Below, follow the three-step plan for building a positive self-concept.

You may be asked to share your plan with a person of your choice in class. Your instructor should tell you if you will be asked to share during class. If you will share during class, do not include anything you do not wish to share. Write in the space provided, using additional pages if needed. Write a separate personal plan for yourself, if you do not want to share it.

Step 1. Identify your strengths and areas for improvement.

What do I like about myself?

What can I do well? (Reflect on some of your accomplishments.)

What skills and abilities do I have to offer people and organizations?

What are the things about myself or behaviors that could be improved to help me build a more positive self-concept?

Step 2. Set goals and visualize them.

Based on your area(s) for improvement, write down some goals in a positive affirmative format. Three to five is recommended as a start. Once you achieve them go on to others.

For example:

1. I am positive and successful (not—I need to stop thinking/worrying about failure).

2. I enjoy listening to others (not—I need to stop dominating the conversation).

Visualize yourself achieving your goals. For example, imagine yourself succeeding without worrying, or visualize having a conversation you know you will have, without dominating it.

Step 3. Develop a plan and implement it.

For each of your goals, state what you will do to achieve it. What specific action will you take to improve your self-concept through changing your thoughts or behavior? Number your plans to correspond with your goals.

**In-Class
Building a More
Positive Self-
Concept**

*Procedure 1
(2–4 minutes)*

*Procedure 2
(10–20 minutes)*

Objective: To build a more positive self-concept.

SCANS: The SCANS competencies of interpersonal skills and information and the foundations of basic and thinking qualities, and especially the personal quality of self-esteem, are developed through this exercise.

Preparation: You should have completed the three-step action plan for building a positive self-concept on the preceding pages.

Experience: In groups of two, you will share your plan to build a more positive self-concept.

Break into teams of two. You may make a group of three if you prefer. Try to work with someone with whom you feel comfortable sharing your plan. Make one group of three if necessary.

Using your preparation plan, share your answers one at a time. It is recommended that you both share on each step/question before proceeding to the next. The choice is yours, but be sure you get equal air time. For example, one person states, "what I like about myself." The other person follows with his or her response. After both share, go on to cover "what I do well," and so on. During your sharing, you may offer each other helpful suggestions but do so in a positive way; remember you are helping one another build a more positive self-concept. Avoid saying anything that could be considered a put-down.

Conclusion: The instructor may lead a class discussion and/or make concluding remarks.

Application: (2–4 minutes): Will I implement my plan? If so, will I succeed at developing a more positive self-concept? What have I learned through this experience?

SKILL-BUILDING EXERCISE 3–3

**In-Class
Giving and Accept-
ing Compliments**

*Procedure 1
(2 minutes)*

Objective: To give and accept compliments as a means to improving self-concept.

SCANS: The SCANS competencies of interpersonal skills and information and the foundations of basic and thinking qualities, and especially the personal quality of self-esteem, are developed through this exercise.

Preparation: Recall that one of the human relations guidelines is to help others. One way to help others is to give them compliments that will help them to develop and maintain a positive self-concept. Also, as stated in this chapter, never minimize compliments but accept them with a thank you. This exercise is based on these two points.

Experience: In groups you will give and accept compliments.

Break into groups of four to six, preferably with people you know.

Procedure 2
(4–8 minutes)

Each person in the group thinks of a sincere positive compliment they can give to each group member (for instance, make a comment on why you like them). When everyone is ready, one person volunteers to receive first. All the other members give that person a compliment. Proceed until everyone, one at a time, has received a compliment from everyone else.

Procedure 3
(3–6 minutes)

Each group discusses the following questions.

1. How did it feel to receive the compliments? Did you, or were you tempted to, minimize a compliment?

2. How do you feel about the people who give you compliments versus those who give you criticism? Or, is there a difference in your human relations between people in these two groups?

3. How did it feel to give the compliments?

4. What is the value of giving compliments?

5. Will you make an effort to compliment yourself, and others?

Conclusion: The instructor may lead a class discussion and/or make concluding remarks. In Chapter 6, SB 6–2 Giving Praise, you can develop the skill of giving compliments.

Application: Write out your answer to question 5 above as the application question.

Communication Skills: The Foundation of Human Relations

Interpersonal Communication

4

Learning Objectives

After completing this chapter, you should be able to:

1. Explain why communication skills are important.
2. List and explain the four steps in the communication process.
3. List the three primary message transmission media.
4. List the steps in the message-sending process.
5. Explain how to give effective criticism.
6. Explain three levels of listening.
7. Describe how to be an active projective listener.
8. Describe how to give and receive feedback.
9. Explain six response styles and know when to use each.
10. Define the following 11 key terms (in order of appearance in the chapter):

communication	**media**
paraphrasing	**nonverbal communication**
goals of communication	**message-sending process**
encoding	**empathic listening**
message	**feedback**
decoding	

Chapter Outline

Sara, a manager at Sears, needs a report typed. She has decided to assign the task to David following the five steps in the message-sending process, which you will learn more about in this chapter. Here's how Sara and David communicated for each step.

Step 1. Develop rapport.

SARA: David, how are you doing today?

DAVID: OK. How about you?

SARA: Fine, thanks. Is the work on schedule?

DAVID: Yes, things are running smoothly.

Step 2. State the communication objective.

SARA: David, I have a report that I'd like you to type for me.

DAVID: Let's see it.

Step 3. Transmit the message.

SARA: Here are five handwritten pages. Please type the first page on my letterhead and the others on regular bond. Place the exhibit on a separate page; it will probably be on page 3. Then run the rest.

DAVID: It sounds easy enough.

SARA: I need it for a presentation to Paul at two o'clock today, and I'd like some time to review it before then. How soon will you have it ready?

DAVID: Well, it's 10 now, and I go to lunch from 12 to 1. I've got to finish what I'm working on now, but I should have it by noon.

SARA: Good. That will allow me to look it over at noon and get it back to you at one o'clock if it needs changes.

Step 4. Check understanding.

SARA: I want to make sure I clearly explained what I need so that it will not need to be redone. Will you please tell me how you are going to do the job?

DAVID: Sure. I'm going to type it on regular bond. I'll run it until I get to the exhibit; the exhibit will be on its own page; then I will run the rest of it.

SARA: Did I mention that I wanted the first page to be on my letterhead?

DAVID: I don't remember, but I'll put page one on your letterhead.

SARA: Good!

Step 5. Get a commitment and follow up.

SARA: So you agree to type it as directed and deliver it to my office by noon today.

DAVID: Yea, I'll get it to you before noon.

SARA: (thinking to herself as she walks back to her office): I'm confident he'll do it. But I'll follow up. If David doesn't show up by 11:55, I will be back, and he'll do it during his lunchtime.

How would you have communicated the typing job? The five steps in the message-sending process above are part of the communication process that you will learn in this chapter. Keep in mind that a diversity of people may use different communication styles.

The Importance of Communication Skills

● Organization
● Group
● Individual

Some of the reasons communication skills are important include:

- At all organizational levels, at least 75 percent of each workday is consumed by talking and listening. However, 75 percent of what we hear we hear incorrectly, and 75 percent of what we hear accurately we forget within three weeks. Various research studies have revealed that as much as 70 percent of all business communication fails to achieve the intended purposes.

- Communication skills are important in your personal life[1] and to career success.[2] In fact, the most important skill employers look for in new graduates applying for entry-level jobs is oral communication skills.[3] Lee Iacocca, the top executive credited with saving Chrysler from bankruptcy said, "The most important thing I learned in school was how to communicate."[4] Unfortunately, a Small Business Advisory Committee said that the biggest thing lacking from most college graduates is their ability to communicate with customers, both on the phone and in person.[5] As a result, today, communication skills are among the most popular subjects in employee training.[6]

Learning Objective

1. Explain why communication skills are important

- To get what you want in your career, stop talking and start listening and observing. Learn how others communicate. When you learn how to listen, you can then learn how to fully service your customer.[7] Customers don't just refer to people who buy your product, but include anyone you have to work with. In this chapter, you can develop your communication skills in a variety of areas. Communication skills top the list of personal qualities sought by employers.[8]

WORK APPLICATIONS

1. Give reasons why communication skills are important in organizations. Do not give reasons stated in the text.

Defining Communication and Its Goals

Like other management terms, the term communication has no universal definition.

Defining Communication

For our purposes, **communication** *is the process of a sender transmitting a message to a receiver with mutual understanding.* The important element in the communication process is the transmission of the message with mutual understanding. If people do not agree on the meaning of the message, communication has not taken place.

Mutual Understanding

After transmitting the message, the sender has two options. The sender can either (1) simply assume that the receiver understands the message and that there is mutual understanding (this is known as one-way communication) or (2) check to see if the message has been understood with mutual understanding. Questioning and paraphrasing are two techniques that can be used to ensure mutual understanding. **Paraphrasing** *is the process of having the receiver restate the message in his or her own words.* A third technique is encouraging employees to offer comments and to make suggestions on communication (These are two-way communication methods). You will learn how to use questioning and paraphrasing later in this chapter.

WORK APPLICATIONS

2. Do you use paraphrasing now? Will you use it more, less, or with the same frequency in the future? Why?

The Goals of Communication

There are at least three major goals of communication. *The* **goals of communication** *are to influence, inform, and/or to express feelings.* However, when sending a message, a person may achieve all three goals simultaneously.

The Goal of Human Relations and Communication

Communication is the foundation of human relations.[9] If managers want subordinates to meet expectations and objectives, they must effectively communicate these objectives.[10] Creating a win-win situation requires effective two-way communication.

How Communication Affects Behavior, Human Relations, and Performance

What we have to communicate often affects our behavior. For example, if you are disciplining an employee who has broken a rule (influence and/or express feelings), you behave differently than when you give praise for a job well done (inform and/or express feelings). Human relations are also affected by our communication. Relations are different during discipline and praise.

Our behavior during communication also affects other people's behavior and human relations. Communication is the foundation on which human relations are built. For example, if you are polite and friendly, chances are the other person will behave in a similar way. However, if you are rude, the other person may retaliate. People who communicate in a friendly manner, following the guidelines for human relations, tend to have good human relations, while those who do not have poor human relations.

Managers get the job done through employees and through communication. The quality of communication has a direct effect on performance.[11] Effective free and open communication contributes to better performance, and personal communication improves earnings.[12] In the opening case, if Sara did a good job of communicating, David should do the task correctly; if not, the task may not be done correctly and have to be done a second time.

WORK APPLICATIONS

3. Give a specific example of how communication affected your behavior, human relations, and performance.

● Organization
● Group
● Individual

The Communication Process

Communication requires a sender to encode a message and transmit the message to a receiver who decodes it. Let's examine these three components separately.

The Sender

The sender of the message is the source or person who initiates the communication. Once people have a reason (to influence, inform, and/or to express feelings) to communicate, they encode the message. **Encoding** *is the sender's process of putting the message into a form that the receiver will understand.* The sender should consider who the receiver of the message is and determine the best way to encode it for mutual understanding to take place. For example, supervisors who are highly knowledgeable in their field must remember that when encoding a message to a new, inexperienced employee, they must explain technical terms in a way that the receiver can relate to and understand. After having performed a task over the years, people forget what it is like being new to a situation. What seems simple and routine is often very complicated to the novice.

Message Transmission

The **message** *is the physical form of the encoded information.* The message can be transmitted in three major ways—orally, in writing, and/or nonverbally. The sender should determine the most appropriate media or channel of transmission to meet the needs of the situation. The next section discusses recommended transmission media for different messages. Workers send and receive an average of 201 messages of all types each day.[13]

The Receiver

The person receiving the message decodes it. **Decoding** *is the receiver's process of translating the message into a meaningful form.* The receiver interprets what the sender is communicating.

An example of the above stages of the communication process would be a professor preparing for a class and encoding by preparing a lecture. The message (lecture) is transmitted orally during class. The students (receivers) decode the lecture (message) by listening and/or taking notes in a way that is meaningful for them. Students generally select from the lecture what to write down in notes. The notes are usually decoded rather than taken verbatim.

Steps in the Communication Process

People listen, analyze, and speak. On a more complex level, the four steps in the communication process are (1) select transmission media, (2) send the message,

(3) receive the message, and (4) respond to the message. Not all messages require a response. During a conversation, the sender and receiver can reverse roles several times. Exhibit 4–1 illustrates the communication process.

EXHIBIT 4–1   **THE COMMUNICATION PROCESS**

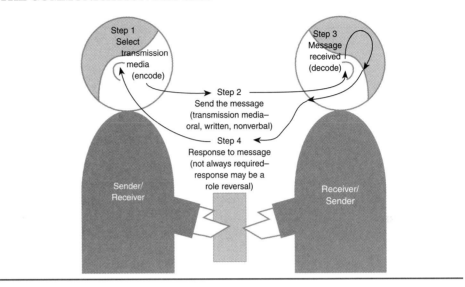

Learning Objective

2. List and explain the four steps in the communication process

IE 4–1
IE 4–2

● Organization
● Group
● Individual

In the opening case, Sara is the sender of an oral message of a handwritten report to be typed. David was the receiver of the message, who responded to the message by agreeing to finish the report by noon. Now you will learn the details of each step in the communication process in separate sections of this chapter.

Message Transmission Media

When encoding the message, the sender should give careful consideration to selecting media.[14] **Media** *are the forms of the transmitted message.* In this section, you will learn the three primary media you can use when transmitting messages: oral, written, and nonverbal.

Oral Communication

Oral communication is most people's preferred media for sending messages. Four common media for oral communication include face-to-face; telephone; meetings; and presentations. Below you will learn the appropriate use of each.

Face-to-Face

Much of a manager's communication time is spent one-on-one, face-to-face with employees. The late Sam Walton, founder of Wal-Mart Stores, the largest discount store chain in the world, relied on face-to-face communication to keep the firm growing. Top executives visit 6 to 12 stores each week. Thus, conversational skills are important.[15]

It is the appropriate medium for delegating tasks, coaching, disciplining, instructing, sharing information, answering questions, checking progress toward objectives, and developing and maintaining human relations.

Telephone

The amount of time spent on the telephone varies greatly with the job. No matter how much time you spend on the phone, before making a call, set an objective and write down what you plan to discuss. Use the paper to write notes during the call.

The telephone is the appropriate medium for quick exchanges of information and checking up on things. It is especially useful for saving travel time. However, it is inappropriate for personal matters like discipline.

Meetings

There are a variety of types of meetings, which will be discussed in Chapter 10. The manager's most common meeting is the brief, informal get-together with two or more employees. It is appropriate for coordinating employee activities, delegating a task to a group, and resolving employee conflicts. (Conflict resolution is covered in Chapter 8.)

Presentations

IE 4–3

Public speaking skills are considered to be an important part of communication skills.[16] On occasion, you may be required to make a formal presentation. Prepare your presentations,[17] and be sure they have the following three parts: beginning, middle, end. For example, Jamal is making a sales presentation to his superiors requesting another employee for his department. Jamal begins by stating that his department needs a new employee. He then moves to the middle of his presentation by explaining all the reasons for needing the employee and how the company will benefit. Jamal ends with a quick summary and a request that his superiors grant his request for a new employee. Presentation skills can help you get what you want.[18]

Written Communication

With the increasing use of e-mail, the need for writing skills has increased.[19] However, writing skills have deteriorated over the years to the point where it is a major skill problem.[20] Do you like writing, receiving, and reading written communications? The higher up in the organization you plan to go, the more important writing skills are to get there.[21] Probably nothing else can reveal your weaknesses more clearly than poor writing. People judge you on your ability to write your thoughts effectively and correctly. When you put your ideas on paper, things become more apparent. Writing helps you become more systematic in your thinking.

IE 4–4

Written communication is appropriate for sending general information; for messages requiring future action; for sending formal, official, or long-term messages; and when the message affects several people in a related way. Common forms of written communication include memos, letters, reports, bulletin board notices, posters, computers/e-mail, and facsimiles/fax.

Nonverbal Communication

Every time you use oral face-to-face communication, you also use nonverbal communication. **Nonverbal communication** *is the facial expressions, vocal qualities, gestures, and posture used while transmitting messages.* Nonverbal communication can be anything that sends a message. The old adage, "Actions speak louder than words," is true. For example, if Amy, a supervisor, tells employees to do a quality job but does not do a quality job herself and does not reward quality performance, employees will most likely ignore the quality message. This is referred to as a *mixed message* since the supervisor says to do a quality job orally, but her nonverbal behavior does not support her oral message.

Media Selection

AS 4–1

Select the most appropriate media for each message.

A. One-on-one   C. Meeting   E. Memo   G. Report

B. Telephone   D. Presentation   F. Letter   H. Poster

_____ 1. The supervisor has to assign a new customer order to Karen and Ralph.

_____ 2. The supervisor is expecting needed material for production this afternoon. She wants to know if it will arrive on time.

_____ 3. Employees have been leaving the lights on when no one is in the stockroom. The manager wants this practice to stop.

_____ 4. The boss asked for the production figures for the month.

_____ 5. An employee has broken a rule and needs to be discouraged from doing it again.

WORK APPLICATIONS

4. Give a specific example of when someone's nonverbal communication did not support the verbal message.

Nonverbal communication is important in sending and understanding others' messages. In fact, people communicate mainly in nonverbal language and only secondarily in verbal language.[22] Studies have shown that although people may not realize it, they pay much more attention to a person's nonverbal communication than verbal when interpreting (decoding) the message being sent. In fact, saying nothing at all often sends a message.[23] Therefore, it is important to pay attention to nonverbal communication.[24]

Below you will learn about common interpretations of nonverbal communication techniques. However, even though they are generally accepted, be careful because there are always exceptions to the rule. By reading others' nonverbal communication, you can often find out how they feel about you. You should change your communication style if you can read that it is interpreted to be negative by others, or if others tell you it is.[25] To really improve human relations, you can read others' verbal and nonverbal communication, understand their preferred means of communicating, and use it when communicating with them.[26] If you work at it, you can improve your ability to give and interpret nonverbal communications.

Facial Expressions: It is commonly thought that a person with a smile is happy and friendly, while a frown conveys unhappiness and displeasure. Raised eyebrows are interpreted as disbelief or amazement. Pursed lips are interpreted as a sign of anger. The use of eye contact shows interest; not using eye contact shows disinterest. When people lie, they tend to avoid eye contact. Biting one's lips is considered a sign of nervousness.

Sometimes people communicate using only facial expressions. Have you ever done something wrong and had a parent, teacher, or boss give you a dirty look, or a look of disapproval? Or made an error and gotten a look of disappointment?

Vocal: The proper use of voice is important for effective communication.[27] You need to monitor the sound of your voice to make sure it isn't too high pitched, whiny, breathy, cute, or mumbly. Your vocal quality enables others to recognize your voice. It is made up of (1) tone, the attitude in your voice (warm, friendly, upset, etc.); (2) pitch, highness or lowness of sound; (3) volume, loud to soft; (4) pace, fast or slow; and (5) pauses, how you manage silence. Adjusting any of these components changes vocal quality. Without any changes in voice, your speech is monotonous. Try to avoid annoying vocal repetition of junk words like "y'know," "alright," "man," and "etc."

To determine your vocal quality, tape (preferably videotape so you can see your other nonverbal communication techniques as well) conversations or speeches and ask others about your voice quality and how to improve it.

Gestures: To a large extent the old adage "you speak with your hands" is true. Putting a hand over your mouth and placing your head in hand while seated are generally interpreted as signs of objection or boredom. Placing hands on hips is considered a sign of anger or defensiveness.[28] Hands uplifted outward show disbelief, puzzlement, or uncertainty. Folded arms is interpreted as being closed to communication and change, or preparation to speak. Arms by your side is considered being open to communication, suggestions, and relaxed. Pointing your finger shows authority, displeasure, or lecturing. Try to avoid the overuse of any gesture;[29] it becomes annoying and distracting to others. We are often unaware of our gestures and their effects. Ask your friends whether you have any annoying gestures.

Posture: Seating oneself on the edge of a chair and leaning slightly forward is a sign of interest. Slouching in a chair is a sign of boredom or lack of interest. Fidgeting and doodling are signs of boredom. Shrugging your shoulders is considered a sign of indifference. Shifting and jiggling money are interpreted as nervousness.

Another important part of posture is the use of space. How close we get while communicating affects the results. If you get too close to someone, you can make them uncomfortable. On the other hand, being too far away can be interpreted as not caring. In the United States, close friends and loved ones tend to communicate from actually touching to about 1½ feet apart. People who are friends, or while conducting personal business, tend to communicate from a distance of 1½ to 4 feet. When conducting impersonal business like shopping for clothes or meeting a new client, people communicate from 4 to 12 feet apart.

Watch for people coming toward you because you are too far away, or backing away because you are too close. If you move, also, you can end up dancing around. When working in a global environment, you will be dealing with people from other cultures. Be aware that the Eastern Europeans, Latin Americans, and Arabs all prefer a closer distance for communications. Therefore, they may tend to get closer to you. Refer back to Chapter 2, nonverbal communication, for a review of eye contact and hand shake.

Nonverbal communication techniques are used together and may send different messages. For example, a person may be smiling (a sign of openness to communication) while having his arms and legs crossed (a sign of being closed to communication).

It is important for you to be aware of your nonverbal communication techniques and to make sure they are consistent with your oral and/or written communication. You can use nonverbal communication, such as a nod of the head, to facilitate face-to-face communication. Be aware of other people's nonverbal communication techniques. They tell you their feelings and attitudes toward the communication and toward you as a person/manager.

APPLICATION SITUATIONS

Nonverbal Communication

AS 4–2

State if the behavior indicates that the person is open or closed to communications.

A. Open   B. Closed

_____ 6. The receiver has his arms crossed and is gripping his biceps.

_____ 7. The receiver is fidgeting and is not using eye contact.

_____ 8. The receiver is sitting on the edge of the chair leaning slightly forward.

Combining Media

As stated above, nonverbal communication is always combined with face-to-face communication. The manager can also combine oral and written communication. Repetition is often needed to ensure that the message has been conveyed with mutual understanding. It is common for a manager to give an oral message followed by a written message to reinforce it. For example, the manager could conduct a safety program orally with the support of a written manual. Posters could also be placed in the work area to remind employees to follow the safety rules.

Oral communication followed by written communication is appropriate for the development of objectives and plans; to communicate new or changed standing plans; when praising employees; when delegating complex tasks; to communicate safety, quality, and good housekeeping; and when reporting progress toward departmental objectives. In the opening case, Sara is assigning David a task, using verbal and written communication, and she has prepared a presentation to be given to Paul.

Before you send a message, be sure to select the best media. Exhibit 4–2 lists the major media sources from which to select.

EXHIBIT 4–2

Learning Objective

3. List the three primary message transmission media

MESSAGE TRANSMISSION MEDIA

Oral Communication Media	Written Communication Media	Nonverbal Communication Media
1. Face-to-face	1. Memos	1. Facial expressions
2. The telephone	2. Letters	2. Vocal quality
3. Meetings	3. Reports	3. Gestures
4. Presentations	4. Bulletin boards	4. Posture
	5. Posters	
	6. Computers/e-mail	
	7. Fax	

WORK APPLICATIONS

5. Which message transmission medium is your strongest and weakest? How will you improve your ability to communicate with your weakest medium?

● Organization
● Group
● Individual

Sending Messages

Have you ever heard a manager say, "This isn't what I asked for"? When this happens, it is usually the manager's fault. Managers often make incorrect assumptions and do not take 100 percent of the responsibility for ensuring the message is transmitted with mutual understanding. To transmit messages effectively, managers must state exactly what they want, how they want it done, and when they need it done.

Sending the message is the second step in the communication process. Before you send a message, you should carefully select the media and plan how you will send the message.

Planning the Message

Before sending a message you should plan:

"What" is the goal of the message? What do you want as the end result of the communication? Set an objective. "Who" should receive the message? With the receiver(s) in mind, plan "how" you will encode the message so that it will be understood. "When" will the message be transmitted? Timing is important. Decide "where" the message will be transmitted.

Sending the Message, Face-to-Face

Skill at sending a face-to-face message influences your success.[30] It is helpful to follow the steps in the **message-sending process:** *step 1, develop rapport; step 2, state the communication objective; step 3, transmit the message; step 4, check understanding; and step 5, get a commitment and follow up.*

In the opening case, Sara followed the five steps in the message-sending process. Below is a discussion of the five steps. After reading them, return to the opening case and review the process.

Step 1. Develop Rapport: Put the receiver at ease. It is usually appropriate to begin communication with small talk related to the message. It helps prepare the employee to receive the message.[31]

Step 2. State the Communication Objective: In business communication with the goal of influencing, it is helpful for the receiver to know the end result of the communication before getting to all the details.

Step 3. Transmit the Message: If the communication goal is to influence, tell the people what you want them to do, give instructions, and so forth. And be sure to set deadlines for completing tasks. If the goal is to inform, tell the people the information. If the goal is to express feeling, do so.[32] Avoid talking too fast and giving too much detail; they are the main mannerisms hindering career advancement.[33]

Step 4. Check Understanding: About the only time you may not want to check understanding is when the goal is to express feelings. When influencing and giving information, one should ask direct questions, and/or use paraphrasing.[34] To simply ask "Do you have any questions?" does not check understanding.

Step 5. Get a Commitment and Follow Up: When the goal of communication is to inform or express feelings, a commitment is not needed. However, when the goal of communication is to influence, it is important to get a commitment to the action. Managers should make sure that employees can do the task and have it done by a certain time or date.[35] In situations in which the employee does not intend to get the task done, it is better to know when sending the message, rather than to wait until the deadline to find out. When employees are reluctant to commit to the necessary action, managers can use persuasive power within their authority. When communicating to influence, follow up to ensure that the necessary action has been taken.

Exhibit 4–3 lists the five steps in the message-sending process.

Skill-Building
4–2

EXHIBIT 4–3	THE MESSAGE-SENDING PROCESS MODEL
Learning Objective	Step 1. Develop rapport
4. List the steps in the message-sending process	Step 2. State the communication objective
	Step 3. Transmit the message
	Step 4. Check understanding
	Step 5. Get a commitment and follow up

Criticizing Others

Most people do not enjoy criticizing others. In fact, some people don't like to use the word criticizing and prefer the word critiquing.[36] But objectives are the same. Part of the job of a manager, teacher, and parent is to criticize others to improve their performance. How criticism is given makes a difference in how it is accepted. The goal of criticism should be to change undesirable behavior while maintaining human relations, not to get even or to show superiority. When criticizing others, follow these guidelines:

Give More Praise Than Criticism: As a manager, try to praise 80 percent of the time and give criticism 20 percent. When employees receive above-average amounts of negative criticism, it generally harms, rather than improves, performance. Praise produces better results. For example, a manager praised an employee for setting up the display nice and straight, rather than criticizing the employee for being too slow. The praise resulted in improved performance. Criticism probably would not have worked. Rewarding employees for meeting expectations encourages them to repeat the behavior. (This is reinforcement theory, discussed in Chapter 6.)

Criticize Immediately: Criticism should be given as soon after the performance as is feasible. Criticism loses its impact with time. Give feedback immediately, unless people are emotional. When people are emotional, for example, angry, following the other criticism guidelines is difficult.

Criticism Should Be Performance Oriented: Focus on the task, not the person. Distinguish between the employee and his or her performance. For example, do not say things like "you are lazy," which is an attack on the person. It would be more useful to the employee to hear "Your rate of production is 10 percent slower than the standard," or "You are letting our group down by only doing five, while we all do seven."

Give Specific and Accurate Criticism: Generalities are of little use to employees. The more descriptive the feedback the more useful it is to the receiver. For example, do not say things like "you always make mistakes." It would be more useful to the employee to hear "Your work has three errors; they are . . ." Giving inaccurate information can cause problems and embarrassment.

Open on a Positive Note and Close by Repeating What Action Is Needed: People remember longest what was said first and last. The opening statement sets the stage for the criticism, and the conclusion the reinforcement of it. Try to let the employee realize that you like and value him or her as a person, and that it is some small aspect of their behavior that needs to be changed.

 Skill-Building
4–3

WORK APPLICATIONS

6. Give a specific example of when a manager should give an employee criticism (do not simply say for good or poor performance).

Learning Objective

5. Explain how to give effective criticism

 Goal of
Human Relations

Generally, employees are open to criticism. Employees prefer to be told when they are not performing adequately, rather than to receive no criticism at all. They cannot improve performance without the necessary praise or criticism. However, employees do not like to be criticized in a negative way. Chastising, sarcasm, and joking should not take place when giving criticism. This type of behavior generally makes things worse.

Praise and criticism are keys to high levels of performance. Following these guidelines will help you do a better job of criticizing others, and it will help them to do a better job. This creates a win-win situation.

Exhibit 4–4 lists the guidelines for giving effective criticism.

EXHIBIT 4-4   GUIDELINES FOR GIVING EFFECTIVE CRITICISM

- Give more praise than criticism.
- Criticize immediately.
- Criticism should be performance oriented.
- Give specific and accurate criticism.

WORK APPLICATIONS

7. Give an example of criticism you received from a manager. List all five guidelines from the text, stating whether or not each was followed. If you can't think of an example, interview someone and report another person's example.

Receiving Messages

The most important oral communication skills are following instructions and listening.[37] This was illustrated in the opening case. Complete Self-Assessment Exercise 4–1 to determine how good a listener you are.

Self-Assessment Exercise 4–1

Listening Skills

Select the response that best describes the frequency of your actual behavior. Place the letter A, U, F, O, or S on the line before each of the 15 statements.

Almost always	Usually	Frequently	Occasionally	Seldom
A	U	F	O	S

_____ 1. I like to listen to people talk. I encourage them to talk by showing interest, by smiling and nodding, etc.

_____ 2. I pay closer attention to speakers who are more interesting or similar to me.

_____ 3. I evaluate the speaker's words and nonverbal communication ability as they talk.

_____ 4. I avoid distractions; if it's noisy, I suggest moving to a quiet spot, etc.

_____ 5. When people interrupt me to talk, I put what I was doing out of sight and mind and give them my complete attention.

_____ 6. When people are talking, I allow them time to finish. I do not interrupt, anticipate what they are going to say, or jump to conclusions.

_____ 7. I tune people out who do not agree with my views.

_____ 8. While the other person is talking or the professor is lecturing, my mind wanders to personal topics.

_____ 9. While the other person is talking, I pay close attention to the nonverbal communication to help me fully understand what the sender is trying to get across.

_____ 10. I tune out and pretend I understand when the topic is difficult.

_____ 11. When the other person is talking, I think about what I am going to say in reply.

_____ 12. When I feel there is something missing or contradictory, I ask direct questions to get the person to explain the idea more fully.

_____ 13. When I don't understand something, I let the sender know.

_____ 14. When listening to other people, I try to put myself in their position and see things from their perspective.

_____ 15. During conversations I repeat back to the sender what has been said in my own words (paraphrase) to be sure I understand correctly what has been said.

If you were to have people to whom you talk regularly answer these questions about you, would they have the same responses that you selected? Have friends fill out the questions for you and compare answers.

To determine your score, give yourself 5 points for each A, 4 for each U, 3 for each F, 2 for each O, and 1 for each S for statements 1, 4, 5, 6, 9, 12, 13, 14, and 15. Place the numbers on the line next to your response letter. For items 2, 3, 7, 8, 10, and 11, the score reverses; 5 points for each S, 4 for each O, 3 for each F, 2 for each U, and 1 for each A. Place these scores on the lines next to the response letters. Now add your total number of points. Your score should be between 15 and 75. Place your score here _____ and on the continuum below. Generally, the higher your score, the better your listening skills.

Poor listener   15 ---- 25 ---- 35 ---- 45 ---- 55 ---- 65 ---- 75   Good listener

● Organization
● Group
● Individual

Step 3 of the communication process is message received. Communication does not take place unless the message is received with mutual understanding. The message cannot be received accurately unless the receiver listens. When asked, "Are you a good listener?" most people say yes. In reality, 75 percent of what people hear they hear imprecisely and 75 percent of what they hear accurately they forget within three weeks. In other words, most people are poor listeners. Poor listening is caused in part by the fact that people speak at an average rate of 120 words per minute, while they are capable of listening at a rate of over 500 words per minute. Also, most people are not taught how listening works.[38] The ability to comprehend words more than four times faster than the speaker can talk often results in minds wandering.

Levels of Listening

To be a successful communicator you need to be an effective listener. There are at least three levels of listening: marginal, evaluative, and projective.[39] See Exhibit 4–5.

1. With marginal listening, as the sender speaks, the receiver does not pay attention. Have you ever talked to someone and realized that his or her mind was "a million miles away"? The use of marginal listening results in misunderstanding and errors.[40]

2. Evaluative listening requires the listener to pay reasonably close attention to the speaker. The receiver evaluates the speaker's remarks as correct or not and determines if he or she will continue to really listen. Once the receiver hears something he or she does not accept, listening stops, and the rebuttal is formed. Now, two ideas develop, neither of which is really communicated, rather than one idea being transmitted with mutual understanding between the sender and receiver. Evaluative listening is common when the receiver feels threatened.

3. Projective listening holds the greatest potential for mutual understanding of the message. It is important to stop talking and start listening.[41] Receivers listen carefully, utilizing their time to project themselves into the position of the sender to understand what is being said from the speaker's viewpoint. Evaluation is postponed until the message is mutually understood. The receiver's attempt to stand in the sender's shoes is also called *empathic listening*. To listen with empathy does not mean you have to agree with the person. **Empathic listening** *is the ability to understand and relate to another's situation and feelings.* Most messages have two components—feelings and content. Try to relate to both. Learning how to respond with empathy to emotional employees is also covered in the last section under the reflective response style.

EXHIBIT 4–5   **LEVELS OF LISTENING**

3. Projective
The receiver listens without evaluation to the full message,
attempting to understand the sender's viewpoint.

2. Evaluation
The receiver listens carefully until hearing
something that is not accepted. Listening
ends and the response to the incomplete
message is developed.

1. Marginal
The receiver does not listen
carefully. The message is
not heard or understood
with mutual
agreement.

Learning Objective

6. Explain three levels
   of listening

Dealing with Emotional Employees

As a manager and an employee, you should understand emotions and how to deal with them.

Emotional Intelligence

In Chapter 2 we talked about the personality trait of stability, which is based on emotions. How well do you control your emotions? How well do you deal with emotional people? *Emotional intelligence* is your ability to successfully deal with your emotions and those of others. *Emotional quotient (EM)* is a measure of emotional intelligence, similar to intelligence quotient (IQ). Some people say that EM is at least as important as IQ, if not more so, to job success. Understanding nonverbal communications is an important part of emotional intelligence. We now focus on how you can successfully deal with emotional employees.

Understanding Feelings

You should realize that:

1. Feelings are subjective; they tell you people's attitudes and needs.
2. Feelings are usually disguised as factual statements. For example, when people are hot, they tend to say, "It's hot in here," rather than "I feel hot."
3. And most importantly, feelings are neither right nor wrong.

We cannot choose our feelings, or control them. However, we can control how we express them. For example, if Vern, an employee, says "You *!!" (pick a swear word that would make you angry) to Bonnie, his supervisor, she will feel its impact. However, Bonnie can express her feelings in a calm manner, or she can yell, hit, or give Vern a dirty look, and so on. Supervisors should encourage employees to express their feelings in a positive way. But they shouldn't allow employees to go around yelling, swearing, or hitting others. And they should not get caught up in others' emotions. You need to pay attention to nonverbal communications of how people are saying things, rather than simply to what they say.[42]

Calming the Emotional Person

When an emotional employee comes to you, NEVER make statements like, "You shouldn't be angry"; "Don't be upset"; "Be a man/woman, not a baby"; "Just sit down and be quiet"; or "I know how you feel." (No one knows how anyone else feels. Even people who experience the same thing at the same time don't feel the same.) These types of statements only make the feelings stronger. While you may get the employee to shut up, communication will not take place. The problem will still exist,[43] and your human relations with the employee will suffer because of it, as will your relations with others who see or hear about what you said and did. When the employee complains to peers, he or she will tend to feel you were too hard or easy on the person. You lose either way.

Empathic Listening

To calm emotional employees, don't argue with them. Encourage them to express their feelings in a positive way. Show them that you understand how they feel;[44] we all want to be understood. Do not agree or disagree with the feelings; simply identify them verbally. Paraphrase the feeling to the employee. Use statements like "you were *hurt* when you didn't get the assignment." "You *resent* Bill for not doing his share of the work; is that what you mean?" "You are *doubtful* that the job will be done on time; is that what you're saying?"

After you deal with emotions, you can go on to work on content (solving problems). It may be wise to wait until a later time when emotions cool down. You will find that understanding one's feelings is often the solution.

Active Projective Listening Tips

The key to effective human relations is listening.[45] People want to be listened to and understood, and if you do not listen to and understand others, they will avoid you.

To improve your listening skills, focus your attention on listening for a week by concentrating on what other people say and their nonverbal communication when they speak. Notice if their verbal and nonverbal communication are consistent. Does the nonverbal communication reinforce the speaker's words or detract from them? Talk only when necessary so that you can listen and see what others are saying. If you follow the 13 tips below, you will improve your listening skills. The tips will be presented in the sequence of the face-to-face communication process: we listen, we analyze, we speak.

Listening

1. Pay attention. When people interrupt you to talk, stop what you are doing and give them your complete attention immediately. Quickly relax and clear your mind so that you are receptive to the speaker. This will get you started correctly. If you miss the first few words, you may miss the message. Commit to listening.[46]

2. Avoid distractions. Keep your eye on the speaker. Do not fiddle with pens, papers, or other distractions. Let your answering machine answer the phone. If you are in a noisy or distracting place, suggest moving to another spot.

3. Stay tuned in. While the other person is talking or the professor is lecturing, do not let your mind wander to personal topics. If it does, gently bring it back. Do not tune out the speaker because you do not like something about him or disagree with what she is saying. If the topic is difficult, do not tune out, ask questions. Do not think about what you are going to say in reply; just listen.[47]

4. Do not assume and interrupt. Do not assume you know what the speaker is going to say or listen at the beginning and jump to conclusions. Most listening mistakes are made when people hear the first few words of a sentence, finish it

in their own minds, and miss the second half. Listen to the entire message without interrupting the speaker.[48]

5. Watch for nonverbal cues. Understand both the feelings and the content of the message. People sometimes say one thing and mean something else. So watch as you listen to be sure that the speaker's eyes, body, and face are sending the same message as the verbal message.[49] If something seems out of place, clarify by asking questions.

6. Ask questions. When you feel there is something missing or contradictory, or you just do not understand, ask direct questions to get the person to explain the idea more fully.[50]

7. Take notes. Part of listening is writing important things down so you can remember them later, and to document them when necessary. This is especially true when listening to instructions. You should always have something to write with such as a pen and a notebook or some index cards.

8. Convey meaning. The way to let the speaker know you are listening to the message is to use verbal clues[51] such as, "you feel . . . ," "uh huh," "I see," "I understand." You should also use nonverbal communication such as eye contact, appropriate facial expressions, nodding of the head, sitting on the edge of the chair, and leaning slightly forward to indicate you are interested and listening.

Analyzing

9. Think. To help overcome the discrepancy in the speed between your ability to listen and people's rate of speaking, use the speed of your brain positively. Listen actively by organizing, summarizing, reviewing, interpreting, and critiquing often. These activities will help you to actively listen at the projective level.

10. Evaluate after listening. When people try to listen and analyze/evaluate what is said at the same time, they tend to miss part or all of the message. You should just listen to the entire message, then come to your conclusions.

11. Evaluate facts presented. When you evaluate the message, base your conclusion on the facts presented rather than on stereotypes and generalities.

Speaking

Skill-Building
4–1

Learning Objective

7. Describe how to be an active projective listener

12. Paraphrase first. Begin speaking by paraphrasing the message back to the sender. When you can paraphrase the message back correctly, you convey that you have listened and understood the other person.[52] Now you are ready to offer your ideas, advice, solution, or decision in response to the sender of the message.

13. Watch for nonverbal cues. As you speak, pay attention to the other person's nonverbal communication. If the person does not seem to understand what you are talking about, clarify the message before finishing the conversation.

Do you talk more than you listen? To be sure your perception is correct ask your boss, coworkers, and friends who will give you an honest answer. If you spend more time talking than listening, you are probably failing in your attempt to communicate. Regardless of how much you listen, if you follow these 13 guidelines, you will improve your communication ability and become a person that people want to listen to, instead of a person they feel they have to listen to. To become an active projective listener, take 100 percent of the responsibility for ensuring mutual understanding. Work to change your behavior to become a better active projective listener.

WORK APPLICATIONS

8. Refer to Self-Assessment Exercise 4–1 and the 13 tips to improve your listening skills. What is your weakest listening skill? How will you improve your listening ability?

● Organization
● Group
● Individual

Responding to Messages

The fourth and last step in the communication process is responding to the message. Not all messages require a response, such as messages to inform. However, when you are communicating a message face-to-face, the best way to ensure mutual understanding is to get feedback from the receiver, as Sara did in the opening case.

Feedback

Giving feedback is an important communication skill.[53] **Feedback** *is the process of verifying messages.* Questioning, paraphrasing, and allowing comments and suggestions are all forms of feedback. Feedback when giving and receiving messages facilitates job performance.[54] Feedback and job performance are discussed in this section.

360-Degree Feedback

The performance feedback method known as 360-degree feedback has gained wide popularity in the corporate world to the point of being used by most of the large Fortune 500 companies.[55] The 360-degree method provides performance feedback in four directions: downward from the supervisor, laterally from peers or coworkers, upwards from subordinates, and inwardly from the person getting the feedback.[56] When appropriate, customers and suppliers also provide feedback on different aspects of performance.[57] Unfortunately, feedback is not always as effective as is typically assumed,[58] and not so much the concept but the implementation of 360-degree feedback has been criticized.[59] Although it should be, but it is not necessarily a part of 360-degree feedback, feedback to and within teams affects team performance.[60]

Getting Feedback

The best way to make sure communication has taken place is to get feedback from the receiver of the message through questioning and paraphrasing.

The Common Approach to Getting Feedback on Messages and Why It Doesn't Work

The most common approach to getting feedback is to send the entire message, followed by asking "Do you have any questions?" Feedback usually does not follow because people have a tendency not to ask questions. There are three good reasons why people do not ask questions:

1. They feel ignorant. To ask a question, especially if no one else does, is considered an admission of not paying attention or not being bright enough to understand the issue.

2. They are ignorant. Sometimes people do not know enough about the message to know whether or not it is incomplete, incorrect, or subject to interpretation. There are no questions because what was said sounds right. The receiver does not understand the message, or does not know what to ask.

3. Receivers are reluctant to point out the sender's ignorance. This is very common when the sender is a manager and the receiver is an employee. The employee fears that asking a question suggests that the manager has done a poor job of preparing and sending the message. Or it suggests that the manager is wrong. Regardless of the reason, the end result is the same: employees don't ask questions; generally, students don't either.

After managers send their messages and ask if there are questions, they proceed to make another common error. They assume that no questions means communication is complete, that there is mutual understanding of the message. In reality, the message is often misunderstood. When "this isn't what I asked for" is the result, the task has to be repeated. The end result is often wasted time, materials, and effort.

The most common cause of messages not resulting in communication is the sender's lack of getting feedback that ensures mutual understanding. The proper use of questioning and paraphrasing can help you ensure that your messages are communicated. This is the topic discussed next.

How to Get Feedback on Messages

Below are four guidelines managers should use when getting feedback on their messages. They are also appropriate for nonmanagers.

Be Open to Feedback: First of all, managers must be open to feedback,[61] and ask for it.[62] The open-door policy encourages feedback. When an employee asks a question, the manager needs to be responsive and patiently answer questions and explain things. There are no dumb questions, only dumb answers. Make the employee feel comfortable.

Be Aware of Nonverbal Communication: Managers must also be aware of their nonverbal communication and make sure that they encourage feedback. For example, if managers say they encourage questions, but they look at employees as though the employees are stupid or they act impatient when employees ask questions, employees will learn not to ask questions. The manager must also be aware of employees' nonverbal communications. For example, if Moe, the manager, is explaining a task to Larry, the employee, and Larry has a puzzled look on his face, he is probably confused but may not be willing to say so. In such a case, Moe should stop and clarify things before going on.[63]

Ask Questions: When you send messages, it is better to know whether or not the messages are understood before action is taken, so that the action will not have to be changed or repeated. Direct questions dealing with the specific information you have given will indicate if the receiver has been listening and whether or not he or she understands enough to give a direct reply. If the response is not accurate, repeating, giving more examples, or elaborating on the message is needed. The manager can also ask indirect questions to attain feedback. The manager could ask "how do you feel?" questions about the message. The manager could also ask "if you were me" questions, such as "if you were me, how would you explain how to do it?" Or the manager can ask third-party questions, such as "how will employees feel about this?" The response to indirect questions will reveal the employee's attitude, and can convey misunderstandings.

Paraphrasing: The most accurate indicator of understanding is paraphrasing—asking the receiver to restate the message in his or her own words. How the manager asks the employee to paraphrase will affect his or her attitude. For example, the manager saying "John, tell me what I just said so that I can be sure you will not make a mistake as usual," would probably result in defensive behavior on John's part. John would probably make a mistake in fulfillment of the Pygmalion effect (as discussed in Chapter 3). Below are two examples of proper requests for paraphrasing:

- "Now tell me what you are going to do so we will be sure that we are in agreement."
- "Would you tell me what you are going to do so that I can be sure that I explained myself clearly?"

Notice that the second statement takes the pressure off the employee. The supervisor is asking for a check on his or her ability, not that of the employee. These types of requests for paraphrasing should result in a positive attitude toward the message and the manager. They show concern for the employee and for communicating effectively, as feedback builds self-esteem.

WORK APPLICATIONS

9. Describe how your present or past boss used feedback. How could his or her feedback skills be improved?

Response Styles

Before learning about response styles, complete Self-Assessment Exercise 4–2 to determine your preferred response style.

Determining Your Preferred Response Style[64]

Select the response that you would actually make as the supervisor in the five situations.

_____ 1. I cannot work with Paul. That guy drives me crazy. He is always complaining about me and everyone else, including you, boss. Why does he have to be my job partner? We cannot work together. You have to assign someone else to be my partner.

    A. I'm sure there are things that you do that bother Paul? You'll have to work things out with him.

    B. What has he said about me?

    C. Can you give me some examples of the specific things that he does that bothers you?

    D. I'll talk to Paul. I'm sure we can improve or change the situation.

    E. So Paul is really getting to you.

_____ 2. We cannot make the deadline on the Procter Project without more help. We've been having some problems. A major problem is that Betty and Phil are recent college grads, and you know they don't know nothing. I end up doing all the work for them. Without another experienced person, my team will not get the job done on time.

    A. Tell me more about these problems you are having.

    B. Did you see the game last night?

    C. You are really concerned about this project aren't you?

    D. You will have to stop doing the work, and train the new people. They will come through for you if you give them a chance.

    E. Don't worry. You're a great project leader. I'm sure you will get the job done.

_____ 3. Congratulations on being promoted to supervisor. I was wondering about what to expect. After all, we go back five years as good friends in this department. It will seem strange to have you as my boss.

    A. Things will work out fine, you'll see.

    B. I take it that you don't like to see things change. Is that what you mean?

    C. Just do a good job and there will not be any problems between us.

    D. Is Chris feeling any better.

    E. Tell me how you think things will change.

_____ 4. I wish you would do something about Gloria. With those short tight clothes, the men are always finding some excuse to come by here. She loves it; you can tell the way she is always flirting with all the guys. Gloria could turn this place into a soap opera if you don't do something.

    A. So you think this situation is indecent, is that it?

    B. I cannot tell Gloria how to dress. Why don't you turn your desk so you don't have to watch.

    C. Don't let it bother you. I'm sure it's innocent and that nothing is really going on. You know how these younger kids are these days.

    D. What do you think I should do?

    E. Are you feeling well today?

_____ 5. I cannot take it anymore. I've been running around like a fool waiting on all these customers and all they do is yell at me and complain.

    A. Are you going to the party tonight?

    B. What is the most irritating thing the customers are doing?

    C. With Erin being out today, it's been crazy. But, tomorrow she should be back and things should be back to normal. Hang in there, you can handle it.

    D. The customers are really getting to you today, hey?

    E. I told you during the job interview that this is how it is. You have to learn to ignore the comments.

To determine your preferred response style, below, circle the letter you selected in situations 1–5. The column headings indicate the style you selected.

Evaluating & Confronting	Diverting	Probing	Reassuring	Reflecting
1. A	B	C	D	E
2. D	B	A	E	C
3. C	D	E	A	B
4. B	E	D	C	A
5. E	A	B	C	D
Total				

Add up the number of circled responses per column. The total column should equal 5. The column with the highest number represents your preferred response style. The more evenly distributed the numbers are between the styles, the more flexible you are at responding.

As the sender transmits a message, how you as the receiver respond to the message directly affects communication. There is no one best response style. The response should be appropriate for the situation. You will learn six response styles. For each alternative you will be given an example of a response to an employee message: "You supervise me so closely that you disrupt my ability to do my job."

Evaluating

People tend to feel obligated to make a judgment about a message they receive. An evaluative response accepts or rejects, passes judgment, or offers advice. Such a response tends to close, limit, or direct the flow of communication.

Evaluative responses used during the early stages of receiving the message may cause the sender to become defensive. People often feel the need to justify the message.

Appropriate Use of Evaluative Responses: The evaluative response is particularly appropriate when the situation calls for an autocratic or consultative supervisory style. Situations in which you are asked for advice, direction, or your opinion call for an evaluative response.

An example of a supervisor's evaluative response to the employee's message above is: "You need my supervision; you lack experience."

Confronting

Confronting responses tend to challenge the sender to clarify the message, usually by pointing out inconsistencies in the message. They tend to reject the message and close, limit, or direct the flow of communication.

Confronting responses used during the early stages of receiving a message may cause the sender to become defensive. They are generally more useful after trust and acceptance have occurred.

Appropriate Use of Confronting Responses: Confrontation is most appropriate when the sender is not aware of the mistake or omission in the message, or when clarity is needed.

An example of a supervisor's confronting response to the employee's message above is: "I disagree. You need my direction to do a good job."

Diverting

Diverting responses switch the focus of the communication to a message of the receiver. The receiver becomes the sender of a different message. It is often called *changing the subject*. Diverting responses tend to redirect, close, or limit the flow of communication.

Diverting responses used during the early stages of receiving the message may cause the sender to feel that his or her message is not worth discussing, or that the other party's message is more important.

Appropriate Use of Diverting Responses: The diverting response is appropriate when using the autocratic or consultative supervisory style. When you want the job done your way, you must convey that message. Diverting responses may be helpful when they are used to share personal experiences of feelings that are similar to those of the sender.

An example of a supervisor's diverting response to the employee's message above is: "You've reminded me of a supervisor I once had who . . ."

Probing

A probing response asks the sender to give more information about some aspect of the message. It is useful to get a better understanding of the situation. When probing, "what" questions are preferred to "why" questions.

Appropriate Use of Probe Responses: Probing is appropriate during the early stages of the message to ensure understanding. It is used with the consultative and participative supervisory styles.

An example of a supervisor's probing response to the employee's message above is: "What do I do to cause you to say this?" Not: "Why do you feel this way?"

Reassuring

A reassuring response is given to reduce the intensity of the emotions associated with the message. Essentially you're saying, "Don't worry; everything will be OK." You are pacifying the sender.

Appropriate Use of Reassuring Responses: Reassuring is appropriate to use when the other person lacks confidence. Encouraging responses can help employees develop.

An example of a supervisor's reassuring response to the employee's message is: "I will not do it for much longer."

Reflecting

Video
4–1
BM–4

The reflective response is used by the empathic projective listener. Most messages have two components—feelings and content. A reflective response paraphrases the message back to the sender to show him or her that the receiver understands and values and accepts him or her. The sender can then feel free to explore the topic in more depth. Empathizing has been found to significantly affect employees' attitudes and behavior in positive ways.

The empathic responder deals with content, feelings, and the underlying meaning being expressed in the message (generally in that order). Carl Rogers, a noted psychology expert, believes that reflective responses should be used in the beginning stages of most communication. Reflective responses lead to mutual understanding, while developing human relations. They should be used with the consultative and participative supervisory styles.

The examples of statements used to calm an emotional employee are reflective responses. An example of a supervisor's reflective response to the employee's message above is: "My checking up on you annoys you!"

WORK APPLICATIONS

10. Give situations in which any two of the six response styles would be appropriate. Give the sender's message and your response. Identify its style.

APPLICATION SITUATIONS

Identifying Response Styles

AS 4–3

Below are two situations with 12 responses. Identify each as:

A. Evaluating   C. Diverting   E. Reassuring

B. Confronting   D. Probing   F. Reflecting

MS. WALKER: Mr. Tomson, do you have a minute to talk?

MR. TOMSON: Sure, what's up?

MS. WALKER: Can you do something about all the swearing the men use around the plant? It carries through these thin walls into my work area. It's disgusting. I'm surprised you haven't done anything.

MR. TOMSON:

_____ 9. I'm surprised to hear you say this. You've worked here for five years and never complained about it before.

_____ 10. I didn't know anyone was swearing. I'll look into it.

_____ 11. You don't have to listen to it. Just ignore it.

_____ 12. Are you feeling well today?

_____ 13. What kind of swear words are they using?

_____ 14. You find this swearing offensive?

JIM: Mary, I have a complaint.

MARY: Sit down and tell me about it.

JIM: Being the A. D. (Athletic Director), you know that I use the weight room after the football team. Well, my track team has to return the plates to the racks, put the dumbbells back, and so forth. I don't get paid to pick up after the football team. After all, they have the use of the room longer than we do. I've complained to Ted (the football coach), but all he says is that's the way he finds it, or that he'll try to get the team to do a better job. But nothing happens.

MARY:

_____ 15. Before I forget, congratulations on beating Harvard.

_____ 16. Don't you think you're being a bit picky about this?

_____ 17. You feel it's unfair to pick up after them?

_____ 18. How long has this been going on?

_____ 19. Are you sure you're not jealous because they get to use the weight room longer than you do?

_____ 20. Thanks for telling me about it; I'll talk to Ted.

In the above two situations, which response is the most appropriate?

Learning Objective

9. Explain six response styles and know when to use each

In this chapter, you were presented with ways to help you improve your communications skills. Begin using these techniques to improve your skill level today.

REVIEW

Select one or more methods: (1) Fill in the missing key terms from memory; (2) match the key terms from the end of the review with their definitions below; and/or (3) copy the key terms in order from the key terms at the beginning of the chapter.

Communication skills are important because they are required in performing the five functions of management. _____ is the process of a sender transmitting a message to a receiver with mutual understanding.

_____ is the process of having the receiver restate the message in his or her own words. The _____ are to influence, inform, and/or to express feelings. Communication is the foundation of human relations. Effective communication has positive effects on behavior, human relations, and performance.

The sender initiates the communication, beginning by _____ , which is the sender's process of putting the message into a form that the receiver will understand. The sender then transmits the _____ , the physical form of the encoded information, to the receiver, who in turn goes through _____ , the receiver's process of translating the message into a meaningful form. If the sender and receiver don't mutually agree on the message, communication has not been successful. The four steps in the communication process are (1) select transmission media, (2) send the message, (3) receive the message, and (4) respond to the message. Not all messages require a response. During a conversation, the sender and receiver can reverse roles several times.

_____ are the forms of the transmitted message. The major forms of media include oral (face-to-face, telephone, meetings, and presentations); written (memos, letters, reports, bulletin board notices, posters, fax machines, and computers); and _____ , the facial expressions, vocal qualities, gestures, and posture used while transmitting messages.

The sender should plan the message by predetermining what, who, when, and where the message will be transmitted. The _____ steps include: step 1, develop rapport; step 2, state the communication objective; step 3, transmit the message; step 4, check understanding; and step 5, get a commitment and follow up. When criticizing others, follow these guidelines: give more praise than criticism, criticize immediately, make the criticism performance oriented, give specific and accurate criticism, open on a positive note, and close by repeating what action is needed.

The three levels of listening are marginal, evaluative, and projective. _____ is the ability to understand and relate to another's situation and feelings. Use empathy when dealing with emotional employees. Be an active projective listener by implementing the 13 tips in the chapter.

_____ is the process of verifying messages. After sending a message, verify mutual understanding by asking questions and having the other person paraphrase the message. When responding to a message, the receiver has six styles to choose from: evaluating, confronting, diverting, probing, reassuring, and reflecting.

KEY TERMS

communication   115
decoding   116
empathic listening   125
encoding   116
feedback   129

goals of
    communication   115
media   117
message   116
message-sending process   122

nonverbal
    communication   118
paraphrasing   115

OBJECTIVE CASE

M. Douglas Ivester:
Coca-Cola

M. Douglas Ivester took over as chairman of the board and CEO of Coca-Cola, replacing the late Cuban born Roberto Goizueta. Some questioned if Ivester could fill Goizueta's shoes, as Goizueta was very successful at leading Coca-Cola to new record sales and profits. Ivester did not get much of a honeymoon as Coke's earnings were hammered by overseas economic woes, and its community credibility has been hurt by a racial-discrimination lawsuit, European Union officials' suspicions that Coke used its dominant market position to shut out competitors, and the contamination scare in Belgium and France.

CEO Ivester was also criticized for his communications in the Belgium and France crises, in June 1999, in which over 200 people in several Belgian and French towns reported illness, complaining of headaches, stomachaches, and nausea after drinking Coca-Cola products. The French consumer-affairs minister, Marylise Lebranchu, complained it took Coke 48 hours to provide information on how to identify which soft drink cans might pose further risks. She said that 48 hours was too long; the delay forced France to order the removal from store shelves of all canned Coke products to avoid risking further illnesses. Coke products were also removed from Belgium; the Netherlands and Luxembourg restricted sales of certain Coke products; and Coke had to recall bottles of water in Poland. The French and Belgian government officials scolded the company for not offering enough information on what caused the illness; Coke had to be asked to bring back more data to provide a satisfactory and conclusive explanation for the illnesses. The U.S. press questioned why it took Ivester a week to apologize and whether or not CEO Ivester could turn things around.

After only two years as CEO of Coke, Ivester stepped down and recommended Douglas Daft take his place, which the board approved. Ivester said he thought it was time for "a change" and "fresh leadership." Despite these problems, the Coca-Cola Company is clearly the global soft-drink industry leader. Since 1998, average sales of all Coke products exceed 1 billion servings per day.[64]

Go to the Internet: For more updated information about M. Douglas Ivester and his successor Douglas Daft and Coca-Cola, go to the Web. Do a name search on the Internet and visit the Coke website at *http://www.cocacola.com.* For ideas on using the Internet with cases, see Appendix C.

Support your answer to the following questions with specific information from the case and text, or other information you get from the web or other source.

1. Ivester was the handpicked successor of Goizueta. What led to his early retirement?

2. What was the goal of communications of the Belgian and French governments? What was Coke's problem in meeting the governments' request?

3. What message transmission media would you have recommended Ivester use for providing the information the governments asked for and to make the apology?

4. Which response style did the governments use when it finally did get information from Coke about the reason for the illnesses?

Cumulative Case
Questions

5. Does Ivester have a stronger surgency or agreeableness personality? Did his personality affect his communications (Chapter 2)?

6. Is stress an issue in the case (Chapter 2)?

7. How do you think the general public perceived (Chapter 2) Ivester's attitude and values (Chapter 3) about the illness situation?

Communication?

In the following dialogue, Chris is the manager and Sandy is his or her employee. (*Note:* Students may role-play, giving instructions.)

CHRIS: I need you to get a metal plate ready for the Stern job.

SANDY: OK.

CHRIS: I need a ¾-inch plate. I want a ½-inch hole a little off center. No, you better make it ⅝. In the left corner I need about a ⅜ hole. And on the right top portion, about ⅞ of an inch from the left side, drill a ¼-inch hole. You got it?

SANDY: I think so.

CHRIS: Good, I'll be back later.

Later.

CHRIS: Do you have the plate ready?

SANDY: It's right here.

CHRIS: This isn't what I asked for. I said a ½-inch hole a little off center; this is too much off center. Do it again so it will fit.

SANDY: You're the boss. I'll do it again.

Answer the following questions. Then in the space between questions, state why you selected that answer.

_____ 1. Chris and Sandy communicated.

       a. true   *b.* false

_____ 2. Chris's primary goal of communication was to:

       a. influence   *b.* inform   *c.* express feelings

_____ 3. Chris was the:

       a. sender/decoder   *c.* sender/encoder
       b. receiver/decoder   *d.* receiver/encoder

_____ 4. Sandy was the:

       a. sender/decoder   *c.* sender/encoder
       b. receiver/decoder   *d.* receiver/encoder

_____ 5. The message transmission medium was:

       a. oral   *c.* nonverbal
       b. written   *d.* combined

_____ 6. Chris followed _____ guidelines to getting feedback on messages.

       a. open to feedback   *c.* ask questions
       b. awareness of nonverbal   *d.* paraphrasing
          communication   *e.* none of these

_____ 7. Which step(s) did Chris follow in the message-sending process? (You may select more than one answer.)

       a. step 1   *c.* step 3   *e.* step 5
       b. step 2   *d.* step 4

_____ 8. Sandy was an active listener.

   a. true   *b.* false

_____ 9. Sandy's response style was primarily:

   a. evaluating   *c.* diverting   *e.* reassuring
   b. confronting   *d.* probing   *f.* reflecting

_____ 10. Chris used the _____ situational supervisory style.

   a. autocratic   *c.* participative
   b. consultative   *d.* laissez-faire

11. In Chris's situation, how would you have given the instructions to Sandy?

INTERNET EXERCISES

Interpersonal Communications Skills (IE 4–1)

Online Internet Exercise 4–1 (Self-Assessment)

The objective of this Internet exercise is to assess your interpersonal communication skills as poor to excellent. Use the information from Appendix B and IE 1–2 and 1–3 as you do the following:

1. Go to the Body-Mind QueenDom website homepage—*www.queendom.com*
2. Click "Tests" and scroll down to the Relationships tests section and Click "Communication Skills" and take the test by clicking your selections then click score to get your score and interpretation (your instructor may ask you to make a copy of it to bring to class).
3. Questions: (1) What was your score? (2) Do you have poor, moderate, or excellent interpersonal communication skills? (3) What can you do to improve your communication skills? (Your instructor may ask you to type and print your answer and bring them to class.)

In-Class Internet Exercises 4–1, IE 4–2, IE 4–3, and IE 4–4

The instructor selects one of the six options from Appendix B page 589.

Communication (IE 4–2)

Online Internet Exercise 4–2

The objective of this exercise is to learn some tips about interpersonal communications that you can use in your personal and professional lives to improve your communication skill. Using the information in Appendix B and IE 1–2 and 1–3 as you do the following:

1. Go to the homepage of Innovission—*www.innovis.com*
2. Click "Articles & Tips" and search around and find an article of interest to you. Click the title and read it (your instructor may ask you to print it).
3. Questions: (1) What is the title? (2) Identify tips that can improve your communications—do's and don'ts. (3) How can you use this information in your personal or professional life to improve you communications? (Your instructor may require you to type and print out your answers.)

Presentations— Message Media (IE 4–3)

Online Internet Exercise 4–2 (Self-Assessment)

The objective of this exercise is to learn tips on giving presentations to develop your skills at speaking to a group. Using the information in Appendix B and IE 1–2 and 1–3 as you do the following:

1. Go to the Leadership Strategies homepage—*www.leaderx.com*
2. Click "Test Yourself" then click "Test Your Presentation Style." Test your presentation style, then click "submit" it for scoring. Print your customized report with feedback on important presentation advice.
3. Read your report. Read it a second time, highlighting the most valuable tips that can help you develop your presentation skills. (Your instructor may require your highlighted printout.)

E-Mail—Message Media (IE 4–4)

Online Internet Exercise 4–4

The objective of this exercise is to learn tips on how to effectively use e-mail to increase your skill at using this message transmission media. Using the information in Appendix B and IE 1–2 and 1–3 as you do the following:

1. Go to the homepage of Webfoot—*www.webfoot.com*
2. Click "Beginner's Guide to Effective Email."
3. Click at least two of the topics from the contents near the top of the page and read the e-mail information. (Your instructor may require a copy).

4. Questions: (1) Who is the author and what are the titles of the contents you read? (2) Identify tips that can improve your e-mail communications—do's and don'ts. (3) How can you use this information in your personal or professional life to improve your communications? (Your instructor may require you to type and print out your answers.)

 Preparation

Nonverbal Communication and Listening

During class you will be given the opportunity to practice using effective nonverbal communication and listening skills. This will be done while you are getting acquainted with someone whom you do not know, or do not know well.

In preparation, make sure you have read the chapter and completed Self-Assessment Exercise 4–1. Review the feedback sheet below, which you will be using during the exercise to analyze how well you used the text material.

Feedback on Nonverbal Communication and Listening Skills

You and your partner will discuss the feedback areas below. After the discussion, using feedback from your partner, rate yourself by putting an *X* in the blank next to the word(s) that best describe the communication you used during the discussion.

Nonverbal Communication:

Facial expressions

1. I _____ smiled _____ frowned.
2. I _____ did _____ did not use eye contact effectively. It was _____ too frequent _____ about right _____ not frequent enough.
3. My facial expressions conveyed:

Vocal

4. My pitch was _____ high _____ about right _____ low.
5. My volume was _____ loud _____ about right _____ soft.
6. My pace was _____ fast _____ about right _____ slow.
7. My pause and silence was _____ too frequent _____ about right _____ too infrequent.
8. I _____ did _____ did not use repetitive words like "y'know."
9. Tone, the attitude in my voice, was:

10. I _____ did _____ did not vary my vocal qualities enough.

Gestures

11. List gestures that you used and indicate whether they were used too frequently.

12. My gestures conveyed:

Posture

13. I _____ sat in my chair leaning slightly forward _____ slouched.

14. Our distance was _____ 0–1½ feet _____ 1½–4 feet _____ 4–7 feet apart.

15. I _____ did _____ did not make my partner comfortable with the distance between us.

Combined

16. My nonverbal and verbal communications _____ were _____ were not consistent.

Self-Evaluations: Evaluate your listening ability without your partner's feedback. However, you may ask each other questions if you want to.

Listening Skills: Mark the following statements true or false by placing the letter T or F on the line before each statement.

_____ 1. I liked listening to my partner talk. I encouraged him or her to talk by showing interest, by smiling and nodding, etc.

_____ 2. I paid close attention to my partner. I did not stereotype him or her. If the person were more interesting or similar to me, I would not have listened differently.

_____ 3. I did not evaluate my partner's words and/or nonverbal communication ability as he or she talked.

_____ 4. I avoided the distractions in the class.

_____ 5. I gave my partner my complete attention. I put everything else out of sight and mind.

_____ 6. I allowed my partner time to finish talking. I did not interrupt, anticipate what he or she was going to say, or jump to conclusions.

_____ 7. I did not tune out my partner because he or she did not agree with my views.

_____ 8. While my partner talked, my mind did not wander to other personal topics.

_____ 9. While my partner talked, I paid close attention to the nonverbal communication cues to help me fully understand what he or she was trying to get across.

_____ 10. I did not tune out and pretend I understood when the topic was difficult or not interesting.

_____ 11. When my partner was talking, I did not think about what I was going to say in reply.

_____ 12. When I felt there was something missing or contradictory, I asked direct questions to get my partner to explain the idea more fully.

_____ 13. When I didn't understand something, I let my partner know it in an effective way.

_____ 14. When listening to my partner, I tried to put myself in his or her position and see things from his or her perspective.

_____ 15. During the conversation, I repeated back to my partner what had been said in my own words to be sure I understood correctly what had been said so far (paraphrase). I paraphrased _____ too often _____ about right _____ not enough.

If all 15 statements were answered T (true), you used the listening skills effectively. If you answered F (false) to any statements, you may want to work on improving this area(s). Overall, how can I improve my listening skills?

SKILL-BUILDING EXERCISE 4-1

**In-Class
Nonverbal
Communication
and Listening**

Objectives: To increase your awareness of the effects nonverbal communication has on conversations. To practice and develop listening skills.

SCANS: The SCANS competencies of interpersonal skills and information and the foundations of basic, thinking, and personal qualities are developed through this exercise.

Preparation: You should have completed the preparation on the preceding pages.

Experience: You will have a personal discussion while trying to be aware of nonverbal communication and listening actively. After the conversation, you will analyze the nonverbal communication and listening skills you and your team member used.

*Procedure 1
(2–4 minutes)*

Pair off with someone you don't know, or don't know well. If there is an odd number in the class, have one group of three people, or have an observer.

*Procedure 2
(5–10 minutes)*

Group members have a conversation to get to know one another better. Possible topics include school activities, present/summer jobs, career goals, nonacademic interests, and so on. Or they can share how they are feeling.

*Procedure 3
(5–10 minutes)*

Turn to the preparation feedback sheet and give each other feedback on your use of nonverbal communication and listening skills. To be useful, the feedback must be honest, specific, and accurate.

Conclusion: The instructor leads a class discussion and/or makes concluding remarks.

Application (2–4 minutes): What did I learn from this experience? How will I use this knowledge in the future?

Sharing: Volunteers give their answers to the application section.

SKILL-BUILDING EXERCISE 4-2

**In-Class
Giving
Instructions**

Objective: To develop your ability to give and receive messages (communication skills).

SCANS: The SCANS competencies of resources, especially interpersonal and information, and the foundations of basic, thinking, and personal qualities are developed through this exercise.

Experience: You will plan, give, and receive instructions for the completion of a drawing of three objects.

Preparation: No preparation is necessary except reading the chapter. The instructor will provide the original drawings that must be drawn.

Procedure 1
(3–7 minutes)

Read all of procedure 1 twice. The task is for the manager to give an employee instructions for completing a drawing of three objects. The objects must be drawn to scale and look like photocopies of the originals. You will have 15 minutes to complete the task.

The exercise has four separate parts or steps.

1. The manager plans.
2. The manager gives the instructions.
3. The employee does the drawing.
4. Evaluation of the results takes place.

Rules: The rules are numbered to correlate with the four parts above.

1. Planning. While planning, the manager may write out instructions for the employee but may not do any drawing of any kind.
2. Instructions. While giving instructions, the manager may not show the original drawing to the employee. (The instructor will give it to you.) The instructions may be given orally, and/or in writing, but no nonverbal hand gestures are allowed. The employee may take notes while the instructions are being given but cannot do any drawing with or without a pen. The manager must give the instructions for all three objects before drawing begins.
3. Drawing. Once the employee begins the drawing, the manager should watch but no longer communicate in any way.
4. Evaluation. When the employee is finished or the time is up, the manager shows the employee the original drawing. Discuss how you did. Turn to the integration section and answer the questions. The manager writes down the answers.

Procedure 2
(2–5 minutes)

Half of the class members will act as the manager first and give instructions. Managers move their seats to one of the four walls (spread out). They should be facing the center of the room with their backs close to the wall.

Employees sit in the middle of the room until called on by a manager. When called on, bring a seat to the manager. Sit facing the manager so that you cannot see any manager drawing.

Procedure 3
(15–20 minutes)

The instructor gives each manager a copy of the drawing. Be careful not to let any employees see it. The manager plans the instructions. When managers are ready, they call an employee and give the instructions. It may be helpful to use the message-sending process. Be sure to follow the rules. The employee should do the drawing on the page entitled Employee Drawing. If you use written instructions, use nonbook paper. You have 15 minutes to complete the drawing, and possibly five minutes for integration (evaluation). When you finish the drawing, turn to the evaluation questions in the integration section below.

Procedure 4
(15–20 minutes)

The employees are now the managers and sit in the seats facing the center of the room. New employees go to the center of the room until called upon.

Follow procedure 3, with the instructor giving a different drawing. Do not work with the same person; then change partners.

Integration

Evaluating Questions: You may select more than one answer.

_____ 1. The goal of communication was to:

   a. influence   *b.* inform   *c.* express feelings

_____ 2. Feedback was:

   a. immediate   *c.* performance oriented
   b. specific and accurate   *d.* positive

_____ 3. The manager transmitted the message:

    a. orally   *c.* nonverbally

    b. in writing   *d.* combined

_____ 4. The manager spent _____ time planning.

    a. too much   *b.* too little   *c.* the right amount of

The following five questions relate to the message-sending process.

_____ 5. The manager developed rapport. (Step 1)

    a. true   *b.* false

_____ 6. The manager stated the communication objective. (Step 2)

    a. true   *b.* false

_____ 7. The manager transmitted the message: (Step 3)

    a. effectively   *b.* ineffectively

_____ 8. The manager checked understanding by using: (Step 4)

    a. direct questions   *c.* both

    b. paraphrasing   *d.* neither

    The amount of checking was:

    a. too frequent   *b.* too infrequent   *c.* about right

_____ 9. The manager got a commitment and followed up. (Step 5)

    a. true   *b.* false

_____ 10. The manager and/or employee got emotional.

    a. true   *b.* false

_____ 11. The primary response style used by the manager was:

    a. evaluating   *c.* diverting   *e.* reassuring

    b. confronting   *d.* probing   *f.* reflecting

_____ 12. The primary response style used by the employee was:

    a. evaluating   *c.* diverting   *e.* reassuring

    b. confronting   *d.* probing   *f.* reflecting

_____ 13. The manager used the _____ supervisory style.

    a. autocratic   *c.* participative

    b. consultative   *d.* laissez-faire

_____ 14. The appropriate style was:

    a. autocratic   *c.* participative

    b. consultative   *d.* laissez-faire

15. Were the objects drawn to approximate scale? If not, why not?

16. Did you follow the rules? If not, why not?

17. If you could do this exercise over again, what would you do differently?

Conclusion: The instructor leads a class discussion and/or makes concluding remarks.

Application   (2–4 minutes): What did I learn from this experience? How will I use this knowledge in the future?

Sharing: Volunteers give their answers to the application section.

EMPLOYEE DRAWING

**Preparation
Giving Criticism**

In class, you will be given the opportunity to role-play giving criticism. Think of a job situation in which you or another employee should have been criticized to improve performance. If you prefer, you can act as criticizer in a nonjob situation in which criticism is warranted. Below, briefly state the situation; then write some notes on what you would say when giving the criticism. Be sure to follow the five guidelines in Exhibit 4–4, p. 124, for giving effective criticism. Remember to maintain human relations while criticizing.

You will get more from the exercise if you think of your own situation. However, if you cannot think of your own situation after making a serious effort, you may use this situation: The employee is a waiter or waitress in an ice cream shop. He or she knows that the tables should be cleaned up quickly after customers leave so that the new customers do not have to sit at a dirty table. It is a busy night. You as the manager notice customers seated at two dirty tables. The employee responsible for clearing the tables is socializing with some friends at one of the tables. Employees are supposed to be friendly. When criticized, the employee may use this fact as an excuse for the dirty tables.

**In-Class
Giving Criticism**

Objective: To develop your skill at improving performance through giving criticism while maintaining human relations.

SCANS: The SCANS competencies of resources, especially interpersonal and information, and the foundations of basic, thinking, and personal qualities are developed through this exercise.

Preparation: You should have developed criticism to role-play in class.

Experience: You will give criticism, be criticized, and observe criticism following the guidelines for giving effective criticism.

*Procedure 1
(2–4 minutes)*

Break into groups of three. Make one or two groups of two if necessary. It is recommended that only one person per group use the example given in the preparation. The other two should have their own situation.

Each member selects a number from one to three to determine the order of giving, receiving, and observing criticism.

*Procedure 2
(5–8 minutes)*

Number 1 will give the criticism to number 2, and number 3 will be the observer. Number 1 explains the situation to numbers 2 and 3. If the person criticized would most likely make some comment in response, tell number 2 what it is so that he or she can make it. When numbers 2 and 3 understand the situation, number 1 role-plays giving the criticism while number 3 observes and takes notes on the observer sheet. When the role play is finished, the observer leads a discussion on how well number 1 criticized number 2 using the observer sheet.

Do not go on to the next criticism until asked to do so. If you finish early, wait for the others to finish.

Observer Sheet

For each question, think of what was done well and how the criticizer could improve. Telling others how to improve is criticism. The person criticized and observer now criticize the criticizer.

1. Was criticism given immediately (if appropriate)?

2. Was the criticism performance oriented?

3. Was the criticism specific and accurate?

4. Did the criticizer open on a positive note?

5. Did the criticizer close by repeating what action is needed (if appropriate).

6. Do you think the person criticized will change the behavior? Why or why not?

7. Was criticism given in a way that will maintain human relations? Explain your answer.

Procedure 3
(5–8 minutes)

Number 2 will give the criticism to number 3, and number 1 will be the observer. Number 2 explains the situation to numbers 1 and 3. If the person criticized would most likely make some comment, tell number 3 what it is so that he or she can make it. When numbers 1 and 3 understand the situation, number 2 role-plays giving the criticism while number 1 observes and takes notes on the observer sheet. When the role play is finished, the observer leads a discussion on how well number 2 criticized number 3 using the observer sheet.

Do not go on to the next criticism until asked to do so. If you finish early, wait for the others to finish.

Procedure 4
(5–8 minutes)

Each person plays the role not yet played, following the same procedures as above.

Conclusion: The instructor leads a class discussion and/or makes concluding remarks.

Application (2–4 minutes): What did I learn from this experience? How will I use this knowledge in the future to give effective criticism while maintaining human relations?

Sharing: Volunteers give their answers to the application section.

Response Styles
VE 4–1
BM–4

Objectives: To better understand the six response styles.

SCANS: The SCANS competencies of interpersonal skills and especially information (evaluating data) and the foundations of basic, thinking, and personal qualities are developed through this exercise.

Preparation: You should understand the six response styles.

Procedure 1
(10–20 minutes)

The instructor shows Video Module 4, Response Styles. As you view each of the six scenes, identify the six response styles being used by the manager.

◆ Video

Scene 1. _____	A. Evaluating
Scene 2. _____	B. Confronting
Scene 3. _____	C. Diverting
Scene 4. _____	D. Probing
Scene 5. _____	E. Reassuring
Scene 6. _____	F. Reflecting

After viewing each of the six scenes, identify/match the style used by the manager by placing the letter of the style on the scene line.

Option A: View all six scenes and identify the style used by the manager. After viewing all six scenes, discuss and/or have the instructor give the correct answers.

Option B: After each scene, the class discusses the style used by the manager. The instructor states the correct answer after each of the six scenes.

Procedure 2
(2–5 minutes)

Select the one style that you would use in this situation. Are other styles also appropriate? Which style would you not use (not appropriate) for this situation? Next to each response style listed above, write the letter *a* for appropriate or *n* for not appropriate.

Discussion:

Option A: In groups of four to six, answer the questions below.

Option B: As a class, answer the questions below.

1. Which style(s) is/are not appropriate to use in this situation?

2. Which style(s) is/are appropriate to use in this situation?

3. Is there one style most appropriate in this situation? If yes, which one?

Conclusion: The instructor may make concluding remarks.

Application (2–4 minutes): What did I learn from this exercise? How will I use this knowledge in the future?

Sharing: Volunteers give their answers to the application section.

Organizational Structure and Communication

5

Learning Objectives

After completing this chapter, you should be able to:

1. Explain six principles of organization.

2. Explain six types of departmentalization.

3. Identify contemporary organization trends.

4. Describe how communication flows through organizations.

5. Explain the advantage the all-channel communication network has over the other networks.

6. List nine common barriers to communication and how to overcome them.

7. Identify your preferred communication style.

8. Explain how to change communication styles to meet the needs of the situation.

9. Define the following 12 key terms (in order of appearance in the chapter):

   organizational structure
   organizational communication
   vertical communication
   horizontal communication
   grapevine
   communication networks
   filtering
   autocratic communication style (S-A)

   departmentalization
   consultative communication style (S-C)
   participative communication style (S-P)
   laissez-faire communication style (S-L)

Chapter Outline

The Digital Equipment Corporation held a "state of the company" meeting for top managers. Senior Vice President Jack Shields was not present at the meeting. Mr. Shields was sometimes mentioned as the likely successor to President Kenneth Olsen. But a new organization chart of U.S. field operations presented at the meeting did not include Mr. Shields. During the meeting, when one of the vice presidents asked Mr. Olsen where Mr. Shields was, Mr. Olsen responded vaguely. The managers present still did not know where Mr. Shields was or why he was not at the meeting.

Rumors that Mr. Shields had resigned or had been fired by Mr. Olsen started moving through the sales force and outside of Digital. The gossip hit Wall Street, raising questions about executive succession at Digital. The price of Digital stock fell more than a point.

Then the media got wind of the story and called Digital to get the story. The company denied the resignation rumors. However, a television show misread a wire story of the denial and reported that Mr. Shields had resigned. Then an electronic bulletin board on Digital's in-house computer network repeated the TV report.

When Mr. Shields heard the news, he invited a reporter to an interview in his office at Digital. Mr. Shields stated that he had no plans to resign or indication he was expected to. He missed the meeting because he was attending the annual meeting of another company for which he was a board member. The organization chart did not show him because it did not go up to the level of the executive committee where he sits. Mr. Olsen could not be reached for comment.

In the last chapter, you learned about interpersonal communication. This chapter explains how communication flows through organizations, and the major barriers causing inaccurate communication at the interpersonal and organizational level. It also explains how to change communication styles to meet the needs of the situation.

● Organization
● Group
● Individual

Organizational Structure

Organizational structure   *refers to the way managers design their firms to achieve their organization's mission and goals.* Effective organization is one of the top-ten challenges to business leaders in the 21st century.[1] Organizational structure affects competitiveness and employer-employee human relations.[2] In this section, we discuss principles of organization, departmentalization, and contemporary organizational designs.

Principles of Organization

Here we present six traditionally accepted principles of organization.

Chain of Command

The chain of command is the line of authority from the top to the bottom of the organization, which is shown in an organization chart. People have a natural tendency to organize in a hierarchy.[3] The common organizational hierarchy chain of command was illustrated in chapter 1 Exhibit 1–1, and it is illustrated in this chapter in Exhibit 5–1 Organization Chart of president, VPs, and managers; the workers are below but are not commonly shown on an organization chart.

Span of Management

The span of management refers to number of employees reporting to a manager. In Exhibit 5–1, the President has three VPs, and the VPs have a span of management of five, three, and four.

EXHIBIT 5–1   **ORGANIZATION CHART**

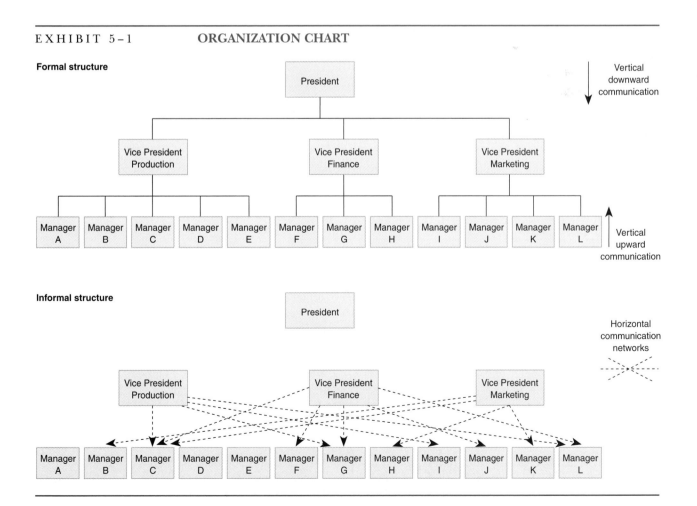

Division of Labor

With the division of labor, employees have specialized jobs. In Exhibit 5–1, labor is divided into production, finance, and marketing jobs.

Coordination

With the division of labor comes the need to coordinate the work of all departments. The production people make the product, the marketing people sell it, and the finance people collect the money. Through the systems effect, if any department is ineffective, it will influence the performance of the other departments and the organization as a whole.

Line and Staff Authority

Line authority is the responsibility to make decisions and issue orders down the chain of command, which includes production, marketing, and finance—as shown in Exhibit 5–1. Staff authority is the responsibility to advise and assist other personnel, which include human resources, information systems, maintenance departments, and so on–not shown in Exhibit 5–1.

Centralized and Decentralized Authority

With centralized authority, top managers make important decisions. With decentralized authority, middle and first-line managers make important decisions.

WORK APPLICATIONS

Learning Objective

1. Explain six principles of organization.

1. Select an organization you work/worked for. Identify the chain of command from your job to the top of the organization. How many people are/were in your boss's span of management? Is/was your job specialized? *How was work coordinated? Was your job line or staff? Was authority centralized or decentralized?*

Departmentalization

An important part of the organizational structure is departmentalization. **Departmentalization** *is the grouping of related activities into units.* Here are six common types of departmentalization:

Functional Departmentalization

Functional departmentalization involves organizing departments around essential input activities, such as production/operations, finance/accounting, marketing/sales, and human resources. Exhibit 5–1 is a functional departmentalization organization chart. Most small businesses are functionally organized.

Product (Service) Departmentalization

Product departmentalization involves organizing departments around goods and services provided. Chrysler in the United States (without Daimler-Benz) could be organized as:

Plymouth	Dodge	Chrysler	Jeep Eagle

Customer Departmentalization

Customer departmentalization involves organizing departments around the needs of different types of customers. Motorola restructured to merge about six business units into two huge divisions—one geared to consumers and the other to industrial customers.

Divisional Departmentalization (M-Form)

When the firm develops independent lines of business, such as Philip Morris with:

Philip Morris cigarettes	Miller Beer	Kraft-General Foods

which operate as separate companies all contributing to the corporation profitability, the design is called divisional departmentalization or (M-Form).

Territory (Geographic) Departmentalization

Territory, also called geographic departmentalization, involves organizing departments in each area in which the enterprise does business. Many retail chains, such as Sears, and the federal government are organized by territory. World Wide Marriage Encounter U.S.A. could be organized as: north, south, east, and west.

Matrix Departmentalization

Matrix departmentalization combines the functional and product departmental structures. The employee works for a functional department and is also assigned to one or more products or projects. The major advantage of the matrix is its flexibility. It allows the firm to temporarily organize for a project, and projects can change fairly quickly. Rank, Xerox, and Boeing use a formal matrix structure.

Combination

Many large companies have more than one than one form of departmentalization. For example, IBM is customer, with divisions, with territories all over the world.

Learning Objective

2. Explain six types of departmentalization.

WORK APPLICATION

2. Draw an organization chart illustrating the type of departmentalization where you work/ed.

Contemporary Organization

Let's discuss some of the contemporary trends in organizational design based on the principles we've talked about. The focus here is not so much on departmentalization, but rather on how to make any form of departmentalization work effectively.

Organization Trends

The hierarchy chain of command is getting *flatter* as organizations have cut layers of management,[4] which has increased the span of management as more employees report to one manager. Organizations are reengineering their structures into team-based forms, in which authority is decentralized to empower lower-level employees.[5] Organizations are focusing more on communications through teams[6] as a means of developing trust and coordination between teams and departments.[7]

Reengineering, Downsizing, and High-Involvement Organization

Reengineering is the redesign of work to combine fragmented tasks into streamlined processes that save time and money. *Downsizing* reduces the size of an organization, often by cutting jobs, to save money. Downsizing commonly is separate from reengineering. Over the past years, the news media has carried stories of thousands of employees getting laid-off at major corporations. The goal of reengineering is not to downsize, however, the redesigned organization often needs fewer employees and less managers. Thus, the two may go together. Reengineering assumes there are no current jobs. Teams develop the process of acquiring the inputs to make the products and services all the way through to transforming them into output products and services.

A form of reengineering is *high-involvement organizations* or *green-fields* that use a team approach to organize a new facility, rather than change a traditional facility. Green-fields are smaller than traditional companies, with between 100 to 200 employees. Cummins Engineering, General Foods, Mead, Procter & Gamble,

Sherwin-Williams, and TRW have developed high-involvement organizations. Reengineering is still being used, but in conjunction with the next three organizational designs, rather than by itself.

The Learning Organization and Community of Practice

The division of labor is still specialized, but not as much as in the past, as firms realize the need for organizational learning (Chapter 2) to continually improve.[8] Some are even calling the learning organization a form of organization,[9] which it is. However, it has no formal structure departmentalization as it is used more as a means of coordination of sharing knowledge throughout the entire organization. Community of practice is used within learning organizations. *Community of practice* is an informal group that gets together to solve common problems. They are a means of sharing information.

The Horizontal Organization

The horizontal organization is currently popular as companies, including AT&T, GE, Motorola, and Xerox are focusing horizontally, rather than on vertical hierarchy. The major focus of everyone in the organization is on directly delivering value to the customer. This is done with an organizational structure that is flat and incorporates reengineering, empowerment (decentralization), and teams.[10] The structure is not based on the functions of production, marketing, and finance but on the important (core) "processes" that are needed to satisfy the customer. Rewards are based on customer satisfaction, rather than stock prices or completing functional tasks. The information system is available to all employees to complete their process and serve the customer. One of the objectives is to reduce the number of times work is passed from one department to another to speed up the process.

Virtual Organizations, Outsourcing, and Core Competency

IE 5–1
IE 5–2

Technology, particularly e-business, is making the virtual organization an increasingly dominant model.[11] *Virtual organizations* are comprised of independent service providers completing a specific task. Many fad products, such as a child's action figure from a movie are produced and marketed through virtual organization. Others are more permanent. For example, Ben Greenfield developed a virtual organization to sell potato chips. First Ben convinced Mystic Seaport Maritime Museum in Connecticut to use their brand name for a royalty fee. He got a Maine processing company to make the potato chips, and a Boston food broker placed the chips in about 300 stores for a fee.

Outsourcing takes place when a firm has a different organization provide a service or product for it. *Core competencies* are the things an organization does well. Many organizations are outsourcing things that are not core competencies. For example, your college's core competency is teaching and learning. The trend has been to outsource bookstores and food services to organizations that specialize in these services.

Contemporary Organization and Human Relations

Learning Objective

3. Identify contemporary organization trends.

To summarize, organization trends include hierarchy being changed, hybridized, in order to increase speed of response, individual accountability, flexibility, knowledge sharing and connectivity.[12] Teams are increasing participating in structuring organizations. The virtual organization and outsourcing clearly require effective communications and human relations to get separate firms to work together. Thus, human relations skill are critically important to designing and operating contemporary organizations, more so than in a traditional organizational structure, that can compete in the diverse, fast-changing, global environment. And communications at the interpersonal level, covered in the last chapter, and organizational level communications, covered next, are the foundation for human relations.

3. Identify contemporary organization trends that are used where you work/ed?

Organizational Communication

● Organization
● Group
● Individual

Managers have the responsibility to tell employees what is going on within the organization. An important management issue is what information should be given to employees and which employees should be given access to what information.[13] With technological advances, such as e-mail and TV monitors, more information is being sent to all employees, and access to information is more available to lower-level employees.[14] Today, information about customer satisfaction and financial performance are being sent to lower-level employees.[15] Effective organizational communications helps to improve human relations and performance and is therefore critical to meeting the goal of human relations.

In general, **organizational communication** *is the compounded interpersonal communication process across an organization.* The interpersonal communication building blocks affect the organization's performance. Communication within an organization flows in a vertical, horizontal, or lateral way throughout the firm. It may also do so through the grapevine, which goes in all directions.

Vertical Communication

One type of communication is **vertical communication,** *the flow of information both up and down the chain of command.* It is often called *formal communication* because it follows the chain of command and is recognized as official. It flows upward and downward.

Downward Communication

When top-level management makes decisions, they are often communicated down the chain of command. It is the process of higher level management telling those below them what to do. Organizational structures tend to facilitate downward flow of communication, so this type of communication generally occurs easily and successfully.

When communicating down the chain of command, management should give careful thought to possible consequences of messages, as is illustrated in the opening case.

Upward Communication

When employees send a message to their manager, they are using upward communications. Hierarchal systems do not facilitate an upward flow of information as they do for the downward flow, and this tends to result in communication failure. To help facilitate upward communications, some organizations like Caterpillar use an open-door policy. Other techniques (which have already been discussed or will be in future chapters) include attitude surveys, suggestion systems, quality circles, and employee meetings.

The Digital Equipment Corporation's "state of the company" meeting when the vice president asked the president why Mr. Shields was absent is an example of upward communication, while Mr. Olsen's response was one of downward communication. Both were examples of vertical communication. For an illustration of downward and upward vertical communication, see Exhibit 5–1.

4. Give a specific example of when you used vertical communication. Identify it as upward or downward.

Status and power are not equal among participants in vertical communication. Managers at higher levels have more status and power, so when they talk employees at lower levels tend to listen and follow their directives. On the other hand, many ineffective managers view themselves as powerful and regard listening to employees and following their advice as giving up some of their power. When upper-level managers are willing to listen, employees will contribute ideas to help the organization develop a mentality of continuous improvement.

Horizontal Communication

Another type of communication, **horizontal communication,** *is the flow of information between colleagues and peers.* It is often called *informal communication* because it does not follow the chain of command and is often not recognized as official. All communication outside the chain of command is horizontal. It is also called *lateral communication.* Most messages processed by an organization are carried via informal channels. Coordination of departments and employees requires communication between colleagues and peers.[16] As an employee, you will often find it necessary to communicate with other department members and members of different departments in order to get them to help you meet your objectives.

The Digital meeting for top managers was a form of both vertical and horizontal communications. Mr. Olsen got the chance to talk to his subordinates, subordinates got to talk to Mr. Olsen, and the vice presidents got to talk to each other.

5. Give a specific example of when you used horizontal communication.

Grapevine Communication

The **grapevine** *is the informal vehicle through which messages flow throughout the organization.* The grapevine is a useful organizational reality that will always exist. It should be considered as much a communication vehicle as the company newsletter or employee meetings. When the grapevine allows employees to know about a management decision almost before it is made, management is doing something right.

Reports on the accuracy of the grapevine vary.[17] Some believe that the grapevine often carries rumors that are usually exaggerated and are almost always wrong. However, others believe that the grapevine is 75 to 95 percent accurate and provides managers and staff with better information than formal communication. Rumors tend to spread out of fear of the unknown; people believe what supports their fears. Rumors often start when management disastrously tries to hide things from employees. At the Digital meeting, when the vice president asked Mr. Olsen where Mr. Shields was, Mr. Olsen responded vaguely. Because Mr. Olsen did not respond to reports, we cannot be sure that he was trying to hide the reason for Mr. Shields's absence. The vagueness could have been because of other reasons such as poor communication skills. In any case, the major reasons for the rumor were that Mr. Olsen did not clearly state why Mr. Shields was not at the meeting and that it was not clear that the new organization chart was incomplete. If Mr. Olsen clearly stated why Mr. Shields was not at the meeting and that the new organization chart doesn't go to his level, employees would not have assumed that Mr. Shields had resigned or was fired by Mr. Olsen.

Rather than ignore or try to repress the grapevine, tune into it. Identify the key people in the organization's grapevine and feed them information. To help prevent incorrect rumors, keep the information flowing through the grapevine as accurate and rumor-free as possible. Share all nonconfidential information with employees; tell them of changes as far in advance as possible. Encourage employees to ask questions about rumors they hear.

Learning Objective

4. Describe how communication flows through organizations

WORK APPLICATIONS

6. Give a specific example of a message you heard through the grapevine. How accurate was it? Was it the exact same message management sent?

Skill-Building

SB 5–3

Be careful when using the grapevine to spread gossip.[18] Gossiping about people can really hurt your human relations with them when they find out what you said about them. In a diverse workplace, it is even more important to be careful about what you say about others different than yourself. The old adage, "if you can't say anything good about someone, don't say anything at all," is a good human relations rule to follow.

APPLICATION SITUATIONS

Communication Flow

AS 5–1

Identify the communication flow as:

A. Vertical-downward   C. Horizontal

B. Vertical-upward   D. Grapevine

_____ 1. Hey, Jim, have you heard Mr. Smith and Cindy went out on a date last night? They went to the . . .

_____ 2. Pete, will you come here and hold this so I can get the plate on straight, the way I do it for you all the time.

_____ 3. Karen, here is the letter you asked me to type. Proofread it and I'll make any necessary changes.

_____ 4. Ronald, I have a new customer here who wants to set up a charge account. Please do the credit check and make the decision soon. I can sell them lots of our merchandise, and you can bill them for it.

_____ 5. Ed, take this over to Carl for me.

Communication Networks

Within organizations, **communication networks** *are sets of employees who have stable contact through which information is generated and transmitted.* Two major types of communication networks are those within organizations and those within departments and small groups.

Networks in Organizations

The formal chain of command illustrates the vertical flow of communications. See Exhibit 5–1.

As the top of Exhibit 5–1 illustrates, the vertical lines represent the formal reporting relationship and flow of vertical communication, both upward and downward. However, the organization chart does not show the networks within the organization.

The vice presidents are responsible for the three major functions within any organization. These functions of operation, finance, and marketing must be coordinated. Yet, within the formal organization structure, you cannot tell who talks to whom to get the job done. The vice president of production may be in an informal horizontal communication network (see informal structure Exhibit 5–1) with managers C, G, I, and L, while the vice president of marketing could be in a communication network with managers B, C, H, and K. Another possible network could include the vice president of finance and managers C, F, G, J, and L. The possible networks are endless. The organization chart does not show the many grapevines within an organization that could start and end with anyone in the organization.

The person in the communications hub tends to have considerable power, regardless of his or her formal position in the organization's structure. In the above example networks, it appears that manager C is in the communications hub, tied into all three communication networks.

Networks in Departments and Small Groups

As within organizations, networks are formed within departments. In order to get the marketing jobs done, managers I, J, K, and L in Exhibit 5–1 may all be involved in a network, while in production the managers may be producing different products that do not require them to work together as a network. Yet, in the finance area, managers F and H may form a network, with G being excluded.

Within departments, smaller groups tend to form networks as well. Within the production area, all of the managers could comprise a network. Managers A, C, and D and managers B and E could form small group networks.

Within the organization and the department, small group communication networks can be developed in a variety of structures. Exhibit 5–2 is an example of the five common network designs, each including five members. The number in the network could be increased or decreased without changing the structure. Notice the wheel, chain, and Y all include a central person, A, through whom much of the communication must pass. The circle and all-channel patterns involve all members equally in exchanges of information.

EXHIBIT 5–2   **SMALL GROUP COMMUNICATION NETWORKS**

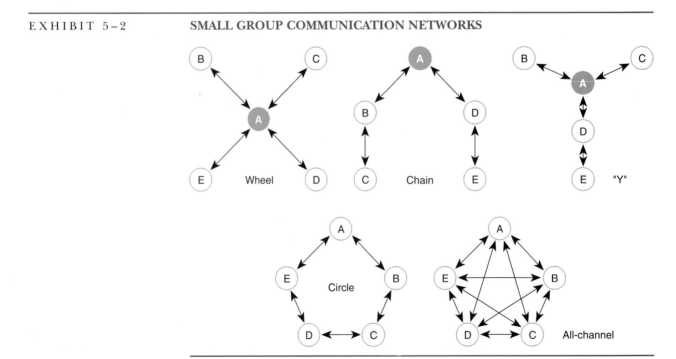

Some network patterns include a central person (A) through whom much of the communication passes; other patterns involve all members equally in the communication exchange.

When small groups work together, they can use any network pattern. However, different patterns work best for different tasks. For simple, routine tasks, the wheel, chain, and Y work fast and accurately; for complex, nonroutine tasks, the circle and all-channel patterns work best where the free flow of communication exists, even though it tends to be slower. In a department setting, the manager would be using an autocratic or consultative supervisory style in the wheel, chain, and Y, with the manager represented by the A member of the group. In the circle and all-channel patterns, the manager would be using the participative or laissez-faire supervisory style.

WORK APPLICATIONS

7. Identify a communication network you are/were a part of. List the other members and their positions within the organization or department.

Information Networks and the Internet

Information networks and the virtual office and telecommuters is the wave of the future.[19] Computer networks are changing the way companies—and their employees—do business.[20] Most jobs today are requiring some computer use.[21] Computer networks centralize control over information access and analysis.[22] Computers do change the way we communicate. However, computers don't replace the need for good human relations skills.[23]

All employees are connected/networked via computer e-mail and other methods.[24] Employees at one site are directly linked to other sites by local-area networks (LAN) and wide-area networks (WAN), which connect multiple sites together via computers using telecommunications or long-range communications devices.[25] Employees can also be networked with customers. Information networks facilitate faster response to customers' problems and needs. Networks to suppliers allow orders to be placed via e-mail, while also providing information on how much to order. Value-added networks (VAN) link manufacturing operations with their external customers and suppliers. The VAN allows for instant transfer of information about current inventories and will automatically place an order for new goods for shipment from operations to retailers when products are low. VANs are controlled through electronic data interchange (EDI) or the scanners cashiers use to ring up your sale at retail stores.[26]

Networks are commonly used to tap into databases, such as online services which may provide access to the Internet and its World Wide Web. Online servicers have led to the increased use of e-mail.[27] Networking is becoming so popular that *Fortune* magazine reports on the 25 "coolest" companies, based on innovative computer networking and information technology advances.[28]

Communication Barriers and How to Overcome Them

Eliminating communication barriers is important for business success.[29] This section discusses some of the major barriers to effective organizational and global communication, and how to overcome them.

Organizational Communication Barriers

When the sender transmits the message, the message is subject to communication barriers.[30] When the message goes to the receiver, it is again subject to these same barriers. See Exhibit 5–3 for an illustration of how barriers affect the communication process.

EXHIBIT 5-3 HOW BARRIERS AFFECT THE COMMUNICATION PROCESS

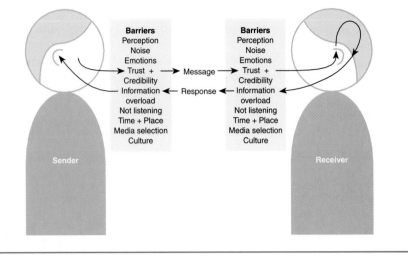

Perception

As messages are transmitted to receivers, they decode them. In the process of decoding, people's background, experience, interest, values, and so forth all affect how the message is interpreted. People usually see the message from their point of view, rather than from that of the sender (Chapter 2).

Another perception problem involves *semantics*. One word often means different things to different people. For example, a manager gives the secretary a letter to type saying "please type this and then burn it." Burn, meaning make a copy, may be interpreted as putting a match to it. Thus, the choice of words is important. Be careful not to use jargon with people who are not familiar with the terminology.

Overcoming Perception Barriers: To overcome perception problems, you need to consider how the other person will most likely perceive the message and try to encode and transmit it appropriately. Checking understanding by asking direct questions and by having the other party paraphrase can help eliminate perception problems.[31]

Noise

As the message is transmitted, noise factors can disturb or confuse communication. For example, there may be a machine making a noise that is distracting; the sender may not speak loud enough for the receiver to hear well; or a radio or TV may distract the receiver, causing him or her to miss the message.

Overcoming Noise Barriers: To overcome noise we need to consider the physical surroundings before transmitting the message. Try to keep noise to a minimum. If possible, stop the noise by shutting off the machine or moving to a location that is quieter.

Emotions

Everyone has emotions, such as anger, hurt, fear, sorrow, happiness, and so on. When you are emotional, it is difficult to be objective and to listen. When communicating, you should remain calm and be careful not to make others emotional by your behavior.[32] For example, if a manager is trying to get an employee to increase productivity and makes a comment like "you're lazy," chances are good that the employee will get angry and defensive (emotional). They may end up arguing, rather than solving the problem through mutual understanding.

Overcoming Emotional Barriers: To avoid emotional problems in communications, you should try not to become emotional. Instead follow the four guidelines to giving effective feedback discussed in Chapter 4 to avoid making others emotional. If you or the other party becomes too emotional, it is usually more productive to postpone the discussion until all parties are calm.

8. Give an example of when perception, noise, or emotions was a barrier to your communication. Explain the situation and how the barrier could have been overcome.

Filtering

Another barrier, **filtering,** *is the process of altering or distorting information in order to project a more favorable image.* For example, when managers are asked to report progress toward objectives, they may stress the positive and deemphasize, or even omit, the negative side of the situation. Employees often filter information as a means of hiding problems from an overly critical boss. Generally, mistakes and errors are discovered eventually, and it's better to find out earlier than later. So encourage full disclosure.[33]

Overcoming Filtering Barriers: To help eliminate filtering, the supervisor should treat errors as a learning experience, rather than as an opportunity to blame and criticize employees. The use of the open-door policy (discussed in Chapter 4) can create and support a two-way communication climate.

Trust and Credibility

When messages are sent, receivers take into account the trust they have in the senders.[34] Trust is a must for leadership.[35] Without trust there would be no followers. Trusting someone does not require liking them, or even agreeing with them. Trust means the leader has integrity and means what he or she says.[36] A receiver may accept or reject a message based on the trust in the sender. If people do not trust you, they will not believe you, or they tend to think you are trying to trick them.

The credibility of the sender also affects acceptance of a message.[37] A person perceived as an expert has a good chance of having his or her message accepted. If the manager is viewed by employees as not being knowledgeable about the department, the employees will not listen to what he or she has to say. They will seek advice from the informal leader or another peer.

The major barrier to communication that caused the false rumor to spread at Digital was the fact that when the vice president asked Mr. Olsen where Mr. Shields was, his response was vague. Being the president of Digital, Mr. Olsen has high credibility. If he had clearly stated why Mr. Shields was not at the meeting, most likely the managers would have believed him. However, because Mr. Olsen did not send a clear message, the trust level was not high. Managers assumed he was covering up Mr. Shields's departure from Digital, and the rumor began.

Overcoming Trust and Credibility Barriers: To improve your trust level, be open and honest with people. If people catch you in a lie, they may never trust you again. To gain and maintain credibility, get the facts straight before you communicate. Send clear, correct messages. Become an expert in your area.

Information Overload

We all have a limit to the amount of information we can decode and understand at any given time. Information overload is common for a new employee during the first few days because he or she is often presented with too much information to comprehend in that period of time. With the widespread use of the Internet and e-mail, there is so much information available managers are often dazzled and don't know what to do with it all.[38]

Overcoming Information Overload: To minimize information overload, send messages in a quantity that the receiver can decode and understand. When sending a message, do not talk for too long without checking to be sure the receiver is decoding the message as you intended; use questioning and paraphrasing. If you talk for too long, the receiver can become bored or lose the thread of the message. For example, if you are explaining a procedure, don't go through it completely, then ask if there are any questions. The receiver may get lost and not know what to ask. Instead, break the procedure down into parts.

WORK APPLICATIONS

9. Give an example of when filtering, trust and credibility, or information overload was a barrier to your communication. Explain the situation and how the barrier could have been overcome.

Not Listening

People usually hear what the sender is saying, but often they do not listen to the message or understand what is being transmitted. Not listening can sometimes be the result of not paying attention. The receiver's mind may wander. Or the receiver may be formulating his or her reply rather than listening. Arguments usually end without communication taking place.

Overcoming Not Listening Barriers: One method to help ensure that people are listening to your message is to question them and have them paraphrase the message back to you. If they can, they have listened to you. If not, keep trying until they can. As you recall, there are 13 tips for listening skills back in Chapter 4.

Time and Place

When and where you send a message affects communication. Selecting a poor time and/or place to send the message often results in missed communication. For example, the professor is about to start class and a student comes to the front of the room to discuss a personal matter. The professor's mind is on starting class and he or she will tend to rush the student. It is better to wait until after class or, better still, go to the professor's office during office hours.

Overcoming Timing Barriers: As a child growing up you learned when it was a good or a bad time to approach parents for permission to do something. The same holds true on the job with your boss and subordinates. Give conscious thought as to when a good time is to send the message and from where it should be sent. For example, Friday near the end of the workday is considered the best time to fire an employee, and the best place is in the manager's office.

Media Selection

Learning Objective

6. List nine common barriers to communication and how to overcome them

The medium used to send the message is also important. It is also interrelated with time and place. Use of an inappropriate medium can result in missed communication. For example, if a supervisor catches an employee in the act of breaking a rule, the best medium selection is one-on-one, face-to-face communications.

Overcoming Media Selection Barriers: Before sending a message, give careful thought to which medium is the most effective. For a full discussion of selecting media, refer back to Chapter 4.

WORK APPLICATIONS

10. Give an example of when not listening, time and place, or media selection was a barrier to your communication. Explain the situation and how the barrier could have been overcome.

Global Communication Barriers

When communicating with people from around the globe in international business, you should be aware that cultural differences can cause barriers to communication.[39]

APPLICATION SITUATIONS

Communication Barriers

AS 5–2

Identify the communication barriers as:

A. Perception   D. Filtering   G. Not listening
B. Noise   E. Trust and credibility   H. Time and place
C. Emotions   F. Information overload   I. Media selection

_____ 6. You shouldn't be upset. Listen to me.

_____ 7. Buddy, last week you took a long break. Don't do it again.

_____ 8. That's a lot to remember; I'm not sure I got it all.

_____ 9. Why did you say the job is going well, when you know it's not? You haven't even finished the . . . or the . . .

_____ 10. I cannot hear you. Shut that thing off! Now, what did you say?

_____ 11. I said I'd do it in a little while. It's only been 10 minutes. Why do you expect it done now?

_____ 12. Why should I listen to you? You don't know what you're talking about.

Some of the major areas include social conventions, language, etiquette and politeness, and nonverbal communication.

Social Conventions

Social conventions can be a barrier to communicating with people of different countries.[40] The directness of how business is conducted varies. North Americans tend to favor "getting down to business" quickly and concisely. If you use this approach with the Arabs or Japanese, you may lose the business because they prefer a more indirect informal chat to begin business meetings. People from the Middle East tend to talk very loudly, but this doesn't mean they are pushy or trying to intimidate you. What constitutes punctuality varies greatly around the world. North Americans and Japanese want you to be on time, while being late for a meeting with an Arab or Latin American is not viewed as negative. A Brazilian who is late for a meeting may be trying to make a proper impression, not showing disrespect.

Language, Etiquette, and Politeness

Even when speaking English to people outside North America, words mean different things,[41] and the same thing may be called by different names (i.e., lift rather than the elevator, and petrol rather than gasoline). What is considered rude in one country may not be rude in another. On an Australian airplane, if you were not in the first-class section and went to take a magazine from that section, a steward would sharply admonish you saying, "First class, mate" rather than the typical explanation given in North America. The steward would be surprised that you would be offended by these words. The Japanese want to maintain interdependence and harmony. They have 16 subtle ways to say no. Rather than saying, "I don't want to buy your product," a Japanese business person would tend to say, "A sale will be very difficult." The Japanese person would think it is clear to the American that he is saying no. The American, however, tends to reply with a statement about how the difficulty can be overcome rather than realizing the deal is off and giving up. Continuing to try to sell is an insult to the Japanese. The French tend to ask lots of questions, Asians do not, during presentations.[42]

Nonverbal Communications

Gestures do not translate well across cultures because they involve symbolism that is not shared. One gesture can mean very different things in different cultures. A raised thumb in the United States is a signal of approval, but in Greece it is an insult, meaning the same as a raised middle finger in the United States. Latin

Americans and Arabs expect extensive eye contact, while the Europeans would be uncomfortable because you are staring at them. Arabs, Latin Americans, and Southern Europeans want to touch, while North Europeans and North Americans don't want to be touched.

Overcoming Global Barriers
IE 5–3

● Organization
● Group
● Individual

This section is not meant to teach you to overcome all the possible barriers to global communication. The objective is to make you realize the importance of learning the culture of other countries if you plan to do business with them successfully. Most major multinational companies train their employees to be sensitive to specific cultural differences when doing business with them.

Situational Communication

People need to change their communication styles to have effective human relations.[43] When you work with people who are outside your department, you have no authority to get them to do something by giving them direct orders. You must use other means to achieve your goal. Situational communication is a model for conducting interpersonal communication with people outside your department, outside the organization, or with people who are peers and managers in higher levels of management than you. The situational communication model will teach you how to analyze a given situation and select the most appropriate style of communication in order to deal with a diversity of people and situations effectively.

In this section we focus on situational communication styles, situational variables, and how to select the most appropriate communication style in a given situation. Begin by determining your preferred communication style by completing Self-Assessment Exercise 5–1.

Self-Assessment
Exercise 5–1

Determining Your Preferred Communication Style

To determine your preferred communication style, select the *one* alternative that most closely describes what you would do in each of the 12 situations below. Do not be concerned with trying to pick the correct answer; select the alternative that best describes what *you* would actually do. Circle the letter *a*, *b*, *c*, or *d*. Ignore the: _____ time _____ information _____ acceptance _____ capability/_____ style and S _____ lines. They will be explained later in this chapter, and will be used during In-Class Skill-Building Exercise 5–1 at the end of the chapter.

_____ 1. Wendy, a knowledgeable person from another department, comes to you, the engineering supervisor, and requests that you design a special product to her specifications. You would: _____ time _____ information _____ acceptance _____ capability/_____ style

   a. Control the conversation and tell Wendy what you will do for her. S _____

   b. Ask Wendy to describe the product. Once you understand it, you would present your ideas. Let her realize that you are concerned and want to help with your ideas. S _____

   c. Respond to Wendy's request by conveying understanding and support. Help clarify what is to be done by you. Offer ideas, but do it her way. S _____

   d. Find out what you need to know. Let Wendy know you will do it her way. S _____

Self-Assessment
Exercise 5–1

_____ 2. Your department has designed a product that is to be fabricated by Saul's department. Saul has been with the company longer than you have; he knows his department. Saul comes to you to change the product design. You decide to: _____ time _____ information _____ acceptance _____ capability/ _____ style

    a. Listen to the change and why it would be beneficial. If you believe Saul's way is better, change it; if not, explain why the original design is superior. If necessary, insist that it be done your way. S _____

    b. Tell Saul to fabricate it any way he wants to. S _____

    c. You are busy; tell Saul to do it your way. You don't have time to listen and argue with him. S _____

    d. Be supportive; make changes together as a team. S _____

_____ 3. Upper management has a decision to make. They call you to a meeting and tell you they need some information to solve a problem they describe to you. You: _____ time _____ information _____ acceptance _____ capability/ _____ style

    a. Respond in a manner that conveys personal support and offer alternative ways to solve the problem. S _____

    b. Respond to their questions. S _____

    c. Explain how to solve the problem. S _____

    d. Show your concern by explaining how to solve the problem and why it is an effective solution. S _____

_____ 4. You have a routine work order. The work order is to be placed verbally and completed in three days. Sue, the receiver, is very experienced and willing to be of service to you. You decide to: _____ time _____ information _____ acceptance _____ capability/ _____ style

    a. Explain your needs, but let Sue make the order decision. S _____

    b. Tell Sue what you want and why you need it. S _____

    c. Decide together what to order. S _____

    d. Simply give Sue the order. S _____

_____ 5. Work orders from the staff department normally take three days; however, you have an emergency and need the job today. Your colleague, Jim, the department supervisor, is knowledgeable and somewhat cooperative. You decide to: _____ time _____ information _____ acceptance _____ capability/ _____ style

    a. Tell Jim that you need it by three o'clock and will return at that time to pick it up. S _____

    b. Explain the situation and how the organization will benefit by expediting the order. Volunteer to help in any way you can. S _____

    c. Explain the situation and ask Jim when the order will be ready. S _____

    d. Explain the situation and together come to a solution to your problem. S _____

_____ 6. Danielle, a peer with a record of high performance, has recently had a drop in productivity. Her problem is affecting your performance. You know Danielle has a family problem. You: _____ time _____ information _____ acceptance _____ capability/ _____ style

    a. Discuss the problem; help Danielle realize the problem is affecting her work and yours. Supportively discuss ways to improve the situation. S _____

    b. Tell the boss about it and let him decide what to do about it. S _____

    c. Tell Danielle to get back on the job. S _____

    d. Discuss the problem and tell Danielle how to solve the work situation; be supportive. S _____

_____ 7. You are a knowledgeable supervisor. You buy supplies from Peter regularly. He is an excellent salesperson and very knowledgeable about your situation. You are placing your weekly order. You decide to: _____ time _____ information _____ acceptance _____ capability/_____ style

    a. Explain what you want and why. Develop a supportive relationship. S _____

    b. Explain what you want and ask Peter to recommend products. S _____

    c. Give Peter the order. S _____

    d. Explain your situation and allow Peter to make the order. S _____

_____ 8. Jean, a knowledgeable person from another department, has asked you to perform a routine staff function to her specifications. You decide to: _____ time _____ information _____ acceptance _____ capability/_____ style

    a. Perform the task to her specifications without questioning her. S _____

    b. Tell her that you will do it the usual way. S _____

    c. Explain what you will do and why. S _____

    d. Show your willingness to help; offer alternative ways to do it. S _____

_____ 9. Tom, a salesperson, has requested an order for your department's services with a short delivery date. As usual, Tom claims it is a take-it-or-leave-it offer. He wants your decision now, or within a few minutes, because he is in the customer's office. Your action is to: _____ time _____ information _____ acceptance _____ capability/_____ style

    a. Convince Tom to work together to come up with a later date. S _____

    b. Give Tom a yes or no answer. S _____

    c. Explain your situation and let Tom decide if you should take the order. S _____

    d. Offer an alternative delivery date. Work on your relationship; show your support. S _____

_____ 10. As a time-and-motion expert, you have been called in regard to a complaint about the standard time it takes to perform a job. As you analyze the entire job, you realize the one element of complaint should take longer, but other elements should take less time. The end result is a shorter total standard time for the job. You decide to: _____ time _____ information _____ acceptance _____ capability/_____ style

    a. Tell the operator and foreman that the total time must be decreased and why. S _____

    b. Agree with the operator and increase the standard time. S _____

    c. Explain your findings. Deal with the operator and/or foreman's concerns, but ensure compliance with your new standard. S _____

    d. Together with the operator, develop a standard time. S _____

_____ 11. You approve budget allocations for projects. Marie, who is very competent in developing budgets, has come to you. You: _____ time _____ information _____ acceptance _____ capability/_____ style

    a. Review the budget, make revisions, and explain them in a supportive way. Deal with concerns, but insist on your changes. S _____

    b. Review the proposal and suggest areas where changes may be needed. Make changes together, if needed. S _____

    c. Review the proposed budget, make revisions, and explain them. S _____

    d. Answer any questions or concerns Marie has and approve the budget as is. S _____

_____ 12. You are a sales manager. A customer has offered you a contract for your product with a short delivery date. The offer is open for two days. The contract would be profitable for you and the organization. The cooperation of the production department is essential to meet the deadline. Tim, the production manager, and you do not get along very well because of your repeated requests

**Self-Assessment
Exercise 5–1** *continued*

for quick delivery. Your action is to: _____ time _____ information _____ acceptance _____ capability/_____ style

  a. Contact Tim and try to work together to complete the contract. S _____

  b. Accept the contract and convince Tim in a supportive way to meet the obligation. S _____

  c. Contact Tim and explain the situation. Ask him if you and he should accept the contract, but let him decide. S _____

  d. Accept the contract. Contact Tim and tell him to meet the obligation. If he resists, tell him you will go to his boss. S _____

To determine your preferred communication style, below, circle the letter you selected as the alternative you chose in situations 1–12. The column headings indicate the style you selected.

	Autocratic (S-A)	Consultative (S-C)	Participative (S-P)	Laissez-Faire (S-L)
1.	a	b	c	d
2.	c	a	d	b
3.	c	d	a	b
4.	d	b	c	a
5.	a	b	d	c
6.	c	d	a	b
7.	c	a	b	d
8.	b	c	d	a
9.	b	d	a	c
10.	a	c	d	b
11.	c	a	b	d
12.	d	b	a	c
Total				

Add up the number of circled items per column. Adding the numbers in the total row should equal 12. The column with the highest number represents your preferred communication style. There is no one best style in all situations. The more evenly distributed the numbers are between the four styles, the more flexible your communication style is. A total of 0 or 1 in any column may indicate a reluctance to use the style(s). You could have problems in situations calling for the use of this style.

Learning Objective

7. Identify your preferred communication style

Situational Communication Styles

Following is the process used with each of the four situational supervisory styles. Notice that behavior can be characterized as a combination of two dimensions— task and relationship. In task behavior, the sender tells the receiver what to do and how to do it; performance is closely supervised. In relationship behavior, the sender listens to the other person in an effort to develop support, trust, and respect; performance is not closely supervised. Both task and relationship can be described as high or low depending on the amount of emphasis placed on each of the two dimensions during communication.

One style, **autocratic communication style (S-A),** *demonstrates high task–low relationship behavior* (HT–LR), *initiating a closed presentation.* The other party has little, if any, information and is low in capability.

- Initiation/Response. You initiate and control the communication with minimal, if any, response.

- Presentation/Elicitation. You make a presentation letting the other parties know they are expected to comply with your message; there is little, if any, elicitation.
- Closed/Open. You use a closed presentation; you will not consider the receiver's input.

The **consultative communication style (S-C)** *demonstrates high task–high relationship behavior (HT–HR), using a closed presentation for the task with an open elicitation for the relationship.* The other party has moderate information and capability.

- Initiation/Response. You initiate the communication by letting the other party know that you want him or her to buy into your influence. You desire some response.
- Presentation/Elicitation. Both are used. You use elicitation to determine the goal of the communication. For example, you may ask questions to determine the situation and follow up with a presentation. When the communication goal is known, little task elicitation is needed. Relationship communication is elicited in order to determine the interest of the other party and acceptance of the message. The open elicitation should show your concern for the other party's point of view and motivate him or her to follow your influence.
- Closed/Open. You are closed to having the message accepted (task), but open to the person's feelings (relationship). Be empathetic.

The **participative communication style (S-P)** *demonstrates low task–high relationship behavior (LT–HR), responding with open elicitation, some initiation and little presentation.* The other party is high in information and capability.

- Initiation/Response. You respond with some initiation. You want to help the other party solve a problem or get him or her to help you solve one. You are helpful and convey personal support.
- Presentation/Elicitation. Elicitation can occur with little presentation. Your role is to elicit the other party's ideas on how to reach objectives.
- Closed/Open. Open communication is used. If you participate well, the other party will come to a solution you can accept. If not, you may have to reject the other party's message.

Another style, **laissez-faire communication style (S-L),** *demonstrates low task–low relationship behavior (LT–LR), responding with the necessary open presentation.* The other party is outstanding in information and capability.

- Initiation/Response. You respond to the other party with little, if any, initiation.
- Presentation/Elicitation. You present the other party with information, structure, and so forth, that the sender wants.
- Closed/Open. Open communication is used. You convey that the other party is in charge; you will accept the message.

WORK APPLICATIONS

11. Which of the four situational communication styles does/did your boss use most often? Explain his or her behavior.

Situational Variables

When selecting the appropriate communication style, you should consider four variables: time, information, acceptance, and capability. Answering the questions related to each variable below can help you select the appropriate style for the situation.

Time

Do I have enough time to use two-way communication? When there is no time, the other three variables are not considered; the autocratic style is appropriate. When time is available, any of the other styles may be appropriate, depending on the other variables. Time is a relative term; in one situation a few minutes may be considered a short time period, while in another a month may be a short period of time.

Information

Do I have the necessary information to communicate my message, make a decision, or take action? When you have all the information you need, the autocratic style may be appropriate. When you have some of the information, the consultative style may be appropriate. When you have little information, the participative or laissez-faire style may be appropriate.

Acceptance

Will the other party accept my message without any input? If the receiver will accept the message, the autocratic style may be appropriate. If the receiver will be reluctant to accept it, the consultative style may be appropriate. If the receiver will reject the message, the participative or laissez-faire style may be appropriate to gain acceptance. There are situations where acceptance is critical to success, such as in the area of implementing changes.

Capability

Capability has two parts:

Ability: Does the other party have the experience or knowledge to participate in two-way communication? Will the receiver put the organization's goals ahead of personal needs or goals?

Motivation: Does the other party want to participate?

When the other party is low in capability, the autocratic style may be appropriate; moderate in capability, the consultative style may be appropriate; high in capability, the participative style may be appropriate; outstanding in capability, the laissez-faire style may be appropriate.

Capability levels can change from one task to another. For example, a professor may have outstanding capability in classroom teaching, but be low in capability for advising students.

Selecting Communication Styles

Successful managers understand different styles of communication[44] and select communication styles based on the situation. There are three steps to follow when selecting the appropriate communication style in a given situation.

Step 1. Diagnose the Situation: Answer the questions for each of the four situation variables. In Self-Assessment Exercise 5–1 at the beginning of this section, you were asked to select an alternative to 12 situations. You were told to ignore the section with _____ time _____ information _____ acceptance _____ capability/ _____ style and S_____ lines. Now you will complete this part in the In-Class Skill-Building Exercise 5–1 by placing the style letters (S-A, S-C, S-P, S-L) on the lines provided for each of the 12 situations.

Step 2. Select the Appropriate Style for the Situation: After analyzing the four variables, select the appropriate style for the situation. In some situations, where variables support conflicting styles, select the style of the most important variable for the situation. For example, capability may be outstanding (C-4), but you have all the information needed (S-A). If the information is more important, use the autocratic style even though the capability is outstanding. When doing Skill-Building Exercise 5–1, place the letters (S-A, S-C, S-P, S-L) for the appropriate styles on the _____ Style lines.

Step 3. Implement the Appropriate Communication Style: During Skill-Building Exercise 5–1, you will identify one of the four communication styles for each alternative action; place the S-A, S-C, S-P, or S-L on the S_____ lines. Select the alternative *a, b, c, or d* that represents the appropriate communication for each of the 12 situations.

Exhibit 5–4 summarizes the material in this section. Use it to determine the appropriate communication style in situation 1 and during Skill-Building Exercise 5–1.

EXHIBIT 5–4   **SITUATIONAL COMMUNICATIONS MODEL**

Step 1. Diagnose the Situation

Resource	Use of Resource Style
Time	No S-A
	Yes S-A, S-C, S-P, or S-L
Information	All S-A
	Some S-C
	Little S-P or S-L
Acceptance	Accept S-A
	Reluctance S-C
	Reject S-P or S-L
Capability	Low S-A
	Moderate S-C
	High S-P
	Outstanding S-L

Step 2. Select the Appropriate Style for the Situation

Autocratic (S-A)

High task–low relationship

Initiate a closed presentation.

Consultative (S-C)

High task–high relationship

Initiate a closed presentation for the task. Use open elicitation for feelings and relationship.

Participative (S-P)

Low task–high relationship

Respond with open elicitation, some initiation, and little presentation.

Laissez-faire (S-L)

Low task–low relationship

Respond with the necessary open presentation.

Step 3. Implement the Appropriate Communication Style

During Skill-Building Exercise 5–1, you will identify each communication style and select the alternative (*a, b, c,* or *d*) that represents the appropriate style.

WORK APPLICATIONS

12. Does/did your boss change communication styles? If yes, which other style(s) does/did he or she use?

Determining the Appropriate Communication Style for Situation 1:

Step 1. Diagnose the situation.   Answer the four variable questions from the model, and place the letters on the four variable lines below.

1. Wendy, a knowledgeable person from another department, comes to you, the engineering supervisor, and requests that you design a special product to her specifications. You would:

   time _____ information _____ acceptance _____ capability/_____ style

   a. Control the conversation and tell Wendy what you will do for her. S_____

   b. Ask Wendy to describe the product. Once you understand, you would present your ideas. Let her realize that you are concerned and want to help with your ideas. S_____

   c. Respond to Wendy's request by conveying understanding and support. Help clarify what is to be done by you. Offer ideas, but do it her way. S_____

   d. Find out what you need to know. Let Wendy know you will do it her way. S _____

Step 2. Select the appropriate style for the situation.   Review the four variables. If they are all consistent, select one style. If they are conflicting, select the most important variable as the style to use. Place its letters (S-A, S-C, S-P, or S-L) on the style line.

Step 3. Select the appropriate action.   Review the four alternative actions. Identify the communication style for each, placing its letters on the S_____ line, then check the appropriate match alternative.

   Let's see how you did.

1. **Time** is available; it can be either S-C, S-P, or S-L. **Information.** You have little information, so you need to use a participative or laissez-faire style to find out what Wendy wants done: S-P or S-L. **Acceptance.** If you try to do it your way rather than Wendy's way, she will most likely reject it. You need to use a participative or laissez-faire style: S-P or S-L. **Capability.** Wendy is knowledgeable and is highly capable: S-P.

2. Reviewing the four variables, you see that there is a mixture of S-P and S-L. Since you are an engineer, it is appropriate to participate with Wendy to give her what she needs. Therefore, the choice is S-P.

3. *Alternative a* is S-A; this is the autocratic style, high task–low relationship. *Alternative b* is S-C; this is the consultative style, high task–high relationship. *Alternative c* is S-P; this is the participative style, low task–high relationship. *Alternative d* is S-L; this is laissez-faire, low task–low relationship behavior.

If you selected *c* as your action, you chose the most appropriate action for the situation. This was a three-point answer. If you selected *d* as your answer, this is also a good alternative; it scores two points. If you selected *b*, you get one point for overdirecting. If you selected *a*, you get zero points; this is too much directing and will most likely hurt communication.

The better you match your communication style to the situation, the more effective you will be at communicating. In Skill-Building Exercise 5–1, we will apply the model to the other 11 situations in Self-Assessment Exercise 5–1 to develop your ability to communicate as a situational communicator.

Video
5–1
BM–5
Skill-Building
5–1

Learning Objective

8. Explain how to change communication styles to meet the needs of the situation

WORK APPLICATIONS

13. Which situational communication style do you prefer to use most and least often? Why?

APPLICATION SITUATIONS

Identifying Situational Communication Styles

AS 5–3

Below are two situations with eight communication styles being used. Identify each style as:

A. Autocratic   B. Consultative   C. Participative   D. Laissez-faire

Your department is a real team with people who work well together. Your department is one of the top performers in the organization. Because of traffic problems, the president okayed staggered hours for departments. You can keep the same hours or change them. Several of your employees have suggested different changes.

_____ 13. Explain the situation and answer questions they may have, while allowing the group to decide the hours.

_____ 14. Decide on new hours, explain why you chose them, and invite questions.

_____ 15. Conduct a meeting to get your employees' ideas; then select the new hours.

_____ 16. Send around a memo stating that your department will not change hours.

Helen has an excellent performance record for the last five years. Recently you have noticed a drop in the quality and quantity of her work. You know she has a family problem.

_____ 17. Tell Helen that her problem is affecting her work, and she has to get back to being productive.

_____ 18. Discuss the problem with Helen. Help her realize her personal problem is affecting her work. Discuss ways to improve the situation. Be supportive and encourage her.

_____ 19. Discuss the problem with Helen, but let her work it out.

_____ 20. Discuss the problem with Helen. Make her realize you are willing to help her, but that she must maintain her performance.

After reading this chapter, you should have a better understanding of organizational structure and communication, barriers to communication and how to overcome them, and how to be a situational communicator.

REVIEW

Select one or more methods: (1) Fill in the missing key terms from memory; (2) match the key terms from the end of the review with their definitions below; or (3) copy the key terms in order from the key terms at the beginning of the chapter.

_____ refers to the way managers design their firms to achieve their organization's mission and goals. Six principles of organization include: chain of command, span of management, division of labor, coordination, line and staff authority, and centralized and decentralized authority.

_____ is the grouping of related activities into units. Six types are: functional, product, customer, divisional, territory, and matrix, and they can be combined. Contemporary organizational trends include flat structures with wider spans of management using teams to design organizations with reengineering. The learning organization, horizontal organization, and virtual organizations are the current trends in organizational structure.

_____is the compounded interpersonal communications process across an organization._____ is the flow of information both up and down the chain of command, while _____ is the flow of information between colleagues and peers. The _____ is the informal vehicle through which messages flow throughout the organization. Provide as much information as possible to keep incorrect rumors to a minimum. _____ are sets of employees who have stable contact through which information is generated and transmitted. The organization chart illustrates the vertical flow of communication, but not the horizontal or grapevine flow of communication. Communication networks are formed within organizations as a whole as well as within departments and small groups.

Common barriers to organizational communication include perception, noise, emotions, _____ (altering or distorting information in order to project a more favorable image), trust and credibility, information overload, not listening, time and place, and media selection. Global barriers include social convention, language, etiquette and politeness, or nonverbal communication.

The four situational communication styles are: _____, High task–low relationship behavior (HT-LR), initiating a closed presentation. _____, High task–high relationship behavior (HT-HR), using a closed presentation for the task with an open elicitation for the relationship. _____, Low task–high relationship behavior (LT-HR), responding with open elicitation, some initiation and little presentation. _____, Low task–low relationship behavior (LT-LR), responding with the necessary open presentation. To determine the appropriate communication style to use in a situation, the person should diagnose the situation by considering the variables of time, information, acceptance, and capability.

KEY TERMS

autocratic communication
  style (S-A)   171
communication
  networks   161
consultative communication
  style (S-C)   172
departmentalization   156
filtering   165
grapevine   160

horizontal
  communication   160
laissez-faire communication
  style (S-L)   172
organizational
  communication   159
organizational
  structure   155

participative
  communication
  style (S-P)   172
vertical
  communication   159

Sam and Rob Walton: Wal-Mart Stores

Back in the 1950s, Sam Walton visited discount stores all over the United States to learn about this industry. Walton asked employees questions and wrote in his little notebook. In 1963, Sam opened his first Wal-Mart store. Before Sam retired, there were several hundred Wal-Mart stores, with headquarters in Bentonville, Arkansas. Sam would visit all Wal-Mart stores at least once a year. He also continued to visit hundreds of competitors. Sam was always looking for ideas to improve operations. Sam would simply walk through the store and talk to the employees, who are called associates, and customers. He continued to write in a notebook. Sam required all executives to visit stores. Every day at least one hundred stores are visited. Sam wanted all employees involved in continuous improvements, so all managers ask every associate what he or she can do to improve store operations. All associates have access to complete financial results to keep them focused on the bottom line.

Sam Walton died in April 1992. The same year, Wal-Mart became the largest retailer in the nation. Wal-Mart, which also owns Sam's Warehouse Club, Super-Centers, and Hypermarts, grew by more than 30 percent a year for more than 20 years to over 1,900 stores. In 1999, Wal-Mart also became the largest seller of toys, overtaking Toys R Us.

Wal-Mart is now managed by Sam's son, Rob, as chairman of the board and David Glass as CEO. However, Sam's original communication system is still used today, and management is committed to continuing it. When Glass is not personally visiting stores, he maintains communication through a six-channel satellite system. The communication goal is to link every store by voice and video to facilitate store-to-store and store-to-home-office communications. The satellite also gathers store data for the master computers. The computerized inventory control system, along with strong negotiation power, helps Wal-Mart keep its costs lower than competitors.

By satellite, Walton, Glass, and other executives can talk via video to every store at the same time as often as they want to. They can also communicate with only a few stores. When associates come up with suggestions for improving operations, such as ideas for increasing sales or decreasing costs, the information is quickly transmitted to all stores via the satellite system. The major advantage of the satellite is in the use of merchandising, which follows the old saying: A picture is worth a thousand words. A buyer can go on video and make an announce such as, "These are the new items for Department 12. Here is how you should display them." Associates can see the how the merchandise is displayed and copy it.

Go to the Internet: For more information on Rob Walton and Wal-Mart and to update the information provided in this case, do a name search on the Internet and visit Wal-Mart's website at *http://www.wal-mart.com.* For ideas on using the Internet with cases, see Appendix C.

Support your answer to the following questions with specific information from the case and text, or other information you get from the Web or other source.

Chapters 4 and 5

1. What part would you say communication has played in Wal-Mart's success?
2. Which level(s) of communication is illustrated in this case?
3. What message do you think Wal-Mart executives send to associates when they visit stores?
4. Which transmission media(s) does the satellite use?
5. The satellite helps with which principle of organization, and which contemporary organization is most associated with its merchandising?
6. The satellite is primarily used with which flow of organizational communications?
7. When an executive visits stores to talk to customers and associates, which situational communications style is most appropriate?

Cummulative Case

8. How do executive attitudes during store visits affect associate attitudes, job satisfaction, and self-concept and organizational performance (Chapter 3)?

I've Got a Complaint

The following monologue takes place when Lowell storms into the office of his boss, Liza. (*Note:* This situation can be role-played in class.)

Lowell: (*Speaking in a loud voice, talking fast without stopping.*) Liza, you told me you were giving me a $1-an-hour raise, effective the first of the month. My friend in payroll tells me that you only put through for a half-dollar-an-hour raise. How can you stab me in the back like that? I thought we were friends. You told me I was getting a $1-an-hour raise and I need it. I just went out and bought a new motorcycle, counting on the money to make my payment. My brother is a lawyer and he told me that this is a breach of contract. I'll sue the company for it if you don't give it to me. Am I going to get my $1-an-hour raise the easy or hard way?

Answer the following questions. Then in the space between questions, state why you selected that answer.

_____ 1. The monologue was a _____ flow of communication.

      a. vertical-downward   *c.* horizontal
      b. vertical-upward   *d.* grapevine

_____ 2. Lowell's statements are based on information he got through _____ communication flow.

      a. vertical-downward   *c.* horizontal
      b. vertical-upward   *d.* grapevine

_____ 3. Lowell and Liza are members of a communication network.

      a. true   *b.* false

_____ 4. Lowell began his monologue with a _____ barrier to communication.

      a. perception   *c.* emotional
      b. noise   *d.* filtering

_____ 5. Lowell's third statement indicates a _____ barrier to communication.

      a. perception   *c.* trust
      b. emotional   *d.* information overload

_____ 6. The place Lowell selected _____ appropriate for the message.

      a. was   *b.* was not

_____ 7. Lowell's selection of one-on-one, face-to-face media _____ appropriate for the message.

      a. was   *b.* was not

_____ 8. Lowell used the _____ communication style.

      a. autocratic   *c.* participative
      b. consultative   *d.* laissez-faire

_____ 9. Liza's decision to wait until Lowell finished before she began to speak shows her selection of the _____ communication style.

      a. autocratic   *c.* participative
      b. consultative   *d.* laissez-faire

_____ 10. So far, Lowell handled this situation in an _____ manner.

     a. effective   *b.* ineffective

11. If you were in Lowell's situation, what would you do or say?

12. Assume you are in Liza's position and that you thought you authorized a $1-an-hour raise. A change or error could have been made somewhere. But at the moment you don't know how it was changed, if it in fact was changed. You only have Lowell's word that it was. Lowell is standing in front of you. What do you do and say to him?

_____

Fiscal Fairy Tale #9: Henny Money

Following the steps to getting to read a fiscal fairy tale, go to the MG website (*www.mgeneral.com*) and read *Fiscal Fairy Tale #9: Henny Money* (your instructor may ask you to print a copy and bring it to class). Answer these questions from Chapters 4 and 5 (your instructor may ask you to type them and bring them to class):

Online MG Webzine Exercise 5

Questions Relating to the Tale Only

1. As stated at the end of the tale, in 50 words or so, what is your response to this tale? You may send it to MG.

2. Have you, or anyone you know, ever had a hunch about something and told people about it, but they would not listen to you? Explain.

3. What makes a person successful in influencing others? How have you successfully influenced or persuaded others?

4. Some people believe in astrology, biorhythms, numerology, and psychics. Why do some people believe, yet others don't? How can we tell a true indicator from a false one?

Questions Relating the Tale to the Chapter Concepts

5. Which communication process roles (Exhibit 4–1) were played by Henny and the people she warned?

6. Which of the five steps in the message-sending process was the major reason for Henny not influencing others with her warning?

7. Which barrier to communications was the major reason the other people would not accept Henny's message?

8. Which response style was first used by Sal Sales, and which response style was used in his second response to Henny's warning? Which response style was first used by Paula People about the warning? Which response style was used in her second response as Henny stepped back out of the door?

9. What was the flow of communications between Henny and Inny Vinny, Sal Sales, Paula People, and Sue Visor?

10. Which situational communication style was Henny using to warn others?

11. Paul People read Henny's nonverbal communication of fright in her face and voice. Thus, she realized that she was dealing with an emotional employee. Could Paula have done a better job of handling an emotional employee? If yes, how?

In-Class MG Webzine Exercise 5

The instructor selects one of the six options from Appendix B page 589.

INTERNET EXERCISES

Identifying Organizational Structure (IE 5–1)

Online Internet Exercise 5–1

The objective of this exercise is to better understand organizational structure. Use the information in Appendix B and IE 1–2 and 1–3 as you do the following:

1. Select an organization you would like to work for that has a website. Find the organization's Web address, if you don't know it, using a search engine (IE 1–2) and go to its homepage.

2. Click "About Us," "Company Overview," "Corporate Profile," or other descriptive that would contain the organization's structure information. Find a verbal, and preferably an organization chart and print it.

3. Questions: (1) Identify the chain of command, the span of management of the CEO/president, division of labor, coordination, line and staff positions, and authority. (2) What type of departmentalization does the organization have? (3) Which contemporary organization ideas does the organization use? (Your instructor may require typed answers.)

In-Class Internet Exercise 5–1, IE 5–2, and IE 5–3

The instructor selects one of the six options from Appendix B page 589.

Organizational Structure (IE 5–2)

Online Internet Exercise 5–2

The objective of this exercise is to learn more about organizational structure. Use the information in Appendix B and IE 1–2 and 1–3 as you do the following:

1. Go to Change Technologies—*www.city-net.com/changetech* or Mackenzie and Company—*www.orgdesign.com*

2. Read the consultants information about organizational structure. (Your instructor may require a copy of what you read.)

3. Question: In 2 to 3 paragraphs, what did you learn about organization structure from the website? (Your instructor may require a written report.)

Communications: MG Ezzay (IE 5–3)

Online Internet Exercise 5–3

The objective of this exercise is to get ideas on how to improve communications. Use the information in Appendix B and IE 1–2 and 1–3 as you do the following:

1. Go to the MG homepage—*www.mgeneral.com*

2. Click "Leaders (Opinion Ezzays)" then a year.

3. Click "Clickdex (index)" then communications (from the 15 categories).

4. Click the name of the author/title and read the Ezzay (your instructor may require you to print it) relating to communications.

5. Questions: (1) Who is the author and what is the title and year of the Ezzay? (2) What are the primary communication ideas? (3) How can you use these ideas to improve communication in your personal and professional life? (Your instructor may require you to type and print your answers.)

VIDEO EXERCISE

◆ **Situational**
Communication

VE 5–1
BM-5

Objectives: To better understand the four communication styles.
SCANS: The SCANS competencies of interpersonal skills and especially information and the foundations of basic, thinking, and personal qualities are developed
through this exercise.
Preparation: You should understand the four communication styles.

Procedure 1
(10–20 minutes)

The instructor shows Video Module 5, Situational Communication. As you view
each of the four scenes, identify the communication style being used by the training manager.

Scene 1. _____   A. Autocratic (S-A)

Scene 2. _____   B. Consultative (S-C)

Scene 3. _____   C. Participative (S-P)

Scene 4. _____   D. Laissez-faire (S-L)

After viewing each of the four scenes, identify/match the style used by the manager by placing the letter of the style on the scene line.
   Option A: View all four scenes and identify the style used by the manager. After
viewing all four scenes, discuss and/or have the instructor give the correct
answers.
   Option B: After each scene, the class discusses the style used by the manager.
The instructor states the correct answer after each of the four scenes.

Procedure 2
(2–5 minutes)

Select the one style that you would use in this situation. Are other styles also appropriate? Which style would you not use (not appropriate) for this situation. Next to
each style listed above, write the letter A for appropriate or N for not appropriate.

Discussion:
   Option A: In groups of four to six, answer the questions below.
   Option B: As a class answer the questions below.

1. Which style(s) is/are not appropriate to use in this situation?

2. Which style(s) is/are appropriate to use in this situation?

3. Is there one style most appropriate in this situation? If yes, which one?

Conclusion: The instructor may make concluding remarks.

Application (2–4 minutes):   What did I learn from this exercise? How will I use this
knowledge in the future?

Sharing: Volunteers give their answers to the application section.

This video exercise serves as a behavior model for In-Class Skill-Building Exercise
5–1, Situational Communication.

SKILL-BUILDING EXERCISE 5–1

**In-Class
Situational
Communication**

BM–5

Objectives: To develop your ability to communicate using the appropriate style for the situation.

SCANS: The SCANS competencies of interpersonal skills systems, and especially information (interpreting and communicating) and the foundations of basic, thinking, and personal qualities are developed through this exercise.

Preparation: You should have completed the 12 situations in Self-Assessment Exercise 5–1. In the self-assessment, you were selected the alternative of what "you" would do in the situation. In this skill-building exercise, you are trying to select the "most" appropriate alternative that will result in the most effective communication. Thus, you may be selecting different answers.

Experience: You will work at selecting the appropriate style for the 12 situations in Self-Assessment Exercise 5–1. On the time, information, acceptance, and capability lines, place the letters S-A, S-C, S-P, or S-L, whichever is appropriate for the situation. Based on your diagnoses, select the one style you would use. Place the letters S-A, S-C, S-P, or S-L on the style line. On the four "S" lines write the letters S-A, S-C, S-P, or S-L to identify each style being used.

Procedure 1
(3–8 minutes)

The instructor reviews the Situational Communication Model and explains how to apply it to determine the appropriate style for situation 1.

Procedure 2
(6–8 minutes)

Turn to situation 2. Using the model, select the appropriate style. If you have time, identify each alternative style (3–4 minutes). The instructor goes over the recommended answers (3–4 minutes).

Procedure 3
(20–50 minutes)

A. Break into groups of two or three. As a team, apply the model to situations 3 through 7 (15–20 minutes). The instructor will go over the appropriate answers when all teams are done or the time is up (4–6 minutes).

B. (Optional) Break into new groups of two or three and do situations 8 through 12 (15–20 minutes). The instructor will go over the appropriate answers (4–6 minutes).

Conclusion: The instructor leads a class discussion and/or makes concluding remarks.

Application (2–4 minutes):   What did I learn from this experience? How will I use this knowledge in the future?

Sharing: Volunteers give their answers to the application section.

SKILL-BUILDING EXERCISE 5-2

● **In-Class Communication Networks**

Objective: To better understand how communication networks affect performance.

SCANS: The SCANS competencies of resources, interpersonal skills, information, and especially systems and the foundations of basic, thinking, and personal qualities are developed through this exercise.

Preparation: No preparation is necessary for this exercise.

Experience: Fifteen of the class members will form three teams that will try to put a puzzle together using different communication networks.

Procedure 1

Set up three teams of five members. The members should be seated in the network positions shown below. All other class members should form a circle around the three groups and observe them work.

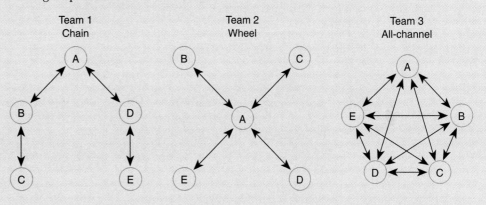

Team 1 Chain   Team 2 Wheel   Team 3 All-channel

The arrows represent the communication flow. In team 1, A can only talk to B or D; B can only talk to A or C; C can only talk to B; D can only talk to A or E; and E can only talk to D. In team 2, A can talk to B, C, D, or E individually but not as a group. B, C, D, and E cannot talk to each other, only to A. In team 3, anyone can talk to anyone.

The instructor gives each team member one of the 5" × 5" square puzzle pieces. Wait until told to start before making the puzzle.

Procedure 2 (5 minutes)

Each team has up to five minutes to finish the puzzle following its communication network.

Procedure 3 (2–3 minutes)

The instructor gives each team a copy of the completed puzzle to check accuracy, or to show them how to do it.

Questions:

1. Each team tells the class how they felt about following their communication network.

2. Did any team finish? Which was first?

3. How did the communication network affect the performance of the team?

4. Which structure was most appropriate for this task?

Conclusion: The instructor leads a class discussion and/or makes concluding remarks.

Application (2–4 minutes):   What did I learn from this experience? How will I use this knowledge in the future?

Sharing: Volunteers give their answers to the application section.

SKILL-BUILDING EXERCISE 5–3

In-Class
The Grapevine

Objective: To better understand organizational communication flow of rumors.

SCANS: The SCANS competencies of resources, interpersonal skills, systems, and especially information (interpreting and communicating) and the foundations of basic, thinking, and personal qualities are developed through this exercise.

Preparation: No preparation is necessary for this exercise.

Experience: You will observe a rumor being spread and determine its accuracy.

Procedure 1
(2–3 minutes)

Six students volunteer or are selected to spread a rumor. Each student has a number 1 through 6. Number 1 remains in the classroom while numbers 2 through 6 leave the room so they cannot overhear the discussion. They may stand in the hall with the door closed. All students should spread the rumor as accurately as possible.

Procedure 2
(2–5 minutes)

Student 1 and the class read the rumor below. When student number 1 is ready, he or she goes to the front of the room.

Rumor

Rumor has it that Chris Wilson, the president of Wilson Company, a fifty-five-year-old married man with four children, is having an affair with a sixteen-year-old girl, Betty Harris. Jean Fleaming saw Chris with Betty in a bar and told Rick Jones about it; Rick told her that he saw them in a hotel on 5th Street. Carlos Veldas, the chairperson of the board of directors, is investigating and may ask Chris to resign, or he may fire him. If this happens, Vice President Katty Likert will probably be named president.

Procedure 3
(1–3 minutes)

Student 1 tells student 2 the rumor loud enough for the class to hear. The rest of the class observe and take notes in the spaces provided on the next page. The instructor may record the rumor spreading.

Procedure 4
(5–10 minutes)

Student 2 spreads the rumor to student 3; 3 to 4; 4 to 5; 5 to 6. Student 6 writes the rumor on the board. After spreading the rumor, students return to their seats, read the rumor, and become observers.

Discussion Questions:

1. How accurately was the rumor spread? Is the rumor verified? Was it distorted as it spread? If so, how was it distorted? Was it longer and more complex, or was it shortened?

2. What could be done to improve the accuracy of the rumor?

3. Does spreading rumors like this help the organization?

4. If Chris Wilson hears about the rumor, what should he do? Would the answer be different if the rumor is true or false?

Conclusion: The instructor may make concluding remarks.

Application (2–4 minutes):   What have I learned through this exercise? How will I use this knowledge in the future?

Sharing: Volunteers give their answers to the application section.

RUMOR OBSERVATION SHEET

Students	Accuracy: Correct Statements	Errors: Distortions, Additions, Deletions
1–2		
2–3		
3–4		
4–5		
5–6		

Other Skills Influencing Behavior, Human Relations, and Performance

Part

3

6   MOTIVATION

7   LEADERSHIP

8   TRANSACTIONAL ANALYSIS, ASSERTIVENESS, AND CONFLICT RESOLUTION

Motivation

Learning Objectives

After completing this chapter, you should be able to:

1. Explain the motivation process and the three factors affecting performance.
2. Describe four content motivation theories.
3. Describe two process motivation theories.
4. State how reinforcement is used to increase performance.
5. List the four steps in the giving praise model.
6. Identify the four parts of the writing objectives model.
7. Explain the three steps of managing by objectives.
8. State ways to enrich, design, and simplify jobs.
9. Explain possible limitations of using motivation theories outside North America.
10. Define the following 16 key terms (in order of appearance in the chapter):

motivation	**equity theory**
performance formula	**reinforcement theory**
content motivation theories	**giving praise**
needs hierarchy	**objectives**
two-factor theory	**management by objectives (MBO)**
manifest needs theory	**job enrichment**
process motivation theories	**job design**
expectancy theory	**job simplification**

Chapter Outline

Latoia Henderson was recently promoted to a management position at State Potato Chip Co. She is enthusiastic about her work. Generally things are going well, but Latoia is having a problem with Hank. Hank is often late for work, and even though he can do a good job, he does not regularly perform to expectations. Latoia had a talk with Hank to find out what the problem was. Hank said the money and benefits were okay, and the people in the department were nice, but the job was boring. He complained that he didn't have any say about how to do his job and that Latoia was always checking up on him. Hank believes he is treated fairly because of the union, which gives him job protection. But because everyone is paid the same, working hard is a waste of time. If you were in Latoia's position, how would you motivate Hank? This chapter examines specific motivation theories and techniques that can be used to motivate Hank and employees in all organizations. There are many motivation theories that can be used with a diversity of people on a global basis. What motivates some people will not motivate all diversities of people.

● Organization
● Group
● Individual

The Importance of Motivation

In this section, we discuss what motivation is and why it is important, and how motivation affects behavior, human relations, and performance.

What Is Motivation and Why Is It Important?

The term **motivation** *means the internal process leading to behavior to satisfy needs.* Have you ever wondered why people do the things they do? The primary reason people do what they do is to meet their needs or wants. The process people go through to meet their needs is:

Need → Motive → Behavior → Satisfaction or Dissatisfaction

For example, you are thirsty (need) and have a drive (motive) to get a drink. You get a drink (behavior) that quenches (satisfaction) your thirst. However, if you could not get a drink, or a drink of what you really wanted, you would be dissatisfied. Satisfaction is usually short-lived. Getting that drink satisfied you, but soon you will need another drink.

Managers often view motivation as an employee's willingness to put forth effort to achieve organizational objectives. Latoia is concerned because Hank is not motivated to work hard.

WORK APPLICATIONS

1. Give an example of how you have gone through the motivation process. Identify the need, motive, behavior, and satisfaction or dissatisfaction.

Why Knowing How to Motivate Employees Is Important

IE 6–1

How Motivation Affects Behavior and Human Relations

Some of the many reasons include:

- Business has come to realize that a motivated and satisfied workforce contributes significantly to the bottom line.[1] Self-motivation is one of the most important skills companies look for when hiring an employee.[2] Motivation is a major part of a manager's job.[3] Much of Pizza Hut/KFC's success is credited to CEO David Novak's ability to motivate employees.[4]

- The old belief was that if you paid people adequately they would be motivated.[5] However, today we realize that money is not the prime motivator. The global environment requires new ways of motivating employees.[6] Thus, organizations are training managers to motivate employees.[7]

How Motivation Affects Behavior, Human Relations, and Performance

All behavior is motivated by some need. However, needs and motives are complex; we don't always know what our needs are or why we do the things we do. Have you ever done something and not known why you did it? Understanding needs will help you understand behavior.

We cannot observe motives; we can observe behavior and infer what the person's motive is. However, it is not easy to know why a person behaved the way he or she did because people do the same thing for different reasons. And people often attempt to satisfy several needs at once. However, understanding behavior can help you to motivate people.[8]

People with Theory X and Theory Y attitudes have different motives and human relations. Personality also affects motivation to have effective human relations. Generally, people with a Big Five agreeableness personality are highly motivated to work at having effective human relations to satisfy their need for affiliation.

Generally, an employee who is motivated will try harder to do a good job than one who is not motivated. However, performance is not simply based on motivation. The level of performance attained is determined by three interdependent factors: ability, motivation, and resources. This relationship can be stated as a **performance formula:** *Performance = Ability × Motivation × Resources.*

For performance levels to be high, all three factors must be high. If any one is low or missing, the performance level will be adversely affected. For example, Mary Lou, a very intelligent student, has the books, but because she does not care about grades, she does not study (low motivation) and does not get an A.

As an employee and manager, if you want to attain high levels of performance, you must be sure that you and your employees have the ability, motivation, and resources to meet objectives. When performance is not at the standard level or above, you must determine which performance factor needs to be improved, and improve it. In the opening case, Hank has the ability and resources, but he lacks motivation.

APPLICATION SITUATIONS

The Performance Formula

AS 6–1

Identify the factor contributing to low performance in the five situations below.

A. Ability   B. Motivation   C. Resources

_____ 1. In recent years, the U.S. steel industry has not been as productive as the foreign competition.

_____ 2. I don't think you produce as much as the other department members because you're lazy.

_____ 3. I practice longer and harder than my track teammates Heather and Linda. I don't understand why they beat me in the running races.

_____ 4. I could get all A's in school if I wanted to. But I'd rather relax and have a good time in college.

_____ 5. The government would be more efficient if it cut down on waste.

Goal of Human Relations

When employee needs are not met through the organization, employees are dissatisfied and are generally lower performers. This is the case with Hank; he finds the job boring and is not performing to expectations. To increase Hank's performance, Latoia must meet the goal of human relations. She must create a win-win situation so that Hank's needs are met to motivate him to perform to her expectations. As each motivation theory and technique is presented, you will learn how Latoia can apply it to motivate Hank or others.

Learning Objective

1. Explain the motivation process and the three factors affecting performance

There is no single universally accepted theory of how to motivate people.[9] In this chapter you will learn seven major motivation theories and how you can use them to motivate yourself and others. After studying all of the theories, you can select one theory to use, or take from several to make your own theory, or apply the theory that best fits the specific situation.

● Organization
● Group
● Individual

Goal of Human Relations

Content Motivation Theories

A satisfied employee is usually more productive. Job satisfaction is the primary motivator.[10] If an organization wants to increase performance, it must meet employees' needs. Each year hundreds of millions of dollars are spent on employee need satisfaction programs to increase productivity. To increase performance, managers must know their own needs and their employees' needs, and they must satisfy them. This is the goal of human relations.

The **content motivation theories** *focus on identifying people's needs in order to understand what motivates them.* You will learn four content motivation theories: (1) needs hierarchy, (2) ERG theory, (3) two-factor theory, and (4) manifest needs theory; and how organizations use them to motivate employees.

Needs Hierarchy

The **needs hierarchy** *is Maslow's theory of motivation that is based on five needs.* In the 1940s, Abraham Maslow developed one of the most popular and widely known motivation theories.[11] His theory is based on three major assumptions:

- People's needs are arranged in order of importance (hierarchy), going from basic needs (physiological) to more complex needs (self-actualization).
- People will not be motivated to satisfy a higher-level need unless the lower-level need(s) has been at least minimally satisfied.
- People have five classifications of needs. Listed below are these five needs in order of importance to the individual.

Physiological Needs: These are people's primary or basic needs. They include air, food, shelter, sex, and relief or avoidance of pain. In an organizational setting, these needs include adequate salary, breaks, and working conditions.

Safety Needs: Once the physiological needs are met, the individual is concerned with safety and security. In the organizational setting, these needs include safe working conditions, salary increases to meet inflation, job security, and fringe benefits that protect the physiological needs. However, jobs are less secure today,[12] and less benefits are given.

Social Needs: After establishing safety, people look for love, friendship, acceptance, and affection. In the organizational setting, these needs include the opportunity to interact with others, to be accepted, and to have friends.

Esteem Needs: After the social needs are met, the individual focuses on ego, status, self-respect, recognition for accomplishments, and a feeling of self-confidence and prestige. In the organizational setting, these needs include titles, the satisfaction of completing the job itself, merit pay raises, recognition, challenging tasks, participation in decision making, and the chance for advancement.

Self-Actualization: The highest level of need is to develop one's full potential. To do so, one seeks growth, achievement, and advancement. In the organizational setting, these needs include the development of one's skills, the chance to be creative, achievement and promotions, and the ability to have complete control over one's job.

Many research studies do not support Maslow's hierarchy theory. However, it has a sound foundation and is still used today. In fact, Maslow's work serves as a basis for several other theories. Today, organizations still strive to meet self-actualization needs.[13]

See Exhibit 6–1, Needs Hierarchy and ERG Theory, for an illustration of Maslow's five needs.

ERG Theory

The classification of needs has been debated. Some say there are only two needs, while others claim there are seven. Several researchers have combined categories to simplify the theory. ERG is a well-known simplification. As Exhibit 6–1 illustrates, Clayton Alderfer reorganizes Maslow's needs hierarchy into three levels of needs: existence (physiological and safety needs), relatedness (social), and growth (esteem and self-actualization). Alderfer maintains the higher- and lower-order needs. He agrees with Maslow that unsatisfied needs motivate individuals. In the opening case, Hank's performance was poor, but he can be motivated to meet Latoia's expectations if his performance results in satisfying his needs.

Motivating with Needs Hierarchy and ERG Theory

Based on Maslow's work, we conclude that the major recommendation to managers is to meet employees' lower-level needs so that they will not dominate the employees' motivational process. Managers should get to know and understand people's needs and meet them as a means of increasing performance. How organizations meet needs is discussed in a later section.

EXHIBIT 6–1   **NEEDS HIERARCHY AND ERG THEORY**

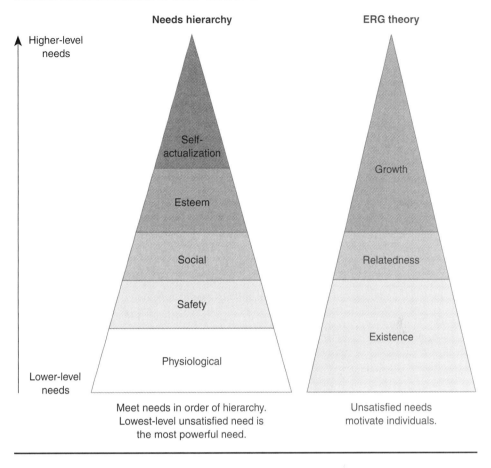

To use ERG theory, answer six questions: (1) What need does the individual have? (2) What needs have been satisfied? (3) Which unsatisfied need is the lowest in the hierarchy? (4) Have some higher-order needs been frustrated? If so, how? (5) Has the person refocused on a lower-level need? (6) How can the unsatisfied needs be satisfied? Latoia observed Hank and took the time to talk to him to determine his needs. Hank's need for existence and relatedness have been met. However, his need for growth has been frustrated. To motivate Hank, Latoia must meet his need for growth. In this chapter, you will learn ways to satisfy growth needs.

Two-Factor Theory

The **two-factor theory** *is Herzberg's classification of needs as hygienes and motivators.* Before learning Herzberg's theory, complete Self-Assessment Exercise 6–1 to learn what motivates you.

In the 1950s, Frederick Herzberg and associates interviewed 200 accountants and engineers.[14] They were asked to describe situations in which they were satisfied or motivated and dissatisfied or unmotivated. Their findings disagreed with the traditional view that satisfaction and dissatisfaction were at opposite ends of a continuum.

While Maslow classifies five needs and Alderfer classifies three needs, Herzberg classifies two needs that he calls *factors*. Herzberg combines lower-level needs (physiological, safety, and social/existence and relatedness) into one classification he calls *hygienes;* and higher-level needs (esteem and self-actualization/growth) into one classification he calls *motivators*. Hygienes are also called *extrinsic factors* because attempts to motivate come from outside the job itself, such as pay,[15] job security,

Motivators or Hygienes

Below are 12 job factors that contribute to job satisfaction. Rate each according to how important it is to you. Place the number 1 to 5 on the line before each factor.

Very important		Somewhat important		Not important
5	4	3	2	1

_____ 1. An interesting job

_____ 2. A good boss

_____ 3. Recognition and appreciation for the work I do

_____ 4. The opportunity for advancement

_____ 5. A satisfying personal life

_____ 6. A prestigious or status job

_____ 7. Job responsibility

_____ 8. Good working conditions (nice office)

_____ 9. Sensible company rules, regulations, procedures, and policies

_____ 10. The opportunity to grow through learning new things

_____ 11. A job I can do well and succeed at

_____ 12. Job security

To determine if hygienes or motivators are important to you, place the numbers 1 to 5 that represent your answers below.

Hygiene Factors Score	Motivational Factors Score
2. ——	1. ——
5. ——	3. ——
6. ——	4. ——
8. ——	7. ——
9. ——	10. ——
12. ——	11. ——
Total points ——	Total points ——

Add each column vertically. Did you select hygienes or motivators as being important to you? Now we'll find out what the difference is and their significance.

and job title; working conditions; fringe benefits; and relationships. Motivators are called *intrinsic factors* because motivation comes from the job itself, such as achievement, recognition, challenge, and advancement.[16] See Exhibit 6–2 below, Two-Factor Theory, for an illustration of Herzberg's theory.

Herzberg contends that providing maintenance factors keeps people from being dissatisfied, but it does not motivate people. For example, if people are dissatisfied with their pay and they get a raise, they will no longer be dissatisfied. They may even be satisfied for a short period of time.[17] However, before long they get accustomed to the new standard of living and will no longer be satisfied. They need another raise to be satisfied again. The vicious cycle goes on. If you got a pay raise, would you be motivated and be more productive? How many people do you know who increased their level of productivity and maintained it until the next pay raise?

To motivate, Herzberg says that you must first ensure that hygiene factors are adequate. Once employees are satisfied with their environment, they can be motivated through their jobs. Today, many organizations are striving to provide meaning in meaningless work.[18]

Review Self-Assessment Exercise 6–1. According to Herzberg, if you seek and attain these job factors, you may not be dissatisfied, but you may not be satisfied

EXHIBIT 6–2   **TWO-FACTOR THEORY**

Hygiene Factors (Needs)
(physiological, safety, and social/existence and relatedness needs)

Extrinsic Factors

Dissatisfaction (Environment) No Dissatisfaction

• Pay • Status • Job security • Fringe Benefits • Policies and administrative practices • Human Relations

Motivator Factors (Needs)
(esteem and self-actualization/growth needs)

Intrinsic Factors

No Job Satisfaction (The Job Itself) Job Satisfaction

• Meaningful and challenging work • Recognition for accomplishments
• Feeling of achievement • Increased responsibility • Opportunity for growth
• Opportunity for advancement

either. Do not expect external rewards for everything you are asked to do. To be satisfied you must seek and attain internal rewards to be self-motivated.[19]

WORK APPLICATIONS

2. In Self-Assessment Exercise 6–1, did you select motivators or hygienes as being important to you? Explain.

Using Two-Factor Theory to Motivate Employees

Skill-Building

6–1

In the opening case, Hank said he was not dissatisfied with hygiene factors. He lacked job satisfaction. If Latoia is going to motivate him, she will have to focus on intrinsic motivation, not hygiene. Since Hank says the job is boring, will a pay raise or better working conditions make the job more interesting and challenging? Motivation comes from doing what you like and enjoy doing. According to Herzberg, the best way to motivate employees is to build challenge and opportunity for achievement into the job itself. Herzberg develops a method for increasing motivation, which he calls *job enrichment*. Under the Motivation Techniques section of this chapter, you will learn about job enrichment and how Latoia could use it to motivate Hank.

Manifest Needs Theory

Like Maslow, Alderfer, and Herzberg, manifest needs theorists believe people are motivated by their needs. However, they classify needs differently. **Manifest needs theory** *of motivation is primarily McClelland's classification of needs as achievement, power, and affiliation.* McClelland does not have a classification for lower-level needs. His affiliation needs are the same as social and relatedness, and power and achievement are related to esteem and self-actualization and growth. See Exhibit 6–3 for a comparison of the need classifications of the four theories of motivation.

Manifest needs theory was originally developed by Henry Murry,[20] then adapted by John Atkinson[21] and David McClelland.[22] Unlike Maslow, they believe that needs

EXHIBIT 6–3   **CLASSIFICATION OF NEEDS BY FOUR THEORIES OF MOTIVATION**

Maslow Needs Hierarchy Theory	Alderfer ERG Theory	Herzberg Two-Factor Theory	McClelland Manifest Needs Theory
Self-actualization	Growth	Motivators	Power
Esteem			Achievement
Social	Relatedness	Hygiene	Affiliation
Safety	Existence		
Physiological			

are based on personality and are developed as people interact with the environment. All people possess the need for achievement, power, and affiliation, but to varying degrees. One of these three needs tends to be dominant in each one of us and motivates our behavior. Before getting into the details of each need, complete Self-Assessment Exercise 6–2, on the next page, and determine your dominant or primary need.

Now that you have a better understanding of your needs, you will learn more about all three needs.

The Need for Achievement (n Ach)

People with a high n Ach tend to be characterized as: Wanting to take personal responsibility for solving problems. Goal oriented; they set moderate, realistic, attainable goals. Seeking a challenge, excellence, and individuality. Taking calculated, moderate risk. Desiring concrete feedback on their performance. Willing to work hard.

People with a high n Ach think about ways to do a better job, how to accomplish something unusual or important, and career progression. They perform well in nonroutine, challenging, and competitive situations, while people low in n Ach do not perform well in these situations.

McClelland's research shows that only about 10 percent of the U.S. population has a dominant need for achievement. There is evidence of a correlation between high achievement need and high performance. People with a high n Ach tend to enjoy sales and entrepreneurial-type positions. Managers tend to have a high, but not a dominant, n Ach.

Motivating Employees with a High n Ach: Give them nonroutine, challenging tasks in which there are clear attainable objectives. Give them fast and frequent feedback on their performance. Continually give them increased responsibility for doing new things.

The Need for Power (n Pow)

▲ Goal of Human Relations

People with a high need for power tend to be characterized as: Wanting to control the situation. Wanting influence or control over others. Enjoying competition in which they can win; they do not like to lose. Willing to confront others.

People with high n Pow think about controlling a situation, and others, while seeking positions of authority and status. People with high n Pow tend to have a low need for affiliation. Managers tend to have a dominant need for power. Power is essential for successful supervision. Today, employees want more power to control their jobs.[23]

Motivating Employees with a High n Pow: Let them plan and control their jobs as much as possible. Try to include them in decision making, especially when they are affected by the decision. They tend to perform best alone rather than as team members. Try to assign them to a whole task rather than just a part of a task.

Self-Assessment
Exercise 6–2

Manifest Needs

Identify each of the 15 statements according to how accurately it describes you. Place the number 1 to 5 on the line before each statement.

Like me		Somewhat like me		Not like me
5	4	3	2	1

_____ 1. I enjoy working hard.

_____ 2. I enjoy competition and winning.

_____ 3. I want/have lots of friends.

_____ 4. I enjoy a difficult challenge.

_____ 5. I enjoy leading and being in charge.

_____ 6. I want to be liked by others.

_____ 7. I want to know how I am progressing as I complete tasks.

_____ 8. I confront people who do things I disagree with.

_____ 9. I enjoy frequent parties.

_____ 10. I enjoy setting and achieving realistic goals.

_____ 11. I enjoy influencing other people to get my way.

_____ 12. I enjoy belonging to lots of groups/organizations.

_____ 13. I enjoy the satisfaction of completing a difficult task.

_____ 14. In a leaderless situation I tend to take charge.

_____ 15. I enjoy working with others more than working alone.

To determine your primary need, below place the number 1 to 5 that represents your score for each statement. Each statement/column represents a specific need.

Achievement	Power	Affiliation
1. ____	2. ____	3. ____
4. ____	5. ____	6. ____
7. ____	8. ____	9. ____
10. ____	11. ____	12. ____
13. ____	14. ____	15. ____
Totals ____	____	____

Add up the total of each column. Each column total should be between 5 and 25 points. The column with the highest score is your dominant or primary need.

People are motivated to gain power because having it meets their needs. In the opening case, Hank's primary need seems to be power. Hank wants more say on how to do his job, and wants Latoia to do less checking up on him. If Latoia empowers Hank by giving him more job-related responsibility, it may satisfy Hank's needs and create a win–win situation, resulting in higher performance.

The Need for Affiliation (*n* Aff)

People with a high *n* Aff tend to be characterized as: Seeking close relationships with others. Wanting to be liked by others. Enjoying lots of social activities. Seeking to belong; they join groups and organizations.

People with a high *n* Aff think about friends and relationships. They tend to enjoy developing, helping, and teaching others. They tend to have a low *n* Pow. People with high *n* Aff seek jobs as teachers, in personnel, and in other helping professions. They tend to avoid supervision because they like to be one of the group rather than its leader.

Learning Objective

2. Describe four content motivation theories

Motivating High *n* Aff Employees:
Be sure to let them work as part of a team. They derive satisfaction from the people they work with rather than the task

itself. Give them lots of praise and recognition. Delegate responsibility for orienting and training new employees to them. They make great buddies and mentors.

WORK APPLICATIONS

3. Explain how your personal *n* Ach, *n* Pow, and *n* Aff affect your motivation, behavior, and performance. How can you use manifest needs theory to motivate employees?

● Organization
● Group
● Individual

How Organizations Meet Employee Needs

See Exhibit 6–4, How Organizations Meet Employee Needs, for a list of methods used by organizations to meet employee needs. Note that pay can meet both higher- and lower-level needs.[24] Motivating employees and paying them well affect performance.[25]

EXHIBIT 6–4   **HOW ORGANIZATIONS MEET EMPLOYEE NEEDS**

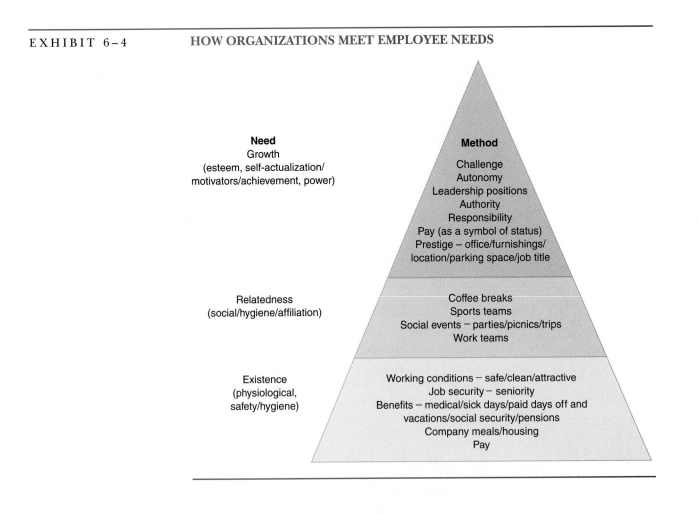

Need
Growth
(esteem, self-actualization/
motivators/achievement, power)

Method
Challenge
Autonomy
Leadership positions
Authority
Responsibility
Pay (as a symbol of status)
Prestige – office/furnishings/
location/parking space/job title

Relatedness
(social/hygiene/affiliation)

Coffee breaks
Sports teams
Social events – parties/picnics/trips
Work teams

Existence
(physiological,
safety/hygiene)

Working conditions – safe/clean/attractive
Job security – seniority
Benefits – medical/sick days/paid days off and
vacations/social security/pensions
Company meals/housing
Pay

● Organization
● Group
● Individual

Process Motivation Theories

Content motivation theory attempts to understand what motivates people while **process motivation theories** *attempt to understand how and why people are motivated.* Its focus is more on behavior than needs.[26] Why do people select certain goals to work toward?[27] Why do people select particular behavior to meet their needs?[28] How do people evaluate need satisfaction? Expectancy and equity theories attempt to answer these questions.

Expectancy Theory

The **expectancy theory,** *which is Vroom's formula, states that Motivation = Expectancy ×* *Valence.* Under Victor Vroom's theory,[29] motivation depends on how much people want something, and how likely they are of getting it. The theory is based on the following assumptions:

- Both internal (needs) and external (environment) factors affect behavior.
- Behavior is the individual's decision.
- People have different needs, desires, and goals.
- People make behavior decisions based on their perception of the outcome.

Two important variables in Vroom's formula must be met for motivation to take place.

Expectancy: Expectancy refers to the person's perception of his or her ability (probability) to accomplish an objective. Generally, the higher one's expectancy, the better the chance for motivation. When employees do not believe that they can accomplish objectives, they will not be motivated to try.

Also important is the "perception" of the relationship between performance and the outcome or reward.[30] Generally, the higher one's expectancy of the outcome or reward, the better the chance for motivation. This is called *instrumentally.* If employees are certain to get a reward or to be successful, they probably will be motivated. When not sure, employees may not be motivated.[31] For example, Dan believes he would be a good supervisor and wants to get promoted. However, Dan has an external locus of control and believes that working hard will not result in a promotion anyway. Therefore, he will not be motivated to work for the promotion.

Valence: Valence refers to the value a person places on the outcome or reward. Generally, the higher the value (importance) of the outcome or reward, the better the chance of motivation. For example, the supervisor, Jean, wants an employee, Sim, to work harder. Jean talks to Sim and tells him that working hard will result in a promotion. If Sim wants a promotion, he will probably be motivated. However, if a promotion is not of importance to Sim, it will not motivate him.

Motivating with Expectancy Theory

Expectancy theory can accurately predict a person's work effort, satisfaction level, and performance,[32] but only if the correct values are plugged into the formula. Therefore, this theory makes accurate predictions in certain contexts but not in others. The following conditions should be implemented to motivate employees:

1. Clearly define objectives and the necessary performance needed to achieve them.[33]

2. Tie performance to rewards.[34] High performance should be rewarded.[35] When one employee works harder to produce more than other employees and is not rewarded, he or she may slow down productivity.

3. Be sure rewards are of value to the employee. The supervisor should get to know his or her employees as individuals. Develop good human relations.

4. Make sure your employees believe you will do as you promise, instrumentality. For example, they must believe you will promote them if they do work hard. And you must do as you promise, so employees will believe you.

Expectancy theory also works best with employees who have an internal locus of control because if they believe they control their destiny, their efforts will result in success. Expectancy theory does not work well with employees who have an external locus of control because they do not believe their efforts result in success. Believing that success is due to fate, or chance, why should they be motivated to work hard?

In the opening case, Hank says that because of the union everyone is paid the same, so working hard is a waste of time. In the expectancy formula, since expectancy is low, there is no motivation. Paying more for higher performance motivates many employees. However, in a union organization, Latoia has no control over giving Hank a raise if he does a better job. However, the chance for advancement to a higher-level job that pays more may motivate him to work harder. Organizations generally do not promote people to a higher-level job unless they are good performers at the present job. Assuming Hank is interested in advancement, Latoia can explain to Hank that if he does a good job, she will recommend him for a promotion when an opportunity arises, provided he does a good job. If a promotion is not important to Hank, Latoia may find some other need to help him meet. If Latoia can find a need with expectancy and valence, Hank will be motivated to perform to expectations, creating a win-win situation for all parties.

▲ Goal of Human Relations

WORK APPLICATIONS

4. Give an example of how expectancy theory has affected your motivation. How can you use expectancy theory to motivate employees?

Equity Theory

The **equity theory** *is primarily Adams's motivation theory, which is based on the comparison of perceived inputs to outputs.* J. Stacy Adams popularized equity theory with his contention that people seek social equity in the rewards they receive (output) for their performance (input).[36] Based on the knowledge of equity, one can predict behavior.[37]

According to equity theory, people compare their inputs (effort, experience, seniority, status, intelligence, and so forth) and outputs (praise, recognition, pay promotions, increased status, supervisor's approval, etc.) to that of relevant others. A relevant other could be a coworker or group of employees from the same or from different organizations, or even from a hypothetical situation. Notice that our definition says perceived and not actual inputs and outputs.[38] Equity may actually exist. However, if employees believe there is inequity, they will change their behavior to create equity.[39] Employees must perceive that they are being treated fairly, relative to others.[40]

Most employees tend to inflate their own efforts or performance when comparing themselves to others. They also overestimate what others earn. Employees may be very satisfied and motivated until they find out that a relevant other is earning more for the same job or earning the same for doing less work. When inequity is perceived, employees attempt to reduce it by reducing input or increasing output.

A comparison with relevant others leads to three conclusions:

Equitably Rewarded: Inputs and outputs are perceived as being equal; motivation exists. Employees may believe that relevant others should have greater outputs when they have more experience, education, and so on.

Underrewarded: When employees perceive that they are underrewarded, they may reduce the inequity by: trying to increase outputs (getting a raise); reducing inputs (doing less work, absenteeism, long breaks, etc.); rationalizing (finding a logical explanation for inequity); changing others' inputs or outputs (getting them to do more, or get less); leaving the situation (getting transferred, or leaving for a better job); changing the object of comparison (they make/get less than I do).

Overrewarded: Being overrewarded is not too disturbing to most employees. However, research suggests that employees may reduce perceived inequity by: increasing inputs (work harder or longer); reducing output (take a pay cut); rationalizing (I'm worth it); trying to increase others' output (give them the same as me).

Motivating with Equity Theory

Using equity theory in practice can be difficult because you don't know who the employee's reference group is, and what their view of inputs and outcomes are. However, it does offer some useful general recommendations:

- The supervisor should be aware that equity is based on perception, which may not be correct. It is possible for the supervisor to create equity or inequity.[41] Some managers have favorite subordinates who get special treatment; others don't.
- Rewards should be equitable.[42] When employees perceive that they are not treated fairly, morale and performance problems occur; resentment and retaliation are common.[43]
- High performance should be rewarded,[44] but employees must understand the inputs needed to attain certain outputs.

Learning Objective

3. Describe two process motivation theories

In the opening case, Hank said that he was equitably treated because of the union. Therefore, Latoia does not need to be concerned about equity theory with Hank. However, it could be an issue with another employee.

WORK APPLICATIONS

5. Give an example of how equity theory has affected your motivation. How can you use equity theory to motivate employees?

- Organization
- Group
- Individual

- Performance
- Human Relations
- Behavior

Reinforcement Theory

Research supports the main effect of reinforcement theory on task performance.[45] Several organizations, including 3M, Frito-Lay, and B. F. Goodrich, have used reinforcement to increase productivity. Michigan Bell had a 50 percent improvement in attendance and above-standard productivity and efficiency level. Emery Air Freight went from 30 percent of employees meeting standard to 90 percent after using reinforcement. Emery estimates that its reinforcement program has resulted in a $650,000 yearly savings.

As you have seen, content motivation theories focus on what motivates people and process motivation theories focus on how and why people are motivated; reinforcement theory focuses on getting people to do what you want them to do.[46] **Reinforcement theory** *is primarily Skinner's motivation theory: Behavior can be controlled through the use of rewards.* It is also called *behavior modification and operant conditioning.*

B. F. Skinner contends that people's behavior is learned through experiences of positive and negative consequences. He believes that rewarded behavior tends to be repeated, while unrewarded behavior tends not to be repeated. The three components of Skinner's framework are:[47]

$$\text{Stimulus} \longrightarrow \underset{\substack{\text{(Behavior/} \\ \text{Performance)}}}{\text{Response}} \longrightarrow \underset{\substack{\text{(Reinforcement/} \\ \text{Positive or Negative)}}}{\text{Consequences}}$$

An employee learns what is, and is not, desired behavior as a result of the consequences for specific behavior. Failure to reinforce behavior can be an inefficient way of motivating employees.[48]

Reinforcement theory is concerned with maintaining desired behavior (motivation) over time. In other words, people behave in ways that are reinforced.[49] For example, if Beth, a student, wants to get an A on an exam, she will study for the outcome. If

Beth gets the A (reward), she will probably study in the same way for the next exam. However, if Beth does not get the A, she will probably change her method of study for the next exam. We tend to learn to get what we want through trial and error. What gets measured/reinforced gets done.[50]

Skinner states that supervisors can control and shape employees' behavior while at the same time making them feel free. The two important concepts used to control behavior are the types of reinforcement and the schedule of reinforcement.

Types of Reinforcement

The four types of reinforcement are:

Positive Reinforcement: A method of encouraging continued behavior is to offer attractive consequences (rewards) for desirable performance. For example, an employee is on time for a meeting and is rewarded by the supervisor thanking him or her. The praise is used to reinforce punctuality. Other reinforcers are pay, promotions, time off, and increased status. Positive reinforcement is the best motivator for increasing productivity.

Avoidance Reinforcement: Avoidance is also called *negative reinforcement*. As with positive reinforcement, avoidance reinforcement encourages continued desirable behavior. The employee avoids the negative consequence. For example, an employee is punctual for a meeting to avoid negative reinforcement, such as a reprimand. Standing plans, especially rules, are designed to get employees to avoid certain behavior.

Extinction: Rather than encourage desirable behavior, extinction (and punishment) attempts to reduce or eliminate undesirable behavior by withholding reinforcement when the behavior occurs. For example, an employee who is late for the meeting is not rewarded with praise. Or a pay raise is withheld until the employee performs to set standards. Supervisors who do not reward good performance can cause its extinction.

Punishment: Punishment is used to provide an undesirable consequence for undesirable behavior. For example, an employee who is late for a meeting is reprimanded. Notice that with avoidance there is no actual punishment; it's the threat of the punishment that controls behavior. Other methods of punishment include harassing, taking away privileges, probation, fining, and demoting. Using punishment may reduce the undesirable behavior, but it may cause other undesirable behavior, such as poor morale, lower productivity, and acts of theft or sabotage. Punishment is the most controversial method and the least effective at motivating employees.

Schedule of Reinforcement

The second reinforcement consideration in controlling behavior is when to reinforce performance. The frequency and magnitude of the reinforcement may be as important as the reinforcement itself.[51] The two major classifications are continuous and intermittent:

Continuous Reinforcement: With a continuous method, each and every desired behavior is reinforced. Examples of this method would be a machine with an automatic counter that lets the employee know, at any given moment, exactly how many units have been produced, piece rate of $1 for each unit produced, or a supervisor who comments on every customer report.

Intermittent Reinforcement: With intermittent reinforcement, the reward is given based on the passage of time or output. When the reward is based on the passage of time, it is called an *interval schedule*. When it is based on output, it is called a *ratio schedule*. When electing to use intermittent reinforcement, there are four alternatives:

1. Fixed interval schedule. (Giving a salary paycheck every week, breaks and meals at the same time every day.)

2. Variable interval schedule. (Giving praise only now and then, a surprise inspection, a pop quiz.)

3. Fixed ratio schedule. (Giving a piece rate or bonus after producing a standard rate.)

4. Variable ratio schedule. (Giving praise for excellent work, a lottery for employees who have not been absent for a set time.)

Ratios are generally better motivators than intervals. The variable ratio tends to be the most powerful schedule for sustaining behavior.

Motivating with Reinforcement

Generally, positive reinforcement is the best motivator. Continuous reinforcement is better at sustaining desired behavior; however, it is not always possible or practical. Some general guidelines include:

- Make sure employees know exactly what is expected of them.[52] Set clear objectives.
- Select appropriate rewards. A reward to one person could be considered a punishment by another. Know your employees' needs.
- Select the appropriate reinforcement schedule.
- Do not reward mediocre or poor performance.
- Look for the positive and give praise, rather than focus on the negative and criticize. Make people feel good about themselves (Pygmalion effect).
- Never go a day without giving praise.
- Do things for your employees, instead of to them, and you will see productivity increases off the scales.

In the opening case, Hank has been coming to work late and performing below expectations. If Latoia offers Hank the possible promotion (expectancy theory), she has used a positive reinforcement with a variable interval schedule. There is no set time before an opening comes up, and Hank doesn't get it after completing a specific amount of work. If the recommendation for a promotion does not change Hank's behavior, Latoia should try some other positive reinforcement such as job enrichment. If positive reinforcement doesn't change Hank's behavior, Latoia can use avoidance reinforcement. Based on her authority, she could tell Hank that the next time he is late or performs below a specific level, he will receive a specific punishment, such as part of his pay being withheld. If Hank does not avoid this behavior, Latoia must follow up and give the punishment. As a manager try the positive first. Positive reinforcement is a true motivator because it creates a win–win situation by meeting both the employee's and the manager's or organization's needs. From the employees' perspective, avoidance and punishment create a lose–win situation. The organization or manager wins by forcing them to do something they really don't want to do.

IE 6–2

Goal of Human Relations

- Organization
- Group
- Individual

Learning Objective

4. State how reinforcement is used to increase performance

Organizational Reinforcement for Getting Employees to Come to Work and to Be on Time

The traditional attempt to get employees to come to work and to be on time has been avoidance and punishment. If employees miss a specific number of days, they don't get paid. If an employee is late, the time card indicates this, and the employee receives punishment.

Many organizations today are using positive reinforcement by offering employees rewards for coming to work and being on time. For example, ADV Marketing Group, a Stamford, Connecticut, company, uses continuous reinforcement by offering prizes simply for showing up and being on time: a $100 dinner certificate after 13 on-time weeks and an $800 vacation plus two days off after a year of on-time performance.

Motivation Theories

AS 6–2

Identify each supervisor's statement of how to motivate employees by the theory behind the statement.

A. Expectancy   C. Needs hierarchy   E. Two factor

B. Equity   D. Manifest needs   F. Reinforcement

_____ 6. I motivate employees by making their jobs interesting.

_____ 7. I make sure I treat everyone fairly.

_____ 8. I know Wendy likes people, so I give her jobs in which she works with other employees.

_____ 9. Paul would yell in the shop because he knew it got to me. So I decided to ignore his yelling, and he stopped.

_____ 10. I got to know all of my employees' values fairly well. Now I can offer rewards that will motivate them.

_____ 11. We offer good working conditions, salaries, and benefits, so I'm working at developing more teamwork.

_____ 12. When my employees do something outstanding, I write them a thank-you note.

_____ 13. I used to try to improve working conditions to motivate employees. But I stopped and now focus on giving employees more responsibility so they can grow and develop new skills.

_____ 14. I set clear objectives that are attainable. And I offer rewards that employees like when they achieve their objectives.

_____ 15. I now realize that I tend to be an autocratic supervisor because it helps fill my needs. I will work at giving some of my employees more autonomy.

Mediatech, a Chicago company, uses variable ratio schedule by holding a lottery. Each week Mediatech puts up $250. On Friday they spin a wheel to determine if a drawing will be held that week. If not, the money goes into the pot for the next week. When a drawing is held, only the employees who have attended on time up to the drawing are included.

A popular technique used by many organizations, which virtually eliminates the problem of being late for work, is flextime. *Flextime* allows employees to determine when they start and end work, provided they work their full number of hours, with certain restrictions on working hours. A typical schedule permits employees to begin work between 6:00 A.M. and 9:00 A.M. and complete their workday between 3:00 P.M. and 6:00 P.M. Flextime helps meet the goal of human relations because it allows employees to schedule their time to accommodate meeting their personal needs and job requirements. Employees at companies that offer flexible work schedules file fewer claims for mental-health benefits.[53] Clearly, employees want more flexible work hours, and organizations also benefit by offering them.[54]

Goal of Human Relations

6. What reinforcement type(s) and schedule(s) does or did your present or past supervisor use to motivate you? Explain each. How can *you* use reinforcement to motivate employees?

● Organization
● Group
● Individual

Motivation Techniques

The previous sections discussed the major motivation theories. Now we examine specific on-the-job techniques to motivate employees: giving praise, MBO, job enrichment, and job design.

Giving Praise

In the 1940s, a survey revealing that what employees want most from a job is full appreciation for work done. Similar studies have been performed over the years with little change in results.[55] Giving recognition to employees motivates them.[56] Workers say they rarely or never get praise from the boss.[57] When was the last time your boss gave you a thank-you or some praise for a job well done? When was the last time your boss complained about your work? If you are a manager, when was the last time you praised or criticized your employees? What is the ratio of praise to criticism?

Goal of
Human Relations

Giving praise develops a positive self-concept in employees and leads to better performance—the Pygmalion effect. Praise is a motivator (not a hygiene) because it meets employees' needs for esteem/self-actualization, growth, and achievement. Giving praise creates a win-win situation. It is probably the most powerful, least-expensive, simplest, and yet most underused motivational technique there is.

Ken Blanchard and Spencer Johnson popularized giving praise through their best-selling book, *The One-Minute Manager.*[58] They developed a technique that involves giving one minute of praise. Exhibit 6–5, Giving Praise Model, is an adaptation. The steps in **giving praise** are as follows: *step 1, tell the person exactly what was done correctly; step 2, tell the person why the behavior is important; step 3, stop for a moment of silence; step 4, encourage repeat performance.* Blanchard calls it one-minute praise because it should not take more than one minute to give the praise. It is not necessary for the employee to say anything. The four steps are illustrated below.

Step 1. Tell the Person Exactly What Was Done Correctly: When giving praise look the person in the eye. Eye contact shows sincerity and concern. It is important to be very specific and descriptive. General statements like "you're a good worker" are not as effective. But, on the other hand, don't talk for too long, or the praise loses its effectiveness.

SUPERVISOR: John, I just overheard you deal with that customer's complaint. You did an excellent job of keeping your cool; you were polite. That person came in angry and left happy.

Step 2. Tell the Person Why the Behavior Is Important: Briefly state how the organization, and/or person, benefits from the action. It is also helpful to tell the employee how you feel about the behavior. Be specific and descriptive.

SUPERVISOR: Without customers we don't have a business. One customer bad-mouthing us can cause hundreds of dollars in lost sales. It really made me proud to see you handle that tough situation the way you did.

Step 3. Stop for a Moment of Silence: This is a tough one. Most supervisors the author trains have trouble being silent. The rationale for the silence is to give the employee the chance to "feel" the impact of the praise. It's like "the pause that refreshes."

Video

BM–6

SUPERVISOR: (*Silently counts to five.*)

Step 4. Encourage Repeat Performance: This is the reinforcement that motivates the employee to keep up performance. Blanchard recommends touching the employee. Touching has a powerful impact. However, he recommends it only if both parties feel comfortable. Others say don't touch employees; touching could lead to a sexual harassment charge.

Skill-Building

6–2

Goal of
Human Relations

■ Performance
■ Human Relations
■ Behavior

SUPERVISOR: Thanks, John, keep up the good work (*while touching John on the shoulder, or shaking hands*).

As you can see, giving praise is easy, and it doesn't cost a penny. Several managers trained to give praise say it works wonders. It's a much better motivator than giving a raise or other monetary reward. One manager stated that an employee was taking his time stacking cans on a display. He gave the employee praise for stacking the cans so straight. The employee was so pleased with the praise that the display went up with about a 100 percent increase in productivity. Notice that the manager looked for the positive and used positive reinforcement, rather than punishment. The manager could have made a comment such as, "Quit goofing off and get the display up faster." That statement would not have motivated the employee to increase productivity. All it would have done was hurt human relations, and could have ended in an argument. Notice that in the above example the cans were straight. The employee was not praised for the slow work pace. However, if the praise had not worked, the manager should have used another reinforcement method.

In the opening case, if Hank is interested in changing behavior to get a promotion, Latoia should give him praise for coming in on time and increasing his performance to encourage him to continue this behavior. Praise is a reinforcement that is very effective when used with a variable interval schedule.

EXHIBIT 6–5

Learning Objective

5. List the four steps in the giving praise model

GIVING PRAISE MODEL

Step 1. Tell the person exactly what was done correctly.

Step 2. Tell the person why the behavior is important.

Step 3. Stop for a moment of silence.

Step 4. Encourage repeat performance.

Objectives and MBO

For many years, writers have been saying that setting difficult objectives leads to higher levels of motivation and performance, and research supports this statement.[59]

The **objectives** *state what is to be accomplished within a given period of time*. Objectives are end results; they do not state how the objective will be accomplished. How to achieve the objective is the plan. Some writers define goals and objectives differently; we do not. You will learn the five criteria objectives should meet, how to write objectives, and how to use management by objectives (MBO).

Criteria for Objectives

To motivate people to high levels of performance, objectives should be:

• Difficult but achievable. Individuals perform better when assigned difficult objectives rather than easy ones, no goals, or simply told "do your best."[60] To motivate people to high levels of performance, objectives must be challenging.[61] However, if people do not believe that the objectives are achievable (expectancy theory), they will not be motivated to work for their accomplishment.

• Observable and measurable. If people are to achieve objectives, they must be able to observe and measure their progress regularly.[62] Individuals perform better when their performance is measured and evaluated.[63]

• Specific, with a target date. To be motivated, employees must know exactly what is expected of them, and when they are expected to have the task completed.[64] Employees should be given specific objectives with deadlines. However, some objectives do not require or lend themselves to target dates. For example, the objectives in the skill-building exercises do not list a target date.

- Participatively set when possible. Groups that participate in setting their objectives generally outperform groups with assigned objectives.[65] Managers should use the appropriate level of participation for the employees' capabilities. The higher the capabilities, the higher the level of participation.
- Accepted. For objectives to be met, employees must accept them. Without acceptance, even meeting the above four criteria can lead to failure. If employees are not committed to strive for the objective, they may not meet it.[66] Using participation helps get employees to accept objectives.[67]

APPLICATION   SITUATIONS

Objectives

AS 6–3

For each objective, state which criterion is not met.

A. Difficult but achievable   C. Specific with a target date

B. Observable and measurable

_____ 16. To increase production of widgets during the fiscal year 20__.

_____ 17. To increase total sales by 40 percent during 20__.

_____ 18. To increase the company's image by June 20__.

_____ 19. To write objectives within two weeks.

_____ 20. To pass this human relations course this semester.

Objectives are actually used outside the context of MBO more than within it because in many situations, like being on a production line, you have to keep up the machine pace, and objectives are not applicable. Most organizations and their departments have objectives.[68]

Writing Objectives

Objectives should be written. To help write objectives that meet the five criteria above, use Max E. Douglas's model shown in Exhibit 6–6.

EXHIBIT 6–6

Learning Objective

6. Identify the four parts of the writing objectives model

WRITING OBJECTIVES MODEL

Objectives Model specific and measurable

Infinitive + Action verb + Singular behavior, + Target date

Example Objectives for a Student:

To + receive + a B as my final grade in human relations + in December/May 20__.

To increase my cumulative grade point average to 3.0 by May 20__.

Example Objectives for a Manager:

To produce 1,000 units per day.

To keep absences to three or less per month.

To decrease accidents by 5 percent during 20__.

Example Objectives for an Organization:

DaimierChrysler will become the world's number-one automaker by 2003.[69]

To cut medical mistake deaths in half by year end 2004.[70]

Coca-Cola's annual volume growth rate is 7% to 8%.[71]

Hyundai will join a foreign partner and become one of the world's top-five automakers by 2010.[72]

Management by Objectives (MBO)

Pointing workers to a common goal is what managers need to do. This is what MBO attempts to do. **Management by objectives (MBO)** *is the process in which managers and their employees jointly set objectives for the employees, periodically evaluate the performance, and reward according to the results.*

For a program to truly be MBO, it should be organizationwide. MBO starts at the top of the management hierarchy and works its way down to the workers. Each level of management's objectives must contribute to the next level's objectives. To be successful, MBO takes a lot of commitment, time, and participation. You can use the MBO process successfully with subordinates if you are truly committed and willing to involve employees.

The three steps of MBO include:

Step 1. Set Individual Objectives and Plans:
Each subordinate jointly sets objectives with the manager. The objectives are the heart of the MBO program and should meet the five criteria discussed earlier.

Step 2. Give Feedback and Evaluate Performance:
Xerox Learning Systems states that giving feedback is the most important management skill. Employees must know how they are progressing toward their objectives. Thus, the manager and employee must meet frequently to review the latter's progress. The frequency of evaluations depends upon the individual and the job performed. However, most managers probably do not conduct enough review sessions.

Step 3. Reward According to Performance:
Employees' performance should be measured against their objectives. Employees who meet their objectives should be rewarded through recognition, praise, pay raises, promotions, and so on.[73] Many organizations now link pay to meeting goals.[74]

MBO is a motivator (not a hygiene) because it meets employees' needs for esteem/self-actualization, growth, and power/achievement. MBO empowers employees to increase responsibility with an opportunity for creating meaningful, challenging work to help them grow and accomplish what *they* and the manager want to accomplish.[75] MBO creates a win-win situation.

In a union situation, such as the opening case, using MBO may not be possible without union consent and input.

Skill-Building

6–3

Goal of Human Relations

Learning Objective

7. Explain the three steps of managing by objectives

Job Enrichment

The term **job enrichment** *is the process of building motivators into the job itself by making it more interesting and challenging.* It differs from job rotation, in which employees learn to perform other employees' jobs, and job enlargement, in which the employee is assigned more tasks of a similar nature.

Job enrichment is an effective motivation tool.[76] Organizations including IBM, AT&T, Polaroid, Monsanto, General Motors, Motorola, Maytag, and The Traveler's Insurance Company have used job enrichment successfully.

Before implementing job enrichment, the manager should be sure that the job is of low motivation potential and that the employees want their jobs enriched. Some people with an external locus of control are happy with the jobs the way they are. Hygienes must also be adequate before using job enrichment.

Some simple ways managers can enrich jobs include:

Delegate More Variety and Responsibility: Give employees challenging assignments that help them to grow and develop new skills. New tasks require the challenge of new learning. The variety of tasks relieves monotony that develops from repetition. Variety gives employees a greater sense of accomplishment because they can perform more tasks. Managers can delegate some of the responsibility and tasks they perform themselves.

Form Natural Work Groups: Allow the team of employees to work together.[77] For example, at AT&T, service-order representatives who prepared service orders to be typed were in separate areas of the office. To enrich the jobs, the service-order representatives were moved to one geographical location and assigned their own typist to work together as a team. As a result, orders typed on time increased from 27 to over 90 percent, with improved accuracy. The work group can also perform their own identifiable work with increased responsibility.

Make Employees Responsible for Their Own Identifiable Work: Let employees make the entire product rather than one part of it. For example, at Motorola, assemblers who worked on one or two components had their jobs enriched. The enriched jobs enabled the assemblers to work on eight different components, and their names were put on the units they assembled. Units not meeting quality control were returned to the person for repair, rather than repaired randomly by assemblers.

Give Employees More Autonomy: Allow employees to plan, schedule, organize, and control their own jobs. For example, at Banker's Trust Company of New York, typists had their jobs enriched by being allowed to schedule their own work and correct their own errors on computer output tape, rather than having a specialist make the change. Making typists responsible for checking their own work eliminated the need for checkers. Job enrichment resulted in an annual savings of $360,000, improved attitudes, and greater job satisfaction.

WORK APPLICATIONS

7. Describe how to enrich a present or past job of yours.

Job Design

Poorly designed jobs cause more performance problems than managers realize. **Job design** *is the employee's system for transforming inputs into outputs.* The more effective and efficient the method, the more productive the employee. The current trend is to have teams design their own jobs, or at least change them to their specifications, which motivate employees to perform at higher levels.[78]

A common approach to job design is work simplification. The idea behind work simplification is to work smarter, not harder. **Job simplification** *is the process of eliminating, combining, and/or changing the work sequence to increase performance.* To motivate employees, have them break the job down into steps and see if they can:

- Eliminate. Does the task have to be done at all? If not, don't waste time doing it. At Intel, they decided it was not necessary to fill out a voucher for expenses amounting to less than $100. Work volume went down by 14 percent in 30 days.

- Combine. Doing more than one thing at a time often saves time. Make one trip to the mail room at the end of the day instead of several throughout the day.

- Change sequence. Often a change in the order of doing things results in a lower total time.

When used appropriately, work simplification can be effective at motivating employees. However, the danger lies in making a job too simple and boring rather than making it more interesting and challenging, as suggested under job enrichment.

8. Describe how to simplify a present or past job of yours. Is it an elimination, combination, or change in sequence that could simplify the job?

Job enrichment and job design are motivators (not a hygiene) because they meet employees' need for esteem/self-actualization, growth, and power/achievement. They empower employees to increase responsibility with an opportunity for creating meaningful, challenging work to help them grow and accomplish what *they* and the manager want to accomplish, creating a win-win situation.

In a union situation like the opening case, job enrichment and/or job design may not be possible without union consent and input. Assuming Latoia can use these techniques, she and Hank could work together to transform Hank's present boring job into a challenging and interesting one. This is the most appropriate motivation technique to use with Hank because it directly addresses the boring job. Hopes of a promotion in the unknown future will not change the present situation; however, if job enrichment is not possible, it may at least make the job tolerable until the promotion comes. If Hank finds his job interesting, he will most likely come to work on time and perform to expectation, creating a win-win situation.

For a review of the major motivation theories, see Exhibit 6–7. For a review of the four steps in the motivation process, see Exhibit 6–8.

Goal of
Human Relations

Learning Objective

8. State ways to enrich, design, and simplify jobs

E X H I B I T   6 – 7   **MOTIVATION THEORIES**

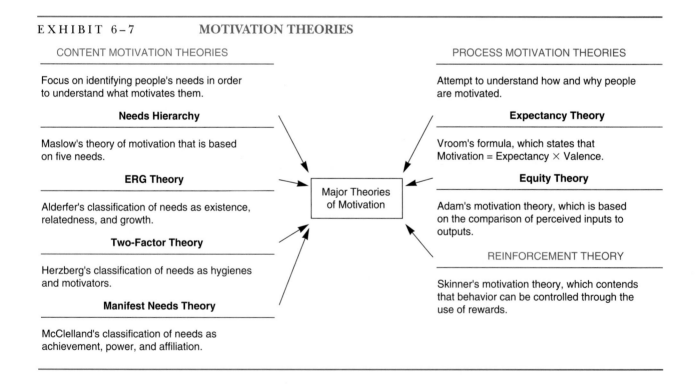

CONTENT MOTIVATION THEORIES

Focus on identifying people's needs in order to understand what motivates them.

Needs Hierarchy

Maslow's theory of motivation that is based on five needs.

ERG Theory

Alderfer's classification of needs as existence, relatedness, and growth.

Two-Factor Theory

Herzberg's classification of needs as hygienes and motivators.

Manifest Needs Theory

McClelland's classification of needs as achievement, power, and affiliation.

PROCESS MOTIVATION THEORIES

Attempt to understand how and why people are motivated.

Expectancy Theory

Vroom's formula, which states that Motivation = Expectancy × Valence.

Equity Theory

Adam's motivation theory, which is based on the comparison of perceived inputs to outputs.

REINFORCEMENT THEORY

Skinner's motivation theory, which contends that behavior can be controlled through the use of rewards.

Major Theories of Motivation

---

9. Which motivation theory is the best? Explain why.
10. What is your motivation theory? What are the major methods, techniques, and so on, you plan to use on the job as a manager to increase motivation and performance?

EXHIBIT 6-9   **THE MOTIVATION PROCESS**

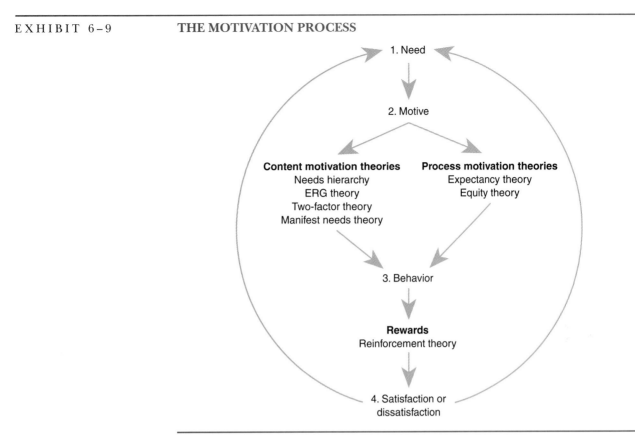

Notice that the motivation process is circular, or ongoing, because meeting our needs is a never-ending process.

● Organization
● Group
● Individual

Do Motivation Theories Apply Globally?

The motivation theories you have learned were developed in North America. As firms become global, they must be aware of the cultural limitations of theories. There is support for the idea that motivational concerns vary across nations.[79] For example, U.S. and Japanese practices vary.[80] There are distinct differences among U.S. salespeople and Japanese and Korean salespeople, but not between salespeople of the two Asian countries.[81] Also, when a U.S. firm in Mexico gave workers a raise to motivate them to work more hours, the raise actually motivated the employees to work less hours. Because they could now make enough money to live and enjoy life (one of their primary values) in less time, why should they work more hours?

One major cultural difference is in the focus on individualistic versus group approaches to business. Individualistic societies (United States, Canada, Great Britain, Australia) tend to value self-accomplishment. Collective societies (Japan, Mexico, Singapore, Pakistan) tend to value group accomplishment and loyalty. Cultural differences suggest that there might not be a hierarchical superiority to self-actualization as a motivator in collective societies. Cultures also differ in the extent to which they value need for achievement. The need for achievement tends to be more group-oriented in Japan and more individualistic in North America. Intrinsic motivation of higher-level needs might be more relevant to wealthy societies than to Third World countries.

Equity theory calls for higher producers to be paid more. This tends to be more of a motivator in individualistic countries than it is in collective countries where people tend to prefer equality where all are paid the same regardless of output.[82]

Learning Objective

9. Explain possible limitations of using motivation theories outside North America

Expectancy theory holds up fairly well cross-culturally because it is flexible. It allows for the possibility that there may be differences in expectations and valences across cultures. For example, societal acceptance may be of higher value than individual recognition in collective societies.

Reinforcement theory also hold up well cross-culturally, as people everywhere tend to use behavior that is reinforced.[83]

Deming's View of North American Motivation Methods

The late Dr. W. Edwards Deming, often credited with making Japan a world business leader, said in an interview with *The Wall Street Journal*:[84]

> We are all born with intrinsic motivation, self-esteem, dignity, an eagerness to learn. Our present system of management crushes that all out. Instead of working for the company, people compete with each other. The Japanese are more successful than the U.S. because they live by cooperation, not competition. American firms will have to learn to support each other, rather than continue with the everybody for himself approach. That's how business should be.

Deming is saying that North America must change from an individualistic society to a collective society if it is to survive in the global economy. He was pessimistic that U.S. business will make the changes he thinks necessary to compete.

WORK APPLICATIONS

11. Do you agree with Deming's statement that to survive in the global economy, the United States must change to the group approach of doing business?

REVIEW

Select one or more methods: (1) fill in the missing key terms from memory; (2) match the key terms, from the end of the review, with their definitions below; and/or (3) copy the key terms in order from the key terms at the beginning of the chapter.

_____ is the internal process leading to behavior to satisfy needs. The process includes need → motive → behavior → satisfaction or dissatisfaction. Generally, motivated people try harder to achieve objectives. Performance is not simply based on motivation. The level of performance is determined by the _____: Performance = Ability × Motivation × Resources. To attain maximum levels of performance, all three determinants must be present.

_____ focus on identifying people's needs in order to understand what motivates them. _____ is Maslow's theory of motivation that is based on five needs. ERG theory is Alderfer's reorganization of Maslow's needs hierarchy into three levels: existence, relatedness, and growth.

_____ is Herzberg's classification of needs as hygienes and

motivators. _____ of motivation is primarily McClelland's classification of needs as achievement, power, and affiliation.

_____ attempt to understand how and why people are motivated. _____ is Vroom's formula, which states that Motivation = Expectancy × Valence. _____ is primarily Adams's motivation theory, which is based on the comparison of perceived inputs to outputs.

_____ is primarily Skinner's motivation theory: Behavior can be controlled through the use of rewards. The types of reinforcement include positive, avoidance, extinction, and punishment. The schedule of reinforcement includes continuous and intermittent (fixed interval, variable interval, fixed ratio, and variable ratio). The steps in _____ are as follows: step 1, tell the person exactly what was done correctly; step 2, tell the person why the behavior is important; step 3, stop for a moment of silence; step 4, encourage repeat performance. _____ state what is to be accomplished within a given period of time. Objectives should be difficult but achievable, observable and measurable, specific, with a target date, participatively set when possible, and accepted. The writing objectives model is infinitive + action verb + singular behavior result + target date. _____ is the process in which managers and their employees jointly set objectives for the employees, periodically evaluate the performance, and reward according to results.

_____ is the process of building motivators into the job itself by making it more interesting and challenging.

_____ is the employee's system for transforming inputs into outputs. _____ is the process of eliminating, combining, and/or changing the work sequence to increase performance.

As firms become global, they must be aware of the cultural limitation to theory generalizations. One major cultural difference is in the focus on the individualistic (U.S.) versus the group approach to business (Japan). Dr. Deming says that to survive in the global economy, the United States must change to the group approach of doing business.

KEY TERMS

content motivation
  theories   193
equity theory   202
expectancy theory   201
giving praise   207
job design   211
job enrichment   210

job simplification   211
management by objectives
  (MBO)   210
manifest needs theory   197
motivation   192
needs hierarchy   194

objectives   208
performance formula   192
process motivation
  theories   200
reinforcement theory   203
two-factor theory   195

Carly Fiorina: Hewlett-Packard (HP)

Carleton Fiorina left Lucent Technology to become president and CEO of Hewlett-Packard (HP) to lead HP's adaptation to the Internet era. HP is not afraid to look at fresh approaches and will do whatever is required to stay on top. Carly is the first outsider to run HP and the first woman to head one of the nation's largest public firms. HP is among the top 20 on the *Fortune* 500 list, as well as among its top-five most admired companies and top-ten best companies to work for in America. Carly's decision-making record at Lucent was a key factor in her getting the CEO position at HP. One challenge any outsider faces taking on a new top-level management job is making peace with the followers, especially with those who wanted the newcomer's job. Carly works relentlessly, but she also has quick wit and a warm way of asserting herself. She feels like she is working all the time—it's relentless; the pace is blistering.

HP was founded in 1939 by Bill Hewlett and Dave Packard and started in a garage. Today HP is one of the world's largest computer companies and the foremost producer of test and measurement instruments. It sells more than 29,000 products used by people for personal use and in industry, business, engineering, science, medicine, and education in more than 120 countries.

The company's management style is called "The HP Way." The achievements of an organization are the result of the combined efforts of each individual in the organization working toward common objectives. These objectives should be realistic, should be clearly understood by everyone in the organization and should reflect the organization's basic character and personality. Seven corporate objectives provide a framework for group and individual goal setting in which all employees participate. Its management objective is: to foster initiative and creativity by allowing the individual great freedom of action in attaining well-defined objectives.[85]

Go to the Internet: For more information about Carleton Fiorina and HP for updated information provided in this case, do a name search on the Internet and visit the HP website at *http://www.hp.com.* For ideas on using the Internet with cases, see Appendix C.

Support your answer to the following questions with specific information from the case and text, or other information you get from the web or other source.

1. How can Carly motivate the people who work for her who wanted her job?

2. What level need is Carly on according to Needs Hierarchy, ERG, and Two-Factor theory?

3. What Manifest Needs profile do you expect Carly to have?

4. Which motivation technique does HP use?

Cumulative Case Questions

5. Review the Chapter 2 Outline. Which concept(s) seemed to be important to Carly as she came to HP to take over as president and CEO?

6. What type of attitude, job satisfaction, and self-concept (Chapter 3) do you think Carly has? Are they important to her success?

7. How does communications relate to this case (Chapters 4 and 5)?

Friedman's Business Technique

The following conversation takes place between Art Friedman and Bob Lussier. In 1970, Art Friedman implemented a new business technique. At that time the business was called Friedman's Appliances. It employed 15 workers in Oakland, California. Friedman's is an actual business that uses the technique you will read about.

BOB: What is the reason for your success in business?

ART: My business technique.

BOB: What is it? How did you implement it?

ART: I called my 15 employees together and told them, "From now on I want you to feel as though the company is ours, not mine. We are all bosses. From now on you decide what you're worth and tell the accountant to put it in your pay envelope. You decide which days and hours you work and when to take time off. We will have an open petty cash system that will allow anyone to go into the box and borrow money when they need it."

BOB: You're kidding, right?

ART: No, it's true. I really do these things.

BOB: Did anyone ask for a raise?

ART: Yes, several people did. Charlie asked for and received a $100-a-week raise.

BOB: Did he and the others increase their productivity to earn their raises?

ART: Yes, they all did.

BOB: How could you run an appliance store with employees coming and going as they pleased?

ART: The employees made up schedules that were satisfactory to everyone. We had no problems of under- or overstaffing.

BOB: Did anyone steal from the petty cash box?

ART: No.

BOB: Would this technique work in any business?

ART: It did work, it still works, and it will always work!!

In 1976, Art Friedman changed his strategy. Art's present business is Friedman's Microwave Ovens. It is a franchise operation, which utilizes his technique of making everyone a boss. In its first three years, Art's business grew from one store in Oakland to 20 stores, which sold over 15,000 microwaves. In 1988, Art had over 100 stores nationwide. Friedman's now sells around 125,000 microwaves per year.

Answer the following questions, supporting your answers in the space between questions.

_____ 1. Art's business technique increased performance.

        a. true   *b.* false

_____ 2. Art focused on the _____ factor in the performance formula.

        a. ability   *b.* motivation   *c.* resources

_____ 3. Art's employees seem to be on the _____ needs level.

        a. physiological   *c.* social   *e.* self-actualization
        b. safety   *d.* esteem

———— 4. Art's technique has less emphasis on meeting _____ needs.

     a. achievement   *b.* power   *c.* affiliation

———— 5. Herzberg would say Art is using

     a. hygienes   *b.* motivators

———— 6. Victor Vroom would say that Art uses expectancy motivation theory.

     a. true   *b.* false

———— 7. Adams would say Art has

     a. equitable rewards   *b.* underrewards   *c.* overrewards

———— 8. Art uses _____ reinforcement.

     a. positive   *c.* extinction

     b. avoidance   *d.* punishment

———— 9. Art's technique is most closely associated with

     a. giving praise   *c.* job enrichment

     b. MBO   *d.* job design

———— 10. Art's technique focuses most on

     a. delegating variety   *c.* making work identifiable

     b. forming natural work groups   *d.* giving autonomy

11. Do you know of any organizations that use any of Art's or other unusual techniques? If yes, what is the organization's name? What does it do?

12. Could Art's technique work in all organizations? Explain your answer.

13. In a position of authority, would you use Art's technique? Explain your answer.

Motivation

In this video, three motivation theories are briefly explained (Maslow's Needs Hierarchy, Herzberg's Two-Factor Theory, and McGregor's Theory X and Y). Tellabs employees talk about the importance of motivation to its company success.

Critical Thinking Questions:

1. What is the major difference and similarity between Maslow's Needs Hierarchy and Herzberg's Two-Factor Theory?

2. Is Tellabs more Theory X or Theory Y oriented? Give specific reasons for your answer.

3. What is the relationship between motivation and performance?

4. What motivation techniques does Tellabs use?

5. Which of Tellabs' motivation technique seems to be most important to the company?

6. Tellabs did not talk about using process motivation theories or reinforcement theory. Does this mean that it does not use these theories?

Fiscal Fairy Tale #10: Little Tim Soldier

Following the steps to getting to read a fiscal fairy tale in MG Webszine Exercise 1 in Chapter 1 page 34, go to the MG website and read *Fiscal Fairy Tale #10: Little Tim Soldier* (your instructor may ask you to print a copy and bring it to class). Answer these questions (your instructor may ask you to type them and bring them to class):

Online MG Webzine Internet Exercise 6

Questions Relating to the Tale Only

1. As stated at the end of the tale, in 50 words or so, what is your response to this tale? You may send it to MG.

2. Have you, or anyone you know, work/ed for an organization that keeps requiring more and more of its employees? Give some examples of things the organizational managers do/did.

3. Many people today are reachable at all hours of the day by pagers and cell phones. Is this a status symbol? Is it a mistreatment by the organization?

4. Does the organization show any regard for Tim's personal needs? What would you do if you were in Tim's situation?

Questions Relating the Tale to the Chapter Concepts

5. Which hierarchy of needs level is Tim on?

6. Which factor of the Two-factor Theory is the company using to motivate Tim?

7. Which manifest need motivation is dominant for Tim?

8. Does equity theory hold true in this tale? Explain.

9. Give two examples of how Tim's boss used objectives to motivate Tim.

10. Which of the two parts of expectancy theory could have failed to motivate Tim in this tale?

11. The boss's call at the end of the tale uses which "type" and which "schedule" of reinforcement? Would this praise motivate you?

12. Does Tim's boss follow all the steps in the giving praise model?

In-Class MG Webzine Internet Exercise 6

The instructor selects one of the six options from Appendix B page 589.

Motivation Fallacy or Fact (IE 6–1)

Online Internet Exercise 6–1

The objective of this exercise is to better understand how to motivate people. Use the information in Appendix B and IE 1–2 and 1–3 as you do the following:

1. Go to the Recognition Plus website homepage—*www.recognition-plus.com*
2. Click "Motivation Tips" and read the Motivation Fallacy and Fact columns (your instructor may require you to print a copy).
3. Questions: (1) Which fallacy were you least knowledgeable of or disagree with? (2) Which motivation fact is most relevant to you? Why? (3) How can you use this information to be more effective at motivating yourself and/or others? (Your instructor may ask you to type and print your answers).
4. Surf the site for other information.

In-Class Internet Exercise 6–1, IE 6–2, and IE 6–3

The instructor selects one of the six options from Appendix B page 589.

Recognition (IE 6–2)

Online Internet Exercise 6–2

The objective of this exercise is to get low-cost recognition tips that you can use to motivate others. Use the information in Appendix B and IE 1–2 and 1–3 as you do the following:

1. Go to Bob Nelson's website homepage—*www.nelson-motivation.com*
2. Click "Recognition Resources."
3. Click "Low-cost recognition ideas" and read the ideas (your instructor may require you to print a copy).
4. Questions: (1) Which three recognition ideas do you like best? (2) How can you use the ideas to be more effective at motivating yourself and/or others? (Your instructor may ask you to type and print your answers).

Motivation: MG Leader-Lines (IE 6–3)

Online Internet Exercise 6–3

The objective of this exercise is to get ideas on how you can motivate others. Use the information in Appendix B and IE 1–2 and 1–3 as you do the following:

1. Go to the MG website homepage—*www.mgeneral.com*
2. Click "Leader.Lines (News Features)," Search, find, and read an interview about motivation (your instructor may require you to print a copy).
3. Questions: (1) Who was interviewed and what was the title of the news feature? (2) In 50 words or less, what was the interview about? (3) How can you use the ideas to more effectively motivate yourself and/or others? (Your instructor may ask you to type and print your answers).

SKILL-BUILDING EXERCISE 6–1

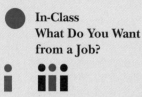

In-Class
What Do You Want
from a Job?

Objectives: To help you better understand how job factors affect motivation. To help you realize that people are motivated by different factors. What motivates you may turn someone else off.

SCANS: The SCANS competencies of resources, interpersonal skills, information, and systems and the foundations of basic, thinking, and personal qualities are developed through this exercise.

Preparation: You should have completed Self-Assessment Exercise 6–1.

Experience: You will discuss the importance of job factors.

Procedure 1
(8–20 minutes)

Break into groups of five or six, and discuss job factors selected by group members in Self-Assessment Exercise 6–1. Come to a consensus on the three factors that are most important to the group. They can be either motivators or hygienes. If the group mentions other job factors not listed, such as pay, you may add them.

Procedure 2
(3–6 minutes)

A representative from each group goes to the board and writes its group's three most important job factors.

Conclusion: The instructor leads a class discussion and/or makes concluding remarks.

Application (2–4 minutes):   What did I learn from this experience? How will I use this knowledge in the future?

Sharing: Volunteers give their answers to the application section.

SKILL-BUILDING EXERCISE 6–2

Preparation
Giving Praise

BM–6

Think of a job situation in which you did something well, deserving of praise and recognition. For example, you may have saved the company some money, you may have turned a dissatisfied customer into a happy one, and so on. If you have never worked or done something well, interview someone who has. Put yourself in a supervisory position and write out the praise you would give to an employee for doing what you did.

Briefly describe the situation:

Step 1. Tell the employee exactly what was done correctly.

Step 2. Tell the employee why the behavior is important.

Step 3. Stop for a moment of silence. (Count to five silently to yourself.)

Step 4. Encourage repeat performance.

**In-Class
Giving Praise**

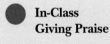
SB 6–1

Procedure (12–17 minutes)

Objective: To develop your skill at giving praise.

SCANS: The SCANS competencies of information and especially interpersonal skills and the foundations of basic, thinking, and especially personal qualities are developed through this exercise.

Preparation: You will need your prepared praise.

Experience: You will give and receive praise.

Break into groups of five or six. One at a time, give the praise.

1. Explain the situation.

2. Select a group member to receive the praise.

3. Give the praise. (Talk; don't read it off the paper.) Try to select the position you would use if you were actually giving the praise on the job. (Both standing, both sitting, etc.)

4. Integration. The group gives the giver of praise feedback on how he or she did:

- Step 1. Was the praise very specific and descriptive? Did the giver look the employee in the eye?
- Step 2. Was the importance of the behavior clearly stated?
- Step 3. Did the giver stop for a moment of silence?
- Step 4. Did the giver encourage repeat performance? Did the giver of praise touch the receiver [optional]?
- Did the praise take less than one minute? Was the praise sincere?

Conclusion: The instructor leads a class discussion and/or makes concluding remarks.

Application (2–4 minutes):   What did I learn from this experience? How will I use this knowledge in the future?

Sharing: Volunteers give their answers to the application section.

SKILL-BUILDING EXERCISE 6–3

 Preparation Setting Objectives

In Chapter 1, you were asked to write five course objectives. Rewrite the five objectives, or new ones, using the Douglas model below:

Infinitive + action verb + singular behavior, specific and measurable + target date

1.

2.

3.

4.

5.

Also, write two personal objectives and two career objectives using the model:

Personal

1.

2.

Career

1.

2.

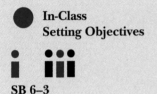

In-Class
Setting Objectives

SB 6–3

Procedure (2–12 minutes)

Objective: To gain skill at setting objectives.

SCANS: The SCANS competencies of resources and information and the foundation of basic and thinking qualities are developed through this exercise.

Preparation: A. You should have written nine objectives in the preparation for the exercise.

Break into groups of five to six people and share your objectives. One person states one objective and the others give input to be sure it meets the criteria of effective objectives. A second person states one objective, followed by feedback. Continue until all group members have stated all their objectives or the time runs out.

Conclusion: The instructor may lead a discussion and/or make concluding remarks.

Leadership

7

Learning Objectives

After completing this chapter, you should be able to:

1. Explain what leadership is and how it affects behavior, human relations, and performance.
2. Describe leadership trait theory.
3. List and describe four behavioral leadership theories.
4. List and describe four contingency leadership theories.
5. Explain four situational supervisory styles.
6. Identify three characteristics that substitute for leadership.
7. Define the following 13 key terms (in order of appearance in the chapter):

leadership
leadership trait theory
behavioral leadership theories
Leadership Grid®
contingency leadership theories
contingency leadership theory

leadership continuum
normative leadership theory
situational leadership
autocratic style
consultative style
participative style
laissez-faire style

Chapter Outline

Leadership
Why Leadership Skills Are Important
Leadership and Management Are Not the Same
How Leadership Affects Behavior, Human Relations, and Performance

Leadership Trait Theory
The Ghiselli Study
Current Studies

Behavioral Leadership Theories
Basic Leadership Styles
Two-Dimensional Leadership Styles
The Leadership Grid®
Transformational Leadership

Contingency Leadership Theories
Contingency Leadership Theory
Leadership Continuum
Normative Leadership Theory
Situational Leadership

Situational Supervision
Defining the Situation
Using the Appropriate Supervisory Style
Applying the Situational Supervision Model

Putting the Leadership Theories Together

Substitutes for Leadership

Diversity of Global Leadership

mike Templeton is a branch manager at the Westfall Bank. Mike has authority over subordinates to make decisions regarding hiring and firing, raises, and promotions. Mike gets along well with his subordinates. The branch atmosphere is friendly. His boss has asked for a special report about the loans the branch has made so far this year. Mike could have done the report himself, but he thought it would be better to delegate the task to one of the three loan officers. After thinking about the qualifications of the three loan officers, Mike selected Jean. He called her into his office to talk about the assignment.

MIKE: Hi, Jean, I've called you in here to tell you that I've selected you to do a year-to-date loan report for the branch. It's not mandatory; I can assign the report to someone else. Are you interested?

JEAN: I don't know; I've never done a report before.

MIKE: I realize that, but I'm sure you can handle it. I selected you because of my faith in your ability.

JEAN: Will you help me?

MIKE: Sure. There is more than one way to do the report. I can give you the details on what must be included in the report, but you can use any format you want, as long as I approve it. We can discuss the report now; then as you work on it, you can come to me for input. I'm confident you'll do a great job. Do you want the assignment?

JEAN: Okay, I'll do it.

Mike and Jean discuss how she will do the report together.

What leadership style would you use to get the report done? This chapter explains 11 leadership theories. Each theory will be applied to the loan report. There are many leadership theories that can be used with a diverse global work force. A style that is effective with one group may not be effective with other groups.

● Organization
● Group
● Individual

Leadership

Leadership is one of the most talked-about, researched, and written-about management topics. Ralph Stogdill's well-known *Handbook of Leadership* contains over 3,000 references on the topic, and Bass's revision of it contains well over 5,000 references.[1] Academics and practitioners alike agree that leadership is the most important topic of all within the realm of organizational behavior/human relations.[2] **Leadership** *is the process of influencing employees to work toward the achievement of objectives.*

In this section, we explain why leadership skills are important; the difference between leadership and management; and how leadership affects behavior, human relations, and performance.

Why Leadership Skills Are Important

Leadership qualities can propel a person to a successful and happy career.[3] Job satisfaction stems from leadership.[4] However, employees feel managers are failing to develop leadership skills[5] and the main reason for employee failure is poor leadership.[6] We need more and better leaders.[7]

Strong leadership is needed.[8] With today's focus on teamwork, leadership ability is important to everyone in the organization, not just managers.[9] The definition of leadership does not suggest that influencing employees is the task of the manager alone; employees influence other employees.[10] Anyone can be a leader within any group/department, and everyone in a team is expected to be a leader.[11] Part of team training includes leadership skills development.[12]

WORK APPLICATIONS

1. Give detailed reasons why leadership skills are important to a specific organization.

Leadership and Management Are Not the Same

People tend to use the terms *manager* and *leader* interchangeably. However, this is not correct. Management and leadership are different but related concepts. Leadership is one of the five management functions. The five functions include planning, organizing, staffing, leading, and controlling. Someone can be a manager without being a true leader. There are managers—you may know of some—who are not leaders because they do not have the ability to influence others. They tell employees to do something, but the employees don't do it. There are also good leaders who are not managers.[13] The informal leader, an employee group member, is a case in point. You may have worked in a situation where one of your peers had more influence in the department than the manager. Managers are sparing leadership responsibility.[14]

- Performance
- Human Relations
- Behavior

How Leadership Affects Behavior, Human Relations, and Performance

There are different styles of leadership. The leader's style affects the leader's behavior.[15] In other words, the leader's behavior actually makes the leader's style.[16] An autocratic leader displays different behavior than a democratic leader. The human relations between leader and follower will differ according to the leadership style.[17] This will be explained in more detail throughout the chapter.

Leadership does have a causal impact on performance. However, it is difficult to demonstrate the direct relationship between performance and leadership because of the number of variables influencing performance.

Leadership can make a difference in performance, though it does not always do so. The leader's behavior can have a positive or negative impact on others' performance. Truly outstanding leaders tend to elicit highly effective performance from others.[18] However, the number of such leaders is small. These outstanding leaders are called *transformational leaders;*[19] we will discuss them later in this chapter.

For years researchers have been trying to answer the questions: "What does it take to be an effective leader?" and "What is the most effective leadership style?" There is no universal agreement about the answers to these questions. We will now turn to a chronological review of how researchers have tried to answer these questions. After studying the major leadership theories, you can select the one you like best or develop your own.

Learning Objective

1. Explain what leadership is and how it affects behavior, human relations, and performance

- Organization
- Group
- Individual

Leadership Trait Theory

In the early 1900s, an organized approach to studying leadership began. The early studies were based on the assumption that leaders are born, not made. It was later called the "great man" theory of leadership. Researchers wanted to identify a set of characteristics or traits that distinguished leaders from followers or effective from ineffective leaders. **Leadership trait theory** *assumes that there are distinctive physical and psychological characteristics accounting for leadership effectiveness.* Researchers analyzed traits, or qualities, such as appearance, aggressiveness, self-reliance, persuasiveness, and dominance in an effort to identify a set of traits that all successful leaders possessed. The list of traits was to be used as a prerequisite for promotion of candidates to leadership positions. Only candidates possessing all the identified traits were to be given leadership positions.

Inconclusive Findings: In 70 years, over 300 trait studies were conducted.[20] However, no one has come up with a universal list of traits that all successful leaders possess. In all cases, there were exceptions. For example, several lists identified successful leaders as being tall. However, Napoleon was short. In addition, some people were successful in one leadership position but not in another.

People also questioned whether traits like assertiveness and self-confidence were developed before or after one became a leader. It is practically impossible to uncover a universal set of traits. Indeed, if leaders were simply born and not made (or in other words, if leadership skills could not be developed), there would be no need for courses in management and human relations.

The Ghiselli Study

Probably the most widely publicized trait theory study was conducted by Edwin Ghiselli.[21] His study concluded that there are traits important to effective leadership, though not all are necessary for success. Ghiselli identified the following six traits, in order of importance, as being significant traits for effective leadership:

1. *Supervisory ability.* Getting the job done through others. Basically, the ability to perform the five functions of management. You develop skills in this course.

2. *Need for occupational achievement.* Seeking responsibility. The motivation to work hard to succeed (Chapter 6).

3. *Intelligence.* The ability to use good judgment, reasoning, and thinking capacity (Chapter 2).

4. *Decisiveness.* The ability to solve problems and make decisions competently (Chapter 10).

5. *Self-assurance.* Viewing oneself as capable of coping with problems. Behaving in a manner that shows others that you have self-confidence (Chapter 3).

6. *Initiative.* Self-starting in getting the job done with a minimum of supervision from one's boss (Chapter 6).

In the opening case, Mike appears to have supervisory ability. He is getting the job done through Jean, using the supervisory process. Based on the case, one cannot determine if Mike has traits two through six.

Current Studies

Even though it is generally agreed that there is no universal set of leadership traits/qualities, people continue to study and write about leadership traits. For example, in *The Wall Street Journal*/Gallup survey, 782 top executives in 282 large corporations were asked, "What are the most important traits for success as a supervisor?"[22] Before the results are revealed, complete Self-Assessment Exercise 7–1 to determine if you have the qualities necessary to be a successful manager.

IE 7–1

Self-Assessment Exercise 7–1

Supervisory Traits

Select the response that best describes the frequency of your actual behavior. Place the number 1–5 on the line before each statement.

Almost always	Usually	Frequently	Occasionally	Seldom
5	4	3	2	1

_____ 1. I am trustworthy. If I say I will do something by a set time, I do it.

_____ 2. I am loyal. I do not do or say things that hurt my friends, relatives, coworkers, boss, etc.

_____ 3. I can take criticism. If people tell me negative things about myself, I give them serious thought and change when appropriate.

_____ 4. I am honest. I do not lie, steal, cheat, etc.

_____ 5. I am fair. I treat people equally. I don't take advantage of others.

_____ 6. I want to be successful. I do things to the best of my ability.

_____ 7. I am a self-starter. I get things done without having to be told to do them.

_____ 8. I am a problem solver. If things aren't going the way I want them to, I take corrective action to meet my objectives. I don't give up easily.

_____ 9. I am self-reliant. I don't need the help of others.

_____ 10. I am hardworking. I enjoy working and getting the job done.

_____ 11. I enjoy working with people. I prefer to work with others rather than working alone.

_____ 12. I can motivate others. I can get people to do things they may not really want to do.

_____ 13. I am respected. People enjoy working with me.

_____ 14. I am cooperative. I strive to help the team do well, rather than to be the star.

_____ 15. I am a leader. I enjoy teaching, coaching, and instructing people.

Self-Assessment
Exercise 7–1 *continued*

To determine your score, transfer the numbers 1–5 that represent your responses below. The column headings represent the trait/quality listed in each statement. Total each column and the total of the three columns.

Integrity	Industriousness	Ability to Get Along with People	
____ 1.	____ 6.	____ 11.	
____ 2.	____ 7.	____ 12.	
____ 3.	____ 8.	____ 13.	
____ 4.	____ 9.	____ 14.	
____ 5.	____ 10.	____ 15.	
____ Total	____ Total	____ Total	____ Grand Total

Your score for each column will range from 5–25, and your grand total will range from 15 to 75. In general, the higher your score, the better your chances of being a successful manager. If you are interested in being (or are) a manager, you can work on improving your integrity, industriousness, and ability to get along with others. As a start, review the list of traits. In which were you strongest (5)? Weakest (1)? Set objectives and develop plans to improve.

The Wall Street Journal/Gallup survey answers revealed integrity, industriousness, and the ability to get along with people as the three most important traits for success. The survey also identified traits that lead to failure in a managers: having a limited viewpoint, not being able to understand others, not being able to work with others, being indecisive, lacking initiative, not assuming responsibility, lacking integrity, lacking the ability to change, reluctance to think independently, inability to solve problems, and wanting to be popular.

It is clear that certain traits can help you to be a successful manager, professional, or worker. You should try to develop these traits. The important thing is how you use these traits on the job. During this course, you should develop your abilities through the skill-building approach the text takes.

Learning Objective

2. Describe leadership trait theory

WORK APPLICATIONS

2. What are your views on leadership trait theory? Recall a manager you have or had. Which of Ghiselli's six traits does the person have? Which traits does the person lack?

● Organization
● Group
● Individual

Behavioral Leadership Theories

By the late 1940s, most of the leadership research had changed from trait theory and focused on what the leader did. In the continuing quest to find the one best leadership style in all situations, studies attempted to identify the differences in the behavior of effective leaders versus ineffective leaders. **Behavioral leadership theories** *assume that there are distinctive styles that effective leaders use consistently, or, that good leadership is rooted in behavior.*[23]

In this section, you will learn the basic leadership styles, two-dimensional leadership styles, the Managerial Grid, System 4, and transformational leadership.

Basic Leadership Styles

In the 1930s, before behavioral theory became popular, studies at the University of Iowa concentrated on the manner or style (behavior) of the leader. Their studies identified three basic leadership styles: *Autocratic:* The leader makes the decisions and closely supervises employees; *Democratic:* The leader allows participation in decisions and does not closely supervise employees; *Laissez-Faire:* The leader takes a leave-the-employees-alone approach.

The studies concluded that the democratic style was the most desirable and productive. However, later research revealed cases in which the democratic style was not more productive. The Iowa studies contributed further to the human relations movement and ushered in an era of attention to behavior rather than trait research.

In the opening case, Mike is using the democratic style because he is allowing Jean to participate in the format of the report.

Two-Dimensional Leadership Styles

Structuring and Consideration Styles

In 1945, Ohio State University began a study to determine effective leadership styles. In the attempt to measure leadership styles, they developed an instrument known as the Leader Behavior Description Questionnaire (LBDQ). Respondents to the questionnaire perceived their leaders' behavior toward them on two distinct dimensions:[24]

- *Initiating structure.* The extent to which the leader takes charge to plan, organize, direct, and control as the employee performs the task.
- *Consideration.* The extent to which the leader communicates to develop trust, friendship, support, and respect.

Job-Centered and Employee-Centered Styles

At approximately the same time the Ohio State studies began, the University of Michigan's Survey Research Center began leadership studies. Their research also identified the same two dimensions or styles of leadership behavior. However, they called the two styles:[25]

- *Job centered.* This is the same as initiating structure. The managerial grid (to be discussed next) refers to this dimension as concern for production.
- *Employee centered.* This is the same as consideration. The managerial grid refers to this dimension as concern for people.

Using Leadership Styles

When interacting with employees, the supervisor can engage in directive (initiating structure, job centered, concern for production) and/or supportive (consideration, employee centered, concern for people) behavior. In an attempt to determine how these two variables affect employee satisfaction and performance, various studies were conducted. The studies concluded that, generally, high support leads to high employee satisfaction. However, the performance results were inconclusive. Some managers with low support (concern for employees) had high performance levels.

Different combinations of the two dimensions of leadership result in four leadership styles, illustrated in Exhibit 7–1, Two-Dimensional Leadership Models.

In the opening case, Mike is using the high-consideration (employee-centered) and low-structure (job-centered) style, box three, because he is telling Jean what needs to be in the report, but how she does the report is up to her. Mike also offers supportive statements.

The Leadership Grid®

Robert Blake and Jane Mouton developed the Managerial Grid® and published it in 1964,[26] updated it in 1978[27] and 1985,[28] and in 1991 it became the Leadership Grid® with Anne Adams McCanse replacing Mouton.[29] The Leadership Grid was recently applied to project management by different researchers.[30]

EXHIBIT 7–1   **TWO-DIMENSIONAL LEADERSHIP MODELS**

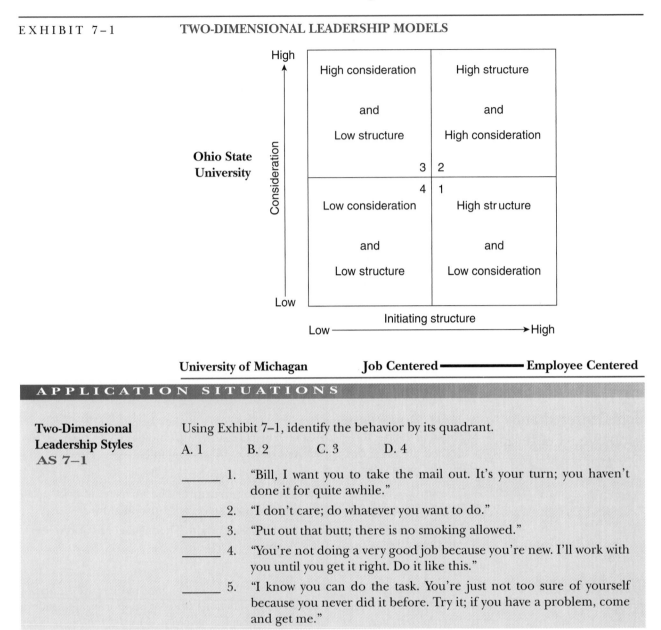

Ohio State University

University of Michagan   Job Centered ————————— Employee Centered

---

APPLICATION SITUATIONS

Two-Dimensional Leadership Styles AS 7–1

Using Exhibit 7–1, identify the behavior by its quadrant.

A. 1   B. 2   C. 3   D. 4

_____ 1. "Bill, I want you to take the mail out. It's your turn; you haven't done it for quite awhile."

_____ 2. "I don't care; do whatever you want to do."

_____ 3. "Put out that butt; there is no smoking allowed."

_____ 4. "You're not doing a very good job because you're new. I'll work with you until you get it right. Do it like this."

_____ 5. "I know you can do the task. You're just not too sure of yourself because you never did it before. Try it; if you have a problem, come and get me."

The Leadership Grid is based on the two leadership dimensions called *concern for production* and *concern for people*. The **Leadership Grid** *is Blake and Mouton's model identifying the ideal leadership style as having a high concern for both production and people.* The grid has 81 possible combinations of concern for production and people. However, they identify five major styles:[31]

(1,1) *The impoverished manager.* This leader has low concern for both production and people. The leader does the minimum required to remain employed in the position.

(9,1) *The sweatshop manager.* This leader has a high concern for production and a low concern for people. The leader uses position power to coerce employees to do the work. People are treated like machines.

(1,9) *The country club manager.* This leader has a high concern for people and a low concern for production. The leader strives to maintain relations and a friendly atmosphere.

(5,5) *The organized-person manager.* This leader has balanced, medium concern for both production and people. The leader strives to maintain satisfactory middle-of-the-road performance and morale.

(9,9) *The team manager.* This leader has a high concern for both production and people. This leader strives for maximum performance and employee satisfaction. Participation, commitment, and conflict resolution are emphasized.

The horizontal axis of the grid (see Exhibit 7–2) represents the concern for production, and the vertical axis represents the concern for people. Each axis is on a 1–9 point scale. The 1 indicates low concern, while the 9 indicates high concern.

Through grid training, which is still being used today, managers fill in an instrument that indicates what they would do in certain situations. The results are scored to indicate where they are on the Leadership Grid, one of the 81 combinations of concern for production and people. They go through training designed to help them become ideal 9,9 managers, having a high concern for both production and people.

EXHIBIT 7-2   **THE LEADERSHIP GRID**

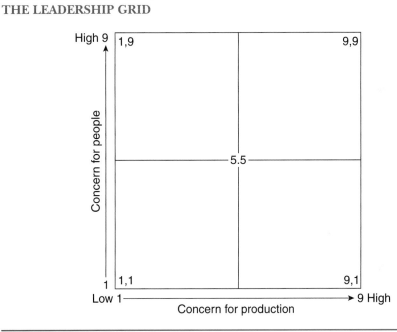

Source: The Leadership Grid® Figure (adapted from *Leadership Dilemmas—Grid Solutions* by Robert R. Blake and Anne Adams McCanse. Houston: Gulf Publishing Company, p. 29. Copyright © 1991, by Scientific Methods, Inc.

In the opening case, Mike has a high concern for getting the report done and a high concern for Jean. If you had to select one of the five major styles, you would probably choose the 9,9 team leader. However, Mike is giving more support to Jean than direction for doing the report. Mike is actually using closer to a 9,7 leadership style.

WORK APPLICATIONS

3. What are your views on the Leadership Grid? Recall a manager you have or had. Which of the five styles does the manager use?

Transformational Leadership

Transformational leadership, a contemporary view of leadership, is a behavioral theory because it focuses on the behavior of successful leaders. Studies conducted

The Leadership Grid

AS 7–2

Identify the five statements by their leader's style. (Exhibit 7–2)

A. 1,1 (impoverished)   C. 9,1 (sweatshop)   E. 9,9 (team manager)
B. 1,9 (country club)   D. 5,5 (organized)

_____ 6. The group has very high morale; they enjoy their work. Productivity in the department is one of the lowest in the company.

_____ 7. The group has adequate morale. They have an average productivity level.

_____ 8. The group is one of the top performers. They have high morale.

_____ 9. The group has one of the lowest levels of morale. It is one of the top performers.

_____ 10. The group is one of the lowest producers. It has a low level of morale.

looked at successful leaders to determine the behavior they use to make their organizations successful.[32] The focus of transformational leadership is on top-level managers, primarily chief executive officers of large organizations.

Transformational leadership is about change, innovation, and entrepreneurship.[33] Transformational leaders perform, or take the organization through, three acts, on an ongoing basis:[34]

Act 1. Recognizing the need for revitalization: The transformational leader recognizes the need to change the organization in order to keep up with the rapid changes in the environment and to keep ahead of the global competition, which is becoming more competitive all the time.

Act 2. Creating a new vision: The transformational leader visualizes the changed organization and motivates people to make it become a reality.

Act 3. Institutionalizing change: The transformational leader guides people as they make the vision become a reality.

Learning Objective

3. List and describe five behavioral leadership theories

Some of the characteristics or traits of transformational leaders include: (1) they see themselves as change agents; (2) they are courageous individuals who take risks; (3) they believe in people and motivate them; (4) they are value driven; (5) they are life-long learners; (6) they have the ability to deal with complexity, ambiguity, and uncertainty; (7) and they are visionaries. These traits are evident during leader-member exchanges.[35]

Transformational leaders include: Mary Ann Lawlor, CEO, Drake Business Schools; Michael Blumenthal, CEO, Burroughs Corporation; Jeffery Campbell, president, Burger King; James Sparks, CEO, Whirlpool Corporation; Jack Welch, Chairperson, General Electric; and James Renier, vice-chairperson, Honeywell. Although Martin Luther King, Jr., was not viewed as an organizational leader, his "I Have a Dream" speech can be considered an example of transformational leadership.

Charismatic Leadership

Transformational leaders can also be charismatic leaders. There is a theory of charismatic leadership.[36] Charismatic leaders inspire loyalty, enthusiasm, and high levels of performance. But they may not take the organization through the three acts.

Transactional Leadership

Transactional leadership has been contrasted with transactional leadership.[37] The transaction is based on the principle of "you do this work for me and I'll give this reward to you." Transactional leadership focuses more on middle and first-line managers who help the transformational leader take their unit through the three acts.

IE 7–2

▲ Goal of
  Human Relations

● Organization
● Group
● Individual

In the opening case, Mike is not a transformational leader as he is not a top-level manager capable of changing the entire bank. Mike is a middle-level branch manager, and he is a transactional leader.

Behavioral leadership theories attempt to create a win–win situation. In general, behavioral theories suggest a high concern for employees, allowing them to participate in decision making that meets their higher-level needs. Participation is a motivator (not a hygiene) because it meets employees' needs for esteem/self-actualization, growth, and power/achievement.

Contingency Leadership Theories

Both the trait and behavioral leadership theories were attempts to find the one best leadership style in all situations. In the late 1960s, it became apparent that there is no one best leadership style in all situations. Both the Ohio State and University of Michigan studies revealed that no set of leader behaviors is effective in all situations. **Contingency leadership theories** *assume that the appropriate leadership style varies from situation to situation.*

In this section, you will learn some of the most popular contingency leadership theories, including contingency leadership theory, leadership continuum, normative leadership theory, and situational leadership.

Contingency Leadership Theory

In 1951, Fred E. Fiedler began to develop the first situational leadership theory. He called the theory "Contingency Theory of Leader Effectiveness."[39] Fiedler believed that one's leadership style is a reflection of one's personality (trait theory oriented) and is basically constant. Leaders do not change styles. **Contingency leadership theory** *is Fiedler's model used to determine if one's leadership style is task or relationship oriented, and if the situation matches the leader's style.* If there is no match, Fiedler recommends (and trains people to) change the situation, rather than their leadership styles.

Leadership Style: The first major factor is to determine whether one's leadership style is task or relationship oriented. To do so, the leader fills in the Least Preferred Coworker (LPC) scales. This is followed by determining the favorableness of the leader's situation.

Situational Favorableness: Situation favorableness refers to the degree to which a situation enables the leader to exert influence over the followers. The three variables, in order of importance, are:

1. *Leader-member relations.* Is the relationship good or poor? Do the followers trust, respect, accept, and have confidence in the leader? Is it a friendly, tension-free situation? Leaders with good relations have more influence. The better the relations, the more favorable the situation.

2. *Task structure.* Is the task structured or unstructured? Do employees perform routine, unambiguous, standard tasks that are easily understood? Leaders in a structured situation have more influence. The more structured the jobs are, the more favorable the situation.

3. *Position power.* Is position power strong or weak? Does the leader have the power to assign work, reward and punish, hire and fire, and give raises and promotions? The leader with position power has more influence. The more power, the more favorable the situation.

Determining the Appropriate Leadership Style: To determine whether task or relationship leadership is appropriate, the user answers the three questions pertaining to situational favorableness, using the Fiedler contingency theory model. See Exhibit 7–3 for an adapted model. The user starts with question 1 and follows the decision tree to determine the situation (1–7) and appropriate leadership style (task or relationship).

One of the criticisms is the view that the leader should change his or her style rather than the situation. The other contingency writers in this chapter take this position. Fiedler has thus helped contribute to the other contingency theories.

In the opening case, Mike has good relations with Jean, the task is unstructured, and Mike's position power is strong. This is situation 3, in which the appropriate leadership style is task (Exhibit 7–3). However, Mike is using a relationship style. Fiedler would suggest that Mike change the situation to meet his preferred relationship style.

EXHIBIT 7–3	FIEDLER'S CONTINGENCY THEORY MODEL

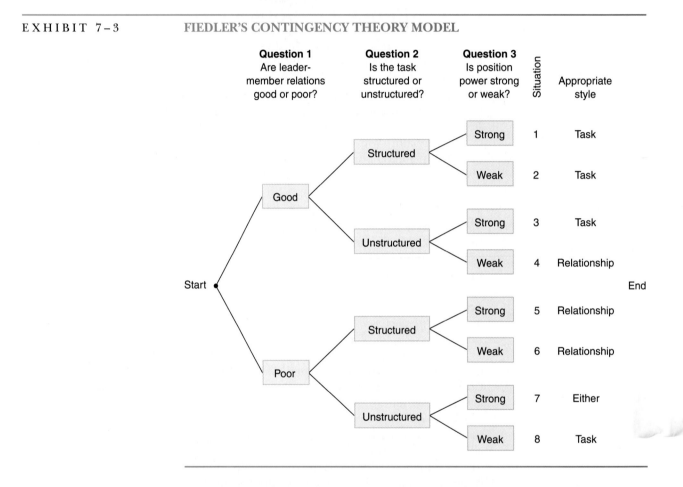

WORK APPLICATIONS

4. What are your views on contingency leadership theory? Do you agree with Fiedler's recommendation to change the situation rather than the leader's style?

Skill-Building

7–2A

Leadership Continuum

Robert Tannenbaum and Warren Schmidt stated that leadership behavior is on a continuum from boss-centered to employee-centered leadership. Their model focuses on who makes the decisions. They identify seven major styles the leader can choose from. Exhibit 7–4 is an adaptation of their model, which lists the seven styles.[39] **Leadership continuum** *is Tannenbaum and Schmidt's model that identifies seven leadership styles based on one's use of boss-centered versus employee-centered leadership.*

APPLICATION SITUATIONS

Contingency Leadership Theory

AS 7–3

Using Exhibit 7–3, determine the situation number with its corresponding appropriate leadership style. Select two answers.

A. 1   B. 2   C. 3   D. 4   E. 5   F. 6   G. 7   H. 8

A. Task oriented   B. Relationship oriented

_____ 11. Ben, the supervisor, oversees the assembly of mass-produced containers. He has the power to reward and punish. Ben is viewed as a hard-nosed supervisor.

_____ 12. Jean, the manager, is from the corporate planning staff. She helps the other departments plan. Jean is viewed as being a dreamer; she doesn't understand their departments. People tend to be rude in their dealings with Jean.

_____ 13. Ron, the supervisor, oversees the processing of canceled checks for the bank. He is well liked by the employees. Ron's boss enjoys hiring and evaluating his employees' performance.

_____ 14. Connie, the principal of a school, assigns teachers to classes and other various duties. She hires and decides on tenure appointments. The school atmosphere is tense.

_____ 15. Len, the chairperson of the committee, is highly regarded by its volunteer members from a variety of departments. They are charged with recommending ways to increase organizational performance.

EXHIBIT 7–4   CONTINUUM OF LEADERSHIP BEHAVIOR

Leader makes decision and announces it	Leader "sells" decision	Leader presents ideas and invites questions	Leader presents tentative decision subject to change	Leader presents problem, gets suggestions, and makes decision	Leader defines limits and asks group to make decision	Leader permits subordinates to function within limits defined by leader
1	2	3	4	5	6	7

Autocratic style / Participative style

Before selecting one of the seven leadership styles, the user must consider the following three factors or variables:

The Manager: What is the leader's preferred style, based on experience, expectation, values, background, knowledge, feeling of security, and confidence in the subordinates?

The Subordinates: What is the subordinates' preferred style for the leader, based on experience, expectation, and so on as above? Generally, the more willing and able the subordinates are to participate, the more freedom to participate should be given, and vice versa.

The Situation: What are the environmental considerations, such as the organization's size, structure, climate, goals, and technology? Upper-level managers also influence leadership styles.

As you read about the situational variables, you will realize that they are descriptive; the model does not state which style to use in a situation. The leadership styles discussed in the next two sections developed models that tell the leader which style to use in a given situation.

In the opening case, Mike began the discussion using style 4, in which the leader presents a tentative decision subject to change. Jean did not have to do the report. Mike would have given it to another employee if she did not want to do it. Mike also used style 5, leader presents problem—need for report and what must be included in report—and told Jean he would allow her to select the form, subject to his final decision of approval.

WORK APPLICATIONS

5. What are your views on the leadership continuum? Recall a manager you have or had. Which of the seven styles does or did the manager use?

APPLICATION SITUATIONS

Leadership Continuum

AS 7–4

Using Exhibit 7–4, identify the five statements by their style.

A. 1   B. 2   C. 3   D. 4   E. 5   F. 6   G. 7

_____ 16. "Samantha, I selected you to be transferred to the new department, but you don't have to go if you don't want to."

_____ 17. "Sally, go clean off the tables right away."

_____ 18. "From now on, this is the way it will be done. Does anyone have any question about the procedure?"

_____ 19. "These are the two weeks we can go on vacation. You select one."

_____ 20. "I'd like your ideas on how to stop the bottleneck on the line. But I have the final say on the solution we implement."

Normative Leadership Theory

Based on empirical research into managerial decision making, Victor Vroom and Philip Yetton attempted to bridge the gap between leadership theory and managerial practice. To do so they developed a model that tells the manager which leadership style to use in a given situation.[40] **Normative leadership theory** *is Vroom and Yetton's decision-tree model that enables the user to select one of five leadership styles appropriate for the situation.*

Leadership Styles

Vroom and Yetton identify five leadership styles. Two are autocratic (AI and AII), two are consultative (CI and CII), and one is group oriented (GII).

AI. The leader makes the decision alone using available information.

AII. The leader gets information from subordinates but makes the decision alone. Subordinates may or may not be told what the problem is. They are not asked for input into the decision.

CI. The leader meets individually with subordinates, explains the situation, and gets information and ideas on how to solve the problem. The leader makes the final decision alone. The leader may or may not use the subordinates' input.

CII. The leader meets with subordinates as a group, explains the situation, and gets information and ideas on how to solve the problem. The leader makes the decision alone after the meeting. Leaders may or may not use the subordinates' input.

GII. The leader meets with the subordinates as a group, explains the situation, and allows the group to make the decision.

Determining the Appropriate Leadership: To determine the appropriate style for a specific situation, the user answers eight questions. The questions are based on two major variables, quality and acceptance of the decision. Questions 1–3 and 8 relate to quality of the decision, while Questions 4–7 relate to the acceptance of the decision. The questions are sequential and are presented in a decision-tree format similar to the Fiedler model in Exhibit 7–3. The eight questions are:

1. Is there a quality requirement such that one solution is likely to be more rational than another?

2. Do I have sufficient information to make a high-quality decision?

3. Is the problem structured?

4. Is acceptance of a decision by subordinates critical to effective implementation?

5. If I were to make the decision by myself, is it reasonably certain that it would be accepted by my subordinates?

6. Do subordinates share the organizational goals to be attained in solving the problem?

7. Is conflict among subordinates likely in the preferred solution (not relevant to individual problems)?

8. Do subordinates have sufficient information to make a high-quality decision?

Normative leadership has developed to the point of having four models to chose from based on the decision. Is the decision individual or group? Is it time or developmental driven? With four models, five leadership styles, and eight decision-diagnostic questions to answer, normative leadership is the most complex contingency theory. There is now a computerized version using mathematical functions.[41]

In the opening case, Mike used the CI consultative individual style. Mike told Jean that she could select the style subject to his approval. Mike makes the final decision based on Jean's input.

> ### WORK APPLICATIONS

6. What are your views on normative leadership theory? Recall a manager you have or had. Which of the five styles does or did the manager use?

Situational Leadership

The term **situational leadership** *is Hersey and Blanchard's model for selecting one of four leadership styles that matches the employees' maturity level in a given situation.* For the most part, situational leadership[42] takes the two-dimensional leadership styles, four quadrants (see Exhibit 7–1), and develops four leadership styles, which they call telling (lower-right quadrant—high structure, low consideration); selling (upper-right quadrant—high structure, high consideration); participating (upper-left quadrant—high consideration, low structure); and delegating (lower-left quadrant—low consideration, low structure). Situational leadership is also based on the life-cycle theory of leadership.[43] Hersey and Blanchard went beyond the behavioral theory by developing a model that tells the leader which style to use in a given situation. To determine the leadership style, one determines the followers' maturity level. If it is low, the leader uses a telling style; if it is moderate to low, the leader uses a selling style; if it is moderate to high, the leader uses the participating style; and if it is high, the leader uses a delegating style.

Hersey and Blanchard's model is also different in another way. The situational model uses the same four quadrants as the Ohio State model with the same two leadership dimensions using the same four styles of leadership, but using different names (task and relationship rather than structure and consideration). However, within the four quadrants, they place a bell-shaped curve, and below the four quadrants they list the four maturity levels going from left (mature) to right (immature). Exhibit 7–5 is an adaptation.

EXHIBIT 7–5   SITUATIONAL LEADERSHIP MODEL

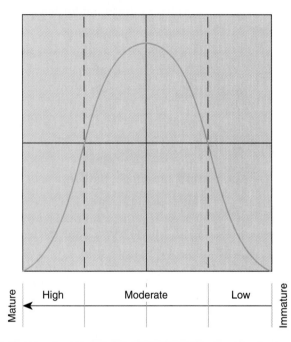

IE 7–3

Learning Objective

4. List and describe four contingency leadership theories

Organization

Group

Individual

In the opening case, Mike used the participative style with Jean. Since Mike had a higher concern for Jean than for the task, he gave Jean more support than directions. Mike gave her the specifics of what had to be included, but he let her decide on the format, subject to his approval.

In general, contingency leadership theories attempt to create a win-win situation by giving the follower(s) the support and direction they need. Overdirecting can frustrate the employee with a need for esteem/growth/power. Not providing enough support can frustrate the employee with a need for social/relatedness/affiliation-achievement.

See Exhibit 7–6 for a review of the major theories of leadership.

Situational Supervision

In this section we discuss situational supervision, which is an adaptation of Hersey and Blanchard's situational leadership model. The primary differences between the two approaches are the terms used and the model itself. It is similar to the situational communication model in Chapter 5. It begins with Self-Assessment Exercise 7–2, which identifies preferred leadership styles. Next follows a presentation of the situational supervision theory. Application of this model produces situational supervisors who change leadership styles to meet the capability level of their followers. Using a variety of leadership styles with a diverse work force is often necessary.[44]

EXHIBIT 7–6 **LEADERSHIP THEORIES**

LEADERSHIP TRAIT THEORY

Assumes that there are distinctive physical and psychological characteristics accounting for leadership effectiveness.

BEHAVIORAL LEADERSHIP THEORIES

Assumes that there are distinctive styles that effective leaders use consistently.

Basic Leadership Styles

Autocratic, democratic, laissez-faire.

Two-Dimensional Leadership Styles

Structuring/job-centered and consideration/employee-centered styles.

Managerial Grid

Blake and Mouton's model identifying the ideal leadership style as having high concern for both product and people.

Transformational Leadership

Take the organization through three acts on an ongoing basis.

Major Theories of Leadership

CONTINGENCY LEADERSHIP THEORIES

Assume that the appropriate leadership style varies from situation to situation.

Contingency Leadership Theory

Fiedler's model used to determine if one's leadership style is task or relationship oriented, and if the situation matches one's style.

Leadership Continuum

Tannenbaum and Scmidt's model that identifies seven leadership styles based on the use of boss-centered versus employee-centered leadership.

Normative Leadership Theory

Vroom and Yetton's decision-tree model that enables the user to select one of five leadership styles that is appropriate for the situation.

Situation Leadership

Hersy and Blanchar's model for selecting one of four leadership styles that matches the employee's maturity level in a given situation.

Self-Assessment Exercise 7–2

Determining Your Preferred Supervisory Style

This exercise is designed to determine your preferred supervisory style. Below are 12 situations. Select the *one* alternative that most closely describes what you would do in each situation. Don't be concerned with trying to pick the right answer; select the alternative you would really use. Circle the letter *a, b, c,* or *d.* Ignore the C ____ and S ____, which will be explained later in this chapter and used in class in Skill-Building Exercise 7–1.

C _____ 1. Your rookie crew seems to be developing well. Their need for direction and close supervision is diminishing. Do you:

    a. Stop directing and overseeing performance unless there is a problem. S ____

    b. Spend time getting to know them personally, but make sure they maintain performance levels. S ____

    c. Make sure things keep going well; continue to direct and oversee closely. S ____

    d. Begin to discuss new tasks of interest to them. S ____

C _____ 2. You assigned Joe a task, specifying exactly how you wanted it done. Joe deliberately ignored your directions and did it his way. The job will not meet the customer's standards. This is not the first problem you've had with Joe. You decide to:

   a. Listen to Joe's side, but be sure the job gets done right away. S ____

   b. Tell Joe to do it again the right way and closely supervise the job. S ____

   c. Tell him the customer will not accept the job and let Joe handle it his way. S ____

   d. Discuss the problem and what can be done about it. S ____

C _____ 3. Your employees work well together. The department is a real team. It's the top performer in the organization. Because of traffic problems, the president okayed staggered hours for departments. As a result, you can change your department's hours. Several of your workers have suggested changing. The action you take is to:

   a. Allow the group to decide the hours. S ____

   b. Decide on new hours, explain why you chose them, and invite questions. S ____

   c. Conduct a meeting to get the group members' ideas. Select new hours together, with your approval. S ____

   d. Send around a memo stating the hours you want. S ____

C _____ 4. You hired Bill, a new employee. He is not performing at the level expected after one month's training. Bill is trying; but he seems to be a slow learner. You decide to:

   a. Clearly explain what needs to be done and oversee his work. Discuss why the procedures are important; support and encourage him. S ____

   b. Tell Bill that his training is over and it's time to pull his own weight. S ____

   c. Review task procedures and supervise his work closely. S ____

   d. Inform Bill that his training is over, to feel free to come to you if he has any problems. S ____

C _____ 5. Helen has had an excellent performance record for the last five years. Recently you have noticed a drop in the quality and quantity of her work. She has a family problem. Do you:

   a. Tell her to get back on track and closely supervise her. S ____

   b. Discuss the problem with Helen. Help her realize her personal problem is affecting her work. Discuss ways to improve the situation. Be supportive and encourage her. S ____

   c. Tell Helen you're aware of her productivity slip and that you're sure she'll work it out soon. S ____

   d. Discuss the problem and solution with Helen and supervise her closely. S ____

C _____ 6. Your organization does not allow smoking in certain areas. You just walked by a restricted area and saw Joan smoking. She has been with the organization for 10 years and is a very productive worker. Joan has never been caught smoking before. The action you take is to:

   a. Ask her to put it out, then leave. S ____

   b. Discuss why she is smoking and what she intends to do about it. S ____

   c. Encourage Joan not to smoke in this area again, and check up on her in the future. S ____

   d. Tell her to put it out, watch her do it, and tell her you will check on her in the future. S ____

C _____   7. Your department usually works well together with little direction. Recently a conflict between Sue and Tom has caused problems. As a result you:

  a. Call Sue and Tom together and make them realize how this conflict is affecting the department. Discuss how to resolve it and how you will check to make sure the problem is solved. S ____

  b. Let the group resolve the conflict. S ____

  c. Have Sue and Tom sit down and discuss their conflict and how to resolve it. Support their efforts to implement a solution. S ____

  d. Tell Sue and Tom how to resolve their conflict and closely supervise them. S ____

C _____   8. Jim usually does his share of the work with some encouragement and direction. However, he has migraine headaches occasionally and doesn't pull his weight when this happens. The others resent doing Jim's work. You decide to:

  a. Discuss his problem and help him come up with ideas for maintaining his work; be supportive. S ____

  b. Tell Jim to do his share of the work and closely watch his output. S ____

  c. Inform Jim that he is creating a hardship for the others and should resolve the problem by himself. S ____

  d. Be supportive but set minimum performance levels and ensure compliance. S ____

C _____   9. Bob, your most experienced and productive worker, came to you with a detailed idea that could increase your department's productivity at a very low cost. It is a new product/service. He can do his present job plus this new assignment. You think it's an excellent idea and you:

  a. Set some goals together. Encourage and support his efforts. S ____

  b. Set up goals for Bob. Be sure he agrees with them and sees you as being supportive of his efforts. S ____

  c. Tell Bob to keep you informed and to come to you if he needs any help. S ____

  d. Have Bob check in with you frequently so that you can direct and supervise his activities. S ____

C _____   10. Your boss asked you for a special report. Fran, a very capable worker who usually needs no direction or support, has all the necessary skills to do the job. However, Fran is reluctant because she has never done a report. You:

  a. Tell Fran she has to do it. Give her direction and supervise her closely. S ____

  b. Describe the project to Fran and let her do it her own way. S ____

  c. Describe the benefits to Fran. Get her ideas on how to do it and check her progress. S ____

  d. Discuss possible ways of doing the job. Be supportive; encourage Fran. S ____

C _____   11. Jean is the top producer in your department. However, her monthly reports are constantly late and contain errors. You are puzzled because she does everything else with no direction or support. You decide to:

  a. Go over past reports, explaining exactly what is expected of her. Schedule a meeting so that you can review the next report with her. S ____

  b. Discuss the problem with Jean and ask her what can be done about it; be supportive. S ____

  c. Explain the importance of the report. Ask her what the problem is. Tell her that you can expect the next report to be on time without errors. S ____

  d. Remind Jean to get the next report in on time without errors. S ____

C _____ 12. Your workers are very effective and like to participate in decision making. A consultant was hired to develop a new method for your department using the latest technology in the field. You:

    a. Explain the consultant's method and let the group decide how to implement it. S ____

    b. Teach them the new method and closely supervise them. S ____

    c. Explain the new method and why it is important. Teach them the method and make sure the procedure is followed. Answer questions. S ____

    d. Explain the new method and get the group's input on ways to improve and implement it. S ____

To determine your supervisory style:

1. In the box below, circle the letter you selected for each situation. The column headings (S-A through S-L) represent the supervisory style you selected.

	S-A	S-C	S-P	S-L
1	c	b	d	a
2	b	a	d	c
3	d	b	c	a
4	c	a	d	b
5	a	d	b	c
6	d	c	b	a
7	d	a	c	b
8	b	d	a	c
9	d	b	a	c
10	a	c	d	b
11	a	c	b	d
12	b	c	d	a
Total				

S-A Autocratic
S-C Consultative
S-P Participative
S-L Laissez-Faire

2. Add up the number of circled items per column. The highest is your preferred supervisory style. Is this the style you tend to use most often?

Your Supervisory Flexibility: The more evenly distributed the numbers are between S-A and S-L, the more flexible your style is. A score of 1 or 0 in any column may indicate a reluctance to use the style.

NOTE: There is no "right" leadership style. This part of the exercise is designed to enable you to better understand the style you tend to use or prefer to use.

Defining the Situation

Having determined a preferred supervisory style, it is time to learn the four supervisory styles and when to use each. As mentioned, no one "best" supervisory style exists for all situations.[45] Instead, the effective supervisor adapts his or her style to meet the capabilities of the individual or group.[46] Supervisor–employee interactions fall into two distinct categories: directive and supportive.

- *Directive behavior.* The supervisor focuses on directing and controlling behavior to ensure that the task gets done. The supervisor tells employees what, when, where, and how to do the task and oversees performance.

- *Supportive behavior.* The supervisor focuses on encouraging and motivating behavior. He or she explains things and listens to employee views, helping employees make their own decisions.

In other words, when a supervisor interacts with employees, the focus can be on directing (getting the task done), supporting (developing relationships), or both.

These definitions lead us to the question: "What style should I use and why?" The answer is, "It depends on the situation." And the situation is determined by the capability of the employee(s). There are two distinct aspects of capability:

- *Ability*—Do the employees have the experience, education, skills, and so on, to do the task without direction from the supervisor?
- *Motivation*—Do the employees want to do the task? Will they perform the task without a supervisor's encouragement and support?

Determining Employee Capability: Employee capability may be measured on a continuum from low to outstanding, which the supervisor will determine by selecting the one capability level that best describes the employee's ability and motivation for the specific task. These levels are as follows:

- *Low (C-1)*—The employees can't do the task without detailed directions and close supervision. Employees in this category may have the ability to do the task, but lack the motivation to perform without close supervision.
- *Moderate (C-2)*—The employees have moderate ability and need specific direction and support to get the job done properly. The employees may be highly motivated but still need direction, support, and encouragement.
- *High (C-3)*—The employees are high in ability but may lack the confidence to do the job. What they need most is support and encouragement to motivate them to get the task done.
- *Outstanding (C-4)*—The employees are capable of doing the task without direction or support.

Most people perform a variety of tasks on the job. It is important to realize that their capability may vary depending on the specific task. For example, a bank teller may be a C-4 for routine transactions, but be a C-1 for opening new or special accounts. Employees tend to start working with a C-1 capability and needing close direction. As their ability to do the job increases, supervisors can begin to be supportive and hopefully stop supervising closely. A supervisor must gradually develop employees from C-1 levels to C-3 or C-4 over time.

Using the Appropriate Supervisory Style

As mentioned, the "correct" supervisory style depends on the situation.[47] And the situation, in turn, is a function of employee capability. Each of the supervisory styles, discussed in greater detail below, also involves varying degrees of supportive and directive behavior.

The four supervisory styles—autocratic, consultative, participative, and laissez-faire—are summarized in Exhibit 7–7 in relation to the different levels of employee capability.

The **autocratic style** (S-A) *involves high-directive/low-supportive behavior (HD–LS) and is appropriate when interacting with low-capability employees (C-1)*. When interacting with employees, the supervisor gives very detailed instructions, describing exactly what, when, where, and how to perform the task. He or she also closely oversees performance. The supportive style is largely absent. The supervisor makes decisions without input from the employees.

Using **consultative style** (S-C) *involves high-directive/high-supportive behavior (HD–HS) and is appropriate when interacting with moderate-capability employees (C-2)*. Here, the supervisor would give specific instructions, telling employees what, when, where, and how to perform the task, as well as overseeing performance at all major stages through completion. At the same time, the supervisor would support the employees by explaining why the task should be performed as requested and answering their questions. Supervisors should work on relationships as they "sell" the benefits of completing the task their way. When making decisions, they may

EXHIBIT 7–7   **SITUATIONAL SUPERVISION MODEL**

Capability Levels (C)	Supervisory Styles (S)
(C-1) Low The employees are unable and/or unwilling to do the task without direction.	**(S-A) Autocratic** *High directive/low supportive* Tell employees what to do and closely oversee performance. Give little or no support. Make decisions by yourself.
(C-2) Moderate The employees have moderate ability and are motivated.	**(S-C) Consultative** *High directive/high supportive* Sell employees on doing the job your way and oversee performance at major stages. You may include their input in your decision. Develop a supportive relationship.
(C-3) High The employees are high in ability but may lack self-confidence or motivation.	**(S-P) Participative** *Low directive/high supportive* Provide little or general direction. Let employees do the task their way. Spend limited time overseeing performance. Focus on end results. Make decisions together, but you have the final say.
(C-4) Outstanding The employees are very capable and highly motivated.	**(S-L) Laissez-Faire** *Low directive/low supportive* Provide little or no direction and support. Let employees make their own decisions.

consult employees, but they have the final say. Once a supervisor makes the decision, which can incorporate employees' ideas, he or she directs and oversees their performance.

The **participative style** (S-P) *is characterized by low-directive/high-supportive behavior (LD–HS) and is appropriate when interacting with employees with high capability (C-3).* When interacting with employees, the supervisor gives general directions and spends limited time overseeing performance, letting employees do the task their way and focusing on the end result. The supervisor should: support the employees by encouraging them and building up their self-confidence; if a task needs to be done, not tell them how to do it, but ask them how they will accomplish it; make decisions together with employees or allow employees to make the decision subject to the supervisor's limitations and approval.

The **laissez-faire style** (S-L) *entails low-directive/low-supportive behavior (LD–LS) and is appropriate when interacting with outstanding employees (C-4).* When interacting with these employees, they should merely be informed about what needs to be done. The supervisor answers their questions, but provides little, if any, direction. It is not necessary to oversee performance. These employees are highly motivated and need little, if any, support. The supervisor allows these employees to make their own decisions subject to the supervisor's limitations although approval by the supervisor will not be necessary.

Exhibit 7–7 summarizes the four supervisory styles.

 Skill-Building

7–2B

Learning Objective

5. Explain four situational supervisory styles

Applying the Situational Supervision Model

The situation below is the same as that in Self-Assessment Exercise 7–2. Now the information in Exhibit 7–7 will be applied to this situation.

To begin, identify the employee capability level each situation describes. These are listed in the left-hand column of the exhibit. Indicate the capability level (1 through 4) on the line marked "C" to the left of the situation. Next, determine the management style that each response (*a, b, c, or d*) represents. Indicate that style (A, C, P, or L) on the line marked "S" at the end of each response. Finally, identify the most appropriate response by placing a check mark (**U**) next to it.

C____1. Your rookie crew seems to be developing well. Their need for close supervision is diminishing. Do you:

    a. Stop directing and overseeing performance, unless there is a problem. S ____

    b. Spend time getting to know them personally, but make sure they maintain performance levels. S ____

    c. Make sure things keep going well; continue to direct and oversee closely. S ____

    d. Begin to discuss new tasks of interest to them. S ____

Let's see how well you did.

1. The capability was C-1 but they have now developed to the C-2 level. If you put the number 2 on the (C 2) C line, you were correct.

2. *Alternative a* is S <u>L</u>, the laissez-faire style. There is no direction or support. *Alternative b* is S <u>C</u>, the consultative style. There is both direction and support. *Alternative c* is S <u>A</u>, the autocratic style. There is direction but no support. *Alternative d* is S <u>P</u>, the participative style. There is low direction and high support (in discussing employee interests).

3. If you selected *b* as the match, you were correct. However, in the business world, there is seldom only one way to handle a problem successfully. Therefore, in this exercise, you receive points based on how successful your behavior would be in each situation. In situation 1, *b* is the most successful alternative because it involves developing the employees gradually; it's a three-point answer. Alternative *c* is the next best alternative, followed by *d*. It is better to keep things the way they are now rather than trying to rush employee development, which would probably cause problems. So, *c* is a two-point answer, *d* a one-point answer. Alternative *a* is the least effective because you are going from one extreme of supervision to the other. This is a zero-point answer because the odds are great that this style will cause problems that will affect supervisory success.

The better a supervisor is at matching his or her supervisory style to employees' capabilities, the greater the chances of being a successful supervisor.

During In-Class Skill-Building Exercise 7–1, Situational Supervision, participants will apply the model to the remaining situations and be given feedback on their success at applying the model as they develop their situational supervision skills.

Video

7–1
BM–7

Skill-Building

7–1

WORK APPLICATIONS

7. What are your views on situational supervision? Recall a manager you have or had. Which of the four styles does or did the manager use? Would you use the model on the job?

8. Which of the four supervisory styles would you like your boss to use with you? Why would you prefer this particular style?

Putting the Leadership Theories Together

This chapter has presented ten different leadership theories. Exhibit 7–8 puts the 10 leadership theories together, converted into four leadership style categories. A review of this exhibit should lead to a better understanding of the similarities and differences among these leadership theories.

9. Which leadership theory/model do you prefer? Why?
10. Describe the type of leader you want to be.

Substitutes for Leadership

The leadership theories presented assume that some leadership style will be effective in each situation. Kerr and Jermier[48] argue that certain individual, task, and organizational variables prevent leaders from affecting subordinates' attitudes and behaviors. Substitutes for leadership, or characteristics that negate or substitute for leadership influence, are those that structure task (directive) for followers or give them positive strokes (support) for their action. Rather than the leader providing the necessary direction and support, the subordinates, task, or organization may provide them.

With the virtual office (Chapter 1 and 14), employees are usually not within the manager's direct supervision. Thus, comes "virtual leadership," since employees must be managed differently.[49] And employees have a greater need to be self-motivated and lead, as we all have leadership responsibility.[50]

The following may substitute for leadership by providing direction and/or support:

I. *Characteristics of Subordinates:*

- Ability, knowledge, experience, training.
- Need for independence.
- Professional orientation.
- Indifference toward organizational rewards.

II. *Characteristics of Task:*
- Clarity and routine.
- Invariant methodology.
- Provision of own feedback concerning accomplishment.
- Intrinsic satisfaction.

III. *Characteristics of the Organization:*

- Formalization (explicit plans, goals, and areas of responsibility).
- Inflexibility (rigid, unbending rules and procedures).
- Highly specified and active advisory and staff functions.
- Closely knit, cohesive work groups.
- Organizational rewards not within the leader's control.
- Spatial distance between superior and subordinates.

Learning Objective

6. Identify three characteristics that substitute for leadership

These substitutes may replace leadership. A study of nursing work indicated that the staff nurses' education, the cohesion of the nurses, and work technology substituted for the head nurse's leadership behavior in determining the staff nurses' performance.[51]

11. Do you agree that characteristics of subordinates, task, and the organization can substitute for leadership direction and support? Explain your answer.

EXHIBIT 7–8   **LEADERSHIP STYLES**

Behavioral Leadership Theories

Basic Leadership Styles	Four Leadership Style Categories			
	Autocratic	Democratic		Laissez-Faire
Two-dimensional leadership styles	High structure/job centered. Low consideration/ employee centered.	High structure/job centered. High consideration/ employee centered.	High consideration/ employee centered. Low structure/job centered.	Low consideration/ employee centered. Low structure/job centered.
Leadership Grid	High concern for production. Low concern for people. (9,1 sweatshop manager)	High concern for both production and people. (9,9 team manager)	High concern for people. Low concern for production. (1,9 country club manager)	Low to moderate concern for both people and production. (1,1 impoverished + 5,5 organized managers)
Transformational leadership	Three acts; no actual style.			

Contingency Leadership Theories

Contingency Leadership Theory	Task		Relationship	
Leadership continuum	1. Make decision and announce it.	2. Sell decision. 3. Present ideas and invite questions.	4. Present tentative decision subject to change. 5. Present problem, get suggestions and make decision.	6. Define limits and ask group to make decision. 7. Permit group to function within limits defined by leader.
Normative leadership theory	AI. Make decision alone using available information.	AII. Get information from subordinates, make decision alone.	CI. Meet individually (CII Group) with subordinates, explain the situation, get information and ideas on how to solve the problem, make final decision alone.	GII. Meet with subordinates as a group, explain the situation, and allow the group to make decision.
Situational leadership	High task. Low relationship (Telling).	High task. High relationship (Selling).	High relationship. Low task (Participating).	Low relationship. Low task (Delegating).
Situational supervision	High directive. Low support (Autocratic).	High directive. High support (Consultative).	High support. Low directive (Participative).	Low support. Low directive (Laissez-faire).

Leadership Trait Theory

Based on traits of leader; no actual style.

Diversity of Global Leadership

Thinking globally[52] and global leadership skills[53] are essential to effective leadership. In the 1970s, Japan's productivity rate was increasing faster than that of the United States. Research was conducted to determine why the Japanese were more productive, and it became apparent that Japanese firms were managed and led differently than U.S. organizations. Seven major differences between the two countries were identified. The Japanese (1) have a longer length of employment, (2) use more collective decision making, (3) use more collective responsibility, (4) evaluate and promote employees more slowly, (5) use more implicit mechanisms of control, (6) have more unspecialized career paths, and (7) have a more holistic concern for employees.[54] Over the years many U.S. companies have adopted more collective decision making and responsibilities, and have taken a more holistic view of employees (total person approach—Chapter 1). Furthermore, the number of firms using total quality management (TQM) techniques from Japan and self-directed work teams increased.

Within Europe there is a diversity of management models, which raises a range of management education issues. European managers deal more with cultural than technical issues in the context of diverse value systems and religious backgrounds. Management is organized more as a language than as a set of techniques. Companies are looking more for graduates with an international openness who can master the complexity of the global economy.

American, European, and Japanese executives realize that they must manage and lead their business units in other countries differently than at home. Toyota and Honda run their plants in the United States somewhat differently than in Japan. Similarly IBM's management style in Japan differs from its style in the United States.

Europeans travel between countries the way Americans travel between states. Many countries and states cater heavily to tourism. Most large companies in the United States conduct business in many parts of the world. This makes cultural awareness and diversity in leadership necessary for business success in the increasingly global business environment. Chapter 13 will discuss cultural awareness.

This chapter presents 10 leadership theories and a theory of leadership substitution. You may select one for use, combine some, or develop your own theory of leadership.

REVIEW

Select one or more methods: (1) Fill in the missing key terms from memory; (2) match the key terms from the end of the review with their definitions below; and/or (3) copy the key terms in order from the key terms at the beginning of the chapter.

_____ is the process of influencing employees to work toward the achievement of objectives. Leadership and management are not the same; leadership is one of the five management functions. Leadership, although mediated by a host of intervening variables, does have a causal impact on performance.

_____ assumes that there are distinctive physical and psychological characteristics accounting for leadership effectiveness. The Ghiselli Study concluded that there are traits important to effective leadership (supervisory ability being the most important), though not all are necessary for success. Trait theory, though not very popular, is still being studied and written about.

_____ assume that there are distinctive styles that effective leaders use consistently. The three basic leadership styles are autocratic, democratic, and laissez-faire. Two-dimensional leadership styles are called *structuring* and *consideration styles* (Ohio State University) and *job-centered* and *employee-centered styles* (University of Michigan). The _____ is Blake and Mouton's model identifying the ideal leadership style as having a high concern for both production and people. Transformational leaders take the organization through three acts on an ongoing basis: act 1, recognizing the need for revitalization; act 2, creating a new vision; and act 3, institutionalizing change.

_____ assume that the appropriate leadership style varies from situation to situation. _____ is Fiedler's model used to determine if one's leadership style is task or relationship oriented, and if their situation matches their style. If not, leaders change the situation rather than their style. _____ is Tannenbaum and Schmidt's model that identifies seven leadership styles based on one's use of boss-centered versus employee-centered leadership. The variables to consider when selecting a style include the manager, subordinates, and the situation. _____ is Vroom and Yetton's decision-tree model that enables the user to select one of five leadership styles that is appropriate for the situation. Its user answers a series of eight questions in a decision tree to determine which style to use.

_____ is Hersey and Blanchard's model for selecting one of four leadership styles that matches the employees' maturity level in a given situation.

The four situational supervision styles are: _____, which involves high-directive/low supportive behavior and is appropriate when interacting with low-capability employees; _____, which involves high-directive/high-supportive behavior and is appropriate when interacting with moderate-capability employees; _____, which is characterized by low-directive/high-supportive behavior and is appropriate when interacting with employees with high capability; and _____, which entails low-directive/low-supportive behavior and is appropriate when interacting with outstanding employees.

It has been proposed that characteristics of subordinates, task, and the organization can substitute for leadership directive and support.

Executives manage and lead differently across the global economy.

KEY TERMS

autocratic style   247
behavioral leadership
  theories   232
consultative style   247
contingency leadership
  theories   237

contingency leadership
  theory   237
laissez-faire style   248
leadership   229
leadership continuum   238
Leadership Grid®   234

leadership trait theory   230
normative leadership
  theory   240
participative style   248
situational leadership   241

Kim Rogers: MONCO

Modern Control, Inc. (MOCON®) is an international company with headquarters in Minneapolis, Minnesota. MOCON is a leading developer, manufacturer, and marketer of high-technology instrumentation designed to test packages and packaging materials, films, and pharmaceutical products. MOCON testing instrumentation is used in research laboratories, production environments, and quality control applications in the food, plastics, medical, and pharmaceutical industries.

MOCON has three major lines of business: (1) Permeation products address the needs of film converters and food packages working on new or better packaging material. (2) Packaging products are used to test for leaks in finished food and snack packages. (3) Weighing and sorting systems serve pharmaceutical capsule and tablet manufacturers.

Kim Rogers worked her way up to become the manager in a department making small parts[55] Kim's job was to supervise the production of one part that is used as a component in other products. Running the machines to make the standard parts is not complicated, and her employees generally find the job to be boring with low pay. Kim closely supervised the employees to make sure they kept production on schedule. Kim believed that if she did not watch the employees closely and keep them informed of their output, they would slack off and miss production goals. Kim's employees viewed her as an OK boss to work for as she did take a personal interest in them, and employees were productive. Kim did discipline employees who did not meet standard productivity, and she ended up firing some workers.

Peter Picnally, the manager of a larger department that designs instruments to customer specifications retired and Kim was given a promotion to manage this department for doing a good job of running her old department. Kim never did any design work herself nor supervise it. The designers are all engineers who are paid well, and who were doing a good job according to their supervisor Peter. As Kim observed workers in her usual manner, she realized that all of the designers did their work differently. So she closely observed them work and looked for good ideas that all her employees could follow. It wasn't long before Kim was telling employees how to do a better job of designing the custom specifications. Things were not going too well, however, as employees told Kim that she did not know what she was talking about. She tried to rely on her authority, which worked while she was watching employees. However, once Kim left one employee to observe another, the workers went back to doing things their own way. Kim's employees were complaining about her being a poor manager behind her back.

The complaints about Kim being a poor manager got to her boss Jose. Jose also realized that performance in the design department has gone down since Kim took over as manager. Jose decided to call Kim into the office to discuss how things are going.

Go to the Internet: For more information on MOCON update the information provided in this case, do a name search on the Internet and visit MOCON's Web site at *www.mocon.com.* For ideas on using the Internet with cases, see Appendix C.

Support your answer to the following questions with specific information from the case and text, or other information you get from the Web or other source.

Cumulative Case Questions

1. Is Kim a manager and/or leader in the parts and design departments?

2. Which leadership theories are illustrated in Kim's success in one department and problems in another department?

3. Using Exhibit 7–3, Fiedler's Contingency Leadership Model, what situation and leadership style are appropriate for the parts production department and for the custom design department?

4. What would Fiedler and Kerr and Jermier recommend that Kim do to improve department performance?

5. Using Exhibit 7–5, which maturity level would Hersey and Blanchard say the employees in the design department are on? Using the text material, which leadership style would they recommend Kim use in this situation to be a successful leader? Is it the style Kim is using?

6. Personality (Chapter 2) is best associated with which leadership theory?

7. What is the role of communication (Chapter 4) and motivation (Chapter 6) in leadership?

8. How was contingency leadership theory presented in Chapter 5?

OBJECTIVE CASE

The Cleanup Job

Brenda is the head meat cutter in the Big K Supermarket. Brenda hires and has fired meat cutters; she also determines raises. Although it has never been said, she speculates that the all-male meat cutting crew isn't friendly toward her because they resent having a female boss. They are all highly skilled.

Once a month the meat and frozen foods cases are supposed to be cleaned by a meat cutter; they are all equally capable of doing it. It is not any one person's job, and no one likes to do it. It's that time of month again, and Brenda has to select someone to clean up. She just happens to see Rif first, so she approaches him.

BRENDA: Rif, I want you to clean the cases this month.

RIF: Why me? I just did it two months ago. Give someone else a turn.

BRENDA: I didn't ask you to tell me when you did it last. I asked you to do it.

RIF: I know, but I'm a meat cutter, not a janitor. Why can't the janitor do it.? Or something more fair?

BRENDA: Do I have to take action against you for not following an order?

RIF: OK, I'll do it.

Answer the following questions, supporting your answers in the space between questions. (Note: Different leadership styles can be role-played in class.)

_____ 1. The basic leadership style Brenda used with Rif was _____.

      a. autocratic   *b.* democratic   *c.* laissez-faire

_____ 2. With Rif, Brenda used the _____ quadrant leadership style, Exhibit 7–1.

      a. 1   *b.* 2   *c.* 3   *d.* 4

_____ 3. With Rif, Brenda should have used the _____ quadrant leadership style, Exhibit 7–1.

      a. 1   *b.* 2   *c.* 3   *d.* 4

_____ 4. The Leadership Grid style Brenda used with Rif was _____, Exhibit 7–2.

      a. 1,1   *b.* 9,1   *c.* 1,9   *d.* 5,5   *e.* 9,9

_____ 5. According to Leadership Grid theory, Brenda used the appropriate leadership style.

      a. true   *b.* false

_____ 6. According to Fiedler's Contingency Theory model, Exhibit 7–3. Brenda is in a _____ situation, and _____ oriented behavior is appropriate.

      a. 1   *b.* 2   *c.* 3   *d.* 4   *e.* 5   *f.* 6   *g.* 7   *h.* 8
      a. task   *b.* relationship

_____ 7. Brenda used the _____ leader continuum style, Exhibit 7–4.

      a. 1   *b.* 2   *c.* 3   *d.* 4   *e.* 5   *f.* 6   *g.* 7

_____ 8. The appropriate normative leadership style to resolve the monthly cleanup job is _____.

     a. AI   *b.* AII   *c.* CI   *d.* CII   *e.* GII

_____ 9. The situational supervision style Brenda used with Rif was _____, Exhibit 7–7.

     a. autocratic   *b.* consultative   *c.* participative   *d.* laissez-faire

_____ 10. The situational supervision style Brenda should use to resolve the monthly cleanup job is _____, Exhibit 7–7.

     a. autocratic   *b.* consultative   *c.* participative   *d.* laissez-faire

11. In Brenda's position/situation, how would you get the cases cleaned each month?

Fiscal Fairy Tale #2:
Snowed White

Go to the MG website (*www.mgeneral.com*) and read *Fiscal Fairy Tale #2: Snowed White* (your instructor may ask you to print a copy and bring it to class). Answer these questions (your instructor may ask you to type them and bring them to class):

Online MG Webzine
Exercise 7

Questions Relating to the Tale Only

1. As stated at the end of the tale, in 50 words or so, what is your response to this tale? You may send it to MG.

2. Do you agree with the decision making process at Apple-A-Day?

3. Should entrepreneurs sell their businesses to big companies?

4. What are some of the positive and negative affects of takeovers?

In-Class MG Webzine
Exercise 7

Questions Relating the Tale to the Chapter Concepts

5. Which basic leadership style did Snowed White use?

6. Which Ohio State leadership style did Snowed White use?

7. Using Fiedler's Contingency Model, Exhibit 7–3, which leadership situation is Snowed White in, thus which style is most appropriate for this situation?

8. Which normative leadership style was Snowed White using?

9. Which situational leadership style was Snowed White using?

10. Was the takeover as situation that enabled substitutes for leadership?

The instructor selects one of the six options from page 589.

INTERNET EXERCISES

Online Internet Exercise 7–1

The objective of this exercise is to better understand contemporary leadership traits and to read about a historic leader. Use the information in Appendix B and IE 1–2 and 1–3 as you do the following:

1. Go to the Leadership Values Website homepage—*www.leader-values.com*
2. Click "4 E's" and quickly read the introductory material on leadership and carefully read the 4 E's—envision, enable, empower, and energize (your instructor may require a printed copy.)
3. Go back to the home page and click "Historic Figures" then click one of them and read about the leadership traits/style of the person.
4. Questions: (1) Which historical figure did you select? (2) What impressed you the most about this leader? (3) How can you use this information to be a better leader? (Your instructor may require your typed answers.)

In-Class Internet Exercise 7–1, IE 7–2, and IE 7–3

The instructor selects one of the six options from page 589.

Online Internet Exercise 7–2 (Self-Assessment)

The objective of this exercise is to learn about your leadership style through a leadership test. Using the information in Appendix B and IE 1–2 and 1–3 as you do the following:

1. Go to the Leadership Strategies homepage—*www.leaderx.com*
2. Click "Test Yourself."
3. Click "Test Your Leadership Style." Test your style then click submit it for scoring. Print your customized report with valuable feedback on leadership.
4. Read your report. Read it a second time highlighting the most valuable tips that can help you develop your leadership. (Your instructor may require your highlighted printout.)
5. Questions: (1) What do you agree and/or not agree with in the report? (2) What, if anything, surprised you in the report? (3) What were the most important findings to you? (4) How can you use this information to be a better leader? (The instructor may require your answers to these questions.)

Online Internet Exercise 7–3

The objective of this exercise is to develop leadership skills through a simulation. You are the supervisor of five employees and face a series of tough human relations issues. The simulation is extensive and will require some time to complete, so complete it when you have less time pressure. Using the information in Appendix B and IE 1–2 and 1–3 as you do the following:

1. Go to the HR Positive Employee Relations Council homepage—*www.perc.net*
2. You can register or Click "Already Registered."
3. Click "The Leadership Challenge Simulation" and do as instructed. (Your instructor may require a copy of some part of the simulation.)
4. Questions: (1) Did you enjoy the simulation? Explain. (2) How well did you do—number of steps, etc.? (3) What are the most important things you learned from the simulation? (4) How can you use this information to be a better leader? (The instructor may require your answers to these questions.)

Situational Supervision

VE 7–1

BM - 7

Procedure 1
(10–20 minutes)

Objectives: To better understand the four situational supervisory styles.

SCANS: The SCANS competencies of resources, interpersonal skills, information, and systems and the foundations of basic, thinking, and personal qualities are developed through this exercise.

Preparation: You should understand the four situational supervisory styles.

The instructor shows Video Module 7, Situational Supervision. As you view each of the four scenes, identify the situational supervisory style being used by the manager.

Scene 1. _____   A. Autocratic (S-A)

Scene 2. _____   B. Consultative (S-C)

Scene 3. _____   C. Participative (S-P)

Scene 4. _____   D. Laissez-faire (S-L)

After viewing each of the four scenes, identify/match the style used by the manager by placing the letter of the style on the scene line.

Option A: View all four scenes and identify the style used by the manager. After viewing all four scenes, discuss and/or have the instructor give the correct answers.

Option B: After each scene the class discusses the style used by the manager. The instructor states the correct answer after each of the four scenes.

Procedure 2
(2–5 minutes)

Select the one style that you would use in this situation. Are other styles also appropriate? Which style would you not use (which is not appropriate) for this situation? Next to each style listed above, write the letter A for appropriate or N for not appropriate.

Discussion:

Option A: In groups of four to six, answer the questions below.

Option B: As a class answer the questions below.

1. Which style(s) are not appropriate for this situation?
2. Which style(s) are appropriate for this situation?
3. Is there one style most appropriate in this situation? If yes, which one?

Conclusion: The instructor may make concluding remarks.

Application (2–4 minutes): What did I learn from this exercise? How will I use this knowledge in the future?

Sharing: Volunteers give their answers to the application section.

This video exercise serves as a behavioral model for In-Class Skill-Building Exercise 7–1, Situational Supervision.

SKILL-BUILDING EXERCISE 7-1

● **In-Class
Situational
Supervision**

BM - 7

Objectives: To learn to use the situational supervision model. To develop your ability to supervise employees using the appropriate situational supervisory style for their capability level.

SCANS: The SCANS competencies of resources, interpersonal skills, information, and systems and the foundations of basic, thinking, and personal qualities are developed through this exercise.

Experience: In groups of two, you will apply the Situational Supervision Model in Exhibit 7–7 to situations 2 through 12 in Self-Assessment Exercise 7–2. After you have finished, your instructor will give you the recommended answers, enabling you to determine your level of success at selecting the appropriate style.

For each situation, use the left-hand column in Exhibit 7–7 to identify the employee capability level the situation describes. Write the level (1 through 4) on the line marked "C" to the left of each situation in Self-Assessment Exercise 7–2. Now identify the supervisory style that each response (*a* through *d*) represents. (These are listed in the right-hand column of the exhibit.) Indicate the style (A, C, P, or L) on the line marked "S" at the end of each response. Finally, choose the management style you think is best for each situation by placing a check mark (**U**) next to the appropriate response (*a, b, c,* or *d*).

*Procedure 1
(3–8 minutes)
Procedure 2
(25–45 minutes)*

The instructor reviews the Situational Supervision Model, Exhibit 7–7, p. 248, and explains how to use the model for situation 1.

To determine how effective you were at supervising, turn to the next page and:
1. Without consulting the model or the answers you gave in class, repeat the exercise, and indicate the responses you would pick on the left-hand side of the table below in the "Without Model" section. On the right-hand side of the table, in the "With Model" section, circle the letter of the alternative you selected using the model in class.

2. Add the number of circles per column and multiply each column total by the number at the top of each column (0, 1, 2, or 3) on the column. Add the four subtotals to get your total score. The range is 0–36. The higher the score, the better the match of style and capability levels. Did your score increase when you used the model? Using the model on a daily basis can improve your performance.

The instructor reviews the situational supervision model and explains how to use the model for situation 1.

Integration (3–5 minutes)

1. Turn to situation 2 in Self-Assessment Exercise 7–2, p. 232, and to Exhibit 7–7, p. 248, Situational Supervision Model. (You may tear the exhibit out of your book.) Apply the model to the situation in an attempt to select the best course of action (3–4 minutes). The instructor will go over the answers/scoring (3–4 minutes).

2. Divide into teams of two; you may have one group of three if there is an odd number in the class. Apply the model as a team to situations 3 through 6. Team members may select different answers if they don't agree (8–12 minutes). Do not do situations 7 through 12 until you are told to do so. Your instructor will go over the answers/scoring for situations 3 through 6 (2–4 minutes).

3. As a team, select your answers to situations 7 through 12 (11–15 minutes). Your instructor will go over the answers/scoring to situations 7 through 12 (2–4 minutes).

Caution: There is no proven relationship between how a person performs on a pencil-and-paper test and how he or she actually performs on the job. People have a tendency to choose the answer they think is correct, rather than what they would actually do. The objective of this exercise is to help you better understand your supervisory style and how to improve upon it.

Source: Adapted from Paul Hersey and Kenneth Blanchard, *LEAD Directions for Self-Scoring and Analysis* (Center for Leadership Studies, 1973).

Conclusion: The instructor leads a class discussion and/or makes concluding remarks.

Application (2–4 minutes): What have I learned from this experience? How will I use this knowledge in the future?

Sharing: Volunteers give their answers to the application section.

● **In-Class
A Leadership Style
Role Play**

Objectives: To experience leadership in action. To identify the leadership style, and how using the appropriate versus inappropriate leadership style affects the organization.

SCANS: The SCANS competencies of resources, interpersonal skills, information, and systems and the foundations of basic, thinking, and personal qualities are developed through this exercise.

Preparation: All necessary material is below; no preparation is necessary.

*Procedure 1
(5–10 minutes)*

Break into your groups and select the style (autocratic, consultative, participative, or laissez-faire) your group would use to make the following decision.

You are an office manager with four subordinates who all do typing on regular typewriters. You will be receiving a word processor to replace one of the present typewriters. (Everyone knows about it because several salespeople have been in the office.) You must decide who gets the new word processor. Below is some information about each subordinate.

- Pat—He or she has been with the organization for 20 years, is 50 years old, and presently has a two-year-old typewriter.

- Chris—He or she has been with the organization for 10 years, is 31 years old, and presently has a one-year-old typewriter.

- Fran—He or she has been with the organization for five years, is 40 years old, and presently has a three-year-old typewriter.

- Sandy—He or she has been with the organization for two years, is 23 years old, and presently has a five-year-old typewriter.

Possible Leadership Styles (Instructor selects one option.)

A. Continuum of Leadership Behavior Styles 1–7. See Exhibit 7–4 for definitions of these seven styles.

or

B. S-A Autocratic *a.* Make the decision alone; then tell each subordinate individually your decision and how and why you made it.

b. Make the decision alone; then have a group meeting to announce the decision and how and why you made it. No discussion allowed.

S-C Consultative *a.* Before deciding, talk to the subordinates individually to find out if they want the word processor, and why they think they should get it.

Then make the decision and announce it to the group/individuals.

b. Before deciding, have a group meeting to listen to why each subordinate wants it, and why they think they should get it. Have no discussion between subordinates. Then make the decision and announce it to the group/individuals.

S-P Participative *a.* Tentatively decide to whom you want to give it. Then hold a meeting to tell the group your plans, followed with a discussion that can lead to you changing your mind. After the open discussion, you make the decision and announce it, explaining the rationale for selection.

	b. Call a group meeting and explain the problem. Lead an open discussion about who should get the word processor. After the discussion, make your decision and explain the rationale for it.
S-L Laissez-faire	a. Call a meeting and explain the situation. Tell the group that they have X amount of time (5–7 minutes for the exercise) to make the decision. You do not become a group member; you may or may not stay for the decision. However, if you do stay, you cannot participate.

Procedure 2
(5–10 minutes)

1. Four volunteers from different groups go to the front of the class. Take out a sheet of 8½-by-11-inch paper and write the name of the person you are role playing (in big, dark letters), fold it in half, and place it in view of the manager and class. While the managers are planning, turn to the end of this exercise and read your role, and the roles of your colleagues. Try to put yourself in the person's position and do and say what he or she actually would during the role play. No one but the typist should read this additional subordinate role information.

2. The instructor will tell each group which leadership style their manager will role play; it may or may not be the one selected.

3. The group selects a manager to do the actual role play of making the decision; and the group plans "who, what, when, where, how." The manager will perform the role play. No one should read the additional subordinate role information.

Procedure 3
1–10 minutes)
Procedure 4
(1–5 minutes)

One manager goes to the front of the class and conducts the leadership role play.

The class members (other than the group being represented) vote for the style (1 to 7 or Tell a. b.; Sell a. b.; Participate a. b.; Delegate a. b.) they think the manager portrayed. Then the manager reveals the style. If several class members didn't vote for the style portrayed, a discussion of why can take place.

Procedures 3 & 4
(25–40 minutes)
Procedure 5
(2–3 minutes)

Continue to repeat procedures 3 and 4 until all managers have their turn or the time runs out.

The entire class individually determines the style they would use when making the decision. The class votes for the style the class would use in this situation. The instructor gives his or her recommendation and/or the author's.

Conclusion: The instructor leads a class discussion and/or makes concluding remarks.

Application (2–4 minutes): What did I learn from this experience? How will I apply this knowledge in the future?

Sharing: Volunteers give their answers to the integration and/or application section.

Subordinate Roles

Additional information (for subordinates' role playing only)

Pat	You are happy with the way things are now. You do not want to learn how to use a word processor. Be firm and assertive in your stance.
Chris	You are bored with your present job. You really want to learn how to run a word processor. Being second in seniority, you plan to be aggressive in trying to get the word processor. You are afraid that the others will complain because you got the last new typewriter, so you have a good idea. You will take the word processor and Sandy can have your typewriter.
Fran	You are interested in having the word processor. You spend more time each day typing than any of the other employees. Therefore, you believe you should get the word processor.
Sandy	You want the word processor. You believe you should get it because you are by far the fastest typist, and you have the oldest typewriter. You do not want a hand-me-down typewriter.

Transactional Analysis, Assertiveness, and Conflict Resolution

8

Learning Objectives

After completing this chapter, you should be able to:

1. Describe the three ego states of transactional analysis.
2. Explain the three types of transactions.
3. Identify the differences among passive, aggressive, and assertive behavior.
4. List the four steps of assertive behavior.
5. Explain when a conflict exists.
6. State when and how to use five conflict management styles.
7. List the steps of initiating, responding to, and mediating conflict resolutions.
8. Define the following 14 key terms (in order of appearance in the chapter):

transactional analysis
ego states
types of transactions
assertiveness
conflict
forcing conflict style
avoiding conflict style
accommodating conflict style
compromising conflict style
collaborating conflict style
initiating conflict resolution steps
XYZ model
responding to conflict resolution steps
mediating conflict resolution steps

Larry and Helen work together doing the same job at Harvey's Department store. They share a special calculator because it is expensive and it is only used for part of their job. The calculator is generally kept in one's possession until the other person requests it. Recently, the amount of time each has to use the calculator has increased.

When Larry wants the calculator, he says, "I need the calculator now" (in a bold, intimidating voice), and Helen gives it to him, even when she is using it. When Helen needs the calculator, she says, "I don't like to bother you, but I need the calculator." If Larry is using it, he tells Helen that he will give it to her when he is finished with it, and Helen says, "OK." Helen doesn't think this arrangement is fair and is getting upset with Larry. But she hasn't said anything to Larry yet. Larry comes over to Helen's desk and this discussion takes place:

LARRY: I need the calculator right now.

HELEN: I'm sick and tired of your pushing me around. Go back to your desk, and I'll bring it to you when I'm good and ready.

LARRY: What's wrong with you? You've never acted like this before.

HELEN: Just take the calculator and go back to your desk and leave me alone.

LARRY: (Says nothing; just takes the calculator and leaves.)

HELEN: (Watches Larry walk back to his desk with the calculator, feels a bit guilty, and thinks to herself) Why do I let little annoyances build up until I explode and end up yelling at people? It's rather childish behavior to let people walk all over me, then to reverse and be tough and rude. I wish I could stand up for my rights in a positive way without hurting my relations.

Can this be done? It can, and you will learn how in this chapter.

The chapter name may suggest that this chapter will discuss three unrelated topics. However, this is not the case. The major theme of these topics is the development of interpersonal dynamic skills. This chapter focuses on dealing with your emotions and those of others in an effective way. When you interact with people, you respond (transactional analysis): You can let people push you around or you can stand up for your rights (assertiveness). When you are in disagreement with others (conflict), you can decide to ignore, or resolve, your differences. Being able to transact with people on the appropriate level, assertively stand up for your rights, and resolve your conflicts without hurting human relations will improve your effectiveness in organizations and in your personal life. The discussion of interpersonal development skills begins with transactional analysis.

● Organization
● Group
● Individual

Transactional Analysis

Transactional analysis (TA) provides useful models for leadership styles.[1] Eric Berne developed transactional analysis,[2] and it has been applied,[3] and written about ever since.[4] TA has been used with organizational development (chapter 12),[5] and to improve quality of work life (chapter 14).[6] Recently TA has been used to help multinational corporations prepare managers to operate effectively within other cultures[7.] TA is being used within relationship marketing to develop good human relations with customers.[8]

Transactional analysis *is a method of understanding behavior in interpersonal dynamics.* When you talk to someone about anything, you are involved in interpersonal dynamics, and a series of transactions take place. An organization is a product of the process of its human relations.[9]

Organizations have trained their employees in TA to improve their ability to handle difficult personal situations. A few of these companies include Pan American World Airways, the United Telephone Company of Texas, and Pitney Bowes. Studying TA can help you better understand people's behavior, and how to deal with emotions in a more positive way.

Below are three ego states, types of transactions, and life positions and stroking. Keep in mind that people are diverse and you will encounter a variety of ego states.

Ego States

According to Berne, we all have three major ego states that affect our behavior or the way we transact. The three **ego states** *are the parent, child, and adult.* We change ego states throughout the day, and even during a single discussion a series of transactions can take place between different ego states. Your parent, child, and adult ego states interact with other people's parent, child, and adult ego states. Understanding the ego state of the person you are interacting with can help you to understand his or her behavior and how to transact in an effective way.

Parent Ego State

When the parent ego state is in control, people behave from one of two perspectives:

1. Critical parent. When you behave and respond with evaluative responses (Chapter 4) that are critical, judgmental, opinionated, demanding, disapproving, disciplining, and so on, you are in the critical parent ego state. People in the critical parent ego state use a lot of do's and don'ts. Managers using the autocratic style tend to be in the critical parent ego state because they use high task/directive behavior.

2. Sympathetic parent. On the other hand, you can also be a different type of parent. When you behave and respond with reassuring responses (Chapter 4) that are protecting, permitting, consoling, caring, nurturing, and so on, you are in the sympathetic parent ego state. Managers using the consultative and participative styles tend to be in the sympathetic parent state because they are using high supportive/relationship behavior.

Child Ego State

When the child ego state is in control, people behave from one of two perspectives:

1. Natural child. When you behave and respond with probing responses (Chapter 4) that show curiosity, intimacy, fun, joyfulness, fantasy, impulsiveness, and so on, you are in the natural child ego state. Successful managers do not tend to continuously operate from the natural child ego state.

2. Adapted child. When you behave and respond with confronting responses (Chapter 4) that express rebelliousness, pouting, anger, fear, anxiety, inadequacy, procrastination, blaming others, and so on, you are in the adapted child ego state. Managers should avoid behaving from the adapted child ego state because this type of behavior often leads to the employee becoming emotional and behaving in a similar manner. When managers are transacting with an employee in this ego state, they should not react with similar behavior, but should be in the adult ego state.

Adult Ego State

When the adult ego state is in control, people behave in a thinking, rational, calculating, factual, unemotional manner. The adult gathers information, reasons things out, estimates probabilities, and makes decisions with cool and calm behavior. When communicating in the adult ego state, you avoid becoming the victim of the other person by controlling your response to the situation.

Learning Objective

1. Describe the three ego states of transactional analysis

Generally, the most effective behavior, human relations, and performance come from the adult ego state.[10] When interacting with others, you should be aware of their ego state. Are they acting like a parent, child, or adult? Identifying their ego state will help you understand why they are behaving the way they are and help you to determine which ego state you should use during the interaction. For example, if the person is acting like an adult, you most likely should, too. If the person is acting like a child, it may be appropriate for you to act like a parent rather than an adult. And there are times when it is appropriate to act out of the child ego state and have a good time.

Types of Transactions

Within ego states there are three different **types of transactions:** *complementary, crossed, and ulterior.*

Complementary Transactions

A complementary transaction occurs when the sender of the message gets the intended response from the receiver. For example, an employee makes a mistake and, wanting some sympathy, apologizes to the boss. Employee—"I just dropped the thing when I was almost done. Now I have to do it all over again."

Supervisor—"It happens to all of us; don't worry about it." This complementary transaction is illustrated below.

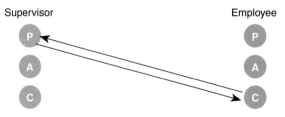

Another example of a complementary transaction is a supervisor who wants a job done and delegates it, expecting the employee to do it. The supervisor behaves on an adult-to-adult level. Supervisor—"Please get this order ready for me by two o'clock." Employee—"I'll have it done before two o'clock, no problem."

Generally, complementary transactions result in more effective communication with fewer hurt feelings and arguments. In other words, they help human relations and performance. Exceptions are if an employee uses an adapted child or critical parent ego state and the supervisor does, too. These complementary transactions can lead to problems.

WORK APPLICATIONS

1. Give an example of a complementary transaction you experienced. Be sure to identify the ego states involved.

Crossed Transactions

Crossed transactions occur when the sender of a message does not get the expected response from the receiver. Returning to our first example: Employee—"I just dropped the thing when I was almost done. Now I have to do it all over again." Supervisor—"You are so clumsy." This crossed transaction is illustrated below.

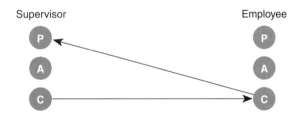

From our second example: Supervisor—"Please get this order ready for me by two o'clock." Employee—"Why do I have to do it? Why don't you do it yourself? I'm busy." This crossed transaction is an adult-adapted-to-child response.

Generally, crossed transactions result in surprise, disappointment, and hurt feelings for the sender of the message. The unexpected response often gets the person emotional, which often results in his or her changing to the adapted child ego state, which causes the communication to deteriorate further. Crossed transactions often end in arguments and hurt human relations.

Crossed transactions can be helpful when the negative parent or child ego response is crossed with an adult response. This crossover may result in the preferred adult-to-adult conversation.

WORK APPLICATIONS

2. Give an example of a crossed transaction you experienced. Be sure to identify the ego states involved.

Ulterior Transactions

Ulterior, or hidden, transactions occur when the words seem to be coming from one ego state, but in reality the words or behaviors are coming from another. For example, after a training program, one of the participants came up to a consultant asking advice on an adult ego state. When the consultant gave advice, the participant twice had quick responses as to why the advice would not work (child rather than adult behavior). The consultant realized that what the participant actually wanted was sympathetic understanding for his situation, not advice. The consultant stopped making suggestions and listened actively, using reflective responses (Chapter 4). The consultant changed from the adult to the sympathetic parent ego state in order to have a complementary transaction.

Sometimes people don't know what they want or how to ask for it in a direct way, so they use ulterior transactions. When possible, it is best to avoid ulterior transactions because they tend to waste time. Avoid making people search for your hidden meaning. Plan your message (Chapter 4) before you send it. When receiving messages look for ulterior transactions and turn them into complementary transactions, as stated above.

WORK APPLICATIONS

3. Give an example of an ulterior transaction you experienced. Be sure to identify the ego states involved.

APPLICATION SITUATIONS

**Transactional
Analysis**

AS 8–1

Identify each transaction as being:

A. Complementary B. Crossed C. Ulterior

_____ 1. "Would you help me move this package over there?" "Sure thing."

_____ 2. "Will you serve on my committee?" "Yes, I think the experience will be helpful to me" (thinking—I want to get to know you, goodlooking).

_____ 3. "Will you help me fill out this report?" "You have done several of them. Do it on your own, then I will check it for you."

_____ 4. "How much will you pay me to do the job?" "$10.00." "What! You're either joking or trying to take advantage of me."

_____ 5. "You're lying." "No, I'm not! You're the one who is lying."

Life Positions and Stroking

Life Positions

As stated in Chapter 3, attitudes affect your behavior and human relations. Within the transactional analysis framework, you have attitudes toward yourself and toward others. Positive attitudes are described as OK, and negative attitudes are described as not OK. The four life positions are illustrated in Exhibit 8–1.

EXHIBIT 8–1   **LIFE POSITIONS**

		Negative	Positive
Attitude toward Oneself	Positive	I'm OK— You're not OK	I'm OK— You're OK
	Negative	I'm not OK— You're not OK	I'm not OK— You're OK

Attitude toward Others

**Goal of
Human Relations**

Stroking

**Skill-Building
8–1**

The most desirable life position is shown in the upper right-hand box: "I'm OK—You're OK." With a positive attitude toward yourself and others, you have a greater chance for having adult-to-adult ego state communication. You can change your attitudes (Chapter 3), and you should, if they are not positive, to create win–win situations. People with a positive self-concept (Chapter 3) tend to have positive attitudes.

Stroking is any behavior that implies recognition of another's presence. Strokes can be positive and make people feel good about themselves, or they can be negative and hurt people in some way.

As discussed in Chapter 6, we all want praise and recognition. Giving praise (positive strokes) is a powerful motivation technique that is easy to use and costs nothing. We should all give positive strokes and avoid giving negative strokes.

Through work and effort, you can learn to control your emotional behavior and transact on an adult-to-adult level in most situations. Skill-Building Exercise 8–1 presents 10 situations in which you are required to identify the ego states being used to help you communicate on an adult-to-adult level.

In the opening case, Larry was behaving out of the critical parent ego state. He showed disapproval of Helen by asking, "What's wrong with you? You never acted like this before." Helen responded to Larry's request for the calculator from the adapted child ego state. Helen was rebellious and showed her anger by saying, "I'm sick and tired of your pushing me around. Go back to your desk and I'll bring it to you when I'm good and ready." They had a crossed transaction because Larry opened in his usual manner but was surprised when Helen did not respond in her typical manner. Larry was in the I'm OK—You're not OK life position; while Helen was in the I'm not OK—You're not OK life position. Both used negative strokes.

WORK APPLICATIONS

4. Identify your present/past boss's life position and use of stroking.

● Organization
● Group
● Individual

Assertiveness

Arnold Lazarus popularized what is known as assertiveness[11] and others have adapted his work.[12] Hundreds of organizations have trained their employees to be assertive[13] including Trans World Airlines Inc., HSBC, Mazda cars, Ford Motor Co., and the U.S. government. Walt Disney Productions trains all of its managers in assertiveness. Through assertiveness training, people learn how to deal with anxiety-producing situations in productive ways. Participants learn to express feelings, ask for favors, give and receive compliments, request behavior changes, and refuse unreasonable requests. Trainees learn to ask for what they want in a direct, straightforward, deliberate, and honest way that conveys self-confidence without being obnoxious or abusive. When people stand up for their rights without violating the rights of others, they are using assertive behavior.

The term **assertiveness** *is the process of expressing thoughts and feelings while asking for what one wants in an appropriate way.* You need to present your message without falling into stereotypical "too pushy" (aggressive) or "not tough enough" (nonassertive-passive) traps. Assertiveness is becoming more global. For example, the employees in Thailand are becoming more assertive,[14] and the Japanese include more strategies of assertiveness.[15]

Being assertive is generally the most productive behavior. However, there are situations in which passive or aggressive behavior is appropriate. These situations are discussed in the section on conflict resolution. Next we discuss passive, aggressive, passive-aggressive, and assertive behavior, and how to be assertive with a diversity of people.

Passive Behavior

Passive or nonassertive behavior comes primarily through the obedient child or supportive parent ego state. Passive people are in an "I'm not OK" life position. Passive behavior is an avoidance of behavior or an accommodation of the other party's wishes without standing up for one's own rights. It involves self-denial and sacrifice.

Nonverbal communication of the passive person includes downcast eyes, soft voice, helpless gestures, and slouched posture. Passive people tend to deny the importance of things. They rationalize things—"It doesn't matter to me"—and take an "it's not my responsibility, let someone else do it" attitude. Passive people are often internally distressed and in pain. Becoming assertive decreases stress.[16]

When people know someone is passive, they tend to take advantage of the person. They make unreasonable requests, knowing the person cannot say no, and refuse to meet the passive person's rare mild request. When the passive person does speak, others tend not to listen and tend to interrupt. In fact, men freely interrupt women and dismiss women's ideas—and many women tolerate this![17]

Passive people often have a poor self-concept and are unhappy. Passivity is often based on fear: fear of failure, fear of rejection, fear of displeasing others, fear of retaliation, fear of hurting others, fear of being hurt, fear of getting into trouble, and so on. Some women are passive due to a lifetime of conditioning in which they were taught to serve others and to give way to men. Many men are also passive; you may know some.

Continued passive behavior is usually unproductive for both the individual and the organization. If you are continuously passive, determine what really is important, and stand up for your rights in an assertive way.

Aggressive Behavior

Aggressive behavior comes primarily through the adapted child and the critical parent ego state. Aggressive people are demanding, tough, rude, and pushy. They insist on getting their own way and use force to gain control. They are very competitive, hate to lose to the point of cheating, and tend to violate the rights of others to get what they want.[18]

Nonverbal communication used by aggressive people includes glaring and frowning to convey coldness. Aggressive people tend to speak loudly and quickly with threatening gestures and an intimidating posture.

When faced with aggressive behavior, the other party often retaliates with aggressive behavior (fight back) or withdraws and gives in (flight). People often avoid contact with the aggressive person or prepare themselves for a fight when transacting.[19]

Aggressive people seem to be self-confident, but their behavior is more often the result of a poor self-concept. They are in an "I'm not OK" life position, but consistently try to prove they are OK by beating and controlling others. They must win to prove their self-worth, and because they violate others' rights, they are often unhappy and feel guilty. They seem to have a complaint about everything. Some women become aggressive because they feel it is behavior necessary to compete in the business world. No one should feel as though he or she has to be aggressive to be taken seriously; assertiveness is more effective.

Continuous use of aggressive behavior is usually destructive to the individual and the organization.[20] If you are continually aggressive, work at becoming more sensitive to the needs of others. Learn to replace aggressive behavior with assertive behavior.

Violence in the Workplace

Violence is clearly aggressive behavior at the extreme level. Violence in the workplace has become the number-one security concern.[21] Human resources managers have reported increased violence,[22] stating it can happen anywhere.[23] Women commit nearly a quarter of all threats or attacks.[24] Aggression is increasing personal injury, property damages, stress, absenteeism, and turnover while decreasing morale and productivity, all of which affect the bottom-line profits of the firm.[25]

People tend to copy, or model, others' behavior.[26] For example, children who have been abused (emotionally and/or physically) are more likely, as parents, to abuse their children. If employees see others being violent, and nothing is done about it, they are more apt to also use violent behavior at work. From the manager's perspective, it is very important to take quick disciplinary action against employees who are violent at work. Otherwise, aggression will spread in the organization and it will be more difficult to stop.[27] Managers especially need to avoid using aggression at work because employees more readily copy managers' behavior than other employees.[28] This practice of copying violent behavior is one of the reasons why social-conscious groups complain about too much violence on television and in the movies. Women's groups are especially concerned about men abusing women. Some groups and individuals claim that television and movie producers are a cause of increased violence in society.

Passive-Aggressive Behavior

Passive-aggressive behavior is displayed in three major ways:

1. The person uses both types of behavior sporadically. For example, a manager may be very aggressive with subordinates, yet passive with superiors.[29] Or the person may be passive one day or moment and aggressive the next. This type of person is difficult to work with because no one knows what to expect.

2. The person uses passive behavior during the situation, then shortly after uses aggressive behavior. For example, an employee may agree to do something, then leave and slam the door or yell at the next person he or she sees.

3. The person uses passive behavior but inside is building up hostility. After the repeated behavior happens often enough, the passive person becomes aggressive.[30] Too often the person who was attacked really doesn't understand the full situation and blames everything on the exploder, rather than examining his or her self-behavior, and changing. The person who becomes aggressive often feels guilty. The end result is usually hurt human relations and no change in the situation. For example, during a meeting, Carl interrupted June three times when she was speaking. June said nothing each time, but was building up hostility. The fourth time Carl interrupted June, she attacked him by yelling at him for being so inconsiderate of her. He simply said, "What's wrong with you?" It would have been better for June to assertively tell Carl not to interrupt her the first time he did it.

If you use passive-aggressive behavior, try to learn to be assertive on a consistent basis and you will be easier to work with, and you will get the results you want more often.

WORK APPLICATIONS

5. Recall an example of when you used/observed passive-aggressive behavior. How did it affect human relations?

Assertive Behavior

Assertive behavior comes through the adult ego state, with an "I'm OK—You're OK" life position. As stated earlier, the assertive person expresses feeling, thoughts, and asks for things without aggressive behavior. The person stands up for his or her rights without violating the rights of others.

The nonverbal communication of the assertive person includes positive facial expressions like smiling and eye contact, pleasant voice qualities, firm gestures, and erect posture.

People who use assertive behavior tend to have a positive self-concept. They are not threatened by others, and they do not let others control their behavior. When others are out of the adult ego state, people using assertive behavior continue to transact in an adult ego state. Assertive people project a positive image (Chapter 3) of being confident, friendly, and honest. Using assertive behavior wins the respect of others. Use it on a consistent basis.

Learning Objective

3. Identify the differences among passive, aggressive, and assertive behavior

Being Assertive

Assertive behavior is generally the most effective method of getting what you want while not taking advantage of others. Being assertive can create a win–win situation. To better understand the differences among passive, aggressive, and assertive behavior, see Exhibit 8–2. The phrases can be thought of as do's and don'ts. Do make assertive phrases and don't make passive and aggressive phrases. But remember, there are times when passive and aggressive behavior are appropriate. You will learn when later in this chapter.

Below is an example that puts it all together. When a person who is talking is interrupted, he or she could behave:

1. Passively. The person would say and do nothing.

2. Aggressively. The person could say, "I'm talking; mind your manners and wait your turn," in a loud voice, while pointing to the interrupter.

3. Assertively. The person could say, "Excuse me; I haven't finished making my point," with a smile and in a friendly but firm voice.

The passive behavior will most likely lead to the person being cut off and not listened to on a regular basis. The aggressive behavior will most likely lead to hurt human relations and could lead to an argument, while the assertive response will most likely lead to the interrupted person getting to finish now and in the future, without hurting human relations.

We will further explain how to be assertive in the next section. *In-Class Skill-Building Exercise 8-2* requires you to identify passive, aggressive, and assertive behavior in 10 different situations. With the trend toward increased use of teamwork, organizations are focusing on how to be assertive within teams to improve human relations and performance.[31]

In the opening case introduction, before the conversation took place, Helen used passive behavior, while Larry used aggressive behavior. During the confrontation Helen used aggressive behavior, but when Larry responded with aggressive behavior, she returned to passive behavior, giving him the calculator.

WORK APPLICATIONS

6. Recall an actual conflict you faced. Identify a passive, aggressive, and assertive response to the situation.

Assertiveness Steps

Below are the four assertive steps that Helen, in the opening case, could have used. These steps are summarized in Exhibit 8–3.

EXHIBIT 8-2   **PASSIVE, ASSERTIVE, AND AGGRESSIVE PHRASES**

Passive Phrases

Passive speakers use self-limiting qualifying expressions without stating their position/needs.

- I don't know/care (when I do).
- It doesn't matter (when it does).
- Either one/way is fine with me (when I have a preference).
- I'm sorry (when I don't mean it).
- It's just my opinion . . .
- I don't want to bother you, but . . .
- It's not really important, but ...

Assertive Phrases

Assertive speakers state their position/needs without violating the rights of others.

- I don't understand . . .
- I need/want/prefer . . .
- I would like . . .
- No, I won't be able to . . .
- I'd prefer that you don't tell me these jokes anymore.
- My opinion is . . .
- I need some of your time to . . .
- I thought that you would like to know . . .

Aggressive Phrases

Aggressive speakers state their position/needs while violating the rights of others using "you-messages" and absolutes.

- You don't need/want . . .
- Your opinion is wrong.
- You don't know what you're talking about.
- You're doing it wrong.
- That won't work!
- You have to . . .
- You need to know . . .

EXHIBIT 8-3   **ASSERTIVENESS STEPS**

Learning Objective

4. List the four steps of assertive behavior

Step 1. Set an objective.

Step 2. Determine how to create a win-win situation.

Step 3. Develop an assertive phrase(s).

Step 4. Implement your plan persistently.

Goal of Human Relations

Step 1. Set an Objective: Specify what you want to accomplish. Helen's objective could have been "to tell Larry that I will give him the calculator after I'm finished with it."

Step 2. Determine How to Create a Win–Win Situation:
Assess the situation in terms of meeting your needs and the other person's needs. Larry's needs are already being met by Helen's giving him the calculator any time he wants it. Presently, there is a win–lose situation. Helen needs to be assertive to meet her own needs to get her work done as well as Larry's. Equitably sharing the use of the calculator will create a win–win situation. The present system of giving it to each other when done may work fine if Helen finishes using it before giving it to Larry.

Step 3. Develop an Assertive Phrase(s):
Before confronting Larry, Helen could have developed a statement like "I'm using it now, and I'll give it to you as soon as I'm finished with it."

Step 4. Implement Your Plan Persistently:
Helen could have used the above statement. If Larry continued to use aggressive behavior to get the calculator, Helen could persistently repeat the phrase again until it sinks in, and Larry leaves without it. It is not necessary, but Helen could explain why she feels the situation is not fair and that she will continue to give the calculator to Larry when she is done with it.

Skill-Building

8–2

A P P L I C A T I O N   S I T U A T I O N S

Assertiveness

AS 8–2

Identify each response to a supervisor's request for the employee to make a personal purchase for him on company time:

A. Passive B. Aggressive C. Assertive

_____ 6. I'm not doing that, and I'll report you to the union if you ask again.

_____ 7. Is that a part of my job description?

_____ 8. I'll get on it just as soon as I finish this.

_____ 9. You know I'm not going to do a stupid thing like that. Do your own shopping.

_____ 10. Your request is unreasonable because it is not part of my job. I will not do it because we could both get in trouble.

● Organization
● Group
● Individual

Conflict Management Styles

We begin by defining conflict and stating why managing conflict skills are important. We also discuss reasons for conflicts and five conflict management styles.

A **conflict** *exists whenever two or more parties are in disagreement.* Conflict is an inherent element of any organization.[32] It cannot be avoided because individual basic traits, ideas, and beliefs are always clashing.[33] Personality conflicts will always exist,[34] and a conflict-free environment is essentially nonexistent.[35] Conflict can be detrimental to productivity.[36] However, conflict and competition can breed creativity,[37] and trying to completely eliminate it from the workplace may cause harm to the organization.[38]

Reasons for Conflict and Avoiding Conflicts

All human relations rely on unwritten, implicit expectations by each party. Often, we are not aware of our expectations until they have not been met. Communications problems or conflicts arise for three primary reasons: (1) We fail to make our expectations known to other parties; (2) We fail to find out the expectations of other parties; (3) We assume that the other parties have the same expectations that we have.

In any relationship, to avoid conflict, share information and assertively discuss expectations early, before the conflict escalates. Unfortunately, avoiding is easier said than done. As stated, we don't always know our expectations until they are not met, and they change over time. At this point we are in conflict. However, making expectations clear early can help resolve conflicts before they escalate.

In the opening case, Larry expected Helen to give him the calculator when he wants it, which he made explicit to Helen. Larry failed to find out Helen's expectations (probably did not care), and may have assumed that she did not mind giving him the calculator whenever he wanted it. Helen's expectation was that Larry would share the calculator, and she found out his expectations were not the same as hers. However, she did not assertively tell Larry this early. Thus, they are in conflict and need to talk about their expectations. Also, there are times when the other party is not being reasonable, like Larry, making conflict more common and more difficult to resolve. Helen is going to need to be assertive with Larry.

Conflict Has Positive Benefits

People often think of conflict as fighting and view it as disruptive. Conflict, however, can be beneficial.[39] The question today is not whether conflict is good or bad but rather how to manage conflict to benefit the organization.[40] A balance of conflict is essential to all organizations.[41] Too little or too much conflict is usually a sign of management's unwillingness or inability to adapt to a diversified environment. Challenging present methods and presenting innovative change causes conflict, but can lead to improved performance.[42]

Constructive conflict skills are one of the most important skills you can acquire.[43] How well you handle conflict affects your job satisfaction and success.

WORK APPLICATIONS

7. Describe a conflict you observed in an organization, preferably an organization with which you are/were associated. Classify the conflict by the people involved and the reasons for the conflict.

Learning Objective

5. Explain when a conflict exists

Before examining the five conflict management styles, complete *Self-Assessment Exercise 8–1* to determine your preferred style.

Self-Assessment Exercise 8–1

Determining Your Preferred Conflict Management Style

Below are four situations. Rank all five alternative actions from 1, the first approach you would use (most desirable), to 5, the last approach you would use (least desirable). Don't try to pick a best answer. Select the alternative that best describes what you would actually do in the situation based on your past experiences.

1. You are the general manager of a manufacturing plant. The purchasing department has found a source of material at a lower cost than the one being used. However, the production manager says the current material is superior, and he doesn't want to change. The quality control manager says that both will pass inspection with similar results. You would:

_____ *a.* Do nothing; let the purchasing and production managers work it out between themselves.

_____ *b.* Suggest having the purchasing manager find an alternative material that is cheaper but acceptable to the production manager.

_____ *c.* Have the purchasing and production managers compromise.

_____ *d.* Decide who is right and make the other comply.

_____ *e.* Get the purchasing and production managers together and work out an agreement acceptable to both parties.

2. You are a professor at a college. You have started a consulting organization and have the title of director of consulting services, which the dean has approved. You run it through the business department, using other faculty and yourself to consult. It has been going well. Randy, the director of continuing education, says that your consulting services should come under his department and not be a separate department. You would:

_____ *a.* Suggest that some services be under continuing education, but that others, like your consulting service, remain with you in the business department.

_____ *b.* Do what you can to stop the move; you go to the dean and request that the consulting services stay under your direction in the business department, as the dean OK'd originally.

_____ *c.* Do nothing. The dean will surely see through this "power grab" and turn Randy down.

_____ *d.* Go and talk to Randy. Try to come up with an agreement you are both satisfied with.

_____ *e.* Go along with Randy's request. It's not worth fighting about; you can still consult.

3. You are a branch manager for a bank. One of your colleagues cut you off twice during a managers' meeting which just ended. You would:

_____ *a.* Do nothing; it's no big deal.

_____ *b.* Discuss it in a friendly manner, but try to get the colleague to stop this behavior.

_____ *c.* Don't do or say anything because it might hurt your relations, even if you're a little upset about it.

_____ *d.* Forcefully tell the colleague that you put up with being cut off, but will not tolerate it in the future.

_____ *e.* Tell the colleague that you will listen without interrupting if he or she does the same for you.

4. You are the human resources/personnel manager. You have decided to have visitors sign in and wear guest passes. However, only about half of the employees sign their guests in before taking them to their offices to do business. You would:

_____ *a.* Go talk to the general manager about why employees are not signing in visitors.

_____ *b.* Try to find a method that will please most employees.

_____ *c.* Go to the general manager and request that he require employees to follow your procedures. If the general manager says to do it, employees will.

_____ *d.* Do not require visitors to sign in; only require them to wear guest passes.

_____ *e.* Let employees do things the way they want to.

To determine your preferred conflict management style, place your numbers 1–5 on the lines below.

Situation 1	**Situation 2**
_____ *a.* Forcing	_____ *a.* Compromising
_____ *b.* Avoiding	_____ *b.* Forcing
_____ *c.* Accommodating	_____ *c.* Avoiding
_____ *d.* Compromising	_____ *d.* Collaborating
_____ *e.* Collaborating	_____ *e.* Accommodating

Situation 3	**Situation 4**
_____ *a.* Avoiding	_____ *a.* Collaborating
_____ *b.* Collaborating	_____ *b.* Accommodating
_____ *c.* Accommodating	_____ *c.* Forcing
_____ *d.* Forcing	_____ *d.* Compromising
_____ *e.* Compromising	_____ *e.* Avoiding

Self-Assessment
Exercise 8–1 *continued*

Now place your ranking numbers 1–5 that correspond to the styles from the four situations in order; then add the four numbers.

Situation 1	Situation 2	Situation 3	Situation 4		
____ A.	____ B.	____ D.	____ C.	= ____	total, Forcing style
____ B.	____ C.	____ A.	____ E.	= ____	total, Avoiding style
____ C.	____ E.	____ C.	____ B.	= ____	total, Accommodating style
____ D.	____ A.	____ E.	____ D.	= ____	total, Compromising style
____ E.	____ D.	____ B.	____ A.	= ____	total, Collaborating style

The total with the lowest score is your preferred conflict management style. There is no one best conflict style in all situations. Like situational supervision and communications, the best style depends upon the situation. The more even the totals are, the more flexible you are at changing conflict management styles. Very high and very low totals indicate less flexibility.

It is also helpful to identify others' preferred styles in order to plan how to resolve conflicts with them.

The five conflict management styles—forcing, avoiding, accommodating, compromising, and collaborating—will be presented next. See Exhibit 8-4 for an overview of the five styles.

Forcing Conflict Style

The **forcing conflict style** *user attempts to resolve the conflict by using aggressive behavior.* The forcer uses the critical parent or adapted child ego state with aggressive behavior. The forcing approach uses an uncooperative, autocratic attempt to satisfy one's own needs at the expense of others, if necessary. A win–lose situation is created. Forcers use authority, threaten, intimidate[44] and call for majority rule when they know they will win. For example, a manager tells an employee "if you don't do it now, you're fired!"

Advantages and Disadvantages of the Forcing Style

The advantage of the forcing style is that better organizational decisions will be made (assuming the forcer is correct) rather than less effective compromised decisions. The disadvantage is that overuse of this style leads to hostility and resentment toward its user.[45]

Appropriate Use of the Forcing Style

The forcing style is appropriate to use when (1) the conflict is about personal differences (particularly values that are hard to change); (2) maintaining close, supportive relationships is not critical; and (3) conflict resolution is urgent.

Avoiding Conflict Style

The **avoiding conflict style** *user attempts to passively ignore the conflict rather than resolve it.* The avoider uses the obedient child or sympathetic parent ego state, with passive behavior. Its user is unassertive and uncooperative, and wants to avoid or postpone confrontation. A lose-lose situation is created because the conflict is not resolved. People avoid the conflict by refusing to take a stance, physically leaving it, or escaping the conflict by mentally leaving the conflict.

Advantages and Disadvantages of the Avoiding Conflict Style

The advantage of the avoiding style is that it may maintain relationships that would be hurt through conflict resolution. The disadvantage of this style is the fact that conflicts do not get resolved. An overuse of this style leads to conflict within the

EXHIBIT 8–4   **MANAGEMENT CONFLICT STYLES**

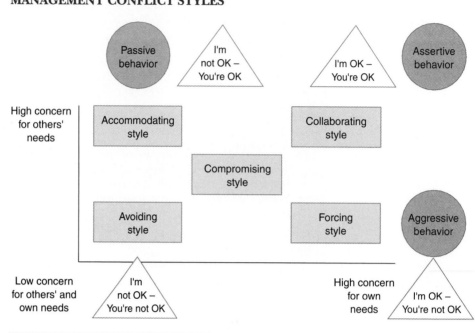

individual. People tend to walk all over the avoider. Supervisors use this style when they allow employees to break rules without confronting them. Avoiding problems usually does not make them go away; the problems usually get worse.

Appropriate Use of the Avoiding Conflict Style

The avoiding style is appropriate to use when (1) one's stake in the issue is not high; (2) confrontation will damage a critical working relationship; and (3) a time constraint necessitates avoidance. Some people use the avoiding style out of fear that they will handle the confrontation poorly, making the situation worse rather than better. After studying this chapter and following its guidelines, you should be able to handle confrontations effectively.

Accommodating Conflict Style

The **accommodating conflict style** *user attempts to resolve the conflict by passively giving in to the other party.* The user is in the obedient child or sympathetic parent ego state, using passive behavior. The accommodating approach is unassertive and cooperative. It attempts to satisfy the other party while neglecting one's own needs. A win–lose situation is created, with the other party being the winner.

Advantages and Disadvantages of the Accommodating Conflict Style

The advantage of the accommodating style is that relationships are maintained. The disadvantage is that giving in to the other party may be counterproductive. The accommodated person may have a better solution. An overuse of this style leads to people taking advantage of the accommodator, and the relationship the accommodator tries to maintain is often lost.

Appropriate Use of the Accommodating Conflict Style

The accommodating style is appropriate when: (1) maintaining the relationship outweighs all other considerations; (2) the changes agreed to are not important to the accommodator, but are to the other party; and (3) the time to resolve the conflict is limited. This is often the only style one can use with an autocratic boss.

Compromising Conflict Style

The **compromising conflict style** *user attempts to resolve the conflict through assertive give-and-take concessions.* Its user is in the adult ego state, using assertive behavior. It attempts to meet one's need for harmonious relationships. An I-win-part-I-lose-part situation is created through compromise, making the compromising style intermediate in assertiveness and cooperation. It is used in negotiations.[46]

Advantages and Disadvantages of the Compromising Conflict Style

The advantage of the compromise style is that the conflict is resolved quickly and relationships are maintained. The disadvantage is that the compromise often leads to counterproductive results (suboptimum decisions). An overuse of this style leads to people playing games such as asking for twice as much as they need in order to get what they want. It is commonly used during management and labor collective bargaining.[47]

Appropriate Use of the Compromising Conflict Style

The compromise style is appropriate to use when (1) the issues are complex and critical, and there is no simple and clear solution; (2) all parties have a strong interest in different solutions; and (3) time is short.

Collaborating Conflict Style

The **collaborating conflict style** *user assertively attempts to jointly resolve the conflict with the best solution agreeable to all parties.* It is also called the *problem-solving style.* Its user is in the adult ego state, using assertive behavior. The collaborating approach is assertive and cooperative. The collaborator attempts to fully address the concerns of all. The focus is on finding the best solution to the problem that is satisfactory to all parties. Unlike the forcer, the collaborator is willing to change if a better solution is presented. This is the only style that creates a win-win situation.

 Goal of Human Relations

Advantages and Disadvantages of the Collaborating Style

The advantage of the collaborating style is that it tends to lead to the best solution to the conflict using assertive behavior. One great disadvantage is that the time and effort it takes to resolve the conflict is usually greater and longer than the other styles.

Appropriate Use of the Collaborating Conflict Style

The collaborating style is appropriate when (1) maintaining relationships is important; (2) time is available; and (3) it is a peer conflict. To be successful, one must confront conflict. The collaborating conflict style is generally considered to be the best style because it confronts the conflict assertively, rather than passively ignoring it or aggressively fighting one's way through it.

The situational perspective states that there is no one best style for resolving all conflicts. A person's preferred style tends to meet his or her needs. Some people enjoy forcing, while others prefer to avoid conflict, and so forth. Success lies in one's ability to use the appropriate style to meet the situation. Of the five styles, the most difficult to implement successfully (and probably the most underutilized when appropriate) is the collaborative style. Therefore, the collaborative style is the only one that will be given detailed coverage in the next section of this chapter.

In the opening case, Larry consistently used the forcing conflict resolution style, while Helen began using the accommodating style, changed to the forcing style, and returned to the accommodating style. To create a true win-win situation for all parties, Helen could have used the collaborating conflict management style.

Learning Objective

6. State when and how to use five conflict management styles

WORK APPLICATIONS
---

8. Give an example of a conflict situation you face/faced and identify and explain the appropriate conflict management style to use.

APPLICATION SITUATIONS

**Selecting Conflict
Management Styles**

AS 8–3

Identify the most appropriate conflict management style as:

A. Forcing   C. Compromising   E. Collaborating

B. Avoiding   D. Accommodating

_____ 11. You are in a class that uses small groups for the entire semester. Under normal class conditions the most appropriate style is:

_____ 12. You have joined a committee in order to meet people. Your interest in its function itself is low. While serving on the committee, you make a recommendation that is opposed by another member. You realize that you have the better idea. The other party is using a forcing style.

_____ 13. You are the supervisor of a production department. An important order is behind schedule. Two of your employees are in conflict, as usual, over how to meet the deadline.

_____ 14. You are on a committee that has to select a new computer. The four alternatives will all do the job. It's the brand, price, and service that people disagree on.

_____ 15. You are a sales manager. One of your competent salespersons is trying to close a big sale. The two of you are discussing the next sales call she will make. You disagree on strategy.

_____ 16. You are on your way to an important meeting. You're late. As you turn a corner, at the end of the shop you see one of your employees goofing off instead of working.

_____ 17. You have a department crisis. Your boss calls you up and tells you, in a stern voice, to get up here right away.

_____ 18. You are in a special one-hour budget meeting with your boss and fellow supervisors. You have to finalize the total budget for each department.

_____ 19. You and a fellow supervisor are working on a report. You disagree on the format to use.

_____ 20. You're over budget for labor this month. It's slow today so you asked a part-time employee to go home early. He tells you he doesn't want to go because he needs the money.

● Organization
● Group
● Individual

Resolving Conflicts with the Collaborating Conflict Style

When a conflict exists, determine the appropriate style to use. Collaboration is not always appropriate in supervisor–employee conflicts. However, it is generally the appropriate style for conflict between colleagues and peers.

The objective of this section is to develop your ability to assertively confront (or be confronted by) people you are in conflict with, in a manner that resolves the conflict without damaging interpersonal relationships. This section examines the roles of initiator, responder, and mediator in conflict resolution.

Initiating Conflict Resolution

An initiator is a person who confronts another person(s) about a conflict. The initiator's attitude will have a major effect on the outcome of the confrontation. We tend to get what we are looking for. If you go into a confrontation expecting to argue and fight, you probably will. If you expect a successful resolution, you will probably get it. (See self-fulfilling prophecy in Chapter 2.)

To resolve conflicts, you should develop a plan of action.[48] When initiating a conflict resolution using the collaborating style, the **initiating conflict resolution steps** *are: step 1, plan to maintain ownership of the problem using the XYZ model; step 2, implement your plan persistently; step 3, make an agreement for change.*

Step 1. Plan to Maintain Ownership of the Problem Using the XYZ Model

Part of the reason confronters are not successful at resolving conflict is that they wait too long before confronting the other party, and they do it in an emotional state without planning (passive-aggressive behavior). People end up saying things they don't mean because they haven't given thought to what it is they want to say and accomplish through confrontation. You should realize that when you are upset and frustrated, the problem is yours, not the other party's. For example, you don't smoke and someone visits you who does smoke. The smoke bothers you, not the smoker. It's your problem. Open the confrontation with a request for the respondent to help you solve your problem. This approach reduces defensiveness and establishes an atmosphere of problem solving.

Know what you want to accomplish, your expectations, and say it ahead of time. Be descriptive, not evaluative. Avoid trying to determine who is to blame.[49] Both parties are usually partly to blame. Fixing blame only gets people defensive, which is counterproductive to conflict resolution. Keep the opening statement short. The longer the statement, the longer it will take to resolve the conflict. People get defensive when kept waiting for their turn to talk. Use the XYZ model.[50] The **XYZ model** *describes a problem in terms of behavior, consequences, and feelings:* When you do X (behavior), Y (consequences) happens, and I feel Z (feelings). For example, when you smoke in my room (behavior), I have trouble breathing and become nauseous (consequence), and I feel uncomfortable and irritated (feeling). Vary the sequence and start with a feeling or consequence to fit the situation and to provide variety.

As stated in Chapter 5, timing is also important. Don't confront people when they are involved in something else. If the other party is busy, set an appointment to discuss the conflict. In addition, don't confront a person on several unrelated issues at once.

WORK APPLICATIONS

9. Use the XYZ model to describe a conflict problem you face/faced.

Step 2. Implement Your Plan Persistently

After making your short, planned XYZ statement, let the other party respond. If the confronted party acknowledges the problem and says he or she will change, you may have succeeded. Often people do not realize there is a conflict and when approached properly are willing to change. However, if the other party does not understand or avoids acknowledgment of the problem, persist. You cannot resolve a conflict if the other party will not even acknowledge its existence. Repeat your planned statement several times, and/or explain it in different terms, until you get an acknowledgment or realize it's hopeless. But don't give up too easily, and be sure to listen to the other party and watch nonverbal clues.[51]

When the other party acknowledges the problem, but is not responsive to resolving it, appeal to common goals. Make the other party realize the benefits to him or her and the organization as well.

Step 3. Make an Agreement for Change

Try to come to an agreement of specific action you will both take to resolve the conflict.[52] Remember that you are collaborating, not forcing. If possible, get a commitment statement describing the change.

Below is an example conflict resolution:

PAM: Hi, Bill! Got a few minutes to talk?

BILL: Sure, what's up?

PAM: Something's been bothering me lately, and I wanted you to know about it. When you come to class without doing your homework [*behavior*], I get irritated [*feeling*], and our group has to wait for you to read the material, or make a decision without your input [*consequences*].

BILL: Hey, I'm busy!

PAM: Do you think the rest of the group isn't?

BILL: No.

PAM: Are grades important to you?

BILL: Yeah, if I don't get good grades I can't play on the football team.

PAM: You get a grade for doing your homework, and we all get the same group grade. Your input helps us all to get a better grade.

BILL: You're right; sometimes I forget about that. Well, sometimes I don't do it because I don't understand the assignment.

PAM: I'll tell you what; when you don't understand it call me, or come over, and I'll explain it. You know my number and address.

BILL: I'd appreciate that.

PAM: So you agree to do your homework before class, and I agree to help you when you need it.

BILL: OK, I'll do it from now on.

Video

BM–8

Skill-Building

8–3

Responding to Conflict Resolution

A responder is a person confronted by an initiator. Here's how to handle the role of the responder to a conflict.

Most initiators do not follow the model above. Therefore, the responder must take responsibility for successful conflict resolution by following the conflict resolution model. The **responding to conflict resolution steps** *are: step 1, listen to and paraphrase the problem using the XYZ model; step 2, agree with some aspect of the complaint; step 3, ask for, and/or give, alternative solutions; step 4, make an agreement for change.* These steps are also presented in Exhibit 8–5.

Mediating Conflict Resolution

Frequently, conflicting employees cannot resolve their dispute. In these cases, the manager should mediate to help them resolve their differences.[53]

Before bringing the conflicting parties together, the manager should decide whether to start with a joint meeting or conduct individual meetings. If one employee comes to complain, but has not confronted the other party, or if there is a serious discrepancy in employee perceptions, the manager should meet one-on-one with each party before bringing them together. On the other hand, when both parties have a similar awareness of the problem and motivation to solve it, the manager can begin with a joint meeting when all parties are calm. The manager should be a mediator, not a judge. Make employees realize it's their problem, not yours, and that they are responsible for solving it.[54] Get the employees to resolve the conflict,[55] if possible. Remain impartial, unless one party is violating company policies. Don't belittle the parties in conflict. Don't make parent comments like "I'm disappointed in you two; you're acting like babies."

When bringing conflicting parties together, follow the mediating conflict model. The **mediating conflict resolution steps** *are: step 1, have each party state his or her complaint using the XYZ model; step 2, agree on the problem(s); step 3, develop alternative solutions; step 4, make an agreement for change and follow up.* These steps also appear in Exhibit 8–5.

EXHIBIT 8–5

CONFLICT RESOLUTION

Initiating Conflict Resolution

Step 1. Plan to maintain ownership of the problem using the XYZ model.

Step 2. Implement your plan persistently.

Step 3. Make an agreement for change.

Responding to Conflict Resolution

Step 1. Listen to and paraphrase the problem using the XYZ model.

Step 2. Agree with some aspect of the complaint.

Step 3. Ask for, and/or give, alternative solutions.

Step 4. Make an agreement for change.

Mediating Conflict Resolution

Learning Objective

7. List the steps of initiating, responding to, and mediating conflict resolutions

Step 1. Have each party state his or her complaint using the XYZ model.

Step 2. Agree on the problem(s).

Step 3. Develop alternative solutions.

Step 4. Make an agreement for change and follow up.

IE 8–1
IE 8–2

In the assertiveness section, there was an example of how Helen could have been assertive with Larry in the opening case. In addition to being assertive with Larry, Helen could have used the collaborating conflict style to resolve the calculator problem. Helen could have suggested to Larry that the two of them go to the boss and ask for another calculator so that they could each have their own. A second calculator could create a win-win situation for all parties. Helen and Larry would both win because they would not have to wait for the calculator. The department would win because productivity would increase; there would be less time wasted getting and waiting for the calculator. The organization wins because the department performs efficiently. Obtaining a second calculator is a good conflict resolution. However, the department/organization may not have the money in the budget to buy a new calculator, or the idle time may actually be cheaper. If this is the case, Helen can be assertive and keep the calculator until she is finished—this is a win–win situation; or they could work out some other collaborative agreement, such as each having the calculator during specific hours. If Larry is not willing to collaborate, their boss will have to mediate the conflict resolution.

WORK APPLICATIONS

10. Describe an actual situation in which the initiating, responding, and/or mediating conflict resolution model would be appropriate.

● Organization
● Group
● Individual

Interpersonal Dynamics

Interpersonal dynamics are the behavior used during our human relations,[56] and interpersonal dynamics grow increasing complex as more people interact.[57] TA, assertiveness, and conflict management are all interpersonal skills that can help you develop good human relations. Let's discuss how these three skills fit together to create interpersonal dynamic styles, and how they affect behavior, human relations, and performance.

Putting It All Together

Goal of
Human Relations

To see the relationship between TA, assertiveness, and conflict management, see Exhibit 8–6. Notice that the first two columns come from conflict management, the third is from assertiveness, the fourth and fifth come from TA, and the last column relates to the goal of human relations. The last column shows the order of priority of which interpersonal behavior to use to meet the goal of human relations. However, remember that this is general advice. As stated in the chapter, at times other behavior is appropriate. In the majority of your human relations, you should strive to have a high concern for meeting your needs while meeting the needs of others. You should use an assertive, adult, collaborating style to create a win–win situation for all parties.

EXHIBIT 8–6   **INTERPERSONAL DYNAMICS STYLES**

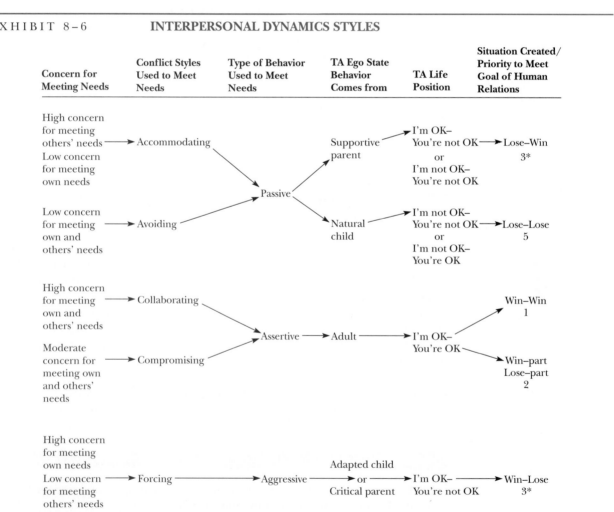

---

*The win-lose and lose-win situations are equal in priority to the group/organization because both an individual and the group/organization lose. The individual's loss is more important to the loser than to the group.

■ Performance
■ Human Relations
■ Behavior

Goal of
Human Relations

Goal of
Human Relations

How Interpersonal Dynamics Affect Behavior, Human Relations, and Performance

In reviewing Exhibit 8–6, you should see that people using the passive, accommodating–avoiding conflict styles behave the opposite of the people who use the aggressive, forcing conflict style. Assertive people use the collaborative conflict style, and their behavior is between the other two extremes.

You should also understand that people using the passive, accommodating-avoiding conflict styles tend to have opposite human relations than people using the aggressive, forcing conflict style. The passive person tends to shy away from making friends and being actively involved, while the aggressive person tries to take over and is offensive to the group. Assertive people use the collaborating style and tend to be friendly and outgoing as they work to create win–win situations for all parties. Generally, people who are passive don't get their needs met; they get walked over by the aggressive people. Aggressive people are disliked because they violate the rights of others. Assertive people tend to have the best human relations.

No clear relationship exists between individual performance and the interpersonal dynamic style used. Many passive people work well alone, and so do aggressive people. Aggressive people are sometimes more productive than passive people because they can take advantage of passive people. This happened in the opening case. When it comes to group/organizational performance, the assertive person is generally the most responsible for the group effort because passive people may have great ideas on how to do a good group job, but they don't say how. Aggressive people only look out for themselves. If someone offers a different idea than theirs, they are not willing to collaborate for the good of all. The assertive group member collaboratively shares ideas but is willing to change to a better alternative to create a win–win situation for all.

By following the guidelines in this chapter, you can develop assertive collaborating skills.

REVIEW

Select one or more methods: (1) fill in the missing key terms from memory; (2) match the key terms from the end of the review with their definitions below; and/or (3) copy the key terms in order from the key terms at the beginning of the chapter.

_____ is a method of understanding behavior in interpersonal dynamics. The three _____ are the parent, child, and adult. The parent includes the critical parent and sympathetic parent, while the child ego state includes the natural and adapted child. The three _____ are complementary, crossed, and ulterior. Complementary adult-to-adult discussions are generally more productive in organizations. There are four life positions, and giving positive strokes is desirable.

Passive behavior is an avoidance of behavior or an accommodation of the other party's wishes without standing up for one's rights. Aggressive behavior is the forcing of one's will on others without regard for their rights. Passive-aggressive behavior is the use of both types of behavior. _____ is the process of expressing thoughts and feelings while asking for what one wants in an appropriate way. Generally, assertive behavior is most productive; however, there are situations in which passive and aggressive behavior is appropriate.

The steps in being assertive are: step 1, set an objective; step 2, determine how to create a win–win situation; step 3, develop an assertive phrase(s); step 4, implement your plan persistently.

_____ exists whenever two or more parties are in disagreement. Conflict management skills are important to interpersonal relations.

There are two methods of classifying types of conflict: (1) constructive and destructive, and (2) by the people involved—conflict within the individual, interpersonal conflict, conflict between an individual and a group, intragroup conflict, and conflict between organizations. These sources of conflict include personal differences, information, different objectives, and environmental factors. The conflict management styles are: The _____ user attempts to resolve the conflict by using aggressive behavior. The _____ user attempts to passively ignore the conflict rather than resolve it. The _____ user attempts to resolve the conflict by passively giving in to the other party. The _____ user attempts to resolve the conflict through assertive give-and-take concessions. The _____ user assertively attempts to jointly resolve the conflict with the best solution agreeable to all parties. Each style has its advantages and disadvantages, and each is appropriate in certain situations.

The _____ are: step 1, plan to maintain ownership of the problem using the XYZ model; step 2, implement your plan persistently; step 3, make an agreement for change. The _____ describes a problem in terms of behavior, consequences, and feelings. The _____ are: step 1, listen to and paraphrase the problem using the XYZ model; step 2, agree with some aspect of the complaint; step 3, ask for, and/or give, alternative solutions; step 4, make an agreement for change. The _____ are: step 1, have each party state his or her complaint using the XYZ model; step 2, agree on the problem(s); step 3, develop alternative solutions; step 4, make an agreement for change and follow up.

Interpersonal dynamics are the behavior used during our human relations. People who are passive and aggressive use opposite behavior, while assertive people behave between these two extremes. Generally, the people who use assertive behavior, from the adult ego state, have a high concern for meeting their own needs and the needs of others. They tend to use the collaborate conflict style and use the most appropriate behavior, which contributes to creating a win–win situation. Exhibit 8–6, Interpersonal Dynamics Styles, summarizes TA, assertiveness, and conflict management; return to it as a review.

KEY TERMS

CASE

Andrea Cunningham: Cunningham Communication

Andrea Cunningham started her own public relations (PR) firm in Santa Clara, California. Andrea believed that any PR firm could package and disseminate information. Her mission gave Cunningham a competitive advantage (keeping clients apprised of how they were perceived by the market, To live the mission, Cunningham keeps tabs on the financial community, the press, consultants, customers, and even employees within the firm. High-quality employees are critical to PR success because the client must have extreme confidence in the PR people in charge of their account because they oftentimes have to give the client bad news based on the data they gather. Client turnover is high at most PR agencies, and employee job-hopping is also common as PR representatives search for higher pay and new challenges.

Cunningham acquired some of Silicon Valley's best clients including Borland International and Aldus Corporation software makers and Hewlett-Packard and Motorola. Andrea's Cunningham Communication revenues grew to over $3 million annually with 24 employees. However, Andrea made a common entrepreneurial error. She tried to make all the decisions herself without delegating authority. As a result, managers were constantly fighting, morale was very low, turnover of both clients and employees was very high, and Andrea faced the threat of losing money for the first time since she started the business.

Faced with problems, Andrea knew changes were needed. Her first attempt was to assign clients to individual teams and to give bonuses based on profitability. Unfortunately, internal competition became fierce. Turf wars developed, employees refused to share information, and there was no cooperation between teams. Andrea realized that teams were a good idea, but the team system needed to be changed.

Andrea came to the realization that she had to delegate authority if she was going to have a turnaround. Andrea decided to develop a goal-driven system with a cooperative management program called input teams. Andrea set annual objectives for each team that developed the necessary plans and budgets to achieve the objectives. Every employee was a member of at least one team that meet for five hours per week. Andrea also realized that her human resource practices had to support the Cunningham mission and new management system. Working with her human resource manager and others they developed the following program.

To attract and retain employees, called associates, they developed a career path system. A career path is a sequence of job assignments that leads to more responsibility with raises and promotions. The career path system was designed to develop associates to a level of competence that inspired the confidence of clients. New associates were oriented to the organizational culture, which is called the Cunningham Culture. They are taught about the input teams and develop team skills, the various departments, and develop time-management skills. New associates attend Cunningham Communications Inc. University for a formal three-day training session.

The compensation system was also changed. All associates receive a set pay for the year and a bonus based on meeting objectives. Each associate determines his or her responsibilities, objectives, and pay. Andrea says that associates rarely request compensation that they are not worth. Frequent advisory sessions give associates feedback from their bosses on how well they are meeting expectations. On occasion when associates fall short of their objectives, compensation has been withheld without complaint. To increase compensation, associates have to generate more revenue.

Some of Andrea's productive senior employees complained about the new system. They did not want to be included with a team. However, Andrea stayed firm in keeping the system, even when senior people started to quit. Within six months of implementing the above changes, all but three members of the senior staff voluntarily terminated employment at Cunningham. Andrea was sad to see them go, but felt they were not right for the new management system. On the positive side, the company became profitable and continues to grow; the number of associates went from 24 to 59 under the new system.

Go to the Internet: For more information on Andrea Cunningham and Cunningham Communications, Inc. to update the information provided in this case, do a name search on the Internet and visit *www.ccipr.com.* For ideas on using the Internet with cases, see Appendix C.

Support your answer to the following questions with specific information from the case and text, or other information you get from the web or other source.

1. How is assertiveness illustrated in this case?

Cumulative Case Questions

2. Identify at least two conflict situations at Cunningham.

3. Which conflict management style did Andrea use with the senior staff?

4. Did Andrea Cunningham effectively resolve the two conflicts you identified in Question 2?

5. What are the learning organization issues in this case (Chapter 2)?

6. What happened to job satisfaction through the change to teams (Chapter 3)?

7. What is the role of organizational structure and communications in this case (Chapters 4 and 5)?

8. Which two motivation techniques did Andrea primarily use in the new teams (Chapter 6)?

9. Which situational supervision style did Andrea use in this case in developing the team system and team objectives? Which situational supervision style did she use on an individual basis (Chapter 7)?

Bill and Saul's Conflict

The following conversation takes place over the telephone between Bill, the salesperson, and Saul, the production manager. (*Note:* This conversation can be role-played in class.)

BILL: Listen, Saul, I just got an order for 1,000 units and promised delivery in two days. You'll get them out on time, won't you?

SAUL: Bill, you know the normal delivery time is five days.

BILL: I know, but I had to say two days to get the order, so fill it.

SAUL: We don't have the capability to do it. You should have checked with me before taking the order. The best I can do is four days.

BILL: What are you—my mother, or the production manager?

SAUL: I cannot have 1,000 units ready in two days. We have other orders that need to be filled before yours. Four days is the best I can do on short notice.

BILL: Come on, Saul, you cannot do this to me, I want to keep this account. It can mean a lot of business.

SAUL: I know, Bill; you've told me this on three other orders you had.

BILL: But this is a big one. Don't you care about sales?

SAUL: Yes, I do, but I cannot produce the product as fast as you sales reps are selling it lately.

BILL: If I don't meet my sales quota, are you going to take the blame?

SAUL: Bill, we are going in circles here. I'm sorry, but I cannot fill your request. The order will be ready in five days.

BILL: I was hoping you would be reasonable. But you've forced me to go to Mr. Carlson. You know he'll be telling you to fill my order. Why don't you just do it and save time and aggravation?

SAUL: I'll wait to hear from Mr. Carlson. In the meantime, have a good day, Bill.

Answer the following questions. Then in the space between the questions, state why you selected that answer.

_____ 1. Bill was transacting from the ____ ego state.

      a. critical parent   *c.* adult   *e.* adapted child
      b. sympathetic parent   *d.* natural child

_____ 2. Saul was transacting from the ____ ego state.

      a. critical parent   *c.* adult   *e.* adapted child
      b. sympathetic parent   *d.* natural child

_____ 3. The telephone discussion was a(n) ____ transaction.

      a. complementary   *b.* crossed   *c.* ulterior

_____ 4. Bill's life position seems to be:

      a. I'm OK—You're not OK   *c.* I'm not OK—You're not OK
      b. I'm OK—You're OK   *d.* I'm not OK—You're OK

_____ 5. Bill's behavior was:

      a. passive   *b.* aggressive   *c.* assertive

_____ 6. Saul's behavior was:

    a. passive   *b.* aggressive   *c.* assertive

_____ 7. Bill and Saul have an ____ conflict.

    a. individual   *c.* individual/group
    b. interpersonal   *d.* intragroup

_____ 8. Their source of conflict is:

    a. personal differences   *c.* objectives
    b. information   *d.* environment

_____ 9. Bill used the ____ conflict style.

    a. forcing   *c.* accommodating   *e.* collaborating
    b. avoiding   *d.* compromising

10. Saul used the ____ conflict style.

    a. forcing   *c.* accommodating   *e.* collaborating
    b. avoiding   *d.* compromising

11. What would you have done if you were Bill?

12. Assume you are Mr. Carlson, the boss. What would you do if Bill called?

Fiscal Fairy Tale # 1:
Jak and the Bean Counter

Following the steps to getting to read a *Fiscal Fairy Tale* in MG 1 in Chapter 1 page 34, go to the MG website and read *Fiscal Fairy Tale # 1: Jak and the Bean Counter* (your instructor may ask you to print a copy and bring it to class). Answer these questions (your instructor may ask you to type them and bring them to class):

Online MG Webzine
Exercise 8

Questions Relating to the Tale Only

1. As stated at the end of the tale, in 50 words or so, what is your response to this tale? You may send it to MG.

2. Have you, or anyone you know, worked with people who are number conscious? Give some examples of things the employees and organizational managers count.

3. Do you understand what is going on in the executive suite, or is it mysterious and unknown to you? Explain.

4. Who really owns the firm you worked for?

Questions Relating the Tale to the Chapter Concepts

5. When the Giant asked questions of Jak, in what ego state was the Giant?

6. Was Jak's behavior with the Giant and taking the envelope passive, aggressive, or assertive?

7. When Jak was in the Giant's office talking, was there a conflict?

In-Class MG Webzine
Exercise 8

The instructor selects one of the six options from Appendix B page 589.

INTERNET EXERCISES

Assertiveness (IE 8–1)

Online Internet Exercise 8–1 (Self-Assessment)

The objective of this Internet exercise is to assess your use of assertiveness as low to high. Use the information from Appendix B and IE 1–2 and 1–3 as you do the following:

1. Go to the Body-Mind QueenDom website homepage—*www.queendom.com*
2. Click "Tests" and scroll down to the Career/Jobs tests section and Click "Assertiveness" and take the test by clicking your selections then click score to get your score and interpretation (your instructor may ask you to make a copy of it to bring to class).
3. Questions: (1) What was your score? (2) Do you have a low, moderate, or high assertiveness? (3) What can you do to improve your assertiveness? (Your instructor may ask you to type and print your answer and bring them to class.)

In-Class Internet Exercise 8–1, IE 8–2, and IE 8–3

The instructor selects one of the six options from Appendix B page 589.

Conflict (IE 8–2)

Online Internet Exercise 8–2

The objective of this exercise is to learn more about conflict by using a supersite. A supersite is a website with links to other websites. Essentially, you go to one site that links/directs you to another website. Thus, for this exercise, you will actually visit two websites. Use the information in Appendix B and IE 1–2 and 1–3 as you do the following:

1. Go to the Work911 website homepage—*www.work911.com*
2. Scroll down to find a list of articles under the heading "Community and Conflict Related" and Click "view" for the one you want to read. You will be taken to another website where you read the article (your instructor may require you to make a copy of it).
3. Questions: (1) What is the name of the website you went to? (2) Who is the author and what is the title of the article you read. (3) What is the basic message of the article you read? (4) How can you use this information to help resolve conflicts in your personal and professional life? (Your instructor may require you to type and print your answers.)

Select a Concept: MG Search (IE 8–3)

Online Internet Exercise 8–3

The objective of this exercise is to learn more about a concept of your choice. Use the information in Appendix B and IE 1–2 and 1–3 as you do the following:

1. Go to the MG homepage—*www.mgeneral.com*
2. Click "Search (Site Map)."
3. Click the "Concept" button/circle to use the concept search mode then type in a concept from this or another chapter that you want to learn more about.
4. Click the resource you want to learn more about (your instructor may require you to print it).
5. Questions: (1) Who is the author and what is the title and year of the resource? (2) What are the primary concept ideas? (3) How can you use these ideas in your personal and professional life? (Your instructor may require you to type and print your answers.)

● **Preparation Transactional Analysis**

Below are 10 situations. For each situation:

1. Identify the sender's communication ego state as:

    CP Critical Parent

    SP Sympathetic Parent

    NC Natural Child

    AC Adapted Child

    A Adult

2. Place the letters CP, SP, NC, AC, or A on the S ____ to the left of each numbered situation.

3. Identify each of the five alternative receiver's ego states as in instruction 1 above. Place the letters CP, SP, NC, AC, or A on the R.

4. Select the best alternative to achieve effective communication and human relations. Circle the letter *a, b, c, d,* or *e.*

S ____ 1. Ted delegates a task, saying, "It's not much fun, but someone has to do it. Will you please do it for me?" Sue, the delegatee, says:

    a. "A good boss wouldn't make me do it."   R ____

    b. "I'm always willing to help you out, Ted."   R ____

    c. "I'm not cleaning that up."   R ____

    d. "You're not being serious, are you?"   R ____

    e. "I'll get right on it."   R ____

S ____ 2. Helen, a customer, brought a dress to the cleaners and later she picked it up, paid, and went home. At home she opened the package and found that the dress was not clean. Helen returned to the cleaners and said, "What's wrong with this place? Don't you know how to clean a dress?" The cleaning person, Saul, responds:

    a. "It's not my fault. I didn't clean it personally."   R ____

    b. "I'm sorry this happened. We'll do it again right now."   R ____

    c. "I can understand your disappointment. Were you planning on wearing it today? What can I do to make this up to you?"   R ____

    d. "These are stains caused by your carelessness, not ours."   R ____

    e. "Gee whiz, this is the first time this has happened."   R ____

S ____ 3. In an office, Bill drops a tray of papers on the floor. Mary, the manager, comes over and says, "This happens once in awhile to all of us. Let me help you pick them up." Bill responds:

    a. "Guess I slipped, ha ha ha."   R ____

    b. "This wouldn't have happened if people didn't stack the papers so high."   R ____

    c. "It's not my fault; I'm not picking up the papers."   R ____

    d. "Thanks for helping me pick them up, Mary."   R ____

    e. "It will not take long to pick them up."   R ____

S ____ 4. Karl and Kelly were talking about the merit raise given in their branch of the bank. Karl says: "I heard you did not get a merit raise." Kelly responds:

   a. "It's true; how much did you get?"   R ____

   b. "I really don't need a raise anyway."   R ____

   c. "The branch manager is unfair."   R ____

   d. "The branch manager didn't give me a raise because he is prejudiced. The men got bigger raises than the women."   R ____

   e. "It's nice of you to show your concern. Is there anything I can do to help you out?"   R ____

S ____ 5. Beckie, the store manager, says to an employee: "Ed, there is no gum on the counter; please restock it." Ed responds:

   a. "Why do I always get stuck doing it?"   R ____

   b. "I'd be glad to do it. I know how important it is to keep the shelves stocked for our customers."   R ____

   c. "I'll do it just as soon as I finish this row."   R ____

   d. "I'll do it if I can have a free pack."   R ____

   e. "Why don't we buy bigger boxes so I don't have to do it so often?"   R ____

S ____ 6. Carol, the manager, asked Tim, an employee, to file some forms. Awhile later Carol returned and asked Tim why he hadn't filed the forms. Tim said: "Oh, oh! I forgot about it." Carol responds:

   a. "I've told you before; write things down so you don't forget to do them."   R ____

   b. "It's OK. I know you're busy and will do it when you can."   R ____

   c. "Please do it now."   R ____

   d. "What's wrong with you?"   R ____

   e. "You daydreaming or what?"   R ____

S ____ 7. Joan just finished making a budget presentation to the controller, Wayne. He says: "This budget is padded." Joan responds:

   a. "I'm sorry you feel that way. What is a fair budget amount?"   R ____

   b. (*laughing*) "I don't pad any more than the others."   R ____

   c. "You don't know what you're talking about. It's not padded."   R ____

   d. "What items do you believe are padded?"   R ____

   e. "You can't expect me to run my department without some padding for emergencies, can you?"   R ____

S ____ 8. Jill, a computer repair technician, says to the customer: "What did you do to this computer to make it malfunction like this?" The customer responds:

   a. "Can you fix it?"   R ____

   b. "I take good care of this machine. You better fix it fast."   R ____

   c. "I'm sorry to upset you. Are you having a rough day?"   R ____ *d.* "I'm going to tell your boss what you just said."   R ____

       e. "I threw it down the stairs, ha ha."   R ____

S ____ 9. Pete is waiting for his friend, Will, whom he hasn't seen for some time. When Will arrives, Pete says, "It's good to see you," and gives Will a hug, spinning him around. Will responds:

       a. "Don't hug me on the street; people can see us."   R ____

       b. "I'm not late; you got here early."   R ____

       c. "Sorry I'm late. Is there anything I can do to make it up to you? Just name it."   R ____

       d. "Let's go party, party, party."   R ____

       e. "Sorry I'm late; I got held up in traffic."   R ____

S ____ 10. Sally gives her secretary, Mike, a note saying: "Please, type this when you get a chance." About an hour later, Sally returns from a meeting and asks: "Mike, is the letter I gave you done yet?" Mike responds:

       a. "If you wanted it done by 11, why didn't you say so?"   R ____

       b. "I'm working on it now. It will be done in about 10 minutes." R ____

       c. "You said to do it when I got a chance. I've been too busy doing more important things."   R ____

       d. "Sure thing, boss lady, I'll get right on it."   R ____

       e. "I'm sorry, I didn't realize how important it was. Can I type it right now and get it to you in about 15 minutes?"   R ____

● **In-Class Skill Transactional Analysis**

SB 8–1

Procedure

Objective: To improve your ability to use transactional analysis.

SCANS: The SCANS competencies of resources, interpersonal skills, and information and the foundations of basic thinking, and personal qualities are developed through this exercise.

Preparation: You should have completed the preparation (10 situations) for this exercise.

Select one option.

1. The instructor goes over the recommended answers to the 10 situations.

2. The instructor asks students for their answers to the situations, followed by giving the recommended answers.

3. Break into groups of two or three and together follow the three-step approach for two to three situations at a time, followed by the instructor going over the recommended answers. Discuss the possible consequences of each alternative response in the situation. Would it help or hurt human relations and performance? How?

Conclusion: The instructor leads a class discussion and/or makes concluding remarks.

Application: What have I learned from this experience? How will I use this knowledge in the future?

Sharing: Volunteers give their answers to the application section.

SKILL-BUILDING EXERCISE 8-2

 **Preparation
Assertiveness**

In this exercise are 10 situations with 5 alternative statements or actions. Identify each as assertive (A), aggressive (G), or passive (P). Place the letter A, G, or P on the line before each of the five alternatives. Circle the letter (*a–e*) of the response that is the most appropriate in the situation.

1. In class, you are in small groups discussing this exercise; however, two of the members are talking about personal matters instead. You are interested in this exercise.

    ____ *a.* "Don't you want to learn anything in this class?"

    ____ *b.* Forget the exercise, join the conversation.

    ____ *c.* "This is a valuable exercise. I'd really appreciate your input."

    ____ *d.* "This exercise is boring, isn't it?"

    ____ *e.* "Stop discussing personal matters, or leave the class!"

2. You and your roommate do not smoke. Smoke really bothers you. However, your roommate has friends over who smoke in your room regularly.

    ____ *a.* Throw them out of your room.

    ____ *b.* Purposely cough repeatedly saying, "I cannot breathe."

    ____ *c.* Ask your roommate to have his guests refrain from smoking, or meet at a different place.

    ____ *d.* Complain to your favorite professor.

    ____ *e.* Do and say nothing.

3. Your boss has repeatedly asked you to go get coffee for the members of the department. It is not part of your job responsibility.

    ____ *a.* "It is not part of my job. Why don't we set up a rotating schedule so that everyone has a turn?"

    ____ *b.* "Go get it yourself."

    ____ *c.* Continue to get the coffee.

    ____ *d.* File a complaint with personnel/union.

    ____ *e.* "Why don't we skip coffee today?"

4. You are riding in a car with a friend. You are nervous because your friend is speeding, changing lanes frequently, and passing in no-passing zones.

    ____ *a.* "Are you trying to kill me?"

    ____ *b.* "What did you think of Professor Lussier's class today?"

    ____ *c.* "Please slow down and stay in one lane."

    ____ *d.* Try not to look where you are going.

    ____ *e.* "Stop driving like this or let me out right here."

5. You are in a department meeting that is deciding on the new budget. However, some of the members are going off on tangents and wasting time. Your boss hasn't said anything about it.

    ____ *a.* Don't say anything. After all, it's your boss's meeting.

    ____ *b.* "So far we agree on XYZ, and we still need to decide on ABC. Does anyone have any ideas on these line items?"

_____ *c.* "Let's stop wasting time and stay on the subject."

_____ *d.* "Let's just vote so we can get out of here."

_____ *e.* "Excuse me, I have to go to the bathroom."

6. One of your coworkers repeatedly tries to get you to do his or her work with all kinds of excuses.

_____ *a.* Do the work.

_____ *b.* "I have no intention of doing your work, so please stop asking me to do it."

_____ *c.* "Buzz off. Do it yourself, freeloader."

_____ *d.* "I'd like to do it for you, but I'm tied up right now."

_____ *e.* "Get away from me and don't bother me again."

7. You bought a watch. It doesn't work so you return to the store with the receipt. The salesclerk says you cannot exchange it.

_____ *a.* Insist on the exchange. Talk to the person's boss and his or her boss if necessary.

_____ *b.* Leave with the watch.

_____ *c.* Drop the watch on the counter and pick up a new watch and walk out.

_____ *d.* Come back when a different salesclerk is there.

_____ *e.* Create a scene, yell, and get other customers on your side. Disrupt business until you get the new watch.

8. You are about to leave work and go to see your child/friend perform in a play. Your boss comes to you and asks you to stay late to do a report she needs in the morning.

_____ *a.* "Sorry, I'm on my way to see a play."

_____ *b.* "I'd be happy to stay and do it."

_____ *c.* "Are you sure I cannot do it tomorrow?"

_____ *d.* "I'm on my way to see a play. Can I take it home and do it later tonight?"

_____ *e.* "Why should I get stuck here? Why don't you do it yourself?"

9. You believe that cheating is wrong. Your roommate just asked you if he or she could copy the homework you spent hours preparing.

_____ *a.* "Here you go."

_____ *b.* "I don't help cheaters."

_____ *c.* "OK, if you don't copy it word for word."

_____ *d.* "I'd like to help you. You're my friend, but in good conscience I cannot let you copy my homework."

_____ *e.* "You go out and have a good time, then you expect me to be a fool and get you off the hook? No way."

10. Some people you know stop by your dorm room. One of them pulls out some drugs, takes some, and passes it along. You don't take drugs.

_____ *a.* "I don't approve of taking drugs. You can get me into trouble. Please put them away or leave."

_____ *b.* Grab them and get rid of them.

_____ *c.* Take some drugs because you don't want to look bad.

_____ *d.* Pass them along without taking any.

_____ *e.* "Are you trying to kill yourselves? Get out of here with that stuff."

SKILL-BUILDING EXERCISE 8–2

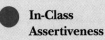

In-Class Assertiveness

Procedure

Objective: To improve your ability to be assertive.

SCANS: The SCANS competencies of resources, and interpersonal skills, and information and the foundations of basic thinking, and personal qualities are developed through this exercise.

Preparation: You should have completed the preparation (10 situations) for this exercise.

Select one option.

1. The instructor goes over the recommended answers to the 10 situations.

2. The instructor asks students for their answers to the situations, followed by giving the recommended answers.

3. Break into groups of two or three and together follow the three-step approach for 2–3 situations at a time, followed by the instructor going over the recommended answers. Discuss the possible consequences of each alternative response in the situation. Would it help or hurt human relations and performance? How?

Conclusion: The instructor leads a class discussion and/or makes concluding remarks.

Application: What have I learned from this experience? How will I use this knowledge in the future?

Sharing: Volunteers give their answers to the application section.

SKILL-BUILDING EXERCISE 8–3

Preparation Initiating Conflict Resolution

During class you will be given the opportunity to role-play a conflict you face, or have faced, in order to develop your conflict skills. Fill in the information below and also record your answers on a separate sheet of paper.

Other party(ies) (You may use fictitious names) ____
    Define the situation:

1. List pertinent information about the other party (e.g., relationship with you, knowledge of the situation, age, background).

2. State what you wish to accomplish (objective) as a result of the conflict confrontation/discussion.

3. Identify the other party's possible reaction to your confrontation (resistance to change: intensity, source, focus).

    How will you overcome this resistance to change?
    Using the three steps in initiating conflict resolution, write out your plan to initiate the conflict resolution. Write your plan on a separate sheet of paper and bring it to class.

For In-Class Use
SB 8–3

Feedback for _____

Try to have positive improvement comments for each step in initiating conflict resolution. Remember to be DESCRIPTIVE and SPECIFIC, and for all improvements have an alternative positive behavior (APB) (i.e., if you would have said/done. . ., it would have improved the conflict resolution by. . .).

Positive   Improvement

Step 1. Did the initiator maintain ownership of the problem?

Did he or she have and implement a well-thought-out XYZ *plan?*

Step 2. Did he or she *persist* until the confrontee acknowledged the problem?

Step 3. Did the initiator get the confrontee to *agree* to a change/solution?

(In-Class)
SB 8–3

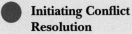 **Initiating Conflict Resolution**

BM 8–1

Procedure 1 (2–3 minutes)

Procedure 2 (8–15 minutes)

Procedure 3 (8–15 minutes)

Procedure 4 (8–15 minutes)

◆ BM 8–2 Mediating Conflict may be shown.

Objective: To experience and develop skills in resolving a conflict.

SCANS: The SCANS competencies of information and especially interpersonal skills and the foundations of basic thinking through problems, and personal qualities are developed through this exercise.

Preparation: You should have completed the questionnaire in the preparation for this exercise.

Experience: You will initiate, respond to, and observe a conflict role play, and then evaluate the effectiveness of its resolution.

Break into as many groups of three as possible. If there are any people not in a triad, make one or two groups of two. Each member selects the number 1, 2, or 3. Number 1 will be the first to initiate a conflict role play, then 2, followed by 3.

1. Initiator number 1 gives his or her information from the preparation to number 2 (the responder) to read. Once number 2 understands, role-play (see number 2 below). Number 3 is the observer.

2. Role-play the conflict resolution. Number 3, the observer, writes his or her observations on the feedback sheet.

3. Integration. When the role play is over, the observer leads a discussion on the effectiveness of the conflict resolution. All three should discuss the effectiveness. Number 3 is not a lecturer. Do not go on until told to do so.

Same as procedure 2, only number 2 is now the initiator, number 3 is the responder, and number 1 is the observer.

Same as procedure 2, only number 3 is the initiator, number 1 is the responder, and number 2 is the observer.

Conclusion: The instructor leads a class discussion and/or makes concluding remarks.

Application (2–4 minutes): What did I learn from this experience? How will I use this knowledge in the future?

Sharing: Volunteers give their answers to the application section.

Team Behavior, Human Relations, and Performance

Part 4

Power, Politics, and Ethics

Learning Objectives

After completing this chapter, you should be able to:

1. Describe seven bases of power.
2. List techniques to increase your power bases.
3. Discuss the necessity of political behavior and how to use ethical politics to help you achieve your objectives.
4. State the Human Relations Guide to Ethical Decision Making.
5. Identify techniques to develop effective human relations with superiors, subordinates, peers, and members of other departments.
6. State how power, politics, and ethics affect behavior, human relations, and performance.
7. Define the following 16 key terms (in order of appearance in the chapter):

power	**information power**	**Type I ethics**
coercive power	**expert power**	**Type II ethics**
connection power	**politics**	**ethical politics**
reward power	**reciprocity**	**unethical politics**
legitimate power	**ethics**	**open-door policy**
referent power		

Chapter Outline

Bob and Sally are at the water fountain talking.

BOB: "I'm sorry the Peterson account was not assigned to you. You deserved it. Roger's claim of being more qualified to handle the job is not true. I'm really surprised that our boss, Ted, believed Roger's claim."

SALLY: "I agree. Nobody likes Roger because he always has to get his own way. I can't stand the way Roger puts down coworkers and members of other departments to force them to give him his own way. Roger has pulled the old emergency routine so many times now that purchasing and maintenance ignore his requests. This hurts our department."

BOB: "You're right. Roger only thinks of himself; he never considers other people or what's best for the company. I've overheard Ted telling him he has to be a team player if he wants to get ahead."

SALLY: "The way he tries to beat everyone out all the time is sickening. He'll do anything to get ahead. But the way he behaves, he will never climb the corporate ladder."

Besides good work, what does it take to get ahead in an organization? You will have to gain power and utilize ethical political skills with your superiors, subordinates, peers, and members of other departments.

● Organization
● Group
● Individual

Power

To be effective in an organization, you must understand how power is used.[1] In this section, we discuss the importance of power in organizations, bases of power and how to increase your power, and how power affects behavior, human relations, and performance. Begin by completing Self-Assessment Exercise 9–1, Power Base, to determine your preferred use of power.

Self-Assessment
Exercise 9–1

Power Base

When you want to get something and need others' consent or help, which approach do you use more often? Think of recent specific situation(s) in which you tried to get something. If you cannot develop your own example, assume you and a coworker both want the same job assignment for the day. How would you get it? Rank all seven approaches below from 1, the first approach you would most commonly use, to 7, the last approach you would most commonly use. Be honest.

_____ I did/would somehow use a form of *coercive power*—pressure, blackmail, force, threat, retaliation, and so forth—to get what I want.

_____ I did/would use the influential *connection power* I have. I'd refer to my friend, or actually have the person tell the person with authority to do it (like your boss).

_____ I did/would use *reward power* by offering the coworker something of value to him or her as part of the process, or in return for compliance.

_____ I did/would convince the coworker to give me what I want by making a *legitimate* request (like referring to your seniority over the coworker).

_____ I did/would convince the coworker using *referent power*—relying on our relationship. Others comply because they like me, or are my friends.

_____ I did/would convince my coworker to give me what I want with *information power*. The facts support the reason why he or she should do what I want. I have information my coworker needs.

_____ I did/would convince my coworker to give me what I wanted by making him or her realize that I have the skill and knowledge. Since I'm the *expert*, it should be done my way.

Your selection rank (1–7) prioritizes your preferred use of power. Each power base is a key term and will be explained in this chapter.

● Organization
● Group
● Individual

IE 9–1

Organizational Power

Some people view power as the ability to make people do what they want them to do, or the ability to do something to people or for people. These definitions may be true, but they tend to give power a manipulative, negative connotation, as does the old adage "Power corrupts and absolute power corrupts absolutely." Within an organization, power should be viewed in a positive sense.[2] Without power, managers could not achieve organizational objectives.[3] Employees are not influenced without a reason, and the reason is often related to the power a manager wields over them. People do not actually have to use power to influence others. Often it is the perception of power, rather than the actual power, that influences employees.[4] Leadership and power go hand in hand. For our purposes, **power** *is a person's ability to influence another person's behavior.*

Power generally begins at the top of an organization and works its way down the hierarchy (Chapter 5).[5] The buzzword for giving more power to employees is *empowerment.*[6] Empowerment enables employees to participate in management.[7] With the trend toward larger global business, power is an important topic.[8]

Bases of Power and How to Increase Your Power

Amital Etzioni differentiated two sources of power—position power and personal power, which are commonly used today.[9] Position power is derived from top-level management and is delegated down the chain of command. Personal power is derived from the follower. Everyone has personal power to varying degrees.[10] Personal power is largely attributed to one's personality. Leaders with personal power get it from followers because they meet their needs.

EXHIBIT 9–1   SOURCES AND BASES OF POWER WITH SITUATIONAL
                     COMMUNICATION STYLES

Personal power ————————————————————▶ ◀————————————————————
                                                              Position power

Expert	Referent	Reward	Coercive
Information	Legitimate	Connection	
Laissez-faire	*Participative*	*Consultative*	*Autocratic*

WORK APPLICATIONS

1. Of the many suggestions for increasing your power bases, which two are
   your highest priority for using on the job? Explain.

APPLICATION SITUATIONS

Using Power

AS 9–1

Identify the appropriate power to use in each situation.

A. Coercive   C. Reward or legitimate   E. Information or expert

B. Connection   D. Referent

_____ 1. Carl is one of the best workers you supervise. He needs little direc-
            tion, but he has slowed down his production level. You know he has a
            personal problem, but the work needs to get done.

_____ 2. You want a new personal computer to help you do a better job.

_____ 3. José, one of your best workers, wants a promotion. He has asked you
            to help prepare him for when the opportunity comes.

_____ 4. Your worst employee has ignored one of your directives again.

_____ 5. Wonder, who needs some direction and encouragement to maintain
            production, is not working to standard today. Wonder claims to be ill,
            as she does occasionally.

Performance
Human Relations
Behavior

Video
9–1
BM–11

How Power Affects Behavior, Human Relations, and Performance

In an organizational setting, your boss has a direct influence over your behavior.[24]
For example, Ted's boss asked him to do a special report for the department, which
he did. Ted was influenced to do something he would not have done otherwise. As
you know, not everyone does what the manager wants them to. Some employees
behave in direct defiance of management. But in either case, managers in power
influence employee behavior. Our coworkers also influence our behavior, though
you may not be as willing to behave as they request as you are for your boss.
Employees often behave differently with their coworkers than they do with their
boss. Coworkers tend to have personal friendship relations, while superior and subordinate often have a professional relationship. Many managers do not socialize
with employees because it may interfere with the power they have with them.

    Some people want and seek power, while others wouldn't take it if you offered it
to them. You discovered the reason for this in Chapter 6, Motivation, where you
learned about McClelland's manifest needs theory, which includes a person's need

Skill-Building

9–1

for power, and determined your own need for power. Do you want power? Do you plan to follow the suggestions in the book to increase your power base?

2. Give two examples, preferably from an organization you work(ed) in, of people using power. Identify the power base and describe the behavior and how it affected human relations and performance.

● Organization
● Group
● Individual

Self-Assessment
Exercise 9–2

Organizational Politics

You will learn the nature of politics and how to develop political skills. Begin by determining your use of political behavior by completing Self-Assessment Exercise 9–2.

Political Behavior

Select the response that best describes your actual or planned use of the following behavior on the job. Place the number 1–5 on the line before each statement.

(5) Usually   (4) Frequently   (3) Occasionally   (2) Seldom   (1) Rarely

____ 1. I get along with everyone, even those recognized as difficult. I avoid or delay giving my opinion on controversial issues.

____ 2. I try to make people feel important and compliment them.

____ 3. I compromise when working with others and avoid telling people they are wrong; instead, I suggest alternatives that may be more effective.

____ 4. I try to get to know the managers and what is going on in as many of the other departments as possible.

____ 5. I take on the same interests as those in power (watch or play sports, join the same clubs, etc.).

____ 6. I purposely seek contacts and network with higher-level managers so they will know who I am by name and face.

____ 7. I seek recognition and visibility for my accomplishments.

____ 8. I form alliances with others to increase my ability to get what I want.

____ 9. I do favors for others and use their favors in return.

____ 10. I say I will do things when I am not sure I can deliver; if I cannot meet the obligation, I explain why it was out of my control.

To determine your political behavior add the 10 numbers you selected as your answers. The number will range from 10 to 50. The higher your score, the more political behavior you use. Place your score here ____ and on the continuum below.

Nonpolitical   10 _ _ _ 20 _ _ _ 30 _ _ _ 40 _ _ _ 50   Political

---

The Nature of Organizational Politics

Politics is critical to your career success.[25] You cannot keep out of politics and be successful.[26] Politics is a fact of organizational life.[27] In our economy, money is the medium of exchange; in an organization, politics is the medium of exchange. Managers are, and must be, political beings in order to meet their objectives.[28] Politics is the network of interactions by which power is acquired, transferred, and exercised upon others. **Politics** *is the process of gaining and using power.* As you can see from the definition, power and politics go hand in hand.

Managers cannot meet their objectives without the help of other people[29] and departments over which they have no authority or position power. For example, Tony, a production department supervisor, needs materials and supplies to make the product, but he must rely on the purchasing department to acquire them. If Tony does not have a good working relationship with purchasing, he may not get the materials when he needs them.

Goal of Human Relations

Using **reciprocity** *involves creating obligations and debts, developing alliances, and using them to accomplish objectives.* When people do something for you, you incur an obligation that they may expect to be repaid. When you do something for people, you create a debt that you may be able to collect at a later date when you need a favor.[30] Over a period of time, when the trade-off results in both parties getting something they want, an alliance usually develops to gain group power in attaining mutually desirable benefits.[31] You should work at developing a network of alliances that you can call on for help in meeting your objectives.[32] When the trade-off of help with alliances creates a win-win situation for all members of the alliances and the organization, the goal of human relations is met.[33]

Like power, politics often has a negative connotation due to people who abuse political power.[34] Mahatma Gandhi called politics without principle a sin. However, ethical politics helps the organization by meeting the goal of human relations without negative consequences.[35] Few areas of corporate life are more universally despised than politics, yet few have more impact on a manager's career.[36] The amount and importance of politics varies from organization to organization. However, larger organizations tend to be more political; and the higher the level of management, the more important politics becomes. In the global context, political skills are even more important.[37]

As you can see, organizational politics is an integral part of everyday corporate life. You should develop your political behavior to take advantage of political realities that can help you and the organization and to avoid being hurt by politics.[38] Developing political skills is the next topic.

WORK APPLICATIONS

3. Give an example of reciprocity, preferably from an organization you work(ed) for. Explain the trade-off.

Organization
Group
Individual

Developing Political Skills

Yes, you can be good at politics without being a jerk.[39] If you want to progress, you should develop your political skills. Human relations skills are critical to political success in organizations. Following the nine human relations guidelines can help you develop political skills. More specifically, review the 10 statements in Self-Assessment Exercise 9–2 and consciously increase your use of these behaviors, especially any that had a low frequency of use. However, use number 10, saying you will do something when you are not sure you can, sparingly and don't use the word "promise." You don't want to be viewed as a person who doesn't keep his or her word. Developing trust is very important.[40] And being honest builds trust.[41]

Use reciprocity. When you want something, determine who else will benefit and create alliance power to help you, the other party(s), and the organization to benefit.[42] Ongoing alliances are also known as political coalitions.[43] Networking is a form of politics.[44]

Successfully implementing these behaviors results in increased political skills. However, if you don't agree with one of the political behaviors, don't use it. You may not need to use all of the political behaviors to be successful. Learn what it takes in the diverse organization where you work.

4. Of the 10 political behaviors in Self-Assessment Exercise 9–2, which two need the most effort on your part? Which two need the least? Explain your answers.

● Organization
● Group
● Individual

Business Ethics and Etiquette

Ethical behavior is a popular topic.[45] Organizations seek employees with integrity.[46] Are all power and political behavior ethical? What is the relationship between ethics and politics? In this section, we discuss Type I and Type II ethics, ethical and unethical politics, and a simple guide to ethical decisions. First complete Self-Assessment Exercise 9–3.

Self-Assessment Exercise 9–3

Ethical Behavior?

Below are 15 statements. Identify the frequency of which you do, have done, or would do these things in the future when employed full time. Place the numbers 4, 3, 2, or 1 on the line before each statement.

(4) Regularly   (3) Occasionally   (2) Seldom   (1) Never

_____ 1. I come to work late and get paid for it.

_____ 2. I leave work early and get paid for it.

_____ 3. I take long breaks/lunches and get paid for it.

_____ 4. I call in sick to get a day off, when I'm not sick.

_____ 5. I use the company phone to make personal long distance calls.

_____ 6. I do personal work while on company time.

_____ 7. I use the company copier for personal use.

_____ 8. I mail personal things through the company mail.

_____ 9. I take home company supplies or merchandise.

_____ 10. I give company supplies or merchandise to friends, or allow them to take them without saying anything.

_____ 11. I put in for reimbursement for meals and travel or other expenses that I did not actually eat or make.

_____ 12. I use the company car for personal business.

_____ 13. I take my spouse/friend out to eat and charge it to the company expense account.

_____ 14. I take my spouse/friend on business trips and charge the expense to the company.

_____ 15. I accept gifts from customers/suppliers in exchange for giving them business.

Total your score. It will be between 15 and 60. Place it here _____ and an X on the continuum below that represents your score.

Ethical   15 ___ 20 ___ 25 ___ 30 ___ 35 ___ 40 ___ 45 ___ 50 ___ 55 ___ 60   Unethical

All of these items are considered unethical behavior by most organizations. However, many of these actions happen regularly in organizations. If many employees do them, does that make it all right for you to do them too?

There has been increased emphasis on business ethics and the need to use power in a socially responsible manner.[47] Companies are being judged on their ethics and social responsibility.[48] In addition, there is a daily radio audience offering advice on ethics and moral responsibility.[49] Some experts distinguish between moral behavior and ethical behavior. Morals refers to absolute worldwide standards of right and wrong behavior, such as "Thou shalt not commit murder." Ethical behavior, on the other hand, reflects established customs and mores that may vary throughout the world and that are subject to change from time to time. For our purpose we combine the two: **ethics** *is the moral standard of right and wrong behavior.* Mahatma Gandhi called business without morality a sin.

Right behavior is considered ethical behavior, while wrong behavior is considered unethical behavior. In the business world, the difference between right and wrong behavior is not always clear. Many unethical behaviors are illegal, but not all. In the diversified global workplace, people have different values, which leads to behaviors that some people view as ethical while others do not. Ethics is also considered to be relative. In one situation, people may feel certain behavior is ethical while the same behavior in a different situation is unethical. For example, giving someone a gift is legal, but giving a gift as a condition of attaining business (a bribe) is illegal. A gift versus a bribe is not always clear.

In your daily life, you face decisions in which you can make ethical or unethical choices. You make your choices based on your past learning from parents, teachers, friends, coworkers, and so forth. Our combined past experiences make up what many refer to as our *conscience,* which helps us to choose right from wrong.

Type I and Type II Ethics

Behavior known as **Type I ethics** *refers to behavior that is considered wrong by authorities, yet not accepted by others as unethical.* The number of people who do not accept authorities' decisions on wrong behavior affects people's decision to behave in unethical ways. In Self-Assessment Exercise 9–3, these behaviors are considered unethical by most organizations, yet many employees do not agree and perform these behaviors. Generally, the more people disagree with specific behavior as being unethical, the more people will perform the behavior. People tend to rationalize, "Everyone does it; it's okay to do it." People also tend to exaggerate the numbers. Often the number "everyone" is actually a small percentage of the population. Employee theft costs stores $10 billion annually.[50]

A person who knowingly conducts unethical behavior because he or she does not agree with authority's view on ethical behavior is guilty of Type I ethics. For example, the company rules say there shall be no smoking in a specific area, yet the employee does not believe smoking is dangerous and smokes anyway.

Another behavior, **Type II ethics,** *refers to behavior that is considered wrong by authorities and the individual, yet conducted anyway.* A person who agrees that the behavior is unethical yet conducts the behavior anyway is guilty of Type II ethics. To continue the smoking example above, the employee knows smoking is not allowed and agrees that it is dangerous, yet smokes anyway.

Why are managers unethical? Some of the many reasons include to gain power, money, advancement, recognition, and anger at the system.

WORK APPLICATIONS

5. Give an example of Type I and Type II ethics behavior, preferably from an organization you work(ed) for.

Type I and
Type II Ethics

AS 9–2

Identify each statement as:

A. Type I ethics   B. Type II ethics

_____ 6. Bill just let another toy go as acceptable quality, when it's not. He agrees that it's wrong to do this, so why does he?

_____ 7. Carla told me it's okay to take home company pens and things; everyone does it.

_____ 8. Wayne is spreading stories about coworkers again. Why doesn't he agree that this is unethical?

_____ 9. Danielle is making copies of directions to the party she is having. I told her it was wrong, and she agreed with me, but she did it anyway.

_____ 10. Mike just left work early again. He says he is underpaid, so it's okay.

Ethical and Unethical Politics

Goal of
Human Relations

Politics can be helpful or harmful to an organization depending upon the behavior. We classify political behavior into two categories: ethical and unethical. **Ethical politics** *includes behavior that benefits both the individual and the organization.* Ethical politics creates a win-win situation, meeting the goal of human relations. On the other hand, **unethical politics** *includes behavior that benefits the individual and hurts the organization.* Unethical politics creates a win-lose situation; Unethical politics also includes management behavior that helps the organization, but hurts the individual. Behavior that helps the individual but does not hurt the organization is also considered ethical. The term *organization* includes people because if employees are hurt, so is the organization. When dealing with people outside the firm, use the *stakeholders* approach to ethics,[51] Creating a win-win situation for all relevant parties, it increases firm financial performance.[52]

The 10 political behavior statements in Self-Assessment Exercise 9–2 are generally ethical. Another example of ethical political behavior includes Tom, the computer manager, who wants a new computer. He talks to several of the powerful managers and sells them on the benefits to them. They form an alliance and attain the funds to purchase the computer. Tom benefits because he now manages a new and more powerful computer. He also looks good in the eyes of the other managers who will also benefit through the use of the new computer. Overall, the organization's performance increases.

Examples of unethical behavior that hurt the organization include the following: (1) Karl, a production manager, wants to be promoted to the general manager's position. To increase his chances, he spreads untrue gossip about his main competitor. (2) There is a vacant office, which is large and well furnished. Sam, a sales manager who spends most of his time on the road, sees the office as prestigious, so he requests it, even though he knows that Cindy, a public relations manager, wants it and will get better use from it. Sam speaks to his friends in high-level management positions and he gets the office. (3) A person lies on his or her resume.[53] (4) A manager asks the secretary (or other employee) to lie.[54]

Ethical political behavior pay?[55] Good business and good ethics are synonymous; ethics is at the heart and center of business, and profits and ethics are intrinsically related.[56] At first, one may be richly rewarded for knifing people in the back, but retaliation follows, trust is lost, and productivity declines. This is illustrated in the opening case. Roger uses unethical politics in hopes of getting ahead. But according to his peers, he will not climb the corporate ladder. It is difficult to get ahead when people don't like you and you make a lot of enemies. Unethical behavior and stress appear to be linked. Exercising good human relations skills is exercising good ethics.

Skill-Building

9–2
Learning Objective

3. Discuss the necessity of political behavior and how to use ethical politics to help you achieve your objectives

6. Give an example of ethical and unethical politics, preferably from an organization you work(ed) for. Describe the behavior and consequences for all parties involved.

APPLICATION SITUATIONS

Ethical and Unethical Politics

AS 9–3

Identify each statement as:

A. Ethical politics   B. Unethical politics

____ 11. Pete goes around telling everyone about any little mistake his peer Sue makes.

____ 12. Tony is taking tennis lessons so he can challenge his boss.

____ 13. Carol delivers her daily figures at 10:00 each day because she knows she will run into Ms. Big Power on the way.

____ 14. Carlos goes around asking about what is happening in other departments during his work time.

____ 15. Frank sent a copy of his department's performance record to three high-level managers to whom he does not report.

Codes of Ethics

A good code of ethics establishes guidelines that clearly describe ethical and unethical behavior.[57] Most organizations consider ethics codes to be important,[58] and many have developed codes of ethics.[59] Exhibit 9–2 is an example of a code of ethics as it relates to its employees.[60]

EXHIBIT 9–2

CODE OF ETHICS*

- We will treat our employees fairly with regard to wages, benefits, and working conditions.
- We will never violate the legal or moral rights of employees in any way.
- We will never employ children in our facilities, nor will we do business with any company that makes use of child labor.
- We are committed to an ongoing program of monitoring all our facilities and those of companies with whom we do business.

---

*Excerpts from the Philips-VanHeusen statement of Corporate Responsibility.

IE 9-2
IE 9-3

To be ethically successful, organizations must audit the ethical behavior of its employees[61] and confront and discipline employees who are unethical.[62] Top managers need to lead by ethical example,[63] they need to be honest with employees,[64] and they need to build trust.[65] Does ethics education lead to successful work ethics? Yes, to some extent it has a positive effect, but other factors also influence ethics,[66] such as a person's basic values and ethical beliefs before, during, and after the ethics education.

Do Ethics Programs Work?: We've just stated how to make ethics programs effective. However, are ethics programs working? Like many ethical situations, there is no clear right or wrong answer.

On the positive side, American businesses are investing in formal ethics programs. A recent survey of large U.S. corporations found that 78% of responding companies had codes of ethics, 51% had telephone lines for reporting ethical concerns, and 30% had offices for dealing with ethics and legal compliance. Corporate ethics officers now have their own professional association—the Ethics Officers Association—with more than 300 major corporations represented.[67]

On the negative side, misrepresentation by tobacco executives about the addictive properties of nicotine, misstatements of earning by Phar-Mor, Inc., and allegations against hospital executives for misrepresenting Medicare claims can only add to concerns about unethical behavior.[68] A recent study stated that ethics programs are not stopping employee misconduct. More than 75% of respondents said they had observed violation of the law or company standards in the previous last 12 months, and 61% thought management wouldn't administer impartial discipline. People are not reporting unethical behavior, known as *whistle blowing*, because they are not encouraged to do so,[69] or there is no reinforcement motivation (Chapter 6).

Can Ethics Programs be Improved?:   Have you observed unethical behavior at college and work? Did you report it? Why or why not? If managers really encourage reporting ethics violations, positively reinforce the whistle-blowers and negatively reinforce the violators, will people report ethics violations? Will business ethics improve?

Human Relations Guides to Ethical Decisions

Goal of Human Relations

Learning Objective

4. State the Human Relations Guide to Ethical Decision Making

When making decisions, try to meet the goal of human relations by creating a win–win situation for all parties. Some of the stakeholder relevant parties, include peers, your boss, subordinates, other department members, the organization, and people/organizations outside the organization you work for as well. The stakeholder will often change from situation to situation. The higher up in the organization, the more relevant parties there are to deal with. For example, if you are not a manager, you will not have any subordinates to deal with. *If, after making a decision, you are proud to tell all these relevant parties your decision, the decision is probably ethical. If you are embarrassed to tell others your decision, or you keep rationalizing the decision, it may not be ethical.*

A second simple guide is the golden rule: "Do unto others as you want them to do unto you." Or, "Don't do anything to anyone that you would not want them to do to you." A third guide is the Rotary International four-way test: (1) Is it the truth? (2) Is it fair to all concerned? (3) Will it build goodwill and better friendship? (4) Will it be beneficial to all concerned?

The rest of this chapter will focus on how to use ethical politics with your boss, subordinates, peers, and members of other departments.

WORK APPLICATIONS

7. Give an example, preferably from an organization you work(ed) for, of an individual creating a win–win situation for all parties involved. Identify all parties involved and how they won. Use Exhibit 9–3, Human Relations Guide to Ethical Decision Making, to help you answer the question.

Etiquette

Etiquette is the socially accepted standard of right and wrong behavior. It includes manners beyond simply saying please and thank you. Notice the similarity in our definition of ethics and etiquette. Etiquette is very important to your career success.[70] However, unlike with ethics, organizations don't usually have codes or any formal training in etiquette.

Many organizations weigh etiquette during the job interview as part of the selection criteria. In fact, some managers will take the job candidate out to eat and observe etiquette, including table manners. Candidates with poor etiquette are not offered the job. You may be thinking that it is unfair to judge job candidates by their etiquette, and you may be right. However, the reality of the business world is that firms do not want employees representing their organization who do not project a favorable image for the organization. Recall that customers, suppliers, and everyone the organization comes into contact with judge the organization based on individual behavior. Organizations do not want employees who will embarrass them.

Organizations assume that people are taught etiquette at home or that it is learned through experience or observation. However, this is not always the case. Etiquette skills can be improved.[71] If you haven't been concerned with business etiquette, start now. We'll give you some tips to improve now.

Job Interview Etiquette:
The career service department at your college may offer job interview training. Take advantage of its services. Here are some dos and don'ts of job interviewing.

- Do research the organization before the interview so that you can talk intelligently about it. For example, what products/services does it offer. How many employees and locations does it have? What is the company's financial status, such as revenues and net profit last year? What are its strategic plans? Much of this information can be found in the company annual report.

- Do go to the job interview properly dressed (Chapter 2, first impressions).

- Do be sure to get there a little early. Allow plenty of time for traffic and parking. If you are more than 10 minutes early, you can relax and wait before going to the receptionist.

- Do bring extra copies of your resume and other material you may need in a briefcase or nice folder.

- Do get the last name and proper pronunciation of the person who will be interviewing you and greet the interviewer by last name. For example, "How do you do, Mr. Smith?"

- Don't call the interviewer by first name unless told to do so by the interviewer.

- Do firmly shake hands and make eye contact if the interviewer extends his or her hand to you, but don't make the first move.

- Do state the interviewer's name a few times during the job interview. For example, "That is a good question, Mr. Smith."

- Don't sit down until the interviewer invites you to sit, and wait for the interviewer to sit first.

- Do be careful of your nonverbal communication (Chapter 4). Don't sit back and slouch. Sit up straight leaning a bit forward in the seat and maintain adequate eye contact to show your interest. You may cross your legs, but crossed arms are a sign of defensiveness or being closed.

- Do not be the first one to bring up salary and benefits. If asked what you expect for a salary, give a range below and above the actual figure you expect. Part of your research prior to the interview should be to find out the salary range for the job you are interviewing for.

- Do take a little time to think about your answers. Talk clearly and loud enough while watching your vocabulary to include proper English; avoid street talk or jargon.

- Do thank the interviewer for his or her time at the close of the interview. If the interviewer does not tell you how long it will take to make a decision, ask when you can expect an answer.

- Do send a short followup written thank-you for the interview letter with another copy of your resume the same day or the next, if you want the job. Include any other information in the letter that you thought about after the interview and state that you look forward to the selection decision by XXX (state the date given by the interviewer).

- Do call back if you do not hear whether you got the job by the decision date given by the interviewer.

Table Manners:

Let's give a few simple tips in case you are taken out to eat during the job interview. If you get the job and take others out to eat, you are the interviewer role even if it's not a job interview. Many of the tips also apply to eating with others during your lunch breaks.

- Don't go out to eat starving and letting the interviewer realize that you are by pigging out.
- Do follow the lead of the interviewer; don't take charge.
- Do let the interviewer sit first.
- Do place your napkin on your lap after the interviewer does and repeat other behavior. For example, if there are dip and crackers, the interviewer will not double-dip bitten crackers, so you don't either.
- If the server asks if you want a drink, do wait for the interviewer to respond. Don't ask for alcohol if you are underage, even if you have a fake id; you don't want the interviewer to know this.
- Don't order alcohol unless asked if you want a drink by the interviewer. If asked, ask the interviewer if he or she will be having a drink. If the interviewer say yes, have one; if no, don't have a drink. However, don't have a drink if you will feel its effects. You want to be in top form for the interview questions and discussion, and you want to maintain your proper etiquette.
- Do expect to order an appetizer, main course, and dessert. However, you don't have to order them all, especially if the interviewer does not. For example, if the interviewer asks if you would like an appetizer/dessert, ask the interviewer if he or she is having one. If the server asks, wait for the interviewer lead.
- Don't begin to eat any serving until everyone at the table is served and the interviewer starts.
- Do try to eat at the same pace as the interviewer so that you are not done eating each serving too much faster or slower than the interviewer.
- Don't talk with food in your mouth. Take small bites to help avoid this problem.
- Don't take the last of anything that you are sharing. It is also polite to leave a little food on your plate, even if you are still hungry.
- Do start using the silverware from the outside in. Again, follow the interviewer's lead when in doubt.
- Do not offer to pay part or all of the bill. The general rule is whoever invites the other out to eat pays the bill, unless otherwise agreed before going to eat.
- Do thank the interviewer for the meal. Also, be polite (say please and thank you) to the server.

Telephone Etiquette:

After you get the job, you may use the telephone as part of your job. These tips assume you are not a telephone operator, a position which should get proper training.

Etiquette when you call others:

- Do have a written outline/plan of the topics you want to discuss. Do write notes on the plan sheet as you talk. Don't use a small piece of scrap paper; a notebook works well to keep track of your calls.
- Do leave a "brief" message if the person does not answer. Do state (1) your name, (2) the reason for the call and message, (3) the telephone number to call back,

and (4) the best time for the return call. Do speak loud and clear enough and speak slowly, especially when leaving your number. Don't use voice mail for bad news, sensitive/confidential information, and complicated information and instructions. Do control your emotions; don't leave emotional messages that can be played back for the entertainment of others or against you in any way, such as a complaint against you to a boss.

- Do ask if the person has time to talk. If he or she busy, set up a time to call back.
- Do call the person back if you get disconnected; it's the caller's responsibility to call back.
- Don't eat while on the phone.
- Don't talk to others while you or they are on the phone.
- Do be the first to hang up, and do hang up gently.

Etiquette when others call you:

- Do try to answer the phone within three rings.
- Do say hello followed by your name (not a nickname) and department or organization.
- If people are calling you at a bad time, and did not ask if you have time to talk, do tell them you do not have time to talk now. Do give them a time when you will call them back, and be sure to call back on time.
- If you have to put people on hold for more than a minute, such as if you have to look up information, do offer to call them back.
- Don't take multiple calls at one time keeping people on hold. Do let the voice mail take a message and call back the person waiting.
- Do keep paper (telephone notebook) and pencil ready. Do write down the person's name immediately when you don't know them and call them by name during the conversation as you jot down notes.
- Don't give out personal information about others over the phone.
- Do be the last one to hang up.
- Do leave a "brief" message on your voice mail for callers. Do include: (1) your name, (2) your organization, (3) invite the caller to leave a message, and (4) suggest a good time to call. Do remember to send calls directly into your voice mail when you are not in, so people don't have to wait to leave their message.
- Do call people back within 24 hours.

Etiquette for pagers and cellular phones:

- Don't interrupt others with your messages. Do use a vibrating pager rather than audio. But even with a vibrating pager, don't interrupt meetings and other activities that are not true emergencies.
- Don't disrupt others with your cellular phone conversations, such as talking in meeting and public places (walking down the street, in a theater, restaurant, or classroom). Do leave to a private place.
- Do be extra careful when talking on the phone while driving for your own safety and that of others, as many accidents are phone related.

E-mail Etiquette:

- Do use e-mail for short messages, two-page max. Do get to the point quickly and clearly; don't ramble.
- Do use attachments for sending long messages, three or more pages. However, do send the attachment so that it is readable to the receiver.
- Do use the spelling and grammar checkers. People place more value on what you say when it is said correctly.
- Do avoid Internet and other jargon that others may not know.

- Don't say anything in an e-mail that you don't want others to know about. It is possible for organizations to read your e-mail, even the ones you delete can be read by some systems.
- Don't send emotional messages, for the same reasons as leaving phone messages.
- Do avoid junk e-mail. Don't send needless messages. Don't "cc:" (carbon copy) people who don't need to know your message.

Meeting etiquette: If you are running a meeting, follow the guidelines in Chapter 11 on managing meeting skills. Below is etiquette for attendees of meetings.

- Do arrive on time.
- Do come to the meeting properly prepared. Do any reading and assignments before the meeting.
- If you are late, do apologize. But do not give a reason for being late. Excuses only take up meeting time and are often not believed anyway.
- Don't be a problem member. Problem members are discussed in Chapter 11 with meeting skills.

Hoteling etiquette: *Hoteling* is the sharing of workspace and equipment, such as desks, computers, phones, fax machines, copiers, eating areas, refrigerators, coffee machines, water coolers, and so on.

- Do follow the general golden rule—do unto others as you would have them do to you.
- Do clean up after yourself and make sure the equipment is ready for the next person to use when you are done, even if you find the area cluttered or dirty, the machine without paper, the coffee pot without coffee, etc. Do assertively confront others who do not clean up or make ready the equipment.
- Do pay your fair share of any expenses, such as coffee or water money, splitting the bill for lunch, chipping in for employee presents, and so on. Don't take other people's food and drinks without permission. And if they give it to you, return the favor.
- Do respect others privacy. Don't read anything on anyone's desk, computer screen, messages, or fax. It's like opening and reading their mail, which is a don't.
- Don't monopolize shared workspace and equipment; share it equitably.

WORK APPLICATIONS

8. Give a job example of when someone behaved with improper etiquette.

● Organization
● Group
● Individual

Vertical Politics

Vertical politics are relations with superiors and subordinates. Your superiors are persons in the organization who are on a higher level than you. Your subordinates are persons who are on a lower level than you. Your boss and the employees you supervise and who report to you are the most important persons with whom to develop effective relations.[72]

Relations with Your Boss

Your relationship with your boss will affect your job satisfaction and can mean the difference between success or failure on the job. Not getting along with your boss can make life miserable for you. Needless to say, you should work at developing a good working relationship with your boss.[73]

Analyze your boss's style and, if necessary, change your style to match it. For example, if your boss is very businesslike and you are very informal and talkative, be businesslike when you are with your boss. Remember, people generally like people who behave like themselves.

Knowing your boss can lead to better human relations between the two of you. It is helpful to know your boss's primary responsibility, what your boss regards as good performance, how your performance will be evaluated, and what your boss expects of you.

Common Expectations of Bosses

Your boss will most likely expect loyalty, cooperation, initiative, information, and openness to criticism.

Loyalty: Executives value loyalty most in subordinates.[74] You will be expected to carry out the organization's standing plans and any special orders with the proper attitude. You should not talk negatively about your boss behind his or her back,[75] even if others are doing so. Regardless of how careful you are, or how trustworthy the other person is, gossip always seems to get back to the boss. When it does, it can seriously hurt your relationship. Your boss may never forget it or forgive you for doing it. The benefits, if any, don't outweigh the cost of not being loyal. In fact, you should never talk negatively about anyone; it can only get you into trouble. The old adage "If you can't say anything good about someone, don't say anything at all" is a good one to follow. It's proper etiquette. Continuing to listen to, and especially agreeing with, negative statements only encourages others to continue this behavior. The discussion between Bob and Sally is an example of negative talk about others. If people are talking negatively about others, encourage them to stop in a nice way, change the subject, or leave them. For example, "Complaining about Roger really doesn't change anything. Why don't we talk about the things we can change like . . ." "Did you/anyone see the movie/game on TV last night?"

Cooperation: Your boss expects you to be cooperative with him or her and with everyone you must work with. If you cannot get along with others, you can be an embarrassment to your boss. And bosses don't like to be embarrassed. Roger is not cooperative; his boss Ted has told him that if he wants to get ahead he will have to be a team player.

Initiative: Your boss will expect you to know your responsibility and authority and to act without having to be told to do so. If there is a problem, the boss may expect you to solve it, rather than bring it to him or her to solve. If it is appropriate to include the boss in solving a problem, at least analyze the situation and have a recommended solution to present.

Information: Your boss expects you to keep him or her informed about what your objectives are and how you are progressing. If there are problems, your boss expects you to tell him or her about them.[76] You should not cover up your mistakes, your employees' mistakes, or your boss's mistakes. You can cause your boss the embarrassment of looking stupid by finding out from others what's going on in his or her department. Bosses don't like to be surprised.

Openness to Criticism: We all make mistakes; part of your boss's job is to help you avoid repeating them. When your boss criticizes you, try not to become defensive and argumentative. Remember that criticism is a means of improving your skills; be open to it even though it may hurt. Don't take it personally.

If you use the nine guidelines to effective human relations (Chapter 1), get to know your boss, and meet his or her expectations, you should develop a good relationship. If you meet your boss's expectations, he or she will most likely be willing to help you meet your needs. Meeting your boss's expectations can help you meet the goal of human relations by creating a win-win situation for both of you.

Goal of Human Relations

If you don't get along with your boss, your chances of promotion may be hurt, and you could be transferred to a dead-end job.[77] Also, be careful about going over his or her head (to your boss's boss) because you may be viewed as a betrayer of loyalty and as unethical.[78] Or going to complain about your boss can create more problems for you than solutions.[79]

WORK APPLICATIONS

9. Of the five common expectations of bosses, which is your strongest area? Your weakest area? Explain your answers.

Relations with Subordinates

If the goal of human relations is to satisfy employee needs while achieving organizational objectives, why are poor human relations common? One reason is the fact that the manager must consider the work to be accomplished as ultimately more important than the needs and desires of those doing the work, including the manager's own needs. Managers get so busy getting the job done that they forget about the needs of the employees doing the work. Employees tend to start a job enthusiastically, but the manager does not take the time to develop the human relations necessary to maintain that enthusiasm. As a manager, you must take the time to develop effective human relations.[80]

Developing Manager–Employee Relations

In developing manager–employee relations, one should follow the nine guidelines to human relations discussed in Chapter 1. Perfect human relations probably don't exist. The manager should strive for harmonious relations where differences of opinion are encouraged and settled in a peaceful manner. Morale should be kept at high levels, but don't try to please all of the people all of the time. As a manager, you may face resentment from an employee who resents you for *what* you are (the manager), rather than for *who* you are. Others may not like you for any number of reasons. A manager can have good human relations without being well liked personally or being popular.

Friendship

The relationship between manager and employee cannot be one of "real" friendship. The nature of supervision excludes true friendship because the manager must evaluate the employee's performance; true friends don't evaluate or judge each other in any formal way. The manager must also give employees directions; friends don't order each other around. The manager must also get the employee to change; friends usually don't seriously try to change each other.

Trying to be friends may cause problems for you, the employee, and the department. Will your friend try to take advantage of your friendship to get special favors? Will you be able to treat your friend like the other members of the department? The other employees may say you play favorites. They may resent your friend(s) and ostracize him or her. Your friendship could adversely affect department morale.

Managers not being true friends to employees does not mean that they should not be friendly. If the manager takes an "I'm the boss" attitude, employees may resent him or her and morale problems could result. As in most cases, there are exceptions to the rule. Some managers are friends with employees and are still very effective managers.

10. Assume you are hired for or promoted to a management position. Will you develop a relationship with your employees based on friendship? Describe the relationship you plan to develop.

The Open-Door Policy

The **open-door policy** *is the practice of being available to employees.* Your management ability is directly proportional to the amount of time your door is open, both literally and figuratively. For effective human relations, you must be available to employees to give them the help they need, when they need it. If employees view the manager as too busy or not willing to help them, poor human relations and low morale can result. Wal-Mart credits part of its success to its open-door policy. An open-door policy does not mean that you must stop everything whenever an employee wants to see you. For nonemergencies the employee should make an appointment. You should prioritize spending time with an employee, along with other responsibilities. Managers are also using an open e-mail policy.

11. Does your present or past boss use the open-door policy? Explain.

Goal of Human Relations

Following the above guidelines should help you develop effective human relations with your subordinates. Use your power wisely to meet the goal of human relations. Remember, as a manager your success depends upon your subordinates.[81] If you want employees to meet your expectations, create a win-win situation. Help your subordinates meet their needs while attaining the high performance that will make you a success. When you ask subordinates to do something, answer their unasked question, "What's in it for me?" The Professor Smith–student aide example under reward power is a superior subordinate win-win situation example.

● Organization
● Group
● Individual

Horizontal Politics

Horizontal politics are your relations with your peers and members of other departments. Your peers are the people who are on the same level in the organizational hierarchy as you. Your direct peers also report to your boss. You will learn how to develop effective horizontal politics.

Relations with Peers

To be successful you must cooperate, compete with, and sometimes even criticize your peers.

Cooperating with Peers

Your success as an employee is linked to other employees in the organization.[82] If you are cooperative and help them, they should have a positive attitude toward you and be willing to help you meet your objectives. If you don't cooperate with your peers, your boss will know it.

Competing with Peers

Even though you are cooperative with your peers, you are still in competition with them. Your boss will compare you to them when evaluating your performance, giving raises, and granting promotions. Like a great athlete, you must learn to be a team player and help your peers to be successful, but at the same time you have to look good as well.

Criticizing Peers

Do not go looking for faults in your peers. But if your peers do something they shouldn't, you owe it to them to try to correct the situation or prevent it from recurring in the future. Tactfully and sincerely telling a peer of a shortcoming is often appreciated. Sometimes peers are not aware of the situation. But there are people who don't appreciate criticism or unsolicited advice. In Chapter 8 are the details on how to approach peers, and others, to resolve conflicts, and Chapter 4 gives suggestions for giving criticism.

Do not go to the boss unless it is a serious offense, such as disregarding safety rules that endanger the welfare of employees. Unless your own safety is in danger, tell the boss only after discussing it with the peer and warning him or her of the consequences of continuing the behavior. Do not cover for a peer in trouble—you will only make things worse for everyone involved. And don't expect or ask others to cover for you.

Roger violates peer relations. He always has to get his own way. Roger is uncooperative, too competitive, and criticizes coworkers and members of other departments to force them to give him his own way.

WORK APPLICATIONS

12. Give an example, preferably from an organization you work(ed) for, of a situation in which you had good human relations with your peers. Describe how you cooperated, competed, and/or criticized your peers.

Relations with Members of Other Departments

You will most likely need the help of other departments and organizations.[83] You will need personnel to hire new employees, accounting to approve budgets, purchasing to get materials and supplies, maintenance to keep the department's equipment running efficiently, quality control to help maintain the quality of the product, payroll to okay overtime pay, and so forth.

Learning Objective

5. Identify techniques to develop effective human relations with superiors, subordinates, peers, and members of other departments

Some of these departments have procedures you should follow. Develop good human relations through being cooperative and following the guidelines set by the organization.[84] It is also advisable to develop good relations with people in other organizations.[85]

Roger's "pulling the old emergency routine" so many times has resulted in purchasing and maintenance ignoring him. This is an embarrassment for Ted and the department, and it is hurting performance.

Following the guidelines in the text should help you to develop effective human relations with others. Make your peers and members of other departments your friends and allies.[86] Use your power wisely to meet the goal of human relations. Your success depends upon others. When you want something, remember to use effective horizontal politics to create a win-win situation for all involved. Answer people's unasked question, "What's in it for me?" Tom, the computer manager in the example under ethical politics, used horizontal politics to get the new computer.

Goal of
Human Relations

WORK APPLICATIONS

13. Give an example, preferably from an organization you work(ed) for, of a situation in which you had good human relations with members of other departments. Describe how your relations affected your performance, the other departments, and the organization as a whole.

Relations with Others

AS 9–4

Identify the other party being mentioned in each statement.

A. Subordinate   C. Peers

B. Superior   D. Other departments

____ 16. "As a supervisor, I report to a middle manager named Kim."

____ 17. "The guys in sales are always trying to rush us to ship the product."

____ 18. "Willy is reluctant to accept the task I delegated to him."

____ 19. "That's the owner of the company."

____ 20. "The supervisors are getting together for lunch. Will you join us?"

- Performance
- Human Relations
- Behavior

How Politics and Ethics Affect Behavior, Human Relations, and Performance

People who are politically inclined tend to use different behavior than those who do not use politics. In reviewing the 10 statements in Self-Assessment Exercise 9-2, Political Behavior, you can see the difference in behavior between political people and nonpolitical people.

People who are ethical behave differently than those who are not ethical. Roger behaves differently than Bob and Sally. Think about the highly ethical and unethical people you have worked with. How does their behavior differ?

Generally, people who use ethical politics have good human relations, while those who use unethical political behavior tend to have poor human relations. People who are ethical and unethical deal with people differently. People using unethical politics tend to lie, cheat, and break the rules. In time people recognize unethical people and distrust them. Bob and Sally don't have effective human relations with Roger because of his political behavior. The purchasing and maintenance department members ignore Roger's request because of his behavior, while Bob and Sally have good relations with these departments. Roger is not meeting Ted's expectations because of his political behavior.

Human relations affect performance.[87] Generally, people who use ethical politics are more productive in the long run than people who use unethical politics.[88] People who use unethical politics may get short-run performance results, but in the long run, performance will be lower. Roger's use of emergencies may have worked for a while, but the purchasing and maintenance departments now ignore his emergency requests. As a result of Roger's behavior, his performance, his peers' performance, his boss Ted's performance, other departments' performance, and the performance of the organization as a whole are affected negatively.

Unethical behavior can get you fired, which will stop your performance within an organization completely, and can also result in your going to prison.

See Exhibit 9–3 for an illustration that puts the concepts of power, politics, and ethics together. You start in the center with the goal of human relations to create a win–win situation through horizontal politics with your peers and people in other departments and through vertical politics with your superiors and subordinates. You also use appropriate power with your politics.

Learning Objective

6. State how power, politics, and ethics affect behavior, human relations, and performance

REVIEW

Select one or more methods: (1) fill in the missing key terms from memory; (2) match the key terms, from the end of the review, with their definitions below; and/or (3) copy the key terms in order from the key terms at the beginning of the chapter.

EXHIBIT 9–3   **HUMAN RELATIONS GUIDE TO ETHICAL DECISION MAKING**

If you are proud to tell all relevant parties your decision, it is probably ethical.

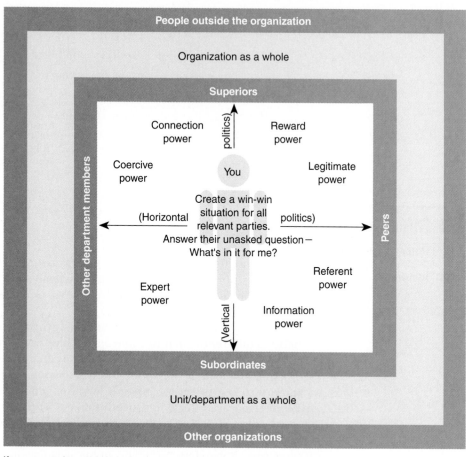

If you are embarrassed to tell all the relevant parties your decision or keep rationalizing, it is probably unethical.

In addition to having good performance, if you want to be successful, you will have to gain power and utilize ethical political skills with your superiors, subordinates, peers, and members of other departments.

_____ is a person's ability to influence another person's behavior. Generally, the higher the organizational level, the more power one has. The two sources of power are position power and personal power, while the seven bases of power include: _____, based on threats and/or punishment to influence compliance; _____, based on the user's relationship with influential people; _____, based on the user's ability to influence others with something of value to them; _____, based on the user's position power; _____, based on the user's personal power; _____, based on the user's information being desired by others; and _____, based on the user's skill and knowledge.

The use of power affects behavior, human relations, and performance. The power used should be appropriate for the situation.

_____, the process of gaining and using power, is an important part of meeting organizational objectives. _____ involves creating obligations and debts, developing alliances, and using them to accomplish objectives.

_____ is the moral standard of right and wrong behavior. _____ refers to behavior that is considered wrong by authorities, yet not accepted by others as unethical; while _____ refers to behavior that is considered wrong by authorities and the individual, yet conducted anyway. _____ includes behavior that benefits both the individual and the organization, while _____ includes behavior that benefits the individual and hurts the organization. The human relations guide to ethical decisions seeks to meet the goal of human relations by creating a win-win situation for all parties including superiors, subordinates, peers, members of other departments, and people and organizations outside the organization. If you are proud to tell all relevant parties your decision, that decision is probably ethical; if you are, embarrassed to tell or if you rationalize, it is probably unethical behavior. Etiquette is the socially accepted standard of right and wrong behavior.

Relations with your superiors and subordinates, vertical politics, are important to career success. Get to know your boss and his or her expectations. Common expectations of bosses include loyalty, cooperation, initiative, information, and openness to criticism. With your employees develop a professional relationship, rather than friendship, and use the _____, the practice of being available to employees.

Relations with peers and other departments, horizontal politics, are also important to career success. Learn to cooperate and compete with your peers and criticize them when necessary. Be cooperative and follow company guidelines in working with other departments.

In general, ethical politics have a positive effect on behavior, human relations, and performance in the long run. In the short run, unethical behavior may increase performance, but in the long run, it tends to have a negative effect on behavior, human relations, and performance.

KEY TERMS

coercive power   309
connection power   309
ethical politics   316
ethics   315
expert power   310
information power   310

legitimate power   310
open-door policy   325
politics   313
power   308
reword power   309
reciprocity   313

referent power   310
reward power   309
Type I ethics   315
Type II ethics   315
unethical politics   316

CASE

Carlton Petersburg: Department of Leadership

Carlton Petersburg is a tenured professor of leadership at a small teaching college in the Midwest. The Department of Leadership (DL) has nine faculty members; it is one of 10 departments in the School of Arts and Sciences (SAS). The leadership department chair is Tina Joel, who is in her first year as chair. Six faculty members, including Carlton, have been in the department for longer than Tina. She likes to have policies so that faculty members have guides for their behavior. On the college-wide level, there is no policy about the job of graduate assistants. Tina asked the dean of the SAS what the policy was. The dean stated that there is not policy, and he had spoken to the v.p for academic affairs. The V.P and the dean suggested letting the individual departments develop their own policy regarding what graduate assistants can and cannot do. So Tina put use of graduate assistants on the department-meeting agenda.

During the DL meeting, Tina asked for members' views on what graduate assistants should and should not be allowed to do. Tina was hoping that the department would come to a consensus on a policy. Carlton Petersburg was the only faculty member who was using graduate assistants to grade exams. All but one of the other faculty members spoke out against the use of graduate assistants grading exams. Other faculty members believed it is the job of the professor to grade the exams. Carlton made a few statements in hopes of not having to correct his own exams. Carlton stated that his exams were objective, thus there being a correct answer, it was not necessary for him to personally correct the exams. He also pointed out that across the campus, and across the country, other faculty members are using graduate assistants to teach entire courses and to correct subjective papers and exams. Carlton stated that he did not think it would be fair to tell him that he could not use graduate assistants to grade objective exams when others could do so. He also stated that the department did not need to have a policy, and requested that the department not set a policy. However, Tina stated that she wanted a policy. He held a single minority view during the meeting. However, after the meeting, one other member, Fred Robbinson, of the department, who said nothing during the meeting, told Carlton that he agreed that it was not fair to deny him the use of a graduate assistant.

There was no department consensus, as Tina hoped there would be. Tina said that she would draft a department policy, which would be discussed at a future DI meeting. The next day, Carlton sent a memo to department members asking if it was ethical and legal to deny him the use of the same resources as others across the campus. He also stated that if the department set a policy stating that he could no longer use graduate assistants to correct objective exams, he would appeal the policy decision to the dean v.p. and president.

Go to the Internet: This case actually did happen. However, the names have been changed for confidentiality. Thus, you cannot go to the college website where the case really happened. Therefore, go to your own college website and get information about your college that you did not know.

Support your answer to the following questions with specific information from the case and text, or information you get from other source.

1. What source of power does Tina have, and what type of power is she using during the meeting?

2. (a) What source of power does Carlton have, and (b) what type of power is he using during the meeting? (c) Is the memo a wise political move for Carlton? What may be gained and lost by sending it?

3. What would you do if you were Tina? (a) Would you talk to the dean letting him know that Carlton said he would appeal the policy decision? (b) Which political behavior would the discussion be? (c) Would you draft a policy directly stating that graduate assistants cannot be used to grade objective exams? (d) Would your answer to c be influenced by your answer to a?

4. If you were Carlton, (a) knowing you had no verbal supporters during the meeting, would you have continued to defend your position or agree to stop using a graduate assistant? (b) What do you think of Carlton sending the memo? (c) As a tenured full professor, Carlton is secure in his job. Would your answer change if you/Carlton had not received tenure or promotion to the top rank?

5. If you were Carlton, and Tina drafted a policy and department members agreed with it, what would you do? (a) Would you appeal the decision to the dean? (b) Again, would your answer change if you/Carlton had not received tenure or promotion to the top rank?

6. If you were the dean of SAS, knowing that the v.p. does not want to set a college-wide policy, and Carlton appealed to you, what would you do? Would you develop a school-wide policy for SAS?

7. At what level (college wide, by schools, or by departments within each school) should a graduate-assistant policy be set?

8. (a) Should Fred Robbinson have spoken up in defense of Carlton during the meeting? (b) If you were Fred, would you have taken Carlton's side against the other seven members? (c) Would your answer change if you were and were not friends with Carlton, and if you were and were not a tenured full professor?

Cumulative Case Questions

9. What is the role of perception (Chapter 2) and attitudes and values (Chapter 3) in this case?

10. What type of communications were used in this case (Chapters 4–5)? What was the major barrier to communications?

11. Which motivation theory was Carlton using to defend his position to use graduate assistance?

12. Which situational supervisory leadership style was Tina using (Chapter 7) to set the policy?

13. Which conflict management style (Chapter 7) did Tina and Carlton use in setting the policy? Which conflict management style would you have used if you were in Carlton's situation?

OBJECTIVE CASE

Politicking

Karen Whitmore is going to be promoted in two months. She will be replaced by her subordinate Jim Green or Lisa Fesco. Both Jim and Lisa know they are competing for the promotion. Their years of experience and quality and quantity of work are about the same. Below is some of the political behavior each used to help them get the promotion.

Lisa has been going to night classes and company training programs in management to prepare herself for the promotion. Lisa is very upbeat; she goes out of her way to be nice to people and compliment them. She gets along well with everyone. Knowing that Karen was an officer in a local businesswomen's networking organization, Lisa joined the club six months ago and now serves on a committee. At work Lisa talks regularly to Karen about the women's organization. Lisa makes an effort to know what is going on in the organization. One thing Karen doesn't like about Lisa is the fact that when she points out Lisa's errors, she always has an answer for everything.

Jim is good at sports and has been playing golf and tennis with upper-level managers for over a year now. In the department, especially with Karen, Jim refers to conversations with managers all the time. When Jim does something for someone, they can expect to do a favor in return. Jim really wants this promotion, but he fears that with more women being promoted to management positions, Lisa will get the job just because she is a woman. To increase his chances of getting the job, Jim stayed late and made a few changes—errors—in the report Lisa was working on. Jim sees nothing wrong with making the changes to get ahead. When Lisa passed in the report, without checking prior work, Karen found the errors. The one thing Karen doesn't like about Jim is the fact that, on occasion, she has to tell him what to do before he acts.

Answer the following questions. Then in the space between the questions, state why you selected that answer. (*Note:* Meetings between Lisa and Jim, Karen and Jim or all three may be role-played in class.)

_____ 1. We know that Karen has ____ power.

      a. position   *b.* personal

_____ 2. To be promoted Lisa is stressing ____ power. Refer to the opening statement about Lisa.

      a. coercive   *c.* reward   *e.* referent   *g.* expert
      b. connection   *d.* legitimate   *f.* information

_____ 3. To be promoted Jim is stressing ____ power. Refer to the opening statement about Jim.

      a. coercive   *c.* reward   *e.* referent   *g.* expert
      b. connection   *d.* legitimate   *f.* information

_____ 4. ____ appears to use reciprocity the most.

      a. Lisa   *b.* Jim

_____ 5. Lisa ____ conducted unethical political behavior.

      a. has   *b.* has not

_____ 6. Jim ____ conducted unethical political behavior.

      a. has   *b.* has not

_____ 7. Jim has committed ____ behavior in changing the report.

     a. Type I   *b.* Type II

_____ 8. Who was *not* affected by Jim changing the report?

     a. supervisors   *c.* peers   *e.* other departments
     b. subordinates   *d.* Karen's department   *f.* the organization

_____ 9. Lisa does not meet Karen's expectation of

     a. loyalty   *c.* initiative   *e.* openness to criticism
     b. cooperation   *d.* information

_____ 10. Jim does not meet Karen's expectation of

     a. loyalty   *c.* initiative   *e.* openness to criticism
     b. cooperation   *d.* information

11. In Lisa's situation, she suspects Jim made the changes in the report but she has no proof. What would you do?

12. In Karen's situation, she suspects Jim made the changes in the report, but she has no proof. What would you do?

Fiscal Fairy Tale # 7: The Three Pugs

Go to the MG website (*www.mgeneral.com*) and read *Fiscal Fairy Tale # 7: The Three Pugs* (your instructor may ask you to print a copy and bring it to class). Answer these questions (your instructor may ask you to type them and bring them to class):

Online MG Webzine Exercise 9

Questions Relating to the Tale Only

1. As stated at the end of the tale, in 50 words or so, what is your response to this tale? You may send it to MG.
2. Have you, or anyone you know, been sold something you did not need, more than you needed, or something that you could not afford to buy?

3. Do you generally trust salespeople?

4. Does it pay to be unethical?

Questions Relating the Tale to the Chapter Concepts

5. What base of power did Wick Wolf use to sell the three houses to the pugs?

6. Based on which power base did the three pugs go to Wick Wolf to buy a house?

7. Which characters in the tale used ethical and unethical behavior?

8. Is Wick Wolf on the Type I or Type II ethics?

In-Class MG Webzine Exercise 9

The instructor selects one of the six options from Appendix B page 589.

Influencing (IE 9–1)
Online Internet Exercise
9–1 (Self-Assessment)

The objective of this exercise is to learn more about influencing. Influencing is an important part of power. In this exercise you will learn more about influencing without a discussion of power bases. Use the information in Appendix B and IE 1–2 and 1–3 as you do the following:

1. Go to the Influence at Work website homepage—*www.influencatwork.com*

2. Click "NQ" to learn what your influencing quotient is (your instructor may require you to make a copy of it). On a sheet of paper, write down the answers you select for the questions/situations. When you are done,

3. Click "Check Your Answers" and determine your score—how many did you get correct? Read the questions/situation and try to understand why a specific answer is the best method of influencing, gaining power.

4. Questions: (1) What was your NQ? (2) Do you disagree with the recommended answers? State which and why you disagree. (3) How can you use this information to help you influence others in your personal and professional life? (Your instructor may require you to type and print your answers.)

5. At the end of the NQ there is a link to an *introduction to influence*. You may go and read more about influencing. There is also a subsection on Ethics I and Ethics II.

The instructor selects one of the six options from Appendix B page 589.

In-Class Internet
Exercise 9–1, IE 9–2,
and IE 9–3

Codes of Ethics (IE 9–2)
Online Internet
Exercise 9–2

The objective of this exercise is to learn more about codes of ethics by reading them. Use the information in Appendix B and IE 1–2 and 1–3 as you do the following:

1. Go to the Center for Study of Ethics in the Professions subsite of Illinois Institute of Technology—*http://csep.itt.edu/codes/codes.html*

2. Click one of the professional categories and read al least three of the codes of ethics (your instructor may require you to make a copy of the codes).

3. Questions: (1) What were the professions/organizations of the three codes of ethics? (2) Which code of ethics did you like best? Why? (3) What were some of the similarities and differences between the codes of ethics? (4) If you are or go into this profession, do you believe it would be helpful to your career if you followed these codes of ethics? Explain. (5) How can you use this information to help you be ethical in your personal and professional life? (Your instructor may require you to type and print your answers.)

Corporate Citizens
(IE 9–3)
Online Internet
Exercise 9–3

The objective of this exercise is to learn more about corporate citizenship. Ethical companies try to create win–win situations for all stakeholders. The Business Ethics Website rates corporations on corporate citizenship in five areas: environment, community relations, employee relations, diversity, and customer relations. Use the information in Appendix B and IE 1–2 and 1–3 as you do the following:

1. Select a large corporation that you believe will be ranked in the top-100 companies for corporate citizenship because they do a good job in the five areas of citizenship listed above. If you work/worked or would like to work for a large corporation, you can select it.

2. Go to the Business Ethics website—*www.business-ethics.com*

3. Click "100 Best Corporate Citizens" then Click "accompanying chart" or scroll down to see the list of all 100 companies and how they rate in the five areas.

4. Questions: (1) What corporation did you select and why? (2) Did the company make the top-100? If yes, what place did they get? (3) How can a company benefit by making the list and placing high on this and similar lists?

Ethics: Arthur Anderson

This video presents separate short cases.

Vignette 1: The High-Bid Dilemma

A purchasing agent and his assistant are reviewing bids from seven companies. They disagree on who to give the contract to. Place yourself in the role of the assistant.

Critical Thinking Questions:

1. Is there a conflict of interest in this case?

2. From the purchasing manager's view, is this Type I or II ethical behavior.

3. Should you, as the assistant, agree with the purchasing agent and give the business to Spin Cast or disagree and object to giving the business to Spin Cast?

4. Would you, as the assistant, be proud to tell all relevant parties your decision or would you be embarrassed? Would you be rationalizing your decision?

5. If you, as the assistant, disagree with your boss, should you go to your bosses' boss and explain the situation and/or should you report this biding process to outside sources (whistleblowing)?

6. Should you, as the assistant, go to the Spin Cast party?

Critical Thinking Questions:

Vignette 5: Creative Expense Reporting

Jim, a salesperson, asks a colleague Ken for information on expenses. Jim tells Ken of his creative expense reporting to claim entertainment expenses. Place yourself in both roles.

1. From Jim's view, is this Type I or II ethical behavior.

2. Should Jim have told Ken about his creative expense reporting?

3. Should Ken have told Jim that adding money to lunch and dinner to pay for entertainment is wrong and suggest that he not pad the expense report? Should Ken say to Jim that he will report this creative expense reporting to the boss, if he does it?

4. Would you, as Jim, be proud to tell all relevant parties your decision or would you be embarrassed? Would you be rationalizing your decision?

5. If you, as Ken, disagree with Jim's behavior, should you go to your boss and explain the situation and/or should you report this to outside sources (whistleblowing)?

VIDEO EXERCISE

◆ **Bases of Power**

VE 9–1
BM–10

Procedure 1
(10–20 minutes)

Objectives: To better understand the seven bases of power and when to use each.
SCANS: The SCANS competencies of resources, interpersonal skills, information, and systems and the foundations of basic, thinking, and personal qualities are developed through this exercise.
Preparation: You should understand the seven bases of power.
The instructor shows video module 10, Power. As you view each of the seven scenes, identify the power base being used by the manager.

_____ Scene 1. ____   A. coercive power

_____ Scene 2. ____   B. connection power

_____ Scene 3. ____   C. reward power

_____ Scene 4. ____   D. legitimate power

_____ Scene 5. ____   E. referent power

_____ Scene 6. ____   F. information power

_____ Scene 7. ____   G. expert power

    After viewing each of the seven scenes, identify/match the power base used by the manager by placing the letter of the power base on the scene line.
Option A: View all seven scenes and identify the power base used by the manager. After viewing all seven scenes, discuss and/or have the instructor give the correct answers.

Option B: After each scene the class discusses the power base used by the manager. The instructor states the correct answer after each of the seven scenes.

Procedure 2
(2–5 minutes)

Select the one power base you would use to get the employee to take the letter to the mail room. Which other power bases are also appropriate? Which power bases would you not use (are not appropriate) for this situation? Next to each power base listed above, write the letter *a* for appropriate or *n* for not appropriate.

Discussion:
Option A: In groups of four to six, answer the questions below.
Option B: As a class, answer the questions below.

1. Which power bases are not appropriate to use in this situation?

2. Which power bases are appropriate to use in this situation?

3. Is there one base of power most appropriate in this situation?

Conclusion: The instructor may make concluding remarks.

Application   (2–4 minutes): What did I learn from this exercise? How will I use this knowledge in the future?

Sharing: Volunteers give their answers to the application section.

SKILL-BUILDING EXERCISE 9-1

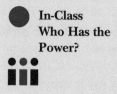

**In-Class
Who Has the
Power?**

Note: This exercise is designed for permanent groups that have worked together at least twice.

Objective: To better understand power and how people gain power.

SCANS: The SCANS competencies of resources, interpersonal skill, information, and systems and the foundations of basic, thinking, and personal qualities are developed through this exercise.

Preparation: You should have read and understood the text chapter.

Experience: Your group will discuss power within the group.

Procedure 1 (5–10 minutes)

Permanent teams get together and decide which member has the most power at this time (greatest ability to influence group members' behavior). Power can change with time. Before discussion, all members select the member they believe has the most power. You may select yourself. Write the most powerful person's name here _____. After everyone has made their selection, each member should state who was selected and explain why. Record the names of those selected below.

Procedure 2 (7–12 minutes)

Come to an agreement on the one person with the most power. Write the group's choice here. _____

Was there a struggle for power?

Why is this person the most powerful in the group? To help you answer this question, as a group, answer the following questions about your most powerful person.

1. Which of the nine human relations guidelines does he or she follow: (1) be optimistic, (2) be positive, (3) be genuinely interested in other people, (4) smile and develop a sense of humor, (5) call people by name, (6) listen to people, (7) help others, (8) think before you act, and (9) create win-win situations.

2. How does this person project a positive image? What type of image does his or her appearance project? What nonverbal communication does this person project that sends a positive image? What behavior does this person use that gains him or her power?

3. The primary source of this person's power is: (position/personal).

4. The primary base for this person's power in the group is: (coercive, connection, reward, legitimate, referent, information, expert).

5. This person uses which of the following political behaviors (gets along with everyone, makes people feel important and compliments them, compromises and avoids telling people they are wrong)?

6. This person uses (ethical/unethical) politics.

7. This person (cooperates with, competes with, criticizes) group members.

Overall, why is this person the most powerful? (Agree and write the reason below.)

Share the feeling you experienced doing this exercise. How did you feel about not being, or being, selected as the most powerful group member? Who wanted power and who didn't? Is it wrong or bad to want and seek power?

Optional:

1. A spokesperson from each group tells the class which member was selected the most powerful, and the overall reason why the person is the most powerful.

2. A spokesperson from each group does not tell the class which member was selected the most powerful, but does state the overall reason why the person is the most powerful.

Conclusion: The instructor leads a class discussion and/or makes concluding remarks.

Application (2–4 minutes): What did I learn from this exercise? How will I use this knowledge in the future?

Sharing: Volunteers give their answers to the application section.

SKILL-BUILDING EXERCISE 9–2

● **Preparation
Ethics**

For each of the following statements, place an "O" on the line if you observed someone doing this behavior. Also place an "R" on the line if you reported this behavior within the organization.

(O) Observed   (R) Reported

_____ 1. Coming to work late and getting paid for it.

_____ 2. Leaving work early and getting paid for it.

_____ 3. Taking long breaks/lunches and getting paid for it.

_____ 4. Calling in sick to get a day off, when not sick.

_____ 5. Using the company phone to make personal long distance calls.

_____ 6. Doing personal work while on company time.

_____ 7. Using the company copier for personal use.

_____ 8. Mailing personal things through the company mail.

_____ 9. Taking home company supplies or merchandise.

_____ 10. Giving company supplies or merchandise to friends or allowing them to take them without saying anything.

_____ 11. Putting in for reimbursement for meals and travel or other expenses that weren't actually eaten or taken.

_____ 12. Using the company car for personal business.

____ 13. Taking spouse/friends out to eat and charging it to the company expense account.

____ 14. Taking spouse/friend on business trips and charging the expense to the company.

____ 15. Accepting gifts from customers/suppliers in exchange for giving them business.

____ 16. A student cheating on homework assignments.

____ 17. A student passing off someone else's term paper as his or her own work.

____ 18. A student cheating on an exam.

____ 19. For items 1–15, select the three which you consider the most severe unethical behavior. Who is harmed and who benefits by these unethical behaviors?

____ 20. For items 16–18, who is harmed and who benefits from these unethical behaviors?

____ 21. If you observed unethical behavior but didn't report it, why didn't you report the behavior? Also, if you did report the behavior, why did you report it? What was the result?

In-Class Ethics

SB 9-2

Procedure 1 (5–30 minutes)

Objective: To better understand ethics and whistle-blowing.

SCANS: The SCANS competencies of resources, interpersonal skills, information, and systems and the foundations of basic, thinking, and personal qualities are developed through this exercise.

Preparation: You should have answered the questions in the preparation.

Experience: You will share your answers to the preparation questions.

Option A: Break into groups of five or six and share your answers to the preparation questions.

Option B: The instructor leads a discussion in which students share their answers to the preparation questions. (The instructor may begin by going over the 18 statements and have students who have observed the behavior raise their hand.) Then the instructor will have them raise their hand if they reported the behavior.

Conclusion: The instructor may lead a class discussion and/or make concluding remarks.

Application (2–4 minutes): What did I learn from this exercise? How will I use this knowledge in the future?

Sharing: Volunteers give their answers to the application section.

Teams and Creative Problem Solving and Decision Making

Learning Objectives

After completing this chapter, you should be able to:

1. Explain the importance of teams.

2. Describe the major types of groups.

3. List the five steps in the problem-solving and decision-making model.

4. Describe five techniques for generating creative alternatives.

5. Explain advantages and disadvantages of group decision making.

6. State when and how to use participation in problem solving and decision making.

7. Define the following 19 key terms (in order of appearance in the chapter):

group/team	**cost-benefit analysis**
functional groups	**creativity**
participative management	**stages in the creative process**
ad hoc committees	**brainstorming**
standing committees	**synetics**
informal groups	**nominal grouping**
problem	**consensus mapping**
problem solving	**Delphi technique**
decision making	**devil's advocate technique**
problem-solving and	
decision-making steps	

ted Williams was asked to serve on the Windy Company's budget committee. Ted looks forward to the change because it will give him a chance to get away from his regular job for a few hours a day over several weeks. But more importantly, Ted knows that the chair of the budget committee is Sonia Windy, president of the company. Ted hopes to do well on the committee so he can impress her in hopes of future advancement. Ted has never served on a committee before and wonders what it will be like.

The budget committee was formed 10 years ago, and its members come from a variety of departments; but membership changes from year to year, except the president remains as chair. The budget committee has the authority to make the actual allocation decision of the budget, but Ted wonders how much participation Sonia will allow from the committee and what supervisory style she will use.

After serving his one-year term on the budget committee, Ted thought about his experience. Sonia had allowed the group members to give their suggestions on how much each department should be given, but no one could speak against the numbers being allocated. After everyone had presented his or her suggested allocation, everyone debated about the figures. After all the debating was over, Sonia made the final decision on how much each department would get. She clearly explained why each department got its allocation.

Organization
Group
Individual

Groups and Teams

The terms *groups* and *teams* are commonly used interchangeably. However, recently groups and teams have been differentiated.[1] In this section, we begin by distinguishing between groups and teams and then stating why team leadership skills are important.

Group and Team Differences

Group and team distinctions and their level of autonomy are presented in Exhibit 10–1. To summarize the differences, they are defined as follows. A *group* is two or more members with a clear leader, who perform independent jobs with individual accountability, evaluation, and rewards. A *team* is a small number of members with shared leadership who perform interdependent jobs with both individual and group accountability, evaluation, and rewards. All teams are groups, but not all groups are teams.[2] Therefore, when the term *groups* is used in this book, it can also refer to a team. It is not always easy to distinguish a team from a group.[3] Therefore, for our purposes a **group/team** *is two or more people interacting to achieve an objective.* Our definition has three important components. The group's objective is what tends to bring its members together—the members interact—as it performs the necessary tasks to achieve the objective.[4] Group members define themselves as members and are defined by others as belonging to the group.[5]

EXHIBIT 10–1   **GROUP AND TEAM DIFFERENCES**

Characteristics	Groups	Teams
Size	Two or more; can be large.	Small number; often 5–12 members.
Leadership	One clear leader making decisions.	Shared leadership and decisions.
Jobs	Members perform one clear independent part of a process.	Members share job responsibility by performing many interdependent tasks.
Accountability and Evaluation	The leader evaluates employees' individual performance.	Members evaluate each other's individual and the group's performance.
Rewards	Based on individual performance only.	Based on individual and group performance.
Objectives	Set by management for the organization.	Organizational and those set by the team.

Level of Autonomy

Group <   *Team*

Management-Directed Semi-Autonomous   Self-Directed

←——→

The use of teams has increased dramatically.[6] Although we do not always make a clear distinction between a group and a team, you should be aware that the trend is toward the use of teams[7] and will need to learn to live with them. Your career may depend on it.[8] Organizations are fitting the person to the job,[9] and they are hiring people with the ability to function within teams.[10]

Some companies attribute huge gains to abandoning assembly lines in favor of teams.[11] Some of the organizations using teams include: AlliedSignal,[12] Honeywell and Dell Computer,[13] the Baltimore County Bureau of Corrections, and Chrysler.[14]

As shown on the bottom of Exhibit 10–1, groups and teams are on a continuum. The terms *management-directed, semi-autonomous,* and *self-directed* (or *managed*) are commonly used to differentiate along the continuum. In line with the trend toward teams, the use of semi-autonomous and self-directed teams is on the increase.[15]

Why Team Leadership Skills Are Important

Below are some of the many reasons why team leadership skills are important to managers and nonmanagers as well.

- Global organizations continue to focus on teams as the major means of increasing productivity.[16]
- Managers report spending 50 to 90 percent of their time in some form of team activity. Managers will spend less time supervising and more time facilitating teams as the trend toward self-directed teams continues.[17]
- It is common knowledge that groups are the backbone of organizations[18] because of the systems effect in which each group/department is affected by at least one other group and each department affects the performance of the total organization.

Learning Objective

1. Explain the importance of teams

WORK APPLICATIONS

1. List some reasons, not mentioned in the text, why team leadership skills are important.

- Organization
- **Group**
- Individual

Types of Groups

In this section, you will learn about the two types of formal groups—functional groups and task groups—and informal groups.

Functional Groups

At all levels in the organization are **functional groups,** *which are ongoing formal groups comprised of managers and their employees.* Each work unit/department makes up a functional group. For example, the marketing, finance, production, and personnel departments make up a number of independent functional groups. Each manager in the organization serves as the link between groups. Ideally, all functional groups coordinate their activities through the aid of the managers who are responsible for linking the activities together. Rensis Likert calls this the *linking pin role.* Exhibit 10–2 illustrates the linking pin concept.

Functional groups are ongoing because they remain in existence indefinitely. The group's objectives and its members may change over time, but the basic functions remain the same. They tend to deal with routine, recurring tasks.

With the growth of participative management, the use of self-directed teams (SDTs) is on the increase.[19] **Participative management** *is the process of the manager and employees working together as a team to set objectives and to plan how to accomplish them.* SDTs are functional groups in which the manager shares the responsibility for planning, scheduling, organizing, staffing, leading, and controlling quality and productivity with the group.[20] SDTs are discussed in more detail in Chapter 14.

So far, the primary focus has been on functional groups in which the manager directs the activities of his or her employees with line authority. Now, you will learn about task groups, in which the manager does not have line authority.

IE 10–1

Task Groups

Task groups are formal groups because they are sanctioned by the organization to perform a specific function. The task force is more commonly called a *committee.* Task groups are an effective problem-solving tool.[21] Unlike functional groups, they

EXHIBIT 10–2   THE LINKING PIN CONCEPT

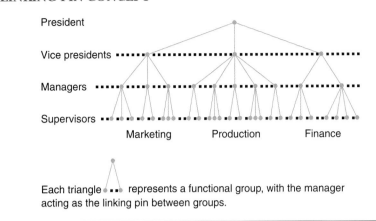

Each triangle ●■▶ represents a functional group, with the manager
acting as the linking pin between groups.

are usually comprised of members from different departments and are thus called
cross-functional teams.[22] Rubbermaid is using cross-functional teams to increase
the speed it takes to get a new product from idea to customer.[23]

While serving on task forces, members usually report to their functional groups
when not meeting with the task force. Serving on task forces is an addition to one's
normal workload.[24] Members work together until the task is completed, or until
their time to serve on the group is ended. Task forces are often created to deal with
nonroutine unique situations, as well as with continuing organizational issues.[25]
They recommend decisions to managers in line positions with the authority to
implement the decisions, or they are given the authority to make the decisions.[26]

The decision-making authority of the group should be clear. In the opening
case, the group had the authority to make the budget allocation decision. However,
the company president was the chair of the committee and made the final decision.

Ad Hoc Committees

The two commonly used classifications for task groups are ad hoc committee and
standing committee. **Ad hoc committees** *are temporary task forces formed for a specific
purpose.* They are temporary because they exist only until the task is accomplished.
Some uses of ad hoc committees include search committees to select or make recommendations on whom to hire, committees to select or recommend equipment
to be purchased, and committees to select or recommend plant locations.

Project Matrix Teams:
Many organizations that make custom-tailored prod-
ucts to meet customer specifications develop project matrix teams. Major defense
contractors are examples. We discussed matrix departmentalization in Chapter 5.

Standing Committees

Standing committees *are permanent groups that exist to deal with continuing organizational issues.* They are permanent because they are ongoing from year to year. Members often serve a term on the committee, and when their term is up, someone else
may take their place. To keep continuity, committees often replace members on a
rotating basis. Many colleges have promotion and tenure committees and curriculum committees to decide which new courses and/or majors to offer. TRW Inc.
uses a variety of teams.[27]

Boards:
Corporations have boards (a type of standing committee) of directors
or trustees whose task is to oversee the management of the organization's assets, to
set or approve policies and objectives, and to review progress toward the objectives.

Public Policy Groups:
With the business environment changing at a more
rapid pace, major companies have developed public policy groups, designed to help
management deal more effectively with the external environmental pressures.[28] The

role of these groups is to be aware of the trends and how they will affect the organization, while at the same time setting policies that will affect the internal environment of the company.

Venture Groups: With the present trend toward the use of entrepreneurial techniques, the use of venture groups has been increasing. Venture groups are responsible for planning entry into new, profitable business or service areas.[29] They are designed to cut the red tape of the complex bureaucratic structure and process. Venture groups tend to be made up of a few skilled experts and managers from various functional groups, under one leader. Organizations that use venture groups include Dow, General Electric, Monsanto, Westinghouse, and Union Carbide. 3M had at least 24 venture groups at one time, and six of its current divisions developed out of these venture groups.

WORK APPLICATIONS

2. Recall a task group you belong/belonged to. Identify it as an ad hoc or standing committee and state the group's name and purpose.

Informal Groups

Task and functional groups are considered formal groups because they are intentionally created by the organization as a means of carrying out its purpose and accomplishing its objectives. Informal groups are not intentionally created by the organization.

Informal groups *are spontaneously created when members join together voluntarily because of similar interests.* Informal groups may be made up of members from formal groups. For example, members of the production department are a functional group during working hours. However, members who get together for breaks, lunch, and after work make up an informal group. Informal groups, sometimes referred to as *cliques,* are often made up of members from different departments. Informal groups may help or hurt the organization as it pursues its objectives. This is discussed in the next chapter.

Learning Objective

2. Describe the major types of groups

WORK APPLICATIONS

3. Identify an informal group you belong to.

APPLICATION SITUATIONS

Types of Groups

AS 10–1

Identify each group as a:

A. Functional group   E. Venture group

B. Ad hoc committee   F. Board

C. Standing committee   G. Public policy

D. Informal group

_____ 1. Class groups that meet to discuss application situations, objective cases, and/or skill-building exercises.

_____ 2. A group that meets to review past performance and plan for future activities of a college.

_____ 3. A college group consisting of department chairpeople and the dean. They meet twice per month to discuss a wide variety of items.

____ 4. A group that meets to determine which books will be published. It consists of editors, marketing people, and general administrators.

____ 5. A group working to find a new and different product to sell.

____ 6. A group that meets to decide on environmental issues.

____ 7. The company-sponsored bowling group.

____ 8. A retail group that is meeting to decide on the purchase (merger) of a clothing manufacturer to supply its clothes.

____ 9. The president and vice presidents that meet to decide which of the committee's recommended manufacturers to buy (merger) to supply them with clothes.

____ 10. A group of top executives and personnel people who meet to decide what to offer the union during labor negotiations.

● Organization
● Group
● Individual

Problem-Solving and Decision-Making Approaches

Surprising but true: Half the decisions in organizations fail.[30] We will begin by discussing problem solving and decision making as it applies to individuals and then to groups. One of the major reasons managers are hired is to make decisions and solve problems. Making bad decisions can destroy companies and careers.[31] Decisions managers make can affect the health, safety, and well-being of consumers, employees, and the community. Managers make poor decisions about 50 percent of the time.[32] Ethical decision making is becoming more important as rapid change continues in the diverse global environment.[33] You should realize that problem-solving and decision-making skills will affect your results. As with all management skills, you can develop problem-solving and decision-making skills.

WORK APPLICATIONS

4. Give reasons why problem-solving and decision-making skills are important. Do not use the reasons stated in the text.

In this section, we discuss decision-making styles and the problem-solving and decision-making model. First, notice what a problem is and the relationship between problem solving and decision making.

A **problem** *exists whenever there is a difference between what is actually happening and what the individual/group wants to be happening.* If your objective is to produce 500 units per day, but only produce 475, there is a problem. A major cause of problems is change. A change in material, tools, and so forth may be the cause of producing 475, rather than 500 units. **Problem solving** *is the process of taking corrective action in order to meet objectives.*

The term **decision making** *is the process of selecting an alternative course of action that will solve a problem.* Decisions must be made when you are faced with a problem. The first decision is whether or not to take action to solve the problem. For example, one can simply change objectives and eliminate the problem. In the above example, you can change the objective to 475 units per day.

Some problems cannot be solved, while other problems are not worth the time and effort to solve. However, since part of a manager's job is to achieve objectives, you will have to attempt to solve most of your problems if you want to be successful. Following the suggestions in this chapter can help you develop your problem-solving and decision-making skills.

> ## WORK APPLICATIONS

5. Give an example of a problem you face now.

Decision-Making Styles

There are different decision-making styles,[34] including: reflexive, consistent, and reflective. To determine your decision-making style, answer the 10 questions in Self-Assessment Exercise 10–1 by selecting the answer 1–3 that best describes how you make decisions.

Self-Assessment Exercise 10–1

Decision-Making Styles

A. Overall I'm ____ to act.

    1. quick   2. moderate   3. slow

B. I spend ____ amount of time making important decisions as I do making less important decisions.

    1. about the same   2. a greater   3. a much greater

C. When making decisions, I ____ go with my first thought.

    1. usually   2. occasionally   3. rarely

D. When making decisions, I'm ____ concerned about making errors.

    1. rarely   2. occasionally   3. often

E. When making decisions, I ____ recheck my work.

    1. rarely   2. occasionally   3. usually

F. When making decisions, I gather ____ information.

    1. little   2. some   3. lots of

G. When making decisions, I consider ____ alternative actions.

    1. few   2. some   3. lots of

H. When making a decision, I usually make it ____ before the deadline.

    1. way   2. somewhat   3. just

I. After making a decision, I ____ look for other alternatives, wishing I had waited.

    1. rarely   2. occasionally   3. usually

J. I regret having made a decision.

    1. rarely   2. occasionally   3. often

To determine your style, add up the numbers 1–3 that represent your answers to the 10 questions. The total will be between 10 and 30. Place an X on the continuum line between 10 and 30 that represents your score.

        Reflexive   Consistent   Reflective

10 – – – – – – – – – – – – – 16 – – – – – – – – – – – – – 23 – – – – – – – – – – – – – 30

A score of 10–16 indicates a reflexive style; 17–23 indicates a consistent style; and 24–30 indicates a reflective style. You have determined your preferred decision-making style. Groups also have a preferred decision-making style, based on how their members make decisions. You could answer the 10 questions, changing the *I* to *we* and referring to a group rather than to yourself.

Reflexive Style

A reflexive decision maker/group likes to make quick decisions ("to shoot from the hip") without taking the time to get all the information that may be needed and without considering all alternatives. On the positive side, reflexive decision makers are decisive; they do not procrastinate. On the negative side, making quick decisions can lead to waste and duplication when a decision is not the best possible alternative. The reflexive decision maker may be viewed by employees as a poor manager if he or she is consistently making bad decisions. If you use a reflexive style, you may want to slow down and spend more time gathering information and analyzing alternatives. Following the steps in the problem-solving and decision-making model can help you develop your skills.

Reflective Style

A reflective decision maker/group likes to take plenty of time to make decisions, taking into account considerable information and an analysis of several alternatives. On the positive side, the reflective type does not make quick decisions that are rushed. On the negative side, he or she may procrastinate and waste valuable time and other resources. The reflective decision maker may be viewed as wishy-washy and indecisive. If you use a reflective style, you may want to speed up your decision making. As Andrew Jackson once said, "Take time to deliberate; but when the time for action arrives, stop thinking and go on."

Consistent Style

A consistent decision maker/group tends to make decisions without rushing or wasting time.[35] He or she tends to know when they have enough information and alternatives to make a sound decision. Consistent decision makers tend to have the most consistent record of good decisions. They tend to follow the problem-solving and decision-making steps below.

The Problem-Solving and Decision-Making Model

This model is also called the rational model, and it is appropriate to use for important nonrecurring decisions. It is not necessary to follow all five steps in the model when making unimportant recurring decisions. In some situations, such as with very limited information, intuitive decisions are appropriate.[36] Intuition can also be used within the steps of the model.

Following the steps in the model will not guarantee success; however, following the model increases the probability of successful problem solving and decision making. Consult others for advice as you progress through the steps. Consciously use the model in your daily life, and you will improve your ability to solve problems and make decisions.

The **problem-solving and decision-making steps** are: *step 1, define the problem; step 2, set objectives and criteria; step 3, generate alternatives; step 4, analyze alternatives and select one; step 5, plan, implement the decision, and control.* Let's examine each step.

Step 1. Define the Problem

Due to time pressure, managers and employees are often in a hurry to solve problems. In haste, we often neglect the first step in problem solving—define the problem. In order to fully define the problem, the employee or group must determine the cause of the problem.[37] "What caused us to produce 475 units rather than 500?" In determining the cause(s) of the problem, people need time to think, preferably quietly, apart from others, reflectively, and with focus. Determining the causes of a problem involves looking back to understand the past, and then forward to predict the future. You must get the necessary information and facts to determine the problem. However, problems are not solved by putting blame on others.[38]

In analyzing a problem, first, distinguish symptoms from the cause of the problem. To do so, list the observable and describable occurrences (symptoms) that indicate a problem exists. Once this is done, you can determine the cause of the problem. After you eliminate the cause, the effects should disappear. For example,

Wayne, an employee of five years' tenure, has been an excellent producer on the job. However, in the last month, Wayne has been out sick and tardy more times than in the past two years. What is the problem? If you say absenteeism or tardiness, you are confusing symptoms and causes. They are symptoms of the problem. If the supervisor simply disciplines Wayne, he may decrease the tardiness and absenteeism, but the problem will not be solved. It would be wiser for the supervisor to talk to the employee and find out the reason (cause) for the problem. The real problem may be a personal problem at home or on the job. The key issue is that the decision maker must define the problem correctly in order to solve it.[39]

Step 2. Set Objectives and Criteria

After the problem has been defined, you are now ready to set an objective and develop the criteria for the decision. The manager should have an objective for solving the problem. Managers with specific objectives generate better operational plans and decisions. Unfortunately, identifying the decision to be made is not as simple as it sounds: the objective must state exactly what is to be accomplished. Refer back to Chapter 6 for a discussion on how to set objectives.

In addition to objectives, you should identify the criteria the decision must meet in order to achieve the objective. It is helpful to specify "must" and "want" criteria. "Must" criteria should be met while "want" criteria are desirable but not necessary. An example of an objective and criteria for a personnel department hiring a manager is as follows: Objective: "To hire a store manager by June 30, 20__." The "must" criteria are a college degree and a minimum of five years' experience as a store manager. The "want" criterion is that the hiree should be a minority group member. The organization wants to hire a minority but will not hire one who does not meet the must criterion.

Continuing the example with Wayne, the objective is to improve Wayne's attendance record. The criterion is his prior good record of attendance.

Step 3. Generate Alternatives

After the problem is defined and objectives and criteria are set, you are ready to generate possible methods/alternatives for solving the problem. There are usually many possible ways to solve a problem; in fact, if you don't have two or more alternatives, you don't have to make a decision. When making routine decisions, the alternatives are fairly straightforward. However, when making nonroutine decisions, new creative solutions are needed.[40] When gathering the information needed to generate alternatives, you should consider the time, energy, action, and cost of the information. You can neither expect nor afford complete information. However, you must get enough information to enable you to make good decisions. When generating alternatives, be creative. Continuing the example with Wayne, some alternatives include to give Wayne a warning, to punish him in some way, or to talk to him to determine the reason for the change.

Step 4. Analyze Alternatives and Select One

After generating alternative solutions to the problem, you must evaluate each in terms of the objectives and criteria. You should not always try to select the optimum alternative. In many cases a satisfactory decision (*satisficing*) will do the job. Think forward and try to predict the outcome of each alternative. One method you can use to analyze alternatives is cost-benefit analysis. **Cost-benefit analysis** *is a technique for comparing the cost and benefit of each alternative course of action.* Each alternative has its positive and its negative aspects, or its cost and benefits. Costs are more than monetary. They may include a sacrifice of time, money, and so forth. To make the best choice, you need to use some intuition,[41] feelings, and judgment when doing a cost-benefit analysis. Cost-benefit analysis has become popular in the nonprofit sector where the benefits are often difficult to determine in quantified dollars.

Continuing the example with Wayne, the alternative selected is to have a talk with him to try to determine why his attendance has changed.

Step 5. Plan, Implement the Decision, and Control

Step 5 in the problem-solving and decision-making process has three separate parts, as the title states. We will discuss each part separately.

Plan: After making the decision, you should develop a plan of action with a schedule for its implementation.

Implement the Decision: After the decision has been made and the plans developed, they must be implemented. Communication of the plan to all employees is critical for the successful implementation of the plan.

Control: As with all plans, controls should be developed while planning. Checkpoints should be established to determine if the decision is solving the problem. If not, corrective action may be needed. You should not be locked into a decision plan and throw good money after bad. When you make a poor decision, you should admit the mistake and change the decision by going back to prior steps in the problem-solving and decision-making model.

Concluding the example with Wayne, the supervisor plans what she will say to him during the meeting, she conducts the meeting, and follows up to be sure that the problem is solved.

Exhibit 10–3 summarizes the five steps in problem solving and decision making. Notice in Exhibit 10–3 that the steps do not simply go from start to end. At any step, you may have to return to a prior step to make changes. For example, if you are in the fifth step and control and implementation are not going as planned, you may have to backtrack to prior steps to take corrective action by generating and selecting a new alternative, or changing the objective. If the problem was not defined accurately, you may have to go back to the beginning.

EXHIBIT 10–3   **PROBLEM-SOLVING AND DECISION-MAKING MODEL**

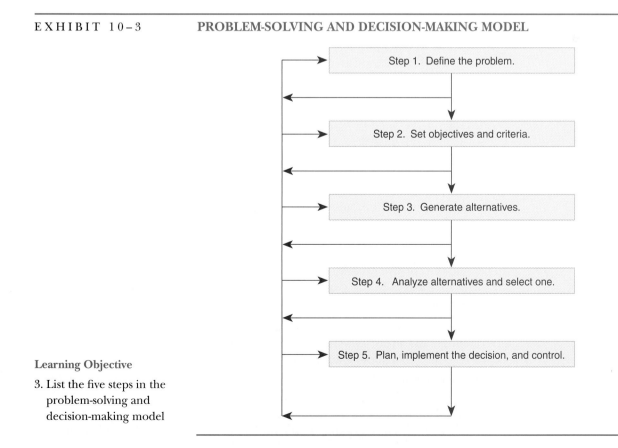

Learning Objective

3. List the five steps in the problem-solving and decision-making model

6. Solve the problem you gave in question 5, following the five steps in the problem-solving and decision-making model. Write it out clearly, labeling each step.

APPLICATION SITUATIONS

Steps in Problem Solving and Decision Making

AS 10–2

Identify the five statements below by their step in the problem-solving and decision-making model:

A. Step 1, define the problem.

B. Step 2, set objectives and criteria.

C. Step 3, generate alternatives.

D. Step 4, analyze alternatives and select one.

E. Step 5, plan, implement the decision, and control.

____ 11. Today we will be using the brainstorming technique.

____ 12. Chuck, is the machine still jumping out of sequence?

____ 13. We should state what it is we are trying to accomplish.

____ 14. What are the symptoms you have observed?

____ 15. I suggest that we use linear programming to help us in this situation.

● Organization
● Group
● Individual

Creative Group Problem Solving and Decision Making

In the last section, problem solving and decision making were presented as it applies to individuals and groups. In this section, we examine creativity and how to generate creative alternatives using groups. Innovation is one of the top 10 challenges business leaders face in the 21st century.[42]

Companies are trying to inspire creativity,[43] as organizational intelligence is developed and related to innovation[44] and creativity.[45] However, intelligent people are not always creative.[46] And it takes seven good ideas to generate a new commercial product.[47]

The term **creativity** *means the ability to develop unique alternatives to solve problems.* An example of creativity was introduced by Adelphi University when it wanted to expand its graduate business program. People perceived that they did not have time to further their education. The alternative Adelphi developed to solve the problem was the "classroom on wheels," which offers classes four days a week on commuter trains into and out of New York. To improve your creativity, follow the stages in the creative process.

The four **stages in the creative process** *are (1) preparation, (2) possible solutions, (3) incubation, (4) evaluation.*

1. Preparation. You must become familiar with the problem. Get others' opinions, feelings, and ideas, as well as the facts. When solving a problem, look for new angles, use imagination and invention, and don't limit boundaries.

2. Possible solutions. Generate as many possible creative solutions as you can think of, without making a judgment.

3. Incubation. After generating alternatives, take a break. It doesn't have to be long, but take time before working on the problem again. During the incubation stage,

you may have an insight to the problem's solution. Have you ever worked hard on a problem and become discouraged, but when you had given up or taken a break, the solution came to you?

4. Evaluation. Before implementing a solution, you should evaluate the alternative to make sure the idea is practical. Evaluation often leads to more creativity.

Everyone has creative capability;[48] Following the above four stages can help you improve your creativity. For a summary of the stages in the creative process, see Exhibit 10–4.

EXHIBIT 10–4

STAGES IN THE CREATIVE PROCESS

Stage 1. Preparation

Stage 2. Possible solutions

Stage 3. Incubation

Stage 4. Evaluation

WORK APPLICATIONS

7. Give an example of how you solved a problem using the stages in the creative process, or use it to solve an existing problem.

How people respond to creative ideas affects the group's action. For a list of responses that kill creativity, see Exhibit 10–5. Avoid these responses and discourage others from using them as well.

EXHIBIT 10–5

RESPONSES THAT KILL CREATIVITY

- It isn't in the budget.
- Don't be ridiculous.
- We've never done it before.
- Has anyone else ever tried it?
- It won't work in our company/industry.
- That's not our problem.
- We tried that before.
- It can't be done.
- It costs too much.
- That's beyond our responsibility.
- It's too radical a change.

- We did all right without it.
- We're doing the best we can.
- We don't have the time.
- That will make other equipment obsolete.
- We're too small/big for it.
- Let's get back to reality.
- Why change it? It's still working OK.
- We're not ready for that.
- You're years ahead of your time.
- Can't teach an old dog new tricks.
- Let's form a committee.

Using Groups to Generate Creative Alternatives

In step 3 of the problem-solving and decision-making process, if you decide to use group input when generating alternatives, there are a variety of techniques you can use. Some of the techniques include brainstorming, synetics, nominal grouping, consensus mapping, and the Delphi technique.

Brainstorming *is the process of suggesting many alternatives, without evaluation, to solve a problem.* When brainstorming, the group is presented with a problem and asked to develop as many solutions as possible to solve it. During brainstorming, employees should be encouraged to suggest wild, extreme ideas. They should build on suggestions made by others, ignoring status differentials. All should have an equal voice. Evaluation of the alternatives should not take place until all alternatives have been generated. Brainstorming can be used for problems requiring creative ideas, such as the naming of a new product or service and how to market it. This process is not appropriate for making decisions under uncertain conditions such as the decision to offer the new product or service. Mediators can use brainstorming to solve conflicts.[49]

Synetics *is the process of generating novel alternatives through role-playing and fantasizing.* Synetics focuses on novel ideas rather than a quantity of ideas. Creativity can come from what seems to be chaos[50] and conflict.[51] At first, in order to expand the group's thinking process, the leader does not state the exact nature of the situation. For example, when Nolan Bushnell wanted to develop a new concept in family dining, he began by discussing general leisure activities. Bushnell then moved toward leisure activities having to do with eating out. The idea that came out of this synetics process was a restaurant-electronic game complex where families could play games and purchase pizza and hamburgers. The restaurant-electronic game complex is called Pizza Time Theatre and its mascot is Chuck E. Cheese, which is also used as the restaurant's name.

Nominal grouping *is the process of generating and evaluating alternatives through a structured voting method.* This process usually involves six steps:

1. Each employee individually generates ideas in writing.
2. The leader records all ideas where everyone can see them.
3. Alternatives are clarified through a guided discussion and any additional ideas are recorded.
4. Each employee rates the ideas and votes; the voting eliminates alternatives.
5. An initial vote discussion takes place for clarification, not persuasion. During this time, it is recommended that employees present the logic behind the reasons they gave for the various alternatives.
6. The final vote is taken to select the alternative solution presented to the leader. Management may or may not implement the decision. (This is the participative supervisory style.)

Consensus mapping *is the process of developing a group consensus solution to a problem.* A consensus is a cooperative attempt to develop a solution acceptable to all employees, rather than a competitive battle in which a solution is forced on some members of the group. It is an extension of nominal grouping. The major difference is that the group categorizes or clusters ideas listed to come to a consensus solution that is the group's rather than voting on one employee's solution. The major benefit of consensus mapping is that since the solution is the group's, members generally are more committed to implementing it.[52] The success of Pizza Hut/KFC is due in part to its CEO's ability to build consensus.[53]

The **Delphi technique** *polls a group through a series of anonymous questionnaires.* The opinions of each round of questionnaires are analyzed and resubmitted to the group in the next round of questionnaires. This process may continue for five or more rounds before a consensus emerges. The Delphi technique is primarily used for technological forecasts, such as what will be the next computer breakthrough, and how will it affect the banking industry? Computers are being used to help people be more creative.[54]

In the opening case, Sonia Windy used brainstorming to generate alternatives. Group members were not allowed to speak against others' allocations until all had made their presentations of figures. For a review of all five creative techniques, see Exhibit 10–6.

Learning Objective

4. Describe five techniques for generating creative alternatives

IE 10-2

EXHIBIT 10–6   **TECHNIQUES FOR GENERATING CREATIVE ALTERNATIVES**

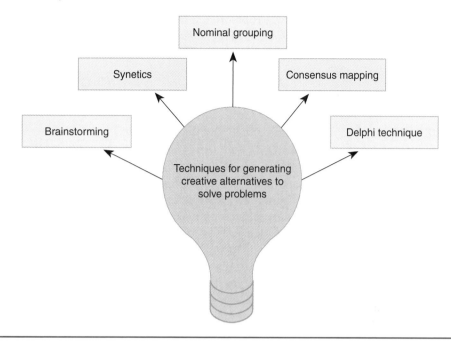

WORK APPLICATIONS

8. Give example situations in which it would be appropriate for a manager to use brainstorming, synetics, nominal grouping, consensus mapping, and the Delphi technique.

APPLICATION SITUATIONS

Using Groups to Generate Alternatives

AS 10–3

In the five situations below, identify the most appropriate group technique to use to generate alternative solutions:

A. Brainstorming   C. Nominal group   E. Delphi
B. Synetics   D. Consensus mapping

_____ 16. The supervisor wants to develop some new and different toys. She is using employees and children together.

_____ 17. The department is suffering from morale problems.

_____ 18. The supervisor must decide on new furniture for the office.

_____ 19. The supervisor wants to reduce waste in the department.

_____ 20. The supervisor wants to project future trends of the business.

● Organization
● Group
● Individual

Determining When to Use Group Problem Solving and Decision Making

The big issue managers must deal with today is no longer whether groups should be used to solve problems and make decisions; they should.[55] The issue today includes *when* managers should use groups and when managers should make the decision alone;[56] and, when a group is used, what level of participation should be used. In this section we discuss the advantages and disadvantages of using groups to solve problems and make decisions, and how to select the appropriate level of participation to meet the needs of the situation.

Advantages and Disadvantages of Group Decision Making

Advantages of Group Problem Solving and Decision Making

Some of the advantages include:

Better Decisions: Participative management is beneficial because groups usually do a better job in solving complex problems.[57] Using groups to solve problems and make decisions is appropriate for nonroutine decisions[58] made under the conditions of risk or uncertainty. Microsoft set up a top decision-making group to improve decision making.[59]

Better decisions result from this synergy. Synergy occurs when the total effect is greater than the sum of the individual effects. With synergy the group solution is superior to that of all individual solutions.

More Alternatives: Diversity is positive because a diverse group offers different points of view and a variety of alternative solutions. A diverse group offers more creativity.[60] Members can build on each other's ideas to improve the quality of alternatives. The leader can use the creative group techniques discussed earlier in this section.

Another approach to improving the quality of decisions is the devil's advocate approach. The **devil's advocate technique** *requires the individual to explain and defend his or her position before the group.* The group critically asks the presenter questions. They try to shoot holes in the alternative solution to determine any possible problems in its implementation. After a period of time, the group reaches a refined solution.[61]

Acceptance: The chances of successfully implementing a decision can be greatly increased if those affected are involved in the decision-making process. How the decision is made often means more than the decision itself. When each member contributes to the decision process, it builds ownership, enthusiasm, and a commitment to action.[62]

Morale: Using participation in problem solving and decision making is tangibly rewarding and personally satisfying to all parties.[63] Participation results in better understanding of why decisions are made and greater job satisfaction.[64] Better communication within the department results when employees are involved in problem solving and decision making.

Disadvantages of Group Problem Solving and Decision Making

Some of the disadvantages of using groups include:

Time: It takes longer for a group to make a decision than for an individual. Employees involved in problem solving and decision making are not on the job producing. Therefore, group problem solving and decision making can cost the organization time and money. Time pressure discourages participation.[65]

Domination: One group member or subgroup may dominate the meeting and nullify the group decision.[66] Subgroups may develop and destructive conflict may result. Conflicting secondary goals may occur (see the discussion on ulterior transactions in Chapter 8). An individual or subgroup may try to win an argument rather than find the best solution, or the individual(s) may put his or her personal needs before the group's needs.

Conformity and Groupthink: Group members may feel pressured to go along with the group's solution without questioning it out of fear of not being accepted or of being ostracized. The group not willing to use the devil's advocate approach nullifies the advantage of diversity. The phenomenon in which conformity clearly has a negative impact on group problem solving and decision making has been labeled *groupthink* by Irving Janis. A charismatic group member may charm others, or an autocratic member may intimidate a group into agreement,[67] especially the shy introverted personality types. With the use of nominal grouping, domination and conformity can be diminished.

Responsibility and Social Loafing: When a group makes a decision, its responsibility is often spread over many people and they can take a less serious attitude knowing they are not personally responsible. However, managers are responsible for decisions, regardless of how they are made. The manager can delegate the authority to the group to make the decision, but she or he retains responsibility. Managers need the necessary skills to effectively use the group.

When the advantages outweigh the disadvantages of using a group, use a group. In the opening case, Sonia decided to use a group. A key question to ask when deciding whether or not to use a group is this: Can the group make a better decision than any one individual? If you feel one individual will make a better decision (the person could be yourself as the manager or a knowledgeable employee), don't use the group. The next part of this section will give you specific guidance on when to use a group, and what level of participation to use.

Determining Which Supervisory Style to Use When Solving Problems and Making Decisions

Managers rely on different leadership styles, according to the type of decisions they must make in their positions.[68] Chapter 7 discussed the situational supervision model. Chapter 5 provided a situational communication model to use when communicating. Now you will learn a similar model to use when deciding which supervisory style to use when solving problems and making decisions. Selecting the appropriate situational supervisory style when solving problems and making decisions includes two steps: step 1, diagnose the situation; and step 2, select the appropriate style.

Step 1. Diagnose the Situation

The first step is to diagnose the situational variables, which include time, information, acceptance, and employee capability level. See Exhibit 10–7 for a list of variables.

EXHIBIT 10–7   VARIABLES INFLUENCING PARTICIPATION

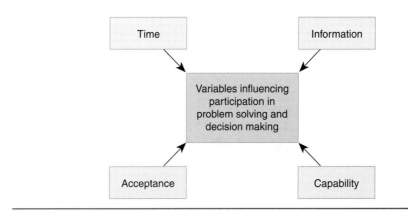

Time: The manager must determine if there is enough time to include the group in decision making.[69] If there is not enough time, managers should use the autocratic style, regardless of their preferred style. In this case the manager should also ignore the other three variables; they are irrelevant if there is no time. If time permits, the manager considers the other three variables and selects the problem-solving and decision-making styles without considering time. When time is short, the manager may use the consultative style, but not the participative or laissez-faire styles. Time, however, is a relative term. In one situation, a few minutes may be considered a short time period, while in another a month may be a short period of time.

Information: Does the manager have enough information to make a quality decision alone? If the manager has all the necessary information, there is no need to use participation. The autocratic style may be appropriate. When the manager has some information but needs more, the consultative style may be appropriate. However, if the manager has little information, the appropriate style may be participative or laissez-faire.

Acceptance: The manager must decide if the group's acceptance of the decision is critical to its implementation.[70] If the manager makes the decision alone, will the group implement it?[71] If so, the appropriate style may be autocratic. If the group will be reluctant, the appropriate style may be consultative or participative. If the group will probably not implement the decision unless consulted in advance, the participative or laissez-faire style may be appropriate.

Capability: The manager must decide if the group has the ability and willingness to be involved in problem solving and decision making.[72] Does the group have the experience and information needed to be involved in problem solving and decision making? Will the group put the organization/department's goals ahead of personal goals? Does the group want to be involved in problem solving and decision making? Employees are more willing to participate when the decisions personally affect them. If the group's level of capability is low, an autocratic style may be appropriate. When a group's capability is moderate, a consultative style may be appropriate. If the group's capability level is high, a participative style may be appropriate. If the group's level of capability is outstanding, the laissez-faire style may be appropriate. Remember that a group's capability level can change from situation to situation.

Exhibit 10–8 summarizes step 1. Diagnose the situation.

Step 2. Select the Appropriate Supervisory Style for the Situation

After considering the four variables, a manager uses the analysis to select the appropriate style for diverse situations. In some situations, all variables suggest the same possible style, while other cases indicate conflicting styles. For example, the manager may have time to use any style and may have all the information necessary (autocratic); employees may be reluctant (consultative or participative); and the capability may be moderate (consultative). In situations where conflicting styles are indicated for different variables, the manager must determine which variable should be given more weight. In the above example, assume it was determined that acceptance was critical for successful implementation of the decision. Acceptance takes precedence over information. Realizing that employees have a moderate capability, the consultative style would be appropriate. See Exhibit 10–8 for an explanation of how the decision is made using each of the four situational supervisory styles.

WORK APPLICATIONS

9. Identify the primary situational problem-solving and decision-making styles used by your present/past boss. Give an example of when the boss used this style. If you've never had a job, interview someone who has.

EXHIBIT 10-8   SITUATIONAL PROBLEM SOLVING AND DECISION MAKING

Step 1. Diagnose the Situation.

Resource	Use of Resource Style
Time	No S-A
	Yes S-A, S-C, S-P, or S-L
Information	All S-A
	Some S-C
	Little S-P or S-L
Acceptance	Accept S-A
	Reluctance S-C
	Reject S-P or S-L
Capability	Low S-A
	Moderate S-C
	High S-P
	Outstanding S-L

Step 2. Select the Appropriate Style for the Situation.

Autocratic (S-A)

The supervisor makes the decision alone and announces it after the fact. An explanation of the rationale for the decision may be given.

Consultative (S-C)

The supervisor consults the group for information, then makes the decision. Before implementing the decision, the supervisor explains the rationale for the decision and sells the benefits to the employees. The supervisor may invite questions and have a discussion.

Participative (S-P)

The supervisor may present a tentative decision to the group and ask for its input. The supervisor may change the decision if the input warrants a change. Or the supervisor presents the problem to the group for suggestions. Based on employee participation, the supervisor makes the decision and explains its rationale.

Laissez-faire (S-L)

The supervisor presents the situation to the group and describes limitations to the decision. The group makes the decision. The supervisor may be a group member.

Applying the Situational Problem-Solving and Decision-Making Model

We will apply the model to the following situation.

Ben, a supervisor, can give one of his employees a merit pay raise. He has a week to make the decision. Ben knows how well each employee performed over the past year. The employees really have no option but to accept getting or not getting the pay raise, but they can complain to upper management about the selection. The employees' capability levels vary, but as a group they have a high capability level under normal circumstances.

Step 1. Diagnose the Situation:

____ time   ____ information   ____ acceptance   ____ capability

Ben, the supervisor, has plenty of time to use any level of participation. He has all the information needed to make the decision (autocratic). Employees have no choice but to accept the decision (autocratic). And the group's level of capability is normally high (participative).

Step 2. Select the Appropriate Style for the Situation: There are conflicting styles to choose from (autocratic and participative):

<u>yes</u> time   <u>S-A</u> information   <u>S-A</u> acceptance   <u>S-P</u> capability

The variable that should be given precedence is information. The employees are normally capable, but in a situation like this, they may not be capable of putting the department's goals ahead of their own. In other words, even if employees know which employee deserves the raise, they may each fight for it anyway. Such a conflict could cause future problems. Some of the possible ways to make the decision include:

- Autocratic (S-A). The supervisor would select the person for the raise without discussing it with any employees. Ben would simply announce the decision and explain the rationale for the selection, after submitting it to the payroll department.

- Consultative (S-C). The supervisor would talk to the employees for information on who should get the raise. Ben would then decide who would get the raise. He would announce the decision and explain the rationale for it. The supervisor may invite questions and discussion.

- Participative (S-P). The supervisor could tentatively select an employee to get the raise, but be open to change if an employee/group convinces him that someone else should get the raise. Or Ben could explain the situation to the group and lead a discussion of who should get the raise. After considering their input, Ben would make the decision and explain the rationale for it.

- Laissez-faire (S-L). The supervisor would explain the situation and allow the group to decide who gets the raise. Ben may be a group member. Notice that this is the only style that allows the group to make the decision.

Selection: The autocratic style is appropriate for this situation because Ben has all the information needed, acceptance is not an issue, and capability is questionable. Doing Skill-Building Exercise 10–1 will help develop your ability to select the appropriate situational problem-solving and decision-making supervisory style.

In the opening case, Sonia used the participative supervisory style to determine the budget allocations. Sonia allowed input from the group but made the final decision based on the group suggestions. Then she explained the rationale for her decision.

Video
10–1
BM–10

Skill-Building
10–1

Learning Objective

6. State when and how to use participation in problem solving and decision making

---

WORK APPLICATIONS

10. Give examples of when the autocratic, consultative, participative, and laissez-faire supervisory styles would be appropriate.

By following the suggestions in this chapter, you can develop your ability to solve problems and make decisions on the individual and group levels.

REVIEW

Select one or more methods: (1) fill in the missing key terms from memory; (2) match the key terms, from the end of the review, with their definitions below; and/or (3) copy the key terms in order from the key terms at the beginning of the chapter.

A _____ is two or more people interacting to achieve an objective. The performance formula (Performance = Ability × Motivation × Resources) also applies to teams. To improve performance, the supervisor can determine which area to work on with the group.

There are two major types of formal groups: (1) _____ are ongoing formal groups comprised of managers and their employees. The current trend is toward more _____, the process of managers and employees working together as a team to set objectives and to plan how to accomplish them. This process is performed by self-directed teams. (2) Task groups are usually comprised of members from different functional areas. The two most commonly used task groups are _____, which are temporary task forces formed for a specific purpose, and _____, which are permanent groups that exist to deal with continuing organizational issues. _____ are spontaneously created when members join together voluntarily because of similar interests.

A _____ exists whenever there is a difference between what is actually happening and what the individual/group wants to be happening. _____ is the process of taking corrective action in order to meet objectives, while _____ is the process of selecting an alternative course of action that will solve a problem. There are three decision-making styles: reflexive, consistent, and reflective. The _____ are step 1, define the problem; step 2, set objectives and criteria; step 3, generate alternatives; step 4, analyze alternatives and select one; and step 5, plan, implement the decision, and control. _____ is a technique for comparing the cost and benefit of each alternative course of action.

_____ is the ability to develop unique alternatives to solve problems. The _____ are (1) preparation, (2) possible solutions, (3) incubation, and (4) evaluation.

Some of the techniques for using groups to generate alternatives are: _____, the process of suggesting many alternatives, without evaluation, to solve a problem; _____, the process of generating novel alternatives through role playing and fantasizing; _____, the process of generating and evaluating alternatives through a structured voting method; _____, the process of developing a group consensus solution to a problem; and the _____, which polls a group of experts through a series of anonymous questionnaires.

There are advantages (better decisions, more alternatives, acceptance, and morale) and disadvantages (time, domination, conformity and groupthink, and responsibility) to using a group when solving problems and making decisions. A technique to help groups make better decisions is the _____, which requires the individual to explain and defend his or her position before the group. When selecting the appropriate situational supervisory style to meet the situation, the four variables include time, information, acceptance, and capability. These four variables are analyzed during step 1, diagnose the situation, while the second step is to select the appropriate style (autocratic, consultative, participative, or laissez-faire) to solve the problem.

KEY TERMS

ad hoc committees   345
brainstorming   353
consensus mapping   354
cost-benefit analysis   350
creativity   352
decision making   347
Delphi technique   354
devil's advocate
    technique   356

functional groups   344
group/team   343
informal groups   346
nominal grouping   354
participative
    management   344
problem   347
problem solving   347

problem-solving and
    decision-making
    steps   349
stages in the creative
    process   352
standing committees   345
synetics   354

Carolyn Blakeslee's *Art Calendar*

In 1986, Carolyn Blakeslee founded *Art Calendar,* a monthly publication for visual artists. *Art Calendar* provides information about grants, shows, and other forums to which artists can submit their work— about 15 pages of them—and some topical freelance columns. The bulk of the periodical is public information. *Art Calendar* was not very professional. It was plain in appearance, without color, contained no advertising, and was mailed second-class, which did little to increase circulation size.

Carolyn started *Art Calendar* as a part-time business in a room in her home, which is near the Potomac in old Virginia. Carolyn believed that half the people who received her first brochure would want to subscribe to her publication. She was heartbroken when only 3 percent subscribed. Later, she was happy to learn that 3 percent is good in publishing. Regardless of her disappointment, every year for the first eight years circulation and revenues doubled. *Art Calendar* grew to become artists' definitive source of information.

Carolyn did not expect the business to become so successful. Over the years, the business became more complex and time-consuming. Without employees, it was no longer possible to read all the mail during her daily five miles on a stationary bike. The part-time hours increased to more than full-time. Carolyn, like many women, wants to have it all. She wanted to meet financial goals and devote time to her family (she really enjoys motherhood, spending time with her husband), her own artwork, and leisure pursuits. Carolyn reached that point in the life of successful small businesses where she had to make a decision based on three major alternatives: 1. maintain, 2. expand, or 3. sell the business. Each alternative with subalternatives for each is presented in the decision tree below.

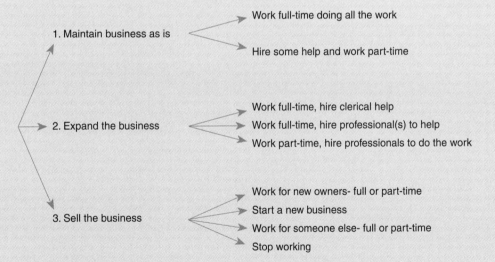

Go to the Internet: For more information on Carolyn Blakeslee and Art Calendar to update the information provided in this case, do a name search on the Internet and visit *http://www.folkart.org.* For ideas on using the Internet with cases, see Appendix C.

Support your answer to the following questions with specific information from the case and text, or other information you get from the web or other source.

1. Should Carolyn use the rational decision-making model to make her decision?

2. Define the problem. What are the causes and symptoms that a problem exists?

3. Should Carolyn set objectives and criteria for this decision?

4. Alternatives are listed in the decision tree; can you generate additional alternatives?

5. Analyze the alternatives and select one. List the pros and cons for each alternative from Carolyn's perspective, which may be different from yours. Be sure to state the risk of not expanding and expanding.

6. What decision would you make if you were in Carolyn's situation? Which alternative would be the most difficult to plan, implement, and control?

7. Should this decision be a group or individual decision?

8. Which Big Five personality type (Chapter 2) is influencing Carolyn's decision? How do perception (Chapter 2), values (Chapter 3), and motivation (Chapter 6) influence this decision?

9. How is organizational structure and communication (Chapter 5) an issue in this case?

10. How might business ethics and etiquette (Chapter 9) be a part of this case?

Department Meeting   Juanita, the check-processing supervisor of the Tenth National Bank, has called her five employees together to try to figure out a way to stop the bottleneck in the processing of checks. Below are some of the statements made during the meeting. (*Note:* The meeting can be role-played in class.)

JUANITA: (*opening statement*) You are all aware of the bottleneck problem we have. I've called this meeting to try to come up with a solution. I feel that this meeting can help bring us together as a team and help increase our job satisfaction by allowing the group to decide how to solve the problem. I'd like you all to suggest possible solutions. One rule is that no one will make any negative comments about any solution. Any crazy idea is acceptable. Who wants to go first? (*After about four or five minutes, Mary, the informal group leader, interrupts the group meeting.*)

MARY: I've already given the best solution. There is no need to keep asking for ideas.

JUANITA: Mary, we are trying to come up with as many creative ideas as possible.

MARY: For what? I've got a good idea.

JUANITA: Let's continue generating ideas. Who will go next? (*Mary looks around the room with an expression that says "be quiet." After waiting three or four minutes, which feel like a hundred, no one makes a suggestion, so Juanita speaks.*)

JUANITA: Let's analyze the seven alternatives we have to determine which is the best.

MARY: Mine is the best.

WILL: Wait a minute, Mary, my idea is as good as yours or better. Tell us why yours is so much better than anyone else's.

MARY: I will if everyone else will.

JUANITA: Wait a minute; these ideas are the group's, not just any one person's. We want to work as a team. (*Will and Mary continue to battle it out. Their two ideas seem to be the most popular. With the battle on, Juanita knows the group will not agree to one solution.*)

JUANITA: We are down to two alternatives. Let's vote for the one to use. (*The vote is four for Mary's idea and two for Will's. Will and Juanita vote for his idea, and the rest go with Mary's alternative.*)

Answer the following questions. Then in the space between the questions, state why you selected that answer.

_____ 1. The six people joined the group primarily because of _.

        a. affiliation   *c.* attraction   *e.* assistance

        b. proximity   *d.* activity

_____ 2. Juanita used participative management during the meeting.

        a. true   *b.* false

_____ 3. The group is a _____ group.

        a. functional   *b.* task   *c.* informal

_____ 4. Mary's decision-making style seems to be _.

        a. reflexive   *b.* consistent   *c.* reflective

_____ 5. The group used the creative process.

        a. true   *b.* false

_____ 6. Will suggested using the ____ technique.

   a. cost-benefit   *c.* Delphi
   b. synetics   *d.* devil's advocate

_____ 7. The major technique Juanita used at the meeting was __.

   a. brainstorming   *c.* nominal grouping   *e.* Delphi
   b. synetics   *d.* consensus mapping

_____ 8. The major benefit of using a group, which Juanita hoped to accomplish was __.

   a. a better decision   *c.* acceptance
   b. more alternatives   *d.* higher morale

_____ 9. The major disadvantage to using a group was __.

   a. time   *c.* conformity and groupthink
   b. domination   *d.* responsibility

_____ 10. Juanita used the ____ problem-solving and decision-making style.

   a. autocratic   *c.* participative
   b. consultative   *d.* laissez-faire

11. If you were in Juanita's situation, would you have used a group to solve the problem? Why or why not?

12. Assume you decided to use a group. In Juanita's position, how would you have handled the meeting?

Organizational Culture and Environment

This video case presents a discussion of how Compaq Computer Corporation built an organization based on TEAMS that would make good decisions by coming up with the right answers.

Critical Thinking Questions:

1. Compaq is a high-technology company. Why does it view its success based on its people and teams rather than on innovative technology?

2. What personality traits (Chapter 2) does Compaq look for in employees?

3. At which level(s), are open communications (Chapters 4 and 5—interpersonal/organizational) important at Compaq?

4. Which motivation technique (Chapter 6—giving praise, MBO, job enrichment, or job design) appears to be used as the driving force at Compaq?

5. Compaq's lead by example is most closely associated with which leadership theory (Chapter 7—trait, behavioral, contingency)?

6. Which base of power appears to be most important at Compaq (Chapter 9—coercive, connection, reward, legitimate, referent, information, expert)?

7. Why does Compaq use teams rather than groups (Chapter 10)?

8. Why was decision making so important to Compaq in its startup years?

9. Which creative problem-solving and decision-making techniques are used at Compaq (Chapter 10)?

Fiscal Fairy Tale # 4: The Ugly Cash Cow

Following the steps to getting to read a fiscal fairy tale in MG Webzine Exercise 1 in Chapter 1, page 34, go to the MG website and read *Fiscal Fairy Tale # 4: The Ugly Cash Cow* (your instructor may ask you to print a copy and bring it to class). Answer these questions (your instructor may ask you to type them and bring them to class):

Online MG Webzine Exercise 10

Questions Relating to the Tale Only

1. As stated at the end of the tale, in 50 words or so, What is your response to this tale? You may send it to MG.

2. Are the sayings, "don't mess with success" and "if it ain't broke, don't fix it" good business philosophies?

3. Have you, or anyone you know, every suggested a change and had the idea rejected because people in the organization did not want to change? Briefly explain the idea and how it was rejected.

In-Class MG Webzine Exercise 10

Questions Relating the Tale to the Chapter Concepts

4. Should the rational decision-making model be used on the farm?

5. What was a major problem and its solution in this tale?

6. Was individual or group decision making most appropriate for this tale?

7. Of the four disadvantages of group decision making, which one is the major problem subsite in this tale?

8. Of the five group decision-making techniques that foster creativity, which one would you recommend for the farm?

The instructor selects one of the six options from Appendix B page 589.

Self-Directed Work Teams (IE 10–1)
Online Internet Exercise 10–1

The objective of this exercise is to learn more about self-directed work teams and to get some tips on working in a SDT. You will be using the supersite subsection, which will link you to another site to read the material. Use the information in Appendix B and IE 1–2 and 1–3 as you do the following:

1. Go to the Self Directed Work Team website—*http://users.ids.net/,brim/ sdwth.html*
2. Click "Sites on Team Basics" and select one of the sites to go visit and read the information (your instructor may require you to make a copy of it).
3. Questions: (1) What website did you visit? (2) Who was the author, and what was the title of what you read? (3) In 50 words or so, what did you learn about SDT? (4) How can you use this information to help you be a better team member and/or leader? (Your instructor may require you to type and print your answers.)

The instructor selects one of the six options from Appendix B page 589.

In Class Internet Exercise 10-1, IE 10-2, and IE 10-3

Creativity Techniques (IE 10–2)
Online Internet Exercise 10–2

The objective of this exercise is to learn a creativity technique. Use the information in Appendix B and IE 1–2 and 1–3 as you do the following:

1. Go to the Brainstorming website—*www.brainstorming.co.uk*
2. Click "Training on Creative Techniques"
3. Click "How Creativity Works" near the top of the page, read it, then click the back arrow to return to the prior page.
4. Click the one "creative technique—training and tutorial" that you want to learn about (your instructor may require you to make a copy of it).
5. Questions: (1) Which creativity technique did you select? (2) How does the technique work? (3) How can you use this information to help you and/or a group be more creative? (Your instructor may require you to type and print your answers.)

Select a Concept: MG Search (IE 10–3)
Online Internet Exercise 10–3

The objective of this exercise is to learn more about a concept of your choice. Use the information in Appendix B and IE 1–2 and 1–3 as you do the following:

1. Go to the MG homepage—*www.mgeneral.com*
2. Click "Search (Site Map)."
3. Click the "Concept" button/circle to use the concept search mode then type in a concept from this chapter that you want to learn more about.
4. Click the resource you want to learn more about (your instructor may require you to print it).
5. Questions: (1) Who is the author and what is the title and year of the resource? (2) What are the primary concept ideas? (3) How can you use these ideas in your personal and professional life? (Your instructor may require you to type and print your answers.)

◆ Situational Superviso-
ry Problem-Solving
and Decision-Making
Styles

Objectives: To better understand the four supervisory decision-making styles.
SCANS: The SCANS competencies of interpersonal skills, systems, and especially
resources and information and the foundations of basic, especially thinking, and
personal qualities are developed through this exercise.
Preparation: You should understand the four supervisory decision-making styles.

VE 10–1

The instructor shows Video Module 11, Situational Problem Solving and Decision
Making. As you view each of the four scenes, identify the supervisory decision-making style being used by the manager.

Procedure 1
(10 minutes)

◆ BM–11

Scene 1. ____   A. Autocratic (S-A)

Scene 2. ____   B. Consultative (S-C)

Scene 3. ____   C. Participative (S-P)

Scene 4. ____   D. Laissez-faire (S-L)

After viewing each of the four scenes, identify/match the style used by the manager
by placing the letter of the style on the scene line.

Option A: View all four scenes and identify the style used by the manager. After
viewing all four scenes, discuss and/or have the instructor give the correct answers.

Option B: After each scene, the class discusses the style used by the manager. The
instructor states the correct answer after each of the four scenes.

Procedure 2
(2–5 minutes)

Select the one style that you would use in this situation. Are other styles also appropriate? Which style would you not use (find not appropriate) for this situation?
Next to each style listed above, write the letter "a" for appropriate or "n" for not
appropriate.

Discussion:

Option A: In groups of four to six, answer the questions below.

Option B: As a class, answer the questions below.

1. Which style(s) are not appropriate to use in this situation?

2. Which style(s) are appropriate to use in this situation?

3. Is there one style most appropriate in this situation? If yes, which one?

Conclusion: The instructor may make concluding remarks.

Application (2–4 minutes):   What did I learn from this exercise? How will I use this
knowledge in the future?

Sharing: Volunteers give their answers to the application section.

This video exercise serves as a model for In-Class Skill-Building Exercise 10–1,
Deciding Which Situational Supervisory Problem-Solving and Decision-Making
Style to Use.

Preparation
Deciding Which
Situational Supervi-
sory Problem-Solv-
ing and Decision-
Making Style to Use

Below are 10 situations calling for a decision. Select the appropriate problem-solving and decision-making style. Be sure to use Exhibit 10–8, p. 359, when determining the style to use. On the time, information, acceptance, and capability lines place the letters S-A, S-C, S-P, or S-L that are appropriate for the situation. Based on your diagnoses, select the one style you would use.

S-A Autocratic   S-C Consultative

S-P Participative   S-L Laissez-faire

_____ 1. You have developed a new work procedure that will increase productivity. Your boss likes the idea and wants you to try it within a few weeks. You view your employees as fairly capable and believe that they will be receptive to the change.

 _____ time _____ information _____ acceptance _____ capability

_____ 2. The industry of your product has new competition. Your organization's revenues have been dropping. You have been told to lay off 3 of your 10 employees in two weeks. You have been the supervisor for over one year. Normally, your employees are very capable.

 _____ time _____ information _____ acceptance _____ capability

_____ 3. Your department has been facing a problem for several months. Many solutions have been tried, but all have failed. You have finally thought of a solution, but you are not sure of the possible consequences of the change required or of acceptance by the highly capable employees.

 _____ time _____ information _____ acceptance _____ capability

_____ 4. Flextime has become popular in your organization. Some departments let each employee start and end work when he or she chooses. However, because of the cooperative effort of your employees, they must all work the same eight hours. You are not sure of the level of interest in changing the hours. Your employees are a very capable group and like to make decisions.

 _____ time _____ information _____ acceptance _____ capability

_____ 5. The technology in your industry is changing so fast that the members of your organization cannot keep up. Top management hired a consultant who has made recommendations. You have two weeks to decide what to do. Your employees are normally capable, and they enjoy participating in the decision-making process.

 _____ time _____ information _____ acceptance _____ capability

_____ 6. A change has been handed down from top management. How you implement it is your decision. The change takes effect in one month. It will personally affect everyone in your department. Their acceptance is critical to the success of the change. Your employees are usually not too interested in being involved in making decisions.

 _____ time _____ information _____ acceptance _____ capability

_____ 7. Your boss called you on the telephone to tell you that someone has requested an order for your department's product with a very short delivery date. She asked you to call her back in 15 minutes with the decision about taking the order. Looking over the work schedule, you realize that it will be very difficult to deliver the order on time. Your employees will have to push hard to make it. They are cooperative, capable, and enjoy being involved in decision making.

____ time ____ information ____ acceptance ____ capability

_____ 8.   Top management has decided to make a change that will affect all of your employees. You know the employees will be upset because it will cause them hardship. One or two may even quit. The change goes into effect in 30 days. Your employees are very capable.

____ time ____ information ____ acceptance ____ capability

_____ 9.   You believe that productivity in your department could be increased. You have thought of some ways that may work, but you are not sure of them. Your employees are very experienced; almost all of them have been in the department longer than you have.

____ time ____ information ____ acceptance ____ capability

_____ 10. A customer has offered you a contract for your product with a quick delivery date. The offer is open for two days. Meeting the contract deadline would require employees to work nights and weekends for six weeks. You cannot require them to work overtime. Filling this profitable contract could help get you the raise you want and feel you deserve. However, if you take the contract and don't deliver on time, it will hurt your chances of getting a big raise. Your employees are very capable

____ time ____ information ____ acceptance ____ capability

**In-Class
Deciding Which
Situational Supervisory Problem-Solving and Decision-Making Style to Use**

SB 10–1

*Procedure 1
(5–12 minutes)*

*Procedure 2
(12–20 minutes)*

10–1 • BM–11
*Procedure 3
(12–20 minutes)*

Objective: To develop your situational supervisory problem-solving and decision-making skills.

SCANS: The SCANS competencies of resources, interpersonal skills, and information and the foundations of basic, especially thinking in the area of decision making, and personal qualities are developed through this exercise.

Preparation: You should have completed the 10 situations from the preparation.

Experience: You will try to select the recommended problem-solving and decision-making style in the 10 preparation situations.

The instructor reviews Exhibit 10–8 and explains how to use it for selecting the appropriate supervisory style for situation 1 of the exercise preparation.

Break into teams of two or three. Apply the model to situations 2–5 as a team. You may change your original answers. It may be helpful to tear the model out of the book so you don't have to keep flipping pages. The instructor goes over the recommended answers and scoring for situations 2–5. Do not continue on to situation 6 until after the instructor goes over the answers to situations 2–5.

In the same teams, select problem-solving and decision-making styles for situations 6–10. The instructor will go over the recommended answers and scoring.

Conclusion: The instructor may lead a class discussion and/or make concluding remarks.

Application (2–4 minutes):   What did I learn from this experience? How will I use this knowledge in the future?

Sharing: Volunteers give their answers to the application section.

SKILL-BUILDING EXERCISE 10–2

● **In-Class
Individual versus
Group Decision
Making**

Objective: To compare individual and group decision making to better understand when and when not to use a group to make decisions.

SCANS: The SCANS competencies of interpersonal skills, systems, and especially resources and information and the foundations of basic, especially thinking, and personal qualities are developed through this exercise.

Preparation: You should have completed Application Situation 10–1 or the 10 questions to the Objective Case, whichever your instructor assigned.

Experience: During class, you will work in a group that will make the same decisions, followed by an analysis of the results.

*Procedure 1
(1–2 minutes)*

Place your individual answers to Application Situation 10–or the Objective Case in the "individual answer" column below.

Application Situation or Objective Case Question	Individual Answer (A-G)	Group Answer (A-G)	Recommended Answer (A-G)	Score 1 Point Each Individual versus Group
1.				
2.				
3.				
4.				
5.				
6.				
7.				
8.				
9.				
10.				
Total score				

*Procedure 2
(18–22 minutes)*

Break into teams of five, making groups of four or six as necessary. As a group, come to an agreement on the answers to Application Situation 10–1. Place the group answers in the group answer column above. Try to use consensus mapping, rather than the nominal group (voting) technique.

*Procedure 3
(4–6 minutes)*

Scoring: The instructor will give the recommended answers to questions 1–10. Determine how many you got right as an individual and as a group. Place the number 1 in the score column for each correct answer you as an individual got. Do the same for the group's answers. Place your individual and the group's total score (1–10) in the total score column.

Averaging: Calculate the average individual score by adding all the individual scores and dividing by the number of group members. Average ____.

Gain or Loss: The difference between the average score and the group score. If the group's score is higher than the average individual score, you have a gain of ____ points; if the group score is lower, you have a loss of ____ points.

Determine the highest individual score ____.

Determine the number of individuals who scored higher than the group's score ____.

Integration (4–8 minutes):   As a group, discuss which advantages and/or disadvantages your group had while making the decisions in this exercise.

Advantages:

- Better decisions. Did your group make better decisions? Was the group's score higher than the highest individual score? If not, why not? Were the knowledgeable members nonassertive, or just not listened to?

- More alternatives. Did the group get members to consider alternatives they did not consider as individuals? Did your group use the devil's advocate approach?

- Acceptance. Did group members accept the answers as a consensus?

- Morale. Were members more satisfied making the decisions/giving the answers in a group?

Disadvantages:

- Time. Did it take the group longer to answer the situation as a group? Was the time spent worth the benefits?

- Domination. Did any one person or subgroup dominate the group? Did everyone participate?

- Conformity. Were members nonassertive in presenting their answers in order to be accepted or due to group pressure to agree with the majority?

- Responsibility. Because no one person was held responsible for the group's answers, did members take an "I don't care" attitude?

Improvements: Overall, were the advantages of using a group greater than the disadvantages of using a group? If your group continues to work together, how could it improve its problem-solving and decision-making ability? Write out the answer below.

Conclusion: The instructor leads a class discussion and/or makes concluding remarks.

Application (2–4 minutes):   What did I learn from this experience? How will I use this knowledge in the future?

Sharing: Volunteers give their answers to the application section.

Team Dynamics and Leadership

11

Learning Objectives

After completing this chapter, you should be able to:

1. Explain the six components of team dynamics and how they affect team performance.
2. Describe the five stages of a team's development.
3. Explain the four situational supervisory styles to use with a group, based on its stage of development.
4. Explain how to plan for and conduct effective meetings.
5. Identify five problem members and explain how to handle them so they do not have a negative effect on your meetings.
6. Define the following 12 key terms (in order of appearance in the chapter):

team dynamics	**maintenance roles**	**group development**
norms	**self-interest roles**	**stage 3**
group cohesive-	**group development**	**group development**
ness	**stage 1**	**stage 4**
status	**group development**	
roles	**stage 2**	
task roles		

Bonnie Sue Swinaski is a machine operator for the Western Pacific Manufacturing Company. In the past, she has recommended ways to increase performance, which management used. As a result, management appointed Bonnie Sue to lead an ad hoc committee charged to recommend ways to increase performance in her work area. Her group has six members, all from her department, who had volunteered to serve on the committee. The committee has been meeting biweekly now for three weeks for one- to two-hour sessions. The members have grown quite close over the weeks, and participation has been fairly equal. Bonnie Sue, however, has not been very pleased with the group's performance. Only three weeks remain before the report presentation to management. She has been thinking about some of the problems and wondering how to handle them. At first the members came to the meeting really enthusiastic and came up with crazy ideas. But over time they lost some of the enthusiasm, even though they were developing better ideas for improving the performance of the department. During meetings, members have been suggesting the need for work to be done outside the meeting, but no one seems to do it. Three of the members cause different kinds of problems in the group. Kirt is destructive—he is constantly putting other people's ideas down, and others have followed his lead. Kirt thinks his way is always better, and he never gives an inch, even when he knows he is wrong. Kirt ends up fighting with members over whose idea is better. Shelby is very pleasant—she tries to keep peace in the group. The problem with Shelby is that she is consistently getting the group off the topic at hand. Carl is the opposite of Shelby—he puts the group back on the

topic. He doesn't believe in wasting any time, but he's a motor mouth. Carl dominates the air time at meetings. What are the issues? If you were in Bonnie Sue's situation, how would you turn the group into a top performer?

The Team Performance Model

A team is like a wristwatch—lots of different parts, but the whole has value only when everyone works together.[1]

The performance of a group or team is based on three major factors and can be listed as a formula.[2] *Group performance* is a function of its structure,[3] dynamics, and development stage, as is illustrated in Exhibit 11–1. The team structure components that affect performance as well as team dynamics and development include the following:

EXHIBIT 11–1   THE TEAM PERFORMANCE MODEL COMPONENTS

| Team Performance | (f)* | Team Structure | + | Team Dynamics | + | Team Development Stage |

*(f) = is a function of.

The team structure components that affect performance as well as team dynamics and development include the following:

1. *Type of group.* As discussed in Chapter 10, there are formal and informal groups. Formal groups include functional and task—ad hoc and standing committees.

2. *Leadership.* Leadership was discussed in Chapter 7 and is expanded in the chapter as it relates to teams, with sections covering leading teams as a situational supervisor based on team development stages and meeting leadership skills.

3. *Composition.* Composition refers to the diversity (multiple chapters) of the team members[4] and their selection.[5] Group composition is important;[6] the greater the diversity, the higher the quality of its decisions.[7]

4. *Problem solving and decision making.* With reengineering, teams are empowered to solve problems and make decisions.[8] It was discussed in Chapter 10.

5. *Conflict.* Conflict can help or hurt team performance.[9] Intergroup (between departments) can hurt organizational performance.[10] Conflict was discussed in Chapter 8.

According to the group performance formula, a formal group with good leadership,[11] with a diversely composed group of individuals, that can solve problems[12] and make effective decisions, and that can resolve its conflict effectively will have a high level of performance; conversely, a team that cannot will have a lower level of performance. Also, the human relations will be different in groups with an autocratic leader who follows clear formal structure for solving problems and decision making and conflict resolution.[13] Team performance is important to organizations.[14] Thus, developing team skills is important to your career, especially in organizations that use team-based work designs.[15] Exhibit 11–2 lists the team structure components.

IE 11–1

● Organization
● Group
● Individual

Team Dynamics

Bill Gates recommends doing projects in college to learn about group dynamics.[16] Group dynamics and interpersonal dynamics (Chapter 8) determine the success or the ultimate demise of teams.[17] Most employees find themselves in teams, but few are actually trained to work in a group.[18] Team members need training in team dynamics to be successful.[19] You will get training in this section.

EXHIBIT 11–2   **TEAM STRUCTURE COMPONENTS**

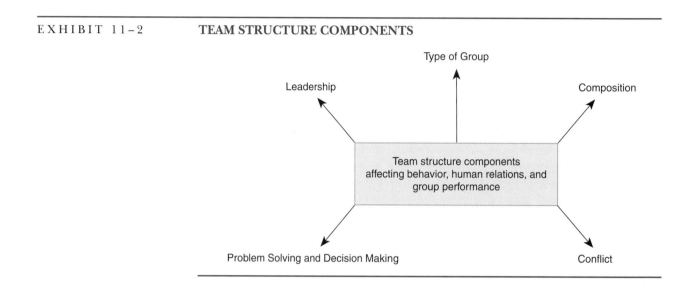

■ Performance
■ Human Relations
■ Behavior

Team dynamics *refers to the patterns of interactions that emerge as groups develop.* It is also called *group process.* When team members work together, how they interact affects their performance as individuals and as a team[20] (the systems affect).

To better understand team dynamics and how it affects group behavior, human relations, and performance, in this section we discuss the six major components of group dynamics: objectives, size, norms, cohesiveness, status, and roles.

Objectives

To be effective, teams must agree on clear objectives and be committed to achieving them.[21] The leader should allow the group to have input in setting objectives, based on its capability to participate.[22]

Implications for Managers

Managers should be certain that their functional groups have measurable objectives[23] and know priorities. As an aid in setting objectives, you should follow the guidelines in Chapter 6 and use the Writing Objectives Model. The team objectives should be coordinated with organizational goals.[24]

When you are a member or follower, rather than the leader, try to get the group to set clear objectives that its members agree to and are committed to. As a member of a team, you have an obligation to help the team be successful. If the team starts out without proper objectives, it will probably not be successful.

WORK APPLICATIONS

For Work Applications 1–8, recall a specific group you belong/belonged to. If you will be doing In-Class Skill-Building Exercise 11–1, do not use your class group for this specific group now.
1. Does the group agree on, and are they committed to, clear objectives? Explain your answer.

Team Size

What is the ideal team size? The number varies, depending on the team's purpose.[25] For functional groups to work well as self-directed teams, Digital uses teams of 12 to 18, but believes the ideal size is 14 or 15. Task groups are often smaller than functional groups. Fact-finding groups can be larger than problem-solving groups. There is no consensus on the ideal size for groups; some say three to nine, others say five, while still others say six to eight. If the group is too small, it tends to be too cautious; if it is too large, it tends to be too slow. But larger groups tend to generate more alternatives and higher-quality ideas as they benefit from diverse participation.

How Size Affects Group Dynamics

Team size affects leadership, members, and its process of getting the job done. The larger the team size, the more formal or autocratic the leadership needs to be to provide direction, and managers tend to be more informal and participative when they have smaller functional groups. Group members are more tolerant of autocratic leadership in large groups. Larger groups tend to inhibit equal participation. Generally, participation is more equal in groups of around five members (and the greater need there is for formal plans, policies, procedures, and rules). Groups of 20 or more tend to be too large to reach consensus on decisions, and they tend to form subgroups.

Implications for Managers

Usually managers have no say in the size of their functional groups. However, the appropriate leadership style may vary with team size. Managers who chair a committee may be able to select the team size. In doing so, the chairperson should be sure to get the right people on the committee, while trying to keep the group size appropriate for the task.

WORK APPLICATIONS

2. How large is the group? Is the size appropriate? Explain.

Team Norms

Functional groups generally have standing plans to help provide the necessary guidelines for behavior, while task groups do not. However, standing plans cannot be complete enough to cover all situations. All groups tend to form their own unwritten rules about how things are done.[26] **Norms** *are the group's shared expectations of its members' behavior.* Norms determine what should, ought, or must be done in order for the group to maintain consistent and desirable behavior.

How Norms Develop

Norms are developed spontaneously as the group members interact through the routine of the team. Each group member has cultural values and past experience. The group's beliefs, attitudes, and knowledge influence the type of norms developed. For example, the group produces 100 units per day. One hundred units become the norm if the group members develop a shared expectation that this behavior is desirable, and they produce it. Norms can change over time to meet the needs of the group.

How Teams Enforce Norms

If a team member does not follow the norm, the other members may try to enforce compliance. The common ways teams enforce norms include ridicule, ostracism, sabotage, and physical abuse. Following the above example, if a member, Sal, produces more than 100 units per day, other members may kid or ridicule him. If Sal continues to break the norm, members could use physical abuse or ostracize him to enforce compliance with the norm. Members could also damage his units or take his tools or supplies to slow down his production.

Implications for Managers

Team norms can be positive, helping the team meet its objective(s), or they can be negative, hindering the group from meeting its objective(s).[27] Continuing the above example, if the company's production standard is 110 units per day, the team's norm of 100 is a negative norm; however, if the standard were 90, it would be a positive norm. Managers should be aware of their group's norms. They should work toward maintaining and developing positive norms, while trying to eliminate negative norms. Managers should confront groups with negative norms and try to work out agreeable solutions to both parties' satisfaction.

WORK APPLICATIONS

3. List at least three of the team's norms. Identify them as positive or negative. How does the team enforce these norms?

Group Cohesiveness

The extent to which a group will abide by and enforce its norms depends upon its degree of cohesiveness. **Group cohesiveness** *is the attractiveness and closeness group members have for themselves and the group.* The more cohesive the group, the more it sticks together as a team.[28] The more desirable group membership is, the more willing the members are to behave according to the team's norms.[29] For example, some team members take drugs, and the team develops a norm of taking drugs. This peer pressure to take drugs often wins out. To be accepted by the team, members will behave in ways they really don't agree with.

Factors Influencing Cohesiveness

Some of the factors include:

Objectives: The stronger the agreement and commitment made to the achievement of the group's objective(s), the greater the cohesiveness of the group.

Size: Generally, the smaller the group, the greater the cohesiveness. The larger the group, the more difficulty there is in gaining consensus on objectives and norms. Three to nine members seems to be a good group size for cohesiveness.

Homogeneity: Generally, the more similar the group members are, the greater the cohesiveness. People tend to be attracted to people who are similar to themselves. However, homogeneity is on the decline. The work force continues to diversify.[30]

Participation: Generally, the more equal the level of participation among group members, the greater the group's cohesiveness. Groups dominated by one or a few members tend to be less cohesive as members are exluded.[31]

Competition: The focus of the competition affects cohesiveness. If the group focuses on intragroup competition and everyone tries to outdo each other, low cohesiveness results. If the group's focus is intergroup, the members tend to pull together as a team to beat the rivals. It is surprising how much a group can accomplish when no one cares who gets the credit.

Success: The more successful a group is at achieving its objectives, the more cohesive it tends to become. Success tends to breed cohesiveness, which in turn breeds more success. People want to be on a winning team. Have you ever noticed that losing teams tend to argue more than winning teams and complain that other members are messing up?

How Cohesiveness Affects Team Performance

Many research studies have compared cohesive and noncohesive teams and concluded that cohesive teams tend to have a higher level of success at achieving their objectives with greater job satisfaction.[32] Cohesive team members tend to miss work less often, are more trusting and cooperative, and have less tension and hostility. S. E. Seashore has conducted one of the most highly recognized studies on this subject. Seashore found that:

- Groups with the highest level of productivity were highly cohesive and accepted management's level of productivity.
- Groups with the lowest levels of productivity were also highly cohesive, but rejected management's level of productivity; they set and enforced their own level below that of management.
- Groups with intermediate levels of productivity were low cohesive groups, irrespective of their acceptance of management's level of productivity. The widest variance of individual group members' performance was among the groups with the lower cohesiveness. They tended to be more tolerant of nonconformity with group norms.

Implications for Managers

Managers should strive to develop cohesive groups that accept their level of productivity. The use of participation helps the group develop cohesiveness while it builds agreement and commitment toward its objective(s).[33] While some intragroup competition may be helpful, managers should focus primarily on intergroup competition. It helps to develop a cohesive winning team, which in turn motivates the group to higher levels of success. Gaining team cohesiveness becomes an increasingly challenging task as the environment becomes more globally diversified.[34]

WORK APPLICATIONS

4. Is the group cohesive? How do the text factors influence the group's cohesiveness? How does the level of cohesiveness affect the group's performance? Explain your answers.

Status within the Team

As team members interact, they develop respect for one another on numerous dimensions.[35] The more respect, prestige, influence, and power a group member has, the higher his or her status within the team. **Status** *is the perceived ranking of one member relative to other members of the group.*

The Development of Status

Status is based on several factors,[36] including a member's job title, wage or salary, seniority, knowledge or expertise, interpersonal skills, appearance, education, race, age, sex, and so on. Diversity training is helping group members increase their status as diversity is viewed as an organizational strength. Group status depends upon the group's objectives, norms, and cohesiveness. Members who conform to the group's norms tend to have higher status than members who do not. A group is more willing to overlook a high-status member breaking the norms, such as President George Bush. High-status members also have more influence on the development of the group's norms. Lower-level members tend to copy high-status members' behavior and standards.

How Status Affects Team Performance

The high-status members have a major impact on the group's performance. In a functional group, the manager is usually the member with highest status.[37] The manager's ability to manage affects group performance. In addition to the manager, high-status employees of the functional group also affect performance. If high-status members support positive norms and high productivity, chances are the group will, too. The informal leader can have a lot of influence on the group.

Another important factor influencing group performance is status congruence. Status congruence is the acceptance and satisfaction members receive from their group status. Members who are not satisfied with their status may feel excluded from the team,[38] and they may not be active team participants. They may physically or mentally escape from the team and not perform to their full potential. Or they may cause team conflict as they fight for a higher status level. Leadership struggles often go on for a long period and/or are never resolved. The group member who is dissatisfied with status and decides on flight or fight leads the group to the same end result, lower performance levels for the group.

Implications for Managers

To be effective, the manager needs to have high status within the functional group. To do so, the manager must perform the five functions of management—planning, organizing, staffing, leading, and controlling—well and have the necessary skills. The manager should maintain good human relations with the group, particularly with the high-status informal leader(s), to be sure they endorse positive norms and objectives. In addition managers should be aware of conflicts that may be the result of lack of status congruence. Managers should use the conflict management techniques discussed in Chapter 8.

WORK APPLICATIONS

5. List each team member in order by their status in the team, including yourself. What are some of the characteristics that lead to high or low status on the team?

Group Roles

As a group works toward achieving its objective(s), it has to perform certain functions. As functions are performed, people develop roles. **Roles** *are shared expectations of how group members will fulfill the requirements of their position.*

How Roles Develop

People develop their roles based on their own expectations, the organizational expectations, and the group's expectations. Individuals come to the organization with expectations about how they should fulfill their positions/roles. When they join the organization, they learn about the organizational expectations through orientations, job descriptions, and managerial supervision. When interacting with the team, they learn the team's expectations of them—norms. As employees internalize the expectations of these three sources, they develop their roles.

People often have multiple roles within the same position.[39] For example, a professor may have the roles of teacher, researcher, writer, consultant, advisor, and committee member. Our roles also expand outside the workplace. The professor may also be a family member, belong to professional and civic organizations, and have different circles of friends, all of which may have very different expectations.

Classifying Group Roles

Chapter 7 stated that when managers interact with employees, they can use directive behavior (structuring, job centered, production and task oriented), supportive behavior (consideration, employee centered, people and relationship oriented), or both. These same two dimensions can also be performed by group members as they interact. When used to relate to group interactions, they are commonly called *task roles* and *maintenance roles*. A third category called *self-interest roles* is often added. Below we will discuss each type of role in more detail.

The group's **task roles** *are the things group members do and say that directly aid in the accomplishment of its objective(s)*. Task roles can be subclassified into:

- Objective clarifiers—their role is to be sure everyone understands the objective.
- Planners—their role is to determine how the objective will be met.
- Organizers—their role is to assign and coordinate the resources.
- Leaders—their role is to influence members through direction as the task is performed.
- Controllers—their role is to take corrective action to ensure the objective is achieved.

The group's **maintenance roles** *are the things group members do and say to develop and sustain group dynamics*. Maintenance roles can be subclassified into:

- Formers—their role is to get the members involved and committed to the group.
- Consensus seekers—their role is to get members' input and agreement on group decisions.
- Harmonizers—their role is to help group members resolve their conflicts so that they do not interfere with group performance.
- Gatekeepers—their role is to see that appropriate norms are developed and enforced.
- Encouragers—their role is to be supportive, friendly, and responsive to the needs of the members.
- Compromisers—their role is to modify or to get others to modify their positions in the interest of cohesiveness.

Video

BM–11

Goal of
Human Relations

The **self-interest roles** *are the things members do and say in order to meet their own needs/objectives at the expense of the team*. Notice that this definition is similar to unethical politicking (Chapter 9) and the forcing conflict style (Chapter 8). When team members use self-interest roles, it is often in association with a hidden agenda. These self-interest seekers often tell the team members how the team and the organization will benefit without coming out and saying what's in it for them personally. They may use unethical politics and the forcing conflict style to push others to get what they want. In other words, they often give the impression that they are concerned about others and the organization when in reality it is a cover to get what they want, and they may do whatever it takes to get it.

As a team member, watch for self-interest roles and hidden agendas as you distinguish between a self-interest that benefits both the individual and the organization (a win–win situation) versus one that benefits the individual and hurts the organization (a win–lose situation). People using self-interest roles are team problem members. You will learn how to handle problem teammates later in the chapter.

Self-interest roles can be subclassified into:

- Aggressors—they deflate others' status through negative criticism or putting members and their ideas down.
- Blockers—they resist the group's efforts and prevent it from achieving its objectives.
- Recognition seekers—they try to take credit for the group's accomplishments.
- Withdrawers—they are physically or mentally involved in personal matters rather than those of the group.

How Roles Affect Team Performance

To be effective, a team must have members who play task roles and maintenance roles,[40] while minimizing self-interest roles. Teams that only have task performers will suffer performance problems because the team does not deal effectively with conflict. Its group process will hurt performance. On the other hand, teams who do not have members playing task roles will not get the job done. Any team that has members playing self-interest roles will not produce to its fullest potential.

Implications for Managers

Managers should make the group aware of the need to play these roles. When in a group, you should be aware of the roles its members play. If the members are not playing the task and/or maintenance role required at a given time, you should play the role.[41] The next section discusses group development and the manager's use of task and maintenance roles as the group develops.

In the opening case, the objective is fairly clear, group size is adequate, and cohesiveness, status, and roles are not major problems. Kirt has been discrediting others' ideas, and others have followed his lead. A negative norm has developed that needs to be addressed by Bonnie Sue as the leader to ensure success of the group. Bonnie Sue can begin the next meeting by stating that the norm has developed and explain how it is destructive to the group. She can interrupt when Kirt and others put ideas down by reminding the group to be positive. The group can also discuss whether there are other negative norms that should be stopped. In addition, they can discuss the development of positive norms that can help the group do a better job. Carl is playing a task role for the group. Shelby is playing a maintenance role for the group. And Kirt is playing a self-interest role. How to handle Kirt, Shelby, and Carl as problem individuals will be discussed near the end of the chapter.

Learning Objective

1. Explain the six components of team dynamics and how they affect team performance

IE 11–2

Skill-Building
11–1

Goal of
Human Relations

WORK APPLICATIONS

6. Using your listing from question 5, identify the major roles played by each group member, including yourself.

To summarize, effective groups should have clear objectives with agreement and commitment to these objectives by its members, appropriate group size to achieve its objectives, positive norms, cohesiveness, status congruence, and members who play task and maintenance roles while minimizing self-interest roles.[42] Developing effective group dynamics that meets the needs of the individuals and the group/organization creates a win-win situation for all parties. See Exhibit 11–3 for an illustration of the six components of group dynamics.

EXHIBIT 11–3   **TEAM DYNAMICS COMPONENTS**

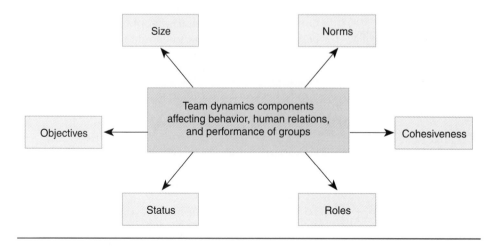

APPLICATION   SITUATIONS

Group Structure

AS 11–1

Identify each of the group structural issues as:

A. Objectives   C. Norms   E. Status

B. Size   D. Cohesiveness F. Roles

_____ 1. "I'm a union man. If it wasn't for the union, we would not be getting
          the pay we do. Collective bargaining really works."

_____ 2. "I could use another employee, but there is no workplace available."

_____ 3. "I wish the administration would make up its mind. One month we
          produce one product, and the next month we change to another."

_____ 4. "When you need advice go see Sharon; she knows the ropes around
          here better than anyone."

_____ 5. "Conrad, you're late for the meeting. Everyone else was on time, so
          we started without you."

APPLICATION   SITUATIONS

Roles

AS 11–2

Identify each statement by the role it fulfills:

A. Task   B. Maintenance   C. Self-Interest

_____ 6. "Wait, we have not heard Kim's idea yet."

_____ 7. "Could you explain why we are doing this again?"

_____ 8. "We tried that before you came here; it does not work. My idea is
          much better."

_____ 9. "What does this have to do with the problem? We are getting
          sidetracked."

_____ 10. "I like that idea better than mine. Let's go with it."

● Organization
● Group
● Individual

Team Development Stages

All teams are unique with dynamics that change over a period of time.[43] However, it
is generally agreed that all groups go through the same stages as they grow from a
collection of individuals to a smoothly operating and effective team, department,
or unit. R. B. Lacoursiere reviewed more than 200 articles and studies of group
dynamics and developed a five-stage model that synthesizes most of what is known
about group development.[44] The five stages include orientation, dissatisfaction, resolution, production, and termination. Although these five stages are described as
separate and distinct, some elements of most group development stages (GDS) can
be found in every other stage. Below we will describe each GDS.

Stage 1: Orientation

This *forming* stage is characterized by low development level (D1), high commitment, and low competence. When people first form a group, they tend to come to
the group with a moderate to high commitment to the group. However, because

they have not worked together, they do not have the competence to achieve the task. When first interacting, members tend to have anxiety over how they will fit in, what will be required of them, what the group will be like, the purpose of the group, and so forth. When task groups are started, this stage is very apparent because the group is new. However, traditional functional groups are rarely started with all new members, but this is becoming common with new self-directed groups.[45] Some functional groups never go beyond this stage. They never resolve these anxiety issues to progress to the next stage of development. If roles[46] and group objectives are never clearly stated and understood by members, it is difficult to develop as a group.

Stage 2: Dissatisfaction

This *storming* stage is characterized by moderate development level (D2), lower commitment, and some competence. As members work together for some time, they tend to become dissatisfied with the group. Members start to question: Why am I a member? Is the group going to accomplish anything? Why don't other group members do what is expected? and so forth. Often the task is more complex and difficult than anticipated; members become frustrated and have feelings of incompetence. However, the group does develop some competence to perform the task. Groups stuck in this stage of development are characterized by demoralization, low motivation, and low productivity. They never progress to being satisfied with the group and learning to perform as a team as long as they are in stage 2. Team building can be effective at this stage.[47]

Stage 3: Resolution

This *norming* stage is characterized by high-development level (D3), variable commitment, and high competence. With time, members often resolve the differences between initial expectations and realities in relation to the objectives, tasks, skills, and so forth. As members develop competence, they often become more satisfied with the group and committed to it.[48] Relationships develop that satisfy group members' affiliation needs. They learn to work together as they develop a group structure with acceptable norms and cohesiveness. Commitment can vary from time to time as the group interacts. During periods of conflict or change, the group needs to resolve these issues.[49] If the group does not deal effectively with group dynamic issues, the group may regress to stage 2, or the group may plateau, fluctuating in commitment and competence. If the group successfully develops a positive group structure, it will develop to the next stage.

Stage 4: Production

This *performing* stage is characterized by outstanding development level (D4), high commitment, and high competence. At this stage, commitment and competence do not fluctuate much. This high commitment enhances productivity and performance,[50] as the high competence skill level also does. The group works as a team with high levels of satisfaction of affiliation needs. The group maintains a positive group structure and dynamics. The fact that members are very productive helps lead to positive feelings. The group dynamics may change with time, but the conflict issues are resolved quickly and easily; members are open with each other.[51]

Stage 5: Termination

In functional groups, the *adjourning* stage is not reached unless there is some drastic reorganization; however, it does occur in task groups. During this stage, members experience feelings about leaving the group. In groups that have progressed through all four stages of group development, the members usually feel sad that the group is ending. However, for groups that did not progress through the stages of development, a feeling of relief is often experienced. The group may talk about its termination over a period of time or only at the last meeting. It tends to vary with the meaningfulness of the relationship, and whether the members will be seeing each other at all after the group terminates.

The two key variables identified through each stage of group development are work on the task (competence) and the socio-emotional tone or morale (commitment). The two variables do not progress in the same manner. Competence tends to continue to increase through each of the first four stages, while commitment tends to start high in stage 1, drops in stage 2, then rises through stages 3 and 4. This is illustrated in Exhibit 11–4.

Learning Objective

2. Describe the five stages of a team's development

EXHIBIT 11–4   **TEAM DEVELOPMENT STAGES**

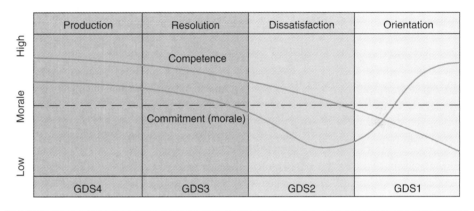

In the opening case, Bonnie Sue's committee is in stage 2—dissatisfaction. The group has had a decrease in commitment and an increase in competence. The group needs to resolve the dissatisfaction to progress to stages 3 and 4 of development. Being an ad hoc committee, the group will go through stage 5—termination—in three weeks. The next section discusses how Bonnie Sue can help the group develop to stages 3 and 4 as a situational supervisor.

WORK APPLICATIONS

7. Identify the group's stage of development and the leader's situational supervisory style used. Does the leader use the appropriate style?
8. What can be done to improve the group's dynamics? Explain.

APPLICATION SITUATIONS

Group Development Stages

AS 11–3

Identify the group's development stage as:

A. 1   B. 2   C. 3   D. 4   E. 5

_____ 11. Members have come to realize that their initial expectations are not a reality and accept the situation.

_____ 12. The ad hoc committee has presented its recommendations to management.

_____ 13. Group members are trying to get to know one another.

_____ 14. The group set a new record level of production.

_____ 15. Members are sitting around and complaining.

Leading Teams as a Situational Supervisor

Before we discuss leading groups as a situational supervisor complete Self-Assessment Exercise 11–1.

Self-Assessment
Exercise 11–1

Determining Your Preferred Group Leadership Style

In the 12 situations below, select the response that represents what you would actually do as the group's leader. Ignore the D _____ and S _____ lines; they will be used as part of Skill-Building Exercise 11–2.

1. Your group works well together; members are cohesive with positive norms. They maintain a fairly consistent level of production that is above the organizational average, as long as you continue to provide maintenance behavior. You have a new assignment for them. To accomplish it you would: D _____

   a. Explain what needs to be done and tell them how to do it. Oversee them while they perform the task. S _____
   b. Tell the group how pleased you are with their past performance. Explain the new assignment, but let them decide how to accomplish it. Be available if they need help. S _____
   c. Tell the group what needs to be done. Encourage them to give input on how to do the job. Oversee task performance. S _____
   d. Explain to the group what needs to be done. S _____

2. You have been promoted to a new supervisory position. The group appears to have little talent to do the job, but they do seem to care about the quality of the work they do. The last supervisor was terminated because of the department's low productivity level. To increase productivity you would: D _____

   a. Let the group know you are aware of its low production level, but let them decide how to improve it. S _____
   b. Spend most of your time overseeing group members as they perform their jobs. Train them as needed. S _____
   c. Explain to the group that you would like to work together to improve productivity. Work together as a team. S _____
   d. Tell the group ways productivity can be improved. With their ideas, develop methods, and make sure they are implemented. S _____

3. Your department continues to be one of the top performers in the organization. It works well as a team. In the past, you generally let them take care of the work on their own. You decide to: D _____

   a. Go around encouraging group members on a regular basis. S _____
   b. Define members' roles, and spend more time overseeing performance. S _____
   c. Continue things the way they are; leave them alone. S _____
   d. Hold a meeting. Recommend ways to improve and get members' ideas as well. After agreeing on changes, oversee the group to make sure it implements the new ideas and does improve. S _____

4. You have spent much of the past year training your employees. However, they do not need as much of your time to oversee production as they used to. Several group members no longer get along as well as they did in the past. You've played referee lately. You: D _____

   a. Have a group meeting to discuss ways to increase performance. Let the group decide what changes to make. Be supportive. S _____
   b. Continue things the way they are now. Supervise them closely and be the referee when needed. S _____
   c. Let the group alone to work things out for themselves. S _____
   d. Continue to supervise closely as needed, but spend more time playing maintenance roles; develop a team spirit. S _____

5. Your department has been doing such a great job that it has grown in numbers. You are surprised at how fast the new members were integrated. The team continues to come up with ways to improve performance on its own. Due to the growth, your department will be moving to a new, larger location. You decide to: D ____

   a. Design the new layout and present it to the group to see if they can improve upon it. S ____

   b. In essence become a group member and allow the group to design the new layout. S ____

   c. Design the new layout and put a copy on the bulletin board so employees know where to report for work after the move. S ____

   d. Hold a meeting to get employee ideas on the layout of the new location. After the meeting, think about it and finalize the layout. S ____

6. You are appointed to head a task group. Because of the death of a relative, you had to miss the first meeting. At the second meeting, the group seems to have developed objectives and some ground rules. Members have volunteered for assignments that have to be accomplished. You: D ____

   a. Take over as a strong leader. Change some ground rules and assignments. S ____

   b. Review what has been done so far, and keep things as is. However, take charge and provide clear direction from now on. S ____

   c. Take over the leadership but allow the group to make the decisions. Be supportive and encourage them. S ____

   d. Seeing that the group is doing so well, leave and do not attend any more meetings. S ____

7. Your group was working at, or just below, standard. However, there has been a conflict within the group. As a result, production is behind schedule. You: D ____

   a. Tell the group how to resolve the conflict. Then closely supervise to make sure it is followed and production increases. S ____

   b. Let the group work it out. S ____

   c. Hold a meeting to work as a team to come up with a solution. Encourage the group to work together. S ____

   d. Hold a meeting to present a way to resolve the conflict. Sell the members on its merits, include their input, and follow up. S ____

8. The organization has allowed flextime. Two of your employees have asked if they could change work hours. You are concerned because all busy work hours need adequate coverage. The department is very cohesive with positive norms. You decide to: D ____

   a. Tell them things are going well; we'll keep things as they are now. S ____

   b. Hold a department meeting to get everyone's input; then reschedule their hours. S ____

   c. Hold a department meeting to get everyone's input; then reschedule their hours on a trial basis. Tell the group that if there is any drop in productivity, you will go back to the old schedule. S ____

   d. Tell them to hold a department meeting. If the department agrees to have at least three people on the job during the busy hours, they can make changes, giving you a copy of the new schedule. S ____

9. You have arrived 10 minutes late for a department meeting. Your employees are discussing the latest assignment. This surprises you because, in the past, you had to provide clear direction and employees rarely would say anything. You: D ____

   a. Take control immediately and provide your usual direction. S ____

   b. Say nothing, just sit back. S ____

   c. Encourage the group to continue, but also provide direction. S ____

   d. Thank the group for starting without you, and encourage them to continue. Support their efforts. S ____

10. Your department is consistently very productive. However, occasionally the members fool around and someone has an accident. There has never been a serious injury. You hear a noise and go to see what it was. From a distance you can see Sue sitting on the floor, laughing, with a ball made from company material in her hand. You: D ____

   a. Say and do nothing. After all, she's OK, and they are very productive; you don't want to make waves. S ____
   b. Call the group together and ask for suggestions on how to keep accidents from recurring. Tell them you will be checking up on them to make sure it does not continue. S ____
   c. Call the group together and discuss the situation. Encourage them to be more careful in the future. S ____
   d. Tell the group that's it; from now on you will be checking up on them regularly. Bring Sue to your office and discipline her. S ____

11. You are at the first meeting of an ad hoc committee you are leading. Most of the members are second- and third-level managers from marketing and financial areas; you are a supervisor from production. You decide to start by: D ____

   a. Working on developing relationships. Get everyone to feel as though they know each other before you talk about business. S ____
   b. Going over the group's purpose and the authority it has. Provide clear directives. S ____
   c. Asking the group to define its purpose. Because most of the members are higher-level managers, let them provide the leadership. S ____
   d. Start by providing both direction and encouragement. Give directives and thank people for their cooperation. S ____

12. Your department has done a great job in the past. It is now getting a new computer, somewhat different from the old one. You have been trained to operate the computer, and you are expected to train your employees to operate it. To train them you: D ____

   a. Give the group instructions, work with them individually, providing direction and encouragement. S ____
   b. Get the group together to decide how they want to be instructed. Be very supportive of their efforts to learn. S ____
   c. Tell them it's a simple system. Give them a copy of the manual and have them study it on their own. S ____
   d. Give the group instructions. Then go around and supervise their work closely, giving additional instructions as needed. S ____

To determine your preferred group leadership style, below, circle the letter you selected in situations 1–12. The column headings indicate the style you selected.

	Autocratic (S-A)	Consultative (S-C)	Participative (S-P)	Laissez-faire (S-L)
1.	*a*	*c*	*b*	*d*
2.	*b*	*d*	*c*	*a*
3.	*b*	*d*	*a*	*c*
4.	*b*	*d*	*a*	*c*
5.	*c*	*a*	*d*	*b*
6.	*a*	*b*	*c*	*d*
7.	*a*	*d*	*c*	*b*
8.	*a*	*c*	*b*	*d*
9.	*a*	*c*	*d*	*b*
10.	*d*	*b*	*a*	*c*
11.	*b*	*d*	*a*	*c*
12.	*d*	*a*	*b*	*c*
Total	____	____	____	____

**Self-Assessment
Exercise 11–1** *continued*

> Add up the number of circled items per column. The total column should equal 12. The column with the highest number represents your preferred group leadership style. There is no one best style in all situations.
>
> The more evenly distributed the numbers are between the four styles, the more flexible you are at leading groups. A total of 0 or 1 in any column may indicate a reluctance to use the style(s). You could have problems in situations calling for this style.
>
> Is your preferred group leadership style the same as your preferred situational supervision style (Chapter 7) and situational communication style (Chapter 5)?

Situational Supervision and Group Development Stages

Situational supervision can be applied to the stages of group development. Chapter 7 presented the situational supervision model. In that chapter, the major focus was on supervising individual employees. Below you will find changes, with the focus on applying the model to the stages of group development. With each stage of group development, a different supervisory style is needed in order to help the group perform effectively at that stage and to develop to the next level.

As stated, when managers interact with their groups, they can perform task roles, maintenance roles, or both. You will learn which role(s) the manager should play during the different stages of group development.

The **group development stage 1,** *orientation—low development D1 (high commitment/low competence), uses the autocratic supervisory style (high task/low maintenance) S-A.* When a task group first comes together, the manager needs to help the group clarify its objectives to provide the direction to be sure the group gets off to a good start. Because the members are committed to joining the group, the manager needs to help the group develop its competence with task behavior.

When managers work with their functional groups, they must be sure that the group has clear objectives and that members know their roles. If the group does not, or when there are complex changes, the manager must play the appropriate task role.

The **group development stage 2,** *dissatisfaction—moderate development D2 (lower commitment/some competence), uses the consultative supervisory style (high task/high maintenance) S-C.* When task and functional groups know their objectives and their roles are clear, its members become dissatisfied. When morale drops, the manager needs to focus on maintenance roles to encourage members to resolve issues. The manager should help the members meet their needs as they develop the appropriate group structure. At the same time, the manager needs to continue to play the task role necessary to help the group develop its level of competence.

The **group development stage 3,** *resolution—high development D3 (variable commitment/high competence), uses the participative supervisory style (low task/high maintenance) S-P.* When the task and functional group members know their objectives and their roles are clear, there is little need to provide task leadership; they know how to do the job.

When commitment varies, it is usually due to some problem in the group's dynamics, such as a conflict or members losing interest. What the manager needs to do is focus on the maintenance behavior to get the group through the issue(s) it faces. If the manager continues to provide task directives that are not needed, the group can become dissatisfied and regress or plateau at this level.

Managers who can develop the type of group structure and dynamics discussed will develop groups to the third or fourth levels. The managers who cannot will have groups that plateau on the second level of group development. Motivating employees and developing and maintaining human relations is an ongoing process. Using the participative style helps the members to develop their commitment, which, in turn, affects their competence.

The **group development stage 4,** *production—outstanding development D4 (high commitment/high competence), uses the laissez-faire supervisory style (low task/low maintenance) S-L.* Groups that develop to this stage have members who play the appropriate task and maintenance roles; the manager does not need to play either role, unless there is a problem.

As a manager, you should determine your group's current level of development and strive to bring it to the next stage of development.

In the opening case, Bonnie Sue's committee is in stage 2—dissatisfaction. Bonnie Sue needs to play both task and maintenance roles to help the group progress to stages 3 and 4. Focusing on solving the negative norm of putting each other's ideas down works on both task and maintenance. Bonnie Sue also needs to provide stronger leadership in the areas of completing meeting assignments and making Kirt, Shelby, and Carl more productive. You will learn how in the next section.

The four stages of group development, along with their appropriate situational supervisory styles, are summarized in Exhibit 11–5.

**Skill-Building
11–2**

EXHIBIT 11–5   **GROUP SITUATIONAL SUPERVISION**

Group Development Stage (D)	Supervisory Styles/Roles (S)
D1 Low Development	**S-A Autocratic**
High commitment/low competence →	**High task/low maintenance**
Members come to the group committed, but they cannot perform with competence.	Provide direction so that the group has clear objectives and members know their roles. Make the decision for the group.
D2 Moderate Development	**S-C Consultative**
Low commitment/some competence →	**High task/high maintenance**
Members have become dissatisfied with the group. They have started to develop competence but are frustrated with results.	Continue to direct the group so it develops task ability. Provide maintenance to regain commitment as the group structure takes place. Include members' input in decisions.
D3 High Development	**S-P Participative**
Variable commitment/high competence →	**Low task/high maintenance**
Commitment changes over time while production remains relatively constant.	Provide little direction. Focus on developing an effective group structure. Have the group participate in decision making.
D4 Outstanding Development	**S-L Laissez-faire**
High commitment/high competence →	**Low task/low maintenance**
Commitment remains constantly high and so does production.	Members provide their own task and maintenance roles. The supervisor is a group member. Allow the group to make its own decisions.

Learning Objective

3. Explain the four situational supervisory styles to use with a group, based on its stage of development

---

Meeting Leadership Skills

Middle managers average 11 hours per week and upper managers average 23 hours per week in meetings.[52]

With the trend toward self-directed teams, meetings in the workplace are taking up an increasing amount of time.[53] Task force meetings are among the most critical these days.[54] Since all level employees' time in meetings is increasing, the need for meeting management skills is stronger than ever.[55] The most common complaints about meetings are: There are too many of them; they are too long; and they are

● Organization
● Group
● Individual

unproductive.[56] Even so, meetings are very important to career success.[57] Careers may be made or broken in the power arenas of meetings. The success or failure of meetings rests primarily with the leader and interpersonal communications.[58] In this section we discuss planning meetings, conducting meetings, and handling problem group members.

Planning Meetings

There are at least five areas where meeting planning is needed: objectives, selecting participants and making assignments, the agenda, the time and place for the meeting, and leadership. A written copy of the plan should be sent to members prior to the meeting.[59]

Objectives

Before getting a group started, determine what is wanted from the team. The single greatest mistake made by those who call meetings is that they often have no clear idea and purpose for the meeting.[60] Leaders should state what they want to happen as a result of the meeting. Before calling a meeting, you should clearly define its purpose and objective.[61]

Participants and Assignments

Before calling the meeting, the leader should decide who is qualified to attend the meeting.[62] The more people who attend a meeting, the lesser the chance that any work will get done.[63] Does the full group/department need to attend? Should some nongroup specialist be invited to provide input? On controversial issues, the leader may find it wiser to meet with the key members before the meeting to discuss and/or vote on an issue.

Participants should know in advance what is expected of them at the meeting. If any preparation is expected (reading material, doing some research, preparing a report, and so forth), they should have adequate advance notice.[64]

Agenda

Before calling the meeting, the leader should identify the activities that will take place during the meeting in order to achieve the objective of the meeting. The agenda tells the members what is expected and how the meeting will progress.[65] Having a set time limit for each agenda item helps keep the group on target; getting off the subject is common to meetings.

Place agenda items in order of priority. Then if the group does not have time to cover every item, the least important items carry forward.[66] At too many meetings, a leader puts all the so-called quick items first. The group gets bogged down and either rushes through the important items or puts them off until later.

Members who are to give reports should do so early in the meeting. The reason for this procedure is that people get anxious and tend to be preoccupied with their report. Once it's over, they are more relaxed and can become more actively involved in the meeting. It is frustrating to prepare to give a report, only to be told "we'll get to it next time." This sends a message that the member and the report are not important.

Date, Time, and Place

In determining which day(s) and time(s) of the week are best for meetings, get members' input. Members tend to be more alert early in the day. Clearly specify the beginning and ending time.[67] Be sure to select an adequate place for the meeting and plan for the physical comfort of the group. Be sure seating provides eye contact for small discussion groups, and plan enough time so that the members do not have to rush. If reservations are needed for the meeting place, make them far enough in advance to get a proper meeting room.

With advances in technology, telephone conferences/meetings are becoming quite common. Video conferences are also gaining popularity. These techniques have saved travel costs and time, and they have resulted in better and quicker decisions. Some of the companies using video conferencing include Arco, Boeing, Aetna, Ford, IBM, TRW, and Xerox. The personal computer has been said to be the most useful tool for running meetings since Robert's Rules of Order. The personal computer can be turned into a large-screen "intelligent chalkboard" that can dramatically change meeting results. Minutes (notes on what took place during the meeting) can be taken on the personal computer and a hard copy distributed at the end of the meeting.

Leadership

The leader should determine the group's level of development and plan to provide the appropriate task and/or maintenance behavior. Each agenda item may need to be handled differently. For example, some items may simply call for disseminating information, while others require a discussion or a vote to be taken; and some items require a report from a member.

An effective way to develop group members' ability is to rotate the role of the group moderator/leader for each meeting, with groups that are capable of doing so.

The Written Plan

After leaders have planned the above five items, they should write them and make copies to be distributed to each member who will attend the meeting. Exhibit 11–6 provides the recommended contents, in sequence, of a meeting plan.

EXHIBIT 11–6

WRITTEN MEETING PLAN

Time: Date, day, place, beginning and ending times

Objectives: A statement of the purpose and/or objective of the meeting

Participants and Assignments: List each participant's name and assignment, if any. If all members have the same assignment, make one assignment statement.

Agenda: List each item to be covered in priority order with its approximate time limit.

Conducting Meetings

Below, you will learn about the group's first meeting, the three parts of each meeting, and leadership, group structure, and emotions.

The First Meeting

At the first meeting, the group is in the orientation stage. The leader should use the high task role; however, the members should be given the opportunity to spend some time getting to know one another. Introductions set the stage for subsequent interactions. If members find that their social needs will not be met, dissatisfaction may occur quickly. A simple technique is to start with introductions, then move on to the group's purpose, objectives, and members' roles. Sometime during or following this procedure, have a break that enables members to interact informally.

The Three Parts of Each Meeting

Each meeting should cover the following:

1. Objectives. Begin the meetings on time; waiting for late members penalizes the members who are on time and develops a norm for coming late. Begin by reviewing progress to date, the group's objectives, and the purpose/objective for the specific meeting. If minutes are recorded, they are usually approved at the beginning of the next meeting. For most meetings it is recommended that a secretary be appointed to take minutes.[68]

2. Agenda. Cover the agenda items. Try to keep to the approximate times, but be flexible. If the discussion is constructive and members need more time, give it to them; however, if the discussion is more of a distractive argument, move ahead.

Learning Objective

4. Explain how to plan for and conduct effective meetings

3. Summarize and review assignments. End the meeting on time. The leader should summarize what took place during the meeting. Were the meeting's objectives achieved? Review all of the assignments given during the meeting. Get a commitment to the task that each member should perform for the next or a specific future meeting. The secretary and/or leader should record all assignments. If there is no accountability and follow-up on assignments, members may not complete them.[69]

Leadership, Group Structure, and Emotions

As stated in the last section, the leadership needed changes with the group's level of development. The leader must be sure to provide the appropriate task and/or maintenance behavior when it is needed.

The leader is responsible for helping the team develop an effective group structure. The leader must focus on the group's process and dynamics as it performs the task and make the team aware of how its process affects its performance and members' commitment. The team needs to create and maintain positive emotions that promote working together effectively. Negative emotions should not be ignored; they should be refocused in a positive direction. Individual members, subgroups, or the entire team may get emotional. Feelings can be caused by the meeting content, the members' perception of the group structure, and the group dynamics. As a member of a team, you need to focus on both verbal and nonverbal communications (see Chapter 4) to help the team understand how its group dynamics are affecting its behavior, human relations, and performance. Do not only look at the speaker, watch others as they listen. When team members show signs of being upset, bring it to the team's attention and discuss it using active listening and conflict resolution skills. Team building (Chapter 12) is an effective technique to help the group develop an effective group structure and dynamics.[70]

WORK APPLICATIONS

9. Recall a specific meeting you attended. Did the group leader plan for the meeting by stating meeting objectives, identifying participants and their assignments, making an agenda, and stating the date, time, and place of the meeting? Did the leader provide a written meeting plan to the members prior to the meeting? Explain your answers and state what you would do differently if you were the leader.

Handling Team Problem Members

As team members work together, personality types tend to emerge. Certain personality types can cause the group to be less efficient than possible. Some of the problem members you may have in your team are the following: silent, talker, wanderer, bored, and the arguer. Below we will discuss how to handle each, in order to make them and the group more effective.

The Silent Member

To be fully effective, all group members should participate. If members are silent, the team does not get the benefits of their input.

It is the leader's responsibility to encourage the silent member to participate without being obvious or overdoing it. Two techniques the leader can use are the nominal group method[71] and the simple rotation method, in which all members take turns giving their input. These methods are generally less threatening than directly calling on members. However, these methods are not appropriate all the time. To build up the silent members' confidence, call on them with questions they can easily answer. When you believe they have convictions, ask them to express them. Watch their nonverbal communications.

If you are a silent type, try to participate more often. Know when to stand up for your views and be assertive. Silent types generally do not make good leaders.

The Talker

Talkers have something to say about everything. They like to dominate the discussion.[72] However, if they do dominate, the other members do not get to participate. The talker can cause intragroup problems.

It is the leader's responsibility to slow talkers down, not to shut them up. Do not let them dominate the group. The nominal group method and simple rotation method are also effective with talkers. They have to wait their turn. When not using a rotation method, gently interrupt the talker and present your own ideas or call on other members to present their ideas.[73] Prefacing questions with statements like "let's give those who have not answered yet a chance" can also slow the talker down.

The penny technique can also be used to slow down the talker and encourage the silent to participate. At the start of the meeting, give each participant five pennies and ask for one back every time a person speaks. When a participant's pennies run out, deny further input. At the end of the meeting, collect the remaining pennies to see who did not participate, to encourage them to do so. This is admittedly a rather clumsy technique, but it works.[74]

If you tend to be a talker, try to slow down. Give others a chance to talk and do things for themselves. Good leaders develop employees' ability in these areas.

The Wanderer

Wanderers distract the team from the agenda items and often like to complain.

The leader is responsible for keeping the group on track. If the wanderer wants to socialize, cut it off. Be kind, thank the member for the contribution, then throw a question out to the group to get it back on track. However, if the wanderer has a complaint that is legitimate and solvable, allow the group to discuss it. Group structure issues should be addressed and resolved; however, if it is not resolvable, get the group back on track. Griping without resolving anything tends to reduce morale and commitment to task accomplishment. If the wanderer complains about unresolvable issues, the leader should make statements like "we may be underpaid, but we have no control over our pay. Complaining will not get us a raise; let's get back to the issue at hand."

If you tend to be a wanderer, try to be aware of your behavior and stay on the subject at hand.

The Bored Member

Your team may have one or more members who are not interested in the task. The bored person may be preoccupied with other issues and not pay attention or participate in the group meeting. The bored member may also feel superior and wonder why the group is spending so much time on the obvious.

The leader is responsible for keeping members motivated.[75] Assign the bored member a task like recording ideas on the board and recording the minutes. Call on bored members; bring them into the group. If you allow them to sit back, things may get worse and others may decide not to participate either. Negative feelings can be carried to other team members.

If you tend to be bored, try to find ways to help motivate yourself. Work at becoming more patient and in control of behavior that can have negative effects on other members.

The Arguer

Like the talker, the arguer likes to be the center of attention. This behavior can occur when you use the devil's advocate approach, which is helpful in developing and selecting alternative courses of action. However, arguers enjoy arguing for the sake of arguing, rather than helping the group. They turn things into a win–lose situation, and they cannot stand losing.

The leader should resolve conflict but not in an argumentative way. Do not get into an argument with arguers; that is exactly what they want to happen. If an

IE 11–3

Conclusion

Learning Objective

5. Identify five problem members and explain how to handle them so they do not have a negative effect on your meetings

argument starts, bring others into the discussion. If it is personal, cut it off. Personal attacks only hurt the group. Keep the discussion moving on target. Try to minimize their opportunity for confrontation.

If you tend to be an arguer, strive to convey your views in an assertive debate format, not as an aggressive argument. Listen to others' views and be willing to change if they have better ideas.

Whenever you work in a team, do not embarrass, intimidate, or argue with any members, no matter how they provoke you. If you do, the result will make a martyr of them and a bully of you to the team. If you have serious problem members who do not respond to the above techniques, confront them individually outside of the team. Get them to agree to work in a cooperative way.

In the opening case, Bonnie Sue's meetings lacked specific assignments. She needs to use more directive leadership and assign tasks to specific members to complete outside the meetings. Recall that the problem members in Bonnie Sue's group were Carl—talker, Shelby—wanderer, and Kirt—arguer. Bonnie Sue needs to use her leadership skills to slow Carl down, to keep Shelby on topic, and to keep Kirt from fighting with others and resolve conflicts quickly.

WORK APPLICATIONS

10. Identify group problem members at a meeting you attended. Was the leader effective in handling them? What would you have done to make them more productive members? Explain in detail.

APPLICATION SITUATIONS

Group Problem People

AS 11–4

Identify the problem type as:

A. Silent   B. Talker   C. Wanderer   D. Bored   E. Arguer

_____ 16. Jesse is always first or second to give his ideas. He is always elaborating on ideas. Because Jesse is so quick to respond, others sometimes make comments to him about it.

_____ 17. Two of the group members are sitting back quietly today for the first time. The other members are doing all the discussing and volunteering for assignments.

_____ 18. As the group is discussing a problem, a member asks the group if they heard about the vice president and the salesclerk.

_____ 19. Eunice is usually last to give her ideas. When asked to explain her position, Eunice often changes her answers to agree with the group.

_____ 20. Hank enjoys challenging members' ideas. He likes to have the group do things his way. When a group member does not agree with Hank, he makes wise comments about the member's prior mistakes.

● Organization
● Group
● Individual

Putting It All Together

Chapters 10 and 11 both cover the topic of teams and group leadership. When putting it all together, you realize that people join groups to meet their needs. The types of groups people join are functional, task, and informal. Organizations use groups to meet performance objectives. As the people in a team interact, they develop group dynamics. The group structure—leadership and ability to solve problems and make decisions—are major determinants of the group's stage of development. The more effective the group structure and dynamics, the higher the stage of development. And the higher the stage of development, the greater the level of performance of the group. The group's performance, in turn, affects its behavior and human relations.[76] Have you ever noticed that behavior and human relations of the same group or team changes when it meets objectives (wins), and when it doesn't (loses)?

When you lead groups in a manner that meets the needs of the individuals while attaining the performance objective of the group, you create a win–win situation.

See Exhibit 11–7 for an illustration of how the factors discussed in this chapter influence teams.

▲ Goal of
Human Relations

EXHIBIT 11–7

THE TEAM PERFORMANCE MODEL

Team Performance (f)*	Team Structure	Team Dynamics	Team Development Stage
High ↔ Low	• Type of group	• Objectives	• 1. Orientation
	• Leadership	• Size	• 2. Dissatisfaction
	• Composition	• Norms	• 3. Resolution
	• Problem solving & decision making	• Cohesiveness	• 4. Production
	• Conflict	• Status	• 5. Termination
		• Roles	

*(f) = is a function of.

■ Performance
■ Human Relations
■ Behavior

IE 11–4

When reading Exhibit 11–7, did you understand that the type of group affects behavior, human relations, and performance? The group's behavior and human relations are influenced by the group's structure and dynamics, as it progresses through stages of development. These, in turn, affect the group's performance. The group's performance also influences group behavior and human relations because the process is an ongoing one, rather than one having a clear starting and ending point.

Learning to develop group dynamics, group leadership, and group problem-solving and decision-making skills will help you to become more effective.

REVIEW

Select one or more methods: (1) fill in the missing key terms from memory; (2) match the key terms, from the end of the review, with their definitions below; and/or (3) copy the key terms in order from the key terms at the beginning of the chapter.

_____ refers to the patterns of interactions that emerge as groups develop. The six components of group structure include objectives, group size, group norms, group cohesiveness, status within the group, and group roles. The group should agree on and be committed to clear objectives. The optimum size of the group varies with the group's purpose. _____ are the group's shared expectations of its members' behavior. _____

is the attractiveness and closeness group members have for themselves and the group. Cohesive groups with positive productive norms tend to have the highest production levels. _____ is the perceived ranking of one member relative to other members of the group. _____ are shared expectations of how group members will fulfill the requirements of their position. Group roles can be classified into _____, the things group members do and say that directly aid in the accomplishment of the group's objective(s); _____, the things group members do and say to develop and sustain group dynamics; and _____, the things members do and say in order to meet their own needs/objectives at the expense of the group.

The five stages of group development, with their appropriate situational supervisory styles are _____, orientation—low development D1 (high commitment/low competence), which uses the autocratic supervisory style (high task/low maintenance) S-A; _____, dissatisfaction—moderate development D2 (lower commitment/some competence), which uses the consultative supervisory style (high task/high maintenance) S-C; _____, resolution—high development D3 (variable commitment/high competence), which uses the participative supervisory style (low task/ high maintenance) S-P; _____, production— outstanding development D4 (high commitment/high competence), which uses the laissez-faire supervisory style (low task/low maintenance) S-L; and stage 5, termination—this happens in task groups, not functional groups.

The five areas in which meeting planning is needed include setting objectives; selecting participants and making assignments; the agenda; the date, time, and place for the meeting; and leadership. A copy of the plan should be sent to members prior to the meetings. The three parts of conducting meetings are (1) reviewing the objectives, (2) going over the agenda items, and (3) summarizing and reviewing the assignments. The meeting leader should help the team develop an effective group structure and use the appropriate leadership style for the group's level of development. Group leaders may encounter group problem members, which include the silent member, whom the leader should get to participate; the talker, whom the leader should slow down; the wanderer, whom the leader should keep on topic; the bored, whom the leader should motivate; and the arguer, whom the leader should keep from arguing.

For a brief summary of topics in Chapters 10 and 11, see Exhibit 11–7.

KEY TERMS

group cohesiveness   380
group development
   stage 1   391
group development
   stage 2   391

group development
   stage 3   391
group development
   stage 4   392
maintenance roles   383
norms   379

roles   382
self-interest roles   383
status   381
task roles   383
team dynamics   378

CASE

**Valena Scientific
Corporation**

In the 1980s, the biotech industry was a rapidly growing sector of the economy. As new discoveries in genetic engineering came to light, companies were formed and heavily financed by venture capitalists to exploit the commercial potential of these new developments. One of these developments with the greatest potential for finding cures to diseases such as cancer and AIDS was in gene splicing.

Valena Scientific Corporation (VSC), a large manufacturer of health-care products saw the trend developing and decided to create a biotech research program. As VSC's senior executives would later remark, the decision to diversify into biotech research was bold and risky. Skilled specialists in microbiology were hard to find given the growth in the industry and the resulting shortage of qualified experts in the field. Also, commercial success, measured in new product introductions from the industry was lacking. Many investors who had high hopes for big margin returns were beginning to lose interest and biotech companies were finding it harder to attract the large amounts of capital needed to sustain research and development efforts. Undeterred, VSC pushed on, believing that it had the solution to overcoming the slow development to market launch problem of the industry.

VSC staffed its program with nine scientists; three were skilled in gene splicing, three in recombination, and three in fermentation. Technicians were also assigned to the program to help the scientists. Top management was convinced that the biotech research program could achieve greater success if the team of scientists and technicians was self-managed. Top management left the scientists alone. Interaction between the three groups was minimal and the workflow was very sequential. For example, the work typically started in the gene-splicing group, followed by work in recombination, and then in fermentation.

VSC's biotech research program was given a special opportunity. Hoffman-LaRoche was developing leukocyte interferon to use as a treatment against cancer. VSC contracted with Hoffman-LaRoche to develop a technique for large-scale interferon production. Six months was all VSC had to come up with a production technology. Scientists in each of the departments (gene splicing, recombination, and fermentation) remained in their departments and began immediately to test ideas relevant to their specialty. A few months later, the informal group leaders met for progress updates and discovered that each group had taken a different research direction. Attempts to find common ground were futile as each subgroup believed their direction was best. Followup meetings were plagued by conflict and did not resolve the issues. When management became aware of the problem they decided to appoint a formal leader to the program. A university professor with extensive research experience in recombinant DNA technology was hired as the chief biologist for VSC's Biotech Research Program. All project members reported to the chief for the duration of the interferon project.

The chief biologist immediately saw the need to transform the three groups into a real team. The strategy was to take the nine scientists on a two-day retreat. The scientists had to talk across their traditional disciplines. The leader facilitated the discussion of their hopes and visions for the project. When a shared vision of the group had been developed, the group turned to scientific issues and in mixed groups discussed the ideas that the VSC subgroups had developed. Gradually a consensus emerged as one approach seemed to have more likelihood of success than the others. As the group return to VSC, the technicians were brought on board and oriented to the new approach and focus of the project. Specific deadlines were set based upon group interdependence.

Major changes were observed in the behavior of the scientists after the retreat. Communication among subgroups became more common. Subgroup leaders exchanged ideas and coordinated many problems among themselves. Informal social gatherings for lunch or coffee breaks involving several members of the subgroups became commonplace. There were daily discussions and cooperation on research matters involving different group leaders and members. Though not the self-managed team that senior executives had envisioned, excitement, motivation, and dedication to the interferon project was high, and team spirit was at its best among project members.

Go to the Internet: For more information on Valena Scientific Corporation (VSC), do a name search on the Internet and visit VSC's website at *http://www.vsc.com.* For ideas on using the Internet, see Appendix C.

Support your answer to the following questions with specific information from the case, or other information you get from the Web or other source.

1. Using the team performance model, Exhibit 11–1, which one function was hurting the research project team performance the most prior to the retreat?

2. Discuss the research project team dynamics for each of the six components prior to the retreat.

3. What stage of development was the research project team on prior to the retreat and after the retreat?

4. What situational supervisory style did top management use with the nine scientist prior to hiring the chief biologist? What situational supervisory style did the chief biologist use during the retreat? Were top management and the chief's styles appropriate for the team development stage?

5. How does the retreat relate to Chapter 11?

Cumulative Questions

6. What are the communications issues in this case (Chapters 4 and 5)?

7. What type of reinforcement (reinforcement theory) did top management use with the research project team prior to the retreat? Which motivational technique was most relevant to getting the members to work as a team (Chapter 6)?

8. How did conflict affect the group prior to the retreat (Chapter 8)?

9. Prior to and after the retreat, were the nine scientists a group or a team? What type of group/team were the nine scientists and leader (Chapter 10)?

Group Performance

Through reorganization, Christen has been assigned three additional departments that produce the same product. Ted, Jean, and Paul are the supervisors of these departments. Christen would like to increase productivity, so she set up a group to analyze the present situation and recommend ways to increase productivity. The group consists of Christen, the three supervisors, an industrial engineer, and an expert on group dynamics from personnel. The group analyzed the present situation in each department as follows:

Group 1: Ted's department produces at or above standard on a regular basis. It averages between 102 and 104 percent of standard on a monthly basis. (Standard is 100 percent.) Members work well together; they often go to lunch together. Members' productivity level is all about the same level.

Group 2: Jean's department produces between 95 and 105 percent on a monthly basis. However, it usually produces 100 percent. The members do not seem to interact too often. Part of the reason for the standard production level is two employees who consistently produce at 115 percent of standard. Jean will be retiring in six months, and they both want to fill her position. There are three members who consistently produce at 80 to 90 percent of standard.

Group 3: Paul's department achieves between 90 and 92 percent of standard on a monthly basis. Betty is a strong informal leader who oversees the productivity level. She lets members know if they produce too much or too little. John is the only member in the department who reaches production standards. The rest of the department members do not talk to John. At times they intentionally keep his level of production down. All other department members produce at about 90 percent of standard.

Answer the following questions. Then in the space between the questions, state why you selected that answer.

_____ 1. Christen, Ted, Jean, and Paul make up a ____ group.

      a. functional   *b.* task   *c.* informal

_____ 2. To increase productivity, Christen set up a ____ group.

      a. functional   *b.* ad hoc committee   *c.* standing committee

_____ 3. Which group(s) has a high agreement and commitment to *its* objectives?

      a. 1   *d.* 1 and 2   *g.* 1, 2, and 3
      b. 2   *e.* 1 and 3
      c. 3   *f.* 2 and 3

_____ 4. Which group has objectives (positive norms) in agreement with that of management?

      a. 1   *d.* 1 and 2   *g.* 1, 2, and 3
      b. 2   *e.* 1 and 3
      c. 3   *f.* 2 and 3

_____ 5. Which group is cohesive?

      a. 1   *d.* 1 and 2   *g.* 1, 2, and 3
      b. 2   *e.* 1 and 3
      c. 3   *f.* 2 and 3

_____ 6. Which group most clearly plays self-interest roles?

   _a._ 1   _b._ 2   _c._ 3

_____ 7. Betty primarily plays a ____ role for her group.

   _a._ task   _b._ maintenance   _c._ self-interest

_____ 8. Group 1 appears to be in stage ____ of group development.

   _a._ 1   _b._ 2   _c._ 3   _d._ 4   _e._ 5

_____ 9. Group 2 appears to be in stage ____ of group development.

   _a._ 1   _b._ 2   _c._ 3   _d._ 4   _e._ 5

_____ 10. Group 3 appears to be in stage ____ of group development.

   _a._ 1   _b._ 2   _c._ 3   _d._ 4   _e._ 5

11. What would you recommend doing to increase productivity in each of the three groups?

Your Team's Response (IE 11–1)

The objective of this exercise is to learn about teams and how to improve their performance through a team test. Using the information in Appendix B and IE 11–2 and 11–3 as you do the following:

Online Internet Exercise 11–1 (Self-Assessment)

1. Select a group/team that you belong/belonged to.
2. Go to the Leadership Strategies homepage—*www.leaderx.com*
3. Click "Test Yourself."
4. Click "Test Your Team's Response." Take the test by answering the questions as they relate to the team you selected in step 1, then click "submit it" for scoring. Print your customized report with valuable feedback.
5. Read your report. Note that this score is not just a reflection of you, as it relates to the team you belong to. The value of the test/score is to give you feedback on how your team can improve. Read the report a second time highlighting the most valuable tips that can help you develop your leadership. (Your instructor may require your highlighted printout.)
6. Questions: (1) What do you agree and/or not agree with in the report? (2) What, if anything, surprised you in the report? (3) What were the most important findings to you? (4) How can your team use this information to improve its performance? (The instructor may require your answers to these questions.)

In-Class Internet Exercise 11–1, IE 11–2, IE 11–3 and IE 11–4

The instructor selects one of the six options from pages 589.

Team Dynamics (IE 11–2)

The objective of this exercise is to better understand team dynamics. You will be using a link to visit another site. Use the information in Appendix B and IE 1–2 and 1–3 as you do the following:

Online Internet Exercise 11–2

1. Go to the supersite of Team Building Plus website—*www.teambuildersplus. com/links.html*
2. Click one of the links to another website and read the material (your instructor may require a printed copy).
3. Questions: (1) What website did you visit? (2) Who was the author and what was the title of the material you read? (3) What did you learn about team dynamics? (4) How can you use this information to be a better team member and leader? (Your instructor may require your typed answers.)

Difficult Employees (IE 11–3)

The objective of this exercise is to better understand how to work with difficult employees. Use the information in Appendix B and IE 1–2 and 1–3 as you do the following:

Online Internet Exercise 11–3

1. Identify a difficult employee that you have to work with. Write a brief description of the behavior of this employee that caused him or her to be a difficult employee (your instructor may require you to type your description).
2. Go to the Work911 website homepage—*www.work911.com*
3. Click "Difficult Employee Help" (your instructor may require a printed copy). Scroll down and you should be in a subsite that has a book contents.

4. Click on at least two sections under any of the first few chapters for more information (your instructor may require a copy).

5. Questions: (1) Who is the author and what is the title of the book? (2) Which chapter (identify title and number) and section (identify it by name) of the chapter did you click to read more information? Identify both. (3) Which chapter (identify title and number) and section (identify it by name) of the chapter best describes the difficult employee you selected in step 1? (4) What did you learn about difficult employees? (5) How can you use this information on the job to help you work with difficult employees?

Team Skills (IE 11–4)

Online Internet Exercise 11–4 (Self-Assessment)

The objective of this exercise is to diagnose/measure your team skills and to develop and implement a plan to improve your team skills. Do the following:

1. Go to the Culture Building website homepage—*www.culture-building.com*

2. Click "Diagnostics," then click "Team Skills—Self-Description," and read about the diagnostics you will get for your team skills, then click "Proceed."

3. To obtain your team skills scores, you must fill in the "team, e-mail, and initials" with your real or fictitious information. If you give your real e-mail address, the diagnostic score will be sent to your e-mail address (an option would be to have the diagnoses e-mailed to your instructor). However, you will get the scores online. You must also answer every question to get your scores.

4. Click your responses to the questions then click "Submit."

5. Generally, the higher your scores (based on 100 percent overall and 10 for subscores) the higher is your level of team skills. Print a copy of your scores (your instructor may require a copy).

6. Questions: (1) What was your total score percentage? (2) What are your highest and lowest subscores? Be sure to list areas and scores for each. (3) How can you improve your team skills in your two weakest areas? Be sure to list specific behavior and to implement your plan.

**Preparation
Team Dynamics**

Note: This exercise is designed for class groups that have worked together for some time. (Five or more hours are recommended.)

Answer the following questions as they apply to your class group.

1. Based on attendance, preparation, and class involvement, identify each group member's level of commitment to the group, including yourself. (Write each member's name on the appropriate line.)

    High commitment _____

    Medium commitment _____

    Low commitment _____

2. Our group size is:

    ____ too large ____ too small ____ OK

    Explain why.

3. List at least five norms your group has developed. Identify each as positive or negative.

    1.
    2.
    3.
    4.
    5.

    What positive norms could the group develop to help it function?

4. Based on the group's commitment, size, homogeneity, equality of participation, intragroup competition and success, identify its cohesiveness level as:

    ____ high ____ medium ____ low

    How does cohesiveness affect performance? What can be done to increase cohesiveness?

5. Identify each group member's status, including your own. (Write each group member's name on the appropriate line.)

    High _____

    Medium _____

    Low _____

    Does the group have status congruence? How can the group improve it?

6. Identify the roles members play. Write the name of each group member who plays each role on the appropriate line. You will most likely use each name several times and have more than one name on each role line, but rank them by dominance.

Task roles

Objective clarifier _____

Planner _____

Organizer _____

Controller _____

Maintenance roles

Consensus seeker _____

Harmonizer _____

Gatekeeper _____

Encourager _____

Compromiser _____

Self-interest roles (if appropriate)

Aggressor _____

Blocker _____

Recognition seeker _____

Withdrawer _____

Which roles should be played more, and which less, to increase effectiveness? Who should and should not play them?

7. Our group is in stage _____ of group development.

1. Orientation
2. Dissatisfaction
3. Resolution
4. Production

What can be done to increase the group's level of development?

8. Identify problem people, if any, by placing their names on the appropriate line(s).

Silent _____

Talker _____

Wanderer _____

Bored _____

Arguer _____

What should be done to help eliminate problem people? Specifically, who should do what?

9. Review the answers to questions 1–8. In priority order, what will the group do to improve its group structure? Specify what each group member will do to help the group's structure.

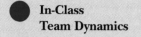

**In-Class
Team Dynamics**

Note: This exercise is designed for groups that have met for some time. (Five or more hours are recommended.)

Objectives: To gain a better understanding of the group structure components and how they affect group performance, and to improve group structure.

SCANS: The SCANS competencies of resource, interpersonal skills, information, and especially systems and the foundations of basic, thinking in the area of problem solving and decision making, and personal qualities are developed through this exercise.

Preparation: You should have answered the preparation questions.

Experience: You will discuss your group's structure and develop plans to improve it.

*Procedure 1
(10–20 minutes)*

Groups get together to discuss their answers to the nine preparation questions. Be sure to fully explain and discuss your answers. Try to come up with some specific ideas on how to improve your group's process and dynamics.

Conclusion: The instructor leads a class discussion and/or makes concluding remarks.

Application (2–4 minutes): What did I learn from this experience? How will I use this knowledge in the future?

Sharing: Volunteers give their answers to the application section.

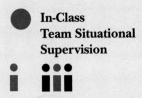

**In-Class
Team Situational
Supervision**

Objectives: To help you understand the stages of group development, and to use the appropriate situational supervision style.

SCANS: The SCANS competencies of resources, interpersonal skills, and information and the foundations of basic, thinking, and personal qualities are developed through this exercise.

Preparation: You should have completed Self-Assessment Exercise 11–1.

Experience: You will discuss your selected supervisory styles for the 12 preparation situations, and you will be given feedback on your accuracy in selecting the appropriate style to meet the situation.

*Procedure 1
(3–10 minutes)*

The instructor reviews the group situational supervision model, Exhibit 11–3, and explains how to apply it to situation 1. The instructor states the group's developmental stage, the supervisory style of each of the four alternative actions, and the scoring for each alternative. Follow the three steps below, as you try to select the most appropriate alternative action for each of the 12 situations.

Step 1. For each situation, determine the team's level of development. Place the number 1, 2, 3, or 4 on the D ____ lines.

Step 2. Identify each supervisory style of all four alternatives *a–d.* Place the letters A, C, P, or L on the S ____ lines.

Step 3. Select the appropriate supervisory style for the team's level of development. Circle its letter, either *a, b, c,* or *d.*

Procedure 2

Option A (3–5 minutes): The instructor gives the class the recommended answers to situations 2–12, as in procedure 1, without any explanation.

Option B (10–30 minutes): Break into teams of two or three and go over the situations chosen by the instructor. The instructor will go over the recommended answers as above.

Conclusion: The instructor leads a class discussion and/or makes concluding remarks.

Application (2–4 minutes): What did I learn from this experience? How will I use this knowledge in the future?

Sharing: Volunteers give their answers to the application section.

Organizational Changes

Part

5

Change: Managing Culture, Diversity, Quality, and Climate

Learning Objectives

After completing this chapter, you should be able to:

1. Explain why managing change skills are important.
2. Describe the four types of changes.
3. State why people resist change and how to overcome it.
4. Explain how to use a change model when making changes.
5. Explain dimensions of an organization's culture.
6. Describe how diversity and quality are dimensions of organizational culture.
7. Explain dimensions of an organization's climate.
8. Describe five OD techniques.
9. Explain the relationship among organizational culture, diversity, quality, climate, and development.
10. Define the following 15 key terms (in order of appearance in the chapter):

types of changes	**organizational**	**morale**
management	**culture**	**organizational**
information	**valuing diversity**	**development**
systems (MIS)	**managing diversity**	**Grid OD**
automation	**total quality man-**	**survey feedback**
resistance to change	**agement (TQM)**	**force field analysis**
	organizational	**team building**
	climate	

ronnie **Linkletter now works for the New York City Insurance Company (NYCIC). Ronnie was the manager of the claims department at Rider, a small insurance company in Danbury, Connecticut, until it was bought by NYCIC. Since the purchase of Rider, Ronnie and his peers don't know what to expect. They know there will be many changes, which they don't look forward to. They have been told by the new managers that they are a part of the NYCIC family. "Family" relates to some kind of organizational culture managers keep talking about, which has developed over many years through an ongoing organizational development program. NYCIC has been concerned about its employees' morale. Ronnie feels confused by all these new buzzwords. He wants to know how these changes will affect him. Ronnie knows that at Rider all the managers were white males, and there were very few minorities. But at NYCIC, there are women and minority managers, and more than half of NYCIC employees are minorities. Is there a way to make changes in organizations so that people don't resist the changes? This is the major topic of Chapter 12.**

● Organization
● Group
● Individual

Why Managing Change Is Important

Change is all about us.[1] Change is good; you have to keep stretching.[2] Plato said, "Change takes place no matter what deters it." In the diverse global business environment, change is a way of life.[3] And it should be evolutionary.[4] The U.S.'s productivity dilemma stems from a lack of understanding of what is required to achieve lasting change and the commitment to change itself.[5] Organizations must learn to change faster to survive and grow.[6] The ability to manage change determines success.[7] Your ability to flexibly change with the diversifying global environment will affect your career success.[8] People with outdated skills are often retrained, unemployed, or underemployed.[9] Your college education should help prepare you to begin a lifelong journey of learning,[10] since organizations stress the need for continuous learning.[11]

WORK APPLICATIONS

1. Give reasons why managing change skills are important to managers in an organization you work/worked for.

Forces for Change

An organization interacts with its external and internal environment. Some of the external environmental forces include increased global competition,[12] consumer taste, government laws,[13] economic conditions, and technological advances.[14]

Some of the internal organizational forces for change include redefined purpose and strategies, financial position, reorganization, and mergers. All of these forces require change, whether it is welcomed or not.[15]

In this section we examine the types of changes, but, first, test your openness to change in Self-Assessment Exercise 12–1.

Types of Changes

Organizations are composed of four interactive variables. The four variables, or **types of changes,** *are technological change, structural change, task change, and people change.* The proper metaphor for the systems affect for managing change is a balanced mobile in which a change in one variable affects the others. Because of the systems affect, you need to consider the repercussions that a change in one variable will have on the other variables, and plan accordingly.[16]

Technological Change

Technological changes, such as the Internet, have increased the rate of speed at which change takes place.[17] Technology is a commonly used method of increasing productivity to gain competitive leverage.[18] For example, Wal-Mart is committed to technology. Wal-Mart's operating costs are less than its nearest competitor, and, consequently, the lower cost structure equals lower prices for customers.

Some of the major areas of technology change include the following:

Machines: New machinery, or equipment, is introduced on an ongoing basis. The computer is a sophisticated machine that is also a part of many other machines. The fax machine and e-mail have increased the speed of doing business.

Process: *Process* refers to how the organization transforms inputs (raw materials, parts, data, and so on) into outputs (finished goods and services, information). The change in the sequence of work in process is a technology change. With the aid of the computer, organizations have changed the way they process information. Management information systems (MIS) *are formal systems for collecting, processing, and disseminating the information necessary to aid managers in decision making.* The MIS attempt to centralize and integrate all or most of the organization's information, such as financial, production, inventory, and sales information. In this way the departments can coordinate their efforts in working with the systems affect.

Openness to Change

Select the response that best describes what you would do in each situation.

1. In my daily life I:

   _____ *a.* Look for new ways of doing things.

   _____ *b.* Like things the way they are.

2. If my friends were opposed to a change:

   _____ *a.* It would not affect my changing.

   _____ *b.* I would resist the change, too.

3. In my work situation I:

   _____ *a.* Do things differently.

   _____ *b.* Do things the same way.

4. If I had the opportunity to learn to use new computer software to help me in school or at work, I would:

   _____ *a.* Take time to learn to use it on my own.

   _____ *b.* Wait until required to use it.

5. I like to know about a change:

   _____ *a.* Anytime. Short notice is OK with me.

   _____ *b.* Well in advance to plan for it.

6. When a work change is required, I:

   _____ *a.* Change as quickly as management wants.

   _____ *b.* Want to move slowly to implement change.

7. When leading others, I:

   _____ *a.* Use the style appropriate for their capability.

   _____ *b.* Use my distinct leadership style.

The more *a* answers you selected, the more open to change you are. The *b* answers show resistance to change. If you tend to be resistant to change, and want to have a successful career, you may want to change your attitude and behavior. You can begin by looking for different ways to do things more productively. Look at your routine for getting ready for school or work. Could you make any changes to save time?

WORK APPLICATIONS

2. Describe the MIS at an organization, preferably one with which you have been associated. If you are not knowledgeable about the MIS, talk with someone who is.

Automation: **Automation** *is the simplification or reduction of human effort to do a job.* Computers and other machines have allowed some jobs, such as inspecting, cleaning, guarding, and assembling parts, to be done by robots. Automation does not take away jobs; it changes the types of jobs. The need for training and higher levels of skills will continue in the future, while the demand for unskilled jobs will continue to decrease.[19] A college education should help you to be flexible and continue to upgrade your skills with technological changes. If you want pay increases and promotions, be the first to volunteer to learn new technologies.

3. Describe an automation change in an organization, preferably one with which you have been associated.

Structural Change

It is important to coordinate structure with technology.[20] *Structure* refers to the type of organization principle and departments used, as discussed in Chapter 5.

Task and People Change

Task refers to the day-to-day things that employees do to perform their jobs. Tasks change with technology and structural changes. As tasks change, people's skills must change. Employee retraining is an ongoing process. In some cases, organizations must hire new people with the necessary skills.

It is people that create, manage, and use technology; therefore, people are the most important resource.[21] What people often resist are the social changes brought about by technological changes. Business success is based on optimizing the integration of both people and technology. This integration is known as *creating a sociotechnical system.* When changing task, structure, or technology, you should never forget the impact of change on people. Changing any of these other variables will not be effective without considering people change. We will talk more about how technology affects behavior in Chapter 14.

In the opening case about Rider Insurance being bought by NYCIC, the primary change is structural. Rider is no longer a separate entity; it is part of NYCIC. NYCIC will most likely change the structure at Rider to match its present structure. With the change in structure, most likely the tasks, technology, and people will also change. See Exhibit 12–1 for a review of the types of changes.

Learning Objective

2. Describe the four types of changes

EXHIBIT 12–1   **TYPES OF CHANGES**

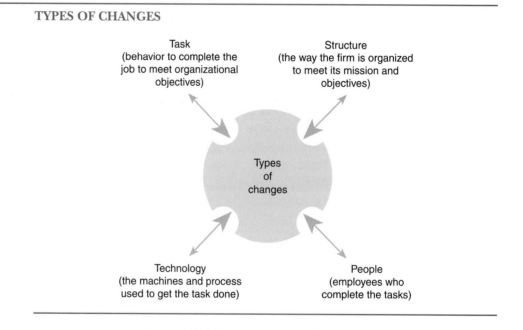

Task
(behavior to complete the job to meet organizational objectives)

Structure
(the way the firm is organized to meet its mission and objectives)

Types of changes

Technology
(the machines and process used to get the task done)

People
(employees who complete the tasks)

---

4. Give one or more examples of a type of change you experienced in an organization. (Identify it as task change, structural change, technological change, or people change.)

Types of Changes

AS 12–1

Identify the type of change as:

A. Task change   C. Technological change

B. Structural change   D. People change

_____ 1. "Jim, from now on, you have to fill in this new form every time you deliver a package."

_____ 2. "Due to the increase in the size of our department, we will now split into two departments."

_____ 3. "Kelly is taking Ray's place, now that he has retired."

_____ 4. "From now on, purchases under $300 will no longer need to be approved by the purchasing manager."

_____ 5. "Kim, report to the training center to learn proper procedures."

Stages in the Change Process

Most people go through four distinct stages in the change process:

1. *Denial.* When people first hear rumors through the grapevine that change is coming, they deny that it will happen at all, or to them. The "it will affect the others, but not me" reaction is common.

2. *Resistance.* Once people get over the initial shock and realize that change is going to be a reality, they resist the change. The next section examines resistance to change and how to overcome it.

3. *Exploration.* When the change begins to be implemented, employees explore the change, often through training,[22] and better understand how it will affect them. Training is an organizational development technique that you will learn about later in this chapter.

4. *Commitment.* Through exploration, employees determine their level of commitment to making the change a success. The level of commitment can change over time.

In the opening case, employees at both Rider and NYCIC will be going through the stages of the change process. How successfully change process is implemented will affect the behavior, human relations, and performance of the two businesses, which are now one company.

Exhibit 12–2 illustrates the stages in the change process. Notice that the stages are in a circular formation because change is an ongoing process, not a linear one, and people can regress as the arrows show.

Resistance to Change and How to Overcome It

About 15% of workers in any firm actively resist change,[23] and their resistance should be overcome.[24] People resist change for a variety of reasons, some of which include: (1) *status quo*[25] (people like things the way they are now, view the change as an inconvenience such as bad timing, or don't agree that a change is needed), (2) uncertainty[26] (people tend to fear the unknown and wonder how the change will affect them), (3) *learning anxiety*[27] (the prospect of learning something new itself produces anxiety) or (4) *fear*[28] (people often fear they may lose their job, the friends they work with may change, or that they will not be successful with learning new ways, and that they may lose control over how they do their jobs, etc.). You will learn why people resist change and how to overcome it.

EXHIBIT 12–2   STAGES IN THE CHANGE PROCESS

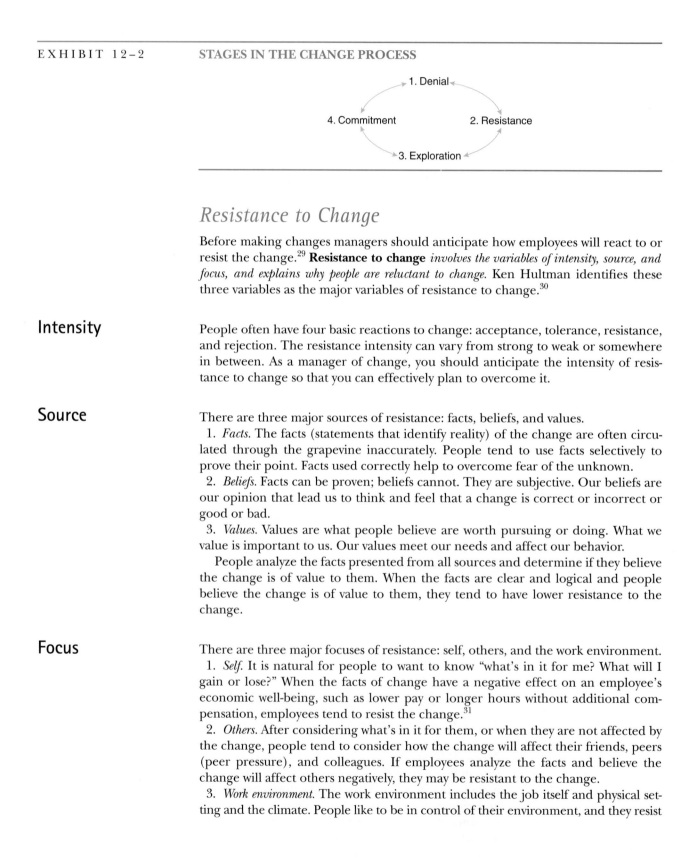

Resistance to Change

Before making changes managers should anticipate how employees will react to or resist the change.[29] **Resistance to change** *involves the variables of intensity, source, and focus, and explains why people are reluctant to change.* Ken Hultman identifies these three variables as the major variables of resistance to change.[30]

Intensity

People often have four basic reactions to change: acceptance, tolerance, resistance, and rejection. The resistance intensity can vary from strong to weak or somewhere in between. As a manager of change, you should anticipate the intensity of resistance to change so that you can effectively plan to overcome it.

Source

There are three major sources of resistance: facts, beliefs, and values.

1. *Facts.* The facts (statements that identify reality) of the change are often circulated through the grapevine inaccurately. People tend to use facts selectively to prove their point. Facts used correctly help to overcome fear of the unknown.

2. *Beliefs.* Facts can be proven; beliefs cannot. They are subjective. Our beliefs are our opinion that lead us to think and feel that a change is correct or incorrect or good or bad.

3. *Values.* Values are what people believe are worth pursuing or doing. What we value is important to us. Our values meet our needs and affect our behavior.

People analyze the facts presented from all sources and determine if they believe the change is of value to them. When the facts are clear and logical and people believe the change is of value to them, they tend to have lower resistance to the change.

Focus

There are three major focuses of resistance: self, others, and the work environment.

1. *Self.* It is natural for people to want to know "what's in it for me? What will I gain or lose?" When the facts of change have a negative effect on an employee's economic well-being, such as lower pay or longer hours without additional compensation, employees tend to resist the change.[31]

2. *Others.* After considering what's in it for them, or when they are not affected by the change, people tend to consider how the change will affect their friends, peers (peer pressure), and colleagues. If employees analyze the facts and believe the change will affect others negatively, they may be resistant to the change.

3. *Work environment.* The work environment includes the job itself and physical setting and the climate. People like to be in control of their environment, and they resist

changes that take away their control. Employees' analysis of the facts about the current versus the changed work environment will affect their resistance to the change.

Exhibit 12–3 is an adapted version of Ken Hultman's resistance matrix with examples of each area of resistance. For instance, in box 1, "facts about self," note that one reason given is "I never did it before." Understanding reasons behind people resisting change will make you better able to anticipate and deal with those reasons. However, resistance may come from more than one focus and source (box). Use the matrix to identify the intensity, source, and focus of resistance. Once you have identified the probable resistance to change, you can work at overcoming it. Overcoming resistance to change is the next topic.

WORK APPLICATIONS

5. Describe a situation in which you were resistant to change. Identify the intensity, source, and focus. Use Exhibit 12–3 to identify the box by number and statement about the resistance.

EXHIBIT 12–3   **RESISTANCE MATRIX**

Sources of Resistance (facts → beliefs → values)

1. Facts about self	4. Beliefs about self	7. Values pertaining to self
I never did it before.	I'm too busy to do it.	I like the job I have now better.
I failed the last time I tried.	I'll do it, but I'll mess up.	I don't want to change; I'm happy.
All my friends are here.	I don't think I can accept the change.	I like working alone.
2. Facts about others	**5. Beliefs about others**	**8. Values pertaining to others**
He's on probation.	She pretends to be busy to avoid extra work.	Let someone else train her; I'm not interested.
She has two children.	He's better at it than I am; let him do it.	What you really think really doesn't matter to me.
Other people told me it's hard to do.	She never understands our side.	I don't give a . . . about him.
3. Facts about the work environment	**6. Beliefs about the work environment**	**9. Values pertaining to the environment**
Why should do it?	This is a lousy place to work.	Who cares what the goals are? I just do my job.
I'm not getting paid extra.	The pay here is terrible.	The salary is more important than the benefits.
I haven't been trained to do it.	It's who you know, not what you know around here that counts.	This job gives me the chance to work outside.
I make less than anyone else in the department.		

Focus of Resistance (self → others → work)

Source: Adapted from Ken Hultman's resistance matrix, *The Path of Least Resistance* (Austin, Tex.: Learning Concepts, 1979).

Identifying Resistance to Change

AS 12–2

Below are five statements made by employees asked to make a change on the job. Identify the source, focus, and intensity of their resistance using Exhibit 12–3. Place the number of the box (1 to 9) that represents and best describes the major resistance.

_____ 6. The police sergeant asked Sue, the patrol officer, to take a rookie cop as her partner. Sue said, "Do I have to? I broke in the last rookie."

_____ 7. The tennis coach asked Bill, the star player, to have Jim as his doubles partner. Bill said, "Come on, Jim is a lousy player. Peter is better; don't break us up." The coach disagreed and forced Bill to accept Jim.

_____ 8. The supervisor realized that Sharon always used the accommodating conflict style. The supervisor told her to stop giving in to everyone's wishes. Sharon said, "But I like people, and I want them to like me, too."

_____ 9. The employee went to Sim, the supervisor, and asked him if she could change the work-order form. Sim said, "That would be a waste of time; the current form is fine."

_____ 10. Ann, an employee, is busy at work. The supervisor tells her to stop what she is doing and begin a new project. Ann says, "The job I'm working on now is more important."

Overcoming Resistance to Change

Below are some of the major methods managers can use to overcome resistance to change.

 Goal of Human Relations

Develop a Positive Climate for Change: Develop and maintain good human relations.[32] Because change and trust are so closely intertwined, the manager's first concern should be to develop mutual trust.[33] Develop cooperation and interdependence within the department. Cooperation carries over into times of change.

Encourage Interest in Improvement: Continually give employees opportunities to develop new skills, abilities, and creativity.[34] Constantly look for better ways to do things. Encouraging employees to suggest changes and listening to and implementing their ideas are important parts of continuous improvement.[35]

Plan: Implementing changes successfully takes good planning. You need to identify the possible resistances to change and plan how to overcome them. Put yourself in the employee's position. Don't consider how you as manager would react because a manager perceives things differently. What seems very simple and logical to you may not be to an employee.[36] Set clear objectives. As stated previously, use a systems approach to planning. A change in one variable like technology will also have effects on social relations, and so forth. The next eight methods should be part of your plan.

Give Facts: Get all the facts and plan how you will present them to the employees. Giving half-answers will only make employees more confused and angry, and hiding things and lying is a disaster.[37] But you can't let bad news dribble out in small pieces because then you'll lose credibility. Giving the facts as far in advance as possible helps to overcome the fear of the unknown. If the grapevine starts to send incorrect information, correct it as quickly as possible.

Clearly State Why the Change Is Needed and How It Will Affect Employees:

As part of giving the facts, you need to remember that employees want and need to know why the change is needed and how it will affect them both positively and negatively.[38] Be open and honest with employees.[39] If employees understand why the change is needed, and it makes sense to them, they will be more willing to change. It is important to create a sense of urgency in order to kill complacency and get employees to want to change.[40]

Create a Win–Win Situation:

Recall that the goal of human relations is to meet the employees' needs while achieving departmental/organizational objectives. To overcome resistance to change, be sure to answer the other parties' unasked question, "What's in it for me?" When people can see the benefits to them, they are more willing to change. If the organization is going to benefit by the change, so should the employees, when possible.

Involve Employees:

To create a win-win situation, involve employees. A commitment to change is usually critical to its successful implementation.[41] Employees who participate in developing changes are more committed to them than employees who have changes assigned to them.[42]

Provide Support:

Allow employees to express their feelings in a positive way. Since training is very important to successful changes, give as much advance notice and training as possible before the change takes place. Giving thorough training helps reduce learning anxiety and helps employees realize they can be successful with the change.[43]

Stay Calm:

Emotional people tend to be defensive. When you are emotional, you may hear, but you don't listen well because you are resistant to change. If managers get emotional, they will likely cause employees to get emotional as well. Try not to do or say things that will make people emotional so that you don't create more resistance to change.[44]

Avoid Direct Confrontation:

Confrontation tends to make people emotional and more resistant to change.[45] A subtle approach is preferable to most people. A confrontational debate is risky. Trying to persuade people that their facts, beliefs, and values are wrong leads to resistance. What if you lose the debate? Avoid statements like "you're wrong; you don't know what you're talking about." "You're just stubborn/lazy."

Use Power and Ethical Politics:

Chapter 9 discussed how to get what you want through the use of power and politics. Getting what you want often involves change. So use your power and ethical political skill to implement changes.[46] Remember that the 10 methods for overcoming change should be a part of your plan for change. Below you will learn about planning for change.

See Exhibit 12–4 for a review of the methods for overcoming resistance to change.

▲ Goal of Human Relations

Learning Objective

3. State why people resist change and how to overcome it

EXHIBIT 12-4   **OVERCOMING RESISTANCE TO CHANGE**

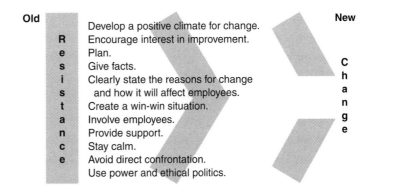

Old

R e s i s t a n c e

Develop a positive climate for change.
Encourage interest in improvement.
Plan.
Give facts.
Clearly state the reasons for change
    and how it will affect employees.
Create a win-win situation.
Involve employees.
Provide support.
Stay calm.
Avoid direct confrontation.
Use power and ethical politics.

New

C h a n g e

Responding to Resistance

Below are classifications of employee resistance types, resistant statements, and responses a manager could make to the employee to help overcome resistance to change. The following are presented to acquaint you with some of the possible resistance you may face, along with some possible responses you could make:

- **The blocker:** "I don't want to do it that way." Manager: "What are your objections to the change? How would you prefer to do it?"
- **The roller:** "What do you want me to do?" Manager: "I want you to . . ." (Be specific and describe the change in detail; use communication skills.)
- **The staller:** "I'll do it when I can." Manager: "What is more important?"
- **The reverser:** "That's a good idea." (But she or he never does it.) Manager: "What is it that you like about the change?"
- **The sidestepper:** "Why don't you have XYZ do it?" Manager: "I asked you to do it because . . ."
- **The threatener:** "I'll do it, but the guys upstairs will not like it." Manager: "Let me worry about it. What are *your* objections?"
- **The politician:** "You owe me one; let me slide." Manager: "I do owe you one, but I need the change. I'll pay you back later."
- **The traditionalist:** "That's not the way we do things around here." Manager: "This is a unique situation; it needs to be done."
- **The assaulter:** "You're a . . . (pick a word)." Manager: "I will not tolerate that type of behavior." Or, "This is really upsetting you, isn't it?"

The above supervisory responses will be helpful in most situations, but not all. If employees persist in resisting the change, they may need to be considered problem employees and handled accordingly.[47]

Change Models

Lewin's Change Model

It is important to know how to implement change.[48] So here are two change models, providing a pro-change orientation.[49] In the early 1950s, Kurt Lewin developed a technique, still used today, for changing people's behavior, skills, and attitudes. Lewin viewed the change process as consisting of three steps:

Step 1. Unfreezing: This step usually involves reducing those forces maintaining the status quo. Unfreezing is sometimes accomplished by introducing information that shows discrepancies between desired performance and actual performance.

Step 2. Moving: This step shifts the behavior to a new level. This is the change process in which employees learn the new desirable behavior, values, and attitudes. Structural, task, technological, and people changes may take place to reach desirable performance levels.

Step 3. Refreezing: The desirable performance becomes the permanent way of doing things. This is the new status quo. Refreezing often takes place through reinforcement and support for the new behavior.

See Exhibit 12–5 for a review of the steps.

Lussier's Change Model

Lewin's model provides a general framework for understanding organizational change. Because the steps of change are broad, the author has developed a more specific model. The model consists of five steps:

Step 1. Define the Change: Clearly state what the change is. Is it a task, structural, technological, or people change? What are the systems effects on the other variables? Set objectives, following the guidelines in Chapter 6.

EXHIBIT 12–5

CHANGE MODELS

Lewin's Change Model	Lussier's Change Model
Step 1. Unfreezing.	Step 1. Define the change.
Step 2. Moving.	Step 2. Identify possible resistance to the change.
Step 3. Refreezing.	Step 3. Plan the change.
	Step 4. Implement the change.
	Give the facts.
	Involve employees.
	Provide support.
	Step 5. Control the change (reinforcement of change).

Step 2. Identify Possible Resistance to the Change: Determine the intensity, source, and focus of possible resistance to the change. Use the resistance matrix in Exhibit 12–3.

Step 3. Plan the Change: Plan the change implementation. Use the appropriate supervisory style for the situation. We will discuss planned change (OD) in more detail later in this chapter.

Step 4. Implement the Change: This step has three parts:

Give facts. Give the facts about the change and explain why it is necessary, as far in advance of the change as possible. Explain how the change will affect the employees. Relate the change to their values.

Involve employees. Use as much employee involvement as you can. But use the appropriate supervisory style for the situation. (Follow the guidelines from Chapter 7.)

Provide support. Allow employees to express their thoughts and feelings in a positive way. Answer their questions openly and honestly. Make sure that they receive proper training in how to implement the changed method(s).

Step 5. Control the Change: Follow up to ensure that the change is implemented, reinforced, and maintained. Make sure the objective is met. If not, take corrective action. For major changes, be sure to change performance appraisals to reflect new jobs accurately.

For a review of the steps, see Exhibit 12–5.

If managers at NYCIC follow the guidelines for overcoming resistance to change and develop an effective plan using the change model, change can be implemented successfully at Rider.

Learning Objective

4. Explain how to use a change model when making changes

WORK APPLICATIONS

6. Give a specific example of when the change model would be helpful to a specific manager.

- Organization
- Group
- Individual

Organizational Culture

You have heard of national cultures, in which citizens of a country behave in certain ways; organizations have cultures, too.[50] For our purposes, **organizational culture** *consists of the shared values and assumptions of how its members will behave.*

Organizations can change and manage cultures.[51] Ford[52] and Navistar[53] are currently changing their cultures, which requires overcoming resistance to change. With the trend toward a diverse global economy, businesses are developing global business cultures that they view as a competitive advantage.[54] A culture of success changes over time, and businesses that fail to change their culture lose competitive advantage.[55] In this section, we examine strong and weak and positive and negative cultures.

Strong and Weak, Positive and Negative Cultures

Organizations that have clear values that are shared to the extent of similar behavior have strong cultures. Organizations that have no stated values and do not enforce behavior have weak cultures. Organizational cultures are created through art, songs, stories, symbols, rites, rituals, slogans, legendary heroes, and mottoes. Some examples of specific organizations with strong cultures include: Ford Motor Co. ("Quality is Job 1") and McDonald's ("Q, S, C, V,—Quality, Service, Cleanliness, and Value"). Other examples of strong cultures include:

IBM: Although IBM had problems and worked to change its culture, IBM is recognized as having a very strong culture. Having a strong culture does not mean the organization is successful. Strong cultures are often difficult to change.[56] Company founder Thomas J. Watson worked to develop IBM's unique culture long before it became popular to do so. IBM policy states that (1) all employees should be respected and treated with dignity; (2) the company should aim to accomplish every task in a superior way; and (3) the customer should be given the best service possible.

PepsiCo, Inc.: Unlike IBM, which stresses excellence, Pepsi's organizational culture stresses competition in every aspect of an employee's work life. Pepsi executives are jointly determined to surpass archrival Coca-Cola, while surpassing rival executives at PepsiCo. Managers are continually pressured to increase market share; a small decline can lead to a manager's dismissal. Pepsi also stresses good physical fitness and has a wellness program to help employees stay in shape.

J. C. Penney Company, Inc.: James Cash Penney established the following seven principles, which serve as its culture base: (1) to serve the public, as nearly as we can, to its complete satisfaction; (2) to expect, from the service we render, a fair remuneration and not all the profit the traffic will bear; (3) to do all in our power to pack the customer's dollar full of value, quality, and satisfaction; (4) to continue to train ourselves and our associates so that the service we give will be more and more intelligently performed; (5) to improve constantly the human factor in our business; (6) to reward men and women in our organization through participation in what the business produces; and (7) to test policy, methods, and act in this manner: "Does it square with what is right and just?"

As you can see, IBM stresses excellence; PepsiCo, competition; and J. C. Penney, fairness. They have different cultures, yet they are all successful organizations, which shows there is no one best organizational culture.

Positive and Negative Cultures

Learning Objective

5. Explain dimensions of an organization's culture

An organizational culture is considered positive when it contributes to effective performance and productivity. A negative organizational culture is a source of resistance and turmoil that hinders effective performance.

The most effective organizational culture that leads to effective performance is strong and positive. Such companies with strong positive cultures, not already listed, include Amdahl, Emerson Electric, Johnson & Johnson, Procter & Gamble, 3M, Dana Corporation, Marriott, Boeing, and Fluor.

Before accepting a job with an organization, you may want to learn about its culture to determine if it is the kind of organization you will enjoy working in. For example, if you are not competitive, you probably will not enjoy working for PepsiCo.

IE 12-1

In the opening case, Ronnie feels that NYCIC has a strong organizational culture, whereas Rider had a weak culture. NYCIC needs to develop the shared values and assumptions of how members behave at Rider. The OD team-building program (discussed later in this chapter) would be an excellent way to develop the NYCIC culture at Rider.

WORK APPLICATIONS

7. Describe the organizational culture at a firm you work/worked for. Does the organization strive to have a strong positive culture? If so, how?

Two popular dimensions of culture are diversity and quality. Organizations are creating cultures to manage and value diversity and cultures of total quality management. This chapter will discuss managing diversity and quality. The next chapter will focus more on valuing diversity.

Managing Diversity

As the global economy increases, the U.S. work force is becoming increasingly diverse. Organizations need to manage diversity to survive since a diverse work force will outperform a homogeneous one.[57]

Valuing Diversity versus Managing Diversity

Valuing diversity focuses on interpersonal qualities, such as race, gender, and age, whereas managing diversity looks at the diverse needs of employees, not their cultural diversity.[58] Managing diversity also requires putting policies and procedures in place to meet the diverse needs of employees.[59] For our purposes, **valuing diversity** *emphasizes training employees of different ages, sexes, and races to function effectively together;* **managing diversity** *emphasizes meeting all employee needs.* Managing diversity goes beyond valuing diversity to focus on the diversity of employees' work-life needs,[60] such as child care, family leave, and flexible work and holiday schedules.

Diversity Policies, Practices, and Training

As a starting point in managing diversity, organizations must develop policies that directly affect how employees are treated.[61] For the organization to truly offer equal employment opportunities, it must actively recruit, train, and promote a diverse work force without discrimination. Policies and procedures must also be developed to handle problems that arise from diversity. For example, if an African-American female complains of not being promoted because of race discrimination, how the complaint is handled will send a message throughout the organization. If excessive burden of proof is placed on the female, she is discouraged from complaining. And if the punishment for discrimination is minor for the guilty party, employees will get the message that discrimination is an accepted practice.

Organizations offer a wide variety of ongoing practices and procedures to meet the diverse needs of their employees. Some of the practices include:

- Diversity training programs help employees value employee differences. Training will be discussed in the organizational development section of this chapter.
- Flexible, often called *cafeteria,* benefits programs allow employees to select their benefit packages.
- Flexible work schedules enable employees to set, within limits, their own beginning and ending work hours.
- Telecommuting lets employees work at home.
- Child-care centers allow employees to bring their children to the job site.
- Family leave allows employees to take time off to care for a child or other relative.

- Counseling helps deal with job and family pressure, and substance abuse.
- Role models and mentoring programs help prepare lower-level employees for progression.
- Wellness programs help employees stay in good health through exercise and diet programs and help them stop smoking.

Some of the many organizations that offer diversity programs include: Levi Strauss & Company, McDonald's Corporation, Nestlé Beverage Company, Avon, Prudential, Hewlett-Packard, and LIMRA.

The Relationship between Culture and Diversity

Managing diversity is a process that must be managed and built into the culture and core value system of the organization through processes that affect everything the organization does. Managing diversity requires an organizational culture that values diversity, and meets the needs of all groups of workers. To be part of the culture, all employees from the top down must value diversity. The way employees know what is valued in the organization is by what management reinforces. Therefore, management must develop policies and practices that reward diversity, if diversity is to be a part of its culture.

WORK APPLICATIONS

8. Does the organization you identified in question 7 value diversity? If so, how? Give examples.

● Organization
● Group
● Individual

Learning Objective

6. Describe how diversity and quality are dimensions of organizational culture

Quality

As the global economy continues to expand, the need to offer quality products and services becomes more important to survival.[62] To offer quality products and services requires a change in culture.[63] A quality culture requires shared vision and values for quality. A quality culture is based on continuous improvement. Continuous improvement must come in every dimension of the organization, not just products and services.[64] A quality culture invites employees to be a part of an ongoing push for improvement. If an organization is to provide quality goods and services, it must have a culture that rewards those who do a good job.[65] Organizations are developing cultures that value quality

Managers tend to blame poor quality on employees. Many people believe workers don't care about quality and don't take pride in their work. Actually, the well-known 85-15 rule is more accurate: 85 percent of what goes wrong is because of the system, which is under the control of management, and only 15 percent of what goes wrong can be attributed to the employees who operate the system. In this section, we discuss total quality management, ISO 9000, and Six Sigma.

Total Quality Management

Quality *is the predetermined standard that the product or service should meet.* The standards vary. For example, the quality of Ford's Lincoln Town Car is higher than its Escort. But both cars meet their respective quality standards. **Total quality management (TQM)** *promotes a culture in which everyone in the organization strives for continual improvement in all dimensions of operations.* The primary focus of TQM is on customer satisfaction. Many organizations strive to exceed customer expectations.

A researcher studied 536 organizations that use TQM and concluded: (1) TQM does improve organizational performance; (2) organizations using TQM for more than three years have been successful in improving operational results, customer satisfaction and retention, and organizational climate; and (3) TQM is still a viable long-term business strategy[66] Some of the organizations using TQM include: Johnson & Johnson, Ford, Honeywell, Unisys, Xerox, Hewlett-Packard, Nasua, Banc One, and Allen-Bradley. L.L. Bean used TQM to increase customer satisfaction and boosted profits at the same time; in doing so, it became the winner of *Personnel Journal*'s Optimas Award for managing change. The most prestigious quality award is the Malcolm Baldrige National Quality Award.

The key to achieving TQM is to establish an agreed-upon set of objectives stated as standards for the product or service to meet. World-class organizations use elements of TQM along with a shared vision and systems thinking. Statistical process control (SPC) is used as a feedback method to statistically maintain consistent quality within narrow limits. With TQM the objectives continually change over time as products or services improve.

Products need to be designed so that they will not fail in the field; that is, quality is a virtue of design. If the product is designed effectively, there will be few defects in the factory and few returned products. Some recommend striving for zero defects as part of the TQM system. However, internal and external customer satisfaction is the primary aim of TQM.

People are the heart of TQM because they are responsible for continual improvements. TQM uses participative management techniques, which will be discussed in Chapter 14. Without effective human relations, TQM will not be effective. The late W. Edwards Deming developed 14 points for creating the TQM environment (see Exhibit 12–6).

ISO 9000

The International Standards Organization (ISO) certifies organizations that meet set quality standards. Manufacturing and service companies seeking ISO 9000 certification are required to document practices that affect the quality of products/services. They need to comply with the applicable guidelines embodied in standards ISO 9000, and higher numbers are now being used. Many companies seek ISO certification because of the benefits associated with being certified, since ISO is the hallmark of excellence. The number of applicants is expected to continue to grow as large companies, including GM and GE, require their suppliers to be certified.

Six Sigma

The cost of poor quality is typically 20–30% of revenues. Six Sigma is a revolutionary quality initiative that is fast becoming a world standard; it is based on the reality that higher levels of unbelievable quality at lower costs are urgently required to compete in the challenging and tough global economy. Six Sigma can reduce costs, rejects, lead times, and capital spending while raising employee skills and strengthen overall financial results.[67]

Six sigma's goal is only 3.4 defects or mistakes per million operations! Sigma is from the Greek alphabet and is used as a statistical term to measure deviations from a standard. Most companies operate at the Three sigma level, or 66,000 defects per million.[68] Six Sigma is grounded in math, statistics, data analysis, finance, and computer skills. It heavily emphasizes measurement sciences and achieving measurable bottom-line results.[69]

Motorola first advanced Six Sigma around 1986.[70] Motorola has saved $15 billion over eleven years, and GE produced more than $2 billion in benefits in 1999 because of the methodology.[71] Weyerhaeuser reduced defects in the customer-service department's product specifications by 85%.[72]

EXHIBIT 12–6   DEMING'S 14 POINTS FOR CREATING THE TOTAL QUALITY ENVIRONMENT

1. Create constancy of purpose toward improvement of product and service, with the aim to become competitive, to stay in business, and to provide jobs.

2. Adopt a new philosophy. We are in a new economic age created by Japan. We can no longer live with commonly accepted styles of American management, nor with commonly accepted levels of delays, mistakes, or defective products.

3. Cease dependence on inspection to achieve quality. Eliminate the need for inspection on a mass basis by building quality into the product in the first place.

4. End the practice of awarding business on the basis of price tag. Instead, minimize total cost.

5. Improve constantly and forever the system of production and service to improve quality and productivity, and thus constantly decrease costs.

6. Institute training on the job.

7. Institute supervision: The aim of supervision should be to help people and machines and gadgets do a better job. Supervision of management is in need of overhaul, as well as supervision of production workers.

8. Drive out fear so that everyone may work effectively for the company.

9. Break down the barriers between departments. People in research, design, sales, and production must work as a team to foresee problems of production and use that may be encountered with the product or service.

10. Eliminate slogans, exhortations, and targets for the work force that ask for zero defects and new levels of productivity. Such exhortations only create adversarial relationships. The bulk of the causes of low productivity belong to the system, and thus lie beyond the power of the work force.

11. Eliminate work standards that prescribe numerical quotas for the day. Substitue aids and helpful supervision.

12. Remove the barriers that rob the hourly worker of his right to pride of workmanship. The responsibility of supervisors must be changed from sheer numbers to quality. Remove the barriers that rob people in management and engineering of their right to pride of workmanship. This means abolishment of the annual rating, or merit rating, and management by objective.

13. Institute a vigorous program of education and retraining.

14. Put everybody in the company to work to accomplish the transformation.

To apply Six Sigma methods requires extensive training. In 1999, over 50,000 people trained in the approach, and the number continues to grow quickly as corporate giants including Citicorp and Johnson & Johnson, and their suppliers, train their employees, as Six Sigma is the hot-button issue of the day.[73]

WORK APPLICATIONS

9. Does the organization you identified in questions 7 and 8 strive for quality? If so, how? Give examples.

● Organization
● Group
● Individual

Organizational Climate

Organizational climate is a broad term. The definition will be explained throughout this section. **Organizational climate** *is the relatively enduring quality of the internal environment of the organization perceived by its members.* Climate is employees' perception of the atmosphere of the internal environment.

The major difference between culture and climate is as follows: Culture is based on shared values and assumptions of "how" things should be done (ideal environment), while climate is based on shared perceptions of the "way" things are done (intangibles of the actual internal environment). An organization can claim to have a strong culture and have a negative climate. Employees can know how things should be, while being dissatisfied with their perception of the way things actually are. For example, in some organizations managers claim that quality is very important; signs are posted telling everyone it is. But if you ask employees if quality is important, they say management only cares about how many units are actually shipped out the door. Successful companies tend to have strong cultures and positive climates.

Organizational climate is important because the employees' perception of the organization serves as the basis for the development of their attitudes toward it. Their attitudes in turn affect their behavior. Climate is concerned with the entire organization or major subunits within it. While the organization has an overall climate, specific work group climates may be different. For example, an entire company may have a positive, friendly climate while one of its departments has a negative climate.

Job satisfaction, discussed in Chapter 3, is primarily based on organizational climate.[74] Morale is also an important part of organizational climate. **Morale** *is a state of mind based on attitudes and satisfaction with the organization.* Morale can be different at various levels within the organization. Morale is commonly measured on a continuum ranging from high to low morale, based on seven dimensions of climate listed below.

Dimensions of Climate

Some of the common dimensions of climate include:

- Structure. The degree of constraint on members—the number of rules, regulations, and procedures.
- Responsibility. The degree of control over one's own job.
- Rewards. The degree of being rewarded for one's efforts and being punished appropriately.
- Warmth. The degree of satisfaction with human relations.
- Support. The degree of being helped by others and of experiencing cooperation.
- Organizational identity and loyalty. The degree to which employees identify with the organization and their loyalty to it.
- Risk. The degree to which risk taking is encouraged.

Learning Objective

7. Explain dimensions of an organization's climate

Climate and Performance

Studies show that poor climate tends to result in lower levels of performance, but not always. Performance tends to be better when climate dimensions are logically consistent with one another. Like plants, employees require a proper climate to thrive. Working in a climate you enjoy will also affect your performance. You can be more innovative and creative in a climate compatible with your needs.[75] Because culture and climate are so important, organizations screen employees to select the ones who fit the culture.[76]

You can develop an effective productive climate by focusing on the dimensions of climate. Often, large companies like NYCIC take over a smaller company like Rider because they are successful. In too many situations, the larger company changes the flexible entrepreneurial climate to one of bureaucracy, resulting in the small company becoming less productive. NYCIC needs to focus on these seven dimensions of climate. For Rider to have a positive climate, NYCIC should provide a structure that minimizes rules and red tape and encourages employees to take risks. Employees should have control over their own jobs and should be rewarded based on performance. The two companies are becoming one; therefore, warm,

■ Performance
■ Human Relations
■ Behavior

supportive human relations should be developed for cooperation and a smooth change. The Rider employees need to shift identity and loyalty to NYCIC.

See Exhibit 12–7 for a list of the dimensions of climate.

EXHIBIT 12–7   **DIMENSIONS OF CLIMATE**

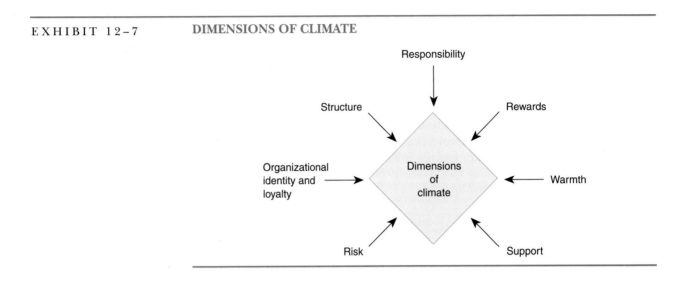

WORK APPLICATIONS

10. Describe the organizational climate at a firm you work/worked for, based on the seven dimensions of climate. Does the organization measure its climate? If so, how?

11. Describe the morale at an organization you work/worked for.

APPLICATION SITUATIONS

Organizational Culture or Climate?

AS 12–3

Identify each statement as being associated with:

A. Organizational culture   B. Organizational climate

_____ 11. Rotary International's motto, "Service above Self."

_____ 12. "Employees were not happy with this year's raise."

_____ 13. "Please fill out this questionnaire and return it to the personnel department when you are done."

_____ 14. "The unwritten dress code is a suit and tie for work."

_____ 15. "From now on, no one but you will check the quality of your work."

● Organization
● Group
● Individual

Organizational Development

Organizations that change and manage culture include: Tektronix, Procter & Gamble, TRW, Polaroid, Pacific Telesis, Pacific Mutual, Fiat, and the City of San Diego. These organizations realize that managing culture and climate is not a program within a few departments with starting and ending dates. It is an ongoing organizationwide process called *organizational development (OD)*. **Organizational development** *is the ongoing planned process of change used as a means of improving the organization's effectiveness in solving problems and achieving its objectives.*

Managing and Changing Culture and Climate through OD

To manage organizational culture, top management must define the attitudes, values, and expectations they want organizational members to share. (Remember IBM's list of three principles and J. C. Penney's list of seven principles discussed earlier.) Current values that organizations are transforming include diversity and quality. After values and expectations are defined, they must be communicated effectively to employees for employees to adopt them.

The first step in organizational development is diagnosis of the problem(s). Indicators that problems exist, such as conflicts between diverse groups, the need for increased quality and productivity, lower profits, and excessive absenteeism or turnover, lead management to call in a change agent to study the problems and needs. A change agent is the person responsible for the OD program. The change agent can use a variety of methods to diagnose problems. Some methods include reviewing records, observation, interviewing individuals and work groups, holding meetings, and/or using questionnaires. After the problem has been diagnosed, OD techniques are used to solve it.

This section examines five OD techniques: training and development, Grid OD, survey feedback, force field analysis, and team building. Training and development is presented first because the other four techniques usually include training.

Training and Development

Training and development commonly follows a five-step process:

Step 1. Needs Assessment: The needs assessment is based on the OD diagnosis of the problem. If the problem is diversity or quality, for example, then the training program will focus on this area.

Step 2. Set Objectives: The key to the training program is well-defined performance-based objectives. Levi Strauss & Company has a $5-million-a-year valuing-diversity educational program designed to get employees to become more tolerant of personal differences.

Step 3. Prepare for Training: With the objectives in hand, the training and development specialist uses prepared activities, or develops activities, to meet the objectives. Activities vary and may include videos, lectures, discussions, and role playing.

Step 4. Conduct the Training: The training takes place as planned.

Step 5. Measure and Evaluate Training Results: During and after the training program, results are measured and evaluated to determine if the objectives were met. If not, continued training may take place. The results of the first group of trainees are often used to improve the results of future groups who go through the training.

Management at NYCIC will have to determine the training needs of Rider employees, set objectives, prepare for training, conduct the training, and evaluate results so that the two units can work effectively as one organization.

Grid OD®

Robert Blake and Jane Mouton developed a "packaged" approach to OD. They developed a standardized format, procedures, and fixed goals. Blake and Mouton, or their associates, conduct the program for organizations. **Grid OD** *is a six-phase program designed to improve management and organizational effectiveness.* The six phases include:[77]

Phase 1. Training: Teams of five to nine managers, ideally from different functional areas, are formed. During a week-long seminar, each team member assesses his or her leadership style by determining where on the grid they are. They work at becoming 9,9 managers by developing skills in the areas of team building, communication, and problem solving.

Phase 2. Team Development:
Managers return to the job and try to use their new skills as 9,9 managers.

Phase 3. Intergroup Development:
Work groups improve their ability to cooperate and coordinate their efforts. This fosters joint problem-solving activities.

Phase 4. Organizational Goal Setting:
Management develops an organization model that it strives to become.

Phase 5. Goal Attainment:
The necessary changes to become the model organization are determined and implemented.

Phase 6. Stabilization:
The first five phases are evaluated to determine and stabilize positive changes, and to identify areas for improvement or alteration.

Survey Feedback

Survey feedback *is an OD technique that uses a questionnaire to gather data that are used as the basis for change.* Different change agents will use slightly different approaches; however, a commonly used survey feedback program would include six steps:

1. Management and the change agent do some preliminary planning to develop an appropriate survey questionnaire.

2. The questionnaire is administered to all members of the organization/unit.

3. The survey data are analyzed to uncover problem areas for improvement.

4. The change agent feeds back the results to management.

5. Managers evaluate the feedback and discuss the results with their subordinates.

6. Corrective action plans are developed and implemented.

A consultant was called by a large manufacturer to discuss training. He met with the managers of industrial engineering and manufacturing engineering. They informed the consultant of a survey that had been conducted (Steps 1–3). The feedback results had shown engineers as being low in organizational performance (Step 4). The three engineering managers had met with their engineers and discussed the reasons for the low rating and ways to change their image (Step 5). They decided to have the engineers go through a human relations/communication skill-building training program to improve their ability to interact more effectively with the organizational members whom they served. The consultant developed and conducted a training program that helped change/correct the situation (Step 6).

Measuring Climate   The survey feedback technique is commonly used to measure the organizational climate.[78] Based on the results, the organization may set up training programs as described above. Some of the signs that an organization may have a climate problem include high tardiness, absenteeism, and turnover. When employees have many complaints, sabotage each other's work, talk about unionization or striking, lack pride in their work, and have low morale, the organization may have a climate problem that should be corrected.

Organizational climate is measured in the same way job satisfaction is (review Chapter 3). Survey feedback is the most common approach. But the dimensions included in the questionnaire vary from organization to organization.

In Skill-Building Exercise 12–2, you are asked to complete a questionnaire. You may want to review it now as a sample climate measurement instrument.

 Skill-Building
12–1

Force Field Analysis

Force field analysis *is a technique that diagrams the current level of performance, the hindering forces toward change, and the driving forces toward change.* The process begins by appraising the current level of performance. The present level of performance is shown in the middle of the diagram. The hindering forces holding back performance are listed in the top part of the diagram. The driving forces keeping performance at this level are listed on the bottom of the diagram. See Exhibit 12–8. After viewing the diagram, you develop strategies for maintaining or increasing the driving forces with simultaneous steps for decreasing hindering forces. For example, in Exhibit 12–8, the solution you select could be to have the salespeople go through a training program. You could spend more time working with the less productive salespeople. Speeding up delivery time could be worked on, while maintaining all of the driving forces could lead to higher sales volume.

EXHIBIT 12–8   **FORCE FIELD ANALYSIS**

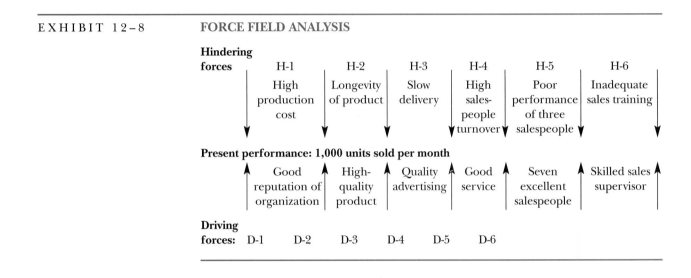

Force field analysis is particularly useful for group problem solving. After group members agree on the diagram, the solution often becomes clear to them.

Video
BM–12

Team Building

Team building is probably the most widely used OD technique today. Individuals work as part of a unit or department, and each small functional group of individuals that works closely and interdependently makes up a team. The effectiveness of each team and all the teams working together directly affects the results of the entire organization.[79] So, in an attempt to develop organizational effectiveness, team building is used.[80] **Team building** *is an OD technique designed to help work groups operate more effectively.*

Team building is widely used as a means of helping new or existing groups that are in need of improving effectiveness. For example, Dr. Miriam Hirsch was called in as a consultant by a medical center and told that there was a restructuring of administrative responsibility. The medical center changed to a three-member team management approach. Doctors were no longer sole decision makers; they had to work with a management nurse and an administrative person. Because these managers were not used to teamwork, the consultant was asked to propose a team-building program to help them develop their skills.

Team-Building Goals

The goals of team-building programs will vary considerably, depending upon the group needs and the change agent's skills. Some of the typical goals are:

- To clarify the objectives of the team and the responsibilities of each team member.
- To identify problems preventing the team from accomplishing its objectives.
- To develop team problem-solving and decision-making, objective-setting, and planning skills.
- To determine a preferred style of teamwork and to change to that style.
- To fully utilize the resources of each individual member.
- To develop open, honest working relationships based on trust and an understanding of group members.

The Change Agent's Responsibilities

Generally, the change agent first meets with the manager to discuss why a team-building program will be conducted. They discuss the goals of the program. The change agent assesses the manager's willingness to get feedback on how the team feels about his or her style and practices. The supervisor's receptiveness to the program will directly affect the potential of the team-building results.

The change agent and manager meet with the team. An atmosphere of openness and trust begins with the change agent describing the goals, agenda, and procedures of the team-building program. The change agent describes the agreement with the manager.

The change agent may interview each team member privately and confidentially to identify group problems. In addition to, or in place of, the interviews, a survey feedback questionnaire may be used. A sample questionnaire appears in Preparation for In-Class Skill-Building Exercise 12–1.

The change agent conducts the team-building program in one or more days, depending upon the problems and the number of members.

Team-Building Program Agenda

The team-building agendas vary with team needs and the change agent's skills. Typical agenda topics include:

1. *Climate building.* The program begins with the change agent trying to develop a climate of trust, support, and openness. He or she discusses the program's purpose and objectives. Team members learn more about each other and share what they would like to accomplish in the session.
2. *Process and structure evaluation.* The team evaluates the strengths and weaknesses of its process. The team explores and selects ideal norms.
3. *Problem identification.* The team identifies its strengths, then its weaknesses or areas where improvement is possible. The problems come from the change agent's interviews and/or the feedback survey. The team first lists several areas where improvement is possible. Then it prioritizes them by importance in helping the team improve performance.
4. *Problem solving.* The team takes the top priority and develops a solution. It then moves to the second priority, followed by the third, then fourth, and so on.
5. *Training.* Team building often includes some form of training that addresses the problem(s) facing the group.
6. *Closure.* The program ends by summarizing what has been accomplished. Follow-up responsibility is assigned. Team members commit to improving performance.

 Skill-Building
12–2
IE 12–2
IE 12–3

At Rider, a good starting place for OD would be team-building sessions. In teams, Rider employees could be made aware of NYCIC's OD program and how Rider will be developed. Through team-building sessions, the planned changes of NYCIC could be implemented at Rider. After a period of months, NYCIC could use survey feedback to determine how the change program at Rider is perceived. The

Learning Objective

8. Describe five OD techniques

survey could serve as the basis for understanding the need for future change at Rider. As the teams develop at Rider, they can use force field analysis to work out problems the new changes bring, and to reach higher levels of performance as part of their team-building program.

WORK APPLICATIONS

12. Identify an OD technique and explain how it is used by a specific organization, preferably one with which you have been associated.

APPLICATION SITUATIONS

OD Techniques

AS 12–4

Below are five situations in which an OD technique would be beneficial. Identify the most appropriate technique for each.

A. Force field analysis   D. Training
B. Survey feedback   E. Team building
C. Grid OD

_____ 16. "We need to teach employees statistical process control techniques."

_____ 17. "We are a progressive company; we believe in developing our people. We'd like to make a good organization even better."

_____ 18. "To improve productivity, we should identify the things that are holding us back and the things that are helping us be productive, too."

_____ 19. "We want an OD program that will enable us to better utilize the input of each manager."

_____ 20. "Morale and motivation are low in our organization. We'd like to know why and change."

● Organization
● Group
● Individual

Learning Objective

9. Explain the relationship among organizational culture, diversity, quality, climate, and development

The Relationship among Organizational Culture, Climate, and Development

Organizational culture, climate, and development are all different, yet related. Climate is a sharing of perceptions of intangibles of the *internal* environment, while culture is the values and assumptions of the *ideal* environment. Thus, culture informs climate. Often the concept of culture encompasses that of climate. However, in recent years, the concern with culture has increased, while the importance of the concept of climate has decreased. At the present time, the focus of culture is on valuing diversity and quality.

Organizational development is commonly used as the vehicle to change culture or climate. Organizational development programs tend to be wider in scope than culture or climate. Culture and climate changes can be a part of an extensive OD program addressing other issues as well.

NYCIC can overcome the resistance to change at Rider through a planned organizational development program involving team building. The OD program can be based on the change model. Through team building, NYCIC can change the culture and climate at Rider to be the same as that of NYCIC.

REVIEW

Select one or more methods: (1) fill in the missing key terms from memory; (2) match the key terms, from the end of the review, with their definitions below; and/or (3) copy the key terms in order from the key terms list at the beginning of the chapter.

Managing change skills are important for the manager when performing the five functions of management. The four major _____ are task change, structural change, technological change, and people change. A change in one variable affects one or more of the other variables.

_____ are formal systems for collecting, processing, and disseminating the information necessary to aid managers in decision making.

_____ is the simplification or reduction of human effort to do a job. The stages in the change process are: (1) denial, (2) resistance, (3) exploration, and (4) commitment.

_____ involves the variables of intensity, source, and focus, and explains why people are reluctant to change. Intensity refers to the level of resistance people have toward the change. There are three sources of resistance: facts, beliefs, and values. The three focuses of resistance to change are self, others, and the work environment. To overcome resistance to change, managers can (1) develop a positive climate for change; (2) encourage interest in improvement; (3) plan; (4) give facts; (5) clearly state the reasons for change and how it will affect employees; (6) create a win-win situation; (7) involve employees; (8) provide support; (9) stay calm; (10) avoid direct confrontation; and (11) use power and ethical politics. The three steps in the Lewin Change Model are (1) unfreezing, (2) moving, and (3) refreezing. The Lussier Change Model has five steps: (1) define the change; (2) identify possible resistance to the change; (3) plan the change; (4) implement the change—give facts, involve employees, and provide support; and (5) control the change.

_____ consists of the shared values and assumptions of how its members will behave. Culture can be strong or weak, positive or negative, and it can be managed and changed. _____ emphasizes training employees of different ages, sexes, and races to function effectively together, whereas _____ emphasizes meeting all employee needs. To manage diversity and quality requires policies, practices, and training.

_____ promotes a culture in which everyone in the organization strives for continual improvements in all dimensions of operations.

Deming developed 14 points of the TQM environment. The International Standards Organization (ISO) certifies firms that meet its set quality standard processes. Six Sigma's goal is only 3.4 defects or mistakes per million operations.

_____ is the relatively enduring quality of the internal environment of the organization perceived by its members.

_____ is a state of mind based on attitudes and satisfaction with the organization. There are seven dimensions of climate that can be measured. They are structure, responsibility, rewards, warmth, support, risk, and organizational identity and loyalty.

_____ is the ongoing planned process of change used as a means of improving the organization's effectiveness in solving problems and achieving its objectives. Five OD techniques are: (1) training and development; (2) _____ , a six-phase program to improve management and organizational effectiveness; (3) _____ , a technique that uses a questionnaire to gather data that are used as the basis for change; (4) _____ , a technique that diagrams the current level of performance, the hindering forces toward change, and the driving forces toward change; and (5) _____ , a technique designed to help work groups operate more effectively.

Organizational culture informs climate and can be changed through organizational development programs. Valuing diversity and quality are currently popular dimensions of culture.

KEY TERMS

automation   415
force field analysis   433
Grid OD   431
management information
   systems (MIS)   414
managing diversity   425
morale   429

organizational climate   428
organizational culture   423
organizational
   development   430
quality   426
resistance to change   418
survey feedback   432

team building   433
total quality
   management
   (TQM)   426
types of changes   414
valuing diversity   425

CASE

Eastman Kodak

Eastman Kodak Company was a very strong leader in the U.S. market in the 1970s. Kodak used the export global strategy of making products for the U.S. market in several plants and shipping them to domestic and foreign customers. Kodak was losing its strong leadership position as competition increased from the Japanese. One of its problem areas of business, best known to the public, was its photographic products. The Japanese came out with the 35-millimeter camera while Kodak ignored the market for too long and gave the first-mover advantage to the Japanese companies. Kodak also unsuccessfully spent years and millions of dollars to develop an instant camera to compete with Polaroid, and got sued in the process for patent infringement. In the film area, it was losing market share to Fuji and other companies. On top of the heavy competition, the price of silver rose dramatically. Kodak was in a crisis because silver was a critical raw material in its photographic products. Today's challenge is the digital camera age, and its change was designed to keep Kodak competitive in the future.

Planning for Change

Top managers identified three major factors contributing to problems at Kodak. First of all, costs were too high. Second, information at the bottom of the operation was not being shared throughout the company, and managers were not being held accountable for performance. Third, strategic planning was developed by staff specialists but not implemented by the line managers. In other words, the planning process was not working. Based on these factors, departmentalization was considered to be the cause of many of Kodak's problems.

Kodak's functional departments focused on manufacturing, marketing, R&D, and finance. However, it seemed to the top managers that the global environment required the company to respond to the environment based on businesses rather than funcitons. With functional departments, no one was responsible for performance. The decision was made to change from functional to divisional departmentalization. The next decision was how to plan and implement the departmental change. A common approach was to have a group of four or five managers make the new organization chart behind closed doors and then dictate the change. Managers were concerned about making the reorganization a success, so they decided to use participative management to implement the change following these steps:

The top three managers developed a new organization. Then they met with the nine line managers, who would be affected by the change, and explain the new organization and the rationale as to why it was required. Part of the rationale was to become more competitive through developing new products at a faster rate. Top managers simply told the nine line managers to go off and think about the reorganization and then come back and discuss it. Line managers were to challenge, question, understand, improve it, and most importantly to feel as though it is "our" reorganization. After four months, the team of 12 had a reorganization plan.

The team of 12 was expanded to the top 50 managers who went through roughly the same process. At the end of five months, 62 managers had a reorganization plan. The 62 widened to the top 150 managers. However, their job was not to rework the departmentalization, they were to develop a specific plan for the divisional implementation.

The next step was to appoint people to the top jobs in the new organization. Appointments were made based first on assessment of talent with seniority second in importance. Most of the top 150 managers involved in the process had new jobs. But more importantly, the large majority of managers supported the reorganization regardless of their new jobs. The preparation for change took 14 months.

Implementing Change

Kodak's reorganization began with a 12 percent reduction of employees over a two-year period. Most left voluntarily for other jobs, retirement, and so on. Over time, the number of managers were reduced by about 25 percent, and Kodak stopped its habit of promoting managers from within. Over a five-year period, nearly 70 percent of the key managers were new to their jobs.

Next, nearly 30 independent business units were created with the responsibility for developing and implementing their own strategy and worldwide profit performance. The export strategy changed, depending upon the business unit, all the way to the direct investment level. The business units were grouped into traditional imaging business, image-intensive information technology, and plastic polymers. Kodak acquired Sterling Drug and expanded into pharmaceuticals as an additional business group.

In order to achieve better focus on the customer, markets, and technology, manufacturing and R&D were split up and distributed into the business units. The relationship between the business units and the different geographic areas where Kodak conducted its business were more clearly articulated. In simple terms, each business unit was responsible for developing the strategic thrust of the business while the geographic unit was responsible for implementing that thrust.

Each business unit was subject to periodic evaluation of its earnings and value. Each one was required to generate a return that exceeded an internally established cost of equity, reflecting its own level of risk and market conditions. Businesses unable to attain the required rate of return were put on probation, and if they did not reach the goal they would be dismanted or divested.

Kodak's reorganization was successful by most measures. It improved its financial, productivity, and market share performance. Kodak's performance improved at a rate four times the U.S. average for several years in a row.

Go to the Internet: For more information on Eastman Kodak, do a name search on the Internet and visit its website at *www.kodak.com.* For ideas on using the Internet, see Appendix C. Select the best alternative for the following questions. Be sure to be able to give an explanation to support your answers.

1. What was the primary type of change made by Kodak?

2. Discuss the systems affect (Chapter 1) of Kodak's change.

3. Which of the 11 methods for overcoming resistance to change did Kodak focus on through its change?

4. It took 14 months to plan the change, and the organizational design (Chapter 5) was not changed dramatically from the original top three managers' plan. Would it have been faster to just have dictated the change? Using hindsight, would you have dictated the change or use participation as Kodak did?

5. Did Kodak use OD? Did Kodak follow the steps in the Lussier change model?

Cumulative Questions

6. What influence do personality, the learning organization, and perception (Chapter 2) and attitudes, job satisfaction, and values (Chapter 3) have in this change?

7. Is the focus of this case interpersonal communications (Chapter 4) or organizational structure and communications (Chapter 5)?

8. Which motivation theory would you say is most relevant to this case?

9. Which situational supervision leadership style (Chapter 7) and situational problem-solving and decision-making style (Chapter 10) did the top executives use during this change process?

10. Which conflict-management style (Chapter 8) was top management using to implement the change knowing that conflict was inevitable?

11. How were power and politics (Chapter 9) handled in this case?

OBJECTIVE CASE

Supervisor Carl's Change

Carl was an employee at Benson's Corporation. He applied for a supervisor job at Hedges Inc., and got the job. Carl wanted to do a good job. He observed the employees at work to determine ways to improve productivity. Within a week Carl thought of a way.

On Friday afternoon he called the employees together. Carl told them that starting on Monday he wanted them to change the steps they followed when assembling the product. He demonstrated the new steps a few times and asked if everyone understood them. There were no questions. So Carl said, "Great. Start it on Monday first thing."

On Monday Carl was in his office for about an hour doing the week's scheduling. When he came out to the shop floor, he realized that no one was following the new procedure he had shown them on Friday. Carl called the crew together and asked why no one was following the new steps.

HANK: We've done it this way for years and it works fine.

SANDY: We are all underpaid for this boring job. Why should we improve productivity? (*Several others nodded.*)

DEBBIE: On Friday at the tavern we were talking about the change, and we agreed that we are not getting paid more, so why should we produce more?

Answer the following questions. Then in the space between the questions, state why you selected that answer. *Note:* The meeting between Carl and the employee may be role-played in class.

_____ 1. The type of change Carl introduced was:

    a. task change   *c.* technological change
    b. structural change   *d.* people change

_____ 2. Using Exhibit 12–3, identify Sandy's major resistance (box) to change.

    a. 1   *c.* 3   *e.* 5   *g.* 7   *i.* 9
    b. 2   *d.* 4   *f.* 6   *h.* 8

_____ 3. Using Exhibit 12–3, identify Debbie's major resistance (box) to change.

    a. 1   *c.* 3   *e.* 5   *g.* 7   *i.* 9
    b. 2   *d.* 4   *f.* 6   *h.* 8

_____ 4. The major step to overcome resistance to change that Carl should have used when implementing his change was:

    a. develop a positive climate   *e.* avoid emotions
    b. encourage improvement interest   *f.* avoid direct confrontation
    c. plan   *g.* involve employees
    d. give facts   *h.* provide support

_____ 5. Hank's response was a _____ resistance statement.

    a. blocker   *d.* reverser   *g.* politician
    b. roller   *e.* sidestepper   *h.* traditionalist
    c. staller   *f.* threatener   *i.* assaulter

_____ 6. The best OD technique for Carl to have used for this change was:

   a. force field analysis   *d.* training
   b. survey feedback   *e.* team building
   c. Grid OD

_____ 7. Carl followed the change model steps.

   a. true   *b.* false

_____ 8. Hank's statement, assuming it is representative of the group, indicates a _____ organizational culture.

   a. positive   *b.* negative

_____ 9. Based on Sandy's response, it appears organizational climate and morale are:

   a. positive   *b.* neutral
   c. in need of improvement

_____ 10. The conflict management style Carl should use in this situation (employees not following the procedures) is:

   a. forcing   *c.* compromising   *e.* collaborating
   b. avoiding   *d.* accommodating

11. Assume you had Carl's job. How would you have made the change?

◆ **Managing Change and Developing Organizations**

Critical Thinking Questions:

This video case presents how Marshall Industries, a leading distributor of electronic components, has managed change within their organization.

1. What are some of the forces for change at Marshall's?

2. What are some of the types of changes Marshall's has made?

3. How does Marshall's overcome resistance to change?

4. What change model do they use at Marshall's and how do they use it?

5. What type of organizational culture have they developed at Marshall's?

6. Does Marshall's use OD as suggested in the text? If yes, how?

7. Which OD technique from the text do they use at Marshall's and how do they use it?

8. Which OD technique not listed in text do they use at Marshall's and how do they use it?

Fiscal Fairy Tale #6: Gridilocks

Go to the MG website (*www.mgeneral.com*) and read *Fiscal Fairy Tale #6: Gridilocks* (your instructor may ask you to print a copy and bring it to class). Answer these questions (your instructor may ask you to type them and bring them to class).

Online MG Webzine Exercise 12

Questions Relating to the Tale Only

1. As stated at the end of the tale, in 50 words or so, what is your response to this tale? You may send it to MG.

2. Have you, or anyone you know, worked for a company that was not open to suggestions for improvements? Give an example of an idea that was rejected.

3. What would you do in this situation if you were Gridilocks?

4. What is the role of creativity in the corporate world?

Questions Relating the Tale to the Chapter Concepts

5. Of the seven major sections of this chapter, which topic is related to the problem in this tale?

6. Which reason for resistance to change do you think is stopping managers from trying Gridilocks' idea?

7. Describe the organizational culture in this tale.

8. Do you think the 85-15 rule applies in this tale?

9. Describe the organizational climate using the seven dimensions.

10. Which OD technique would you recommend be used to change the climate and culture to one that is open to change?

In-Class MG Webzine Exercise 12

The instructor selects one of the six options from Appendix B page 589.

Culture (IE 12–1)

Online Internet Exercise 12–1(Self-Assessment)

The objective of this exercise is to measure an organizational culture; you will get an overall culture score and subscores in eleven areas of culture. Note that these measures go beyond the textbook discussion of culture. Do the following:

1. Select an organization you work/worked for to measure its culture.

2. Go to the Culture Building website homepage—*www.culture-building.com*

3. Click "Diagnostics", then click "Norm Indicator" (which measures culture) and read about the diagnostics you will get for the organization you selected. Then click "Proceed."

4. To obtain your culture score, you must fill in the "organization, e-mail, and initials" with your real or fictitious information. If you give your real e-mail address, the diagnostic score will be sent to your e-mail address (an option would be to have the diagnoses e-mailed to your instructor). However, you will get the scores online. You must also answer every question to get your scores.

5. Click your responses to the questions then click submit.

6. Generally, the higher your scores (based on 100% overall and 10 for subscores) the stronger is the culture. Print a copy of your scores (your instructor may require a copy).

7. Questions: (1) What is the name of the organization for which you measured the culture? (2) What was the total score percentage? (3) What were the highest and lowest subscores? Be sure to list area and score for each. (4) How can an organization use a culture measure like this to improve its culture as an OD intervention? (5) How can the organization you diagnosed improve its culture?

In-Class Internet Exercise 12–1, IE 12–2, and IE 12–3 Team Building OD Intervention Plan (IE 12–2)

Online Internet Exercise 12–2

The instructor selects one of the six options from Appendix B page 589.

The objective of this exercise is to develop some change-agent skills by interviewing a team member and setting goals and an agenda as preparation for team building OD intervention. Do the following:

1. Go to Glenn Parker's website homepage—*www.glennparker.com*

2. Click "Freebies" then "Team Building and Training Activities" and quickly read the introductory information.

3. Print or write down the 11 Team Building Interview Guide Questions.

4. Interview a team member recording the responses to the 11 questions (your instructor may require a written copy). Note that as an actual team building change agent you would interview all team members, not just one (your instructor may require you interview all members). Based on the interview, complete question 5.

5. (1) Write at least one goal for your team building session with this team. (2) Write your agenda plans for the team building session. What will happen during the team building session? (Your instructor may require a typed copy).

Team Building Lessons (IE 12–3)

Online Internet Exercise 12–3

The objective of this exercise is to read lessons learned about work teams. Do the following:

1. Go to the University of North Texas Center for the Study of Work Teams website—*www.workteams.unt.edu*

2. Click "Free Articles and Literature" then "Abstracts and Lessons Learned."

3. Click one of the categories then select and read one of the abstracts and lessons learned (your instructor may require a copy).

4. Questions: (1) Which abstract did you select? (2) As relates to your work experience, what is the most important lesson? (3) How can you use the information in this lesson to improve a work team you belong to or will belong to in the future?

Preparation
Team Building

Note: This exercise is designed for permanent class groups. Below is a survey feedback questionnaire. There is no right or wrong answer. Check off the answer to each question as it applies to your class group. All questions have five (lines) choices.

Strongly Agree	Agree Somewhat	Neutral/ Between	Disagree Somewhat	Strongly Disagree

Conflict or Fight

1. Our group's atmosphere is friendly.

2. Our group has a relaxed (rather than tense) atmosphere.

3. Our group is very cooperative (rather than competitive).

4. Members feel free to say what they want.

5. There is much disagreement in our group.

6. Our group has problem people (silent, talker, bored, wanderer, arguer).

Apathy

7. Our group is committed to its tasks (all members actively participate).

8. Our group has good attendance.

9. Group members come to class prepared. (All assignments are complete.)

10. All members do their share of the work.

11. Our group should consider firing a member for not attending and/or doing his/her share of the work.

Decision Making

12. Our group's decision-making ability is good.

_____|_____|_____|_____

13. All members participate in making decisions.

_____|_____|_____|_____

14. One or two members influence most decisions.

_____|_____|_____|_____

15. Our group follows the five steps of the decision-making model (Chapter 10).

    Step 1. Define the problem.

_____|_____|_____|_____

    Step 2. Set objectives and criteria.

_____|_____|_____|_____

    Step 3. Generate alternatives.

_____|_____|_____|_____

    Step 4. Analyze alternatives (rather than quickly agreeing on one).

_____|_____|_____|_____

    Step 5. Plan, implement the decision, and control.

_____|_____|_____|_____

16. Our group uses the following ideas:

    a. Members sit in a close circle.

_____|_____|_____|_____

    b. We determine the approach to the task before starting.

_____|_____|_____|_____

    c. Only one member speaks at a time, and everyone discusses the same question.

_____|_____|_____|_____

    d. Each person presents answers with specific reasons.

_____|_____|_____|_____

    e. We rotate order for presenting answers.

_____|_____|_____|_____

    f. We listen to others rather than rehearse our own answers.

_____|_____|_____|_____

g. We eliminate choices not selected by group members.

_____|_____|_____|_____|_____

h. All members defend their answers (when they believe they are correct) rather than change to avoid discussion, conflict, or to get the task over with.

_____|_____|_____|_____|_____

i. We identify the answers remaining and reach a consensus on one (no voting).

_____|_____|_____|_____|_____

j. We come back to controversial questions.

17. List other relevant questions.

18. Our group uses the _____ conflict management style:

    a. forcing   *c.* avoiding   *e.* collaborating

    b. accommodating   *d.* compromising

19. Our group _____ resolve its conflicts in a manner that is satisfactory to all.

    a. does   *b.* does not

In-Class Team Building

SB 12–1

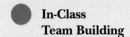

Procedure 1–a (5-30 minutes)

This exercise is designed for groups that have worked together for some time.

Objectives: To experience a team-building session and to improve your group's effectiveness.

SCANS: The SCANS competencies of interpersonal skills, information, and especially systems and the foundations of basic, especially thinking in the area of problem solving, and personal qualities are developed through this exercise.

Experience: This exercise is discussion oriented.

Material: Preparation for Skill-Building Exercise 12–1.

Climate Building

To develop a climate of trust, support, and openness, group members will learn more about each other through a discussion based on asking questions.

Rules:

1. Rotate; take turns asking questions.

2. You may refuse to answer a question as long as you did not ask it (or plan to).

3. You do not have to ask the questions in the order listed below.

4. You may ask your own questions. (Add them to the list.)

As an individual and before meeting with your group, review the questions below and place the name of one or more *group members* whom you want to ask the question. If you prefer to ask the entire group, put *group* next to the question. When everyone is ready, begin asking the questions.

1. How do you feel about this course? _____

2. How do you feel about this group? _____

3. How do you feel about me? _____

4. How do you think I feel about you? _____

5. Describe your first impressions of me. _____

6. What do you like to do? _____

7. How committed to the group are you? _____

8. What do you like most about this course? _____

9. What do you plan to do after you graduate? _____

10. What do you want out of this course? _____

11. How do you react to deadlines? _____

12. Who in the group are you the closest to? _____

13. Who in the group do you know the least? _____

Other _____

Source: Adapted from John E. Jones, "Twenty Five Questions: A Team-Building Exercise," in *A Handbook of Structured Experiences for Human Relations Training* (La Jolla, Calif.: University Associates, 1973), no. 118, pp. 88–91.

When the instructor tells you to do so, get together with your group members and ask each other your questions.

Procedure 1–b (2–4 minutes)   Participants determine what they would like to accomplish during the team-building session. Below are six major goals of team building; you may add to them. Rank them according to your preference.

_____ To clarify the team's objectives.

_____ To identify areas for improving group performance.

_____ To develop team skills.

_____ To determine and utilize a preferred team style.

_____ To fully utilize the resources of each group member.

_____ To develop working relationships based on trust, honesty, and understanding.

_____ Your own goals (list them).

Procedure 1–c (3–6 minutes)
Procedure 2 (3–8 minutes)   Participants share their answers to Procedure 1–b. The group can come to a consensus on its goal(s) if it wants to.

Process and Structure: As a team, discuss strengths and weaknesses in group process (how the group works and communicates). Below, list norms (do's and don'ts) for the group to abide by.

Procedure 3–a
(10–15 minutes)

Problem Identification: As a team, answer the survey feedback questionnaire (Preparation for In-Class Skill-Building Exercise 12–1). Place a *G* on the line to signify the team's answer. Don't rush; fully discuss the issues and how and why they affect the group.

Procedure 3–b
(3–7 minutes)

Based on the above information, list 8 to 10 ways in which the team could improve its performance.

Procedure 3–c
(3–6 minutes)

Prioritize the above list (1=most important).

Procedure 4
(6–10 minutes)

Problem Solving: Take the top priority item. Then:

1. Define the problem.

2. Set objectives.

3. Generate alternatives.

4. Analyze alternatives and select one.

5. Develop an action plan for its implementation.

Follow the same five steps for each area of improvement until time is up. Try to cover at least three areas.

Procedure 5
(1 minute)

Training: Team building often includes training to address the problems facing the group. Because training takes place during most exercises, we will not do any now. Remember that the agendas for team building vary and usually last for one or more full days, rather than one hour.

Procedure 6–a (3 minutes)

Closure Application:

1. I intend to implement the team's solutions. Why?

2. What did I learn from this experience?

3. How can I apply this knowledge in my daily life?

4. How can I apply this knowledge as a manager?

Procedure 6–b
(1–3 minutes)
Sharing
(4–7 minutes)

Group members summarize what has been accomplished and state what they will do (commit) to improve the group.

A spokesperson from each team tells the class the group's top three areas for improvement. The instructor records them on the board.

● **Preparation
Your College
Climate**

A popular method of determining organizational climate is a survey questionnaire. Below is a survey instrument developed by Dr. Roland E. Holstead, former chairperson of the Department of Social Sciences and Human Services at Springfield College, and adapted with his permission. Answer the questions as they apply to your college. Leave unanswered the questions that do not apply to you or your school.

Academic Life

	Very Satisfied	Somewhat Satisfied	Satisfied	Somewhat Dissatisfied	Very Dissatisfied
1. How satisfied are you with your academic program?	_____	_____	_____	_____	_____
2. How satisfied are you with your academic adviser?	_____	_____	_____	_____	_____
3. How satisfied are you with your instructors, in general?	_____	_____	_____	_____	_____
4. How satisfied are you with the following types of courses?	_____	_____	_____	_____	_____
All-college requirements	_____	_____	_____	_____	_____
Major coursess	_____	_____	_____	_____	_____
Elective courses	_____	_____	_____	_____	_____

5. In your experience, what academic departments offer some of the *most* worthwhile courses?

_____

_____

_____

6. In your experience, what academic departments offer some of the *least* worthwhile courses?

_____

_____

_____

7. A. How difficult are the following types of courses for you personally?

	Very Difficult	Somewhat Difficult	About Right	Somewhat Easy	Very Easy
All-college requirements	_____	_____	_____	_____	_____
Major courses	_____	_____	_____	_____	_____
Elective courses	_____	_____	_____	_____	_____

B. How challenging are the following types of courses for you personally?

	Very Challenging	Somewhat Challenging	About Right	Somewhat Unchallenging	Very Unchallenging
All-college requirements	_____	_____	_____	_____	_____
Major courses	_____	_____	_____	_____	_____
Elective courses	_____	_____	_____	_____	_____

C. How interesting are the following types of courses for you personally?

	Very Interesting	Somewhat Interesting	Interesting	Somewhat Uninteresting	Very Uninteresting
All-college requirements	___	___	___	___	___
Major courses	___	___	___	___	___
Elective courses	___	___	___	___	___

D. *For Juniors and Seniors Only:* Some courses are numbered for freshmen-sophomores, others for juniors-seniors, and others for seniors-graduate students. Would you agree that as the course number increases, the difficulty or demand on your performance also increases? In other words, are junior-senior courses generally harder than freshman-sophomore courses?

_____ Yes   _____ No   _____ No difference—numbering system is useless.

8. A. Where do you study most often?

	What Time(s) of Day?
_____ Own room	___
_____ Library	___
_____ Student lounge	___
_____ Empty classrooms	___
_____ Other	___

B. How satisfied are you with your ability to study in each of the following places?

	Very Satisfied	Somewhat Satisfied	Satisfied	Somewhat Dissatisfied	Very Dissatisfied
In your room	___	___	___	___	___
In the library	___	___	___	___	___
In a student lounge	___	___	___	___	___
In empty classrooms	___	___	___	___	___

9. About how many hours a day, if any, do you spend:

Completing assignments _____   Reading _____   Studying _____

10. About how many classes do you cut per week, if any? _____

	Very Satisfied	Somewhat Satisfied	Satisfied	Somewhat Dissatisfied	Very Dissatisfied
11. How satisfied are you with your college's library holdings?	___	___	___	___	___
12. How satisfied are you with the size of (number of students in) your classes?	___	___	___	___	___
13. How satisfied are you with the grading structure?	___	___	___	___	___

What is your major? _____

What is your grade-point average? _____

What is your year in college? _____

Student Services

14. Which of the following services have you ever used, and how satisfied were you with them?

	Very Satisfied	Somewhat Satisfied	Satisfied	Somewhat Dissatisfied	Very Dissatisfied
Dean of Students Office	_____	_____	_____	_____	_____
Housing Office	_____	_____	_____	_____	_____
Counseling Center	_____	_____	_____	_____	_____
Infirmary	_____	_____	_____	_____	_____
Chaplain	_____	_____	_____	_____	_____
Security/Campus Police	_____	_____	_____	_____	_____
Career Planning and Placement Office	_____	_____	_____	_____	_____
Minority Advisement/ Special Advisement	_____	_____	_____	_____	_____

Social Life

15. In general, are you satisfied with the social life at your college? _____

16. Are there enough social activities planned on campus during a typical week? _____ If no, what activities should be increased?

_____

_____

_____

17. In which of the following social activities do you engage on a weekly basis, when available?

_____ Dorm parties   _____ Movies

_____ Private parties   _____ Athletic events on campus

_____ Off-campus activities   _____ Cultural events on campus

18. On what night(s) would you be most likely to attend a social/cultural event on the campus? _____

19. A. How often do you go home (if you are living away from home to go to college)?

_____ Usually weekly (weekends)   _____ At least once a month

_____ Twice monthly   _____ At least once a semester

B. For what reason(s) are you most likely to go home during a school term other than a holiday or term break?

_____

_____

_____

20. What types of events would you like to see available on campus?

_____

_____

_____

21. In which of the following activities do you participate?

_____ Newspaper

_____ Yearbook

_____ Radio station

_____ Varsity athletics

_____ Intramural athletics

_____ Student government

_____ Other clubs

_____ Religious activity

_____ Other (specify)

Dorm Life (Skip questions 22–33 if you do not live in a dorm.)

	Very Satisfied	Somewhat Satisfied	Satisfied	Somewhat Dissatisfied	Very Dissatisfied
22. How satisfied are you with your life in the dorm?	_____	_____	_____	_____	_____
23. How satisfied are you with your Resident director?	_____	_____	_____	_____	_____
Resident assistant?	_____	_____	_____	_____	_____
24. How satisfied are you with your ability to study in your dorm room?	_____	_____	_____	_____	_____
25. How satisfied are you with your ability to sleep in your dorm room?	_____	_____	_____	_____	_____
26. How satisfied are you with the degree of privacy in your dorm?	_____	_____	_____	_____	_____
27. How satisfied are you with the cleanliness of your dorm?	_____	_____	_____	_____	_____

	Very Effective	Somewhat Effective	Ineffective	Somewhat Effective	Very Ineffective
28. How effective is your dorm government?	_____	_____	_____	_____	_____

	Very Fair	Somewhat Fair	Fair	Somewhat Unfair	Very Unfair
29. How fair are your dorm's rules?	_____	_____	_____	_____	_____
30. How fair is the enforcement of your dorm's rules?	_____	_____	_____	_____	_____

31. A. Is there a problem in your dorm with

_____ Drug use   _____ Security

_____ Sexual activity (whether heterosexual or homosexual)   _____ Violence

_____ Sexual harassment   _____ Noise

B. Are there problems in your dorm not identified above? _____ If yes, what are they?

C. To whom did you report any of these problems?

_____ Resident assistant

_____ Resident director

_____ Dean of Students Office

Were you satisfied with the official response to the problem? _____

32. What are the best things about your dorm?

_____

_____

_____

33. If you could change anything about your dorm, what would it be, and why?

_____

_____

_____

In what dorm do you live? _____

Do most of your college friends live in your dorm? _____

● **In-Class
Your College
Climate**

SB 12–2

*Procedure 1 Tabulate the
Class's Survey Responses*

Objectives: To better understand organizational climate and the climate at your college.

SCANS: The SCANS competencies of interpersonal skills, information, and especially systems and the foundations of basic, especially thinking in the area of problem solving, and personal qualities are developed through this exercise.

Preparation: You should have completed the preparation questionnaire.

Experience: Your class will calculate its climate and discuss it.

Option A: Break up into teams of five or six and tabulate team members' responses to each of the questions selected by your instructor. Each group reports its responses to the instructor, who tabulates the total responses for the entire class. He or she summarizes the results on the board.

Option B: The instructor asks students to indicate their responses to selected questions by raising their hands. The instructor totals the responses to each question and writes them on the board.

*Procedure 2 Discuss
School Climate*

1. Climate surveys are usually given to an entire organization or to a major unit. Can you assume that your class is representative of the entire college or university? Why or why not?

2. The survey questions were designed for Springfield College. What sections or individual questions should be changed or added to make it more reflective of the climate at your school?

3. Is your school's climate consistent with your needs (and with the needs of the student body as a whole)?

4. How does your school's climate affect your behavior and attitudes (and the student body's)?

5. How does your school's climate affect your (and the student body's) performance and productivity?

6. Would conducting a climate survey of the entire student body be of value at your college or university? How?

Conclusion: The instructor leads a class discussion and/or makes concluding remarks.

Application (2–4 minutes):   What did I learn from this experience? How will I use this knowledge in the future?

Sharing: Volunteers give their answers to the application section.

Valuing Diversity Globally

13

After completing this chapter, you should be able to:

1. Define prejudice and discrimination and state common areas of employment discrimination in organizations.

2. State major laws protecting minorities and women.

3. Identify what employers can and cannot ask job applicants.

4. List the groups that are legally protected by the EEOC.

5. Explain the six areas of sexual harassment.

6. Explain sexism in organizations and ways to overcome it.

7. List seven areas of global diversity and give examples of differences.

8. List the steps in handling a complaint.

9. Define the following 12 key terms (in order of appearance in the chapter):

prejudice	**sexual harassment**
discrimination	**sexism**
minority	**comparable worth**
bona fide occupational	**multinational company (MNC)**
qualification	**expatriates**
affirmative action programs	**complaint model**
disability	

A small group of white women at the Smith Company was standing around the water cooler talking. These were some of the statements they made: "There is a lot of prejudice and discrimination against women around here." "There are more nonwhite faces around all the time." "We even have handicapped workers now, and its uncomfortable to look at them and work with them." "There are plenty of women in this company, but very few of them hold professional or managerial positions." "We women here in the offices only make a fraction of what the men in the shop are paid; and with the cutbacks, women are not getting into the higher-paying jobs." "My male supervisor recently made sexual advances, and since I shot him down, he's been giving me all the lousy jobs to do." "I've complained to the union about these inequities, but nothing seems to change for us white women."

At the same time, a group of white men were also talking. Some of their statements included these: "There are more nonwhites and women around all the time." "Why can't these minorities learn to speak English like the rest of us?" "These people are always complaining about not being treated fairly, when they *are*." "We've given a few promotions to management, even though they are not qualified." "They don't make good managers anyway." "The way management positions are being eliminated, it's tough enough to compete against the men, let alone these others."

Are these statements, which may have been said in many organizations, based on fact or fiction? Do these attitudes help or hurt the individuals, others, and the organization? You will learn about these, and other valuing-diversity issues, in this chapter.

● Organization
● Group
● Individual

■ Performance
■ Human Relations
■ Behavior

IE 13–1

Prejudice and Discrimination

Although progress has been made, prejudice and discrimination based on race, creed, color, and gender still exists in the United States.[1] The use of discrimination prevents equal employment opportunity. Discrimination is usually based on prejudice. **Prejudice** *is the prejudgment of a person or situation based on attitudes.* As stated in Chapter 2, an attitude is a strong belief or feeling. If someone were to ask you "Are you prejudiced?" you would probably say no. However, we all tend to prejudge people and situations. Recall that Chapter 2 discussed first impressions and the four-minute barrier. In four minutes you don't have time to get to know someone, yet you make assumptions that affect your behavior. Chapter 3 defined stereotyping as the process of generalizing behavior of all members of a group. Your prejudice is often based on your stereotype of the group. To prejudge or stereotype a person or situation in and of itself is not harmful; we all tend to do this. Although prejudice is not always negative, if you discriminate based on your prejudice, you may cause harm to yourself and other parties. **Discrimination** *is behavior for or against a person or situation.*

To illustrate the difference between prejudice and discrimination, assume that Joan is a supervisor and is in the process of hiring a new employee. There are two qualified candidates: Pete, an African-American male and Ted, a white male. Joan is white and has a more positive attitude toward whites. She stereotypes blacks as not being as productive on the job as whites. But she also believes that blacks deserve a break. Joan has a few options.

Joan can discriminate based on her prejudice and hire Ted. Selecting an employee based wholly on race or color is clear illegal discrimination for Ted and against Pete. In the same manner, Joan could be prejudiced for Pete and against Ted.

Joan can be aware of her prejudices, yet try not to let them influence her decision. She can interview both candidates and select the person who is best qualified for the job. Then there would be no discrimination. This option is legal and the generally recommended approach. When selecting employees, you must examine a wide variety of issues and not base the decision on prejudice.

WORK APPLICATIONS

1. Give a situation in which you were discriminated against for some reason.

APPLICATION SITUATIONS

Prejudice or Discrimination

AS 13–1

Identify each statement made by a white male as an example of

A. Prejudice   B. Discrimination

_____1. Here comes Jamal (a tall black), I bet he will talk about basketball.

_____2. I select Pete as my partner, Karen you team up with Betty for this assignment.

_____3. I cannot continue to work with you today, Sue. Is it your time of the month?

_____4. I do not want to work the night shift. Can you force me to change?

_____5. The boss hired a new good-looking blond secretary, I bet she's not very bright.

Common Areas of Employment Discrimination

Historically, the five areas where discrimination in employment is most common include:

- *Recruitment.* People who hire employees fail to actively recruit people from certain groups to apply for jobs with their organization.
- *Selection.* People who select candidates from the recruited applicants fail to hire people from certain groups.
- *Compensation.* White males still make more money than other groups.[2]
- *Upward mobility.* Certain employees do not advance within organizations due to discrimination.[3]
- *Evaluation.* When organizations do not base evaluations on actual job performance, discrimination in compensation and upward mobility occur.

WORK APPLICATIONS

2. Cite an example of employment discrimination in recruitment, selection, compensation, upward mobility, or evaluation, preferably from an organization you work/worked for.

Valuing-Diversity Training

Organizations of all types are training their employees to value employee differences.[4] For example, LIMRA developed a customized diversity seminar with the following objectives:

1. To understand the current and changing demographics of the work force.
2. To view the company's business as part of a global work force and economy.
3. To recognize how prejudice and discrimination can inhibit business success.
4. To recruit from and market to targeted multicultural markets in their territory.

Avon Products began its managing-diversity program in an effort to move away from assimilation as a corporate value and to raise awareness of how negative stereotypes affect the workplace. Avon's success is evident in the number of women who have advanced to management positions. Hewlett-Packard introduced its managing-diversity program as part of the management development curriculum required of all its managers. The program stresses diversity as a competitive advantage. Many other organizations including National Transportation Systems, General Computer, United Communications and Xerox[5] offer diversity training.

Bill Gates advises you to learn to work with people.[6] To have effective human relations with all types of people who are different from you, you need to be tolerant of people's differences, try to understand why they are different, have empathy for them and their situation, and communicate openly with them. Be aware of the human tendency to prejudge and stereotype others and to avoid discriminating based on your prejudices.

WORK APPLICATIONS

3. Have you, or has anyone you know, gone through diversity training? If yes, describe the program.

● Organization
● Group
● Individual

IE 13–2

■ Performance
■ Human Relations
■ Behavior

Equal Employment Opportunity for All

As managing diversity and valuing diversity are different, so are valuing diversity, equal employment opportunity (EEO), and affirmative action (AA). Diversity differs conceptually from equal employment opportunity, which is primarily concerned with racism and prejudice. By valuing work force diversity, management seizes the benefits differences bring.[7] Managers in the coming decade will be challenged to manage a slower-growing labor force comprised of more female, immigrant, minority, and older workers as white men will make up only 45 percent of the labor force by the year 2000[8] and 38 percent by the year 2005.[9] Also, by the year 2030 less than 50 percent of Americans will be white. Affirmative action is a recruitment tool to bring formerly disadvantaged workers into the work force and to help them fit into corporate culture. Valuing differences stresses the understanding, respecting, and valuing of differences among employees.[10] Managing and valuing diversity build on the foundations created by EEO and AA. True diversity, unlike AA, is not about quotas but about finding qualified workers of all races.[11] EEO and AA direct attention to laws that guide recruiting, selecting, compensating, promoting, and evaluating employees.

Laws Affecting Employment Opportunity

You are aware that an organization cannot discriminate against a minority. Who is legally considered a minority? A minority is just about anyone who is not a white male, of European heritage, or adequately educated. The Equal Employment Opportunity Commission (EEOC) **minority** *list includes Hispanics, Asians, African-Americans, Native Americans, and Alaskan natives.* Women are also protected by law from discrimination in employment, but they are not considered to be a legal minority because in some situations they are a majority. Disadvantaged young people, disabled workers, and persons over 40 and up to 70 years of age are also protected.

The EEOC has 47 field offices across the nation. It offers seminars for employees who feel they aren't getting a fair shake, and it operates a WATTS line (1-800-USA-EEOC) and website (uuw.eeoc.gov) around the clock to provide information on employee rights.

EEO, a 1972 amendment to the Civil Rights Act of 1964 and 1991, prohibits employment discrimination on the basis of sex, religion, race or color, or national origin, and applies to virtually all private and public organizations that employ 15 or more employees.

Some of the other laws affecting staffing include the Equal Pay Act of 1963, which requires employers to provide equal pay for substantially equal work regardless of sex; the Age Discrimination in Employment Act of 1967, which prohibits discriminatory employment practices against persons ages 40 through 69; the Vocational Rehabilitation Act of 1973, which requires federal contractors to take affirmative action to hire ("reasonable accommodation") and advance employment of disabled persons; the Vietnam-Era Veterans' Readjustment Assistance Act of 1972 and 1974 (amended in 1980), which requires contractors to take affirmative action to hire disabled individuals and Vietnam-era veterans; and the Pregnancy Discrimination Act of 1978, which prohibits discrimination against women because of pregnancy, childbirth, or related medical conditions, especially in the area of benefits administration. The Americans with Disabilities Act of 1990 is discussed later in this chapter.

Companies suspected of violating any of these laws may be investigated by the EEOC or become defendants in class-action or specific lawsuits.[12]

In 1998, discrimination claims filed with the EEOC escalated,[13] then dropped a little over 1% in 1999.[14] Despite expensive court settlements and negative public relations, organizations continue to have problems embedding the management of

Learning Objective

2. State major laws protecting minorities and women

diversity into their daily practices and procedures.[15] In fact, half of employers say their companies have been sued over employment-related issues.[16] There is no one best way to manage workforce diversity.[17] However, clearly, it is important for you to be familiar with the law and your organization's EEO and AA program guidelines.

Preemployment Inquiries

On the application blank and during interviews, no member of an organization can legally ask discriminatory questions. The two major rules of thumb to follow are:

1. Every question that is asked should be job related. When developing questions, you should have a purpose for using the information. Only ask legal questions you plan to use in your selection process.

2. Any general question that you ask should be asked of all candidates.

Below, we will discuss what you can (lawful information you can use to disqualify candidates) and cannot (prohibited information you cannot use to disqualify candidates) ask during a job interview. Prohibited information is information that does not relate to a bona fide occupational qualification (BFOQ) for the job. A **bona fide occupational qualification** *allows discrimination on the basis of religion, sex, or national origin where it is reasonably necessary to normal operation of a particular enterprise.* In an example of a BFOQ upheld by its supreme court, the state of Alabama required all guards in male maximum-security correctional facilities to be male. People believing that this requirement was sexual discrimination took it to court. The supreme court upheld the male sex requirement on the grounds that 20 percent of the inmates were convicted of sex offenses, and this creates an excessive threat to the security of female guards.

For a list of topics or questions that can and cannot be asked, see Exhibit 13–1.

EXHIBIT 13–1   **PREEMPLOYMENT INQUIRIES**

Name

Can Ask: Current legal name and whether the candidate has ever worked under a different name.

Cannot Ask: Maiden name or whether the person has changed his or her name.

Address

Can Ask: Current residence and length of residence.

Cannot Ask: If the candidate owns or rents his or her home, unless it is a BFOQ.

Age

Can Ask: If the candidate is between specific age groups, 21 to 70, to meet job specifications. If hired, can you furnish proof of age? For example, an employee must be 21 to serve alcoholic beverages.

Cannot Ask: How old are you? Or to see a birth certificate. Do not ask an older person how much longer they plan to work before retiring.

Sex

Can Ask: Only if sex is a BFOQ.

Cannot Ask: If it is not a BFOQ. To be sure not to violate sexual harassment laws, do not ask questions or make comments remotely considered flirtatious.

EXHIBIT 13-1   PREEMPLOYMENT INQUIRIES (*continued*)

Marital and Family Status

Can Ask: If the candidate can meet the work schedule or job and whether the candidate has activities, responsibilities, or commitments that may hinder meeting attendance requirements. The same question(s) should be asked of both sexes.

Cannot Ask: To select a marital status or any questions regarding children or other family issues.

National Origin, Citizenship, Race, or Color

Can Ask: If the candidate is legally eligible to work in the United States, and if this can be proven if hired.

Cannot Ask: To identify national origin, citizenship, race or color (or that of parents and other relatives).

Language

Can Ask: To list languages the candidate speaks and/or writes fluently. The candidate may be asked if they speak and/or write a specific language if it is a BFOQ.

Cannot Ask: The language spoken off the job, or how the applicant learned the language.

Convictions

Can Ask: If the candidate has been convicted of a felony and other information if the felony is job related.

Cannot Ask: If the candidate has ever been arrested. (An arrest does not prove guilt.) For information regarding a conviction that is not job related.

Height and Weight

Can Ask: If the candidate meets or exceeds BFOQ height and/or weight requirements, and if it can be proven if hired.

Cannot Ask: The candidate's height or weight if it is not a BFOQ.

Religion

Can Ask: If the candidate is of a specific religion when it is a BFOQ. If the candidate can meet the work schedules or anticipated absences.

Cannot Ask: Religious preference, affiliations, or denominations.

Credit Ratings or Garnishments

Can Ask: If it is a BFOQ.

Cannot Ask: If it is not a BFOQ.

Education and Work Experience

Can Ask: For information that is job related.

Cannot Ask: For information that is not job related.

References

Can Ask: For the names of people willing to provide references. For the names of people who suggested the candidate apply for the job.

Cannot Ask: For a reference from a religious leader.

Military

Can Ask: For information on education and experience gained that relates to the job.

Cannot Ask: Dates and conditions of discharge. Draft classification or other eligibility for military service. National Guard or reserve units of candidates. About experience in foreign armed services.

EXHIBIT 13–1   **PREEMPLOYMENT INQUIRIES** *(concluded)*

Organizations

Can Ask: To list membership in job-related organizations, like union or professional or trade associations.

Cannot Ask: To identify membership in any non-job-related organization that would indicate race, religion, and so on.

Disabilities/AIDS

Learning Objective

3. Identify what employers can and cannot ask job applicants

Can Ask: If the candidate has any disabilities that would prevent him or her from performing the specific job.

Cannot Ask: For information that is not job related. In states where people with AIDS are protected under disabled discrimination laws, you should not ask if the candidate has AIDS.

WORK APPLICATIONS

4. Have you, or has anyone you know, been asked an illegal discriminatory question during the hiring process? If yes, identify the question(s).

APPLICATION SITUATIONS

Legal Questions

AS 13–2

Identify the five questions below as:

A. Legal (can be asked)   B. Illegal (cannot be asked)

_____ 6. "What is your mother tongue or the major language you use?"

_____ 7. "Are you married or single?"

_____ 8. "Are you a member of the Teamsters Union?"

_____ 9. "Have you been arrested for stealing on the job?"

_____ 10. "Can you prove you are legally eligible to work?"

From Affirmative Action to Valuing Diversity

Affirmative action is a 1977 amendment to Executive Orders of 1965 and 1968, requiring firms doing business with the federal government to make special efforts to recruit, hire, and promote women and members of minority groups.

Affirmative action programs *are planned special efforts to recruit, hire, and promote women and members of minority groups.* AA required that organizations determine their racial and sexual compositions and compare these ratios with those of the available people in the population of the appropriate recruitment area. Based on these numbers, the organization is required to plan and act to obtain the proper percentages according to a complex calculation process.

Under the Reagan and Clinton administrations, support for AA declined. Some of the many reasons that AA went out of favor were the fact that: quotas often worked against minorities, quotas could not be met, and organizations were charged with reverse discrimination. Many believed that forced AA was not the answer to the problem of discrimination. Thus, we went from AA to valuing diversity. Managers now have titles such as manager of diversity at Xerox,[18] and many organizations, including Coca-Cola,[19] have diversity advisory councils. Many successful organizations are not only offering diversity training, but are truly valuing diversity as they realize that a diverse work group increases the quality of decision making,[20] and organizational performance.[21] For example, Denny's Restaurant went from paying 45.7 million to settle a discrimination lawsuit in 1994 to winning a corporate conscience award from the Council on Economic Priorities for being one of the most successfully diverse places to work in America.[22]

With downsizing, maintaining minority rights is a challenge that must be met. With the trend away from AA, reporting statistics on hiring minorities and women is declining.[23] Simply offering diversity programs without advancing these groups proves divisive.[24] The staff of the Marriott Marquis in New York's Time Square is a model of diversity with 1,700 members representing every race, 70 countries, and 47 languages.[25]

WORK APPLICATIONS

5. Describe the affirmative action program at an organization, preferably one for which you work/worked.

The Legally Protected and Sexual Harassment

The last section presented the laws affecting minorities and protected groups. This section discusses minorities, religious beliefs, older workers, the disabled, alcohol and drug abuse and testing, AIDS and AIDS testing, sexual orientation, and women and sexual harassment in more detail.

Minorities

EEO laws prohibit job discrimination on the basis of race, color, national origin, and religion unless it is a BFOQ. Minorities are generally more welcome at the unskilled, nonprofessional, and nonmanagerial levels.[26]

Recall that protected minorities include women, people with religious beliefs, older workers, and the disabled. Therefore, in the following guidelines any of these terms could replace the word *minority*.

Nonminorities should realize that they may unconsciously stereotype minorities,[27] expect them to fail, and set higher performance standards for them; these practices should be consciously avoided. Errors should not be blamed on ethnic background, age, religion, and so on. Nonminorities should realize that minorities may live down to negative expectations. Minorities should not be subject to the negative Pygmalion Effect (Chapter 3) and let others' negative expectations become their self-fulfilling prophecy.

It is also helpful to be open to getting to know people who are different from you. Open, honest communication helps to break down negative stereotypes.[28] When your self-concept is high, it tends to be higher in the minds of others. So project a positive image (Chapter 3).

Religious Beliefs

Employers are required by law to make reasonable accommodations for employees' religious beliefs, without undue hardship on the employer. "Undue hardship" is fairly clear. It involves having to pay premium wages or other costs in order to accommodate an employee's religious rights, defined as "all forms and aspects of religion." However, "reasonable accommodation" is ambiguous. Employers should willingly negotiate with employees and allow them to swap shifts or job dates with consenting colleagues.[29] And employees should be allowed to take religious holidays off in place of other paid days off. Some employers allow employees to select which paid holidays they want to take.[30]

Age

Young and older workers have differences. You will be working with older customers and workers.[31] The fastest growing segment of the population is adults and elders. There are 77 million baby boomers reaching their 50s.

People age 40 and older are protected from age discrimination.[32] However, the EEOC has been criticized as shaky in fighting age bias. Criticism may be based on the fact that hiring and promotion discrimination based on age is one of the most difficult types of discrimination for the victim to prove. People over 50 have a difficult time finding a job. Part of this problem is due to many incorrect stereotypes or myths about older workers.

Some of the myths about older workers include: (1) They cost more for benefits. This is not necessarily true, especially when they are healthy. Younger sickly employees are more costly. (2) They have more absences for sickness. Older workers are as reliable as anyone. Sick leave is more related to a person's lifetime pattern of sick leave. Many organizations find older employees are absent less frequently than younger employees, and recruit them for this reason. (3) They resist change. Older workers are not necessarily more rigid in their thinking than younger persons. With the shrinking work force, many organizations are actively recruiting older workers, particularly for part-time jobs in the retailing and fast-food industries. Thus, early retirement shouldn't be encouraged.[33]

People with Disabilities

In July of 1992, the Americans with Disabilities Act (ADA) went into effect. This act gives equal access to employment, transportation, and buildings to about 43 million people in the United States with physical or mental disabilities. The act is viewed as the most sweeping civil-rights measure in over 25 years. A disability used to be commonly called a *handicap*. People with a **disability** *have significant physical, mental, or emotional limitations.* They include people with prison records, major obesity, or a history of heart disease, cancer, or mental illness (one in five Americans has a mental disorder)[34] since others might view them as disabled. Rehabilitated alcoholics and drug abusers are also considered disabled. The law requires that employers make "reasonable accommodations" to hire the disabled. The disabled can be required to meet the same productivity standards as other employees.

The employment provisions of the ADA affect 9 to 11 percent of the U.S. population between the ages of 16 and 64 who have a work disability.[35] Although the U.S. government is working to place more disabled people to work,[36] most disabled people are not working even though they want to. About two out of three disabled people are not working (this figure is unchanged from 1986), even though 79 percent of them would rather have a job. And many of those that do have jobs say coworkers will not socialize with them.[37] This situation exists despite the fact that in some cases, the disability is an advantage. For example, blind people work well in darkrooms. This is also despite the fact that companies rate disabled employees as good or excellent workers.[38] Most disabled workers want their bosses and coworkers to treat them like everyone else. Open and honest communication is the best policy.

The cost of "reasonable accommodations" to employ the disabled are to be paid for by the employer. However, there is often no cost and the average cost is only $120, plus the government gives a tax credit of up to $5,000 to help pay the costs.

ADA legislation states that reasonable accommodation "may include such areas as job restructuring, part-time or flexible work schedules, acquisition or modification of equipment or devices, the provision of readers or interpreters, and other similar actions." American and Canadian employers who need help in assisting the disabled can obtain information by phone from the President's Committee on Employment of the Handicapped (PCEH). The committee has a Job Accommodation Network

(JAN) that provides free information on how new technologies can help as well as names and phone numbers of employers who have successfully developed programs of accommodation. In Canada, call voice or TDD, 1-800-526-2262; in the United States (except West Virginia), call voice or TDD, 1-800-526-7234; in West Virginia, call voice or TDD, 1-800-526-4698; the commercial phone number is 304-293-7186.

Alcohol and Drug Abuse and Testing

Since October of 1986 when Attorney General Edwin Meese spoke about the responsibility of management to curb drug abuse in the workplace and the government began to administer drug tests, drug abuse has been given much attention. Mr. Meese stated that it cost employers $7,000 per year for each drug-abusing employee. According to Partnership for a Drug-Free America, one in six Americans has a substance abuse problem. Six out of 10 people say they know of someone who has gone to work under the influence of drugs or alcohol.[39] Complete Self-Assessment Exercise 13–1 to see if you may have a potential substance problem.

To help prevent drug abuse, the Federal Drug-Free Workplace Act of 1988 was enacted. Drug testing is on the increase in both the private and public sectors. Almost three-fourths (74.5 percent) of 1,200 companies surveyed said they test employees for drugs.[40] More big companies than small ones test for substances,[41] and more blue collar than white collar employees are tested.[42]

Self-Assessment Exercise 13–1

Substance Problem

For each of the following statements, select the number from 1 to 5 that best describes the frequency of your actual substance (alcohol or drug) use. Place the number on the line before each statement. You will not be asked to share this information in class.

(5) Usually   (4) Frequently   (3) Occasionally   (2) Seldom   (1) Rarely

_____ 1. I take substances in the morning.

_____ 2. I take substances to calm my nerves or to forget about worries or pressure.

_____ 3. I go to work/school under the influence of substances or take them during work/school hours.

_____ 4. I take substances when I'm alone.

_____ 5. I lie about my substance use.

_____ 6. I drive under the influence of substances.

_____ 7. I wake up and don't remember what I did under the influence of substances.

_____ 8. I do things under the influence of substances that I would not do without them.

_____ 9. I'm late for work/school due to substance use.

_____ 10. I miss work/school due to substance use.

_____ 11. I take substances to help me sleep.

_____ 12. I've had financial difficulties due to substances.

_____ 13. My friends take substances.

_____ 14. I plan activities around being able to use substances.

_____ 15. When I'm not under the influence of substances, I think about taking them.

_____ Total

Your score will range from 15 to 75. To determine the degree to which you have a substance problem, place your score total on the continuum below.

No substance problem   15 - - - - - - 30 - - - - - - 45 - - - - - - 60 - - - - - - 75   Substance problem

If you do have a substance problem, you should seek professional help.

6. Have you ever seen any employees under the influence of alcohol or drugs at work? How did their substance use affect their ability to work?
7. How do you feel about drug testing by employers? Why do you feel this way?

AIDS and AIDS Testing

Human immunodeficiency virus (HIV) is the virus that causes AIDS. Acquired immune deficiency syndrome (AIDS) is the name for the condition that occurs after HIV has gradually destroyed a person's immune system, making the person prone to life-threatening infections. AIDS is not a disease only affecting homosexuals; 40 percent of all reported cases have occurred among heterosexuals. According to the World Health Organization (WHO), by the year 2000, more than half of the newly infected adults will be women. The U.N. reported that AIDS has killed 19 million globally.[43]

A person with HIV or AIDS is protected from discrimination under the ADA of 1990 and the Rehabilitation Act of 1973. In 1987, the federal government unveiled a policy barring discrimination against federal government workers who have AIDS. It also authorizes discipline for those who refuse to work with AIDS patients. The ADA approach to contagious diseases is the same as its approach to drug and alcohol abuse. Employers may adopt a standard that disqualifies persons who currently have a contagious disease if they pose a "direct threat to the health or safety of other individuals in the workplace."

There is no clear agreement on how the AIDS virus is transmitted. There is agreement on the four major ways in which it is transmitted: (1) through sex, (2) through shared hypodermic needles, (3) by an infected mother to a fetus, and (4) through blood transfusions. Most medical authorities state that the virus is not transmitted through casual contact. Therefore, there is no risk to coworkers or the public from "normal" social or work contact with an HIV-infected person.

The national Centers for Disease Control (CDC) has a national 24-hour AIDS hotline to assist any manager or employee who desires information about AIDS. The hotline has Spanish speakers and a TDD for deaf callers. The hotline number is 1-800-342 AIDS. The CDC also helps sponsor managing- and valuing-diversity programs through a program called "Business Responds to AIDS." The CDC will help establish workplace AIDS policies, train managers to deal with infected employees, educate workers and their families, and encourage community service.

In some states, including California, Wisconsin, and Florida, it is illegal for employers to test for AIDS. Testing is of questionable use because the test does not reveal whether the individual has AIDS—only whether the individual has been exposed to the AIDS virus. If an employer refuses to hire an employee with AIDS, it may be vulnerable to a charge of disability discrimination.

Learning Objective

4. List the groups that are legally protected by the EEOC

8. How would you feel about working with a person with AIDS? Why?

Sexual Orientation

A newcomer to the list of diversity groups is based on sexual orientation. *Homophobia* (an aversion to homosexuals) is the term used to refer to discrimination based on a person's sexual orientation. In most situations, companies are not responsible for determining right and wrong behavior off the job. However, all organizations are responsible for providing all workers with an environment that is safe and free of threats, intimidation, harrassment, and especially violence.

Although gays and lesbians are not one of the protected groups under the federal EEOC law against illegal discrimination from being hired or discharged from their jobs because of their sexual orientation, some states have enacted laws that do protect gays and lesbians from job discrimination. The state of Vermont was the first to legalize, not a marriage, but a similar civil union between gays and lesbians. Some government, nonprofit, and private organizations extend medical and other benefits to gay and lesbian partners, as well as unmarried heterosexual partners living together. Companies including AT&T, Walt Disney, Polaroid, Lotus, and Xerox are combating homophobia in the workplace.[44]

Women and Sexual Harassment

Women are a legally protected group. The most common issues that prompt sex discrimination complaints, in order by numbers of cases, are discharge, terms and condition of employment, sexual harassment, wages, pregnancy, promotion, hiring, and intimidation and reprisals. Sexual harassment is one of the most sensitive areas of discrimination because it is often a matter of personal judgment. Sexual harassment charges can be made against either sex; however, the vast majority of cases are against men. Same-sex harassment is also becoming a problem.

Until 25 years ago, there was no label for actions that today are considered sexual harrasment. However, it has become an important social and legal concern and managing sexual harrasment at work is important.[45] Although many firms are training workers to avoid sexual harrasment,[46] researchers have reported that as many as 42% of women have been victims of sexual harrasment at work.[47] Part of the problem is that people observe sexual harrasment and don't report it because they don't believe their organizations encourage them to do so,[48] and because complaints fall on deaf ears as organizations lack policies and procedures to resolve the problems. For example, Mitsubishi Motors of America had a long history of harrasment complaint, and it wasn't until it was taken to court that strong action was taken.[49] The number of sexual harrasment cases taken to the EEOC continues to increase.[50]

The most frequent harassment targets include new employees, people who are on probation in their jobs, and the young and inexperienced. People who have recently experienced a personal crisis, like separation or divorce, are frequently victims. Women in traditionally male jobs are also more subject to sexual harassment.

Behaviors considered to be sexual harassment by some are not considered to be harassment by others. To help people know if they have been sexually harassed, the EEO has defined the term. EEO defines *sexual harassment* as follows: Unwelcome sexual advances, requests for sexual favors, and other verbal or physical conduct of a sexual nature constitute sexual harassment when (1) submission to such conduct is made either explicitly or implicitly a term or condition of an individual's employment, (2) submission to or rejection of such conduct by an individual is used as the basis for employment decisions affecting such individual, or (3) such conduct has the purpose or effect of unreasonably interfering with an individual's work performance or creating an intimidating, hostile, or offensive environment.

The federal and state courts have defined sexual harassment in six areas as grounds for lawsuits:

1. Unwelcome sexual advances. An employee who is repeatedly propositioned by a supervisor or coworker trying to establish an intimate relationship, on or off the job, may sue for sexual harassment even if not overtly threatened.

2. Coercion. An employee whose supervisor asks for a date or sexual favor with the stated or unstated understanding that a favor will be bestowed, or a reprisal made, may sue for sexual harassment.

3. Favoritism. Courts have ruled that an employer is liable when employees who submit to sexual favors are rewarded, while others who refuse are denied promotions

or benefits. One federal court ruled that an employee who wasn't asked for sexual favors, while others were, was a victim of sexual harassment.

4. Indirect harassment. Employees who witness sexual harassment on the job can sue even if they are not victims. In a California state court, a nurse complained that a doctor grabbed other nurses in full view of her, causing an environment of sexual harassment.

5. Physical conduct. Employees don't have to be touched. Courts have ruled that unseemly gestures may constitute harassment and create a hostile work environment.

6. Visual harassment. Courts have ruled that graffiti written on men's bathroom walls about a female employee is sexual harassment. The pervasive displays of nude or pornographic pictures constitute sexual harassment.

Learning Objective

5. Explain the six areas of sexual harassment

To keep it simple, Du Pont tells its people, "It's harassment when something starts bothering somebody." For our purposes, **sexual harassment** *is any unwelcomed behavior of a sexual nature.*

When people find themselves in a sexual harassment situation, they often feel overwhelmed, confused, unproductive, afraid, alone, and unable to find the words to confront the harasser. Some workable responses to the harasser, which can be revised to suit the offense, include:

"I am uncomfortable when you touch me. Don't do it again or I will report you for sexual harassment."

"It is inappropriate for you to show me sexually graphic material. Don't do it again."

"I am uncomfortable with off-color jokes. Don't tell one to me again or I will report you for sexual harassment."

IE 13–3

If the behavior is very serious, you may want to report the first offense. If it is less serious, a warning may be given before reporting the offense. If the behavior is repeated, report the offense to your boss or some other authority in the organization. If the people in authority do not take suitable action to stop the harassment, take the complaint to the EEOC.

WORK APPLICATIONS

9. Have you or has anyone you know been sexually harassed? If so, describe the situation(s) (use language acceptable to everyone).
10. How do you feel about groups being legally protected against discrimination?

APPLICATION SITUATIONS

Sexual Harassment

AS 13–3

Identify whether the following behavior is:

A. Sexual harassment   B. Not sexual harassment

_____11. Ted tells Clair she is sexy and he'd like to take her out on a date.

_____12. Sue tells José he will have to go to a motel with her if he wants to get the job.

_____13. Jean's legs are sticking out into the walkway. As Wally goes by, he steps over them and says, "Nice legs."

_____14. For the third time, after being politely told no, Pat says to Chris, "You have a real nice (*fill in the missing sexual words for yourself*). Why don't you and I XXXX?"

_____15. Ray puts his hand on Lisa's shoulder as he talks to her.

The next section continues the discussion of women and how they are discriminated against in the workplace.

Sexism and Work and Family Balance

● Organization
● Group
● Individual

■ Performance
■ Human Relations
■ Behavior

The term **sexism** *refers to discrimination based on sex.* Sexism limits the opportunities of both women and men to choose the lifestyles and careers that best suit their abilities and interests. The Home Depot agreed to pay $65 million to settle a sex discrimination suit against women.[51] Men and women face discrimination when they pursue careers traditionally held by the opposite sex. Males still dominate the construction trades and women nursing, for example. Stereotyping men and women not only hurts the individuals who dare to be different; it also hurts the organization and holds both back from achieving their full potential.

Culture promotes differences in males and females. Children learn these values by the age of 10. Traditional behavior states that men should be aggressive and unemotional, and women are emotional and weak. Men and women will always be different, but their roles can and should be equal. However, traditional roles are changing.

This section examines women in the work force, women managers, overcoming sexism, changing sex roles, and work and family balance. Now determine your attitude toward women at work by completing Self-Assessment Exercise 13–2.

Each of the 10 statements is a commonly held attitude about women at work. However, they have all been shown to be myths through research conducted by various people. Throughout this section, research disproving these attitudes will be cited. There are always exceptions to the rule. However, if you have a negative attitude toward women at work, you are stereotyping them unfairly. You may want to work at

Self-Assessment
Exercise 13–2

Attitude toward Women at Work

For each of the following 10 statements, select the response that best describes your honest belief about women at work. Place the number 1, 2, 3, or 4 on the line before each statement.

(1) Strongly agree   (2) Agree   (3) Disagree   (4) Strongly disagree

_____ 1. Women work to earn extra pocket money.

_____ 2. Women are out of work more often than men.

_____ 3. Women quit work or take long maternity leaves when they have children.

_____ 4. Women have a lower commitment to work than men.

_____ 5. Women lack motivation to get ahead.

_____ 6. Women lack the education necessary to get ahead.

_____ 7. Women working has caused rising unemployment among men.

_____ 8. Women are not strong enough or emotionally stable enough to succeed in high-pressure jobs.

_____ 9. Women are too emotional to be effective managers.

_____10. Women managers have difficulty in situations calling for quick and precise decisions.

_____Total

To determine your attitude score, add up the total of your 10 answers and place it on the total line and on the continuum below.

Negative attitude→   10 ---------- 20 ---------- 30 ---------- 40   ←Positive attitude changing your negative attitude. Negative stereotypes like those above hold women back from gaining salary increases and promotions into management positions, despite EEO, AA and diversity.

Women in the Work Force

We now discuss *women in the work force* as opposed to *working women*. Women who elect to work as homemakers make a great contribution to society. Unfortunately, these women are not commonly referred to as *working women* because they are not rewarded monetarily for their work. However, every female homemaker is a working woman.

How Many Women Are in the Work Force and Why Are They Employed?

Women and minorities are entering the work force in unprecedented numbers.[52] Women currently constitute nearly half of the U.S. labor force.[53] The number of mothers in the work force continues to increase as there are more than 22.3 million mothers with children under 18 years old.[54] The Education Department estimates that there are as many as 15 million latchkey children spending 20–25 hours per week at home alone.[55]

Women work for many different reasons, but they can generally be classified by economic necessity and self-concept needs. With the divorce rate over 50% and the increase in single-parent households, which are mostly women, women work for economic necessity. Married women contribute 25–50% of the household income on average, and women's income is critical to the family support. In general, women today want it all, a job and family, as they are motivated to meet their needs for achievement and affiliation (Chapter 6). Actually, economic and self-concept needs are so highly intertwined that they usually can't be separated.

Do Men and Women Get the Same Pay?

Because of the Equal Pay Act, which is over 30 years old, women and men doing the exact same job generally do get paid the same. However, overall, women's average earnings are 74% of men's,[56] and minorities make less than white men. In fact, U.S. Hispanics earned half of what white workers did it 1998, and many are stuck in menial jobs.[57] However, the pay difference is not simply caused by discrimination as women tend to work in jobs with lower pay, such as childcare,[58] and Hispanics have lower levels of education and don't qualify for many high-paying jobs.

Comparable Worth

The term **comparable worth** *refers to jobs that are distinctly different, but require similar levels of ability, having the same pay scale.* Comparable worth advocates want traditional women's jobs, like secretaries, to be paid comparable to men's jobs, like electricians, when they require the same ability. People opposed to comparable worth claim that it is the supply and demand for labor that sets the pay rates, not discrimination against women.

Comparable worth has received much attention from certain women's groups, with mixed support from government agencies and the courts. The issue was tabled by the Civil Rights Commission in 1984 as unenforceable.

WORK APPLICATIONS

11. How do you feel about making comparable worth a law? Why?

Women Managers

Myths about Women Managers

Two old myths about women managers are that women will leave the job to have children and women are too emotional to be managers. The statistics presented show that women stay on the job. An eight-year study of male and female managers found virtually identical psychological and emotional profiles between the sexes. On all the variables that have to do with good leadership, men and women as a group show no major differences. Men and women are truly equal in management ability. In fact, women executives were rated superior in their ability to meet deadlines, boost productivity, and generate ideas while men scored higher in handling pressure and frustration.[58] Another popular myth is that women are not as committed to the organization as men, they are.

How Women Are Progressing in Management and the Glass Ceiling

Today's successful women managers realize that they do not have to act like a man and become one of the boys to get ahead.[59] They feel free to be, well, women; they are confident about their business and management skills and are not shy about showing it.[60] Women who perceive they will have problems managing solely because of their sex may be creating a self-fulfilling prophecy. Management is about developing strong relationships,[61] and women are very effective at developing unique relationships with each employee.[62]

Women are progressing well, representing around 43%, at the first level and middle levels of management, yet they hold less than 5% of executive positions. Only four of the *Fortune 1000* CEO positions were held by women in 1996[63] (you may want to surf the Internet to see how much progress has been made to date). This lack of progress has been attributed to the *glass ceiling,* an invisible barrier to advancement based on attitudinal or organizational bias. Women executives[64] and human resource professionals[65] state that the glass ceiling is persistent and the U.S. government has a Federal Glass Ceiling Commission to help eliminate the problem.[66] However, in a survey of 325 male CEOs, 82% said lack of experience was the main reason more women executives don't advance.[67] However, women identified male stereotyping of women and women's exclusion from informal communication networks as the key barriers to their advancement.[68] With this male CEO perceptional attitude, and other reasons, female executives, especially CEOs will remain rare for years to come in corporate America.[69]

WORK APPLICATIONS

12. How do you feel about having a female boss? Why?

APPLICATION SITUATIONS

Women

AS 13–4

Identify each of the following statements about women as:

A. Factual   B. Myth

_____16. "Men make better managers than women."

_____17. "Women work because they need the money."

_____18. "Men managers are more committed to their jobs than women managers."

_____19. "Women managers are viewed as more caring for the individual subordinate than men managers."

_____20. "About one out of every three managers is female."

Overcoming Sexism

Hiring and promotion decisions should not be based on sex, though affirmative action plans may be implemented.

Sexist Language and Behavior

Skill-Building
13–1

Skill-Building
13–2

Learning Objective

6. Explain sexism in organizations and ways to overcome it

Men and women should avoid using sexist language. Sexist words such as *mailman* and *salesman* should be replaced with nonsexist terms such as *letter carrier* and *salesperson*. In written form, the use of *he* or *she* is appropriate, but don't overuse the number of times it appears; use neutral language like plurals—*everyone* rather than *gentlemen and ladies*, or *supervisors* rather than *the supervisor*, which tends to end up needing a *he* or *she* as writing progresses.

Call people by name, rather than by sexist terms. Working women are not girls and should not be called *girls* because this word is used to describe children, not grown women.

Be very careful of swearing in the workplace; it is preferable not to use such language. What is really gained through swearing, anyway? Are you impressed by people who swear? Are people who do not swear pressured to do so at work?

If anyone uses language that offends you, assertively state your feelings about the words used. Many times people do not use sexist language intentionally and will not use it if they are requested not to.

Many working men are becoming more sensitive to sexism because they have wives and daughters entering the work force, whom they want to have equal opportunities. Exhibit 13–2 illustrates negative sexist stereotyping that needs to be eliminated: They are examples of stereotypes that are a barrier to women breaking the glass ceiling.[70]

EXHIBIT 13–2

A SEXIST (STEREOTYPICAL) WAY TO TELL A BUSINESSMAN FROM A BUSINESSWOMAN

Man	Woman
A businessman is aggressive.	A businesswoman is pushy.
He is careful about details.	She's picky.
He loses his temper because he's so involved in his job.	She's bitchy.
He's depressed (or hung over), so everyone tiptoes past his office.	She's moody, so it must be her time of the month.
He follows through.	She doesn't know when to quit.
He's firm.	She's stubborn.
He makes wise judgments.	She reveals her prejudices.
He is a man of the world.	She's been around.
He isn't afraid to say what he thinks.	She's opinionated.
He exercises authority.	She's tyrannical.
He's discreet.	She's secretive.
He's a stern taskmaster.	She's difficult to work for.

Sex Roles Are Changing

The traditional family in which the husband works and the wife doesn't work outside the home is no longer the pattern in a majority of American households. Two-income marriages became the norm back in 1994.[71] Dual-career couples generally agree to split housework and child care evenly. Men are gradually putting in more time on such tasks.[72] But their average time contribution is still less than half that of women.

Now men say they want it all too and are spending an average of 2.3 hours a day with their kids, a half-hour increase over 20 years ago.[73] The number of fathers taking time off to care for newborns continues to creep upward, partly because of the

1993 Family and Medical Leave Act's broad mandate of up to 12 weeks of unpaid leave to care for a family member. More fathers routinely stay home to care for their sick children, take them to the doctors, and give them medicine.[74]

Before entering marriage, it is very helpful for couples to discuss and agree on career and family plans and the distribution of household tasks. Many couples elect the split shift, in which one works at home while the other works outside the home, so that outside child-care arrangements are not necessary.

Work and Family Balance

In today's reengineered, reorganized, and downsized companies, the employees who remain are being asked to work longer hours, to work more days each week, and to maintain this place for longer uninterrupted periods.[75] Heavy overtime is straining families.[76] Parents are feeling guilty about using childcare and not getting home for dinner to eat as a family; they want to spend more time at home.[77] People are searching for fulfillment,[78] however, exhausted from nonstop work and family responsibilities, many people realize their life is out of whack.[79]

Many parents enjoy working full-time and choose to do so regardless of family status and income. However, some parents are reevaluating being gone all the time and leaving the kids under other people's supervision. Some are electing to quit work or cut back to part-time while others work at home. However, even though many women and 25% of men would rather stay home and take care of the family than hold a job, as stated, single-parent and dual incomes are needed to finance most households. About 28% of dual-parent households are traditional families, and in around 5% of them men elect to stay home while their wife works full-time. And the percentage of traditional families is not on the rise from 28%.[80]

Men and women want a better balance between work and family,[81] with a stable family life.[82] Researchers have shown that the most important years of a person's life are ages 0–5 as this is when our personalities are developed. Many parents want to be around to shape their children's personalities. Tired of long work hours and short family hours, what job candidates really want to know is: Will I have a life?.[83] Many men between the ages of 20–39 are electing the daddy track as a "family-friendly" schedule is their most important job criteria.[84]

Researchers have clearly debunked the myth that work and family are independent. Family-friendly policies affect employee absenteeism and turnover. Thus, the link between work and family affect organizational performance and family functioning.[85] More managers find a happy staff leads to happy customers and raises financial performance. AC Nielsen is tying managers' bonuses partly to employee-satisfaction scores on a wide range of issues including work-life balance.[86] Family-friendly CEOs are changing cultures at more workplaces.[87] Family-friendly policies, including flexible work schedules,[88] childcare benefits, family leave,[89] and time off to attend family activities win the loyalty of employees.[90] Students get lessons in how to manage a well-balanced life,[91] and organizations, including Navistar, offer training programs on how to balance work and family life.[92]

Work and family balance has become so important that *Fortune, Business Week,* and *Working Mother* publish lists of "best place to work." Companies compete with each other to earn a place on the list and use their placements as recruiting tools.[93] As you have read, managing diversity in the United States is very challenging. With the trend towards larger global businesses, diversity becomes an increasingly complex issue.

● Organization
● Group
● Individual

Global Diversity

Globalization is the number-one challenge to business leaders in the 21st century.[94] Business leaders realize the need to compete globally,[95] and the environment is becoming more complex and diverse.[96] Managing effectively across cultures is

important to global success.[97] It is particularly important to value diversity to get teams from different cultures to work effectively together.[98] Our last topic, work and family balance, is also a global concern.[99] In this section, we discuss multinational companies and cross-cultural relations.

Multinational Company (MNC)

Advances in technology have allowed the world to become smaller through rapid communication and travel. Technology has made it practical to conduct business in more than one country, and competition has made it necessary for the survival of some firms. Hence, countries are becoming more interdependent. A **multinational company (MNC)** *conducts a large part of its business outside the country of its headquarters.*

MNCs link many cultures. They operate in virtually every major country. Sometime during your career, you may be given the opportunity to work with MNCs. You may also be given the opportunity to work for a MNC in a different country.

Expatriates *are people who live and work in a country other than their native country.* Expatriates often experience culture shock, a state of confusion, and anxiety when they are first exposed to an unfamiliar culture. There are changes with any move, but the changes compound tremendously when the move is to another country. U.S. managers using traditional American management styles often fail in an overseas business culture because managing diversity goes well beyond business etiquette. Companies need to train expatriates in language, local culture, and local business practices so they can be successful globally. The trend today is to hire more local managers to run the company unit in their country.

Cross-Cultural Relations

When conducting business with foreign firms, and more importantly in foreign countries, be aware of cultural differences. To have successful human relations, you must be flexible and adapt to other people's ways of behaving; you are the foreigner and cannot expect others to change for you. This section examines diversity in customs, time, work ethics, pay, laws and politics, ethics, and participative management. As you read, realize that you are presented with stereotyped generalizations to which there are exceptions and paradox.[100] The examples are not meant to judge "right" and "wrong" behavior. They are intended to illustrate cross-cultural differences that do affect human relations.

Diversity in Customs

In Japan, they place a high priority on human relations, participative management, and teamwork. If you try to be an individual star, you will not be successful in Japan. However, the French do not place high importance on team effort. If you are very outspoken, you will be considered impolite in Japan. If you refuse to be involved in receiving and giving gifts, you will offend Japanese people. However, don't wrap gifts in white paper as it is a sign of death. Also, don't place chopsticks straight up and down as it imitates an offering to the dead.[101] Many Japanese companies start the day with exercises and company cheers. If you do not actively participate, you will be an outsider.

In Europe, management has more cultural than technical aspects and deals with value systems and religious background; it is organized more as a language than a set of techniques. While power and politics (Chapter 9) are important in the United States, they are even more important in France. It is important for a French manager to be perceived as very powerful. An essential part of the morning routine for many French businessmen is to kiss most of the women of the social class equivalent to themselves. Unexpected kissing could create an embarrassing situation for you.

Americans prefer to speak face-to-face from a greater distance than people of most other countries. If you back away or turn to the side from others, they may follow you and create a dance, and you may be considered cold and standoffish. During face-to-face communication, Latins tend to touch each other more than Americans. Jumping when unexpectedly touched could create an embarrassing situation.

Gestures vary from country to country. For example, Americans prefer eye contact. However, if you talk to young Puerto Ricans they will look down as a mark of respect when speaking to adults because eye contact is rude. So do the Japanese. Look at the knot in a Japanese colleague's tie, or the neck, to show respect.[102] In Australia, making the "V" sign with the hand is considered an obscenity rather than victory. Former President Bush found this out after flashing the V sign to the Australian crowds in 1992.

Diversity in Attitudes toward Time

Americans typically view time as a valuable resource that is not to be wasted, and socializing is often considered a waste of time. However, it would be considered impolite to start a business meeting with Hispanics without engaging in a certain amount of relaxed small talk. If you try to rush business deals without slowly developing personal relationships with Japanese managers, you will not be successful in obtaining Japanese business accounts.

Americans and the Swiss businesspeople usually expect you to be precisely on time for an appointment. However, in several countries, you could find yourself going to an appointment with a manager on time, only to be kept waiting for an hour. If you call a meeting, in some countries, most members will be late and some may not show up at all. When they do show up, they may express that punctuality was not one of their priorities. They may expect you to wait one-half to a full hour for them. If you get angry and yell, you could harm human relations.

Diversity in Work Ethics

The work ethic, viewing work as a central life interest and a desirable goal in life, varies around the world. Generally, the Japanese have a stronger work ethic than Americans and Europeans. With a strong work ethic, and the acceptance of automation, many Japanese plants are the most productive in the world. Although there is not much difference in work ethics between Americans and Europeans, Americans are more productive even though the Europeans are usually better trained.

Americans are relatively good at getting poorly prepared workers to be productive, which is important when working with illiterate people all over the world. However, in some cultures, managers and employees have little interest in being productive. These relaxed attitudes do not do much for the bottom line of global businesses that are trying to change work ethics.

Diversity in Pay

Americans, in general, are no longer the world's highest-paid employees. The Japanese and Europeans have caught up and earn as much as Americans.

Employees in Third World countries are paid much less than employees in developed countries.

Pay systems also vary to meet employee values. One of the pay trends in the United States is pay for performance. However, some cultures value being paid for loyalty and following orders. Paying a salary works well in some countries, but not in others.

Diversity in Laws and Politics

The legal and political environment becomes increasingly complex as multinationals do business all over the world. Employee health and safety laws are generally more protective in developed countries than in Third World countries. Labor laws also vary widely from country to country. Western European nations offer good benefits including a required four- to six-week vacation, paid holidays, and sick and family leave. The amount of time employees work varies from country to country: German auto workers work about 1,600 hours a year, compared to Americans working 2,000 hours and Japanese 2,300 hours. Such differences change the actual labor cost per hour. It is also easier to terminate employees in some countries than in others.

In some countries, government structure and politicians are more stable than in others. A change in government can mean changes in business practices overnight. Some countries have literally taken away the plants and equipment owned by U.S. companies and sent the Americans home without any compensation.

Diversity in Ethics

When conducting global business you must rethink business ethics. In the United States and some other countries, it is illegal to take and give bribes for doing business. However, in some countries, bribing is the standard practice of doing business. For example, an American businessperson complained to a local telephone company manager that the service person showed up and asked for a bribe, which was refused, so the telephone worker left without installing the phone. The businessperson was told by the telephone company manager that the matter would be investigated, for a fee (bribe). MNC are working to develop global ethics codes.[103]

Diversity in Participative Management

Learning Objective

7. List seven areas of global diversity and give examples of differences

IE 13–4

In Third World nations, employees need basic skills training and may not be capable of participating in management decisions. Some cultures, like Japan and the United States, value participation in management whereas others do not. In some cultures employees simply want to be told what to do.

Management-labor relations vary globally. In France relations are more polarized than in the United States, whereas in Japan they are more cooperative. You should realize that management and human relations become more complex as styles change from country to country.

WORK APPLICATIONS

13. Have you experienced any cultural differences in human relations with others? If so, explain.

Handling Complaints

The EEOC's job is to handle complaints that are brought to it, many of which result in lawsuits. Effective management can be measured by the lack of complaints.[104] As a manager, you should strive to meet the goal of human relations by creating a win–win situation for all employees. All employees and customers should be given equal treatment.[105] However, no matter how hard you try to satisfy employees' needs, complaints will arise covering a range of topics which may include discrimination. Use the open-door policy and let employees feel as though they can come to you with a complaint. It is much better to get complaints out in the open and try to resolve them than to have employees complaining to everyone else about you.

You can use the complaint model to help you resolve complaints in either a union or nonunion organization when employees come to you with a complaint. The **complaint model** *involves: step 1, listen to the complaint and paraphrase it; step 2, have the complainer recommend a solution; step 3, schedule time to get all the facts and/or make a decision; and step 4, develop and implement a plan, and follow up.* Each step is discussed below.

Step 1. Listen to the Complaint and Paraphrase It

Listening is probably the most important step.[106] Listen to the full story without interruptions, and paraphrase it to ensure accuracy. When employees come to you with a complaint, try not to take it personally; even the best supervisors have to deal with complaints. Do not become defensive and try to talk the employee out of the complaint.

Step 2. Have the Complainer Recommend a Solution

After the supervisor has paraphrased the complaint and the employee has agreed with the paraphrasing, the supervisor should ask the complainer to recommend a solution that will resolve the complaint. Requesting a solution does not mean that the supervisor has to implement it.

In some cases, the recommended solution may not solve the problem. Or the solution may not be fair to others. Some recommendations may not be possible for the supervisor to implement. In such cases, the supervisor should let the employee know that the solution is not possible, and explain why.

Step 3. Schedule Time to Get All the Facts and/or Make a Decision

Since employee complaints often involve other people, you may find it necessary to check records or to talk to others. It is often helpful to talk to your boss or your peers, who may have had a similar complaint; they may be able to offer you some good advice on how best to resolve the complaint. Even when you have all the facts, it is usually advisable to take some time to weigh the facts and make a decision.

Schedule a specific period of time. In many cases, it does not have to be long. Generally, the more quickly a complaint is resolved, the fewer the negative side effects. Too many supervisors simply say, "I'll get back to you on this," without specifying a time period. This is very frustrating to the employee. Some supervisors are purposely vague because they have no intention of getting back to the employee. They are hoping the employee will forget about the complaint. This tactic may get the employee to stop complaining, but it may also cause productivity and turnover problems.

Step 4. Develop and Implement a Plan, and Follow Up

 Video
BM–4

 Skill-Building
13–3

After getting all the necessary facts and advice from others, the supervisor should develop a plan. The plan may be developed by simply using the complainer's recommended solution. However, when supervisors do not agree with the complainer's solution, they should explain why, and either work with the employee to find an alternative, or present their plan. The level of the employee's participation can change with capability level.

In cases where supervisors decide not to take any action to resolve the complaint, they should clearly explain why they chose not to do so. They should also state that if employees are not satisfied, they can appeal the decision to another level. The complainer should be told how to appeal the decision. In the nonunion organization, the usual step is to go to the supervisor's boss. In the union organization, the next step is often to go to the union steward.

As with all plans, it is important for the supervisor to make sure that the plan is implemented through follow-up methods. It may be appropriate to set a follow-up meeting. It is also advisable to document all meetings and action.

Exhibit 13–3 lists the four steps in the handling complaints model.

EXHIBIT 13-3	**HANDLING COMPLAINTS MODEL**
Learning Objective 8. List the steps in handling a complaint	Step 1. Listen to the complaint and paraphrase it. Step 2. Have the complainer recommend a solution. Step 3. Schedule time to get all the facts and/or make the decision. Step 4. Develop and implement a plan, and follow up.

WORK APPLICATIONS

14. Identify a complaint you brought to a supervisor. If you have never complained, interview someone who has. State the complaint and identify the steps in the complaint model the supervisor did and/or did not follow.

Customer Complaints

Handling a customer complaint is somewhat different than handling an employee when it involves something you and your company did wrong. The steps to follow are:

1. Admit you made a mistake.
2. Agree that it should not have happened.
3. Tell the customer what you are going to do about it. Or, ask what the customer recommends you do about it.
4. Take the action to make it up to the customer.
5. Take precautions to prevent the mistake in the future.

REVIEW

Select one or more methods: (1) fill in the missing key terms from memory; (2) match the key terms, from the end of the review, with their definitions below; and/or (3) copy the key terms in order from the key terms list at the beginning of the chapter.

_____ is the prejudgment of a person or situation based on attitudes. _____ is behavior for or against a person or situation. The five common areas of employment discrimination include recruitment, selection, compensation, upward mobility, and evaluation.

Equal Employment Opportunity and Affirmative Action are the major laws affecting discrimination. The EEOC _____ list includes Hispanics, Asians, African-Americans, Native Americans, and Alaskan natives. Employers must be careful not to ask illegal discriminatory questions during the hiring process. _____ allows discrimination on the basis of religion, sex, or national origin where it is reasonably necessary to normal operation of a particular enterprise. _____ are planned special efforts to recruit, hire, and promote women and members of minority groups.

The legally protected groups include minorities; older workers; the _____, people with significant physical, mental, or emotional limitations; alcohol and drug abusers, people with AIDS, and women.

_____ is any unwelcomed behavior of a sexual nature.

_____ is discrimination based on sex. Both men's and women's sex roles are changing as the majority of women work, and men take on more responsibility for child care. Most women work for economic necessity, and they do not get equal pay. _____ refers to jobs that are distinctly different, but require similar levels of ability, having the same pay scale. Men and women are equally capable of being successful managers. Only about 37 percent of managers are women. Women do not have to act like men to be successful managers. To overcome sexism, organizations should eliminate sexist language and behavior.

When working with people of different cultures, traditional Americans should be empathetic and make efforts to make people feel comfortable. A _____ conducts a large part of its business outside of the country of its headquarters. _____ are people who live and work in a country other than their native country. There is global diversity in the areas of customs, time, work ethics, pay, law and politics, ethics, and participative management.

The _____ involves step 1, listen to the complaint and paraphrase it; step 2, have the complainer recommend a solution; step 3, schedule time to get all the facts and/or make a decision; and step 4, develop and implement a plan, and follow up.

KEY TERMS

affirmative action
   programs   464
bona fide occupational
   qualification   462
comparable worth   472

complaint model   478
disability   466
discrimination   459
expatriates   476
minority   461

multinational company
   (MNC)   476
prejudice   459
sexism   471
sexual harassment   470

OBJECTIVE CASE

**Vance Coffman:
Lockheed Martin**

Vance Coffman, Chief Executive Officer (CEO) of Lockheed Martin since 1996, has gained the admiration and respect of many diversity scholars and diversity advocates. Through his leadership, Lockheed Martin—a highly diversified advanced technology corporation with approximately $30 billion in annualized sales and approximately 190,000 employees—has one of the most successful diversity programs in the nation. Coffman is most admired for his efforts at creating a work environment that fosters greater awareness and sensitivity to the needs of Lockheed's diverse employee population. These efforts include crafting a "mission success" statement that clearly delineates the corporation's commitment to diversity and also hiring executives with the skills and commitment to implementing the corporation's diversity initiatives. Lockheed Martin's core values on its mission statement are ethics, excellence, "can-do," integrity, people, and teamwork. On people, Lockheed maintains that it will embrace lifelong learning, combined with company-sponsored education and development programs. On teamwork, it will multiply the creativity, talents, and contributions by focusing on team goals. Teams will assume collective responsibility, share trust and leadership, embrace diversity, and accept responsibility for prudent risk taking.

At Lockheed Martin, the belief is that to attract the best of the best, the corporation must include all segments of the population. In this respect, the corporation's Equal Opportunity Office, (EOO) has created Workforce Diversity Initiatives that provide guidelines for implementing diversity programs at the business unit levels. The EOO is set up to assist Lockheed Martin companies on how to best achieve diversity. According to Holley, director of EOO, there is no cookie-cutter approach to achieving diversity at Lockheed. Many Lockheed Martin companies have diversity departments charged with ensuring, among other things, that their companies are flexible enough to meet the needs of all employees. A number of Lockheed Martin companies have enhanced their diversity efforts by creating employee councils that serve as the conduits that carry concerns from employees to the councils and from the councils to management. The councils, all of which work on a volunteer basis, carry out the goals and programs suggested by the diversity department and by fellow employees.

Another diversity initiative of Lockheed Martin has been the creation of employee organizations. Examples of social support networks of this kind include members of the Gay, Lesbian or Bisexual at Lockheed Martin (GLOBAL) organization, the Asian American and Pacific-Islander American Lockheed Martin Association (ALMA) and the Black Effectiveness Support Team (BEST). Minority-based social networks such as these are important because they tailor their training and mentoring to the specific issues of a particular subculture, says Paul Ma, research specialist with the Missiles and Space division and chairman or ALMA.

Lockheed Martin has also actively advocated community outreach, which allows employees of the corporation to work with the community to enhance diversity. The corporation awards scholarships to minority students, sponsors and participates in local and national conferences such as the Society of Women Engineers Conference, the Mexican-American Society Conference, the NAACP Intensive Summer Studies Program (ISSP), and the Academic Olympics for African-American students.

Diversity managers and volunteers at companies throughout Lockheed Martin take different approaches to assessing how big a role their diversity initiatives have played in helping current employees feel at home. One of the most quantifiable approaches for self-evaluation is the Diversity Progress Index for measuring improvements in diversity over time. The index, which was first piloted in 1997, evaluates a department's approach to advocacy, assessment, planning, and implementation—as they relate to diversity. The index also allows a department to evaluate the role diversity has played in its business success. Outstanding performers are honored with the prestigious President's Diversity Awards.

Because of strong leadership from Coffman and his executive team and a highly motivated and committed group of lower-level managers, Lockheed Martin has received national attention for its diversity efforts. In the 1997 issue of *Diversity/Careers In Engineering and Information Technology*, the corporation was credited with having a wide-ranging diversity program that emphasizes ties to business activities, employee training and development, the workplace environment, employee support and communication—as well as to a variety of recruitment strategies.

Go to the Internet: For more information on Vance Coffman and Lockheed Martin and to update the information provided in this case, do a name search on the Internet and go to the website at *www.lockheed.com.* For ideas on using the Internet with cases, see Appendix C.

Support your answer to the following questions with specific information from the case and text, or other information you get from the Web or other source.

1. In what ways has Lockheed Martin taken proactive approaches towards supporting and valuing diversity?

2. Is Lockheed Martin a multinational corporation (MNC)?

3. Are cross-cultural relationships important to Lockheed Martin?

Cumulative Questions

4. Why is important for Lockheed Martin to cultivate a learning organization (Chapter 2 and 5)?

5. What do attitudes, self-concept, values (Chapter 3), and leadership (Chapter 7) have to do with this case?

6. Lockheed's Diversity Progress Index best illustrates which motivation theory (content, process, reinforcement—Chapter 6) and OD technique (Chapter 12)?

7. Review Chapter 12 and discuss which concepts relate to this case and how.

OBJECTIVE CASE

Lilly's Promotion

The Carlson Mining and Manufacturing Co. needs a new vice president of human resources. Its headquarters are in Detroit, but the company has mining and manufacturing plants in three states and five different countries. Foreign plants account for about 70 percent of total operations.

The president, Ron Carlson, is meeting with some of the vice presidents and the board of directors to make the decision on who gets promoted to vice president. The following are excerpts from their discussion.

RON: As you know, we are meeting today to promote someone to vice president. Ted, tell us about the candidates.

TED: We have narrowed the decision down to two people. You all know the two candidates. They are Rich Martin and Lilly Jefferson. Rich is 38 and has been with us for 15 years, and he has worked in human resources for 10 years. He has an M.B.A. from a leading business school. Lilly is 44 and has been with us for 10 years. She recently finished her B.S. in business, going to school nights at the local state college.

JIM: Lilly is an African-American female with older children. She is perfect for the job, fitting into two AA classifications. We can meet our AA quotas without promoting Lilly, but it would help. Besides, there are a lot of African-Americans here in Detroit; we could get some great publicity.

ED: Wait a minute. We cannot have any girls at the V. P. level. You know they are emotional and cannot take the pressure of the job.

CARL: Their performance records are about the same, but Rich has been with us longer, and is better educated.

The discussion ended in a vote. Lilly won by a large margin. Off the record: it was because she is a qualified African-American female. If she were a white male, Rich would have been promoted.

Answer the following questions. Then in the space between questions, state why you selected that answer.

_____ 1. Discrimination was used in the promotion process.

      a. true   *b.* false

_____ 2. The primary area discussed in this case is:

      a. recruitment   *c.* compensation   *e.* evaluation
      b. selection   *d.* upward mobility

_____ 3. Affirmative action affected the decision to promote Lilly.

      a. true   *b.* false

_____ 4. Rich may have a case for reverse discrimination.

      a. true   *b.* false

_____ 5. Sexism occurred in this case.

      a. true   *b.*false

_____ 6. Ed's statement was:

      a. factual   *b.* myth

_____ 7. Ed used sexist language.

      a. true   *b.* false

_____ 8. With Lilly being a minority member, she will most likely encounter cross-cultural relations problems.

     a. true   *b.* false

_____ 9. Carlson is a multinational company.

     a. true   *b.* false

_____ 10. The most help Lilly got in getting to the V. P. position was:

a. AAP	*d.* child care	*f.* EAP
b. training	*e.* role models and mentors	*g.* wellness programs
c. flexible work schedule		

11. Who would you have voted for? Why?

12. How would you feel in Lilly's position, knowing that you are qualified for the job, but were selected because you were a minority? Lilly's response can be role-played.

Ethics: Arthur Anderson

*Critical Thinking
Questions:*

Vignette 3: A Very Friendly Fellow
   Vignette 3 illustrates a situation in which you determine if sexual harassment
occurs on the job.

1. Is the male, Bill, sexually harassing the female, Shelly?

2. If you believe Bill is sexually harassing Shelly, which of the six areas as grounds
   for lawsuits exist.

3. If Shelly takes stronger action to stop Bill's behavior, what consequences may
   result?

4. If sexual harassment exists, what can/should Shelly do to stop it?

Fisal Fairy Tale #8: Cindrella

Following the steps to getting to read a fiscal fairy tale in MG Webzine Exercise 1–2 in Chapter 1, page 34 go to the MG website and read *Fiscal Fairy Tale #8: Cindrella* (your instructor may ask you to print a copy and bring it to class). Answer these questions (your instructor may ask you to type them and bring them to class).

Online MG Webzine Exercise 13

Questions Relating to the Tale Only

1. As stated at the end of the tale, in 50 words or so, what is your response to this tale? You may send it to MG.

2. Are you, or anyone you know, different from your fellow workers, with values different from the establishment? How does it feel being different? Explain some of the differences and feelings.

3. Should organizations have these yearly offsite meetings? What are the advantages and disadvantages?

4. What options does Cindrella have? List at least three. What would you do in Cindrella's position?

Questions Relating the Tale to the Chapter Concepts

5. Of the legally protected groups listed in the text, which diversity issue seems to be the focus of the difference in perception of the off-site meeting?

6. Is sexism and work and family balance an issue in this case?

7. Has Cindrella's supervisor done an effective job of handling Cindrella's complaint about not wanting to go to the off-site meeting? Does Cindrella have a legitimate complatint?

In-Class MG Webzine Exercise 13

The instructor selects one of the six options from Appendix B page 589.

INTERNET EXERCISES

Anti-Defamation League (IE 13–1)

Online Internet Exercise 13–1

The objective of this exercise is to learn more about the Anti-Defamation League (ADL) and prejudice and ways to beat it. Do the following:

1. Go to the ADL website homepage—*www.adl.org* At the top of the page it gives a brief explanation of what the ADL is.

2. Click "Search" then type in "Prejudice: 101 ways you can beat it" then click "go" and "101 ideas for building a prejudice-free zone." Read the Citizen's Action Guide definitions. Scroll back up.

3. Next, click one of the zone subsections (education, community, work) you want to learn more about and read the numbered ideas (your instructor may require a copy) and select one as most relevant to you.

4. Questions: (1) What does the ADL do? (2) Which zone subsection did you visit and what number ideas were related to that zone? (3) Which one idea, list it by number and name, did you select as most relevant to you and why? (4) How could this idea be used to beay prejudice in your zone? (Your instructor may require typed answers.)

In-Class Internet Exercise 13–1, IE 13–2, IE 13–3, and IE 13–4

Equal Employment Opportunity Commission (IE 13–2)

The instructor selects one of the six options from Appendix B page 589.

The objective of this exercise is to learn more about the Equal Employment Opportunity Commission (EEOC). Do the following:

Online Internet Exercise 13–2

1. Go to the EEOC Website homepage—*www.eeoc.gov* and review it.

2. Click any of the subsites that you want to learn more about and read the formation (your instructor may require a copy).

3. Questions: (1) Which subsite did you visit and why did you select it? (3) What did you learn about the EEOC, in 50 words or so, that you did not learn in the textbook? (Your instructor may require typed answers.)

The objective of this exercise is to learn more about sexual harassment by taking a quiz. Do the following:

Sexual Harassment (IE 13–3)

1. Go to the Capstone Communications website homepage—*www.capstn.com*

2. Click "Capstone Quiz" and select your answers. As stated, you may place your answers on a sheet of paper and another alternative is to print out the quiz and place your answers on the quiz. Note that this quiz goes beyond the information given in the textbook. Therefore, you are not expected get a high score. Thus, don't be concerned about your score. (Your instructor may require a copy of the quiz and/or answers). As directed, when you finish the quiz

Online Internet Exercise 13–3 (Self-Assessment)

3. Click "check your answers" and score your quiz. However, focus on what you are learning about sexual harassment.

4. Questions: (1) What was your score—how many questions did you get correct? (2) What did you learn about sexual harassment that you did not learn in the textbook? (3) How can you use this information on the job? (Your instructor may require typed answers.)

**Country Information
(IE 13–4)**

**Online Internet
Exercise 13–4**

The objective of this exercise is to learn more about a country of interest to you. Do the following:

1. Go to the Lonely Planet travel guide website homepage—www.lonelyplanet.com.

2. Click "Destinations," and click to select a country you want to learn more about.

3. Read about the "Facts at a Glance," "Culture," and another category to learn more about that country (your instructor may require a copy).

4. Questions: (1) What country did you select? (2) Why is this country of interest to you? (3) What did you learn about this country that you did not already know? (4) How can you use this information in your personal and/or professional life? (Your instructor may require typed answers.)

In-Class Sexism

Objective: To better understand sexist language and behavior, and how it affects human relations.

SCANS: The SCANS competencies of interpersonal skills, especially information and systems and the foundations of especially basic and thinking, and personal qualities are developed through this exercise.

Preparation: None for this exercise.

Experience: You will discuss sexism.

Procedure 1
(7–15 minutes)

Option A: Students give sample words and behaviors found in the workplace that are sexist. (For example, [words] foreman and [behavior] a woman being required to get the coffee.) The instructor or a class member writes the headings "words" and "behavior" on the board and records the class members' examples. Discuss how these sexist words and behaviors affect people's behavior in organizations.

Option B: Break into teams of five or six with as equal representation of male and female as possible. As in Option A, develop a list of sexist words and behaviors and discuss how they affect people's behavior in organizations.

Procedure 2
(7–15 minutes)

Option A: As a class, select a few sexist words and behaviors. Discuss how to overcome this sexism.

Option B: As a group, select a few sexist words and behaviors. Discuss how to overcome this sexism.

Conclusion: The instructor may lead a class discussion and/or make concluding remarks.

Application (2–4 minutes): What did I learn from this exercise? How will I use this knowledge in the future?

Sharing: Volunteers give their answers to the application section.

SKILL-BUILDING EXERCISE 13–2

Preparation
Male and Female
Small Group
Behavior

For this exercise, some of the class members will need to bring tape recorders to class in order to record small group discussions. Small tape recorders are suggested. Your instructor may assign specific people to bring them. If not, bring a tape recorder if you have one.

Source: The idea to develop this exercise came from Susan Morse, University of Massachusetts at Amherst, in "Gender Differences in Behavior in Small Groups: A Look at the OB Class," paper presented at the 25th Annual Meeting of the Eastern Academy of Management, May 12, 1988.

In-Class
Male and Female
Small Group
Behavior

Objective: To see if there are any differences in male and female behavior in small groups.

Preparation: Some of the class members need to bring tape recorders to class to record the small group discussion.

SCANS: The SCANS competencies of interpersonal skills, especially information and systems and the foundations of especially basic and thinking, and personal qualities are developed through this exercise.

Experience: In a small group, you will make a decision that will be tape recorded, and then analyze the tape to determine if there are differences in male and female behavior.

Procedure 1
(15–20 minutes)

Break into teams of five or six. Make the number of males and females as even as possible in each group. Be sure each group has a tape recorder. As a group, you will select a candidate for a job opening. As an individual, read the information below and think about who you would hire in this situation. When all group members are ready, begin your discussion of whom to hire. *Be sure to tape record the conversation.* Discuss each candidate's qualifications fully, coming to a group consensus on whom to hire. Do not vote, unless the time is almost up. You must make a decision by the deadline stated by your instructor. Try not to finish very early, but if you do, wait for the rest of the class to finish before going on to the next procedure.

You are a member of the local school board. The board is making the decision on which candidate to hire for the open position of girls' high school tennis coach. The following is information on each candidate.

Mary Smith: Mary has been a history teacher at a nearby high school for 10 years. She was the tennis coach for one year. It has been five years since she coached the team. Mary says she stopped coaching because it was too time-consuming with her young daughter, but she misses it and wants to return. Mary's performance was rated as 3 on a scale of 1 to 5. Mary never played competitive tennis, but she says she plays regularly. You guess she is about 35 years old.

Tom Jones: Tom works as a supervisor on the 11 P.M. to 7 A.M. shift for a local business. He has never coached before. However, Tom was a star player in high school and college. He still plays in local tournaments, and you see his name in the paper now and then. You guess Tom is about 25 years old.

Wendy Clark: Wendy has been a basketball coach and a teacher of physical education classes for a nearby high school for the past five years. She has a bachelor's degree in physical education. Wendy has never coached tennis, but she did play on the high school team. She says she plays tennis about once a week. You guess she is about 40 years old.

Lisa Williams: Lisa has been an English teacher at your school for the past two years. She has never coached, but she did take a course in college covering how to coach tennis. She is popular with her students. Lisa plays tennis regularly, and you have heard she is a pretty good player. She is African American. You guess Lisa is about 24 years old.

Hank Chung: Hank has been teaching math at your school for seven years. He was a star player in high school in Japan, and he played tennis for a successful U.S. college team. He still plays for fun regularly. He has never coached or had any type of coaching courses. He applied for the job the last time it was open four years ago but was not selected. You guess Hank is about 30 years of age.

Sally Carson: Sally has taught physical education classes at your school for the past four years. She never played competitive tennis but has a master's degree in physical education and has had courses regarding how to coach tennis. Sally taught and coached field hockey at a high school for 15 years before moving to your city. You guess she is about 48 years old.

Procedure 2
(1–2 minutes)

As an individual, answer the following questions. Circle the letter of your response.

1. Who spoke more?
    a. males   *b.* females   *c.* equal time

2. The one individual with the most influence in the group was
    a. male   *b.* female

3. The one individual with the least influence in the group was
    a. male   *b.* female

4. Overall, who had the most influence on the group?
    a. males   *b.* females   *c.* Influence was equal

5. Interruptions came more frequently from
    a. males interrupting females
    b. females interrupting males
    c. equal interruption from both

6. Of the total discussion time, I spoke for about _____ minutes.

Procedure 3
(2–4 minutes)
Procedure 4
(20–30 minutes)

Total the group's answers to the six questions in Procedure 2. All members should write the totals above next to the questions.

Play back the tape-recorded discussion. As it plays, write down who talks and how long they talk for. If one person interrupts another, note it as male interrupts female, or vice versa. When the tape finishes, add up the number of minutes each person spoke. Total the male and female times. As a team, re-answer the six questions in Procedure 2 above. Were the answers the same before and after listening to the tape-recorded discussion?

Conclusion: The instructor may lead a class discussion and/or make concluding remarks.

Application (2–4 minutes): What did I learn from this experience? How can I use this knowledge in the future?

Sharing: Volunteers give their answers to the application section.

● **Preparation
Handling
Complaints**

During class you will be given the opportunity to role-play handling a complaint. Select a complaint. It may be one you brought to a supervisor, one that was brought to you, one you heard about, or one you made up. Fill in the information below for the person who will role-play bringing you a complaint to resolve.

Explain the situation and complaint.

List pertinent information about the other party that will help him or her play the role of the complainer. (Relationship with supervisor, knowledge, years of service, background, age, values, and so on.)

Review Exhibit 13–3 and think about what you will say and do when you handle this complaint.

Complaint Observer Form

During the role play, observe the handling of the complaint. Determine whether the supervisor followed the steps below, and how well. Try to have a positive and improvement comment for each step in the complaint model. Be specific and descriptive. For all improvement comments, have an alternative positive behavior (APB). What could have been done or said that was not?

Step 1. How well did the supervisor listen? Was the supervisor open to the complaint? Did the supervisor try to talk the employee out of the complaint? Was the supervisor defensive? Did the supervisor get the full story without interruptions? Did the supervisor paraphrase the complaint?

(positive)   (improvement)

Step 2. Did the supervisor have the complainer recommend a solution? How well did the supervisor react to the solution? If the solution could not be used, did the supervisor explain why?

(positive)   (improvement)

Step 3. Did the supervisor schedule time to get all the facts and/or make a decision? Was it a specific date? Was it a reasonable length of time?

(positive)   (improvement)

Step 4. Did the supervisor develop and implement a plan, and schedule a follow-up? (This step may not have been appropriate at this time.)

● **In-Class
Handling
Complaints**

SB 13–3

Objective: To experience and develop skills in resolving complaints.

SCANS: The SCANS competencies of information and especially interpersonal skills and the foundations of basic, especially thinking in the area of solving problems, and personal qualities are developed through this exercise.

Preparation: You should have prepared to handle a complaint.

Experience: You will initiate, respond to, and observe a complaint role play. Then you will evaluate the effectiveness of its resolution.

*Procedure 1
(2–3 minutes)*

Break into as many groups of three as possible. (You do not have to be with members of your permanent team.) If there are any people not in a triad, make one or two groups of two. Each member selects a number 1, 2, or 3. Number 1 will be the first to initiate a complaint role play, then 2, followed by 3.

*Procedure 2
(8–15 minutes)*

A. Number 1 (the supervisor) gives his or her preparation for Preparation for In-Class Skill-Building Exercise 13–3, complaint information, to Number 2 (the complainer) to read. Once Number 2 understands, role-play (step B). Number 3 is the observer.

B. Role-play the complaint. Put yourself in this person's situation, ad-lib. Number 3, the observer, writes his or her observations on the complaint observer form, found.

C. Integration. When the role play is over, the observer leads a discussion on the effectiveness of the conflict resolution. All three should discuss the effectiveness; Number 3 is not a lecturer.

Do not go on until told to do so.

*Procedure 3
(8–15 minutes)*

Same as Procedure 2, only Number 2 is now the supervisor; Number 3 is now the complainer; and Number 1 is the observer.

*Procedure 4
(8–15 minutes)*

Same as Procedure 2, only Number 3 is the supervisor; Number 1 is the complainer; and Number 2 is the observer.

Conclusion: The instructor leads a class discussion and/or makes concluding remarks.

Application (2–4 minutes): What did I learn from this experience? How will I use this knowledge in the future?

Sharing: Volunteers give their answers to the application section.

Productivity, Technology, and Participative Management

14

Learning Objectives

After completing this chapter, you should be able to:

1. Explain the three ways to increase productivity.

2. Explain how to increase productivity through resources.

3. Describe the training cycle and how training is used to increase productivity.

4. List and explain the steps in the increasing-productivity (coaching) model.

5. List and explain the five steps of performance appraisals and state how performance appraisals can lead to increased productivity.

6. Discuss some of the ways that technology affects behavior, human relations, and performance.

7. Explain the relationship between suggestion and reward systems.

8. Discuss the differences among quality of work life, quality circles, and work teams.

9. Define the following 15 key terms (in order of appearance in the chapter):

productivity	**participative management**
training	**techniques**
development	**reward systems**
training cycle	**compensation**
job instructional training	**gainsharing**
performance appraisal	**quality of work life (QWL)**
standards	**quality circles**
increasing-productivity model	**work teams**

Cindy Witney had a great idea for a new product, so she started her own small business five years ago today. Over the first four years under her autocratic management style, the company went from 3 employees to 300. But now it's having problems. Competition from two big businesses has moved in on her market. They are producing the same product for less. As much as Cindy hated to do it, she laid 50 people off over the last year, and if things continue the way they are, she will lay off more employees. She asks herself, "Is there any way I can increase my productivity to compete with the big businesses? After all, it was my idea to make the product in the first place. This isn't fair." There are ways to increase productivity; you have learned some of them in other chapters, and you will learn more in this chapter.

● Organization
● Group
● Individual

Goal of
Human Relations

Productivity

Productivity is a major concern of organizations.[1] To compete globally, companies have been pushing for productivity gains.[2] When firms pay employees more and they don't increase productivity, firms generally increase the prices of goods and service, which results in inflation. U.S. productivity has increased.[3] Increased productivity has meant inflation has been low despite pay increases in recent years.[4] If we want to increase our standard of living, we must increase productivity. The major means of increasing productivity is through participative management,[5] which we talked about in prior chapters and will discuss further in this chapter.

If U.S. workers are not productive, they will continue to be put out of work as their jobs are performed in other countries. We need to produce more with less while creating a win–win situation for employees and management in order to compete globally.

By definition, **productivity** *is a performance measure of inputs to outputs.* The inputs include employee's time, materials, equipment, and so forth. The outputs are the products or services produced. Productivity tells managers how efficiently they are utilizing their department's resources. Some organizations have increased their productivity by working better and faster with fewer employees. For example,

Xerox has halved both the number of people and the amount of time needed to design a product. Harley-Davidson, Inc., has reduced total plant employment by 25 percent while cutting the time to make a motorcycle by more than one-half.

Measuring Productivity

Different tasks and products can be measured by dividing the outputs by the inputs. For example, a trucking company wants to measure its energy performance on a delivery. The truck traveled 500 miles and used 50 gallons of gas. Its productivity was 10 miles to the gallon:

$$\frac{\text{Output — 500 miles traveled}}{\text{Inputs — 50 gallons of gas}} = \text{Productivity of 10 MPG}$$

Measuring productivity is not always as straightforward and easy to do.

Increasing Productivity

Measuring productivity is, in itself, insufficient without stressing increases in productivity. There are three ways to increase productivity:

1. Increase the value of the outputs while maintaining the value of the inputs ($\uparrow$O$\leftrightarrow$I). In the opening case, if Cindy can get the same number of employees to produce more products at no additional cost, she will increase productivity.

2. Maintain the value of the outputs while decreasing the value of the inputs ($\leftrightarrow$O$\downarrow$I). If Cindy lays off 50 workers and the remaining employees continue to produce the same number of products, she will increase productivity. The U.S. Postal Service expects to save $300,000 a year by installing 15,000 exit signs that use less electricity.[6] Mortgage Electronic Registration Systems plans to cut paperwork and will save $40 per loan on processing, or up to $200 million a year.[7] Chrysler implemented thousands of cost-saving ideas it got from suppliers, which will boost its profits by $325 million.[8]

3. Increase the value of the outputs while decreasing the value of the inputs ($\uparrow$O$\downarrow$I). If Cindy cuts the work force and they produce more products than before, she gets a double benefit that increases productivity. Teams are being used to redesign the way jobs are performed in order to increase outputs while decreasing inputs.[9]

Learning Objective

1. Explain the three ways to increase productivity

APPLICATION SITUATIONS

Measuring Productivity

AS 14–1

The standard monthly rate of productivity in the department is:

$$\frac{\text{Output 10,000 units}}{\text{Input 5,000 costs}} = 2.00:1 \text{ ratio or } 200\%$$

Calculate the ratio, percentage, and percentage increase or decrease for the next five months.

_____ 1. Month 6, output was 9,500, input cost $5,000.

_____ 2. Month 7, output was 10,300, input cost $5,000.

_____ 3. Month 8, output was 10,000, input cost $5,200.

_____ 4. Month 9, output was 10,000, input cost $4,900.

_____ 5. Month 10, output was 10,200, input cost $4,800.

Increasing Productivity through Resources

Although productivity lies more in its people,[10] resources can and do have a major impact on productivity. Chapter 12 discussed technological changes, including machines and automation, which can increase performance through resources. In Chapter 6, you learned about motivation. Motivating employees increases performance.[11] With the appropriate use of resources, you can enrich and design jobs that increase productivity by focusing on employee behavior.[12]

One area not yet covered is increasing productivity through capital. *Capital* refers to the financial and physical resources of the organization. There are five areas to work on to increase productivity through capital:

Capital Equipment: Capital equipment is a major way of increasing productivity because new equipment can often save time. Organizations should invest in the latest technology that will increase productivity.[13]

Reduce Waste: Not wasting your capital resources can also increase productivity. Most managers can find waste within their departments and reduce it. This is often the major focus of cost cutting. However, too many organizations carry reducing waste and downsizing to the point of decreasing efficiency and productivity.[14]

Inventories: It is expensive to have excess inventories of raw materials, work-in-process (WIP), and finished goods inventories. To keep inventories to a minimum, many organizations are using just-in-time inventory.

Budgets: When developing and spending the budget, managers should get the best value for the department and organization.

Space: Use the department's space as productively as possible.

In the opening case, Cindy can consider buying new equipment as a means of increasing productivity to compete with the big businesses. She can also focus on reducing waste, inventories, budgets, and space. But before rushing out to buy new equipment, Cindy should determine why the big businesses are more productive. She needs to follow the guidelines from Chapter 10 about problem solving and decision making.

Learning Objective

2. Explain how to increase productivity through resources

WORK APPLICATIONS

1. Describe how an organization you work/worked for can increase productivity through better utilization of capital resources.

Increasing Productivity through Training

Training pays,[15] and a lack of training is blamed for the failure of employees.[16] As the diversified global environment continues to expand, the need for continuous learning and training becomes necessary for companies to remain competitive.[17] Successful companies adjust to changes quickly because their employees receive continuing training.[18] Companies are increasing training programs.[19] Consultants, including Performance Innovators Consultant Group, are developing training programs for corporate worldwide. Because, investing in employees pays off.[20]

After a position is staffed, either by a new or an existing employee, there is usually a need to train the person to do the job. **Training** *is the process of developing the necessary skills to perform the present job.* **Development** *is the process of developing the ability to perform both present and future jobs.* Typically, training is used to develop technical skills of nonmanagers, while development is usually less technical and is designed for professional and managerial employees. The terms *training* and *development* are often used together, and interchangeably as well.

The Training Cycle

Following the steps in the training cycle helps ensure that training is done in a systematic way. The **training cycle** *steps include step 1, conduct needs assessment; step 2, set objectives; step 3, prepare for training; step 4, conduct the training; and step 5, measure and evaluate training results.*

Step 1. Conduct Needs Assessment:
Before training begins, someone must determine the employees' training needs. The training needs analysis differs between new and present employees.

In the opening case, Cindy needs to determine if training will make her employees more productive. If her employees are as well trained as her competitors' employees are, training will not solve her productivity problem. If training is a solution, she can proceed to step 2.

Step 2. Set Objectives:
The key to the training program is the well-defined, performance-based objectives. As with all plans, you should begin by determining the end result you want to achieve. The objective criteria discussed in Chapter 6 apply to training objectives. Sample training objectives are: "Assemblers will be able to assemble 10 sets per hour by the end of the one-day training period." "Customer service representatives will service an average of 20 customers per hour by the end of the one-month training period."

Step 3. Prepare for Training:
Before conducting a training session, you should plan the training session and have all the necessary materials ready. Your plans should answer the who, what, when, where, and how questions. If you have ever had an instructor come to class obviously unprepared or who did not understand the material, you know why you need to be prepared before training.

In preparing for a training session, you need to break the task down into steps. What you do as part of a routine task seems simple to you, but to the new employee it may seem very complicated. Write out the steps and go through them to make sure they work. Your steps should be based on the job instructional training (JIT) steps. JIT focuses on procedural aspects of training, and is used globally. The **job instructional training** *steps are: step 1, preparation of the trainee; step 2, trainer presentation of the job; step 3, trainee performance of the job; and step 4, follow-up.* The JIT steps are presented in Exhibit 14–1.

EXHIBIT 14–1

 Video

BM 14–1

JOB INSTRUCTIONAL TRAINING

Step 1. Preparation of the trainee.
Step 2. Trainer presentation of the job.
Step 3. Trainee performance of the job.
Step 4. Follow-up.

Step 4. Conduct the Training:
Follow your plans as you implement the JIT program. Be sure to have your written JIT plan with you and any other materials needed. When you conduct training using other training methods, you should still implement your plans.

Step 5. Measure and Evaluate Training Results:
During and at the end of the training program, you should measure and evaluate the training results to determine whether or not the trainees achieved the objectives of the training program. If objectives were achieved, the training is over. If not, you may have to continue the training until objectives are met, or take the employees off the job if they cannot meet the standards.

Revise your written plans where improvements can be made. File them where you can find them for future use.

Exhibit 14–2 illustrates the training cycle steps.

IE 14–1

EXHIBIT 14–2   THE TRAINING CYCLE

Learning Objective

3. Describe the training cycle and how training is used to increase productivity

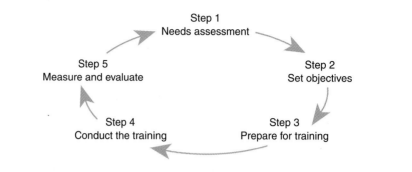

2. State how you were trained to perform a specific job. Explain how the training affected your job performance. How could training at this organization be used to increase productivity?

APPLICATION SITUATIONS

The Training Cycle	Identify each of the five statements below, by its step:

AS 14–2

A. Step 1, conduct needs assessment   D. Step 4, conduct the training

B. Step 2, set objectives   E. Step 5, measure and evaluate results

C. Step 3, prepare for training

_____ 6. "I will now demonstrate the proper technique."

_____ 7. "At the end of this training session, you will be able to operate the machine."

_____ 8. "In reviewing your performance, I've decided that you need more training to increase your speed."

_____ 9. "You passed the test with a perfect score; you're certified."

_____ 10. "Where did I put that JIT sheet? I need to revise it."

Performance Appraisal as a Means of Increasing Productivity

After employees are hired, during and after their training, they must be evaluated. And properly trained employees get better performance reviews.[21] **Performance appraisal** *is the ongoing process of evaluating employee job performance.* Performance appraisal is also called *performance job evaluation, performance review, merit rating,* and *performance audit.* Regardless of the name, because of the relationship between the manager's behavior and the employees performance,[22] performance appraisal is one of the manager's most important, and most difficult, functions.[23] Managers should provide performance feedback as a daily function,[24] and 360-degree feedback (chapter 4) is effective.[25] Conducted properly, performance appraisal can decrease absenteeism and turnover, and increase morale and productivity.

The performance of employees is appraised according to two sets of objectives: (1) developmental and (2) evaluative. Developmental objectives are used as the basis of decisions that improve future performance.[26] Evaluative objectives are used as the basis of administrative decisions that reward or punish past performance, for example, to make compensation decisions (e.g., wage and salary increases, bonus pay); and to make demotion, termination, transfer, and promotion decisions.

The performance appraisal process has five steps. These are shown in Exhibit 14–3 and discussed below.

EXHIBIT 14–3   **PERFORMANCE APPRAISAL STEPS**

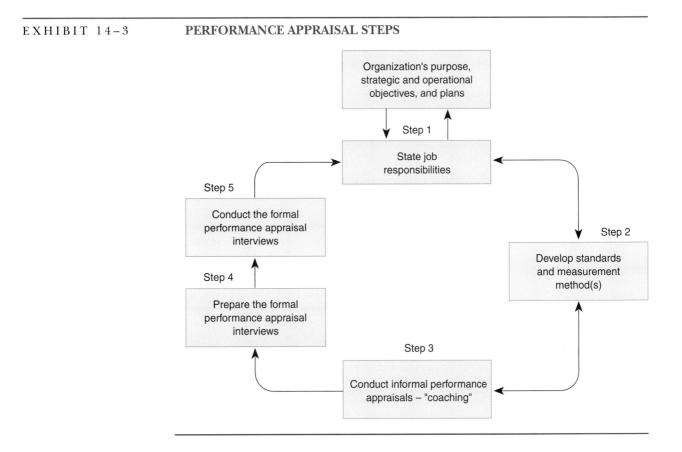

Step 1. State Job Responsibilities

Job responsibilities are usually stated in the employee's job description as the basic tasks and responsibilities of the employee for the job. Job responsibilities should be ranked in order of importance.

Step 2. Develop Standards and Measurement Methods

After you determine what it takes to do the job, you should develop standards and methods for measuring performance.[27] Poor standards are a major problem of performance appraisals. They include vagueness of the performance, poorly defined performance criteria, inappropriate scale measures, and meaningless assessment items.

The term **standards** *describes performance levels in the areas of quantity, quality, time, and cost.* Sample standards for a secretary could be to type 50 words (quantity) per minute (time) with two errors or less (quality) at a maximum salary of $8 per hour (cost). When establishing standards for performance appraisals, you should have a range of performance. For example, the standard range for typing could be 70 words per minute (WPM)—excellent; 60 WPM—good; 50 WPM—average; 40 WPM—satisfactory; 30 WPM—unsatisfactory. Not communicating standards and giving feedback[28] are major problems with performance appraisals. In Exhibit 14–4, several commonly used performance appraisal measurement methods are described.

3. Describe the performance standards for a job you hold/held. How would you improve them?

EXHIBIT 14–4   PERFORMANCE APPRAISAL METHODS

The Critical Incidents File

The critical incidents file is a performance appraisal method in which the manager writes down positive and negative performance behavior of employees throughout the performance period. The critical incidents file is a form of documentation that is needed in this litigious environment.

The Rating Scale

The rating scale is a performance appraisal form on which the manager simply checks off the employee's level of performance. Some of the possible areas evaluated include quantity of work, quality of work, dependability, judgment, attitude, cooperation, and initiative.

Behaviorally Anchored Rating Scales (BARS)

BARS is a performance appraisal method combining rating and critical incidents. It is more objective and accurate than the two methods separately. Rather than having excellent, good, average, and so forth, the form has several statements that describe the employee's performance, from which the manager selects the one that best describes the employee's performance for that task. Standards are clear when good BARS are developed.

Ranking

Ranking is a performance appraisal method that is used to evaluate employee performance from best to worst. Under the ranking method, the manager compares an employee to another employee, rather than comparing each one to a standard measurement. An offshoot of ranking is the forced distribution method, which is similar to grading on a curve. A predetermined percentage of employees are placed in performance categories: for example, excellent—5 percent, above average—15 percent, average—60 percent, below average—15 percent, and poor—5 percent.

Management by Objectives (MBO)

MBO is a process in which managers and their employees jointly set objectives for the employee, periodically evaluate the performance, and reward according to the results (review Chapter 6 for details).

The Narrative Method

The narrative method requires the manager to write a statement about the employee's performance. The system can vary. Managers may be allowed to write whatever they want, or they may be required to answer questions about employees' performance. The narrative is often combined with another method.

Which Performance Appraisal Method Is the Best?

Determining the best appraisal method depends upon the objectives of the system. A combination of the methods is usually superior to any one method. For developmental objectives, critical incidents and MBO work well. For administrative decisions, a ranking method based on rating scales or BARS works well. The real success of performance appraisal does not lie in the method or form used; it depends upon the manager's human relations skills.

---

4. Identify the performance measurement method(s) used to evaluate your job performance. Describe how you would improve the method(s).

APPLICATION SITUATIONS

Performance Appraisal Methods

AS 14–3

Below, select the major performance appraisal method that should be used in each situation

A. Critical incidents   C. BARS   E. MBO
B. Rating scales   D. Ranking F. Narrative

_____ 11. You work for a small organization that does not have a formal performance appraisal system. You are overworked, but you want to develop an evaluation tool/form.

_____ 12. You have been promoted from a supervisory position to a middle-management position. You have been asked to select your replacement.

_____ 13. Wally is not performing up to standard. You have decided to talk to him in order to improve his performance.

_____ 14. You want to develop a system for developing employees.

_____ 15. You have a master's degree in HRD and work in the HRD department. You have been assigned to develop an objective performance appraisal system meeting EEO guidelines for the entire organization.

Step 3. Conduct Informal Performance Appraisals— "Coaching"

Performance appraisals should not merely be formal once-a-year, one-hour sessions. Employees need regular informal feedback on their performance.[29] The employee performing below standard may need daily or weekly coaching to reach increased productivity. The supervisor's new emerging role is that of a coach rather than that of a dictator, as it tended to be in the past.

The increasing-productivity model is designed for use in improving ability and for dealing with motivation problems. The **increasing-productivity model** _involves: step 1, refer to past feedback; step 2, describe current performance; step 3, describe desired performance; step 4, get a commitment to the change; and step 5, follow up._ In order to help you understand each step, dialogue is used to illustrate it. In the dialogue situation, Fran is the supervisor of vending machine repair and Dale is a relatively new vending machine repair technician. Fran is coaching Dale.

Step 1. Refer to Past Feedback: This assumes that the employee was told or trained to do something in the past and never did or no longer does it properly. If the employee has never received feedback, explain the situation.

FRAN: Hi, Dale. I called you into my office because I wanted to discuss your repair record.

DALE: What about it?

FRAN: We haven't discussed your performance since you started, but I've noticed a problem and wanted to correct it quickly.

Step 2. Describe Current Performance: Using specific examples, describe in detail the current performance that needs to be changed.

FRAN: In reviewing the repair reports, I realized that you repaired vending machines at the Big Y Supermarket, the United Cooperative Bank, and the Springfield YMCA. In all three locations, you had to return to repair the same machine within a month.

DALE: That's correct. If you look at my report, you'll see that it was for different problems. I fixed them right the first time.

FRAN: I realize that. That's not the problem. The problem is that the average time before returning for any repair on a machine is three months. Did you realize that?

Dale: Now that you mention it, I did hear it in the training class.

Fran: I want to determine why you have to return to the same machine more frequently than the average. My guess is that it's because when you go to a machine for repair, you only fix the problem, rather than going through the entire machine to perform routine maintenance.

Dale: My job is to fix the machines.

Step 3. Describe Desired Performance:
In detail, tell the employee exactly what the desired performance is. Have him or her tell you why it is important. If a skill is needed, teach it, using job instructional training (JIT). Explain why it is important for the performance to be done differently, and model the behavior.[30]

Fran: At the training program, did they tell you to go through the entire machine for routine maintenance or just to fix it?

Dale: I don't remember them saying that.

Fran: Do you know why it is important to do maintenance rather than just to fix the machines?

Dale: I guess it's so I don't have to go back within a month and repair the same machine.

Fran: That's right. You're more productive. From now on, I want you to go through the machines and perform maintenance rather than just fix them.

Step 4. Get a Commitment to the Change:
If possible, get the employee to commit to changing his or her performance. The commitment is important because if the employee is not willing to commit to the change, he or she will not make the change. It's better to know now that the employee is not going to change than it is to wait and find out later when it may be too late. The employee can commit and not make the change. But at least you have done your job, and you can refer to past commitments without change when you discipline the employee.

Fran: From now on, will you do maintenance, rather than repairs?

Dale: I didn't do it in the past because I didn't realize I was supposed to. But in the future, I will.

Step 5. Follow Up:
The follow-up is important to ensure that the employee realizes that the supervisor is serious about the change. When employees know their performance will be evaluated, they are more likely to make the change. A specific meeting is not always needed. But the employee should be told how the supervisor will follow up.

Fran: In the future, I will continue to review the records for frequent repairs of the same machine. I don't think it will continue, but if it does, I will call you in again.

Dale: It will not be necessary.

Fran: Great. I appreciate your cooperation, Dale. This was the only concern about your work that I had. Other than this one area, you're doing a good job. I'll see you later.

Dale: Have a good one.

During the discussion with the employee, preferably near the end, give positive reinforcement while correcting performance. Being positive helps motivate the employee to make the necessary change. For an example, refer to Fran's last statement above. Exhibit 14–5 lists the five steps to increase employee performance through ability and motivation.

◆ Video
BM 14–2

● Skill-Building
14–1

Learning Objective

4. List and explain the steps in the increasing-productivity (coaching) model

EXHIBIT 14–5   COACHING: INCREASING-PRODUCTIVITY MODEL

Step 1. Refer to past feedback.

Step 2. Describe the current performance.

Step 3. Describe the desired performance.

Step 4. Get a commitment to the change.

Step 5. Follow up.

WORK APPLICATIONS

5. Describe a specific situation in which it would be appropriate to use the increasing-productivity model.

Step 4. Prepare for the Formal Performance Interviews

Step 5. Conduct the Formal Performance Appraisal Interviews

Video
BM 14–3

Video
BM 14–4

Learning Objective

5. List and explain the five steps of performance appraisals and state how performance appraisals can lead to increased productivity

● Organization
● Group
● Individual

Failure to plan for the performance appraisal is planning to fail. Most organizations use a formal measurement tool. The manager should spend time carefully filling it out.

The formal performance appraisal should be conducted effectively. If an employee gets an average, rather than a good rating, the manager should be able to clearly explain why she or he did not get the higher rating. The employee should understand what needs to be done during the next performance period to get the higher rating. Clear standards should eliminate surprises during the formal performance appraisal.

Exhibit 14–3 lists the performance appraisal steps. Notice that steps 1–3 are double-looped (have two-headed arrows) because the development at one step may require the manager to backtrack and make changes. For example, during an informal appraisal, the manager may realize that environmental changes require a change in the employee's job and/or performance standards. Step 5 brings the manager back to step 1.

The opening case does not state whether people are performing to expectations. If they are, performance appraisals will not help solve Cindy's productivity problems. However, if employees are performing below expectations, using performance appraisals and the increasing-productivity model can lead to higher levels of productivity.

Technology and Human Relations

Technology can increase productivity, and managing technology is a top management priority.[31] However, we must remember that people are our most important asset,[32] not technology, as people are the ones who develop and utilize technology. We cannot predict the future, but we know the context in which it will emerge. That context is human nature, those deeply embedded laws of behavior shape technology.[33] Thus, we need to focus on the human side of technology.[34] The major technology focus is the Internet and (electronic) e-business conducted over the Web.[35] However, don't be fooled by the number-1 myth of the Web economy: building a website is not easy—try putting a traditional business online.[36] Although e-commerce is becoming routine at large companies, e-commerce is still in its infancy as 75% of small businesses still don't have websites,[37] and 56% of workers don't have Internet access at work.[38]

In this section, we are going to focus on how technology affects human relations, rather than explain technology itself. We discuss how technology affects human relations by chapters.

Chapter 1:
Above in the introduction to this section, we emphasized the human side of technology. Clearly, technology affects behavior, human relations, and technology. Technology was discussed as one on the major trends and challenges in the field of human relations. Back in the 1950s, it became known that managers need to carefully integrate people and technology (to develop sociotechnical systems). To focus on one without the other leads to lower levels of productivity.

Chapters 2 and 3:
Our Big Five personality trait of openness to experience and our perception and values of technology also affect our attitudes, behavior, human relations, and performance. Are you an "e-believer"? Or is your attitude "e-nough" about technology?[39] Technology can be a threat to one's self-concept, as there is a threat of becoming obsolete, and it can affect job satisfaction. Technology can also cause stress, when it is severe it is called *technostress*—the inability to cope with technologies in a healthy manner. On the positive side, technology enhances the learning organization as sharing knowledge becomes easier[40] and repeating the same mistakes less likely.[41] The challenge is motivating employees to use the technology.[42]

Chapters 4 and 5:
Technology increases the speed of communications globally.[43] E-mail has become a major message transmission media; it's as common as the sticky note in organizations around the world.[44] However, e-mail has also changed human relations away from direct talking to written communications. Technology has played a major role in changing organizational structures. Hierarchy is turned on its head as senior people learn from their juniors and old-timers from newcomers.[45] There is a shift from vertical to horizontal communications. In an e-business, orders issued from the top down are replaced by ideas spreading from any part of the organization.[46] Rumors also spread faster through the grapevine with e-mail. E-business thrives on computer networks. Very small companies gain very large benefits by being linked to wider networks.

Chapters 6 and 7:
Research shows that friendship at work affects behavior, human relations, and performance.[47] People meet their need for affiliation, in part, through friendships at work. Through technology advances, downsizing and reengineering have caused changes in staff and human relations. To take advantage of the potential in e-business, leaders must lead differently.[48] Quick planning, decisio making, and participative management are needed.[49] Today's virtual managers lead from a distance as more employees are at remote locations or telecommute. Voice time and e-mail replace face time as the dominant form of communication.[50]

Chapters 8 and 9:
E-business requires employees with strong negotiation skills and the ability to handle conflict with people (employees, customers, and suppliers) all over the world.[51] Computers give managers the power to constantly oversee employees at work.[52] The FBI e-mail surveillance system secretly searches millions of e-mails a second for messages from crime suspects.[53] Security systems can read all the information on your computer, including deleted files.[54] However, this has a negative effect on our desire for a substantial degree of personal privacy, including private space.[55] The Internet brings us a host of new ethical issues. Is it ethical to use the organization's Internet for personal use?[56] More specifically, is it ethical to visit pornographic websites?[57] Is it ethical to use e-mail for personal use, computers to help children or others do schoolwork or other projects, to play computer games, or to shop using the Internet?[58] Do the answers change if the personal use of the Internet is during working hours or outside of working hours?

Chapters 10 and 11:
Technology enhances creativity and innovation.[59] Decisions can be made more quickly and with more information provided by decision support systems and the Internet. In an e-business, people must work together differently.[60] Team dynamics are different when team members are at different locations. Virtual managers must use new team-building methods for members who

work in different locations, possibly all over the world.[61] Virtual teams enable organizations to become more flexible by providing the impressive productivity of team-based designs in environments where teamwork would have once been impossible.[62]

Chapters 12 and 13:   The Internet has forced the business world to go through a massive unprecedented revolutionary exercise in managing change, with resistance to change. New companies that work solely through the Internet, especially the dot-coms, have a distinctive organizational culture—the e-culture. Although the e-culture is not well defined, some dot-coms have the flavor of a youth cult, rather than a culture, complete with preferred wardrobes and special languages. Employees take pride in pulling all-nighters that resemble communal living in the office. They are convinced that they will change the world and that no one over 30 can be trusted.[63] The Internet makes conducting global business possible for the small business and easier for the large MNC. Doing business over the Internet eliminates some prejudice and discrimination, as people don't see or talk to each other with written communications.

Chapters 14 and 15:   As you know, technology can increase productivity through resources. Technology is being used to improve training. Job training on websites is growing fast as courses are cheaper and more adaptable, and workers can be easily trained on the jobs or at home.[64] The new dress code for training is slippers and pajamas as more employees train at home.[65] Employees are managing their time with e-time management materials, such as computer schedules and to-do lists. More and more organizations are recruiting online.[66] And more people continue to find jobs online. You may have to fill out a job application or submit your resume online during your career searches.[67]

Learning Objective

6. Discuss some of the ways that technology affects behavior, human relations, and performance

---

WORK APPLICATIONS

6. Discuss how technology has affected behavior, human relations, and performance where you work/ed.

● Organization
● Group
● Individual

IE 14–2

Participative Management Techniques

Before reading on, answer the 10 questions in Self-Assessment Exercise 14–1 Participation Level, to determine your preferred level of participation.

According to Edward Lawler, **participative management techniques** *move information, knowledge, rewards, and power farther down the organization.* To be truly effective, all four variables must go down to the lowest level in the organization. Organizations with high levels of management participation outperform those with low levels,[68] as they empower employees to manage themselves.[69] Some of the benefits of participative management techniques include increased motivation, satisfaction, employee retention, skill development, quality, and productivity; decreased supervision and grievances; lower resistance to change; and better problem solving, communications, and coordination.[70] H. J. Heinz Company figures it will generate $200 million in annual savings within four years by listening to teams of employees enlisted to boost productivity and reduce waste.

Few people will argue against the appropriateness of participative management today. If you ask managers whether they use participative management, most will say yes. But are U.S. companies truly using more participative management techniques? The answer is yes. However, are the majority of U.S. businesses truly using participative management at low levels in the organization? The answer is no. Many employees are still being told what to do instead of being asked what should be done.[71]

The United States is unlikely to become dramatically better competitively using traditional management approaches. Better implementation of traditional

Self-Assessment
Exercise 14–1

Participation Level

Circle the letter that best describes what you would *actually* do as a supervisor, rather than choose a general answer.

Usually (U)   Frequently (F)   Occasionally (O)   Seldom (S)

U	F	O	S	1. I would set the objectives for my department alone (rather than with employees' input).
U	F	O	S	2. I would allow employees to do their jobs their own way (rather than my way, as long as they perform to expectations).
U	F	O	S	3. I would ask employees how to make their jobs more interesting and challenging.
U	F	O	S	4. I would allow employees to make decisions (rather than make decisions for employees).
U	F	O	S	5. I would recruit and select new employees alone (rather than include employees' input).
U	F	O	S	6. I would train new employees myself (rather than have employees do it).
U	F	O	S	7. I would tell employees what they need to know (rather than everything I know).
U	F	O	S	8. I would spend time checking the quality of employee work (rather than making it the employee's responsibility).
U	F	O	S	9. I would reward employees for actual performance (rather than give equal salaries to all).
U	F	O	S	10. I would ask employees for ideas on how to improve performance of the department.

To better understand your preferred participation level, score your answers. For items 1, 5, 6, 7, and 8, give yourself one point for each *usually* (U) answer; two points for each *frequently* (F) answer; three points for each *occasionally* (O) answer; and four points for each *seldom* (S) answer. For items 2, 3, 4, 9, and 10, give yourself one point for each *seldom* (S); two points for each *occasionally* (O) answer; three points for each *frequently* (F) answer; and four points for each *usually* (U) answer. Total all points. Your score should be between 10 and 40. Place your score here _____ and place a check mark on the continuum below.

Low   10 ---------- 20 ---------- 30 ---------- 40   High participation

management techniques is very possible, but it is unlikely that it will lead to the kind of improvement needed to improve competitiveness. U.S. business must use participative management techniques at the lowest levels in organizations, instead of doing the old better.[72]

You will learn about eight participative management techniques. Using these techniques can lead to creating win-win situations for both employees and the department/organization by meeting employee needs while increasing productivity. The eight participative management techniques are listed in Exhibit 14–6.

Goal of
Human Relations

WORK APPLICATIONS

7. What was your score on Self-Assessment Exercise 14–1? Should, and will, you become more participative? Explain your answer.

Suggestion Systems

The suggestion box, one of the oldest management tools, is being replaced by e-mail and phone.[73] Suggestion systems send the message that management cares about what its employees think,[74] and they have a positive impact on the bottom line.[75] According to the National Association of Suggestion Systems, organizations spend about $150 million in cash and other awards to implement suggestion systems, and they save over $2 billion a year because of them.[76] A few of the organizations using employee suggestion systems include IBM, Frito-Lay, American Airlines,

EXHIBIT 14–6   PARTICIPATIVE MANAGEMENT TECHNIQUES

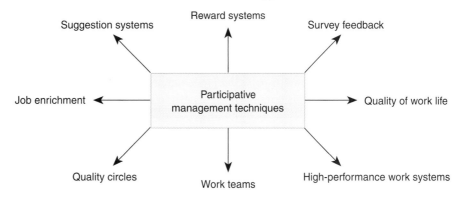

Taxtron, Nippondenso, Time-Life, Calvert, Bank of America, Allied-Signal, Hallmark, BellSouth, United Illumination, American Freightways, and 3M.

As the number of employees participating in suggestion systems rises, so do the cost savings. Therefore, success is based on getting employees involved. Suggestion systems do not have to be companywide or complicated. You can develop a simple system for your department.

WORK APPLICATIONS

8. Explain the suggestion system at an organization you work/worked for. How could the suggestion system be improved?

Reward Systems

Performance appraisal is a part of **reward systems,** *which are the mechanisms for defining, evaluating, and rewarding employee performance.* Performance is appraised on the group and organizational level, as well as the individual level. Rewards can be financial[77] (pay, commission, bonus, profit sharing, pensions, employee stock options, fringe benefits, and so on) or nonfinancial (praise, promotions, status, additional assignments, special awards, commendations, and so on). Reward systems are participative techniques in which employees who participate in increasing productivity get rewarded as part of their compensation.[78] **Compensation** *is the direct and indirect pay that employees receive.* The increase can be in direct pay and/or benefits. Indirect pay, commonly called *benefits,* includes insurance, social security, sick pay, paid vacations, workers' compensation, unemployment benefits, pension plans, tuition payments, child care, and so forth. Indirect costs vary from organization to organization; however, many estimates state that benefits average around 35 percent of employees' direct pay.

Rewards are often part of suggestion systems. However, all organizations have reward systems, but not all use suggestion systems. Rewards for suggestions are called *incentives*[79] and are paid in addition to employee compensation. Incentives include bonuses, profit sharing, stock awards, and so on for increased productivity. Some managers have special recognition parties and give only award certificates. However, it is generally recognized that noncash awards alone are not enough to get employees to exert significant effort toward continuous improvement. A mix of cash and noncash awards is most effective.[80]

Incentives can be given to individuals, teams, or to everyone in the organization. While individual incentives remain popular, with the trend toward more teamwork, team and organizationwide incentives are increasing.[81] Gainsharing is a popular reward method used on an organizationwide basis. **Gainsharing** *involves sharing cost savings with employees using an organizationwide formula.* The percentage of sharing ranges widely as do the formulas used to distribute the savings. Gainsharing plans were designed for manufacturing plants. However, use by the government and the service sector is growing.[82]

With *profit sharing*, a percentage of the profit is given to all employees. Organizations commonly give cash, company stock, and an increase in retirement accounts, or some combination. In addition to giving company stock to employees as part of profit sharing, many companies offer *stock options* that enable employees to buy stock at a reduced rate. Many companies offer payroll deductions for stock purchases.

One thing you should always remember: *What is evaluated and rewarded or punished gets done.* For example, how much time and effort do you put into studying material that the instructor says will not be on a test versus what will be on the test? For this reason, many organizations are focusing on pay for performance,[83] so the good employees get paid more. Most slackers can be pressured into doing the job right, or pressured into leaving voluntarily, or can be fired. As a closing point, reward systems depend on properly using human relations principles.[84]

WORK APPLICATIONS

9. Explain how employees are rewarded at an organization you work/worked for. How could the reward system be improved?

Survey Feedback

Recall that the details of survey feedback were discussed in Chapter 3 in the Measuring Job Satisfaction section, and in Chapter 12 in the section on survey feedback.

Survey feedback can be used as a means of getting suggestions. What is done with the data gathered is important. If management ignores the survey data, employees will not feel as though it is a vehicle of participation. Surveys have revealed that employees believe the organization systems and managers actually stifle their participation in management.[85]

Survey feedback is more commonly used as a tool to facilitate change to a more participative level than as a participative tool in and of itself. Survey feedback is used to diagnose the situation, to plan for increased levels of participation, and to determine effectiveness of the change to participative management.

Job Enrichment

Recall that the details of job enrichment were discussed in Chapter 6 in the Motivation Techniques section. Through participative management, a job is enriched both horizontally (more steps, variety, and so on) and vertically (selection of methods, schedules, quality control responsibility, and so on). And very importantly, the employees doing the work need to have input into how the job is enriched, rather than being dictated to by some efficiency expert. For the job to be enriched in a participative way, employees doing the job must receive more autonomy, feedback, skill variety, and task identity, and the task must be more significant after the changes. As a result, knowledge, information, power, and rewards, but not necessarily financial rewards, move down to the lowest level in the organization. Job enrichment can be used on an individual and team basis.[86] However, job enrichment is best used as part of a broad organizational change rather than as a stand-alone program. Work teams can, and do, perform job enrichment for the group.

IE 14–3

Skill-Building
14–2

Quality of Work Life

The concept of quality of work life (QWL) became popular in the 1960s and has been around ever since. It is not a specific technique; rather, it is more of a philosophy of the condition of work. Quality of work life means different things to diversified employees.[87] For our purposes, **quality of work life (QWL)** *is an organizational attempt to balance business, human, and social needs.* Quality of work life attempts to develop the individual while increasing productivity so that all of society benefits.[88] Organizations are helping employees balance their work and family life (Chapter 13) so that employees and employers benefit.[89] Work at home is a QWL benefit,[90] as half of large companies offer work-at-home or job sharing arrangments.[91] Some of the organizations involved in improving quality of work life include IBM, Kodak, Procter & Gamble, Westinghouse, AT&T, GTE, GM, Martin Marietta, General Foods, Weyerhauser, Cummins Engineering, Mary Kay Cosmetics, and many colleges.

Quality of work life programs tend to push power, information, and knowledge farther down in the organizations. However, they do not tend to move rewards down to lower levels. To be truly effective, QWL programs should include rewards.

Quality Circles

Quality circles *are groups that meet regularly to spot and solve problems in their work area.* In a sense, they are a group dynamics approach to a suggestion system. There are no universal quality circle procedures. Numbers of participants range from 3 to 20. They meet at different intervals. Some meet weekly, some meet biweekly, and others meet monthly. Some organizations pay employees for their suggestions; others do not. Many quality circles follow steps similar to those used in team building (see Chapter 12 for a review).

Quality circles became popular in the United States in the early 1980s after proving their success in Japan. To increase quality, thousands of organizations have used quality circles, typically with good results.[92] Among them are Hewlett-Packard, IBM, Kodak, Procter & Gamble, Ford Motor Co., Control Data, GM, GE, Lockheed, Honeywell, American Airlines, Friendly Ice Cream, and the U.S. government. Over time, any technique loses its effectiveness. Many organizations have extended quality circles to be a part of work team responsibilities. In many respects, quality circles are like team building extended to the work area.

WORK APPLICATIONS

10. Describe how an organization, preferably one you work/worked for, uses quality circles. Be sure to state how employees are rewarded.

Work Teams

Work teams are *self-managed groups.* Work teams are also called *autonomous work groups, semiautonomous work groups,* and *self-directed* or *self-managed teams.* Work teams take over power and authority from management. The work team makes decisions conventionally made by managers.[93] For example, the team sets production and quality objectives; the team is held accountable and responsible for inventory and quality control; the team solves problems and sets schedules; teams develop their own work methods; and the team decides which employees will perform which tasks. Team members are cross-trained so that they can perform each other's jobs.[94] Work teams are the best technique for using the team dynamics concepts (Chapters 10 and 11) to increase productivity.[95] When teams are cohesive, social pressure can play an important role in motivating performance. Teams often have authority to hire, reward, punish, and even fire workers who do not perform to standards set by the group.[96] Work teams have lower absenteeism and turnover rates than conventional departments. Not surprisingly, the members of effective work teams tend to report very high satisfaction.[97] The group setting meets the individual's needs for social interaction and belonging. Effective teams meet members' needs for competence, achievement, and recognition. Work teams create a win–win situation for the department/organization and for individuals who enjoy working in groups. Not everyone does. Some people prefer to work alone.

Goal of Human Relations

Using teams does move power down to lower levels in the organization. However, it is a misconception that if employees are grouped in a team structure they will function as a team and the organization will reap benefits. Team members need training[98] in group dynamics (Chapter 11) and team building (Chapter 12) to be successful.67 However, the cost of training is usually more than offset by higher quality and productivity gains.

The work teams method is based on the idea that everyone should share in leadership.[99] Team work actually incorporates most of the other participative management techniques. Work teams perform the suggestion systems, and quality circles function as part of their ongoing work. Continuous improvement is also a responsibility of work teams. Work teams enrich their jobs through cross-training and changing jobs regularly. As a result, the quality of work life increases. Because the work teams method incorporates the other participative management techniques, it moves more information, knowledge, power, and rewards to lower levels than the other techniques used individually.

Learning Objective

8. Discuss the differences among quality of work life, quality circle, and work teams

WORK APPLICATIONS

11. Describe how an organization, preferably one you work/worked for, uses teams. How would you increase and/or improve the use of teams at this organization?

High-performance Work Systems

High-performance work systems involve employees in participative management by incorporating the other techniques into one system. High-performance work systems are based on work teams, but they are broader in scope. A company can develop work teams for some departments as a stand-alone program. With high performance work systems, the entire facility is structured around and supports work teams. The entire plant is transformed through the input of employees. The high-performance work systems are more commonly implemented in new plants, rather than existing plants. They are often called *greenfields*. The new plant designs have a flat structure (few levels of management), few if any supervisors, a wide span of control (many employees reporting to one boss), and a lean staff (few people who do not actually make the product/service). Employees receive extensive training and participate in designing the new plant's physical layout. Teams are created to produce an entire piece of work or the entire product/service.

Some of the firms with multiple high-performance work systems plants include AT&T, General Foods, PPG Industries, Procter & Gamble, Sherwin-Williams, TRW, Corning, H. J. Heinz, Rockwell, Johnson & Johnson, Mead, and Cummins Engine. The know-how for using this level of participative management is widespread throughout many organizations.

A major limitation of high-performance work systems is their numbers. However, high-performance work systems are the most revolutionary, and most effective, way to move power, information, knowledge, and rewards down to the lowest levels.

In the opening case, Cindy faces very tough competition. Using participative management techniques may be the answer to her problems. Cindy will have to stop using her autocratic style and give employees more information, knowledge, power, and rewards. Cindy should probably bring in a consultant to help her implement a high-performance work system.

If U.S. business wants to be competitive in the global environment, it must increase productivity. It is time to redesign present organizations utilizing high-performance work systems.

APPLICATION SITUATIONS

Participative Management Techniques

AS 14–4

Below, select the participative management technique that is described in each situation.

A. Suggestion systems   D. Job enrichment   G. Work teams

B. Reward systems   E. Quality of work life   H. High-performance

C. Survey feedback   F. Quality circles   work systems

_____ 16. My department has just been changed. The old supervisor is now one of the group. The group determines how the department is run on a daily basis.

_____ 17. Our company has installed a new computer terminal. Employees are encouraged to type in ideas that will increase productivity. If the company accepts your idea, you win a trip.

_____ 18. I've been involved in meetings where we try to come up with ways to help the company while improving the employee situation at the same time.

_____ 19. The president of our company is crazy. He plans to turn the company upside down. He expects us workers to redesign the plant and make the decisions on how to run it on a daily basis.

_____ 20. I volunteered to serve on a committee. Our charge is to come up with ideas on how to increase productivity in the shop. A woman from personnel runs the meetings for our group. We meet once every week during the last hour and a half of work.

REVIEW

Select one or more methods: (1) fill in the missing key terms from memory; (2) match the key terms from the end of the review, with their definitions below; and/or (3) copy the key terms in order from the key terms list at the beginning of the chapter.

_____ is a performance measure of inputs to outputs. The three ways to increase productivity are (1) to increase the value of the outputs while maintaining the value of the inputs, (2) to maintain the value of the outputs while decreasing the value of the inputs, and (3) to increase the value of the outputs while decreasing the value of the inputs.

Ways to increase productivity through capital include (1) capital equipment, (2) reducing waste, (3) inventories, (4) budgets, and (5) space.

_____ is the process of developing the necessary skills to perform the present job. _____ is the process of developing the ability to perform both present and future jobs. The _____ steps include: step 1, conduct needs assessment; step 2, set objectives; step 3, prepare for training; step 4, conduct the training; and step 5, measure and evaluate training results. The _____ steps are step 1, preparation of the trainee; step 2, trainer presentation of the job; step 3, trainee performance of the job; step 4, follow-up.

_____ is the ongoing process of evaluating employee job performance. Performance is appraised for developmental and evaluative reasons. The performance appraisal steps are step 1, state job responsibilities; step 2, develop standards and measurement methods; step 3, conduct informal performance appraisals—"coaching"; step 4, prepare the formal performance interviews; and step 5, conduct the formal performance appraisal interviews.

_____ describe performance levels in the areas of quantity, quality, time, and cost. The _____ involves step 1, refer to past feedback; step 2, describe current performance; step 3, describe desired performance; step 4, get a commitment to the change; and step 5, follow up.

Although technology does increase productivity, employees are the most important asset, as people are the ones who develop and use technology. Technology affects behavior, human relations, and performance. To be successful, people and technology must be carefully integrated to develop a sociotechnical system.

_____ move information, knowledge, rewards, and power farther down the organization. There are eight participative management techniques: (1) With suggestion systems, employees typically place ideas in a box. (2) _____ are the mechanisms for defining, evaluating, and rewarding employee performance. _____ is the direct and indirect pay that employees receive. _____ involves sharing cost savings with employees using an organizationwide formula. (3) Use survey feedback. (4) Use job enrichment. (5) _____ is an organizational attempt to balance business, human, and social needs.

(6) _____ are groups that meet regularly to spot and solve problems in their work area. (7) _____ are self-managed groups. (8) Use high-performance work systems. They move more information, knowledge, rewards, and power down the organization than any other technique because they combine the other participative management techniques into one design for the entire organization.

KEY TERMS

compensation   511
development   500
gainsharing   511
increasing-productivity
   model   505
job instructional
   training   501

participative management
   techniques   509
performance
   appraisal   502
productivity   498
quality circles   513

quality of work life
   (QWL)   513
reward systems   511
standards   503
training   500
training cycle   501
work teams   513

**John Mariotti:
Huffy Bicycles**[1]

This is a case about how we transformed the average Huffy Bicyles plant in Celina, Ohio, into a world-class plant in the early 1980s into the 1990s. It is truly amazing what happens when you treat people like real people, give them respect and preserve their dignity, provide them a chance to learn and then use it to achieve goals they understand and have some equity in—it is like *magic*.

History: In the early 1980s, the Huffy plant was the typical U.S. plant using paternalistic autocratic management with the union versus management mentality—it was us against them. The direct incentive pay system ("piecework") was great for output, but terrible for quality, service, and teamwork. Quality was considered OK at 40 defects per 100 bikes.

Employee experience taught them to come to work, do what they were told, make their rate, and go home. They were used to the opposite of participative management. Each employee had a clearly delineated job and little sharing of work went on— no teamwork. The term "lean and mean" took on literal meaning. The organizational structure of the plant was a traditional grouping of equipment. The departments were largely called by the name of what they did: Wheel Room, Welding Room, Paint Room, Assembly, etc. The term "room" apparently came from the old days when these departments actually were in different "rooms" of the old plant.

As more "enlightened" management took over, successive general managers with no operations experience began making changes. Old leadership was moved aside in favor of "upgraded" management. New management fads were attempted including the current "fad" of quality circles. However, the circles were gripe sessions and did not improve quality or productivity. Not too surprisingly, the workers were mostly just going through the motions.

Bike prices started falling and before stabilising, would fall 25 to 30 percent because of Taiwanese imported bikes flooding into the United States. Their costs allowed imports to have a retail price that was the same as our wholesale price— and with more features, a real problem! Each successive wave of import competition would wipe out more of the U.S. mass-market bike producers, turning them into importers. After this wave, in 1990, only three remained. (After the last wave from China, by 2000, none were left!)

The Transformation: It was clear to me (John Mariotti) that there were several places to start if this plant was to survive and prosper. The first was with the unionized work force. I called a meeting of the union committee, and I still remember it. I told them we could either continue fighting and all go down together, or we could work together, and try to compete. Fortunately, working together, competing was what they chose to do, but it wasn't easy.

Next we continued the upgrade process by evaluating every process and piece of equipment to see if it was—or could be—world-class competitive. Over the next few years, we replaced or significantly upgraded almost every major piece of production equipment in the plant, with the exception of basic items like punch presses. While we were upgrading equipment, we undertook to start changing the culture as well.

Our management team led by the VP of Operations, Doug Dempsey, coined a couple of acronyms, which he wrote on an easel in full view of anyone who came in or near his office. These were related to quality and the old cultural tendency to do it fast (but not necessarily right!). The first acronym was DIRTFT (or "dirt foot" as we called it). This was shorthand for Do It Right The First Time! It was simple, effective and easy to remember. The second one was FIKIF, which stood for "Fix It and Keep It Fixed." With these reminders always in view, we embarked on a quality improvement program.

[1]SOURCE: John Mariotti, former president of Huffy Bicycle plant, wrote this case with editing from the author.

We focused on getting the quality circles to improve quality and productivity. So, we trained a bunch of trainers to manage the circles. We taught them statistical problem-solving techniques and how to facilitate meetings. Quality circles began to respond. One of the things they did was suggest we change the teams' name to "HEIT," to better match their new purpose. This stood for Huffy Employee Involvement Teams. We trained a lot of people in statistical process control and statistical problem solving.

We selectively began to attack other processes and learned why our quality, scrap, and rework were so bad. We began to use the new knowledge to make improvements and reduce variability. The savings from waste and scrap elimination were starting to show.

Another step was a major housekeeping improvement initiative. We felt that if we could get the employees to care more about how the workplace looked and was organized, quality, safety, inventory control, productivity, and morale would all improve. To get this going, we initiated what we called a "dollars for donuts" program. In this case, the VP of Operations personally became the "champion" of the housekeeping "contest," and made a big deal about going out to the winning department with armloads of boxes of donuts to celebrate their "victory!" Of course, as housekeeping improved, so also did many other things in the plant.

While struggling to get inventory under control and the parts documentation needed to improve quality in place, upgrade worn-out equipment, and outsource some major processes, we continued to work on the attitudes and culture of the people.

As we decided which things we had to be good at, which we were good at, and which we weren't so good at, processes began to sort themselves out. We knew we were good at making frames and forks, handlebars and rims. This was fortunate because these make up the structure of the bike and constitute the reference points on which all the other components are assembled. We decided to invest further in these. We formed evaluation teams that included hourly people from the other production areas and obtained proposals from the best specialty fabricators we could find. The ideas and improvements that came about from this process were incredible.

Import bikes at very low prices continued to flood into the U.S. market. Our people knew they were fighting for their jobs, but they also understood (as a result of constant reinforcement) that if we weren't really productive, their jobs would go away anyway, and possibly so would those of a lot of their peers. It was in this environment that our work proceeded at a frenzied pace. We tracked every move of the Taiwan producers. Each new lower-priced imported bike was purchased and put on display in the plant lunchroom next to our closest competitive model. Photos of Taiwanese bike plants were posted prominently for all employees to see. While these faraway competitors made less in several days than our employees made in an hour, the competition for jobs was really on, primarily because of the Taiwanese low cost of wages.

Employee meetings were constant and intense as we communicated the reality of the outside world to our hard-working steelworker union employees. Then we were helped by a stroke of luck. A new subdistrict director of the United Steelworkers, Frank Vickers was assigned to our local. He had seen the pain of closing steel plants far too often. So, when the union contract negotiation bogged down in 1984, he asked if he could bring a company president from a steel service center into the negotiating room and if I would join them. This was an unprecedented move. They told us about a gainsharing plan they had put together to save that company, and the union rep proposed we consider one to get us off our impasse about wages versus productivity. We all knew that we couldn't pay employees more unless they produced more.

This move not only got us a contract settlement, but it set the tone for a whole new level of cooperation. We held an intense series of small group meetings involving well over half of our 2,000 employees. The meetings resulted in them carrying out half-inch thick packets of stories, handouts, and information about gainsharing as a concept and the Improshare plan we haped to use as a specific idea. The Improshare plan was ratified as a supplement to our direct incentive (piecework) hourly pay plan. Now indirect labor employees had a way to earn a bonus, too—and we both (company and employees) could grin all the way to the bank as we met the goal of human relations with a win–win situation.

As the people worked with us, and we upgraded equipment and processes and reconfigured the things we did to those that were strategically critical, our quality also improved, while scrap and rework dropped dramatically. A wonderful thing happened as a result of these efforts. Our capacity limits started to go away! We added about 10 to 15 percent a year to the capacity for 5 years in a row, without any "overt" actions or capital expenditures aimed at increased capacity. It was just the "waste" being wrung out of the system and turning into usable capacity.

Hourly employees, who had for so many years been managed autocratically, enjoyed being asked what they thought and participating in management. They added their considerable experience to the investments in new equipment and improved methods. Over 60 percent of the work force had been building bikes for more than 10 years! We later discovered that the steps we took with our hourly work force and plant management had a name—Total Quality Management (TQM)!

Productivity rose steadily, but quality leaped to another level. Measurements went from defects per hundred bikes to parts per million. Throughput continued to steadily march upward, and the time from material arrival to final production dropped from days or weeks to hours or shifts. Because we promised (and kept the promise) that no one would be laid-off—and lose their job—as a result of coming up with ideas that saved labor, the ideas flowed freely.

Joint teams of management and hourly people called HATs for "Huffy Action Teams" attacked chronic problems. These teams formed, dissected problems, described the solution to the departments involved and disbanded. "Task teams" attacked simpler tasks in short time frames. "Steering teams" directed the efforts and provided coordination. At the highest level, I met regularly with my staff VPs and the local steelworkers union president—and this group made up the "oversight team" to review quality progress and discuss new plant directions.

Such simple, yet effective practices helped build the Huffy Bicycles team or "Huffy's People" into a tightly knit partnership where there was knowledge, mutual respect, and much shared information. The logical extension of these kind of sessions was to share the outcomes of real results—warranty costs, sales program negotiations, field trips, and much more with all the people.

A real partnership is based on open information sharing and that means financial results, too. Although Huffy was a public company, we decided to share both the divisional strategic measures (quality, service, cost improvement, innovation outcomes, etc.) as well as the current financial results—high-level summaries of the income statement and balance sheet. Sharing this information with 2000 United Steelworkers union members meant several things. First, we had to educate them about what the terms meant in a frame of reference they could relate to—their home finances. Next we had to impress them with the need for confidentiality—these results were not disclosed in any of the public documents on a divisional level—just by segments of the corporation. Finally, we had to explain what was being done with the profits, and why profits at the level we aspired to were both necessary and justifiable.

At first it was slow going, but the mere fact that we'd share the info—even if they did not understand it—was worth a lot. As they began to understand it after three to four quarterly sessions, the true value came out. They could see why it was in their best interest to help assure that the company was profitable, and profitable enough to make the RONA (Return On Net Assets) that we set as our goal. There are few substitutes for face-to-face communications. Sharing this information with five meetings of about 400 to 500 hourly employees, and a separate meeting for office employees meant six one-hour meetings in a single day, starting with one at 5:30 A.M. and ending with one just after midnight. Whew, what days those were!

Any time a manufacturer grows and is successful, the challenge becomes "what do you do for an encore"? In the case of Huffy Bicycles, it was to move to a new level of competitive excellence. This involved putting the work force through yet another revolutionary type of training. "Strategic learning" is a strange name for a factory training program, but that is what we called it. To move to the next level, we had to enlist our workers' full talent array. Using an outside consultant's help, classes started in which the union and management learned how to "think outside the box." This was long before Peter Sense's book *The Fifth Discipline* came out, but that book aptly described the process that process that went on in our training.

Supervisors became Area Coordinators and "team leader–technicians" were selected from the hourly work force based on skills and qualifications first, and seniority second (a real concession in a union environment). Teams became increasingly "self-directed," and progress continued. As the threat of the Taiwanese and Korean imports waned because of the weakening U.S. dollar, the new challenge was the landslide shift in product mix from lightweight racing bikes which has been over 50 percent of the line to mountain bikes which were only 5 percent in 1987. Mountain bike volume grew relentlessly until it reached over 55 percent of the volume by 1991. These new bikes offered many opportunities for differentiaion, increased prices, and better margins. Profitability soared, and volume rose to over 4 million units in 1991—limited only by production capacity. In 1992, ten years after this effort started, Huffy held 3 percent of the U.S. bike market and was the acclaimed world leader in bicycle production know-how. But this hard-earned leadership was short-lived.

Top Management Changes:
After all of these great efforts, a series of changes in the top management of the Huffy Bicycles, and a change in the leadership of the local Steelworkers Union during the mid-1990s triggered a resumption of bitter, adversarial relations. Huffy top management, struggling to sustain corporate earnings, demanded that employees take sizable pay cuts (30 percent to preserve their jobs (while corporate officers earned sizable bonuses—a point that is being disputed to this day). Disputes about Pacific Rim dumping of bikes polarized relations with key customers. Another Huffy bike plant was opened in a lower wage area of the United States (in rural Missouri) to put additional pressure on the Steelworkers for still more concessions, then as the Celina plant was cut back dramatically, a third, smaller plant in Mississippi—all to no avail.

The Huffy Bicycle focus became fighting with each other instead of fighting the competitors, serving Wall Street instead of serving its customers. In the face of unprecedented low-cost competition from China, this was a prescription for disaster. Sadly, and ultimately, disaster befell not only the famed Celina plant, but all of the Huffy U.S. plants. The next wave of cheap Chinese bicycles drove down prices still further. During that final wave of imported bikes (1997–1999), Huffy chose to become an importer—and to abandon U.S. production (1999–2000)—marking the end of an era for yet another American manufactured product.

Go to the Internet: For more information on John Mariotti visit his website at *www.mariotti.net* and for Huffy Bikes visit its website at *www.huffy.com*. For ideas on using the Internet with cases, see Appendix C. Answer the following questions. Be sure to be able to give an explanation to support your answers.

1. What was the key to Huffy's success in increasing productivity?

2. What role did technology play in Huffy's success?

3. Which participative management techniques did Huffy use at the Celina plant to increase productivity?

4. What was the relationship between behavior, human relations, and organizational performance at Huffy (Chapters 1–15)?

5. What role did intelligence and learning play in this case (Chapter 2)?

6. What role did attitudes, self-concept, and values play in this case (Chapter 3)?

7. What type of leadership (Chapter 7), motivation (Chapter 6), and conflict resolution (Chapter 8) were used at Huffy?

8. What were power, politics, and ethics like at Huffy (Chapter 9)?

9. Why was Huffy so successful at managing change (Chapter 12)?

**Carlos Increases
Productivity**

Carlos, a production supervisor at Snider Wallet Company, wanted to increase productivity. He knew that the average production rate was 32 wallets per eight-hour day, and that different styles take longer than others.

Carlos's idea was to set a quota that would allow people to leave work once they met the quota. He decided to raise production by about 10 percent to 35 wallets per day. Carlos realized that if workers pushed, they could get out of work around a half hour early.

Carlos sat down with each employee and set the quota for their machine. He told them to go home after they produced their quota.

Things were going well. The production report showed an increase in production of 9 percent over the first two weeks. However, the last few days, April left at 2:30, while the others were leaving around 4:30. 5:00 P.M. was the old quitting time. Carlos had the following conversation with April as she was leaving that day.

CARLOS: April, it's only 2:30. Where are you going?

APRIL: Home. I produced my 35 wallets.

CARLOS: Your machine's hourly output average is only four wallets. You cannot produce 35 wallets in five and one-half hours, April!

APRIL: Wrong. The machine used to produce four per hour before I adjusted it and added this little gadget. It took me two hours to fix the machine, but it was worth it. Have there been any complaints?

CARLOS: No. *(He didn't know what to say or do. As he watched April leave, he wondered if he should change the system.)*

Answer the following questions. Then, in the space between the questions, state why you selected that answer. (Note: Any meetings can be role-played in class.)

_____ 1. Carlos increased productivity by:

      a. increasing the value of the outputs while maintaining input value

      b. maintaining the value of the outputs while decreasing input value

      c. increasing the value of the outputs while decreasing input value

_____ 2. Carlos increased productivity through training.

      a. true   *b.* false

_____ 3. Carlos increased productivity through increasing:

      a. ability   *b.* motivation   *c.* resources

_____ 4. Carlos' objective in sitting down with each employee to set their quota was:

      a. developmental   *b.* evaluative

_____ 5. Carlos set standards in the area(s) of _____. (You may select more than one answer.)

      a. quantity   *b.* quality   *c.* time   *d.* cost

_____ 6. Carlos is primarily using _____ to measure performance.

      a. critical incidents   *c.* BARS   *e.* MBO

      b. rating scales   *d.* ranking   *f.* narrative

_____ 7. Carlos used rewards to increase productivity.

     a. true   *b.* false

_____ 8. Carlos used an incentive pay system to increase productivity.

     a. true   *b.* false

_____ 9. Carlos used the _____ participation technique to increase productivity.

     a. work team   *c.* quality circle   *e.* none of these
     b. suggestion system   *d.* quality of work life

_____ 10. April is getting out of work early through:

     a. resisting controls   *c.* cheating
     b. breaking rules   *d.* creativity

11. Should Carlos continue to let April leave two hours earlier than other employees? If not, what should he do?

**The Management of
Quality**

*Critical Thinking
Questions:*

This video case presents how award winning Xerox and the University of Michigan Hospitals manage quality.

1. What is the relationship between quality and productivity at Xerox and University of Michigan Hospitals (UMH)?

2. UMH primarily increased productivity and quality through which of the three methods discussed in the text?

3. Do Xerox and UMH practice TQM as it is defined in the text (Chapter 12)? If yes, explain how?

4. Do Xerox and UMH implement the TQM techniques for controlling quality (Chapter 12)? If yes, explain how?

5. What is the role of participative management in TQM?

6. Which participative management techniques are the most relevant to Xerox and UMH TQM programs?

● **In-Class**
Increasing
Productivity—
Coaching

Objective: To develop your skill at improving performance through coaching.

SCANS: The SCANS competencies of resources, especially interpersonal skills, information, and systems and the foundations of basic, thinking, and personal qualities are developed through this exercise.

Preparation: You should have read and understood the chapter.

Experience: You will coach, be coached, and observe coaching using the increasing-productivity model.

Procedure 1
(2–4 minutes)

◆ BM 14–2

Break into groups of three. Make one or two groups of two, if necessary. Each member selects one of the three situations below in which to be the supervisor, and a different one in which to be the employee. You will role-play coaching and being coached.

1. Employee 1 is a clerical worker. He or she uses files, as do the other 10 employees. The employees all know that they are supposed to return the files when they are finished so that others can find them when they need them. Employees should only have one file out at a time. As the supervisor walks by, he or she notices that Employee 1 has five files on his or her desk, and another employee is looking for one of the files. The supervisor thinks Employee 1 will complain about the heavy workload as an excuse for having more than one file out at a time.

2. Employee 2 is a server in an ice cream shop. He or she knows that the tables should be cleaned up quickly after customers leave so that the new customers do not have to sit at a dirty table. It's a busy night. The supervisor looks at Employee 2's tables to find customers at two of them with dirty dishes. Employee 2 is socializing with some friends at one of the tables. Employees are supposed to be friendly. Employee 2 will probably use this as an excuse for the dirty tables.

3. Employee 3 is an auto technician. All employees know that they are supposed to place a paper mat on the floor of each car to prevent the carpets from getting dirty. When the service supervisor got into a car Employee 3 repaired, it did not have a mat, and there was grease on the carpet. Employee 3 does excellent work and will probably make reference to this fact when coached.

Procedure 2
(3–7 minutes)

Prepare for coaching to improve performance. Below, each group member writes a basic outline of what she or he will say when coaching Employee 1, 2, or 3, following the steps in improving productivity below:

Step 1. Refer to past feedback.

Step 2. Describe the current performance.

Step 3. Describe the desired behavior. (Don't forget to have the employee state why it is important.)

Step 4. Get a commitment to the change.

Step 5. Follow up.

Procedure 3
(5–8 minutes)

A. Role play. The supervisor of Employee 1, the clerical worker, coaches him or her (use the actual name of the group member role-playing Employee 1) as planned. Talk; do not read your written plan. Employee 1, put yourself in the worker's position. You work hard; there is a lot of pressure to work fast. It's easier when you have more than one file. Refer to the workload while being coached. Both the supervisor and the employee will have to ad-lib.

The person not role-playing is the observer. He or she writes notes on the observer form below about what the supervisor did well and how he or she could improve.

B. Feedback. The observer leads a discussion on how well the supervisor coached the employee. It should be a discussion, not a lecture. Focus on what the supervisor did well and how he or she could improve. The employee should also give feedback on how he or she felt and what might have been more effective in getting him or her to change.

Do not go on to the next interview until told to do so. If you finish early, wait for the others to finish.

Same as Procedure 3, but change roles so that Employee 2, the waiter/waitress, is coached. Employee 2 should make a comment about the importance of talking to customers to make them feel welcome. The job is not much fun if you can't talk to your friends.

Procedure 5
(5–8 minutes)

Same as Procedure 3. But change roles so that Employee 3, the auto technician, is coached. Employee 3 should comment on the excellent work he or she does.

OBSERVER FORM

Try to have positive comments and give areas for improvement. State alternative things the supervisor could have said to improve the coaching session.

Step 1. How well did the supervisor refer to past feedback?

Step 2. How well did the supervisor describe current behavior?

Step 3. How well did the supervisor describe desired behavior? Did the employee state why the behavior is important?

Step 4. How successful was the supervisor at getting a commitment to the change? Do you think the employee would change?

Step 5. How well did the supervisor tell the employee how he or she was going to follow up to ensure the desired behavior was performed?

Conclusion: The instructor leads a class discussion and/or makes concluding remarks.

Application (2–4 minutes): What did I learn from this experience? How will I use this knowledge in the future?

Sharing: Volunteers give their answers to the application section.

**In-Class
Improving the
Quality of
Student Life**

*Procedure 1
(8–15 minutes)*

*Procedure 2
(3–10 minutes)*

*Procedure 3
(5–10 minutes)*

*Procedure 4
(5–20 minutes)*

Objective: To experience the quality circle approach to increasing the quality of student life at your college.

SCANS: The SCANS competencies of resources, interpersonal skills, information, and systems and the foundations of basic, thinking, and personal qualities are developed through this exercise.

Preparation: None needed for this exercise.

Experience: You will experience being a part of a quality circle.

Break into groups of five or six members. Select a spokesperson. Your group is to come up with a list of the three to five most needed improvements at your college. Rank them in order of priority, from 1—most important to 5—least important. When you are finished, or the time is up, the spokesperson will write the ranking on the board. You may refer back to Preparation for Skill-Building Exercise 12–2, for ideas on areas needing improvement.

Option A: The instructor determines the class's top three to five priorities for improvement.

Option B: The class achieves consensus on the top three to five priorities for improvement.

Each group selects a new spokesperson. the group develops solutions that will improve the quality of student life for the class's three to five priority areas.

For the first priority item, each spokesperson states the group's recommendation for improving the quality of student life. The class votes or comes to a consensus on the best way to solve the problem. Proceed to items 2 to 5 until you finish or time is up.

Discussion:

1. Are survey feedback and quality circles effective ways to improve the quality of student life on campus?

2. Did the class consider that quality of student life is a balance between the college, students, and society? Are your solutions going to benefit the college and society as well as the students?

Conclusion: The instructor may lead a class discussion and/or make concluding remarks.

Application   (2–4 minutes): What did I learn from this experience? How will I use this knowledge in the future?

Sharing: Volunteers give their answers to the application section.

Fiscal Fairy Tale # 3:
Rumplsheepskin

Go to the MG website (*www.mgeneral.com*) and read *Fiscal Fairy Tale #3: Rumplsheepskin* (your instructor may ask you to print a copy and bring it to class). Answer these questions (your instructor may ask you to type them and bring them to class):

Online MG Webzine
Exercise 14

Questions Relating to the Tale Only

1. As stated at the end of the tale, in 50 words or so, what is your response to this tale? You may send it to MG.

2. Have you, or anyone you know, worked for an organization that keeps requiring more and more of its employees, while laying them off as there are fewer to keep improving productivity? Give some examples of things the organizational managers do/did.

3. Have you, or anyone you know, worked for an organization that hired consultants? What were the positive and negative results?

4. At what point does economic success become more important than the human element? Who can benefit and who gets hurt when a company cuts costs by reducing is workforce?

Questions Relating the Tale to the Chapter Concepts

5. Which of the three methods for increasing productivity was the major focus of the little man to double productivity?

In-Class MG Webzine
Exercise 14

6. Which methods for "increasing productivity" were used by the little man?

7. Which participative management technique did the little man primarily use to increase productivity?

The instructor selects one of the six options from Appendix B page 589.

INTERNET EXERCISES

Training (IE 14–1)

Online Internet Exercise 14–1

The objective of this exercise is to learn training tips that can help you increase productivity.

1. Go to the American Media website–*www.ammedia.com*

2. Click "Trainer's Room" then "Trainer's Tips" and select a concept to learn more about.

3. Click and read the tips (your instructor may want a copy).

4. Questions: (1) What topic did you select? (2) What training tips did you learn? (3) How can you use these tips to increase performance? (Your instructor may require a typed copy.)

In-Class Internet Exercises 14–1, IE 14–2, and IE 14–3

The instructor selects one of the six options from Appendix B page 589.

Participative Management (IE 14–2)

Online Internet Exercise 14–2

The objective of this exercise is to learn more about participative management by visiting a nonprofit website that has lots of information on broad-based participation programs.

1. Go to the Foundation for Enterprise Development—*www.fed.org*

2. Click "Online Magazine" then an article and read it (your instructor may want a copy). You may select a current article or click back issues and find one there.

3. Questions: (1) Who was the author and what was the title of the article? (2) What did you learn, in 50 words or so? (3) How can you use this information to increase performance? (Your instructor may require a typed copy.)

Quality of Life (IE 14–3)

Online Internet Exercise 14–3 (Self-Assessment)

The objective of this exercise is to diagnose/measure your quality of life and to develop and implement a plan to improve your quality of life. Do the following:

1. Go to the Culture Building website homepage—*www.culture-building.com*

2. Click "Diagnostics" then Click "Quality of Life Checkup" and read about the diagnostics you will get for your life, then click "Proceed."

3. To obtain your quality of life scores, you must fill in the "name and e-mail" with your real or fictitious information. If you give your real e-mail address, the diagnostic score will be sent to your e-mail address (an option would be to have the diagnoses e-mailed to your instructor). However, you will get the scores online. You must also answer every question to get your scores.

4. Click your responses to the questions then click submit.

5. Generally, the higher your scores (based on 100 percent overall and 5 for sub-scores) the higher is your level of quality of life. Print a copy of your scores (your instructor may require a copy).

6. Questions: (1) What was your total score percentage? (2) What are your highest and lowest subscores? Be sure to list areas and scores for each. (3) How can you improve your quality of life in your weakest area? Be sure to list specific behavior and to implement your plan. (Your instructor may require a typed copy.)

Personal Development

Time and Career Management

15

After completing this chapter, you should be able to:

1. Explain how to analyze your use of time with a time log.

2. State the three priority determination questions and when an activity on the to-do list is a high, medium, low, or delegate priority.

3. List and explain the three steps in the time management system.

4. Identify at least three time management techniques you presently do not use but will use in the future (items in the should-use column of Self-Assessment Exercise 15–1).

5. Describe the four career stages.

6. List and explain the five steps in the career planning model.

7. Explain at least three tips to get ahead that you can use to improve your chances of getting a job, raises, and promotions.

8. Define the following 11 key terms (in order of appearance in the chapter):

time management	**time management steps**
time log	**career planning**
priority	**career development**
priority determination	**career planning model**
questions	**career path**
to-do list	**job shock**

Chapter Outline

Whitney and Shane were talking during a coffee break. Whitney was complaining about all the tasks she had to get done. She had all kinds of deadlines to meet. Whitney was a nervous wreck as she listed the many tasks. After a while, Shane interrupted to say that he used to be in the same situation until he took a time management workshop that taught him to get more done in less time with better results. Shane gave Whitney the details so she could take the course. In return, Whitney told Shane about a career development course she took. It helped her to get the job she has now, and helped her know what she wants to accomplish in the future. Have you ever felt as though you have more to do than the time you have to do it in? Do you ever wonder about your career? If you answered yes to either of these two questions, this chapter can help you.

Time Management

Some people question whether time management belongs in a human relations textbook. However, it is here because one of the major reasons managers do not have better human relations is their lack of time. If you manage your time better, you will have more time to spend developing effective human relations and creating win–win situations. Developing time management skills is also an effective way to better balance work–family life,[1] reduce stress (Chapter 2), increase personal productivity, and experience inner peace. It is possible for one to gain control of one's life by controlling one's time. Do you struggle with time management like most people? In the downsized organization with workload expansion, squeezing more productivity out of our workdays, through better time management, seems more critical to career success than ever.[2] The term **time management** *refers to techniques designed to enable people to get more done in less time with better results.* Time is a manager's most valuable resource.[3]

In this section, we examine ways to analyze your present use of time, a priority determination system, how to use a time management system, and time management techniques.

WORK APPLICATIONS

1. Why are time management skills important? How can you benefit by using the time management information discussed in this chapter?

Analyzing Time Use

The first step to successful time management is to determine current time use.[4] People often do not realize how they waste their time until they analyze time use. Professionals say they waste at least an hour daily because they are unorganized.[5] An analysis of how you use your time will indicate areas for improvement.

Time Log

The **time log** *is a daily diary that tracks activities and enables one to determine how time is utilized.* You use one time log for each day. See Exhibit 15–1 for an example. It is recommended that you keep track of your daily time use for one or two typical weeks. Make 5 to 10 copies of Exhibit 15–1; you may need to change the hours to match your working hours. Try to keep the time log with you throughout the day. Fill in each 15-minute time slot, if possible. Try not to go for longer than one hour without filling in the log. Each time shown represents 15 minutes of time. Beside each time write the activity(s) completed. For example, on the 8:15 line record the activity(s) completed from 8:00-8:15.

Analyzing Time Logs:
After keeping time logs for 5 to 10 working days, you can analyze them by answering the following questions:

1. Review the time logs to determine how much time you are spending on your primary responsibilities. How do you spend most of your time?

2. Identify areas where you are spending too much time.

3. Identify areas where you are not spending enough time.

4. Identify major interruptions that keep you from doing what you want to get done. How can you eliminate them?

5. Identify tasks you are performing that you do not have to be involved with. If you are a manager, look for nonmanagement tasks. To whom can you delegate these tasks?

6. How much time is controlled by your boss? How much time is controlled by your employees? How much time is controlled by others outside of your department? How much time do you actually control? How can you gain more control of your own time?

7. Look for crisis situations. Were they caused by something you did or did not do? Do you have recurring crises? How can you plan to eliminate recurring crises?

8. Look for habits, patterns, and tendencies. Do they help or hurt you to get the job done? How can you change them to your advantage?

9. List three to five of your biggest time wasters. What can you do to eliminate them?

10. Determine how you can manage your time more efficiently.

Learning Objective

1. Explain how to analyze your use of time with a time log

The remainder of this section presents ideas to help you improve time management.

WORK APPLICATIONS

2. Identify your three biggest time wasters, preferably with the use of a time log. How can you cut down or eliminate these time wasters?

EXHIBIT 15–1   TIME LOG

Date _____

8:00

8:15

8:30

8:45

9:00

9:15

9:30

9:45

10:00

10:15

10:30

10:45

11:00

11:15

11:30

11:45

12:00

12:15

12:30

12:45

1:00

1:15

1:30

1:45

2:00

2:15

2:30

2:45

3:00

3:15

3:30

3:45

4:00

4:15

4:30

4:45

5:00

5:15

5:30

5:45

Priority Determination

At any given time, you face having to do many different tasks. One of the things that separates successful from unsuccessful people is their ability to do the important things—priorities—first, and the less important things later.[6] A **priority** *is the preference given to one activity over other activities.*

Tasks that you must get done should be placed on a to-do list,[7] and then prioritized to rank the order of performance.[8] After prioritizing tasks, focus only on one at a time.[9] According to Peter Drucker, a few people who seem to do an incredible number of things; however, their impressive versatility is based mainly on doing one thing at a time.

Priority Determination Questions

Set priorities[10] by answering three priority determination questions. The three questions are:

1. Do I need to be personally involved because of my unique knowledge or skills? (yes or no) Although delegation is an important part of the manager's job, there are times when you are the only one who can do the task, and you must be involved.[11]

2. Is the task within my major area of responsibility or will it affect the performance or finances of my department? (yes or no) Managers must oversee the performance of their departments and keep the finances in line with the budget.

3. When is the deadline? Is quick action needed? (yes or no) Should I work on this activity right now, or can it wait? Time is a relative term. In one situation, months or even a year may be considered quick action, while in another situation a matter of minutes may be considered quick action. For example, the decision to earn a college degree may have to be made close to four years in advance. It often takes several months before applicants are told if they are accepted. To the admissions personnel, this may be quick action. On the production line, machine changes to make a different product may take minutes or hours, and this is considered quick action.

To summarize, **priority determination questions** *ask: (1) Do I need to be personally involved? (2) Is the task my responsibility or will it affect the performance or finances of my department? and (3) Is quick action needed?*

Assigning Priorities

Based on the answers to the three questions, a manager can delegate a task or assign it a high, medium, or low priority:

Delegate (D):   The task is delegated if the answer to question 1 (Do I need to be personally involved?) is no. If the answer to question 1 is no, it is not necessary to answer questions 2 and 3 because a priority is not assigned to the task. However, planning the delegation and delegating the task are prioritized.

High (H) Priority: A high priority is assigned if you answer yes to all three questions. You need to be involved, it is your major responsibility, and quick action is needed.

Medium (M) Priority: A medium priority is assigned if you answer yes to question 1 (you need to be involved) but no to question 2 (it is not your major responsibility) or 3 (quick action is not needed; it can wait).

Low (L) Priority: A low priority is assigned if you answer yes to question 1 (you need to be involved) but no to questions 2 and 3. It is not your major responsibility, and quick action is not needed.

The To-Do List

The three priority questions are on the to-do list in Exhibit 15-2, and in Application Situation 15–1 in order to help you develop your ability at assigning priorities. The **to-do list** *is the written activities the individual has to complete.* Feel free to make copies of Exhibit 15–2 and use it on the job. In summary, decide what is really important and find the time to do it.[12]

EXHIBIT 15–2 **TO-DO LIST**

D Delegate—no to #1 H High priority—yes to all three questions (YYY) M Medium priority—yes to #1 and #2 or #3 (YYN or YNY) L Low priority—yes to #1, no to #2 and #3 (YNN)	#1	#2	#3		
Activity	Involvement Needed?	Responsibility\Performance\Finances?	Quick Action\Deadline?	Time Needed?	Priority

Source: Adapted from Harbridge House Training Materials (Boston).

Prioritizing To-Do List Activities

AS 15–1

Prioritize the following 10 activities on the to-do list of a supervisor of a production department in a large company.

Priority Determination	Questions			
	#1	#2	#3	
D Delegate—no to question 1 H High priority—yes to all three questions (YYY) M Medium priority—yes to #1 and #2 or #3 (YYN or YNY) L Low priority—yes to #1, no to #2 and #3 (YNN)	Do I Need to Be Involved?	Is It My Resposbility\ Performance\Finances?	Is Quick Action Needed?	Deadline?	Priority
Activity				
1. John, the sales manager, told you that three customers stopped doing business with the company because your products have decreased in quality.				
2. Your secretary Rita told you that there is a salesperson waiting to see you. He does not have an appointment. You don't do any purchasing.				
3. Jan, a vice president, wants to see you to discuss a new product to be introduced in one month.				
4. John, the sales manager, sent you a memo stating that the sales forecast was incorrect. Sales are expected to increase by 20 percent starting next month. Inventories are as scheduled.				
5. Dan, the personnel director, sent you a memo informing you that one of your employees has resigned. Your turnover rate is one of the highest in the company.				
6. Rita told you that a John Smith called while you were out. He asked you to return his call, but wouldn't state why he was calling. You don't know who he is or what he wants.				
7. Sandy, one of your best workers, wants an appointment to tell you about a situation that happened in the shop.				
8. John called and asked you to meet with him and a prospective customer for your product. The customer wants to meet you.				
9. Tom, your boss, called and said he wants to see you about the decrease in the quality of your product.				
10. In the mail you got a note from Frank, the president of your company, and an article from *The Wall Street Journal.* The note said FYI (for your information).				

Source: Adapted from Harbridge House Training Materials (Boston).

In using the to-do list, write each activity you have to accomplish on one or more lines and assign a priority to it.[13] Remember that priorities may change several times during the day due to unexpected tasks that must be added to your to-do list. Look at the high (H) priority activities and start by performing the most important one. When it's done, cross it off and select the next, until all high-priority activities are done. Then do the same with the medium (M) priorities, then the low (L)

Learning Objective

2. State the three priority determination questions and when an activity on the to-do list is a high, medium, low, or delegate priority

priorities. Be sure to update the priorities. As deadlines come nearer, priorities will change. With time, low priorities often become high priorities.

WORK APPLICATIONS

3. Identify at least three high priorities related to your education.
4. List at least five activities on your to-do list. Based on the three priority determination questions, prioritize each activity as H, M, L, or D.

Time Management System

The problem people face is not a shortage of time, but how to use their time. Experts say that most people waste at least two hours a day.

The time management system that is presented in this section has a proven record of success with thousands of managers. It can also be used by nonmanagers and students. You should try it for three weeks. After that time, you may adjust it to meet your own needs.

The four major parts to the time management system are priorities, objectives, plans, and schedules:

- Priorities. Setting priorities on a to-do list helps increase performance.
- Objectives. Objectives state *what* we want to accomplish within a given period of time. The manager should set objectives,[14] following the guidelines stated in Chapter 6.
- Plans. Plans state *how* you will achieve your objectives. They list the necessary activities to be performed.
- Schedules. Schedules state *when* the activities planned will be carried out. You should schedule each workday.

Time management techniques all boil down to making a plan and sticking to it as much as possible.[15] The **time management steps** *include: step 1, plan each week; step 2, schedule each week; and step 3, schedule each day.*

Step 1. Plan Each Week

On the last day of each week, plan the coming week. Do this each and every week. Using your to-do list and the previous week's plan and departmental objectives, fill in the weekly planning sheet (see Exhibit 15–3). Start by listing the objectives you want to accomplish during the week.[16] The objectives should not be routine tasks you perform weekly/daily. For example, if an employee's annual review is coming due, plan for it.

After setting a few major objectives, list the activities it will take to accomplish each objective.[17] To continue our example, you will need to make an appointment with the employee and plan to complete the performance review form.

The next two columns to fill in are the time needed and the day to schedule. To continue our example, assume it will take you 10 minutes to schedule the performance appraisal and about 1 hour to prepare for it. The day to schedule would be on Tuesday, your relatively quiet day. With time, you will learn how much you can plan for and accomplish in one week. Planning too much becomes frustrating when you cannot get it all done.[18] On the other hand, if you do not plan enough activities, you will end up wasting time and missing deadlines.

Step 2. Schedule Each Week

Scheduling your week gets you "organized" to achieve your important objectives. You may schedule the week at the same time you plan it, or after, whichever you prefer. Planning and scheduling the week should take about 30 minutes. See

EXHIBIT 15–3   **WEEKLY PLANNING SHEET**

Plan for the week of _____

Objectives: (What is to be done, by when) (Preposition *to* + action verb + single behavior result + target data.)

Activities	Priority	Time Needed	Day to Schedule

Total time for the week

Exhibit 15–4 for a weekly schedule. Make copies of Exhibits 15–3 and 15–4 for use on the job. When scheduling your plans for the week, select times when you do not have time commitments such as meetings and so forth. Most managers should leave about 50 percent of the week unscheduled for unexpected events. Your job may require more or less unscheduled time.[20] With practice, you will perfect weekly planning and scheduling. *The key to success is not to prioritize your schedule, but to schedule your priorities weekly and daily.*[21]

Step 3. Schedule Each Day

Successful managers have daily schedules.[22] At the end of each day, you should schedule the next day.[23] Or begin each day by scheduling it.[24] This should take 15 minutes or less. Using your plan and schedule for the week, and your to-do list, schedule each day on the form in Exhibit 15–5. Make copies of it as needed on the job.

Begin scheduling the activities over which you have no control, such as meetings you must attend.

Leave your daily schedule flexible. As stated above, most managers need about 50 percent of their time unscheduled to handle the unexpected events. Don't be too optimistic; schedule enough time to do each task.[25] Many managers find that estimating the time it will take to perform a nonroutine task, and then doubling it, works well. With practice, your time estimation should improve.

Schedule your high-priority items during your prime time. Prime time is the period of time when you perform at your best. For most people this time is early in the morning. Determine your prime time and schedule the tasks that need your full attention then. Do routine things, like checking your mail, during non-prime . . . time hours.[26]

Try to schedule a time for unexpected events. Tell employees to see you with routine matters during a set time like 3:00 P.M. Have people call you, and call them during this set time.[27]

Do not do an unscheduled task before doing a scheduled task without prioritizing it first. If you are working on a high-priority item and a medium-priority item is brought to you, let it wait. Often, the so-called urgent things can wait.[28]

The steps of the time management system bridge the gap between objectives, plans, and their implementation.[29] Keep your daily schedule and to-do list with you.

Forms similar to Exhibits 15–1 to 15–5 can be purchased in pad, book, computerized and Web[30] versions. However, you may copy these exhibits for your own use.

 Skill-Building
15–1

Learning Objective

3. List and explain the three steps in the time management system

Time Management Techniques

In Self-Assessment Exercise 15–1 are 68 time management techniques. Complete the exercise to determine which techniques you presently use and techniques that can help you get more done in less time with better results. Review and

---

APPLICATION SITUATIONS

Time Management

AS 15–2

Identify each time management statement as:

A. Priorities   C. Plans   E. Schedule for the day

B. Objectives   D. Schedule for the week

_____ 11. "I set up my appointments for May 5."

_____ 12. "I know what I want to accomplish."

_____ 13. "I've decided how to get the work done."

_____ 14. "I know my major responsibilities."

_____ 15. "I've planned my week; now I'm going to . . ."

E X H I B I T 1 5 – 4 **WEEKLY SCHEDULE**

Schedule for week of _____

	Monday	Tuesday	Wednesday	Thursday	Friday
8:00 8:15 8:30 8:45					
9:00 9:15 9:30 9:45					
10:00 10:15 10:30 10:45					
11:00 11:15 11:30 11:45					
12:00 12:15 12:30 12:45					
1:00 1:15 1:30 1:45					
2:00 2:15 2:30 2:45					
3:00 3:15 3:30 3:45					
4:00 4:15 4:30 4:45					
5:00 5:15 5:30 5:45					

EXHIBIT 15–5   **DAILY SCHEDULE**

Day _____   **Date** _____

8:00
8:15
8:30
8:45

9:00
9:15
9:30
9:45

10:00
10:15
10:30
10:45

11:00
11:15
11:30
11:45

12:00
12:15
12:30
12:45

1:00
1:15
1:30
1:45

2:00
2:15
2:30
2:45

3:00
3:15
3:30
3:45

4:00
4:15
4:30
4:45

5:00
5:15
5:30
5:45

prioritize the items in the "should" column. Select at least your top priority item now and each week to work on. Write it (them) on your to-do list, and schedule it, if appropriate. Once you have completed the should column, do the same with the items in the "could do" column. Then review the "not applicable" column to be sure they do not apply.

Self-Assessment Exercise 15–1

Time Management Techniques

Below is a list of 68 ideas that can be used to improve your time management skills. Check off the appropriate box for each item.

(1) I should do this.   (3) I do this now.

(2) I could do this.   (4) Does not apply to me.

	Should	Could	Do	N/A
Planning and Controlling				
1. Set objectives—long and short term.				
2. Plan your week, how you will achieve your objectives.				
3. Use a to-do list; write all assignments on it.				
4. Prioritize the items on your to-do list. Do the important things rather than urgent things.				
5. Get an early productive start on your top-priority items.				
6. During your best working hours—prime time—only do high-priority items.				
7. Don't spend time performing unproductive activities to avoid or escape job-related anxiety. It doesn't really work.				
8. Throughout the day ask yourself, "Should I be doing this now?"				
9. Plan before you act.				
10. Plan for recurring crises and plan to eliminate crises.				
11. Make decisions. It is better to make a wrong decision than none at all.				
12. Have a schedule for the day. Don't let your day be planned by the unexpected.				
13. Schedule the next day before you leave work.				
14. Schedule unpleasant or difficult tasks during prime time.				
15. Schedule enough time to do the job right the first time. Don't be too optimistic on the length of time to do a job.				
16. Schedule a quiet hour(s). Only be interrupted by true emergencies. Have someone take a message or ask people to call you back during scheduled unexpected event time.				

	Should	Could	Do	N/A
17. Establish a quiet time for the entire organization, department, etc. The first hour of the day is usually the best time.				
18. Schedule large blocks of uninterrupted (emergencies only) time for projects, etc. If this doesn't work, hide somewhere.				
19. Break large (long) projects into parts (time periods).				
20. If you don't follow your schedule, ask the priority question (is the unscheduled event more important than the scheduled event?).				
21. Schedule a time for doing similar activities (e.g., make and return calls, write letters, memos).				
22. Keep your schedule flexible—allow _____ % of time for unexpected events.				
23. Schedule unexpected event time and answer mail, and do routine things in between events.				
24. Ask people to see/call you during your scheduled unexpected event time only, unless it's an emergency.				
25. If staff members ask to see you—"got a minute?"—tell them you're busy and ask if it can wait until x o'clock (scheduled unexpected time).				
26. Set a schedule time, agenda, and time limit for all visitors, and keep on topic.				
27. Control your time. Cut down on the time controlled by the boss, organization, and your subordinates.				
Organizing				
28. Keep a clean desk.				
29. Rearrange your desk for increased productivity.				
30. All nonwork-related or distracting objects should be removed from your desk.				
31. Do one task at a time.				
32. With paperwork, make a decision at once. Don't read it again later and decide.				
33. Keep files well arranged and labeled.				
34. Have an active and inactive file section.				
35. If you file an item, put a destruction date on it.				
36. Call rather than write, when appropriate.				
37. Have someone else (delegate) write letters, memos, etc.				

	Should	Could	Do	N/A
38. Dictate rather than write letters, memos, etc.				
39. Use form letters and/or form paragraphs.				
40. Answer letters (memos) on the letter itself.				
41. Have someone read things for you and summarize them for you.				
42. Divide reading requirements with others and share summaries.				
43. Have calls screened to be sure the right person handles them.				
44. Plan before calling. Have an agenda and all necessary information ready—take notes on agenda.				
45. Ask people to call you back during your scheduled time (unexpected). Ask when is the best time to call them.				
46. Have a specific objective/purpose for every meeting.				
47. For meetings, invite only the necessary participants and keep them only for as long as they are needed.				
48. Always have an agenda for a meeting and stick to it. Start and end as scheduled.				
49. Conclude each meeting with a summary, and get a commitment on who will do what by when.				
50. Call rather than visit, if possible.				
51. Set objectives for travel. List everyone you will meet with. Send (call) them agendas and have a file folder for each with all necessary data for your meeting.				
52. Combine and/or modify activities to save time.				
Leadership and Staffing				
53. Set clear objectives for subordinates with accountability—give them feedback/evaluate results often.				
54. Use your subordinates' time well. Do you make subordinates wait idly for decisions, instructions, materials, or in meetings?				
55. Communicate well. Do you wait for a convenient time, rather than interrupt your subordinates and waste their time?				
56. Train your subordinates. Don't do their work for them.				
57. Delegate activities in which you personally do not need to be involved.				
58. Delegate nonmanagement functions.				

**Self-Assessment
Exercise 15–1** *continued*

	Should	Could	Do	N/A
59. Set deadlines when delegating.				
60. Set deadlines that are earlier than the actual deadline.				
61. Use the input of your staff. Don't reinvent the wheel.				
62. Teach time management skills to your subordinates.				
63. Don't procrastinate; do it.				
64. Don't be a perfectionist; define acceptable and stop there.				
65. Learn to stay calm. Getting emotional only causes more problems.				
66. Reduce socializing without causing antisociality.				
67. Identify your time wasters and work to minimize them.				
68. If there are other ideas you have that are not listed above, add them here.				

Learning Objective

4. Identify at least three time management techniques you presently do not use but will use in the future

WORK APPLICATIONS

5. From the 68 time management techniques, list the three most important ones you should be using. Explain how you will implement each technique.

● Organization
● Group
● Individual

■ Performance
■ Human Relations
■ Behavior

Career Management

People who effectively manage their time are usually more successful on the job and have a greater chance of career advancement. However, career success depends on hard work and planning.[31] You must take the responsibility for managing your career.[32] If you expect others to give you jobs, raises, and promotions, they may never come your way. In this section, you will learn how to manage your career successfully. The topics covered are career stages, career planning and development, getting a job, and getting raises and promotions.

Career Stages

Before planning your career, you must consider your career stage. As people get older, they have different career stage needs.

The 20s

This is the time when managers are just getting started. The challenge is to prove that you have what it takes to get the job done well—and on time.[33] There is a lot of pressure to be the best. Women and minorities who seek advancement in a world dominated by men tend to feel personal pressure to try harder. One must develop the job skills needed to do the present job and to prepare for advancement. Initiative is needed. Young people often work long, hard hours to get ahead.

Today's young managers have higher expectations. They are impatient as they feel the pressure for quick advancement up the corporate ladder, which is shaky at best (and which is viewed more as a jungle gym than a ladder because you may need to go sideways or even down to find a new route to that goal). Most professionals don't stay at their first job for more than three years.[34] With today's flatter organizations having fewer management positions, it takes longer to progress, and lateral moves are more common than upward promotions.

The 30s

This decade is the time when managers develop an expertise and show their strength as bosses. They try to gain visibility with top management. In their 30s people often question their careers. Where am I going? Should I be here? Am I secure in my position? This time of doubt is especially tough on women, who must decide whether and how to combine children and careers. Men especially feel trapped by financial demands and are frightened of changing careers, which often requires a cut in pay to start at a lower position, even though they are not happy. However, the days of working 20 to 30 years for the same organization are gone for most people. It is common for a manager to work for two to four different organizations during a career; career changes are more common.[35]

The 40s and 50s

By age 45, most managers have weathered a failure or two and know whether or not they have a shot at higher-management jobs. The majority don't make it and must accept that the race is over. In the past, people at this stage would settle into a secure middle-management job. However, times have changed. Many organizations have cut back the number of middle-manager positions and continue to do so. People in their 40s and 50s are sometimes forced to seek new employers or new careers. This can be difficult when trying to cope with growing older. As a means of getting rid of middle managers, some organizations are forcing people to take early retirement.

The 60s and 70s

Learning Objective

5. Describe the four career stages

At this stage, people begin to prepare for retirement. They can pass along what they have learned and provide continuity. People at this stage make good role models and mentors. Mentors can boost young careers, but few employees get them.[36] Get one if you can.

WORK APPLICATIONS

6. Which career stage are you in? Does the information stated about your career stage relate to your career? Explain.

Career Planning and Development

There is a difference between career planning and career development. **Career planning** *is the process of setting career objectives and determining how to accomplish them.* **Career development** *is the process of gaining skill, experience, and education to achieve career objectives.* You must take responsibility for your career, and develop a career plan.[37]

Most colleges and large organizations offer career planning and development services. The career planning counselor's role is not to find people jobs but to help them set realistic career objectives and plans. Many colleges also offer career placement services designed to help students find/get jobs. But it is the students' responsibility to obtain the job offer.

The career planning model can help you develop your own career plan. In preparation for Skill-Building Exercise 15–2, you will find working papers to guide you in the development of your own career plan. The **career planning model** *steps* *are step 1, self-assessment; step 2, career preferences and exploration; step 3, set objectives; step 4, develop a plan; and step 5, control.*

Step 1. Self-Assessment

The starting point in career planning is the self-assessment inventory: Who are you? What are your interests, values, needs, skills, and experience? What do you want to do during your career?

The key to career success is to determine the following: What do you do well? What do you enjoy doing? How do you get a job that combines your interests and skills? To be successful you need to view yourself as successful. To be successful develop some realistic short-term objectives and achieve them.

Step 2. Career Preferences and Exploration

Others can help you get a job, but you are responsible for your career selection and progression. Based on your self-assessment, you must decide what you want from your job and career, and prioritize these wants. Career planning is not just a determination of what you want to do. It is also important to determine why you want to do these things. What motivates you? How much do you want it? What is your commitment to your career? Without the appropriate motivation and commitment to career objectives and plans, you will not be successful in attaining them.

Some of the things you should consider are: (1) what industry you want to work for; (2) what size organization you want to work for; (3) what type of job(s) you want in your career; which functional areas interest you—production/operations, marketing, finance, human resources, and so on; if you want to be a manager, what department(s) you want to manage; (4) what city, state, or country you want to work in; people who are willing to relocate often find more opportunities; and (5) how much income do you expect when you start your career, and 5 years and 10 years from then.

IE 15–1

Once you have made these determinations read about your primary career area.[38] Talk to people in career planning and to people who hold the types of jobs you are interested in. People in these positions can help provide information that you can use in developing your career plan. Get their advice. Determine the requirements and qualifications you need to get a job in the career that interests you. Getting an internship, fieldwork, cooperative job, part-time job, and/or summer job in your field of interest can help you land the job you want after graduation. In the long run, it is often more profitable to take a job that pays less but gives you experience that will help you in your career progression.

Step 3. Set Career Objectives

Set short- and long-range objectives, using the guidelines from Chapter 6. Objectives should not simply be a listing for the next job(s). For example (assuming graduation from college in May 2004):

- To attain a sales position with a large insurance company by June 30, 2004.
- To attain a starting first-year income of $30,000.
- To attain my M.B.A. by June 30, 2006.
- To become a sales manager in the insurance industry by June 30, 2008.
- To attain a salary of $40,000 by June 30, 2009.

Step 4. Develop a Plan

Develop a plan that will enable you to attain your objectives.[39] A college degree is becoming more important to high school graduates for developing skills and earning pay increases.[40] This is where career development fits in. You must determine what skills, experience, and education you need to get to where it is you want to go, and plan to develop as needed. Talking to others can help you develop a career plan. You may find it helpful to use the planning sheet from Skill-Building Exercise 15–2.

You should have a written career plan, but this does not mean that it cannot be changed. You should be open to unplanned opportunities and take advantage of them when it is in your best interest to do so.

Step 5. Control

Learning Objective

6. List and explain the five steps in the career planning model

It is your responsibility to achieve your objectives. You may have to take corrective action. Review your objectives, check your progress at least once a year, and change and develop new objectives and plans. Update your résumé (to be discussed) at the same time.

Exhibit 15–6 lists the steps in the career planning model.

EXHIBIT 15–6

CAREER PLANNING MODEL

Step 1. Self-assessment.

Step 2. Career preferences and exploration.

Step 3. Set career objectives.

Step 4. Develop plan.

Step 5. Control.

WORK APPLICATIONS

7. What career development efforts are you making?

APPLICATION SITUATIONS

Career Planning Steps

AS 15–3

Identify each statement by its step in the career planning model:

A. 1   B. 2   C. 3   D. 4   E. 5

_____ 16. "First, I have to get my degree, then I'll apply for a management trainee position with the major banks in the Midwest."

_____ 17. "I'm very good in math and computers."

_____ 18. "I want to be a partner in a CPA firm within seven years."

_____ 19. "Once a year I sit down and reassess who I am and where I'm going."

_____ 20. "I want to get into the co-op program because I'm not sure what I want to do when I graduate. I figure it will help me to decide."

Getting a Job

It has been said that getting a good job is a job in itself. In attaining any good job, you need to develop a career plan; develop a résumé and cover letter; conduct research; and prepare for the interview.

Career Plan

Interviewers are often turned off by candidates who have no idea of what they want in a job and career. On the other hand, they are usually impressed by candidates with realistic career plans. Having a good career plan gives you a competitive advantage over those who do not. Doing Preparation for Skill-Building Exercise 15–2 will help prepare you for getting a job.

Résumé and Cover Letter

A recruiting executive at Xerox once said that the résumé is about 40 percent of getting a job. The cover letter and résumé are your introduction to the organization you wish to work for. If the résumé is not neat, has errors, or contains mistakes, you may not get an interview.[41] Recruiters tend to believe that a sloppy résumé comes from a sloppy person.

The cover letter should be short, one page. Its purpose is to introduce your résumé and to request an interview. The résumé should also be short; one page is recommended unless you have extensive education and experience. The résumé's primary purpose is to get you an interview.[42] When writing about internships and other work experience be sure to focus on accomplishments and skills that you developed that can be used on other jobs. Also, explain what value you added.[43] How did the organization benefit by having you as an employee? If you offered ideas on how to improve performance, developed new ways of doing things, etc., state them. Exhibit 15–7 has a sample résumé you can follow when developing your own résumé.

The résumé guidelines are designed more for the graduating student who has limited work experience. Experience is important, so take advantage of internships. But, if you have full-time work experience related to the job you seek, you can list the experience before the education section and be less concerned about internships, honors, and activities. Conversely, without full-time experience these activities are important. Getting involved in extracurricular activities can help you get a job. But, don't just list a club. Again, state what skills you developed and value you added to the organization.[44]

IE 15–2

After writing and printing your résumé draft with perfect balance for eye appeal, bold headings, etc., have an English professor proofread it to make sure it contains no spelling or grammar errors. Then have people in the field you want to enter read it for content and suggest improvements. After finalizing, it should be typed/printed/copied on a high-quality bond paper. Having matching personalized stationery for cover letters can impress a recruiter and get you an interview over other equally fine candidates with low quality appearance.

The use of a résumé for part-time and summer employment can also give a positive impression that makes you stand out from the competition. Give copies to friends and relatives to help you get a job.[45]

WORK APPLICATIONS

8. Make a résumé following the chapter guidelines. Bring your résumé to class. Your professor may allow class time for you to see other students' résumés in order to give and receive feedback on résumés.

Research

IE 15–3

You need to research to determine where to send your résumé. Many colleges offer seminars in job-search strategies. There are also a number of articles and books on the subject. Some people take the attitude that they want to make it on their own. It's an honorable thought, but the use of contacts can help you land the job you are looking for. Many people today are finding jobs through networking. However, a friend or relative giving you a lead and recommendation usually does not guarantee that you get the job. You must still go through the interview and land the job yourself. Help wanted ads in newspapers and online are common places to research jobs.

Once you have landed an interview, but before you go to it, you should research the organization. You want to determine as much about the organization as you can. For example, you should know the products and/or services it offers, know about the industry and its trends, know about the organization's profits and future plans. *www.Hoovers.com* may have the company information. For organizations that are publicly owned, you can get an annual report that has

EXHIBIT 15–7   **RÉSUMÉ GUIDELINES**

Name

Address

City, State, Zip

Telephone Number and Area Code

Objective

If you have a specific job, include it here. If your objective is general or covers several areas, omit this section, and, in a cover letter, tailor the objective to the job you are applying for.

Education

Degree/major	College, name, address, city, state, zip, and telephone number. Date of graduation. Minor area (if any). Grade point average (if you are proud of it).
Internship	(if any) List organization name, address, city, state, zip, telephone. State department and specific work activities; state areas of responsibility and other relevant information. List dates employed and supervisor's name and title.
Honors and/or activities	(if any) List any sports, clubs, or other extracurricular activities. Be sure to state any offices held, honors received, and skills, such as leadership, that you developed.

Experience

Title	List any full-time, summer, part-time, or volunteer job held. State organization name, address, city, state, zip, telephone number. List responsibilities and any skills developed, particularly any that relate to the job you are applying for. List dates employed and supervisor's name and title.
Title	Same as above.
Title	Same as above.

Skills/Training/Certification/Etc.

List, under an appropriate heading, any specific skills/training (e.g., computers), foreign language fluency, musical talent, hobbies (e.g., stamp collecting), certification (e.g., lifeguard, CPA, broker), or another talent. Try to present them as job related; even if you cannot, listing them shows successful achievement and motivation. Interviewers may ask about your hobby.

References

Furnished upon request. (Get approval before giving out names. You may be able to file references with your college career department; check with them.)

---

much of this information, they are also online at most company websites. If you know people who work at the organization, talk to them about these issues.

Also, you should develop a list of questions you want to ask the interviewer during, or at the end of, the interview. Asking questions is a sign of intelligence and shows interest in the organization. Two good areas to ask questions about are job responsibilities and career opportunities.

The Interview

The interview is given the most weight in job decisions in most cases, about 60 percent, according to the Xerox recruiter. References and/or the résumé will get you an interview, but how you perform during the interview usually determines if you get the job. It is vital to make a very positive first impression (Chapter 2). This means conveying a relaxed presence and an ability to convey accomplishments and pique the interviewer's interest quickly. Follow job interview etiquette (chapter 9).

Many college career placement services offer workshops on how to interview for a job. Some offer mock interviews on camera that allow you to see how you conduct yourself during an interview. If this service is available, take advantage of it.

After the interview, evaluate how well you did. Make some notes on what you did and did not do well. If you want the job, send a thank-you letter, add anything you forgot to say, state your interest in the job and the fact that you look forward to hearing from the interviewer. Enclose a copy of your résumé.

If you did not get the job, ask the interviewer why. You may or may not be told, but an honest answer can be helpful in preparation for future interviews.

WORK APPLICATIONS

9. Which specific idea(s) on getting a job do you plan to use?

Getting Raises and Promotions

To help you get raises and promotions, this section discusses tips to help you get ahead, career paths, how to prepare for getting a raise or promotion, how to ask for a raise or promotion, changing organizations, and job shock.

Tips to Help You Get Ahead

Below are 10 ways to enhance your chances of career advancement.

- Be a top performer at your present job. If you are not successful at your present job, you are not a likely candidate for a raise or promotion.
- Finish assignments early. When your boss delegates a task, get it done before the deadline.[46] This shows initiative.
- Volunteer for extra assignments. If you can handle additional work, you should get paid more, and you show your ability to take on a new position.
- Keep up with the latest technology. Request the opportunity for training. Take the time to learn to use the latest technology. Use the computer and MIS (management information systems) to full capability. Read publications that pertain to your field.
- Develop good human relations with the important people in the organization. (Follow the ideas throughout this book.)
- Know when to approach your boss. Make requests when your boss is in a good mood; stay clear when the boss is in a bad mood unless you can help resolve the reason for the bad mood.
- Be polite. Say thank you both verbally and in writing. Sending a thank-you note keeps your name in front of people. Saying please and pardon me, and so on, shows concern for others.[47]
- Never say anything negative about anyone. You never know who will find out what you've said. That "nobody" may be a good friend of an important person.
- Be approachable. Smile, and go out of your way to say hi to people. Take time to talk to people who want your help.
- make effective presentations. If you are not effective at speaking before people, get training. Join Toastmasters International.

WORK APPLICATIONS

10. Which of the 10 tips for getting ahead need the most and the least conscious effort on your part? Explain your answer.

Career Paths

A **career path** *is a sequence of job assignments that lead to more responsibility, with raises and promotions.* In organizations that have career paths, it is easier to develop a career plan, because in a sense that's what career paths are. In the fast-food industry, career paths are common. For example, management trainees start out by going to a formal training program for a few weeks, then they are assigned to a store as a trainee for six months, then they go to a different store as an assistant store manager for a year, then they become a store manager. After one year they can be promoted to a larger store. After being a store manager for five years, they are eligible for regional management positions.

Preparation for Getting a Raise or Promotion

It is very important to understand your job responsibilities and how you are evaluated by your boss, both formally and informally. Know your boss's expectations and exceed them, or at least meet them. Do what needs to be done to get a high performance appraisal. If you don't get a good performance appraisal, your chances of getting a raise or promotion will be hurt.

Chapter 14 discussed keeping a critical incident file of the good and poor performances of employees. In reality, most bosses don't keep a written record, or only record the negative. If you want a raise or promotion, it's your responsibility to prove that you deserve one. The way to prove it is through self-documentation.

Keep a critical incident file of every positive thing you do that is not generally required but that helps the organization. Keeping the boss appraised of your success on a regular basis is not bragging. Some of the things to include are:

Learning Objective

7. Explain at least three tips to get ahead that you can use to improve your chances of getting a job, raises, and promotions

- Any additional work you now perform.
- Times when you volunteered/cooperated to help other departments.
- Ideas you suggested that helped the organization.
- Any increases in the performance of your department. Be specific. For example, productivity was up by 5 percent last year, absenteeism was down 10 percent last year, returns were down by 100 units this period, sales increased by $5,000 this quarter.
- If during the last performance appraisal you were told of areas that needed improvement, gather evidence to show how you have improved.

The first four suggestions also apply to getting a job—adding value.[48]

If you plan to ask for a raise, state a specific amount. Check to find out what other people in similar jobs are getting for raises, and what other organizations pay their employees for similar jobs. If your boss is a negotiator, start with a request for a higher raise than you expect to get. This way you can compromise and still get what you feel you deserve.

Asking for a Raise or Promotion

When asking for a raise or promotion, don't catch your boss by surprise. The best time to ask is usually during the performance appraisal process. Present your critical incidents to help you get a good review and raise.

Requests for promotion should be known before a specific position is open. Your boss and the human resources/personnel department should know your career plan. Ask them where you stand, what the chances of promotion are, and when promotion may come. Have them help prepare you for a promotion.

WORK APPLICATIONS

11. Which specific idea(s) do you plan to use to help you get raises and promotions?

Changing Organizations

The choice will be yours. If you are satisfied that you are meeting your career plan with one organization, stay with it. If not, search out new opportunities elsewhere.[49]

However, you should realize that it is not uncommon for a job, particularly your first full-time job, to be frustrating and not meet your expectations. It would be nice, but don't expect to be told you are doing a good job; it is expected of you. Expect to be criticized, and be open to changing.

If you are open to making a career move, have an updated résumé and let your network of contacts know you are willing to make a move if the right opportunity comes along. Don't quit your job until you get another one, and don't publicize that you are looking for a new job with your boss and peers.

Job Shock

Video
BM–15

Skill-Building
15–2

Few jobs, if any, meet all expectations. **Job shock** *occurs when the employee's expectations are not met.* The expectation that the workplace is fair, and good work will always be recognized and rewarded is the leading cause of job shock. It is also common for employers to say, "Don't worry, we'll take care of you," and nothing happens, to your dismay. People also find part or many of their day-to-day tasks boring. Job shock has no quick cure. However, it is helpful to learn to cope with unsettling on-the-job realities by developing a "real world" mindset. Talk to other people to find out if your situation is unique. If it's not, you probably have unrealistic job expectations. People often change jobs only to find the same frustrations they hoped to leave behind. Learn to realize that your unhappiness often springs from unrealistic job expectations. Your real world mindset can help shield you from future shocks.

Through personal development, you can improve your human relations skills and time management skills, and advance in your career. Good luck in doing so.

REVIEW

Select one or more methods: (1) fill in the missing key terms from memory; (2) match the key terms, from the end of the review, with their definitions; and/or (3) copy the key terms in order from the key terms list at the beginning of the chapter.

_____ refers to techniques designed to enable people to

get more done in less time with better results. Analyzing your

_____ , a daily diary that tracks activities and enables one to

determine how time is utilized, reveals how you use your time. It serves as the basis

for determining how to improve your time management. A

_____ is the preference given to one activity over other

activities. The _____ are (1) Do I need to be personally

involved? (2) Is the task my responsibility or will it affect the performance or

finances of my department? (3) Is quick action needed? If you answer no to

question 1, delegate (D) the task. If you answer yes to all three questions, assign

the task a high (H) priority. If you answer yes to question 1 and no to 2 or 3, assign

the task a medium (M) priority. If you answer yes to question 1 and no to 2 and 3,

assign the task a low (L) priority. The _____ is the written

activities that the individual has to complete. The four major parts of the time

management system are priorities, objectives, plans, and schedules. The

_____ are: step 1, plan each week; step 2, schedule each

week; step 3, schedule each day.

As people age, they go through different career stages. _____ is the process of setting career objectives and determining how to accomplish them. _____ is the process of gaining skill, experience, and education to achieve career objectives. The _____ steps are step 1, self-assessment; step 2, career preferences and exploration; step 3, set objectives; step 4, develop a plan; and step 5, control. To attain a job, you should develop a career plan, résumé, and cover letter; conduct research; and prepare for the interview. Some organizations offer a _____, a sequence of job assignments that lead to more responsibility, with raises and promotions. Before asking for a raise or promotion, you should prepare yourself by developing a critical incident file of all the positive contributions you make to the organization. If you are not satisfied with your career progression, change organizations. However, realize that few, if any, jobs will meet all your expectations. _____ occurs when the employee's expectations are not met. Developing a real world mindset can help shield you from future shocks.

KEY TERMS

career development   550
career path   556
career planning   550
career planning model   550
job shock   557

priority   538
priority determination
   questions   538
time log   536

time management   535
time management
   steps   535
to-do list   538

Herb Kelleher:
Southwest Airlines

Southwest Airlines started as a small business with four planes in 1971. But its chairman and CEO, Herb Kelleher, has turned Southwest into a major U.S. carrier. It has been profitable in all but its first two years. What makes this success story ever more remarkable is the fact that companies including TWA, Delta, American, and United were reporting huge losses and retrenching while Southwest had a growth stragegy.

Southwest used a focus and low-cost strategy to get where it is today. Rather than compete head on with major airlines, Southwest selected a niche focus in short-haul point-to-point flights. Its average flight is only fifty-five minutes. Therefore, it essentially has no hubs, does not make connections with other carriers, and it does not have to transfer baggage. Southwest is more limited in the cities it covers, but it offers more frequent flights to those cities than its competitors. For example, it has 78 daily flights between Dallas and Houston, 46 between Phoenix and Los Angeles, and 34 between Las Vegas and Phoenix.

Southwest's cost per available-seat mile was 6.5 cents versus 9 cents at American, and 15 cents at USAir. Southwest's average yearly salary and benefits for each unionized worker was $43,707 versus $58,816 at Delta, and the industry average of $45,692. However, Southwestern is considered a fun place to work. Southwest has one of the lowest debt-to-equity ratios, 49 percent, and the highest Standard & Poor's credit rating among U.S. airlines. Southwest planes spend an average of around 15 minutes at the gate between flights while the industry average was around 60 minutes. Therefore, Southwest planes spent about 11 hours per day in the air while the industry average was 8 hours, despite the fact that it has more frequent shorter flights than the competition.

The mission at Southwest is airline service that is cheap, simple, and focused. Based on its low cost, it offers low fares. Southwest's average fare was under $60. In some areas, the competition was charging $300. Needles to say, competitors had to drop their prices to compete with Southwest, and some decided to get out of Southwest markets because they cannot compete. Southwest is cheaper than comparable intercity bus prices in most of its markets. CEO Kelleher has said that Southwest has created a solid niche making the automobile Southwest's main competition.

To achieve its mission of cheap simple service, Southwest has only one type of plane—the fuel-efficient Boeing 737. This standardization allows lower inventory cost for spare parts, and allows specialization and minimizes training of flight and maintenance crews. Employee turnover is the lowest in the industry at 7 percent.

To keep cost and fares down, Southwest uses a "no frills" approach to operations. There is no first-class or business section. There is no computerized reservations system because there are no reserved seats. Agents issue reusable numbered plastic cards on a first-come first-aboard to pick seats basis. There are no meals or movies. However, low-cost no frills does not mean low quality. In fact, Southwest is the only airline to win the U.S. Department of Transportation's "tripple crown" monthly citation for the best on-time performance, fewest lost bags, and fewest overall complaints. It has won it not once, but eleven times.

Go to the Internet: For more information on Herb Kelleher and Southwest Airlines, do a name search on the Internet and visit its website at *http://www.iflyswa.com*. For ideas on using the Internet with cases, see Appendix C. Select the best alternative for the following questions. Be sure to be able to give an explanation to support your answers.

1. What important concepts from this chapter contribute to Southwest's success?

2. Southwestern is considered a fun place to work. Does this affect careers at Southwestern?

3. In Southwestern pays less than competitors, how can it have the lowest turnover rate?

Cumulative Questions

4. How do Southwest management practices affect behavior, human relations, and performance (Chapter 1 to 14)?

5. How do you assess stress, intelligence, and impressions at Southwest (Chapter 2)?

6. How do you access employee attitudes, job satisfaction, and values at Southwestern (Chapter 3)?

7. How does Southwest's organizational structure differ from its competitors (Chapter 5)?

8. Are teams important at Southwest (Chapters 10 to 11)?

9. What type of culture does Southwest have (Chapter 12)?

10. How do you assess Southwest's productivity and participative management (Chapter 14)?

Overworked?

In the following discussion, Iris is a middle manager and Peggy is a first-line supervisor who reports to her.

Iris: Peggy, I've called you into my office to speak to you again about the late report.

Peggy: I know it's late again, but I'm so busy getting the work out that I don't have time to do it. I'm always the first to arrive for work and the last to go home. I push hard to get the job done. Sometimes I end up redoing employees' work because it's not done properly. I often get headaches and stomach cramps from working so intensely.

Iris: I know you do. Maybe the problem lies in your time management ability. What do you usually do each day?

Peggy: Most of each day is spent putting out fires. My employees constantly need me to help them with their work. The days just seem to speed by. Other than putting out fires, I don't do much.

Iris: So you can't get the reports done on time because of the number of fires. What is your approach to getting the reports done on time?

Peggy: I just wait until there are no fires to put out, then I do them. Sometimes it's after the deadline.

Iris: You are going to have to make some definite changes if you are going to be a successful supervisor. Do you enjoy being a supervisor?

Peggy: For the most part I do. I think I might like to move up the ladder some day. But I like the hands-on stuff; I'm not too thrilled about doing paperwork.

Iris: If you develop your time management skills, I believe you will find that you can get the job done on time with less stress. On Monday the company is offering a time management workshop. I took the course myself; it's excellent. It really helped me a lot when I was in your position, and today. It teaches you a three-step approach. [*It covers the to-do list and the information covered in this chapter.*] Do you want to attend?

Peggy: Yes, but what about the work in my department?

Iris: I'll cover for you. On Tuesday, I want you to come see me first thing in the morning so that we can discuss what you learned and how you are going to apply it on the job.

Answer the following questions, supporting your answers in the space between questions.

_____ 1. Keeping a time log and using a to-do list would be helpful to Peggy.
   a. true   *b.* false

_____ 2. Peggy seems to be effective at setting priorities.
   a. true   *b.* false

_____ 3. Peggy seems to delegate _____ activities.
   a. many   *b.* few

_____ 4. Setting weekly objectives, plans, and schedules would help Peggy get the reports done on time.
   a. true   *b.* false

_____ 5. Peggy seems to have a _____ personality type.

     a. A   *b.* B

_____ 6. Peggy appears to be in the _____ career stage.

     a. 20s   *c.* 40s and 50s
     b. 30s   *d.* 60s and 70s

_____ 7. Peggy has a career plan.

     a. true   *b.* false

_____ 8. The time management workshop is best classified as:

     a. career planning   *c.* career development
     b. career planning model   *d.* career path

_____ 9. From the case information, we can assume that this company has career paths.

     a. true   *b.* false

_____ 10. It appears that Peggy will be a good candidate for raises and promotions.

     a. true   *b.* false

11. How would you conduct the Tuesday morning session with Peggy?

Fiscal Fairy Tale # 5: Tortoise and the Harried

Go to the MG website (*www.mgeneral.com*) and read *Fiscal Fairy Tale # 5: Tortoise & Harried* (your instructor may ask you to print a copy and bring it to class). Answer these questions (your instructor may ask you to type them and bring them to class):

Online Internet Exercise 15

Questions Relating to the Tale Only

1. As stated at the end of the tale, in 50 words or so, what is your response to this tale? You may send it to MG.

2. Have you, or anyone you know, worked with people who are often in a rush? Give some examples of things the employees and organizational managers do/did.

3. Have you, or anyone you know, worked with people who seem to be very busy (activity), yet don't actually get much work done (action)? Give an example.

4. Who sets your work pace (you, coworkers, boss, organization, etc.)?

Questions Relating the Tale to the Chapter Concepts

5. How would you rate the boss's planning ability?

6. What is your assessment of the financial services time management?

7. What appears to be the missing key to successful use of time management at the financial services company?

In-Class MG Webzine Exercise 15

8. How are career planning and career development illustrated in this tale?

The instructor selects one of the six options from Appendix B page 589.

INTERNET EXERCISES

Career Exploration:Occupational Outlook Handbook (IE 15–1)

Online Internet Exercise 15–1

The objective of this exercise is to complete part of a career exploration to help you determine your next job preference using the government Occupational Outlook Handbook.

1. Before going to the website, think about the next job you want. State the occupational title as best you can. If you have no idea, you can select one at the website.

2. Go to the Department of Labor's Bureau of Labor Statistics (BLS), Occupational Outlook Handbook at *www.bls.gov*. Look over the homepage to see how much the BLS has to offer, then

3. Click the Occupational Outlook Handbook (OOH) box. You should now be in the OOH homepage. If you know the specific job, type it in the search box. If you don't have an exact title, look at the occupations and select a category or the A–Z index.

4. After selecting an occupation, read about it (your instructor many require a copy of the occupational information and/or a written report about what you learned about the occupation).

In-Class Internet Exercises 15–1, IE 15–2, IE 15–3 and 15–4

The instructor selects one of the six options from Appendix B page 589.

Resume (IE 15–2)

Online Internet Exercise 15–2 (Self-Assessment)

The objective of this exercise is to write or improve your résumé. If you do not have a written resume, write one during this exercise. If you have a résumé, improve it during this exercise.

1. Go to the Proven Résumés homepage—*www.provenresumes.com*

2. Click "Résumé Strategies that have. . . Workshops" and read the free workshops. Note that this will take quite some time as there is a lot of information that can help you to write or improve your resume. If you are serious about writing or improving your résumé to help you get a job, take your time; if not, at least get ideas for writing or improving your resume and be sure to return when you are serious.

3. Write, rewrite, or edit your résumé using a word processor. You may get offline and go back online for the next step of this exercise.

4. Click "Quiz to Rate Your Résumé" print the quiz and complete it on your copy (your instructor may require a copy).

5. Questions: (1) What is your résumé score? (2) What are your weakest area (lowest scores)? (3) How can you improve your résumé?

6. Edit your résumé and print copies. (Your instructor may require a copy of your answers and/or completed resume.)

Job Search (IE 15–3)
Online Internet
Exercise 15–3

The objective of this exercise is to complete an online job search for a job you would like to have.

1. Before going to the website, think about the next job you want. If you have no idea, you can select one at the website.

2. Go to the Monster website homepage—*www.monster.com*

3. Click "Search Jobs" and follow the search instructions.

4. Click on three of the jobs (one at a time) that sound interesting to you and read the job descriptions (your instructor may require a print out).

5. Questions: (1) What job were you searching for? (2) What did you learn about job searching? (3) How can you use this information to get a job?

Career Information: MG
SuperSite (IE 15–4)

Online Internet
Exercise 15–4

The objective of this exercise is to find out more about careers using the MG Super-Site.

1. Go to the MG homepage—*www.mgeneral.com*

2. Click "SuperSite" then careers "Jumpstart" and read the short description of the websites and select at least one to visit.

3. Click on one of the links and visit the website (be sure you left MG for another website) and read the career information (your instructor may require a copy).

4. Questions: (1) What website did you visit? (2) What did you learn about careers? (3) How can you use this information in your career? (Your instructor may require typed answers.)

SKILL-BUILDING EXERCISE 15–1

● **Preparation**
Time Management
System

Before using the time management system, you will find it helpful, but not necessary, to keep a time log for one or two typical weeks. It is strongly recommended that you keep a time log and analyze it.

Note: For this exercise you will need copies of Exhibits 15–1, 15–3, 15–4, and 15–5. You may make photocopies of the exhibits or make your own copies on sheets of paper. While performing the steps below, refer to the text guidelines.

Step 1. Plan Your Week: Use Exhibit 15–3 to develop a plan for the rest of this week. Begin with today.

Step 2. Schedule Your Week: Use Exhibit 15–4 to schedule the rest of this week. Be sure to schedule a 30-minute period to plan and schedule next week, preferably on the last day of the week.

Step 3. Schedule Your Day: Schedule each day using Exhibit 15–5. Do this each day, at least until the class period for which this exercise is assigned.

Be sure to bring your plans and schedules to class.

● **In-Class**
Time Management
System

Objective: To understand how to use the time management system to enable you to get more done in less time with better results.

SCANS: The SCANS competencies of resources, especially allocating time, interpersonal skills, information, and systems and the foundations of basic, thinking, and personal qualities are developed through this exercise.

Preparation: You need your completed plans and schedules.

Experience: You will share and discuss your plans and schedules for the week and daily schedule(s).

Procedure 1
(5–10 minutes)

Break into groups of five or six and share and discuss your plans and schedules. Pass them around so that you and others can make comparisons. The comparisons serve as a guide to improving future plans and schedules.

Conclusion: The instructor leads a class discussion and/or makes concluding remarks.

Application (2–4 minutes):   What did I learn from this experience? How will I use this knowledge in the future?

Sharing: Volunteers give their answers to the application section.

SKILL-BUILDING EXERCISE 15–2

● **Preparation**
  Career Planning

Answering the following questions will help you develop a career plan. Use additional paper if needed. Do not reveal anything about yourself that you prefer not to share with classmates during the in-class exercise.

Step 1. Self-Assessment

a. List two or three statements that answer the question "Who am I?"

b. Think about two or three of your major accomplishments. (They can be in school, work, sports, hobbies, etc.) List the skills it took to achieve each accomplishment.

c. Identify skills and abilities you already possess that you can use in your career (for example, planning, organizing, communicating, leading).

Step 2. Career Preferences and Exploration

a. What type of industry would you like to work in? (You may list more than one.)

b. What type and size of organization do you want to work for?

c. List by priority the five factors that will most influence your job/career decisions (opportunity for advancement, challenge, security, salary, hours, location of job, travel involved, educational opportunities, recognition, prestige, environment, co-workers, boss, responsibility, variety of tasks, etc.).

d. Describe the perfect job.

e. What type of job(s) do you want during your career (marketing, finance, operations, personnel, and so forth)? After selecting a field, select a specific job—for example, salesperson, manager, accountant.

Step 3. Career Objectives

a. What are your short-range objectives for the first year after graduation?

b. What are your intermediate objectives for the second through fifth years after graduation?

c. What are your long-range objectives?

Step 4. Use the Following Form to Develop an Action Plan to Help You Achieve Your Objectives

---

CAREER PLAN

Objective: _____

Starting date _____ Due date _____

Steps (what, where, how, resources, etc.—subobjectives)	When	
	Start	End

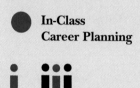

**In-Class
Career Planning**

Objective: To experience career planning; to develop a career plan.

SCANS: The SCANS competencies of resources, interpersonal skills, and information and the foundations of basic, thinking, and personal qualities are developed through this exercise.

Preparation: You will need the completed preparation that serves as your career plan.

Experience: You will share your career plan with one or two classmates to help make improvements in time.

*Procedure 1
(10–20 minutes)*

Break into teams of two or three. One at a time, go through your career plan while the other(s) ask questions and/or make recommendations to help you improve your career plan.

Conclusion: The instructor leads a class discussion and/or makes concluding remarks.

Application (2–4 minutes):   What did I learn from this experience? How will I use this knowledge in the future?

Sharing: Volunteers give their answers to the application section.

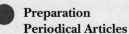

Preparation
Periodical Articles

Select a human relations topic that you would like to learn more about. It can be any topic covered in this book or topics not covered, if they relate to human relations.

Now go to the library (usually the reference section). Find the computer database that has business journals. Search your topic by typing it in the computer. The index should list periodical titles with the name of the author(s) and the name of the periodical in which the article appears with its date and page number(s). You may also get an abstract of the article and a full article in the database, which you can download and/or print. Select one of the articles to read. Be sure the library has the publication in some form.

Write down the following information:

Author's name(s):

Title of article:

Title of the periodical:

Date of publication and page number(s):

Now get the periodical and read the article. Then answer the following questions. (Use additional paper if needed.)

Be sure to write neatly. You may be asked to report to the class, or pass this assignment in to the instructor. Be prepared to give a three-to-five-minute talk on your article.

What did the article say? (Give a summary of the most important information in the article.)

How does this information relate to me and/or my interest?

How will I use this information in the future?

When reading articles of interest to your career, always answer the three questions. Answering these questions will help you to use the information, rather than to forget it, and develop your abilities and skills.

To continue to improve on your human relations skills after the course is over, read more articles of interest to you. When you can afford it, subscribe to a periodical of interest to you. Many employers have copies of periodicals related to their business available to employees, and they are willing to pay for employee subscriptions.

**In-Class
Periodical Articles**

Objectives: To become familiar with various publications. To gain some specific knowledge in a topic of your choice, and the choice of other students in the class.

Scans: The SCANS competencies of resource, interpersonal skills, information, technology (computer search) and possibly systems and the foundations of basic, thinking, and personal qualities are developed through this exercise.

Preparation: You should have read an article of interest to you and answered the three questions in the preparations.

Experience: Class members will share their articles.

*Procedure 1
(5–50 minutes)*

One at a time, students come to the front of the room and give a three-to-seven-minute speech on the article they read.

Conclusion: The instructor leads a class discussion and/or makes concluding remarks.

Applications (2–4 minutes):   What did I learn from this experience? How will I use this knowledge in the future?

Sharing: Voluteers give their answers to the application section.

Applying Human Relations Skills

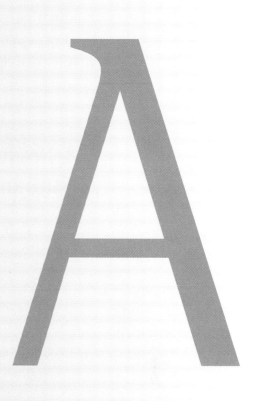

Learning Objectives

After completing this appendix, you should be able to:

1. State why human relations skills are important.
2. Identify the most important human relations concepts from the entire book.
3. Determine your strongest and weakest areas of human relations.
4. Compare your present skills assessment with the one you did in Chapter 1.
5. Explain three options in handling human relations problems.
6. Describe the four steps of changing behavior.
7. Develop your own human relations plan.

Pat O'Conner and David Fredrick, two students nearing completion of a human relations course, were talking about the course:

PAT: This course has a lot of good practical advice that can help me develop effective human relations.

DAVID: I agree. Have you been using the information on a regular basis in your daily life?

PAT: Some of it. I'm so busy that I don't always have time to think about and actually do these things, even though I know they will help me. Have you been using it?

DAVID: Most of it. I figure that if I use these skills now rather than wait until I get a full-time job, I'll be that much ahead of the game.

PAT: Is there a way to do this?

DAVID: Yes, I've already read the appendix. It explains how to develop a human relations plan that you can put into action immediately.

PAT: Guess I'll go read it now.

DAVID: Good luck, see you in class.

Whether you are more like Pat or David, this appendix will help you develop your own human relations plan.

A Review of Some of the Most Important Human Relations Concepts

Let's highlight some of the most important information from each chapter in the book to tie things all together. If you cannot recall the information covered in any of the chapters, please return to the chapter for a review of the material.

Part I: Behavior, Human Relations, and Performance Begin with You

Chapter 1 defined some of the important concepts used throughout the book. Can you define the following: human relations, the goal of human relations, behavior, levels of behavior, group behavior, organizational behavior, and performance? Please return to Chapter 1 and review the first few pages that state the many reasons why human relations are so important.

Can you define and discuss personality, stress, intelligence, learning styles, perception, and first impressions? If not, return to Chapter 2.

Can you define and discuss attitudes, job satisfaction, self-concept, and values? If not, return to Chapter 3.

Part II: Communication Skills: The Foundation of Human Relations

Can you define and discuss the importance of communications; the communication process; message transmission media; and how to send, receive, and respond to messages? If not, return to Chapter 4.

Can you define and discuss organizational structure and communications, communication barriers and how to overcome them, and situational communications? If not, return to Chapter 5.

Part III: Other Skills, Influencing Behavior, Human Relations, and Performance

Can you define and discuss content motivation theories, process motivation theories, reinforcement theory, and motivation techniques? If not, return to Chapter 6.

Can you define and discuss trait leadership theory, behavioral leadership theories, contingency leadership theories, situational supervision, and substitutes for leadership? If not, return to Chapter 7.

Can you define and discuss transactional analysis, assertiveness, conflict management styles, how to resolve conflict with the collaborating conflict style, and interpersonal dynamics? If not, return to Chapter 8.

Part IV: Team Behavior, Human Relations, and Performance

Can you define and discuss power, organizational politics, business ethics, vertical politics, and horizontal politics? If not, return to Chapter 9.

Can you define and discuss three types of groups, problem-solving and decision-making approaches, and creative group problem-solving and decision-making techniques. If not, return to Chapter 10.

Can you define and discuss team dynamics, group development stages and how to lead groups and meetings? If not, return to Chapter 11.

Part V: Organizational Challenges

Can you define and discuss resistance to change and how to overcome it; organizational culture, including managing diversity and quality; organizational climate; and organizational development? If not, return to Chapter 12.

Can you define and discuss prejudice and discrimination, equal employment opportunity, legally protected groups, sexual harassment, sexism in organizations, global diversity and cross-cultural relations, and how to handle complaints? If not, return to Chapter 13.

Can you define and discuss productivity, how to increase productivity, technology, and participative management techniques? If not, return to Chapter 14.

Part VI: Personal Development

● Organization
● Group
● Individual

Can you define and discuss time management and career management? If not, return to Chapter 15.

Assessing Your Human Relations Abilities and Skills

This section of the chapter gives you the opportunity to assess your human relations abilities and skills.

For each of the 43 statements below, score each by selecting the number from 1 to 7 that best describes your level of ability or skill. Record the number in the blank to the left of each statement.

Low ability/skill					High ability/skill	
1	2	3	4	5	6	7

_____ 1. I understand how personality and perception affect people's behavior, human relations, and performance.

_____ 2. I can describe several ways to handle stress effectively.

_____ 3. I know my preferred learning style (accommodator, diverger, converger, assimilator), and how it affects my behavior, human relations, and performance.

_____ 4. I understand how people acquire attitudes, and how attitudes affect behavior, human relations, and performance.

_____ 5. I can describe self-concept and self-efficacy, and how they affect behavior, human relations, and performance.

_____ 6. I can list several areas of personal values, and state how values affect behavior, human relations, and performance.

_____ 7. I can describe the communication process.

_____ 8. I can list several transmission media, and when to use each.

_____ 9. I can identify and use various message response styles.

_____ 10. I understand organizational communications and networks.

_____ 11. I can list barriers to communications and how to overcome them.

_____ 12. I know my preferred communication style, and how to change communication styles to meet the needs of the situation.

_____ 13. I understand the process people go through to meet their needs.

_____ 14. I know several content and process motivation theories, and can use them to motivate people.

_____ 15. I can list and use motivation techniques.

_____ 16. I can identify behavioral leadership theories.

_____ 17. I can identify contingency leadership theories.

_____ 18. I know my preferred leadership style and how to change it to meet the needs of situations.

_____ 19. I can describe transactional analysis.

_____ 20. I can identify the difference between aggressive, passive, and assertive behavior. I am assertive.

_____ 21. I can identify different conflict resolution styles. I understand how to resolve conflicts in a way that does not hurt relationships.

_____ 22. I can identify bases and sources of power. I know how to gain power in an organization.

_____ 23. I can list political techniques to increase success.

_____ 24. I can state the difference between Type I and Type II ethics.

_____ 25. I understand the roles of various types of groups in organizations.

_____ 26. I can help groups make better decisions through consensus.

_____ 27. I know when, and when not, to use employee participation in decision making.

_____ 28. I understand how to plan and conduct effective meetings.

_____ 29. I can identify components of group dynamics and how they affect behavior, human relations, and performance.

_____ 30. I know the stages groups go through as they develop.

_____ 31. I understand why people resist change, and how to overcome it.

_____ 32. I can identify and use organizational development techniques.

_____ 33. I understand how to develop a positive organizational culture and climate.

_____ 34. I understand equal employment opportunity (EEO) and the rights of legally protected groups like minorities, the disabled, alcohol and drug addicts, and people with AIDS.

_____ 35. I can define sexism and sexual harassment in organizations.

_____ 36. I can handle a complaint using the complaint model.

_____ 37. I know how to increase performance.

_____ 38. I can list and describe various participation programs.

_____ 39. I understand total quality management (TQM).

_____ 40. I know how to use a time management system.

_____ 41. I understand how to use time management techniques in order to get more done in less time with better results.

_____ 42. I know how to develop a career plan and manage my career successfully.

_____ 43. I understand how to plan for improved human relations.

To use the profile form, place an X in the box whose number corresponds to the score you gave each statement above.

PROFILE FORM

	Your Score							Parts and Chapters in Which the Information Is Covered in the Book
	1	2	3	4	5	6	7	
								Part I. Behavior, Human Relations, and Performance Begin with You
1.								2. Diversity in Personality, Intelligence, and Perception
2.								
3.								
4.								3. Diversity in Attitudes, Self-Concept, and Values
5.								
6.								

PROFILE FORM (*concluded*)

	Your Score							Parts and Chapters in Which the Information Is Covered in the Book
	1	**2**	**3**	**4**	**5**	**6**	**7**	
								Part II. Communication Skills: The Foundation of Human Relations
7.								4. Interpersonal Communication
8.								
9.								
10.								5. Organizational Structure and Communication
11.								
12.								
								Part III. Other Skills Influencing Behavior, Human Relations, and Performance
13.								6. Motivation
14.								
15.								
16.								7. Leadership
17.								
18.								
19.								8. Transactional Analysis, Assertiveness, and Conflict Resolution
20.								
21.								
								Part IV. Team Behavior, Human Relations, and Performance
22.								9. Power, Politics, and Ethics
23.								
24.								
25.								10. Teams and Creative Problem Solving and Decision Making
26.								
27.								
28.								11. Team Dynamics and Leadership
29.								
30.								
								Part V. Organizational Changes
31.								12. Change: Managing Culture, Diversity, Quality, and Climate
32.								
33.								
34.								13. Valuing Diversity Globally
35.								
36.								
37.								14. Productivity, Technology, and Participative Management
38.								
39.								
								Part VI. Personal Development
40.								15. Time and Career Management
41.								
42.								
43.								Appendix A. Applying Human Relations Skills

Recall that in Chapter 1 you answered these same 43 questions. At that time you were told that you would compare your scores at the beginning and end of the course. Do so now. Turn back to your profile form in Chapter 1. Either tear it out or flip back and forth as you place your scores from Chapter 1 on the profile form here. You were asked to place an X in the boxes above. To distinguish your responses from Chapter 1, place a check or some other mark in the boxes above. If you have the same box marked for both, don't bother to check the box above. You will know it was the same response because there is no check.

When you have finished, you will have your early and present assessment of your human relations abilities and skills on one form. This will allow you to make an easy comparison of your scores, which represent your strong and weak areas of human relations. You will be using your profile form in the next section.

● Organization
● Group
● Individual

Human Relations Planning

In this section, you will learn about handling human relations problems, changing one's behavior, and developing a human relations plan.

Handling Human Relations Problems

In any organization, there are bound to be times when you disagree with other employees. You may be assigned to work with a person whom you do not like. When you encounter these human relations problems, you have to decide either to avoid resolving the problem or to confront the person to solve it. In most cases, it is advisable to solve human relations problems, rather than to ignore them. Problems usually get worse rather than solve themselves. When you decide to resolve a human relations problem, you have at least three alternatives:

1. *Change the other person.* Whenever there is a human relations problem, it is easy to blame the other party, and expect them to make the necessary changes in their behavior to meet our expectations. In reality, few human relations problems can be blamed entirely on one party. Both parties usually contribute to the human relations problem. Blaming the other party without taking some responsibility usually results in resentment and defensive behavior. The more we force people to change to meet our expectations, the more difficult it is to maintain effective human relations.

2. *Change the situation.* If you have a problem getting along with the person or people you work with, you can try to change the situation by working with another person or people. You may tell your boss you cannot work with so and so because of a personality conflict, and ask for a change in jobs. There are cases where this is the only solution; however, when you complain to your boss, the boss often figures that you are the problem, not the other party. Blaming the other party and trying to change the situation enables us to ignore our behavior, which may be the actual cause of the problem.

Goal of
Human Relations

3. *Change yourself.* Throughout this book, particularly Part I, the focus was on personal behavior. In many situations, your own behavior is the only thing you can control. In most human relations problems, the best alternative is to examine the other party's behavior and try to understand why they are doing and saying the things they are, then examine your own behavior to determine why you are behaving the way you are. In most cases, the logical choice is to change your behavior. We are not saying to simply do what other people request. In fact, you should be assertive, as discussed in Chapter 8. You are not being forced to change; you are changing your behavior because you elect to do so. When you change your behavior, the other party may also change. Remember to create a win–win situation for all stakeholders.

Changing One's Behavior

To improve human relations generally requires a change in one's behavior. It is hoped that over the time period of this course, you have made changes in your behavior that have improved your human relations abilities and skills. In changing behavior, it is helpful to follow a four-step approach: step 1, assess your abilities and skills; step 2, develop new skills; step 3, change your behavior; and step 4, get feedback on your change and reward yourself.

Step 1. Assess Your Abilities and Skills

You should consistently be aware of your behavior and assess it. Without becoming aware of your behavior and being committed to changing it, you cannot improve. You may know someone who has annoying behavior. The person is aware of it, yet does nothing to change. Without that commitment this person will not change. Think about your own behavior; others may find you annoying, but do you change? What can you gain from changing? Can you make the change successfully?

In the last section of this chapter, you assessed your human relations abilities and skills at the beginning of the course and at the present time. To continue your assessment, answer the following questions, in the space provided, using your profile form.

1. Did your profile numbers (1–7) get higher at the end of the course than they were at the beginning of the course? Why or why not?

2. Review your five objectives from Chapter 2, following your profile form. Did you meet them? Why or why not?

3. What are your strongest areas of human relations (highest numbers on your profile form)?

4. What are the human relations areas you need to improve the most (lowest numbers on your profile form)?

5. What are the most important abilities and skills you have developed and/or things you have learned through this course?

Step 2. Develop New Skills

The development of new skills can come in a variety of ways. In this course, you had a text to read. This information gives you the basis for new skills. In life, when there is no textbook, you can refer to libraries for periodicals and books that can give you the knowledge you need to change your behavior. You can also refer to friends and experts in the areas you need to improve. There may also be workshops, seminars, and courses in these areas as well.

Step 3. Change Your Behavior

Try to find safe, nonthreatening situations to try out your new behavior. Friends are usually willing to help; try your new behavior on them to see how it works.

Progressively change your behavior as you develop skill and confidence. For example, if you want to develop your ability to speak in front of people, volunteer and speak in class when the instructor gives you the opportunity. Take a speech class or join Toastmasters.

As with anything in life, it takes time to develop new skills. Try not to be discouraged. For example, if you want to develop more positive, or less emotional, behavior, be patient; it will not happen overnight. If you catch yourself acting emotionally, be aware of it and change to more controlled behavior. With time and persistence, you will catch yourself less often.

Step 4. Get Feedback and Reward Yourself

Being aware of people's nonverbal communication will give you feedback on your behavior, as well as their intentional behavior toward you. However, others' direct feedback requested by you is often more accurate and unbiased. After trying new behavior, ask people you trust if they have noticed any difference. Get their advice on what you can do to improve. For example, if you are trying to be more positive and to give less negative feedback to others, ask them if they have noticed any difference. Ask them to recall the last time they remember hearing you make a put-down statement. People are often willing to help you, especially when it benefits them.

You should also reward yourself for your efforts. Notice we said efforts, not total success. Build on small successes; take one step at a time. As the saying goes, "Success by the yard is hard . . . but a cinch by the inch." Your rewards do not have to be big or expensive; you can treat yourself to a snack, take a walk, or do anything you enjoy. For example, you want to stop putting people down, and you catch yourself in the act. You stop yourself in the middle and end by complimenting the person. Focus on the success, not the failure. Reward yourself rather than be disappointed in yourself.

Exhibit A–1 illustrates these four steps.

E X H I B I T A – 1   **CHANGING BEHAVIOR MODEL**

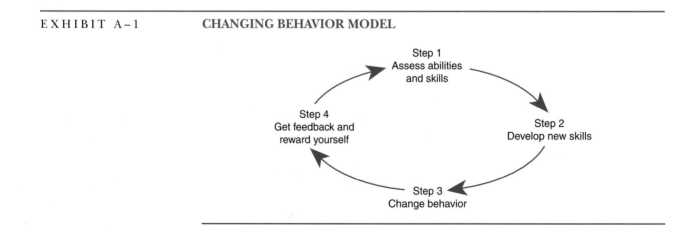

My Human Relations Plan

Follow the changing behavior model and develop a plan to change your behavior. Write in the space provided.

Step 1. Assess Abilities and Skills

Select the one human relations area in most need of improvement. Use the information in question 4 on the facing page under step 1. Write it below.

Step 2. Develop New Skills

Review the material in the text that will help you develop the skill to improve your behavior. You may also talk to others for ideas, and go to the library to find articles and books on the skill. You can even look into taking a workshop or course on the subject. Below, write down some helpful notes on these skills.

Step 3. Change Your Behavior

Describe what you will have to do to change your behavior. Try to be specific.

Step 4. Get Feedback and Reward Yourself

How will you get feedback on your changed behavior? How will you know if you have succeeded in changing your behavior? When will you reward yourself? How will you reward yourself?

Additional Plans: If you feel you can handle working on more than one change in human relations, follow the changing behavior steps and develop another plan. However, don't try to make too many changes too quickly.

Because this chapter presented relatively little new material, it does not include a review, questions, application situations, or objectives case. However, two skill-building exercises follow.

SKILL BUILDING EXERCISE A-1

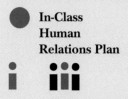

**In-Class
Human
Relations Plan**

Objectives: To share your human relations plan with others in order to get feedback on it.

SCANS: The SCANS competencies of resources, interpersonal skills, information, and systems and the foundations of basic, thinking, and especially personal qualities are developed through this exercise.

Preparation: You should have completed the human relations plan in the chapter.

Experience: This exercise is discussion oriented.

*Procedure 1
(5–15 minutes)*

Break into groups of two to six persons and share your answers to the first four questions under step 1, Assessing your abilities and skills of the human relations plan. You may also look at and discuss each other's profiles, if you wish to do so. Share your human relations plan, offering each other positive feedback on your plans.

Conclusion: The instructor may lead a class discussion and/or make concluding remarks.

Application (2–4 minutes): What did I learn from this experience? How will I use this knowledge in the future?

Sharing: Volunteers give their answers to the application situation.

SKILL-BUILDING EXERCISE A-2

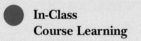

**In-Class
Course Learning**

Objectives: To share your human relations abilities and skills developed through this course.

SCANS: The SCANS competencies of resources, interpersonal skills, information, and systems and the foundations of basic, thinking, and especially personal qualities are developed through this exercise.

Preparation: You should have answered the question. "What are the most important abilities and skills you have developed and/or things you learned through this course?".

Experience: This exercise is discussion oriented.

*Procedure 1
(5–30 minutes)*

Volunteers tell the class the most important abilities and skills developed and/or things they have learned through this course.

Conclusion: The instructor may lead a class discussion and/or make concluding remarks.

Help and Options

This appendix is designed for three reasons. First, we explain why you need to use the Internet. Second, we give the Internet novice some basic information about the Net and some of the basic software features to use. Hopefully, if you have self-training experience with the Internet, you may get a better understanding of what you are doing and hopefully gain a new idea or two to improve your efficiency on the Web. Third, it provides six options for doing all Internet exercises in class.

Why You Need To Use The Internet

Today, we live in a wired world, which is quickly becoming unwired as well. We communicate via dozens of personal voice mails and e-mails. E-commerce now allows people to buy and sell anywhere, anytime, anyplace. One source estimates that 2.8 billion e-mails are sent daily—and that's just the ones related to business! Somewhere on the planet—right now—those who are guiding organizations large and small, global and local are doing so with electronic assistance that is so much a part of their daily lives that to proceed without such help seems unpalatable, if not impossible. The Internet clearly affects our human relations; you will learn more about how it does in Chapter 14.

The "central nervous system" for all the interconnectedness we now enjoy is, of course, the Internet. A countless number of computers are connected via modems and other high-speed access lines so that the world of management and the *world* are one and the same. Via the wonders of hypertext, people with so-called "browsers" can log onto a seemingly endless bounty of electronic information pages.

In Beverly Goldberg's well-written *Overcoming High-Tech Anxiety* (Jossey-Bass, 1999), she notes: "On a personal level, there is time for each of us to decide how much a part of the electronically connected world we want to be." She goes on to note that this vast, interconnected world has forced all of us to adapt: "We must adapt—but adaptation and even mastery of this high-tech world that is constantly developing is not all that frightening if approached in the right way." Our goal is to help you adapt to the Internet through Internet Exercises at the end of all chapters.

All textbooks become outdated quickly and provide a limited view of the author(s) on any topic. Thus, by completing Internet Exercises, you can find up-to-the-minute information on the textbook concepts with a variety of perspectives, while at the same time you improve your skills at using the latest technology—the Internet. Another goal is to get you acquainted with a variety of search engines. For the end-of-chapter Internet exercises, you are asked to use several different search engines to find information. In Chapter 14, the exercise asks you to review different search engines and select the one you find most useful.

Basic Information about the Internet and Its Software

Use This Supplement in Conjunction with the Computer

This information was designed with the idea that a picture is worth a thousand words. So you should use it as a reference while in your browser. For best results, read this information in front of the computer so that you can see what is being talked about on your computer screen.

Access to the Internet and the Browser

Like a computer, you cannot use the Internet without software. The software used to view websites is called a *browser*. Like being in a library or bookstore, browsing (the word for web-viewing software, because this is what it is used for) skimming, or previewing a book for information, *surfing* the Net is done online. If you already use the Net, you already know how to get online. If not, your college will provide you with access to the Net on campus, often in the library and computer labs. Librarians and computer lab instructors often provide Internet training for groups and individuals. You may also be able to access the Internet through the college from your dorm or home.

Off campus, the simplest way to gain access to the Internet is to sign up for an Internet-service provider (ISP) such as pay per month America Online (AOL—www.aol.com) or the Microsoft Network (MSN—www.msn.com) or a free service, such as NetZero (www.netzero.com). Assuming you have found access to the Net, the next questions are, what is a website and how do I get there? Or without access to the browser/Net, as they say, you can't get there from here.

Some Important Basics on Using Your Computer Hardware and Browser on the Web

The Mouse

Do I *click* the left or right button on the mouse? Press the left button on the mouse; you don't really need the right button for basic website use. Do I click once or twice? If you click something once and nothing happens, double-click it, or click another command, such as OK—pressing the Enter key often works, too.

Typing in a Web Site and the Mouse

Another important point is making sure you use the mouse to place the *cursor* (flashing dark vertical line or other symbol) where you want to type. If you type and you cannot see the cursor or words on screen, this may be the problem. So (1) use the mouse and place the hourglass, arrow, or hand into the box and click the button and you will see the cursor. (2) Now type on your keyboard.

The Previous–Back Icon

(1) If you end up somewhere that you don't want to be, try clicking the word [*Previous–Back*] or its *icon* (some type of an ← located at the top left of the screen in your browser). You can retrace your step or several steps to find your error or simply to return to the previous place. (2) You can also use this function in MG if you come to a dead end—no options on screen to select to go to another location. (3) You may also use this function to return to MG (or other site) after clicking a link to go to another web site. However, you may end up with open windows. So to return to MG, use the close function by clicking x (close) at the top right of the window − ☐ X

Full Screen

Once you get to a website subsite you want to surf, click the *square icon* (maximize) between the minus sign (minimize) and the x (close) at the top right of the window − ☐ X so you have better visibility with a larger viewing subsite.

Printing

You may be able to print just about anything you see on your screen from the web using your browser. Click the printer icon (a [picture of a printer]) or click the word "File" at the top of the screen then click "print" from the drop-down box. You will see your printing options: (1) all (just click it), (2) selected page range (type starting and ending page number), (3) current page (click it), (4) *selection*. To use selection (only print some information), first (A) *highlight* (click the mouse button and hold it while you move the mouse to highlight what you want to print). Then (B) click [printer] (or [edit] to get to it) and (C) click the "selection" option. If you want to do a lot of printing of parts of documents/subsites in the site, a browser that will allow you to use the select feature will save you a lot of paper and ink.

(5) Print what is on the screen. If all you want is what you can see, you can also try just pressing your "Print Scrn SysRq" key on the top right row of keys on your keyboard without using the print function at all. Now that you know some basics, let's discuss websites.

Websites

The *World Wide Web (www* or *web)* is a place on the Internet that contains websites. There are over 10 million websites on the web. A *website* is usually a location on the Internet that an organization has set up to disseminate information, usually about itself. Many websites are in business to sell advertising (like commercials on TV and company signs at sporting events) and/or something directly (books at amazon.com) or indirectly (your college to recruit students). A website can be thought of as a book on a computer; the similarities and differences between books and websites is compared here.

Help Getting to the Browser

If you have never been online and are not comfortable with computers, it may be a good idea to get someone to help you get into the browser (again, this is the software you need to use the Web). If you are at your college in a computer lab (or library), someone is usually available to help anyone who needs it. You may need your student ID number to get access to the Net. You can also simply ask a friend or people sitting at other machines if they can help you. It is also helpful, especially if you are using a college computer that you are not familiar with, to write down the steps to get online.

Going to and Leaving a Website

Once you are in the browser, all you usually have to do is just use the mouse and keyboard to type the web address in the box at the top middle of the screen (often to the right of the word "find," or similar word). In this box, it may tell you to type in key words or an address. Then click the word to the right of the box, often "go"; pressing the Enter key may also get you there. With most browsers, it does not matter if you type in UPPER- or lowercase letters, and all you need to type is the address such as *mgeneral.com* (no http://www is needed before it). However, if by chance you are not typing the address in the correct box, or have an older browser, you may need to type the "full" address—http://www.mgeneral.com. To leave the website, just click "[x]" (close) at the top right of the window.

Trouble Getting to a Website

If you attempt to go to the MG (or other) address and do not come to it; you could have made one of two common errors: (1) You typed the address incorrectly; check the spelling. (2) You may not actually be on the web but rather searching within the browser needed to get you online. Try following the instructions on getting to a website.

The Home Page

The *home page* is the first thing that comes on screen when you type in the web address and click "go" or "enter" (unless you by pass the home page by typing additional information following the basic address). The home page is usually designed like a *table of contents* in a book, or it tells you what information is available from this site, or where you can go for more information on specific topics. Each subsite of the website can be thought of as a chapter in a book.

Clicking Links vs. Icons/Toolbar

Unlike a book, on the Web you don't turn the pages, you simply click the link and you are automatically taken to the subsite—chapter pages. From the subsite—chapter—you usually have options to go to other subsites—pages, or even other websites—books. You should also understand that a *link is* usually the <u>underlined</u>

words in a different-colored font that describe the subsite within that website. The cursor will change, usually from an arrow, to a hand with a finger pointing for you to click with. A link is different from an *icon* (which is a picture that represents a short-cut to tell the computer to perform a function, such as print) because an icon is part of the software and the button to click is at the top of the screen on the toolbar. Thus, you will always have the same icons on your toolbars in your browser no matter which website you visit. However, the web links will change from page to page.

Getting to a Web-site Using Favorites

If you use the MG or other website regularly, you can get to it very quickly by using Favorites. Using *favorites* are like placing *bookmarks* in books so that you can get to where you want to be very quickly. Therefore, favorites are also called bookmarks; this feature is provided with your browser. When in the home page, or any subsite within the site you want to return to, try simply pressing the control key and the letter d at the same time [Ctrl] + [D] and many browsers will automatically place the address in the favorites location for you. If this *command* [Ctrl + D] does not automatically set up the favorite, click the "[favorites]" word at the top of the screen to see what keys to press to set a favorite. When this command was tried in AOL it did not work. When favorites was clicked, the command letters to set one were Ctrl++, so some students pressed control [Ctrl] and the key with [+] on it twice, and it did not work. In AOL, you press the [Ctrl] [Shift] [+/=] keys at the same time to set a favorite (or you used to have to if AOL changed it since I wrote this. But it is easy to find out the current keys by clicking favorites.) If you are using a college computer lab or library with multiple computers, favorites may not be a good option.

You find your favorite websites link by clicking the word "[Favorites]" at the top of the screen; it will appear in the drop-down box. The next time you want to return to the site, just click "Favorites" then click the "website" from the drop-down box. You can have different favorites to go to various websites and multiple favorites within oneweb site to bypass the home page and go directly to any of its subsites. In the case of MG, I just have a favorite to go to the home page and select where to go from there.

Search Engines

Search engines may be thought of as card catalogues in a library. A *search engine* is actually a website that retrieves summaries of other websites. Search engines have *links* to the other web site to get the information. You probably have heard of Yahoo (*www.yahoo.com*) as it is a popular overall search engine and it is a directory of websites. However, there are others that are more valuable for business and academic use. The Search Engine Watch Website (*www.searchenginewatch.com*) gives information on several search engines. Internet Exercises 1–2 and 2–3 use this website to help you learn more about search engines and to develop your skill at using them. You can use many search engines for free.

Options For All Exercise Parts "Doing Internet Exercise In Class"

The instructor selects an option to be used in class for a specific MG exercise. Different options may be used with different exercises.

1. (0–60 minutes with another option) Based on how the instructor will include MG Internet Exercises as part of the grading process, students pass in their copies from the MG Website and/or answers to the exercise questions as specified by the instructor. Passing in material may also be a part of any of the other options below. With this option,

(a) the instructor may not discuss the exercise at all in class, or

(b) may discuss only the questions that are not going to be graded, until after grading. With option 1–B, another option below is selected.

2. (5–10 minutes) The instructor gives the answers to the exercise questions without discussion.

3. (10–60 minutes) The instructor asks for volunteers and/or calls on students to give their exercise answers to the entire class. Student "professional" presentations may be scheduled. The instructor will determine if class members may respond to others answers.

4. (10–15 minutes) Students share their exercise answers in small groups of three to seven members. For exercises that allow students to select their own resources, try to have groups in which no two people selected the same material. With all Fiscal Fairy Tales, all students are usually assigned the same questions. There is no class discussion, but the instructor may make concluding remarks and/or give answers to some or all of the questions from the exercise.

5. (20–35 minutes: 10–15 group, 10–20 presentations) This is the same as option 4 with an addition based on the exercise.

(a) With exercises in which students select their own material, each group selects one resource to be shared with the entire class. So each group presents one of its member's resource to the class.

(b) For Fiscal Fairy Tale Exercises, and others that require all students to answer the same questions based on the same material, the instructor assigns different questions to be answered by one or more different groups, based on the number of questions and groups. Each group selects a spokesperson to record the group's answers and to present them to the class.

There is no class discussion following spokesperson presentations, but the instructor may ask questions or make comments following each presentation. The instructor may also make concluding remarks and/or give answers to some or all of the questions from the exercise.

6. (45–60 minutes: 15–20 group, 30–40 presentations and discussion) Same as 5, but class members may ask questions or make comments after each spokesperson's presentation, rather than just listen. The instructor may make concluding remarks and/or give answers to some or all of the questions from the exercise.

How to Research Case Material Using the Internet

Appendix

C

Until the mid-1990s, it was hard to find information regarding a company that was being discussed in a case study. Today, there is a whole new science to conducting research to find company material. It is virtually impossible to go anywhere without hearing about the Internet. A major advantage of the Internet online data search is the fact that you dramatically increase the number of sources available to you. Also, home access to the Net reduces the need to visit a physical library and enables you to be in the comfort of your home or dormitory room.

Web-Skepticism

Students do about 90 percent of their research online, yet few question the accuracy of their sources.[1] You need to remember that anyone can set up a website and write whatever they want to without anyone checking it to make sure it is factually true information. Therefore, you want to search reputable websites for information, such as the Management General Website discussed in Appendix B and the ones recommended in this appendix.

Basic Information about the Internet and Its Software

For basic information about the Internet and its software, see Appendix B, the second section with this heading. This part of Appendix B is designed to give the Internet novice some basic information about the Net and some of the basic software features to use.

Assuming you have found access to the Net, the next question is, "How do I get information about the company in the case?" You may go directly to the website of the case company, access databases, and use search engines using key topics/words.

Business Research Tutorial

The Intellifact International website (*www.intellifact.com*) has a business research tutorial. See Internet Exercise 1–3, Internet Research Tutorial, at the end of Chapter 1 page 000 for more details.

Going Directly to the Company's Website

A website is a location on the Net that a company has set up to disperse information about its company. Information can be gathered by accessing the World Wide Web on your service provider. Pages of company information from financial information to corporate strategies are provided. A great area for current information can usually be found in the press releases section of most large company Web sites.

At the ends of "Cases: Internet" of each chapter are the website addresses of the case company web addresses when the book was published. Simply type in the case company address to access its information. For instance, Nike has an elaborate website that can be accessed by typing in *http://www.nike.com*. With most updated browsers, all you need to type in is *nike.com*.

Limitation of Company Websites and the Need to Cite at Least Two Other Sources

A limitation of company websites is that the company provides the information, and it may be biased and not indicative of what other sources are writing about the company. You should also realize that researching only one journal/magazine/newspaper (no matter which one) is not enough to validate the findings of a company's website. In other words, simply using a company website is not enough. You also need to use at least two, and preferably more written sources of information.

Finding Sources of Company Information on the Internet

Our first choice, which is our first choice for general business research, is to access the library's selected reference source. Through your college library, you should be able to link to Infotrack SearchBank (General BusinessFile), EBSCO Host (Business Premier), or some other reference online databases, which contain articles from several hundred journals/magazines/newspapers by using key topic/word searches. If you have never used the library online database, there is usually a reference librarian who can teach you how to access and used the database. You may need to have your student ID # to access the database.

Other databases such as *marketguide.com* and *hoovers.com* are designed to give investors or researchers information about companies and are a second choice source. Additionally, search engines such as *nlsearch.com, altavista.net, excite.com, lycos.com,* and *yahoo.com* can be accessed to search a desired topic or company. The Search Engine Watch Website (*www.searchenginewatch.com*) gives information on several search engines. Internet Exercises 1–2 and 2–3 uses this website to help you learn more about search engines and to develop your skill at using them.

These types of databases may give you the ability to gain access to complete articles about the company you are researching. The information can be as current as today's issue of whichever source you are searching.

Referencing Internet Material

Finding information on the Internet does not allow you to bypass proper bibliography procedures. Referencing material found on the Net is not quite as straightforward as citing books, journals, and magazines. Databases on the Net can be found anywhere in cyberspace. Material is only acceptable if you can specifically document its origins as if you were writing a traditional reference. You must write:

- The author's name
- Title of the article/subsite
- Name of publication/website
- Date and page numbers

Your instructor will provide you with more details on his or her expectations of how to use Internet material.

Source: Appendix written by Dr. David C. Kimball, Associate Professor of Management, Elms College, Chicopee, Massachusetts.

Notes

CHAPTER 1

1. B. Gates, "My Advice to Students: Get a Sound, Broad, Education," *The Costco Connection* (February, 1999), p. 13.

2. R. Quick, "A Makeover That Began at the Top," *The Wall Street Journal,* May 25, 2000, p. B1.

3. L. Weinberg, "Seeing through Organization: Exploring the Constitutive Quality of Social Relations," *Administration & Society* 28, No. 2 (1996), pp. 177–90.

4. "Learning to Lead," *Business Week,* October 18, 1999, pp. 76–77.

5. S. Zahra, "The Changing Rules of Global Competitiveness in the 21st Century," *Academy of Management Executive* 13, No. 1 (1999), p. 36.

6. "Evaluating Human Capital," *The Wall Street Journal,* September 30, 1999, p. A1.

7. J. Pfeffer and J.F. Veiga, "Putting People First for Organizational Success," *Academy of Management Executive* 13, No. 2 (1999), pp. 37–48.

8. M. Hammer and J. Champy, "Re-Engineering Authors Reconsider Re-Engineering," *The Wall Street Journal,* January 17, 1995, p. B1.

9. Information taken from the FedEx website, www.fedex.com. June 23, 2000.

10. R. Harborne, "Wisdom of the CEO: The Challenge to Business Leadership in the 21st Century," keynote presentation at the New England Business Administration Association International Conference, Southern Connecticut State University, April 28, 2000, Price Waterhouse Coopers.

11. D. Carnegie, "Human Relations Skills Provide Entrepreneurial Breadth," *Training* 34, No. 4 (1997), p. 53

12. "AT&T President," *The Wall Street Journal,* July 17, 1997, p. A1.

13. P.U. Bender, "Frustrated with Work Relationships," *CMA—The Management Accounting Magazine* 70, No. 10 (December–January 1996), p. 8

14. H. Lancaster, "Managing Your Career, How You Can Make Your M.B.A. Degree Even More Valuable," *The Wall Street Journal,* July 16, 1997, p. B1.

15. L. Weinberg, "Seeing through Organization: Exploring the Constitutive Quality of Social Relations," *Administration & Society* 28, No. 2 (1996), pp. 177–90.

16. S.L. Robinson and A.M. O'Leary-Kelly, "Monkey See, Monkey Do: The Influence of Work Groups on the Antisocial Behavior of Employees," *Academy of Management Journal* 41, No. 6, (1998), pp. 658–72.

17. M.E. Furman, "Reverse the 80-20 Rule," *Management Review* 86, No. 1 (1997), pp. 18–21.

18. R. Ackoff, *Redesigning the Future* (New York: Wiley & Sons, 1974), p. 13.

19. J. Gharajedaghi, *Toward a Systems Theory of Organization* (Seaside, Calif.: Intersystems Publication, 1985), p. 12.

20. S.J. Wayne, L.M. Shore, and R.C. Liden, "Perceived Organizational Support and Leader-Member Exchange: A Social Exchange Perspective," *Academy of Management Journal* 40, No. 1 (1997), pp. 82–111.

21. S. Zahra, "The changing Rules of Global Competitiveness in the 21st Century," *Academy of Management Executive* 13, No. 1 (1999), p. 36.

22. Lancaster, "Managing Your Career, M.B.A. Degree," p. B1.

23. H. Lancaster, "Managing Your Career, It's Time to Stop Promoting Yourself and Start Listening," *The Wall Street Journal,* June 10, 1997, p. B1.

24. *Bits & Pieces,* Vol. F, No. 4G, p. 7.

25. P.U. Bender, "Frustrated with Work Relationships," *CMA—The Management Accounting Magazine* 70, No. 10 (December–January 1996), p. 8

26. L. Frankel and A. Fleisher, *The Human Factor in Industry* (New York: The Macmillan Company, 1920), p. 8.

27. F. Roethlisberger and W. Dickson, *Management and the Worker* (Cambridge: Harvard University Press, 1939) pp. 15–86.

28. D. McGregor, *The Human Side of the Enterprise* (New York: McGraw-Hill, 1960).

29. E. Berne, *Games People Play* (New York: Grove Press, 1964).

30. W. Ouchi, *Theory Z—How American Business Can Meet the Japanese Challenge* (Reading, Mass.: Addison-Wesley Publishing, 1981).

31. T. Peters and R. Waterman, *In Search of Excellence: Lessons from America's Best-Run Companies* (New York: Harper & Row, 1982).

32. E. Lawler, *High-Involvement Management* (San Francisco: Jossey-Bass, 1991).

33. R. Quick, "A Makeover That Began at the Top," *The Wall Street Journal,* May 25, 2000, p. B1.

34. " 'Action-Learning' Gains Momentum as a *Method* of Training Managers," *The Wall Street Journal,* September 12, 1996, p. A1.

35. R. Harborne, "Wisdom of the CEO: The Challenge to Business Leadership in the 21st Century," keynote presentation at the New England Business Administration Association International Conference, Southern Connecticut State University, April 28, 2000, Price Waterhouse Coopers.

36. A.S. Tsui, J.L. Pearce, L.W. Porter, and A.M. Tripoli, "Alternative Approaches to the Employee-Organization Relationship: Does Investment in Employees Pay Off?" *Academy of Management Journal* 40, No. 5 (1997), pp. 1089–1121.

37. P. Mirvis, "Human Resource Management: Leaders, Laggards, and Followers," *Academy of Management Executive* 11, No. 2 (February 1997), pp. 43–56.

38. P.U. Bender, "Frustrated with Work Relationships," *CMA—The Management Accounting Magazine* 70, No. 10 (December–January 1996), p. 8

39. "Count Me in Plans 'Microloans' for U.S. Women," *The Wall Street Journal,* March 28, 2000, p. A1.

40. G.L. Stewart and M.R. Barrick, "Team Structure and Performance: Assessing the Mediating Role of Intrateam Process and the Moderating Role of Task Type," *Academy of Management Journal* 43, No. 2 (2000), pp. 135–48.

41. A.S. Tsui, J.L. Pearce, L.W. Porter, and A.M. Tripoli, "Alternative Approaches to the Employee-Organization Relationship: Does Investment in Employees Pay Off?" *Academy of Management Journal* 40, No. 5 (1997), pp. 1089–1121.

42. J.P. Kotter, "Kill Complacency ... Before It Kills You," *Fortune* (August 5, 1996), pp. 168–170

43. G. McNamara and P. Bromily, "Risk and Return in Organizational Decision Making," *Academy of Management Journal* 42, no 3 (1999), pp. 330–39.

44. "The Checkoff," *The Wall Street Journal,* July 2, 1996, p. A1.

45. P. Mirvis, "Human Resource Management: Leaders, Laggards, and Followers," *Academy of Management Executive* 11, No. 2 (February 1997), pp. 43–56.

46. J.H. Fritz, "Men's and Women's Organizational Peer Relationships: A Comparison," *The Journal of Business Communication* 34, No. (1997), pp. 27–46

47. N. Yang, C.C. Chen, J. Choi, and Y. Zou, "Sources of Work-Family Conflict: A Sino-U.S. Comparison of the Effects of Work and Family Demands," *Academy of Management Journal* 43, No. 1 (2000), pp. 113–23.

48. "Count Me in Plans 'Microloans' for U.S. Women," *The Wall Street Journal,* March 28, 2000, p. A1.

49. N. Yang, C.C. Chen, J. Choi, and Y. Zou, "Sources of Work-Family Conflict: A Sino–U.S. Comparison of the Effects of Work and Family Demands," *Academy of Management Journal* 43, No. 1 (2000), pp. 113–23.

50. R. Harborne, "Wisdom of the CEO: The Challenge to Business Leadership in the 21st Century," key note presentation at the New England Business Administration Association International Conference, Southern Connecticut State University, April 28, 2000, Price Waterhouse Coopers.

51. Ibid.

CHAPTER 2

1. R. House and R. Adita, "The Social Scientific Study of Leadership: Quo Vadis?" *Journal of Management* 23, No. 3 (May–June 1997), pp. 409–74.

2. J.M. Nash, "The Personality Genes," *Time* 151, No. 16 (April 1998), pp. 60–62.

3. R.R. Perman, *Hard Wired Leadership: Unleashing the Power of Personality to Become a New Millenium Leader,* (New York: Davis-Black, 1998).

4. G.J. Curpy, *Users Guide and Interpretive Report for the Leadership Personality Survey* (Minneapolis: Personnel Decisions International, 1998).

5. D.F. Caldwell and J.M. Burger, "Personality Characteristics of Job Applicants and Success in Screening Interviews," *Personnel Psychology* 51, No. 1 (Spring 1998), pp. 119–37.

6. S.S.K. Lam, S. Schaubroeck, "The Role of Locus of Control in Reactions to Being Promoted and to Being Passed Over: A Quasi Experiment," *Academy of Management Journal* 43, No. 1 (2000), pp. 66–78.

7. S.H. Chiang and M. Gort, "Personality Attributes and Optimal Hierarchical Compensation Gradients," *Journal of Economic Behavior & Organization* 33, No. 29 (January 1998), pp. 227–41.

8. J. Steininger, "When Personalities Collide, Look for the 'Catbird Seat,' " *The Business Journal-Milwaukee* 14, No. 18 (January 31, 1997), p. 10.

9. D.P. Skarlicki, R.F. Folger, and P. Tesluk, "Personality as a Moderator in the Relationship Between Fairness and Retaliation," *Academy of Management Journal* 42, No. 1 (1999), pp. 100–8.

10. D.F. Caldwell and J.M. Burger, "Personality Characteristics of Job Applicants and Success in Screening Interviews," *Personnel Psychology* 51, No 1 (Spring 1998), pp. 119–37.

11. J. Steininger, "When Personalities Collide, Look for the Catbird Seat," *The Business Journal-Milwaukee* 14, No. 18 (January 31, 1997), p. 10.

12. S. Divita, "Behavior, Not Experience, Guides Productivity," *Marketing News* 31, No. 6 (March 17, 1997), p. 4.

13. T.W. Smith, "Punt, Pass, and Ponder the Questions: In the NFL, Personality Tests Help Teams Judge the Draftees," *New York Times,* April 20, 1997, pp. 13–19.

14. A.M. Ryan, R.E. Ployhart, and L.A. Friedel, "Using Personality Testing to Reduce Adverse Impact: A Cautionary Note," *Journal of Applied Psychology* 83, No. 2 (April 1998), pp. 298–308.

15. R.J. Heckan and B.W. Roberts, "Personality Profiles of Effective Managers Across Functions," *Personality Applications in the Workplace,* 1997, Proceedings of the Industrial and Organizational Psychology, pp. 123–34.

16. J.F. Salgado, "The Five-Factor Model of Personality and Job Performance in the European Community," *Journal of Applied Psychology* 82, No. 1 (1997), pp. 30–43.

17. R.S. DeFrank and J.M. Ivancevich, "Stress on the Job: An Executive Update," *Academy of Management Executive* 12, No. 3 (1998), pp. 55–66.

18. "Absenteeism Has Eased," *The Wall Street Journal,* September 21, 1999, p. A1.

19. "Too Stressed to Work?" *The Wall Street Journal,* November 2, 1999, p. A1.

20. "The Checkoff," *The Wall Street Journal,* December 24, 1996, p. A1.

21. "Stress," *The Wall Street Journal,* December 10, 1996, p. A1

22. "A Study of British Civil Servants," *The Wall Street Journal,* July 25, 1997, p. A1.

23. J. Schaubroeck, D. Ganster, and B. Kemmerer, "Job Complexity, 'Type A' Behavior, and Cardiovascular Disorder: A Prospective Study," *Academy of Management Journal* 37, Iss. 2, (April 1994), pp. 426–439.

24. "Stress," *The Wall Street Journal,* August 20, 1996, p. A1.

25. S. Shellenbarger, "Is the Awful Behavior of Some Bad Bosses Rooted in Their Past?" *The Wall Street Journal,* May 10, 2000, p. B1.

26. B.J. Tepper, "Consequences of Abusive Supervision," *Academy of Management Journal* 43, No. 2 (2000), pp. 178–90.

27. S. Shellenbarger, "From Our Readers: The Bosses That Drove Me to Quit My Job," *The Wall Street Journal,* February 9, 2000, p. B1.

28. "High-Risk Employees Often Require Coaxing to Watch Their Health," *The Wall Street Journal,* September 24, 1996, p. A1

29. B. Dossey, "Help Your Patient Break Free from Anxiety," *Nursing* 26, No. 10 (1996), pp. 52–54.

30. "The MineWorkers' New President Pushes Organizing," *The Wall Street Journal,* January 30, 1996, p. A1.

31. B. Dossey, "Help Your Patient Break Free from Anxiety," *Nursing* 26, No. 10 (1996), pp. 52–54.

32. S. Shellenbarger, "An Overlooked Toll of Job Upheavals: Valuable Friendships," *The Wall Street Journal,* January 12, 2000, p. B1.

33. "Mind Field," *The Wall Street Journal,* July 9, 1997, p. A1.

34. "A Primer on Multiple Intelligences," *NEA Today,* March 1997, p. 17.

35. Y. Ganzach, "Intelligence and Job Satisfaction," *Academy of Management Journal* 41, No. 5 (1998), pp. 526–39.

36. O. Behling, "Employee Selection: Will Intelligence and Conscientiousness Do the Job?" *Academy of Management Executive* Vol. 12, No. 1 (1998), p. 77.

37. B. Gates, "My Advice to Students: Get a Sound, Broad, Education," *The Costco Connection* (February, 1999), p. 13.

38. J. Campbell Quick and J.H. Gavin, "The Next Frontier: Edgar Schein on Organizational Therapy," *Academy of Management Executive* 14. No. 1 (2000), pp. 31–32.

39. The material in this section is adapted from the training material of David Kolb in Learning-Style Inventory (Boston: McBer and Company, 1985); for more information contact McBer at 137 Newbury Street, Boston, Mass. 02116 (617-437-7080).

40. D. Stamps, "Communities of Practice," *Training* 34, No. 2 (February 1997), pp. 34–42.

41. M.A. Glynn, "Innovative Genius: A Framework for Relating Individual and Organizational Intelligences to Innovation," *Academy of Management Review* 21, No. 4 (October 1996), pp. 1081–1112.

42. E.J. Van Slyke, "Facilitating Productive Conflict," *HR Focus* 74, No. 4 (April 1997), pp. 17–18.

43. D. Stamps, "Communities of Practice," *Training* 34, No. 2 (February 1997), pp. 34–42.

44. J. Greenwald, "Where the Jobs Are," *Time* 149, No. 3 (January 20, 1997), pp. 54–60.

45. D. Stamps, "Communities of Practice," *Training* 34, No. 2 (February 1997), pp. 34–42.

46. J. Campbell Quick and J.H. Gavin, "The Next Frontier: Edgar Schein on Organizational Therapy," *Academy of Management Executive* 14. No. 1 (2000), pp. 31–32.

47. B.L. Simonin, "The Importance of Collaborative Know-How: An Empirical Test of the Learning Organization," *Academy of Management Journal* 40, No. 5 (1997), pp. 1150–1174.

48. R. Harborne, "Wisdom of the CEO: The Challenge to Business Leadership in the 21st Century," keynote presentation at the New England Business Administration Association International Conference, Southern Connecticut State University, April 28, 2000, Price Waterhouse Coopers.

49. P. Senge, A. Kleiner, C. Roberts, R. Ross, G. Roth, and B. Smith, *The Dance of Change: The Challenges to Sustaining Momentum in Learning Organizations* (Currency Doubleday, 1999).

50. "Knowledge-Hoarding," *The Wall Street Journal,* October 14, 1999, p. A1.

51. R. Harborne, "Wisdom of the CEO: The Challenge to Business Leadership in the 21st Century," keynote presentation at the New England Business Administration Association International Conference, Southern Connecticut State University, April 28, 2000, Price Waterhouse Coopers.

52. J. Quinn, P. Anderson and S. Finkelstein, "Leveraging Intellect," *Academy of Management Executive* 10, No. 3 (November 1996), pp. 7–27.

53. S.A. Zahra and H.M. O'Neill, "Charting the Landscape of Global Competition: Reflections on Emerging Organizational Challenges and Their Implications for Senior Executives," *Academy of Management Executive* 12, No. 4 (1998), pp. 13–21.

54. Y. Ganzach, "Intelligence and Job Satisfaction," *Academy of Management Journal* 41, No. 5 (1998), pp. 526–39.

55. O. Behling, "Employee Selection: Will Intelligence and Conscientiousness do the Job?" *Academy of Management Executive* 12, No. 1 (1998), p. 77.

56. M.M. Crossan, H.W. Lane, and R.E. White, "An Organizational Learning Framework: From Institution to Institution," *Academy of Management Review* 24, No. 3 (1999), pp. 522–37.

57. A. Edmondson, "Psychological Safety and Learning Behavior in Work Teams," *Administrative Science Quarterly* 44, pp. 350–83.

58. T.A. Saccardi, "The Effects of Hospital Executives' Personality Traits on Their Perceptions and Trust," *Hospital & Health Services Administration* 41, No. 2 (Summer 1996), pp. 197–209.

59. M.A. Carpenter and B.R. Golden, "Perceived Managerial Discretion: A Study of Cause and Effect," *Strategic Management Journal* 18, No. 3 (March 1997), pp. 187–206.

60. G. Ball, L.K. Trevino, and H. Sims, "Just and Unjust Punishment: Influences on Subordinate Performance and Citizenship," *Academy of Management Journal* 37, No. 2, April 1994, pp. 299–322.

61. G.R. Ferris, D.D. Frink, M.C. Galong, J. Zhou, K.M. Kacmar, and J.L. Howard, "Perceptions of Organizational Politics: Prediction, Stress-Related Implications, and Outcomes," *Human Relations* 49, No. 2 (February 1996), pp. 233–66.

62. C.R. Wanberg, L.W. Bunce, and M.B. Gavin, "Perceived Fairness of Layoffs Among Individuals Who Have Been Laid Off: A Longitudinal Study," *Personnel Psychology* 52, Iss. 1 (Spring 1999), pp 59–61.

63. J.H. Dulebohn and G.R. Ferris, "The Role of Influence Tactics in Perceptions of Performance Evaluations' Fairness," *Academy of Management Journal* 42, No. 3 (1999), pp. 288–303.

64. J.C. McElroy, P.C. Morrow, and E.J. Mullen, "Intraorganizational Mobility and Work-Related Attitudes," *Journal of Organizational Behavior* 17, No. 4 (July 1996), pp. 363–74.

65. S.J. Wayne, L.M. Shore, and R.C. Liden, "Perceived Organizational Support and Leader-Member Exchange: A Social Exchange Perspective," *Academy of Management Journal* 40, No. 1 (1997), pp. 82–111.

66. J.T. Delaney and M.A. Hueslid, "The Impact of Human Resource Management Practices on Perceptions of Organizational Performances," *Academy of Management Journal* 39, No. 4 (August 1996), pp. 949–69.

67. N.L. Vasiopoulos, R.R. Reilly, and J.A. Leaman, "The Influence of Job Familiarity and Impression Management on Self-report Measure Scale Scores and Response Latencies," *Journal of Applied Psychology* 85, No. 1 (February 2000), pp. 50–65.

68. L. Zuin and N. Zuin, *Contact—The First Four Minutes* (New York: Ballentine Books, 1972), p. 5.

69. J. Elsea, *The Four-Minute Sell* (New York: Simon & Schuster, 1984), p. 9.

70. L. Zuin and N. Zuin, *Contact—The First Four Minutes* (New York: Ballentine Books, 1972), p. 5.

71. A.D. Brown and M. Jones, "Honourable Members and Dishonourable Deeds: Sensemaking, Impression Management and Legitimation in the 'Arms to Iraq Affair,' " *Human Relations* 53, No. 5 (May 2000), p. 655.

72. W.L. Gardner and B.J. Avolio, "The Charismatic Relationship: A Dramaturgical Perspective," *Academy of Management Review* 23, No. 1 (1998), pp. 32–58.

73. N.L. Vasiopoulos, R.R. Reilly, and J.A. Leaman, "The Influence of Job Familiarity and Impression Management on Self-report Measure Scale Scores and Response Latencies," *Journal of Applied Psychology* 85, No. 1 (February 2000), pp. 50–65.

74. M.C. Bolino, "Citizenship and Impression Management: Good Soldiers or Good Actors?" *Academy of Management Review* 24, No. 1 (1999), pp. 82–83.

75. T. Stirr, "Communication Starts with Rapport," *CMA Magazine* 71, No. 2 (March 1997), p. 8.

76. J.T. Molly, *New Dress for Success* (New York: Warner Books, 1998).

77. Ibid.

78. D.M. Anderson and M. Warshaw, "The Number One Entrepreneur in America," *Success* (March 1995), pp. 32–43.

CHAPTER 3

1. M. Coyle, "Quality Interpersonal Communication— An Overview," *Manage* 44, No. 4, April 1993, pp. 4–5.

2. "Employers Go Beyond Background Checks and Test Employee Attitudes," *The Wall Street Journal*, December 22, 1998, p. A1.

3. R. Taylor, "It's Your Attitude that Counts," *The Financial Times*, February 19, 1997, p. 35.

4. P.M. Podsakoff, S.B. MacKenzie, and W.H. Bommer, "Meta-Analysis of the Relationships between Kerr and Jermier's Substitutes for Leadership and Employee Job Attitudes, Role Perceptions, and Performance," *Journal of Applied Psychology* 81, No. 4 (August 1996), pp. 380–99.

5. P. Chattopadhyay, "Beyond Direct and Symmetrical Effects: The influence of Demographic Dissimilarity on Organizational Citizenship Behavior," *Academy of Management Journal* 42, No. 3 (1999), pp. 273–87.

6. A.E. Schwartz, "How to Handle Conflict," *The CPA Journal* 67, No. 4 (April 1997), pp. 72–3.

7. T.A. Saccardi, "The Effects of Hospital Executives' Personality Traits on Their Perceptions and Trust," *Hospital & Health Services Administration* 41, No. 2 (Summer 1996), pp. 197–209.

8. T. Choi and O. Behling, "Top Managers and TQM Success: One More Look Over, after All These Years," *Academy of Management Executive* 11, No. 1 (February 1997), pp. 37–47.

9. S. Livingston, "Pygmalion in Management," in *Harvard Business Review on Human Relations* (New York: Harper & Row, 1979), p. 181.

10. P.M. Podaskoff, S.B. Mackenzie, and W.H. Bommer, "Meta-Analysis of the Relationships between Kerr and Jermier's Substitutes for Leadership and Employee Job Attitudes, Role Perceptions, and Performance," *Journal of Applied Psychology* 81, No. 4 (August 1996), pp. 380–99.

11. S. Shellenbarger, "More Managers Find a Happy Staff Leads to Happy Customers," *The Wall Street Journal*, March 2, 1998, p. B1.

12. G. Dessler, "How to Earn Your Employees' Commitment," *Academy of Management Executive* 13, No. 2 (1999), p. 58–67.

13. A.E. Schwartz, "How to Handle Conflict," *The CPA Journal* 67, No. 4 (April 1997), pp. 72–3.

14. T. Petzinger, "Peter Drucker: The 'Arch-Guru of Capitalism' Argues that We Need a New Economic Theory and a New Management Model," *The Wall Street Journal*, January 1, 2000, p. R34.

15. J.W. Bishop and K.D. Scott, "How Commitment Affects Team Performance," *HR Magazine* 42, No. 2 (February 1997), pp. 107–11.

16. Ibid.

17. S. Shellenbarger, "More Managers Find a Happy Staff Leads to Happy Customers," *The Wall Street Journal*, March 2, 1998, p. B1.

18. J.W. Bishop, K.D. Scott, "How Commitment Affects Team Performance," *HR Magazine* 42, No. 2 (February 1997), pp. 107–11.

19. J.A.S. Koh, "Exploring the Relationships Between User Information Satisfaction and Job Satisfaction," *International Journal of Information Management* 17, No. 3 (June 1997), pp. 169–77.

20. J.C. McElroy, P.C. Morrow, and E.J. Mullen, "Intra-organizational Mobility and Work-Related Attitudes," *Journal of Organizational Behavior* 17, No. 4 (July 1996), pp. 363–74.

21. T. Petzinger, "Mihali Csikszentmihalyi: A "Happiness" Expert Talks About Suburban Anxiety and the Search for Fulfillment," *The Wall Street Journal*, January 1, 2000, p. R51.

22. V.M. Parachin, "How to Be Happier with Your Job," *Supervision* 58, No. 2 (February 1997), pp. 6–8.

23. J.A. Tannenbaum, "Worker Satisfaction Found to Be Higher at Smaller Companies," *The Wall Street Journal*, May 5, 1997, p. A1.

"Good News, Bad News: Workers Like Their Jobs but Criticize Their Bosses," *The Wall Street Journal*, August 27, 1991, p. A1.

24. V.M. Parachin, "How to Be Happier with Your Job," *Supervision* 58, No. 2 (February 1997), pp. 6–8.

25. J.C. McElroy, P.C. Morrow, and E.J. Mullen, "Intra-organizational Mobility and Work-Related Attitudes," *Journal of Organizational Behavior* 17, No. 4 (July 1996), pp. 363–74.

26. T. Petzinger, "Peter Drucker: The "Arch-Guru of Capitalism" Argues that We Need a New Economic Theory and a New Management Model," *The Wall Street Journal*, January 1, 2000, p. R34.

27. J.W. Bishop and K.D. Scott, "How Commitment Affects Team Performance," *HR Magazine* 42, No. 2 (February 1997), pp. 107–11.

28. Ibid.

29. V.M. Parachin, "How to Be Happier with Your Job," *Supervision* 58, No. 2 (February 1997), pp. 6–8.

30. Y. Ganzach, "Intelligence and Job Satisfaction," *Academy of Management Journal* 41, No. 5 (1998), pp. 526–39.

31. A.S. Koh, "Exploring the Relationships Between User Information Satisfaction and Job Satisfaction," *International Journal of Information Management* 17, No. 3 (June 1997), pp. 169–77.

32. S. Kravetz, "The Checkoff," *The Wall Street Journal*, June 8, 1999, p. A1.

33. J.C. McElroy, P.C. Morrow, and E.J. Mullen, "Intra-organizational Mobility and Work-Related Attitudes," *Journal of Organizational Behavior* 17, No. 4 (July 1996), pp. 363–74.

34. S. Shellenbarger, "More Managers Find a Happy Staff Leads to Happy Customers," *The Wall Street Journal*, March 2, 1998, p. B1.

35. A.S. Koh, "Exploring the Relationships between User Information Satisfaction and Job Satisfaction," *International Journal of Information Management* 17, No. 3 (June 1997), pp. 169–77.

36. S. Shellenbarger, "More Managers Find a Happy Staff Leads to Happy Customers," *The Wall Street Journal*, March 2, 1998, p. B1.

37. T. Petzinger, "Edward O. Wilson: Human Nature, Dr. Wilson Believes, Has Changed Little in Many Millennia. And It Will Change Very Little in the Millennia Ahead," *The Wall Street Journal*, January 1, 2000, p. R16.

38. P. Chattopadhyay, "beyond Direct and Symmetrical Effects: The influence of Demographic Dissimilarity on Organizational Citizenship Behavior," *Academy of Management Journal* 42, No. 3 (1999), pp. 273–87.

39. M. Gist, "Self-Efficacy: Implications for Organizational Behavior and Human Resource Management," *Academy of Management Review*, July 1987, p. 472.

40. T. Peters, "Company Efficiency Tied to Workers' Self-Esteem," *Union-News,* July 4, 1988, pp. 19–21.

41. M. Coyle, "Quality Interpersonal Communication— An Overview," *Manage* 44, No. 4, April 1993, pp. 4–5.

42. C.B. Gibson, "Do They Do What They Believe They Can? Group Efficacy and Group Effectiveness Across Tasks and Cultures," *Academy of Management Journal* 42, No. 2 (1999), pp. 138–52.

43. "Power of Self-Image Psychology," *American Salesman* 41, No. 8 (August 1996), pp. 3–6.

44. J. McCarty and L.J. Shrum, "The Recycling of Solid Wastes: Personal Values," *Journal of Business Research,* 30, No. 1, May 1994, pp. 53–62.

45. C.S. Grizzard Sr., "Family Values at Work," *Fund Raising Management* 27, No. 8 (October 1996), p. 48.

46. "Big Problem for Small Businesses: a Poor Work Ethic," *The Wall Street Journal,* February 8, 2000, p. A1.

47. R. Barrett, "Liberating the Corporate Soul," *HR Focus* 74, No. 4 (April 1997), pp. 15–6.

48. D. Tricket, "How to Use a Values Audit," *Training & Development* 51, No. 3 (March 1997), pp. 34–8.

49. C.S. Grizzard Sr., "Family Values at Work," *Fund Raising Management* 27, No. 8 (October 1996), p. 48.

50. B. Kotey and G. Meredith, "Relationships among Owner/Manager Personal Values, Business Strategies and Enterprise Performance," *Journal of Small Business Management* 35, No. 2 (April 1997), pp. 37–64.

51. T. Petzinger, "Mihali Csikszentmihalyi: A "Happiness" Expert Talks About Suburban Anxiety and the Search for Fulfillment," *The Wall Street Journal,* January 1, 2000, p. R51.

52. Ibid.

53. T. Petzinger, "Edward O. Wilson: Human Nature, Dr. Wilson Believes, Has Changed Little in Many Millennia. And It Will Change Very Little in the Millennia Ahead," *The Wall Street Journal,* January 1, 2000, p. R16.

54. This section was written by Judith Neal, Professor of Management, University of New Haven, and editor, Spirit at Work website (www.spiritatwork.com).

55. K.T. Scott. Leadership and Spirituality: A Quest for Reconciliation, in Spirit at Work, in Jay Conger (ed.), *Discovering the Spirituality in Leadership* (San Francisco: Jossey-Bass, 1994), 63–99.

56. G. Fairholm, *Capturing the Heart of Leadership: Spirituality and Community in the New American Workplace.* (Westport, CT: Praeger), 1997.

57. J. Neal, 1995. Employees Seek Jobs that Nourish Their Souls. *Hartford Courant,* August 8, 1996\5, A12. J. Neal, B. Lichtenstein, and D, Banner. Spiritual Perspectives on Individual, Organizational, and Societal Transformation, *Journal of Organizational Change Management* 12, No. 3, 1999, pp. 175–85.

58. C. Schaefer and J. Darling, "Does Spirit Matter? A Look at Contemplative Practice in the Workplace," *Spirit at Work* newsletter, July 1997.

59. Material is taken from the Federal Express Information Packet available to anyone upon request by calling 901-395-3460.

CHAPTER 4

1. A. Arthur, "Keeping Up Public Appearances: Master the Fine Art of Public-Speaking and Give a Great Presentation Every Time," *Black Enterprise* 27, No. 12 (July 1997), p. 54.

2. R. Taylor, "It's Your Attitude that Counts," *The Financial Times,* February 19, 1997, p. 35.

3. J.D. Maes, T.G. Weldly, and M.L. Icenogle, "A Managerial Perspective: Oral Communication Competency Is Most Important for Business Students in the Workplace," *The Journal of Business Communication* 34, No. 1 (January 1997), pp. 67–80.

4. L. Iacocca, *Iacocca* (New York: Bantam Books, 1985), p. 15.

5. This statement came from a reviewer, who is the chair of the committee, in August 1997.

6. T. McEwen, "Communication Training in Corporate Settings: Lessons and Opportunities for the Academy," *Mid-American Journal of Business* 12, No. 1 (Spring 1997), pp. 49–58.

7. Lancaster, "Managing Your Career, Start Listening," *The Wall Street Journal,* p. B1.

8. A.R. Karr, "The Checkoff," *The Wall Street Journal,* February 8, 2000, p. A1

9. "Become a Better Listener," *Association Management* 52, No. 4 (April 2000), p. 27.

10. L. Cole and M.S. Cole, "Teamwork is Spelled Incorrectly Teamwork = Communication," *Communication World* 17, No. 4 (2000) p. 56.

11. "Guide Readers Through Your Written Communications and Save Them Time," *Marketing to Finishers* 5, No. 12 (October 1999), p 1.

12. D. Turecamo, "Managing Upward," *Supervision,* July 1986, p. 10.

13. "Message Madness," *The Wall Street Journal* (June 22, 1999), p. A1.

14. J.R. Carlson and R.W. Zmud, "Channel Expansion Theory and the Experiential Nature of Media Richness Perceptions," *Academy of Management Journal* 42, No. 2 (1999), pp. 153–70.

15. J.D. Maes, T.G. Weldly, and M.L. Icenogle, "A Managerial Perspective: Oral Communication Competency Is Most Important for Business Students in the Workplace," *The Journal of Business Communication* 34, No. 1 (January 1997), pp. 67–80.

16. A. Arthur, "Keeping Up Public Appearances: Master the Fine Art of Public-Speaking and Give a Great Presentation Every Time," *Black Enterprise* 27, No. 12 (July 1997), p. 54.

17. S. Ober, J.J. Zhao, R. Davis, and M.W. Alexander, "Telling it Like it is: the Use of Certainty in Public Business Discourse," *The Journal of Business Communication* 36, No. 3 (July 1999), pp. 280–82.

18. J.D. Maes, T.G. Weldly, and M.L. Icenogle, "A Managerial Perspective: Oral Communication Competency Is Most Important for Business Students in the Workplace," *The Journal of Business Communication* 34, No. 1 (January 1997), pp. 67–80.

19. T. McEwen, "Communication Training in Corporate Settings: Lessons and Opportunities for the Academy," *Mid-American Journal of Business* 12, No. 1 (Spring 1997), pp. 49–58.

20. Ibid.

21. S. Ober, J.J. Zhao, R. Davis, and M.W. Alexander, "Telling it Like it is: the Use of Certainty in Public Business Discourse," *The Journal of Business Communication* 36, No. 3 (July 1999), pp. 280–82.

22. S. Divita, "It's Not What You Say, But How You Say It," *Marketing News* 30, No. 14 (July 1, 1996), p. 15.

23. L. Cole and M.S. Cole, "Teamwork is Spelled Incorrectly Teamwork = Communication," *Communication World* 17, No. 4 (2000) p. 56.

24. Lancaster, "Managing Your Career, Start Listening," *The Wall Street Journal,* p. B1.

25. J.R. Waddell, "Are We Overstating Things Just a Tad," *Supervision* 58, No. 1 (January 1997), pp. 11–3.

26. T. Stirr, "Communication Starts with Rapport," *CMA Magazine* 71, No. 2 (March 1997), p. 8.

27. Lancaster, "Managing Your Career, Start Listening," *The Wall Street Journal*, p. B1.

28. T. Stirr, "Communication Starts with Rapport," *CMA Magazine* 71, No. 2 (March 1997), p. 8.

29. J.R. Waddell, "Are We Overstating Things Just a Tad," *Supervision* 58, No. 1 (January 1997), pp. 11–3.

30. R.A. Baron and G.D. Markman, "Beyond Social Capital: How Social Skills Can Enhance Entrepreneurs' Success," *Academy of Management Executive* 14, No. 1 (2000), p. 106–8.

31. T. Pollock, "A Personal File of Stimulating Ideas, Little Known Facts and Daily Problems," *Supervision* 58, No. 2 (February 1997) pp. 24–7.

32. T. Stirr, "Communication Starts with Rapport," *CMA Magazine* 71, No. 2 (March 1997), p. 8.

33. S. Kravetz, "Tech Firms Want Talented Employees to Switch Jobs- Not Companies," *The Wall Street Journal*, August 31, 1999, p. A1.

34. Bender, "Frustrated with Work Relationships," p. 8.

35. J.D. Maes, T.G. Weldly, and M.L. Icenogle, "A Managerial Perspective: Oral Communication Competency Is Most Important for Business Students in the Workplace," *The Journal of Business Communication* 34, No. 1 (January 1997), pp. 67–80.

36. Suggestion of a reviewer of the textbook.

37. J.D. Maes, T.G. Weldly, and M.L. Icenogle, "A Managerial Perspective: Oral Communication Competency Is Most Important for Business Students in the Workplace," *The Journal of Business Communication* 34, No. 1 (January 1997), pp. 67–80.

38. Lancaster, "Managing Your Career, Start Listening," *The Wall Street Journal*, p. B1.

39. T. Gunderson, "Listen and Learn," *Restaurant Hospitality* 83, Iss. 3 (March 1999), p. 26.

40. T. Pollock, "A Personal File of Stimulating Ideas, Little Known Facts and Daily Problems," *Supervision* 58, No. 2 (February 1997) pp. 24–7.

41. M.E. Rega, "Developing Listening Skills," *American Salesman* 45, No. 5 (May 2000), p. 3.

42. Lancaster, "Managing Your Career, Start Listening," *The Wall Street Journal*, p. B1.

43. D.H. Weis, "How to Say Nothing and Say It Well," *Getting Results* 41, No. 12 (December 1996), p. 4.

44. Ibid.

45. "Become a Better Listener," *Association Management* 52, No. 4 (April 2000), p. 27.

46. T. Gunderson, "Listen and Learn," *Restaurant Hospitality* 83, No. 3 (March 1999), p. 26.

47. "Become a Better Listener," *Association Management* 52, No. 4 (April 2000), p. 27.

48. Ibid.

49. T. Gunderson, "Listen and Learn," *Restaurant Hospitality* 83, No. 3 (March 1999), p. 26.

50. "Become a Better Listener," *Association Management* 52, No. 4 (April 2000), p. 27.

51. T. Gunderson, "Listen and Learn," *Restaurant Hospitality* 83, No. 3 (March 1999), p. 26.

52. Ibid.

53. J.D. Maes, T.G. Weldly, and M.L. Icenogle, "A Managerial Perspective: Oral Communication Competency Is Most Important for Business Students in the Workplace," *The Journal of Business Communication* 34, No. 1 (January 1997), pp. 67–80.

54. A.S. DeNisi and A.N. Kluger, "Feedback Effectiveness: Can 360-Degree Appraisals be Improved," *Academy of Management Executive* 14, No. 1 (2000), p. 129.

55. J. Ghorpade, "Managing Five Paradoxes of 360-Degree Feedback," *Academy of Management Executive* 14, No. 1 (2000), p. 140.

56. D.A. Waldman, L.E. Atwater, and D. Antonioni, "Has 360 Degree Feedback Gone Amok?" *Academy of Management Executive* 12, No. 2 (1998) pp. 86–92.

57. J. Ghorpade, "Managing Five Paradoxes of 360-Degree Feedback," *Academy of Management Executive* 14, No. 1 (2000), p. 140.

58. A.S. DeNisi and A.N. Kluger, "Feedback Effectiveness: Can 360-Degree Appraisals be Improved," *Academy of Management Executive* 14, No. 1 (2000), p. 129.

59. J. Ghorpade, "Managing Five Paradoxes of 360-Degree Feedback," *Academy of Management Executive* 14, No. 1 (2000), p. 140.

60. J.R. Hollenbeck, D.R. Ilgen, J.A. LePine, J.A. Colquitt, and J. Hedlund, "Extending the Multilevel Theory of Team Decision Making: Effects of Feedback and Experience in Hierarchical Teams," *Academy of Management Journal* 41, No. 3 (1998), pp. 269–82.

61. S. Divita, "It's Not What You Say, But How You Say It," *Marketing News* 30, No. 14 (July 1, 1996), p. 15.

62. R.R. Callister, M.W. Kramer, and D.B. Turban, "Feedback Seeking Following Career Transitions," *Academy of Management Journal* 42, No. 4 (1999), pp. 429–38.

63. J.P. Kotter, "Managing: Ideas & Solutions," *Fortune*, August 5, 1996, pp. 168–70.

64. Information for the opening case is taken from *The Wall Street Journal*, the *New York Times*, and the Coca-Cola Company website www.cocacola.com from June to December 1999.

CHAPTER 5

1. R. Harborne, "Wisdom of the CEO: The Challenge to Business Leadership in the 21st Century," keynote presentation at the New England Business Administration Association International Conference, Southern Connecticut State University, April 28, 2000, Price Waterhouse Coopers.

2. A. Brown, "Transforming Business Structures to Hyborgs," *Employment Relations Weekly* 26, No. 4 (2000), pp. 5–15.

3. T. Petzinger, "Edward O. Wilson: Human Nature, Dr. Wilson Believes, Has Changed Little in Many Millennia. And It Will Change Very Little in the Millennia Ahead," *The Wall Street Journal*, January 1, 2000, p. R16.

4. A.S. Tsui, J.L. Pearce, L.W. Porter, and A.M. Tripoli, "Alternative Approaches to the Employee-Organization Relationship: Does Investment in Employees Pay Off?" *Academy of Management Journal* 40, No. 5 (1997), pp. 1089–1121.

5. G.R. Jones and J.M. George, "The Experience and Evolution of Trust: Implications for Cooperation and Teamwork," *Academy of Management Review* 23, No. 3 (1998), pp. 531–46.

6. L. Cole and M.S. Cole, "Teamwork is Spelled Incorrectly Teamwork = Communication," *Communication World* 17, No. 4 (2000) p. 56.

7. G.R. Jones and J.M. George, "The Experience and Evolution of Trust: Implications for Cooperation and Teamwork," *Academy of Management Review* 23, No. 3 (1998), pp. 531–46.

8. D.P. Ellerman, "Global Institutions: Transforming International Development Agencies Into Learning Organizations," *Academy of Management* 13, No. 1, (1999) pp. 25–36.

9. B.G. Jackson, "A Fantasy theme Analysis of Peter Senge's Learning Organization," *Journal of Applied Behavioral Science* 36, Iss. 2, (June 2000) pp. 193–209.

10. F. Ostroff, *The Horizontal Organization: What the Organization of the Future Actually Looks like and How it Delivers Value to Customers*, (Oxford University Press, 1999), pp.

11. R. Harborne, "Wisdom of the CEO: The Challenge to Business Leadership in the 21st Century," keynote presentation at the New England Business Administration Association International Conference, Southern Connecticut State University, April 28, 2000, Price Waterhouse Coopers.

12. Ibid.

13. M. Schrage, "Net Computers Hinge on Corporate Politics," *Computerworld* 30, No. 50 (December 9, 1996), p. 37.

14. "Employee Newsletters Are Rapidly Becoming Obsolete," *The Wall Street Journal*, March 25, 1997, p. A1.

15. J.P. Kotter, "Managing: Ideas & Solutions," *Fortune*, August 5, 1996, pp. 168–70.

16. R.J. Marsak, T. Keenoy, C. Oswick, and D. Grant, "From Outer Words to Inner Worlds," *Journal of Applied Behavioral Science* 36, Iss. 2, June 2000, pp. 245–58.

17. N.B. Kurland, and L.H. Pelled, "Passing the Word: Toward a Model of Gossip and Power in the Workplace," *Academy of Management Review* 25, No. 2, 2000, pp. 428–38.

18. Ibid.

19. T. Deupi, "Designing for the New Century: Making the Office More Powerful?" *Managing Office Technology* 42, No. 4 (April 1997), pp. 24–5.

20. Lussier, "Management," pp. 61–62.

21. "High-Tech Skills Are Increasingly Required for Low-Skill Work," *The Wall Street Journal*, July 29, 1997, p. A1.

22. M. Schrage, "Net Computers Hinge on Corporate Politics," *Computerworld* 30, No. 50 (December 9, 1996), p. 37.

23. G. Levine, "Finding Time," *Bobbin* 35, Iss. 10, June 1994, pp. 113–14.

24. "Employee Newsletters Are Rapidly Becoming Obsolete," *The Wall Street Journal*, March 25, 1997, p. A1.

25. M. Kramer, "Networking Times They Are a-Changing," *PC Week* 14, No. 18 (May 5, 1997), p. 79.

26. Lussier, "Management," pp. 61–2.

27. R. Liss, "Virtual Places and Virtual Spaces," *National Underwriter Life & Health Financial Services* 101, No. 14 (April 7, 1997), pp. 17–8.

28. B. Schlender, "Cool Companies," *Fortune* 136, No. 1 (July 7, 1997), pp. 84–99.

29. A. Bird, "The Ten Commandments of SuperCommunity Banking," *The Bankers Magazine* 180, No. 1 (January–February 1997), pp. 12–19.

30. F. Whaley, "Shooting For Success: Staff Break Communication Barriers—By Firing Lasers at Each Other," *Asian Business Weekly* 26, No. 2 (2000), p. 48.

31. J. Weisberg, "Listen to Me," *Telemarketing Magazine* 12, No. 9 (March 1994), pp. 69–70.

32. Bender, "Frustrated with Work Relationships," p. 8.

33. "Communication Breakdown," *American Medical News* 43, Iss. 9, (March 6, 2000), p. 18.

34. P.M. Doney, J.P. Cannon, and M.R. Mullen, "Understanding the Influence of National Culture on the Development of Trust," *Academy of Management Review* 23, No. 3 (1998), pp. 601–20.

35. "How Do You Rate as a CyberManager," *The Wall Street Journal*, May 28, 1996, p. B1.

36. P. Drucker, "Leadership: More Doing than Dash," *The Wall Street Journal*, January 6, 1988, p. 19.

37. E.W. Whitener, S.E. Brodt, M.A. Korsgaard, and J.M. Werner, "Managers as Initiators of Trust: An Exchange Relationship Framework For Understanding Managerial Trustworthy Behavior," *Academy of Management Review* 23, No. 3 (1998), pp. 513–30.

38. B. Cole-Gromolski, "Tools for E-Mail Relief," *Computerworld* 31, Iss. 26 (June 30, 1997), p. 2.

39. F. Whaley, "Shooting For Success: Staff Break Communication Barriers- By Firing Lasers at Each Other," *Asian Business Weekly* 26, No. 2 (2000), p. 48.

40. P.M. Doney, J.P. Cannon, and M.R. Mullen, "Understanding the Influence of National Culture on the Development of Trust," *Academy of Management Review* 23, No. 3 (1998), pp. 601–20.

41. K.L. Allen, "Getting It Across," *Across the Board* 37, No. 1 (January 2000), p. 78.

42. Ibid.

43. J.R. Waddell, "Are We Overstating Things Just a Tad," *Supervision* 58, No. 1 (January 1997), pp. 11–3.

44. Lancaster, "Managing Your Career, Start Listening," *The Wall Street Journal*, p. B1.

CHAPTER 6

1. T. Watson, "Linking Employee Motivation and Satisfaction to the Bottom Line," *CMA Magazine* 68, No. 3, April 1994, p. 4.

2. A.R. Karr, "The Checkoff," *The Wall Street Journal*, February 8, 2000, p. A1.

3. G. Dessler, "How to Earn Your Employees' Commitment," *Academy of Management Executive* 13, No. 2 (1999), p. 58–67.

4. R.L. Papiernik, "David Novak: The Pizza Hut/ KFC Quarterback Builds a Better Team on His Drive to Fast-Food Touchdown," *Nation's Restaurant News* 31, No. 4 (January 1997), pp. 170–71.

5. T. Petzinger, "Peter Drucker: The 'Arch-Guru of Capitalism' Argues that We Need a New Economic Theory and a New Management Model," *The Wall Street Journal*, January 1, 2000, p. R34.

6. N. Fitzgerald, "Real Investment," *CA Magazine* 101, No. 1088 (March 1997), pp. 58–59.

7. T. McEwen, "Communication Training in Corporate Settings: Lessons and Opportunities for the Academy," *Mid-American Journal of Business* 12, No. 1 (Spring 1997), pp. 49–58.

8. M.E. Furman, "Reverse the 80-20 Rule," *Management Review* 86, No. 1 (January 1997), pp. 18–21.

9. K. Down and L. Liedtka, "What Corporations Seek in MBA Hires: A Survey," *Selections* 10, Iss. 2, Winter 1994, pp. 34–39.

10. V.M. Parachin, "How to Be Happier with Your Job," *Supervision* 58, No. 2 (February 1997), pp. 6–8.

11. A. Maslow, "A Theory of Human Motivations," *Psychological Review* 50 (1943), pp. 370–396; and *Motivation and Personality* (New York: Harper & Row, 1954).

12. G.P. Zachary, "Workplace, The New Search for Meaning in 'Meaningless' Work," *The Wall Street Journal*, January 9, 1997, p. B1.

13. Ibid.

14. F. Herzberg, "One More Time: How Do You Motivate Employees?" *Harvard Business Review*, January–February 1968, pp. 53–62.

15. T. Petzinger, "Peter Drucker: The 'Arch-Guru of Capitalism' Argues that We Need a New Economic Theory and a New Management Model," *The Wall Street Journal*, January 1, 2000, p. R34.

16. V.M. Parachin, "How to Be Happier with Your Job," *Supervision* 58, No. 2 (February 1997), pp. 6–8.

17. T.R. Mitchell and A.E. Mickel, "The Meaning of Money: An Individual-Difference Perspective," *Academy of Management Review* 24, No. 3 (1999), pp. 568–78.

18. G.P. Zachary, "Workplace, The New Search for Meaning in 'Meaningless' Work," *The Wall Street Journal*, January 9, 1997, p. B1.

19. V.D. Arnold and R.H. Krapels, "Motivation: A Reincarnation of Ideas," *Industrial Management* 38, No. 3 (May–June 1996), pp. 8–9.

20. H. Murry, *Explorations in Personality* (New York: Oxford Press, 1938).

21. J. Atkinson, *An Introduction to Motivation* (New York: Van Nostrand Reinhold, 1964); D. McClelland, *The Achieving Society* (New York: Van Nostrand Reinhold, 1961).

22. D. McClelland, *The Achieving Society* (New York: Van Nostrand Reinhold, 1961); and D. McClelland and D.H. Burnham, "Power Is the Great Motivator," *Harvard Business Review*, March–April 1978, p. 103.

23. G.P. Zachary, Workplace, "The New Search for Meaning in 'Meaningless' Work," *The Wall Street Journal*, January 9, 1997, p. B1.

24. T.R. Mitchell and A.E. Mickel, "The Meaning of Money: An Individual-Difference Perspective," *Academy of Management Review* 24, No. 3 (1999), pp. 568–78.

25. C. Tejada, "Priceless?" *The Wall Street Journal*, May 30, 2000, p. A1.

26. V.D. Arnold and R.H. Krapels, "Motivation: A Reincarnation of Ideas," *Industrial Management* 38, No. 3 (May–June 1996), pp. 8–9.

27. R. Forrester and A.B. Drexler, "A Model for Team-Based Organization Performance," *Academy of Management Executive* 13, No. 3 (1998), pp. 36–49.

28. D.P. Skarlicki, R.F. Folger, and P. Tesluk, "Personality as a Moderator in the Relationship Between Fairness and Retaliation," *Academy of Management Journal* 42, No. 1 (1999), pp. 100–8.

29. V. Vroom, *Work and Motivation* (New York: John Wiley & Sons, 1964).

30. J.C. McElroy, P.C. Morrow, and E.J. Mullen, "Intraorganizational Mobility and Work Related Attitudes," *Journal of Organizational Behavior* 17, No. 4 (July 1996), pp. 363–74.

31. A. Rercens, J. Wanous, and J. Austin, "Understanding and Managing Cynicism about Organizational Change," *Academy of Management Executive* 11, No. 1 (February 1997), pp. 48–58.

32. D. Ilgen, D. Nebeker, and R. Pritchard, "Expectancy Theory Measures: An Empirical Comparison in an Experimental Simulation," *Organizational Behavior and Human Performance* 28, 1981, pp. 189–223.

33. J.K. Klein, and J.S. Kim, "A Field Study of the Influence of Situational Constraints, Leader-Member Exchange, and Goal Commitment on Performance," *Academy of Management* 41, No. 1 (1998), p. 86–95.

34. S.L. Mueller and L.D. Clarke, "Political-Economic Context and Sensitivity to Equity: Differences Between the United States and the Transition economies of Central and Eastern Europe," *Academy of Management Journal* 41, No. 3 (1998), pp. 319–29.

35. R. Quick, "A Makeover That Began at the Top," *The Wall Street Journal*, May 25, 2000, p. B1.

36. S. Adams, "Toward an Understanding of Inequity," *Journal of Abnormal and Social Psychology* 67 (1963), pp. 422–36.

37. M. Bloom, "The Performance Effects of Pay Dispersion on Individuals and Organizations," *Academy of Management Journal* 42, No. 1 (1999), p. 25–40.

38. R.H. Moorman, G.L. Blakely, and B.P. Niehoff, "Does Perceived Organizational Support Mediate the Relationship Between Procedural Justice and Organizational Citizenship Behavior?" *Academy of Management Journal* 41, No. 3 (1998), p. 351–57.

39. K. Seiders and L.L. Berry, "Service Fairness: What is it and Why it Matters," *Academy of Management Executive* 12, No. 2 (1998), pp. 8–20.

40. J.C. McElroy, P.C. Morrow, and E.J. Mullen, "Intraorganizational Mobility and Work Related Attitudes," *Journal of Organizational Behavior* 17, No. 4 (July 1996), pp. 363–74.

41. R.H. Moorman, G.L. Blakely, and B.P. Niehoff, "Does Perceived Organizational Support Mediate the Relationship Between Procedural Justice and Organizational Citizenship Behavior?" *Academy of Management Journal* 41, No. 3 (1998), p. 351–57.

42. M. Bloom, "The Performance Effects of Pay Dispersion on Individuals and Organizations," *Academy of Management Journal* 42, No. 1 (1999), p. 25–40.

43. D.P. Skarlicki, R.F. Folger, and P. Tesluk, "Personality as a Moderator in the Relationship Between Fairness and Retaliation," *Academy of Management Journal* 42, No. 1 (1999), pp. 100–8.

44. R. Quick, "A Makeover That Began at the Top," *The Wall Street Journal*, May 25, 2000, p. B1.

45. A.D. Stajkovic and F. Luthans, "A Meta-Analysis of the Effects of Organizational Behavior Modification on Task Performance, 1975–95," *Academy of Management Journal* 40, No. 5 (1997) pp. 1122–49.

46. S.M. Puffer, "Continental Airlines' CEO Gordon Bethume on Teams and New Product Development," *Academy of Management Executive* 13, No. 3 (1999), pp. 28–35.

47. B.F. Skinner, *Beyond Freedom and Dignity* (New York: Alfred A. Knopf, 1971).

48. Michele Marchetti, "Are Reps Motivated by Bonuses?" *Sales & Marketing Management* 149, No. 2 (February 1997), p. 33.

49. F. Luthans and A.D. Stajkovic, "Reinforce For Performance: The Need to Go Beyond Pay and Even rewards," *Academy of Management Executive* 13, No. 3 (1999), pp. 49–57.

50. M.A. Berry and D.A. Rondinelli, "Proactive Corporate Environmental Management: A New Industrial Revolution," *Academy of Management Executive* 12, No. 2 (1998), pp. 38–50.

51. M.E. Furman, "Reverse the 80-20 Rule," *Management Review* 86, No. 1 (January 1997), pp. 18–21.

52. S.M. Puffer, "Continental Airlines' CEO Gordon Bethume on Teams and New Product Development," *Academy of Management Executive* 13, No. 3 (1999), pp. 28–35.

53. "The Checkoff," *The Wall Street Journal*, December 17, 1996, p. A1.

54. G.P. Zachary, "Workplace, The New Search for Meaning in 'Meaningless' Work," *The Wall Street Journal*, January 9, 1997, p. B1.

55. T. Petzinger, "Edward O. Wilson: Human Nature, Dr. Wilson Believes, Has Changed Little in Many Millennia. And It Will Change Very Little in the Millennia Ahead," *The Wall Street Journal*, January 1, 2000, p. R16.

56. M. Marchetti, "Are Reps Motivated by Bonuses?" *Sales & Marketing Management* 149, No. 2 (February 1997), p. 33.

57. T. Petzinger, "Peter Drucker: The 'Arch-Guru of Capitalism' Argues that We Need a New Economic Theory and a New Management Model," *The Wall Street Journal*, January 1, 2000, p. R34.

58. K. Blanchard and S. Johnson, *The One-Minute Manager* (New York: Wm. Morrow & Co., 1982).

59. J.K. Klein, and J.S. Kim, "A Field Study of the Influence of Situational Constraints, Leader-Member Exchange, and Goal Commitment on Performance," *Academy of Management* 41, No. 1 (1998), p. 86–95.

60. Ibid.

61. J.P. Kotter, "Kill Complacency ... Before It Kills You," *Fortune*, August 5, 1996, pp. 168–70.

62. R. Forrester and A.B. Drexler, "A Model for Team-Based Organization Performance," *Academy of Management Executive* 13, No. 3 (1998), pp. 36–49.

63. C. Shalley and G. Oldham, "Effects of Goal Difficulty and Expected External Evaluation of Intrinsic Motivation," *Academy of Management Journal*, September 1985, p. 56.

64. W.J. Liccione, "Effective Goal Setting: A Prerequisite for Compensation Plans with Incentive Value," *Compensation & Benefits Management* 13, No. 1 (Winter 1997), pp. 19–25.

65. Erez, Zarley, and Hulin, "The Impact of Participation on Goal Acceptance and Performance," *Academy of Management Review*, March 1985, p. 56.

66. G. Dessler, "How to Earn Your Employees' Commitment," *Academy of Management Executive* 13, No. 2 (1999), p. 58–67.

67. Erez, Zarley, and Hulin, "The Impact of Participation on Goal Acceptance and Performance," *Academy of Management Review* March 1985, p. 56.

68. "Super K's Future Overshadowed Again," *Discount Store News* 36, No. 12 (June 23, 1997), pp. 41–43.

69. "DainlerChrisler is Aiming," *The Wall Street Journal*, January 14, 2000, p. A1.

70. "Medical Mistakes Kill," *The Wall Street Journal*, January 30, 1999, p. A1.

71. B. McKay, "Street Seeks Real Thing," *The Wall Street Journal*, January 17, 2000, p. C1.

72. "Hyundai Plans to Link Up," *The Wall Street Journal*, January 11, 2000, p. A1.

73. W.J. Liccione, "Effective Goal Setting: A Prerequisite for Compensation Plans with Incentive Value," *Compensation & Benefits Management* 13, No. 1 (Winter 1997), pp. 19–25.

74. "Cure-All for Hospital Pay," *The Wall Street Journal*, May 28, 1996, p. A1.

75. T. Petzinger, "Peter Drucker: The 'Arch-Guru of Capitalism' Argues that We Need a New Economic Theory and a New Management Model," *The Wall Street Journal*, January 1, 2000, p. R34.

76. G. Dessler, "How to Earn Your Employees' Commitment," *Academy of Management Executive* 13, No. 2 (1999), p. 58–67.

77. R. Forrester and A.B. Drexler, "A Model for Team-Based Organization Performance," *Academy of Management Executive* 13, No. 3 (1998), pp. 36–49.

78. Ibid.

79. S.L. Mueller and L.D. Clarke, "Political-Economic Context and Sensitivity to Equity: Differences Between the United States and the Transition Economies of Central and Eastern Europe," *Academy of Management Journal* 41, No. 3 (1998), pp. 319–29.

80. T. Mroczkowski and M. Hanaoka, "Effective Right Sizing Strategies in Japan and America: Is There a Convergence of Employment," *Academy of Management Executive* 11, No. 1 (February 1997), pp. 57–67.

81. A. Dubinsky, M. Kotabe, C.U. Lim, and R. Michaels, "Differences in Motivational Perceptions among U.S., Japanese, and Korean Sales Personnel," *Journal of Business Research* 30, No. 2 (June 1994), pp. 175–85.

82. S.L. Mueller and L.D. Clarke, "Political-Economic Context and Sensitivity to Equity: Differences Between the United States and the Transition Economies of Central and Eastern Europe," *Academy of Management Journal* 41, No. 3 (1998), pp. 319–29.

83. S.M. Puffer, "Continental Airlines' CEO Gordon Bethume on Teams and New Product Development," *Academy of Management Executive* 13, No. 3 (1999), pp. 28–35.

84. "Deming's Demons," *The Wall Street Journal*, June 4, 1990, pp. R39, 41.

85. Information for the case taken from *The Wall Street Journal*, July 20, 1999, p. 1 and the HP website www.hp.com.

CHAPTER 7

1. B. Bass, *Stogdill's Handbook of Leadership*, rev. ed. (New York: Free Press, 1981).

2. T. Owen, "Elements of Leadership Are Key," *San Diego Business Journal* 21, Iss. 23 (June 5, 2000), p. 82.

3. "Mind Field," *The Wall Street Journal*, July 9, 1997, p. A1.

4. R. Warbington, "New Leadership Breeds new Energy," *Women in Business* 52, Iss. 3 (May 2000), pp. 18–19.

5. J. Kouzes and B. Pusner, "Fad-Resistant Leadership," *Management Review* 85, No. 1 (January 1996), p. 7.

6. M.A. O'Neil, "Developing Leaders," *Supervision* 61, No. 3 (March 2000), p. 3.

7. J. Kouzes and B. Pusner, "Fad-Resistant Leadership," *Management Review* 85, No. 1 (January 1996), p. 7.

8. D. Cottrell, "The Need for Speed in New Millennium Leadership Styles," *Employment Relations Today* 27, No. 1 (2000), pp. 61–71.

9. "Leading Effectively," *Association Management* 52, No. 3 (March 2000), p. 23.

10. A. Oliver, "NLC Summit Will Address Leadership Challenges," *Nation's Cities Weekly* 23, No. 14 (April 10, 2000), p. 1.

11. N. Grund, "From Sage to Artisan: The Many Roles of the Value-Driven Leader," *Academy of Management Executive* 11, No. 2 (February 1997), pp. 94–95.

12. M.A. O'Neil, "Developing Leaders," *Supervision* 61, No. 3 (March 2000), p. 3.

13. "Leading Effectively," *Association Management* 52, No. 3 (March 2000), p. 23.

14. C. Hymowitz, "More Top Executives, Used to Single Life, Are Cohabiting Now," *The Wall Street Journal*, January 5, 1999, p. B1.

15. D. Cottrell, "The Need for Speed in New Millennium Leadership Styles," *Employment Relations Today* 27, No. 1 (2000), pp. 61–71.

16. J. Kouzes and B. Pusner, "Fad-Resistant Leadership," *Management Review* 85, No. 1 (January 1996), p. 7.

17. K.H. Blanchard and P. Hersey, "Great Ideas Revisited," *Training & Development* 50, No. 1 (January 1996), pp. 42–7.

18. "Great Acts To Follow," *Management Today*, March 2000, p. 59.

19. A. Oliver, "NLC Summit Will Address Leadership Challenges," *Nation's Cities Weekly* 23, No. 14 (April 10, 2000), p. 1.

20. B. Bass, *Handbook of Leadership*, (New York: Free Press, 1990).

21. E. Ghiselli, *Explorations in Management Talent* (Santa Monica, Calif.: Goodyear Publishing, 1971).

22. "What Are the Most Important Traits for Success as a Supervisor?" *The Wall Street Journal*, November 14, 1980, p. 33.

23. J. Kouzes and B. Pusner, "Fad-Resistant Leadership," *Management Review* 85, No. 1 (January 1996), p. 7.

24. R. Likert, *New Patterns of Management* (New York: McGraw-Hill, 1961).

25. R.M. Stogdill and A.E. Coons (eds.), *Leader Behavior: Its Description and Measurement* (Columbus: The Ohio State University Bureau of Business Research, 1957).

26. R. Blake and J. Mouton, *The Managerial Grid* (Houston: Gulf Publishing, 1964).

27. R. Blake and J. Mouton, *The New Managerial Grid* (Houston: Gulf Publishing, 1978).

28. R. Blake and J. Mouton, *The Managerial Grid III: Key to Leadership Excellence* (Houston: Gulf Publishing, 1985).

29. R. Blake and A.A. McCanse, *Leadership Dilemmas-Grid Solutions* (Houston, Tex.: Gulf Publishing, 1991). They changed the name from the Mgr Grid to the Leadership Grid.

30. L. Pheng and B. Lee, "Managerial Grid" and Zhuge Liang's "Art of Management": Intergration for Effective Project Management, *Management Decision* 35, No. 5–6 (May–June 1997), pp. 382–392.

31. D.I. Jung and B.J. Avolio, "Effects of Leadership Style and Followers' Cultural Orientation on Performance in Group and Individual Task Conditions," *Academy of Management Journal* 42, No. 2 (1999), pp. 208–18.

32. A. Oliver, "NLC Summit Will Address Leadership Challenges," *Nation's Cities Weekly* 23, No. 14 (April 10, 2000), p. 1.

33. N. Tichy and M.A. Devanna, *The Transformational Leader* (New York: John Wiley & Sons, 1986).

34. R.T. Sparrowe and R.C. Liden, "Process and Structure in Leader-Member Exchange," *Academy of Management Exchange* 22, No. 2 (April 1997), pp. 522–52.

35. W.L. Gardner and B.J. Avolio, "The Charismatic Relationship: A Dramaturgical Perspective," *Academy of Management Review* 23, No. 1 (1998), pp. 32–58.

36. B. Shamir, E. Zakay, E. Breinin, and M. Popper, "Correlates of Charismatic Leader Behavior in Military Units: Subordinates' Attitudes, Unit Characteristics, and Superiors' Appraisals of Leader Performance," *Academy of Management Journal* 41, No. 4 (1998), pp. 387–409.

37. D.I. Jung and B.J. Avolio, "Effects of Leadership Style and Followers' Cultural Orientation on Performance in Group and Individual Task Conditions," *Academy of Management Journal* 42, No. 2 (1999), pp. 208–18.

38. F. Fiedler, *A Theory of Leadership Effectiveness* (New York: McGraw-Hill 1967).

39. R. Tannenbaum and W. Schmidt, "How to Choose a Leadership Pattern," *Harvard Business Review* (May–June 1973), p. 166.

40. V. Vroom and P. Yetton, *Leadership and Decision Making* (Pittsburgh: University of Pittsburgh Press, 1973).

41. R. Lussier and C. Achua, *Leadership: Theory, Applications, Skill Development* (Cincinnati: South-Western, 2001), pp. 176–78.

42. P. Hersey and K. Blanchard, *Management of Organizational Behavior: Utilizing Human Resources*, 4th ed. (Englewood Cliffs, N.J.: Prentice Hall, 1982).

43. K.H. Blanchard and P. Hersey, "Great Ideas Revisited," *Training & Development* 50, No. 1 (January 1996), pp. 42–47.

44. D. Cottrell, "The Need for Speed in New Millennium Leadership Styles," *Employment Relations Today* 27, No. 1 (2000), pp. 61–71.

45. R. Barner, "Five Steps to Leadership Competencies," *Training & Development* 54, No. 3 (March 2000), p. 47.

46. "How Situational Leadership Fits into Today's Organizations," *Supervisory Management* 41, No. 2 (February 1996), p. 1–3.

47. K.H. Blanchard and P. Hersey, "Great Ideas Revisited," *Training & Development* 50, No. 1 (January 1996), pp. 42–47.

48. S. Kerr and J.M. Jermier, "Substitutes for Leadership: The Meaning and Measurement," *Organizational Behavior and Human Performance* 22 (1978), pp. 375–403.

49. "How Do You Rate as a CyberManager?" *The Wall Street Journal*, May 28, 1996, p. B1.

50. N. Grund, "From Sage to Artisan: The Many Roles of the Value-Driven Leader," *Academy of Management Executive* 11, No. 2 (February 1997), pp. 94–95.

51. J.E. Sheridan, D.J. Vredenburgh, and M.A. Abelson, "Contextual Model of Leadership Influence in Hospital Units," *Academy of Management Journal* 27 (1984), pp. 57–78.

52. "Leading Effectively," *Association Management* 52, No. 3 (March 2000), p. 23.

53. J.A. Petrick, R.F. Scherer, J.D. Brodzinski, J.F. Quinn, and M.F. Ainina, "Global Leadership Skills and Reputational Capital: Intangible Resources for Sustainable Competitive Advantage," *Academy of Management Executive* 13, No. 1 (1999), pp. 58–69.

54. W. Ouchi, *Theory Z—How American Business Can Meet the Japanese Challenge* (Reading, Mass.: Addison-Wesley, 1981).

55. MOCON is a successful company. However, Kim Rogers is not the actual name of a manager at MOCON. She is used to illustrate contingency leadership.

CHAPTER 8

1. J. Hay, "Creating Community: The Task of Leadership," *Leadership & Organizational Development* 14, No. 7, 1993, pp. 12–17.

2. E. Berne, *Transactional Analysis in Psychotherapy* (New York: Grove Press, 1961).

3. E. Berne, *Games People Play* (New York: Grove Press, 1964).

4. N. Nykodym, L.D. Freedman, J.L. Simonetti, W.R. Nielsen, and K. Battles, "Mentoring: Using Transactional Analysis to help Organizational Members Use Their Energy in More Productive Ways," *Transactional Analysis Journal* 25, No. 2 (1995), p. 170.

5. N. Nykodym, W.R. Nielson, and J.C. Christen, "Can Organization Development Use Transactional Analysis?" *Transactional Analysis Journal* 15, No. 4 (October 1985), p. 278.

6. N. Nykodym, C.O. Longenecker, and W.N. Ruud, "Improving Quality of Work Life with Transactional Analysis as an Intervention Change Strategy," *Applied Psychology: An International Review* 40, No. 4 (1991), pp. 395–404.

7. H. Park and K. Harrison, "Enhancing Managerial Cross-Cultural Awareness and Sensitivity: Transactional Analysis Revisited," *Journal of Management Development* 12, No. 3, 1993, pp. 20–29.

8. R. Bennett, "Relationship Formation and Governance in Consumer Markets: Transactional Analysis Versus the Behaviorist Approach," *Journal of Marketing Management* 12, No. 5 (July 1996), pp. 417–35.

9. L. Weinberg, "Seeing through Organization: Exploring the Constitutive Quality of Social Relations," *Administration & Society* 28, No. 2 (1996), pp. 177–90.

10. H. Park and K. Harrison, "Enhancing Managerial Cross-Cultural Awareness and Sensitivity: Transactional Analysis Revisited," *Journal of Management Development* 12, No. 3, 1993, pp. 20–29.

11. A. Lazarus, He first published a paper in the late 1960s "On Assertive Behavior: A Brief Note," *Behavior Therapy* 4 (October 1973), pp. 697–99.

12. K. Aquino, S.L. Grover, M. Bradford, and D.G. Allen, "The Effects of Negative Affectivity, Hierarchival Status, and Self-Determination on Workplace Victimization," *Academy of Management Journal* 42, No. 2 (1999), pp. 260–72.

13. A. Chaudhuri, "The New Boy Network," *The Guardian*, May 26, 1999, p. T6–7.

14. G. Fairclough, "Feeling Squeezed: Thailand's Economic Woes Fuel Worker Unrest," *Far Eastern Economic Review* 160, No. 2 (January 9, 1997), p. 8.

15. A. Rao and K. Hashimoto, "Intercuteral Influences: A Study of the Japanese Expatriate Managers in Canada," *Journal of International Business Studies* 27, No. 3 (Fall 1996), pp. 443–66.

16. B. Dossey, "Help Your Patient Break Free from Anxiety," *Nursing* 26, No. 10 (1996), pp. 52–4.

17. B.J. Tepper, "Consequences of Abusive Supervision," *Academy of Management Journal* 43, No. 2 (2000), pp. 178–90.

18. D.P. Skarlicki, R.F. Folger, and P. Tesluk, "Personality as a Moderator in the Relationship Between Fairness and Retaliation," *Academy of Management Journal* 42, No. 1 (1999), pp. 100–8.

19. S.L. Robinson and A.M. O'Leary-Kelly, "Monkey See, Monkey Do: The Influence of Work Groups on the Antisocial Behavior of Employees," *Academy of Management Journal* 41, No. 6, (1998), pp. 658–72.

20. B.J. Tepper, "Consequences of Abusive Supervision," *Academy of Management Journal* 43, No. 2 (2000), pp. 178–90.

21. "Workplace Violence," *The Wall Street Journal*, April 4, 2000, p. A1.

22. A.G. Podolak, "Is Workplace Violence in Need of Refocusing?" *Security Management* 44, No. 6 (June 2000), pp. 152–53.

23. C. Garvey, "Looking for Chinks in the Armor," *HRMagazine* 45, No. 6 (June 2000), pp. 161–62

24. "Put Up Your Dukes," *The Wall Street Journal*, August 13, 1996, p. A1.

25. L. Goulet, "Modeling Aggression in the Workplace: The Role of Role Models," *Academy of Management Executive* 11, No. 2 (February 1997), pp. 84–5.

26. S.L. Robinson and A.M. O'Leary-Kelly, "Monkey See, Monkey Do: The Influence of Work Groups on the Antisocial Behavior of Employees," *Academy of Management Journal* 41, No. 6, (1998), pp. 658–72.

27. L. Goulet, "Modeling Aggression in the Workplace: The Role of Role Models," *Academy of Management Executive* 11, No. 2 (February 1997), pp. 84–85.

28. B.J. Tepper, "Consequences of Abusive Supervision," *Academy of Management Journal* 43, No. 2 (2000), pp. 178–90.

29. Ibid.

30. D.P. Skarlicki, R.F. Folger, and P. Tesluk, "Personality as a Moderator in the Relationship Between Fairness and Retaliation," *Academy of Management Journal* 42, No. 1 (1999), pp. 100–8.

31. K.A. Smith-Jentsch, E. Salas and D.P. Baker, "Training Team Performance-Related Assertiveness," *Personal Psychology* 49, No. 4 (Winter 1996), pp. 909–36.

32. J.M. Brett, D.L. Shapiro, and A.L. Lytle, "Breaking the Bonds of Reciprocity in Negotiations," *Academy of Management Journal* 41, No. 4 (1998), pp. 410–24.

33. G. Labianca, D.J. Brass, and B. Gray, "Social Networks and Perceptions of Intergroup Conflict: The Role of Negative Relationships and Third Parties," *Academy of Management Journal* 41, No. 1 (1998), pp. 55–67.

34. J. Steininger, "When Personalities Collide, Look for the 'Catbird Seat,'" *The Business Journal—Milwaukee* 14, No. 18 (January 31, 1997), p. 10.

35. T. Pollock, "A Personal File of Stimulating Ideas, Little Known Facts and Daily Problems," *Supervision* 58, No. 2 (February 1997) pp. 24–7.

36. J.M. Brett, D.L. Shapiro, and A.L. Lytle, "Breaking the Bonds of Reciprocity in Negotiations," *Academy of Management Journal* 41, No. 4 (1998), pp. 410–24.

37. T.L. Simons and R.S. Peterson, "Task Conflict and Relationship Conflict in Top Management Teams: The Pivotal Role of Intragroup Trust," *Journal of Applied Psychology* 85, No. 1 (2000), pp. 102–11.

38. S. Berglas, "Boom! There's Nothing Wrong with You or Your Business That a Little Conflict Wouldn't Cure," *Inc.* 19, No. 6 (May 1997), pp. 56–58.

39. E.J. Van Slyke, "Facilitating Productive Conflict," *HR Focus* 74, No. 4 (April 1997), pp. 17–8.

40. D. Lynch, "Unresolved Conflicts Affect the Bottom Line," *HR Magazine* 42, No. 5 (May 1997), pp. 49–50.

41. T.L. Simons and R.S. Peterson, "Task Conflict and Relationship Conflict in Top Management Teams: The Pivotal Role of Intragroup Trust," *Journal of Applied Psychology* 85, No. 1 (2000), pp. 102–11.

42. J.F. Brett, G.B. Northcraft, and R.B. Pinkley, "Stairways to Heaven: An Interlocking Self-Regulation Model of Negotiation," *Academy of Management Review* 24, No. 3 (1999), pp. 435–51.

43. T. Pollock, "A Personal File of Stimulating Ideas, Little Known Facts and Daily Problems," *Supervision* 58, No. 2 (February 1997) pp. 24–7

44. B.J. Tepper, "Consequences of Abusive Supervision," *Academy of Management Journal* 43, No. 2 (2000), pp. 178–90.

45. Ibid.

46. J.T. Polzer, E.A. Mannix, and M.A. Neale, "Interest Alignment and Coalitions in Multiparty Negotiation," *Academy of Management Journal* 41, No. 1 (1998), pp. 42–54.

47. J.F. Brett, G.B. Northcraft, and R.B. Pinkley, "Stairways to Heaven: An Interlocking Self-Regulation Model of Negotiation," *Academy of Management Review* 24, No. 3 (1999), pp. 435–51.

48. A.E. Schwartz, "How to Handle Conflict," *The CPA Journal* 67, No. 4 (April 1997), pp. 72–3.

49. D. Lynch, "Unresolved Conflicts Affect the Bottom Line," *HR Magazine* 42, No. 5 (May 1997), pp. 49–50.

50. T. Gordon, *Parent Effectiveness Training* (New York: Wyden, 1970).

51. T. Pollock, "A Personal File of Stimulating Ideas, Little Known Facts and Daily Problems," *Supervision* 58, No. 2 (February 1997) pp. 24–7.

52. A.E. Schwartz, "How to Handle Conflict," *The CPA Journal* 67, No. 4 (April 1997), pp. 72–3.

53. D.E. Conlon and D.P. Sullivan, "Examining the Actions of Organizations in Conflict: Evidence from the Delaware Court of Chancery," *Academy of Management Journal* 42, No. 3 (1999), pp. 319–29.

54. T. Gunderson, "It's Not My Problem," *Restaurant Hospitality* 81, No. 5 (May 1997), p. 46.

55. E.J. Van Slyke, "Facilitating Productive Conflict," *HR Focus* 74, No. 4 (April 1997), pp. 17–8.

56. L. Weinberg, "Seeing through Organization: Exploring the Constitutive Quality of Social Relations," *Administration & Society* 28, No. 2 (1996), pp. 177–90.

57. J.T. Polzer, E.A. Mannix, and M.A. Neale, "Interest Alignment and Coalitions in Multiparty Negotiation," *Academy of Management Journal* 41, No. 1 (1998), pp. 42–54.

CHAPTER 9

1. C.W. Moon and A.A. Lado, "MNC-Host Government Bargaining Power Relationship: A Critique and Extension Within the Resource-Based View," *Journal of Management* 26, No. 1 (January 2000), p. 85.

2. "Criterion: Arming Management With the Power of Information," *Dallas Business Journal* 23, No. 39 (May 19, 2000), p. 18c.

3. T. Gautschi, "Don't Confuse Authority, Power, and Politics," *Design News* 52, No. 9 (May 5, 1997), pp. 202–3.

4. M.A. Carpenter and B.R. Golden, "Preceived Managerial Discretion: A Study of Cause and Effect," *Strategic Management Journal* 18, No. 3 (March 1997), pp. 187–206.

5. D.E. Conlon and D.P. Sullivan, "Examining the Actions of Organizations in Conflict: Evidence from the Delaware Court of Chancery," *Academy of Management Journal* 42, No. 3 (1999), pp. 319–29.

6. A. Bird, "The Ten Commandments of SuperCommunity Banking," *The Bankers Magazine* 180, No. 1 (January–February 1997), pp. 12–9.

7. H.P. Guzda, "The Business of Employee Empowerment: Democracy and Ideology in the Workplace," *Monthly Labor Review* 123, No. 2 (February 2000), p. 49.

8. Pascarella, "Thinking Globally," pp. 58–60.

9. G.P. Zachary, "Workplace, The New Search for Meaning in 'Meaningless' Work," *The Wall Street Journal*, January 9, 1997, p. B1.

10. M.A. Carpenter and B.R. Golden, "Perceived Managerial Discretion: A Study of Cause and Effect," *Strategic Management Journal* 18, No. 3 (March 1997), pp. 187–206.

11. J. French and B. Raven, "A Comparative Analysis of Power and Preference," in J.T. Tedeschi, ed., *Prospectives on Social Power* (Hawthorne, N.Y.: Adline Publishing, 1974).

12. S.S.K. Lam, "Social Power for Compliance of Middle Managers and Front-Line Workers with Quality Improvment Policies," *Journal of Management Development* 15, No. 9 (September 1996), pp. 13–7.

13. D.E. Conlon and D.P. Sullivan, "Examining the Actions of Organizations in Conflict: Evidence from the Delaware Court of Chancery," *Academy of Management Journal* 42, No. 3 (1999), pp. 319–29.

14. C.S. Katsikeas, M.M.H. Goode, and E. Katsikea, "Sources of Power in International Marketing Channels," *Journal of Marketing Management* 16, No. 1–3 (January 2000), p. 185.

15. "Managing Your Career" or "You Can Be Good at Office Politics without Being a Jerk," *The Wall Street Journal*, March 18, 1997, p. A1.

16. C.S. Katsikeas, M.M.H. Goode, and E. Katsikea, "Sources of Power in International Marketing Channels," *Journal of Marketing Management* 16, No. 1–3 (January 2000), p. 185.

17. Ibid.

18. H.P. Guzda, "The Business of Employee Empowerment: Democracy and Ideology in the Workplace," *Monthly Labor Review* 123, Iss. 2 (February 2000), p. 49.

19. "Criterion: Arming Management With the Power of Information," *Dallas Business Journal* 23, No. 39 (May 19, 2000), p. 18c.

20. M. Schrage, "Net Computers Hinge on Corporate Politics," *Computerworld* 30, No. 50 (December 9, 1996), p. 37.

21. M.I. Reed, "Expert Power and Control in Late Modernity: An Empirical Review and Theoretical Synthesis (Special Issue: Change as an Underlying Theme in Professional Service Organizations)," *Organizational Studies* 17, No. 4 (Fall 1996), pp. 573–97.

22. C.W. Moon and A.A. Lado, "MNC-Host Government Bargaining Power Relationship: A Critique and Extension Within the Resource Based View," *Journal of Management* 26, No. 1 (January 2000), p. 85.

23. C. Oswick and D. Grant, "Personnel Management in the Public Sector: Power, Roles and Relationships," *Personnel Review* 25, No. 2 (February 1996), pp. 4–18.

24. Pascarella, "Thinking Globally," pp. 58–60.

25. M.A. Reed-Woodard, "Campaigning for Office," *Black Enterprise* 30, No. 9 (2000), p. 68.

26. G.R. Ferris, D.D. Frink, M.C. Galang, J. Zhou, K.M. Kacmar and J.L. Howard, "Perceptions of Organizational Politics: Prediction, Stress-Related Implications, and Outcomes," *Human Relations* 49, No. 2 (February 1996), pp. 233–66.

27. M. Schrage, "Net Computers Hinge on Corporate Politics," *Computerworld* 30, No. 50 (December 9, 1996), p. 37.

28. T. Gautschi, "Don't Confuse Authority, Power, and Politics," *Design News* 52, No. 9 (May 5, 1997), pp. 202–3.

29. R.G. Cook and D.R. Fox, "Resources, Frequency, and Methods," *Business and Society* 39, No. 1 (March 2000), pp. 94–113.

30. J.M. Brett, D.L. Shapiro, and A.L. Lytle, "Breaking the Bonds of Reciprocity in Negotiations," *Academy of Management Journal* 41, No. 4 (1998), pp. 410–24.

31. J. Steininger, "When Personalities Collide, Look for the 'Catbird Seat,' " *The Business Journal—Milwaukee* 14, No. 18 (January 31, 1997), p. 10.

32. Managing Your Career, "You Can Be Good at Office Politics without Being a Jerk," *The Wall Street Journal*, March 18, 1997, p. B1.

33. R.T. Sparrowe and R.C. Liden, "Process and Structure in Leader-Member Exchange," *Academy of Management Exchange* 22, No. 2 (April 1997), pp. 522–53.

34. M. Valle and P.M. Perrewe, "Do Politics Relate to Political Behavior? Test of an Implicit Assumption and Expanded Model," *Human Relations* 53, No. 3 (March 2000), p. 359.

35. T. Gautschi, "Don't Confuse Authority, Power, and Politics," *Design News* 52, No. 9 (May 5, 1997), pp. 202–3.

36. Managing Your Career, "You Can Be Good at Office Politics without Being a Jerk," *The Wall Street Journal*, March 18, 1997, p. B1.

37. M.I. Reed, "Expert Power and Controll in Late Modernity: An Empirical Review and Theoretical Synthesis (Special Issue: Change as an Underlying Theme in Professional Service Organizations)," *Organizational Studies* 17, No. 4 (Fall 1996), pp. 573–97.

38. Ibid.

39. Managing Your Career, "You Can Be Good at Office Politics without Being a Jerk," *The Wall Street Journal*, March 18, 1997, p. B1.

40. E.J. Walsh, "Leadership in an Age of Distrust," *Industry Week* 246, No. 13 (July 7, 1997), pp. 78–83.

41. N. Fitzgerald, "Real Investment," *CA Magazine* 101, No. 1088 (1997), pp. 58–60.

42. J. Steininger, "When Personalities Collide, Look for the 'Catbird Seat,' " *The Business Journal–Milwaukee* 14, No. 18 (January 31, 1997), p. 10.

43. J.T. Polzer, E.A. Mannix, and M.A. Neale, "Interest Alignment and Coalitions in Multiparty Negotiation," *Academy of Management Journal* 41, No. 1 (1998), pp. 42–54.

44. "Finding a Niche in Networking," *Women in Business* 49, No. 1 (January–February 1997), p. 6.

45. D.J. Brass, K.D. Butterfield, and B.C. Skaggs, "Relationships and Unethical Behavior: A Social Network Perspective," *Academy of Management Review* 23, No. 1 (1998) pp. 14–31.

46. T.B. Becker, "Integrity in Organizations: Beyond Honesty and Conscientiousness," *Academy of Management Review* 23, No. 1, pp. 154–61.

47. J. Vidal, "The Real Politics of Power (Growing Power of Large Corporations; Excerpt from McLibel: Burger Culture on Trial; Society)," *The Guardian* (April 30, 1997), pp. 54–55.

48. R. Barrett, "Liberating the Corporate Soul," *HR Focus* 74, No. 4 (April 1997), pp. 15–16.

49. J.M. Schrof, "No Whining! (Profile of Talk Show Host Laura Schlessinger)," *US News & World Report* 123, No. 2 (July 14, 1997), pp. 48–53.

50. Business Bulletin, "A Special Background Report on Trends in Industry and Finance," *The Wall Street Journal*, April 17, 1997, p. B1.

51. S.G. Scott and V.R. Lane, "A Stakeholder Approach to Organizational Identity," *Academy of Management Review* 25, No. 1 (2000) pp. 43–62.

52. S. Berman, A.C. Wicks, S. Kotha, and T.M. Jones, "Does Stakeholder Orientation Matter? The Relationship Between Stakeholder Management Models and Firm Financial Performance," *Academy of Management Journal* 42, No. 5, pp. 488–506.

53. "Liars Index," *The Wall Street Journal*, February 1, 2000, p. A1.

54. "Lying for the Boss," *The Wall Street Journal*, November 30, 1999, p. A1.

55. J.F. Harrison and R.E. Freeman, "Stakeholders, Social Responsibility, and Performance: Empirical Evidence and Theoretical Perspectives," *Academy of Management Journal* 42, No. 5 (1999), pp. 479–85.

56. S. Berman, A.C. Wicks, S. Kotha, and T.M. Jones, "Does Stakeholder Orientation Matter? The Relationship Between Stakeholder Management Models and Firm Financial Performance," *Academy of Management Journal* 42, No. 5, pp. 488–506.

57. L.A. Gjertsen, "Future of Insurance Relies on Ethics (How Insurance Companies Can Encourage Ethical Behavior in Employees)," *National Underwriter Property & Casualty—Risk & Benefits Management* 101, No. 24 (June 16, 1997), pp. 9–10.

58. "Most Companies Consider (Ethics Codes Important But Few Back Them Up)," *The Wall Street Journal*, May 14, 1996, p. A1.

59. G.R. Weaver, L.K. Trevino, and P.L. Cochran, "Corporate Ethics Programs as Control Systems: Influences of Executive Commitment and Environmental Factors," *Academy of Management Journal* 42, No. 1 (1999), pp. 41–57.

60. W. Bounds, "Critics Confront CEO Dedicated to Human Rights," *The Wall Street Journal*, February 24, 1997, p. B1.

61. B. Heller, "Growing Pains: APOR to Explore Ethics, Standardization (Association for Pharmacoeconomics and Outcomes Researches Major Objectives for 1997)," *Drug Topics* 141, No. 10 (May 19, 1997), p. 47.

62. D. Lempert, "Holding Accountable the Powers That Be: Protecting Our Integrity and the Public We Serve," *Public Administration Review* 57, No. 4 (July–August 1997), pp. 11–4.

63. S.L. Robinson and A.M. O'Leary-Kelly, "Monkey See, Monkey Do: The Influence of Work Groups on the Antisocial Behavior of Employees," *Academy of Management Journal* 41, No. 6, (1998), pp. 658–72.

64. D. Carnegie, "Human Relations Skills Provide Entrepreneurial Breadth," *Training* 34, No. 4 (1997), p. 53.

65. "How Do You Rate as a CyberManager," *The Wall Street Journal*, May 28, 1996, p. B1.

66. D.C. Menzel, "Teaching Ethics and Values in Public Administration: Are We Making a Difference?" *Public Administration Review* 57, No. 3 (May–June 1997), pp. 224–30.

67. G.R. Weaver, L.K. Trevino, and P.L. Cochran, "Corporate Ethics Programs as Control Systems: Influences of Executive Commitment and Environmental Factors," *Academy of Management Journal* 42, No. 1 (1999), pp. 41–57.

68. A. Tenbrunsel, "Misrepresentation and Expectations of Misrepresentation in an Ethical Dilemma: The Role of Incentives and Temptation," *Academy of Management Journal* 41, No. 3 (1998), pp. 330–39.

69. P.S. Ridge, "Ethics Programs Aren't Stemming Employee Misconduct, a Study Indicates," *The Wall Street Journal*, May 11, 2000, p. A1.

70. R.A. Baron and G.D. Markman, "Beyond Social Capital: How Social Skills Can Enhance Entrepreneurs' Success," *Academy of Management Executive* 14, No. 1 (2000), p. 106–8.

71. Ibid.

72. Lancaster, Managing Your Career, "Start Listening," *The Wall Street Journal*, p. B1.

73. M. Lynn, "How to Manage Your Boss," *Management Today*, January 2000, p. 66.

74. "Blind Devotion Wanted?" *The Wall Street Journal*, July 22, 1997, p. A1.

75. M. Lynn, "How to Manage Your Boss," *Management Today* (January 2000), p. 66.

76. Ibid.

77. Managing Your Career, "You Can Be Good at Office Politics without Being a Jerk," *The Wall Street Journal*, March 18, 1997, p. B1.

78. H. Lancaster, Managing Your Career, "Pick Your Fights before Going Over Your Boss's Head," *The Wall Street Journal*, June 17, 1997, p. B1.

79. M. Lynn, "How to Manage Your Boss," *Management Today*, January 2000, p. 66.

80. C.S. Grizzard Sr., "Family Values at Work," *Fund Raising Management* 27, No. 8 (October 1996), p. 48.

81. M. Lynn, "How to Manage Your Boss," *Management Today*, January 2000, p. 66.

82. Lancaster, "Managing Your Career, Start Listening," *The Wall Street Journal*, p. B1.

83. D.L. Swanson, "Toward an Integrative Theory of Business and Society: A Research Strategy for Corporate Social Performance," *Academy of Management Review* 24, No. 3 (1999), pp. 506–21.

84. T. O'Toole and B. Donaldson, "Relationship Governance Structures and Performance," *Journal of Marketing Management* 16, No. 4 (May 2000), p. 327.

85. Managing Your Career, "You Can Be Good at Office Politics without Being a Jerk," *The Wall Street Journal*, March 18, 1997, p. B1.

86. Lancaster, Managing Your Career, "Start Listening," *The Wall Street Journal*, p. B1.

87. T. O'Toole and B. Donaldson, "Relationship Governance Structures and Performance," *Journal of Marketing Management* 16, No. 4 (May 2000), p. 327.

88. B. Kotey and G.G Meredith, "Relationships among Owner/Manager Personal Values, Business Strategies and Enterprise Performance," *Journal of Small Business Management* 35, No. 2 (April 1997), pp. 37–65.

CHAPTER 10

1. Lussier, "Management," p. 419.

2. Ibid.

3. B.L. Kirkman and B. Rosen, "Beyond Self-Management: Antecedents and Consequences of Team Empowerment," *Academy of Management Journal* 42, No. 1 (1999), pp. 58–74.

4. P.R. Earley and E. Mosakowski, "Creating Hybrid Team Cultures: An Empirical Test of Transnational Team Functioning," *Academy of Management Journal* 43, No. 1 (2000), pp. 26–49.

5. J.R. Hollenbeck, D.R. Ilgen, J.A. LePine, J.A. Colquitt, and J. Hedlund, "Extending the Multilevel Theory of Team Decision Making: Effects of Feedback and Experience in Hierarchical Teams," *Academy of Management Journal* 41, No. 3 (1998), pp. 269–82.

6. M.J. Waller, "The Timing of Adaptive Group Responses to Non-Routine Events," *Academy of Management Journal* 42, No. 2 (1999), pp. 127–37.

7. Mirvis, "Human Resource Management," pp. 43–56.

8. H. Lancaster, Managing Your Career, "That Team Spirit Can Lead Your Career to New Victories," *The Wall Street Journal*, January 14, 1997, p. B1.

9. S. Divita, "Behavior, Not Experience, Guides Productivity," *Marketing News* 31, No. 6 (March 17, 1997), p. 4.

10. T.R. Zenger and C.R. Marshall, "Determinants of Incentive Intensity in Group-Based Rewards," *Academy of Management Journal* 43, No. 2 (2000), pp. 149–63.

11. Work Week, "A Special News Report About Life on the Job—And Trends Taking Shape There," *The Wall Street Journal*, May 28, 1996, p. B1.

12. A. Hendershot, "How We Brought Teamwork to Marketing, Manager's Journal," *The Wall Street Journal*, August 26, 1996, p. B1.

13. Work Week, "A Special News Report About Life on the Job—And Trends Taking Shape There," *The Wall Street Journal*, May 28, 1996, p. B1.

14. "Chrysler Is Expecting to Announce that Thousands of Cost Savings Ideas Will Boost 1997 Profit by $325 Million," *The Wall Street Journal*, June 5, 1997, p. A1.

15. V.D. Arnold and R.H. Krapels, "Motivation: A Reincarnation of Ideas," *Industrial Management* 38, No. 3 (May–June 1996), pp. 8–9.

16. G.L. Stewart and M.R. Barrick, "Team Structure and Performance: Assessing the Mediating Role of Intrateam Process and the Moderating Role of Task Type," *Academy of Management Journal* 43, No. 2 (2000), pp. 135–148.

17. B.L. Kirkman and B. Rosen, "Beyond Self-Management: Antecedents and Consequences of Team Empowerment," *Academy of Management Journal* 42, No. 1 (1999), pp. 58–74.

18. M.J. Waller, "The Timing of Adaptive Group Responses to Non-Routine Events," *Academy of Management Journal* 42, No. 2 (1999), pp. 127–37.

19. H. Lancaster, Managing Your Career, "That Team Spirit Can Lead Your Career to New Victories," *The Wall Street Journal*, January 14, 1997, p. B1.

20. B.L. Kirkman and B. Rosen, "Beyond Self-Management: Antecedents and Consequences of Team Empowerment," *Academy of Management Journal* 42, No. 1 (1999), pp. 58–74.

21. R.S. Dooley and G.E. Fryxell, "Attaining Decision Quality and Commitment From Dissent: The Moderating Effects of Loyalty and Competence in Strategic Decision-Making Terms," *Academy of Management Journal* 42, No. 4 (1999), pp. 389–402.

22. A.R. Jassawalla and H.C. Sashittal, "Building Collaborative Cross-Functional New Product Teams," *Academy of Management Executive* 13, No. 3 (1998), pp. 50–63.

23. "The Excellent Files," Public Television program viewed September 2, 1997.

24. H. Lancaster, Managing Your Career, "That Team Spirit Can Lead Your Career to New Victories," *The Wall Street Journal*, January 14, 1997, p. B1.

25. A. Edmondson, "Psychological Safety and Learning Behavior in Work Teams," *Administrative Science Quarterly* 44, pp. 350–83.

26. M. Uhl-Bien and G.B. Graen, "Individual Self-Management: Analysis of Professionals' Self-Managing Activities in Functional and Cross-Functional Work teams," *Academy of Management Journal* 41, No. 3 (1998), pp. 340–50.

27. "Good Teamwork Merits a Team Bonus, Right? Not Necessarily," *The Wall Street Journal*, February 6, 1997, p. A1.

28. A. Edmondson, "Psychological Safety and Learning Behavior in Work Teams," *Administrative Science Quarterly* 44, pp. 350–83.

29. G. McNamara and P. Bromily, "Risk and Return in Organizational Decision Making," *Academy of Management Journal* 42, No. 3 (1999), pp. 330–39.

30. P.C. Nutt, "Surprising But True: Half the Decisions in Organizations Fail," *Academy of Management Executive* 13, No. 4 (1999), pp. 75–90.

31. T. Petlinger, "So Long Supply and Demand," *The Wall Street Journal*, January 1, 2000, p. R31.

32. "Decisions Go Sour," *The Wall Street Journal*, June 25, 1996, p. A1.

33. K.D. Elsbach and G. Elofson, "How the Packaging of Decision Explanations Affects Perceptions of Trustworthiness," *Academy of Management Journal* 43, No. 1 (2000), pp. 80–89.

34. L.A. Burke and M.K. Miller, "Taking the Mystery Out of Intuitive Decision Making." *Academy of Management Executive* 13, No. 4 (1999), pp. 91–9.

35. A. Bird, "The Ten Commandments of SuperCommunity Banking," *The Bankers Magazine* 180, No. 1 (January–February 1997), pp. 12–19.

36. L.A. Burke and M.K. Miller, "Taking the Mystery Out of Intuitive Decision Making." *Academy of Management Executive* 13, No. 4 (1999), pp. 91–9.

37. P.C. Nutt, "Surprising But True: Half the Decisions in Organizations Fail," *Academy of Management Executive* 13, No. 4 (1999), pp. 75–90.

38. D. Lynch, "Unresolved Conflicts Affect the Bottom Line," *HR Magazine* 42, No. 5 (May 1997), pp. 49–50.

39. P.C. Nutt, "Surprising But True: Half the Decisions in Organizations Fail," *Academy of Management Executive* 13, No. 4 (1999), pp. 75–90.

40. Ibid

41. L.A. Burke and M.K. Miller, "Taking the Mystery Out of Intuitive Decision Making." *Academy of Management Executive* 13, No. 4 (1999), pp. 91–9.

42. R. Harborne, "Wisdom of the CEO: The Challenge to Business Leadership in the 21st Century," keynote presentation at the New England Business Administration

Association International Conference, Southern Connecticut State University, April 28, 2000, Price Waterhouse Coopers.

43. "Be Creative Now! (Companies Try to Inspire Creativity in a Leaner Workplace)," *The Wall Street Journal*, June 13, 1996, p. A1.

44. M.A. Glynn, "Innovative Genius: A Framework for Relating Individual and Organizational Intelligences to Innovation," *Academy of Management Review* 21, No. 4 (October 1996), pp. 1081.

45. T. McEwen, "Communication Training in Corporate Settings: Lessons and Opportunities for the Academy," *Mid-American Journal of Business* 12, No. 1 (Spring 1997), pp. 49–58.

46. "Mind Field," *The Wall Street Journal*, July 9, 1997, p. A1.

47. Business Bulletin, "A Special Background Report on Trends in Industry and Finance," *The Wall Street Journal*, May 1, 1997, p. B1.

48. "Mind Field," *The Wall Street Journal*, July 9, 1997, p. A1.

49. E.J. Van Slyke, "Facilitating Productive Conflict," *HR Focus* 74, No. 4 (April 1997), pp. 17–8.

50. T. Petzinger Jr., "How Creativity Can Take Wing Act Edge of Chaos, The Front Lines," *The Wall Street Journal*, October 18, 1996, p. B1.

51. S. Berglas, "Boom! There's Nothing Wrong with You or Your Business That a Little Conflict Wouldn't Cure," *Inc.* 19, No. 6 (May 1997), pp. 56–8.

52. J.R. Hollenbeck, D.R. Ilgen, J.A. LePine, J.A. Colquitt, and J. Hedlund, "Extending the Multilevel Theory of Team Decision Making: Effects of Feedback and Experience in Hierarchical Teams," *Academy of Management Journal* 41, No. 3 (1998), pp. 269–82.

53. R.L. Papiernik, "David Novak: The Pizza Hut/ KFC Quarterback Builds a Better Team on His Drive to Fast-Food Touchdown," *Nation's Restaurant News* 31, No. 4 (January 1997), pp. 170–1.

54. B. Schlender, "Cool Companies," *Fortune* 136, No. 1 (July 7, 1997), pp. 84–99.

55. T.R. Zenger and C.R. Marshall, "Determinants of Incentive Intensity in Group-Based Rewards," *Academy of Management Journal* 43, No. 2 (2000), pp. 149–63.

56. A. Bird, "The Ten Commandments of SuperCommunity Banking," *The Bankers Magazine* 180, No. 1 (January–February 1997), pp. 12–9.

57. R.S. Dooley and G.E. Fryxell, "Attaining Decision Quality and Commitment From Dissent: The Moderating Effects of Loyalty and Competence in Strategic Decision-Making Terms," *Academy of Management Journal* 42, No. 4 (1999), pp. 389–402.

58. M.J. Waller, "The Timing of Adaptive Group Responses to Non-Routine Events," *Academy of Management Journal* 42, No. 2 (1999), pp. 127–37.

59. "Microsoft Set Up a New Top Decision-Making Group and Shifted Responsibilities of Two Rising Stars," *The Wall Street Journal*, December 4, 1996, p. A1.

60. T. Petlinger, "So Long Supply and Demand," *The Wall Street Journal*, January 1, 2000, p. R31.

61. P.C. Nutt, "Surprising But True: Half the Decisions in Organizations Fail," *Academy of Management Executive* 13, No. 4 (1999), pp. 75–90.

62. K.D. Elsbach and G. Elofson, "How the Packaging of Decision Explanations Affects Perceptions of Trustworthiness," *Academy of Management Journal* 43, No. 1 (2000), pp. 80–9.

63. T.R. Zenger and C.R. Marshall, "Determinants of Incentive Intensity in Group-Based Rewards," *Academy of Management Journal* 43, No. 2 (2000), pp. 149–63.

64. K.D. Elsbach and G. Elofson, "How the Packaging of Decision Explanations Affects Perceptions of Trustworthiness," *Academy of Management Journal* 43, No. 1 (2000), pp. 80–9.

65. P.C. Nutt, "Surprising But True: Half the Decisions in Organizations Fail," *Academy of Management Executive* 13, No. 4 (1999), pp. 75–90.

66. Ibid.

67. Ibid.

68. K.D. Elsbach and G. Elofson, "How the Packaging of Decision Explanations Affects Perceptions of Trustworthiness," *Academy of Management Journal* 43, No. 1 (2000), pp. 80–9.

69. "How Situational Leadership Fits into Today's Organizations," *Supervisory Management* 41, No. 2 (February 1996), pp. 1–3.

70. Ibid.

71. K.D. Elsbach and G. Elofson, "How the Packaging of Decision Explanations Affects Perceptions of Trustworthiness," *Academy of Management Journal* 43, No. 1 (2000), pp. 80–9.

72. "How Situational Leadership Fits into Today's Organizations," *Supervisory Management* 41, No. 2 (February 1996), pp. 1–3.

CHAPTER 11

1. S.M. Puffer, "Continental Airlines' CEO Gordon Bethume on Teams and New Product Development," *Academy of Management Executive* 13, No. 3 (1999), pp. 28–35.

2. Lussier, "Management," p. 419.

3. G.L. Stewart and M.R. Barrick, "Team Structure and Performance: Assessing the Mediating Role of Intrateam Process and the Moderating Role of Task Type," *Academy of Management Journal* 43, No. 2 (2000), pp. 135–48.

4. "Good Teamwork Merits a Team Bonus, Right? Not Necessarily," *The Wall Street Journal*, February 6, 1997, p. A1.

5. K.A. Smith-Jentsch, E. Salas, and D.P. Baker, "Training Team Performance-Related Assertiveness," *Personal Psychology* 49, No. 4 (Winter 1996), pp. 909–36.

6. P. Chattopadhyay, "Beyond Direct and Symmetrical Effects: The influence of Demographic Dissimilarity on Organizational Citizenship Behavior," *Academy of Management Journal* 42, No. 3 (1999), pp. 273–87.

7. T. Petlinger, "So Long Supply and Demand," *The Wall Street Journal*, January 1, 2000, p. R31.

8. G.R. Jones and J.M. George, "The Experience and Evolution of Trust: Implications for Cooperation and Teamwork," *Academy of Management Review* 23, No. 3 (1998), pp. 531–46.

9. T.L. Simons and R.S. Peterson, "Task Conflict and Relationship Conflict in Top Management Teams: The Pivotal Role of Intragroup Trust," *Journal of Applied Psychology* 85, No. 1 (2000), pp. 102–11.

10. G. Labianca, D.J. Brass, and B. Gray, "Social Networks and Perceptions of Intergroup Conflict: The Role of Negative Relationships and Third Parties," *Academy of Management Journal* 41, No. 1 (1998), pp. 55–67.

11. J. Wallace Bishop, and K. Dow Scott, "How Commitment Affects Team Performance," *HR Magazine* 42, No. 2 (February 1997), pp. 107–11.

12. K.A. Smith-Jentsch, E. Salas, and D.P. Baker, "Training Team Performance-Related Assertiveness," *Personal Psychology* 49, No. 4 (Winter 1996), pp. 909–36.

13. R.T. Sparrowe and R.C. Liden, "Process and Structure in Leader-Member Exchange," *Academy of Management Exchange* 22, No. 2 (April 1997), pp. 522–52.

14. Work Week, "A Special News Report About Life on the Job—And Trends Taking Shape There," *The Wall Street Journal*, May 28, 1996, p. A1.

15. Mirvis, "Human Resource Management," pp. 43–56.

16. B. Gates, "My Advice to Students: Get a Sound, Broad, Education," *The Costco Connection* (February, 1999), p. 13.

17. Lussier, "Management," p. 419.

18. T. McEwen, "Communication Training in Corporate Settings: Lessons and Opportunities for the Academy," *Mid-American Journal of Business* 12, No. 1 (Spring 1997), pp. 49–58.

19. K.A. Smith-Jentsch, E. Salas, and D.P. Baker, "Training Team Performance-Related Assertiveness," *Personal Psychology* 49, No. 4 (Winter 1996), pp. 909–36.

20. T.L. Simons and R.S. Peterson, "Task Conflict and Relationship Conflict in Top Management Teams: The Pivotal Role of Intragroup Trust," *Journal of Applied Psychology* 85, No. 1 (2000), pp. 102–111.

21. J. Wallace Bishop and K. Dow Scott, "How Commitment Affects Team Performance," *HR Magazine* 42, No. 2 (February 1997), pp. 107–11.

22. Lussier, "Management" p. 419.

23. R. Forrester and A.B. Drexler, "A Model for Team-Based Organization Performance," *Academy of Management Executive* 13, No. 3 (1998), pp. 36–49.

24. P. Chattopadhyay, "Beyond Direct and Symmetrical Effects: The influence of Demographic Dissimilarity on Organizational Citizenship Behavior," *Academy of Management Journal* 42, No. 3 (1999), pp. 273–87.

25. T.R. Zenger and C.R. Marshall, "Determinants of Incentive Intensity in Group-Based Rewards," *Academy of Management Journal* 43, No. 2 (2000), pp. 149–63.

26. D. Stamps, "Communities of Practice," *Training* 34, No. 2 (February 1997), pp. 34–42.

27. S.L. Robinson and A.M. O'Leary-Kelly, "Monkey See, Monkey Do: The Influence of Work Groups on the Antisocial Behavior of Employees," *Academy of Management Journal* 41, No. 6, (1998), pp. 658–72.

28. J. Wallace Bishop and K. Dow Scott, "How Commitment Affects Team Performance," *HR Magazine* 42, No. 2 (February 1997), pp. 107–11.

29. P.P. Shah, "Who Are Employees' Social Referents? Using a Network Perspective to Determine Referent Others," *Academy of Management Journal* 41, No. 3 (1998), pp. 249–68.

30. P.R. Earley and E. Mosakowski, "Creating Hybrid Team Cultures: An Empirical Test of Transnational Team Functioning," *Academy of Management Journal* 43, No. 1 (2000), pp. 26–49.

31. R.T. Sparrowe and R.C. Liden, "Process and Structure in Leader-Member Exchange," *Academy of Management Exchange* 22, No. 2 (April 1997), pp. 522–53.

32. B.L. Kirkman and B. Rosen, "Beyond Self-Management: Antecedents and Consequences of Team Empowerment," *Academy of Management Journal* 42, No. 1 (1999), pp. 58–74.

33. J. Wallace Bishop and K. Dow Scott, "How Commitment Affects Team Performance," *HR Magazine* 42, No. 2 (February 1997), pp. 107–11.

34. P.R. Earley and E. Mosakowski, "Creating Hybrid Team Cultures: An Empirical Test of Transnational Team Functioning," *Academy of Management Journal* 43, No. 1 (2000), pp. 26–49.

35. T. Petzinger, "Peter Drucker: The 'Arch-Guru of Capitalism' Argues that We Need a New Economic Theory and a New Management Model," *The Wall Street Journal*, January 1, 2000, p. R34.

36. K. Aquino, S.L. Grover, M. Bradford, and D.G. Allen, "The Effects of Negative Affectivity, Hierarchival Status, and Self-Determination on Workplace Victimization," *Academy of Management Journal* 42, No. 2 (1999), pp. 260–72.

37. J.R. Hollenbeck, D.R. Ilgen, J.A. LePine, J.A. Colquitt, and J. Hedlund, "Extending the Multilevel Theory of Team Decision Making: Effects of Feedback and Experience in Hierarchical Teams," *Academy of Management Journal* 41, No. 3 (1998), pp. 269–82.

38. R.T. Sparrowe and Robert C. Liden, "Process and Structure in Leader-Member Exchange," *Academy of Management Exchange* 22, No. 2 (April 1997), pp. 522–53.

39. N. Grund, "From Sage To Artisan: The Many Roles of the Value-Driven Leader," *Academy of Management Executive* 11, No. 2 (February 1997), pp. 94–95.

40. Bender, "Frustrated with Work Relationships," pp. 8(1).

41. N Grund, "From Sage to Artisan: The Many Roles of the Value-Driven Leader," *Academy of Management Executive* 11, No. 2 (February 1997), pp. 94–95.

42. Hal Lancaster, "Managing Your Career, 'That Team Spirit Can Lead Your Career to New Victories', " *The Wall Street Journal*, January 14, 1997, p. B1.

43. C.B. Gibson, "Do They Do What They Believe They Can? Group Efficacy and Group Effectiveness Across Tasks and Cultures," *Academy of Management Journal* 42, No. 2 (1999), pp. 138–52.

44. R.B. Lacoursiere, *The Life Cycle of Groups: Group Development Stage Theory* (New York: Human Service Press, 1980).

45. B.L. Kirkman and B. Rosen, "Beyond Self-Management: Antecedents and Consequences of Team Empowerment," *Academy of Management Journal* 42, No. 1 (1999), pp. 58–74.

46. N. Grund, "From Sage to Artisan: The Many Roles of the Value-Driven Leader," *Academy of Management Executive* 11, No. 2 (February 1997), pp. 94–95.

47. *The Excellent Files*, 1997.

48. J.W. Bishop and K.D. Scott, "How Commitment Affects Team Performance," *HR Magazine* 42, No. 2 (February 1997), pp. 107–11.

49. L. Cole and M.S. Cole, "Teamwork is Spelled Incorrectly Teamwork = Communication," *Communication World* 17, No. 4 (2000) p. 56.

50. J.W. Bishop and K.D Scott, "How Commitment Affects Team Performance," *HR Magazine* 42, No. 2 (February 1997), pp. 107–11.

51. T.L. Simons and R.S. Peterson, "Task Conflict and Relationship Conflict in Top Management Teams: The Pivotal Role of Intragroup Trust," *Journal of Applied Psychology* 85, No. 1 (2000), pp. 102–11.

52. C.S. Frings, "Managing Meetings Effectively," *Medical Laboratory Observer* 32, No. 6 (2000), p. 34.

53. G.L. Stewart and M.R. Barrick, "Team Structure and Performance: Assessing the Mediating Role of Intrateam Process and the Moderating Role of Task Type," *Academy of Management Journal* 43, No. 2 (2000), pp. 135–48.

54. B. Orton, "Meetings: Entrepreneur Style," *Los Angeles Business Journal* 22, No. 26 (2000), p. 60.

55. C.S. Frings, "Managing Meetings Effectively," *Medical Laboratory Observer* 32, No. 6 (2000), p. 34.

56. B. Orton, "Meetings: Entrepreneur Style," *Los Angeles Business Journal* 22, No. 26 (2000), p. 60.

57. C.S. Frings, "Managing Meetings Effectively," *Medical Laboratory Observer* 32, No. 6 (2000), p. 34.

58. T. McEwen, "Communication Training in Corporate Settings: Lessons and Opportunities for the Academy," Mid-American Journal of Business 12, No. 1 (Spring 1997), pp. 49–58.

59. B. Orton, "Meetings: Entrepreneur Style," *Los Angeles Business Journal* 22, No. 26 (2000), p. 60.

60. C.S. Frings, "Managing Meetings Effectively," *Medical Laboratory Observer* 32, No. 6 (2000), p. 34.

61. "The Perfect Meeting May Be the One that Never Takes Place," The Wall Street Journal, August 22, 1996, p. A1.

62. C.S. Frings, "Managing Meetings Effectively," *Medical Laboratory Observer* 32, No. 6 (2000), p. 34.

63. B. Orton, "Meetings: Entrepreneur Style," *Los Angeles Business Journal* 22, No. 26 (2000), p. 60.

64. C.S. Frings, "Managing Meetings Effectively," *Medical Laboratory Observer* 32, No. 6 (2000), p. 34.

65. B. Orton, "Meetings: Entrepreneur Style," *Los Angeles Business Journal* 22, No. 26 (2000), p. 60.

66. C.S. Frings, "Managing Meetings Effectively," *Medical Laboratory Observer* 32, No. 6 (2000), p. 34.

67. B. Orton, "Meetings: Entrepreneur Style," *Los Angeles Business Journal* 22, No. 26 (2000), p. 60.

68. C.S. Frings, "Managing Meetings Effectively," *Medical Laboratory Observer* 32, No. 6 (2000), p. 34.

69. Ibid.

70. The Excellent Files, 1997.

71. M. Finley, "Subduing the Loudmouth: How to Keep Dominating People from Dominating Meetings," *Manage* 44, No. 3 (1993), pp. 7–9.

72. Ibid.

73. Ibid.

74. D. Hodson, "A Penny for Your Thoughts," *The Wall Street Journal*, June 17, 1997, p. A1.

75. T. McEwen, "Communication Training in Corporate Settings: Lessons and Opportunities for the Academy," *Mid-American Journal of Business* 12, No. 1 (1997), pp. 49–58.

76. D.I. Jung and B.J. Avolio, "Effects of Leadership Style and Followers' Cultural Orientation on Performance in Group and Individual Task Conditions," *Academy of Management Journal* 42, No. 2 (1999), pp. 208–18.

CHAPTER 12

1. A. Rercens, J. Wanous, and J. Austin, "Understanding and Managing Cynisism About Organizational Change," *Academy of Management Executive* 11, No. 1 (1997), pp. 48–58.

2. R. Quick, "A Makeover That Began at the Top," *The Wall Street Journal*, May 25, 2000, p. B1.

3. B. Mullins and B. Mullins, "Coaching Winners," *Canadian Insurance* 99, No. 1 (1994), p. 34.

4. *The Excellent Files*, 1997.

5. A.J. Hoffman, "Institutional Evolution and Change: Environmentalism and the U.S. Chemical Industry," *Academy of Management Journal* 42, No. 4 (1999), pp. 351–71.

6. "Learning to Lead," *Business Week*, October 18, 1999, pp. 76–77.

7. T. Petzinger Jr., "How Creativity Can Take Wing Act Edge of Chaos," "The Front Lines," *The Wall Street Journal*, October 18, 1996, p. B1.

8. E.W. Morrison and C.C. Phelps, "Taking Charge at Work: Extrarole Efforts to Initiate Workplace Change," *Academy of Management Journal* 42, No. 4 (1999), pp. 403–19.

9. T. Mroczkowski and Masao Hanaoka, "Effective Right Sizing Strategies in Japan and America: Is There A Convergence of Employment?" *Academy of Management Executive* 11, No. 1 (1997), pp. 57–67.

10. *The Excellent Files*, 1997.

11. D.L. Wiley, "Recommended Reading," *Online* 24, Iss. 4 (2000), p. 101.

12. T. Mroczkowski and Masao Hanaoka, "Effective Right Sizing Strategies in Japan and America: Is There a Convergence of Employment?" *Academy of Management Executive* 11, No. 1 (1997), pp. 57–67.

13. A.J. Hoffman, "Institutional Evolution and Change: Environmentalism and the U.S. Chemical Industry," *Academy of Management Journal* 42, No. 4 (1999), pp. 351–71.

14. R. Harborne, "Wisdom of the CEO: The Challenge to Business Leadership in the 21st Century," keynote presentation at the New England Business Administration Association International Conference, Southern Connecticut State University, April 28, 2000, Price Waterhouse Coopers.

15. L. Hirschhorn and L. May, "The Campaign Approach to Change," *Change* 32, No. 3 (2000), p. 31.

16. J. Nirenberg, *Power Tools* (Upper Saddle River, NJ: Prentice Hall, 1997).

17. "Learning to Lead," *Business Week*, October 18, 1999, pp. 76–77.

18. J. Nirenberg, *Power Tools* (Upper Saddle River, NJ: Prentice Hall, 1997).

19. L. Goff, "Building Blocks to Managing Change," *Computerworld*, February 14, 2000, p. 54.

20. *The Excellent Files*, 1997

21. R. Quick, "A Makeover That Began at the Top," *The Wall Street Journal*, May 25, 2000, p. B1.

22. "Learning to Lead," *Business Week*, October 18, 1999, pp. 76–77.

23. "Dream On, Kid," *The Wall Street Journal*, October 12, 1999, p. A1.

24. M. Haseltine, "What Competition Means to You," *Management Today*, July 28, 1999, p. 28.

25. J. Nirenberg, "Overcoming Hammurabi's Curse," *Old Practitioner* 30, No. 1 (1998), pp. 6–14.

26. Ibid.

27. J. Campbell Quick and J.H. Gavin, "The Next Frontier: Edgar Schein on Organizational Therapy," *Academy of Management Executive* 14. No. 1 (2000), pp. 31–32.

28. J. Nirenberg, "Overcoming Hammurabi's Curse," *Old Practitioner* 30, No. 1 (1998), pp. 6–14.

29. N. Fitzgerald, "Real Investment," *CA Magazine* 101, No. 1088 (1997), pp. 58–60.

30. K. Hultman, *The Path of Least Resistance* (Austin, Tex.: Learning Concepts, 1979).

31. J. Nirenberg, "Overcoming Hammurabi's Curse," *Old Practitioner* 30, No. 1 (1998), pp. 6–14.

32. Ibid.

33. N. Fitzgerald, "Real Investment," *CA Magazine* 101, No. 1088 (1997), pp. 58–60.

34. Ibid.

35. L. Goff, "Building Blocks to Managing Change," *Computerworld*, February 14, 2000, p. 54.

36. J. Nirenberg, *Power Tools* (Upper Saddle River, NJ: Prentice Hall, 1997).

37. Ibid.

38. Ibid.

39. N. Fitzgerald, "Real Investment," *CA Magazine* 101, No. 1088 (1997), pp. 58–60.

40. J.P. Kotter, "Managing: Ideas & Solutions," *Fortune*, August 5, 1996, pp. 168–70.

41. L. Hirschhorn and L. May, "The Campaign Approach to Change," *Change* 32, No. 3 (2000), p. 31.

42. L. Goff, "Building Blocks to Managing Change," *Computerworld,* February 14, 2000, p. 54.

43. J. Campbell Quick and J.H. Gavin, "The Next Frontier: Edgar Schein on Organizational Therapy," *Academy of Management Executive* 14, No. 1 (2000), pp. 31–32.

44. J.P. Kotter, "Managing: Ideas & Solutions," *Fortune,* August 5, 1996, pp. 168–170.

45. J. Nirenberg, "Overcoming Hammurabi's Curse," *Old Practitioner* 30, No. 1 (1998), pp. 6–14.

46. Ibid.

47. "Dream On, Kid," *The Wall Street Journal,* October 12, 1999, p. A1.

48. J.P. Kotter, "Managing: Ideas & Solutions," *Fortune,* August 5, 1996, pp. 168–170.

49. *The Excellent Files,* 1997

50. A. Brown, "Transforming Business Structures to Hyborgs," *Employment Relations Weekly* 26, No. 4 (2000), pp. 5–15.

51. M. Beer and N. Nohria, "Cracking the Code of Change," *Harvard Business Review* 78, No. 3 (2000), p. 133.

52. R.L. Simison, "Ford Rolls Out New Model of Corporate Culture," *The Wall Street Journal,* January 13, 1999, p. B1.

53. "Daily Grind," *The Wall Street Journal,* March 2, 1999, p. A1.

54. D.L. Wiley, "Recommended Reading," *Online* 24, No. 4 (2000), p. 101.

55. P. Senge, A. Kleiner, C. Roberts, R. Ross, G. Roth, and B. Smith, *The Dance of Change: The Challenges to Sustaining Momentum in Learning Organizations* (Currency Doubleday, 1999).

56. R.L. Simison, "Ford Rolls Out New Model of Corporate Culture," *The Wall Street Journal,* January 13, 1999, p. B1.

57. T. Petlinger, "So Long Supply and Demand," *The Wall Street Journal,* January 1, 2000, p. R31.

58. J.A. Gilbert and J.M. Ivancevich, "Valuing Diversity: A Tale of Two Organizations," *Academy of Management Executive* 14, No. 1 (2000), p. 93.

59. L.E. Winter, "Companies Try a New Tool to Bring Diversity Home," *The Wall Street Journal,* January 6, 1999, p. B1.

60. "Daily Grind," *The Wall Street Journal,* March 2, 1999, p. A1.

61. J. Pfeffer and J.F. Veiga, "Putting People First for Organizational Success," *Academy of Management Executive* 13, No. 2 (1999), pp. 37–48.

62. J.A. DeFeo, "Be a Six Sigma Leader!" *MG Webzine* (www.mgeneral.com) July 2, 2000 issue.

63. A. Fusco, "Translating TQM into TQS," *Quality Progress* 27, Iss. 5, May 1994, pp. 105–8.

64. H. Lancaster, "Managing Your Career," *The Wall Street Journal,* September 14, 1999, p. B1.

65. *The Excellent Files,* 1997

66. J. Kendrick, "Study Looks at TQM," *Quality* 32, No. 5 (1993), p. 13.

67. J.A. DeFeo, "Be a Six Sigma Leader!" *MG Webzine* (www.mgeneral.com) July 2000 issue.

68. Ibid.

69. H. Lancaster, "Managing Your Career," *The Wall Street Journal,* September 14, 1999, p. B1.

70. Ibid.

71. J.A. DeFeo, "Be a Six Sigma Leader!" *MG Webzine* (www.mgeneral.com) July 2000 issue.

72. H. Lancaster, "Managing Your Career," *The Wall Street Journal,* September 14, 1999, p. B1.

73. Ibid.

74. J. Ang, S. Koh, "Exploring the Relationships between User Information Satisfaction and Job Satisfaction," *International Journal of Information Management* 17, No. 3 (June 1997), pp. 169–77.

75. J. Ang, S. Koh, "Exploring the Relationships Between User Information Satisfaction and Job Satisfaction," *International Journal of Information Management* 17, No. 3 (June 1997), pp. 169–77.

76. *The Excellent Files,* 1997.

77. R. Blake and J. Mouton, *The Managerial Grid III: Key to Leadership Excellence* (Houston: Gulf Publishing, 1985).

78. S. Shellenbarger, "More Managers Find a Happy Staff Leads to Happy Customers," *The Wall Street Journal,* March 2, 1998, p. B1.

79. *The Excellent Files,* 1997.

80. F. Whaley, "Shooting For Success: Staff Break Communication Barriers—By Firing Lasers at Each Other," *Asian Business Weekly* 26, No. 2 (2000), p. 48.

CHAPTER 13

1. "The EEOC Steps Up Litigation, Irritating Business Groups," *The Wall Street Journal,* April 1, 1997, p. A1.

2. "Women Beware: You Can Still Get Shortchanged in Some Careers," *The Wall Street Journal,* January 16, 1996, p. A1.

3. Work Week, "A Special News Report About Life on the Job—And Trends Taking Shape There," *The Wall Street Journal,* December 24, 1996, p. B1.

4. "Diversity Study's Printing Error Lives On and On as Fact," *The Wall Street Journal,* October 29, 1996, p. A1.

5. L.E. Winter, "Companies Try a new tool to Bring Diversity Home," *The Wall Street Journal,* January 6, 1999, p. B1.

6. B. Gates, "My Advice to Students: Get a Sound, Broad, Education," *The Costco Connection* (February, 1999), p. 13.

7. M.A. Reed-Woodard, "Campaigning for Office," *Black Enterprise* 30, Iss. 9 (2000), p. 68.

8. "The Checkoff," *The Wall Street Journal,* July 2, 1996, p. A1.

9. "Diversity Study's Printing Error Lives On and On as Fact," *The Wall Street Journal,* October 29, 1996, p. A1.

10. O.C. Richard, "Radical Diversity, Business Strategy, and Firm Performance: A Resource-Based View," *Academy of Management Journal* 43, No. 2 (2000), pp. 164–77.

11. "Workplace Diversity Wins Labor Department Praise," *The Wall Street Journal,* September 24, 1996, p. A1.

12. "EEOC Gets More Money for Victims," *The Wall Street Journal,* June 17, 1997, p. A1.

13. "Bias Claim Escalates in Face of Employers' Attempts to Head Them Off," *The Wall Street Journal,* December 12, 1998, p. A1.

14. "Filing a Discrimination Suit? More Workers Cite Emotional Disabilities," *The Wall Street Journal,* January 5, 1999, p. A1.

15. J.A. Gilbert and J.M. Ivancevich, "Valuing Diversity: A Tale of Two Organizations," *Academy of Management Executive* 14, No. 1 (2000), p. 93.

16. S. Kravetz, "Tech Firms Want Talented Employees to Switch Jobs- Not Companies," *The Wall Street Journal,* August 31, 1999, p. A1.

17. P. Dass and B. Parker, "Strategies for Managing Human Resource Diversity: From Resistance to Learning," *Academy of Management Executive* 13, No. 2 (1999), pp. 68–80.

18. L.E. Winter, "Companies Try a New Tool to Bring Diversity Home," *The Wall Street Journal*, January 6, 1999, p. B1.

19. "Coca-Cola's Diversity Advisory Council Co-Chairman Carl Ware, Said He Plans to Retire at End of 2000," *The Wall Street Journal*, November 3, 1999, p. A1

20. T. Petlinger, "So Long Supply and Demand," *The Wall Street Journal*, January 1, 2000, p. R31.

21. P. Dass and B. Parker, "Strategies for Managing Human Resource Diversity: From Resistance to Learning," *Academy of Management Executive* 13, No. 2 (1999), pp. 68–80.

22. "A Corporate Conscience Award Goes to Denny's in a Comeback Role," *The Wall Street Journal*, April 27, 2000, p. A1.

23. Work Week, "A Special News Report About Life on the Job—And Trends Taking Shape There," *The Wall Street Journal*, December 24, 1996, p. B1.

24. A. Markels, Workplace, "A Diversity Program Can Prove Divisive," *The Wall Street Journal*, January 30, 1997, p. B1.

25. A. Markels, Management, "How One Hotel Manages Staff's Diversity," *The Wall Street Journal*, November 20, 1996, p. B1.

26. T.Simons, L.H. Pelled, and K.A. Smith, "Making Use of Difference: Diversity, Debate, and Decision Comprehensiveness in Top Management Teams," *Academy of Management Journal* 42, No. 6 (1999), pp. 662–73.

27. A. Mehra, M. Kilduff, and D.J. Brass, "At the Margins: A Distinctiveness Approach to the Social Identity and Social Networks of Underrepresented Groups," *Academy of Management Journal* 41, No. 4 (1998), pp. 441–52.

28. P. Chattopadhyay, "Beyond Direct and Symmetrical Effects: The influence of Demographic Dissimilarity on Organizational Citizenship Behavior," *Academy of Management Journal* 42, No. 3 (1999), pp. 273–87.

29. "Religious Diversity Spurs Many High-Tech Firms to Allow Holiday Diversity," *The Wall Street Journal*, April 18, 2000, p. A1.

30. "Holiday Flex Time," *The Wall Street Journal*, January 28, 1997, p. A1.

31. P. Chattopadhyay, "Beyond Direct and Symmetrical Effects: The Influence of Demographic Dissimilarity on Organizational Citizenship Behavior," *Academy of Management Journal* 42, No. 3 (1999), pp. 273–87.

32. A.R. Karr, "The Checkoff," *The Wall Street Journal*, April 18, 2000, p. A1.

33. "Early Retirement Shouldn't ...," *The Wall Street Journal*, August 5, 1997, p. A1.

34. "U.S. Immigration Officials Met," *The Wall Street Journal*, December 14, 1999, p. A1.

35. E. Freeburg, "Employment Provisions of the Americans with Disabilities Act: Implications for HRD Practices," *Human Resource Development Quarterly* 5, Iss. 1 (1994), pp. 93–98.

36. "Chambermaids Face a New Wrinkle as a Hotel Chain Changes Bed-Making," *The Wall Street Journal*, August 31, 1999, p. A1.

37. E. Freeburg, "Employment Provisions of the Americans with Disabilities Act: Implications for HRD Practices," *Human Resource Development Quarterly* 5, No. 1 (1994), pp. 93–98.

38. R.N. Lussier, K. Say, and J. Corman, "Improving Job Satisfaction of Employees Who are Deaf and Hearing," *Mid-American Journal of Business* 14, No. 1 (1999), pp. 69–73.

39. "The Checkoff," *The Wall Street Journal*, October 22, 1996, p. A1.

40. R. Ledman and D. Brown, "The Americans with Disabilities Act: The Cutting Edge of Managing Diversity," *SAM Advanced Management Journal* 58, No. 2 (1993), pp. 17–20.

41. "Big Companies May Boost the Risk of Employee Drug Use at Small Business," *The Wall Street Journal*, May 13, 1997, p. A1.

42. "Chances Are if You Are White Collar, You Aren't Being Drug-Tested," *The Wall Street Journal*, August 19, 1997, p. A1.

43. "House Republicans Agreed to Relax Food and Medicine Sanctions on Cuba," *The Wall Street Journal*, June 28, 2000, p. A1.

44. B.L. Reece and R. Brandt, *Effective Human Relations* 7/e (Boston: Houghton Mifflin, 1999).

45. A.M. O'Leary-Kelly, R.L. Paetzold, and R.W. Griffin, "Sexual Harassment as Aggressive Behavior: An Actor Based Perspective," *Academy of Management Review* 25, No. 2 (2000), pp. 372–88.

46. "Training New Workers to Avoid Sexual Harassment is a Summer Priority," *The Wall Street Journal*, June 29, 1999, p. A1.

47. S.L. Robinson and A.M. O'Leary-Kelly, "Monkey See, Monkey Do: The Influence of Work Groups on the Antisocial Behavior of Employees," *Academy of Management Journal* 41, No. 6, (1998), pp. 658–72.

48. P.S. Ridge, "Ethics Programs Aren't Stemming Employee Misconduct, a Study Indicates," *The Wall Street Journal*, May 11, 2000, p. A1.

49. E. Peirce, C.A. Smolinski, and B. Rosen, "Why Sexual Harassment Complaints Fall on Deaf Ears," *Academy of Management Executive* 12, No. 3 (1998), p. 41–54.

50. "Bias Claim Escalates in Face of Employers' Attempts to Head Them Off," *The Wall Street Journal*, December 12, 1998, p. A1.

51. "Home Depot's Results Could Be Cut by 21% for the Third Quarter Following Its Agreement to Pay $65 Million to Settle a Sex-Discrimination Suit," *The Wall Street Journal*, September 22, 1997, p. A1.

52. A. Mehra, M. Kilduff, and D.J. Brass, "At the Margins: A Distinctiveness Approach to the Social Identity and Social Networks of Underrepresented Groups," *Academy of Management Journal* 41, No. 4 (1998), pp. 441–52.

53. B.R. Ragins, B. Townsend, and M. Mattis, "Gender Gap in the Executive Suite: CEOs and Female Executives Report on Breaking the Glass Ceiling," *Academy of Management Executive* 12, No. 1 (1998), p. 28.

54. J.R. Gordon and K.S. Whelan, "Successful Professional Women in Midlife: How Organizations Can More Effectively Understand and Respond to the Challenges," *Academy of Management Executive* 12, No. 1 (1998), p. 8.

55. "Throwing in the Towel," *The Wall Street Journal*, April 18, 2000, p. A1.

56. "Women Beware: You Can Still Get Shortchanged in Some Careers," *The Wall Street Journal*, January 16, 1996, p. A1.

57. "GM, Ford, and DaimlerChrysler," *The Wall Street Journal*, July 5, 2000, p. A1.

58. "Gender Wage Gaps Begin in High School, and Girls Earn Less," *The Wall Street Journal*, June 22, 1999, p. A1.

59. "Many Women Execs Take Up Golf, Invading the 'Man's World,' " *The Wall Street Journal*, July 29, 1997, p. A1.

60. E.J. Pollack, "In Today's Workplace, Women Feel Freer to be, Well, Women," *The Wall Street Journal*, February 7, 2000, p. A1.

61. "Japanese Tips," *The Wall Street Journal*, August 13, 1996, p. A1.

62. F.J. Yammarino, A.J. Dubinski, L.B. Comer, and M.A. Jolson, "Women and Transformational Contingent Reward Leadership: A Multiple-Levels-of-Analysis Perspective," *Academy of Management Journal* 40, No. 1 (February 1997), p. 205–22.

63. B.R. Ragins, B. Townsend, and M. Mattis, "Gender Gap in the Executive Suite: CEOs and Female Executives Report on Breaking the Glass Ceiling," *Academy of Management Executive* 12, No. 1 (1998), p. 28.

64. Ibid.

65. "The Glass Ceiling," *The Wall Street Journal*, July 13, 1999, p. A1.

66. Work Week, "A Special News Report about Life on the Job—And Trends Taking Shape There" *The Wall Street Journal*, December 24, 1996, p. B1.

67. G. Burkins, "The Checkoff," *The Wall Street Journal*, March 24, 1998, p. A1.

68. J.S. Lublin, Workplace, "Women at Top Still Are Distant from CEO Jobs," *The Wall Street Journal*, February 28, 1996, p. B1.

69. J.S. Lublin, Workplace, "Women at Top Still Are Distant from CEO Jobs," *The Wall Street Journal*, February 28, 1996, p. B1.

70. J.S. Lublin, Workplace, "Women at Top Still Are Distant from CEO Jobs," *The Wall Street Journal*, February 28, 1996, p. B1.

71. "Two-Income Marriages Are Now the Norm," *The Wall Street Journal*, June 13, 1994, p. B1.

72. "Doctor Dad: A Recent Survey by the Council on Family Health Found that 35% of the 251 Working Fathers Interviewed Said They Routinely Stay Home to Care for Their Sick Children," *The Wall Street Journal*, June 17, 1997, p. A1

73. "Salaried Pharmacists Sue a Company Over Hourly-Wage Dispute," *The Wall Street Journal*, January 19, 1999, p. A1.

74. "Doctor Dad: A Recent Survey by the Council on Family Health Found that 35% of the 251 Working Fathers Interviewed Said They Routinely Stay Home to Care for Their Sick Children," *The Wall Street Journal*, June 17, 1997, p. A1

75. S. Babbar and D.J. Aspelin, "The Overtime Rebellion: Symptom of a Bigger Problem?" *Academy of Management Executive* 12, No. 1 (1998), p. 68.

76. "Count Me in Plans "Microloans" for U.S. Women," *The Wall Street Journal*, March 28, 2000, p. A1.

77. M. Beck, "Never Home for Dinner? New Strategies Might Help You Get There," *The Wall Street Journal*, March 1, 2000, p. B1.

78. T. Petzinger, "Mihali Csikszentmihalyi: A "Happiness" Expert Talks About Suburban Anxiety and the Search for Fulfillment," *The Wall Street Journal*, January 1, 2000, p. R51.

79. S. Shellenbarger, "Three Harried Workers Get a Wake-Up Call and Make Big Changes," *The Wall Street Journal*, December 15, 1999, p. B1

80. S. Shellenbarger, "The Heralded Return of Traditional Families is Not What it Seems," *The Wall Street Journal*, May 31, 2000, p. B1.

81. "Work and Family," *The Wall Street Journal*, April 23, 1997, p. A1.

82. S. Shellenbarger, Work & Family, "Work Gets Wilder as Employees Insist on Stable Family Life," *The Wall Street Journal*, July 16, 1997, p. B1.

83. S. Shellenbarger, "What Job Candidates Really Want to Know: Will I Have a Life?" *The Wall Street Journal*, November 17, 1999, p. B1.

84. "Computational Biology," *The Wall Street Journal*, May 11, 2000, p. A1.

85. J.R. Edwards and N.P. Rothbard, "Mechanisms Linking Work and Family: Clarifying the Relationship Between Work and Family Constructs," *Academy of Management Review* 25, No. 1 (2000), pp. 178–99.

86. S. Shellenbarger, "More Managers Find a Happy Staff Leads to Happy Customers," *The Wall Street Journal*, March 2, 1998, p. B1.

87. S. Shellenbarger, "Family-Friendly CEOs Are Changing Cultures at More Workplaces," *The Wall Street Journal*, September 15, 1999, p. B1.

88. "Uncle Sam Wants You, as Government Feels the Labor Squeeze," *The Wall Street Journal*, April 11, 2000, p. A1.

89. "Family Leave Riles Many Employers, but Others Use it to Keep Workers," *The Wall Street Journal*, April 18, 2000, p. A1.

90. S. Shellenbarger, "To Win the Loyalty of Your Employees, Try a Softer Touch," *The Wall Street Journal*, January 26, 2000, p. B1.

91. S. Shellenbarger, "Students Get Lessons in How to Manage a Well-Balanced Life," *The Wall Street Journal*, February 24, 1999, p. B1.

92. "Daily Grind," *The Wall Street Journal*, March 2, 1999, p. A1.

93. S. Shellenbarger, Work & Family, "Businesses Compete to Make the Grade as Good Workplaces," *The Wall Street Journal*, August 27, 1997, p. B1.

94. R. Harborne, "Wisdom of the CEO: The Challenge to Business Leadership in the 21st Century," keynote presentation at the New England Business Administration Association International Conference, Southern Connecticut State University, April 28, 2000, Price Waterhouse Coopers.

95. S. Zahra, "The Changing Rules of Global Competitiveness in the 21st Century," *Academy of Management Executive* 13, No. 1 (1999), p. 36.

96. R. Saner, L. Yiu, and M. Sondergaard, "Business Diplomacy Management: A Core Competency for Global Companies," *Academy of Management Executive* 14, No. 1 (2000), p. 80.

97. S.M. Puffer, "Continental Airlines' CEO Gordon Bethune on Teams and New Product Development," *Academy of Management Executive* 13, No. 3 (1999), pp. 28–35.

98. D.I. Jung and B.J. Avolio, "Effects of Leadership Style and Followers' Cultural Orientation on Performance in Group and Individual Task Conditions," *Academy of Management Journal* 42, No. 2 (1999), pp. 208–18.

99. N. Yang, C.C. Chen, J. Choi, and Y. Zou, "Sources of Work-Family Conflict: A Sino–U.S. Comparison of the Effects of Work and Family Demands," *Academy of Management Journal* 43, No. 1 (2000), pp. 113–23.

100. J.S. Osland and A. Bird, "Beyond Sophisticated Stereotyping: Cultural Sensemaking in Context," *Academy of Management Executive* 14, No. 1 (2000) p. 65.

101. "Japanese Tips," *The Wall Street Journal*, August 13, 1996, p. A1.

102. Ibid.

103. "Saxophones and Trumpets Lead Back-to-school Business at Music Stores," *The Wall Street Journal*, August 19, 1999, p. A1.

104. Ted Pollock, "A Personal File of Stimulating Ideas, Little Known Facts and Daily Problems," *Supervision* 58, No. 2 (1997) pp. 24–27.

105. K. Seiders and L.L. Berry, "Service Fairness: What Is It and Why It Matters," *Academy of Management Executive* 12, No. 2 (1998), pp. 8–20.

106. T. Pollock, "A Personal File of Stimulating Ideas, Little Known Facts and Daily Problems," *Supervision* 58, No. 2 (1997) pp. 24–7.

CHAPTER 14

1. " 'Organizational Health' Plays a Growing Role in a Company's Productivity," *The Wall Street Journal,* April 6, 2000, p. A1.

2. "Workers Feel Impact of Employers' Persistent Productivity Push," *The Wall Street Journal,* June 29, 1999, p. A1.

3. A.R. Karr, "The Checkoff," *The Wall Street Journal,* September 21, 1999, p. A1.

4. "Working Smarter," *The Wall Street Journal,* May 21, 1997, p. A1.

5. This statement was taken from a reviewer of this book.

6. "The Checkoff," *The Wall Street Journal,* January 28, 1997, p. A1.

7. "A Mortgage Clearinghouse Intended to Cut Paperwork and Cost Is Backed by Mortgage Bankers Association and Three Federal Agencies," *The Wall Street Journal,* January 30, 1997, p. A1.

8. "Chrysler Is Expecting to Announce that Thousands of Cost Savings Ideas Will Boost 1997 Profit by $325 Million," *The Wall Street Journal,* June 5, 1997, p. A1.

9. Mirvis, "Human Resource Management," pp. 43–56.

10. J. Quinn, P. Anderson, and S. Finkelstein, "Leveraging Intellect," *Academy of Management Executive* 10, No. 3 (November 1996), pp. 7–27.

11. C. Tejada, "Priceless?" *The Wall Street Journal,* May 30, 2000, p. A1.

12. S. Divita, "Behavior, Not Experience, Guides Productivity," *Marketing News* 31, No. 6 (March 17, 1997), p. 4.

13. R. Harborne, "Wisdom of the CEO: The Challenge to Business Leadership in the 21st Century," keynote presentation at the New England Business Administration Association International Conference, Southern Connecticut State University, April 28, 2000, Price Waterhouse Coopers.

14. P.P. Shah, "Network Destruction: The Structural Implications of Downsizing," *Academy of Management Journal* 43, No. 1 (2000), pp. 101–112.

15. "Training Pays," *The Wall Street Journal,* May 7, 1996, p. A1.

16. "Think about It: Your Brainpower May Be Vastly Underused on the Job," *The Wall Street Journal,* February 11, 1997, p. A1.

17. " 'Action-Learning' Gains Momentum as a Method of Training Managers," *The Wall Street Journal,* September 12, 1996, p. A1.

18. T. McEwen, "Communication Training in Corporate Settings: Lessons and Opportunities for the Academy," *Mid-American Journal of Business* 12, No. 1 (Spring 1997), pp. 49–58.

19. "Learning to Lead," *Business Week,* October 18, 1999, pp. 76–77.

20. A.S. Tsui, J.L. Pearce, L.W. Porter, and A.M. Tripoli, "Alternative Approaches to the employee-Organization Relationship: Does Investment in Employees Pay Off?" *Academy of Management Journal* 40, No. 5 (1997), pp. 1089–1121.

21. "Training Pays," *The Wall Street Journal,* May 7, 1996, p. A1.

22. P.M. Podsakoff, S.B. MacKenzie, and W.H. Bommer, "Meta-Analysis of the Relationships between Kerr and Jermier's Substitutes for Leadership and Employee Job Attitudes, Role Perceptions, and Performance," *Journal of Applied Psychology* 81, No. 4 (1996), pp. 380–99.

23. H. Lancaster, "Performance Reviews: Some Bosses Try a Fresh Approach," *The Wall Street Journal,* December 1, 1998, p. A1.

24. Work Week, "A Special News Report about Life on the Job—And Trends Taking Shape There," *The Wall Street Journal,* August 26, 1997, p. B1.

25. J. Ghorpade, "Managing Five Paradoxes of 360-Degree Feedback," *Academy of Management Executive* 14, No. 1 (2000), p. 140.

26. J.H. Dulebohn and G.R. Ferris, "The Role of Influence Tactics in Perceptions of Performance Evaluations' Fairness," *Academy of Management Journal* 42, No. 3 (1999), pp. 288–303.

27. H. Lancaster, "Performance Reviews: Some Bosses Try a Fresh Approach," *The Wall Street Journal,* December 1, 1998, p. A1.

28. A.S. DeNisi and A.N. Kluger, "Feedback Effectiveness: Can 360-Degree Appraisals be Improved," *Academy of Management Executive* 14, No. 1 (2000), p. 129.

29. Work Week, "A Special News Report about Life on the Job—And Trends Taking Shape There," *The Wall Street Journal,* August 26, 1997, p. B1.

30. S.L. Robinson and A.M. O'Leary-Kelly, "Monkey See, Monkey Do: The Influence of Work Groups on the Antisocial Behavior of Employees," *Academy of Management Journal* 41, No. 6, (1998), pp. 658–72.

31. G.M. Scott, "Top Priority Management Concerns About New Product Development," *Academy of Management Executive* 13, No. 3 (1999), pp. 77–84.

32. J. Pfeffer and J.F. Veiga, "Putting People First for Organizational Success," *Academy of Management Executive* 13, No. 2 (1999), pp. 37–48.

33. T. Petzinger, "Edward O. Wilson: Human Nature, Dr. Wilson Believes, Has Changed Little in Many Millennia. And It Will Change Very Little in the Millennia Ahead," *The Wall Street Journal,* January 1, 2000, p. R16.

34. R.M. Kanter, "Are You Ready to Lead the E-Cultural Revolution?" *Inc.,* February 2000, p. 43.

35. R. Harborne, "Wisdom of the CEO: The Challenge to Business Leadership in the 21st Century," keynote presentation at the New England Business Administration Association International Conference, Southern Connecticut State University, April 28, 2000, Price Waterhouse Coopers.

36. E. Barker, A.M. Borrego, and M. Hofman, "I Was Seduced by the Web Economy," *Inc.,* February 2000.

37. F.M. Biddle, "E-Commerce," *The Wall Street Journal,* October 26, 1999, p. A1.

38. C. Tejada, "Unwired," *The Wall Street Journal,* August 29, 2000, p. A1.

39. R.M. Kanter, "Are You Ready to Lead the E-Cultural Revolution?" *Inc.,* February 2000, p. 43.

40. R. Harborne, "Wisdom of the CEO: The Challenge to Business Leadership in the 21st Century," keynote presentation at the New England Business Administration Association International Conference, Southern Connecticut State University, April 28, 2000, Price Waterhouse Coopers.

41. G.G. Dess and J.C. Picken, "Creating Competitive (Dis)advantage: Learning From Food Lion's Freefall," *Academy of Management Executive* 13, No. 3 (1999), pp. 97–111.

42. P.S. Ridge, "Knowledge Sharing Isn't Always Best Handled by the Technology-Minded," *The Wall Street Journal,* March 23, 2000, p. A1.

43. D. Cottrell, "The Need for Speed in New Millennium Leadership Styles," *Employment Relations Today* 27, No. 1 (2000), pp. 61–71.

44. J.R. Carlson and R.W. Zmud, "Channel Expansion theory and the Experimental Nature of Media Richness Perceptions," *Academy of Management Journal* 42 (1999), pp. 153–70.

45. R.M. Kanter, "Are You Ready to Lead the E-Cultural Revolution?" *Inc.,* February 2000, p. 43.

46. Ibid.

47. S. Shellenbarger, "An Overlooked Toll of Job Upheavals: Valuable Friendships," *The Wall Street Journal,* January 12, 2000, p. B1.

48. R.M. Kanter, "Are You Ready to Lead the E-Cultural Revolution?" *Inc.,* February 2000, p. 43.

49. D. Cottrell, "The Need for Speed in New Millennium Leadership Styles," *Employment Relations Today* 27, No. 1 (2000), pp. 61–71.

50. C. Hymowitz, "Remote Managers Find Ways to Narrow the Distance Gap," *The Wall Street Journal,* June 6, 1999, p. A1.

51. R.M. Kanter, "Are You Ready to Lead the E-Cultural Revolution?" *Inc.,* February 2000, p. 43.

52. M.J. McCarthy, "Virtual Mortality: A New Workplace Quandry," *The Wall Street Journal,* October 21, 1999, p. B1.

53. "An FBI E-mail Surveillance System is Stirring Alarm by Privacy Advocates," *The Wall Street Journal,* July 11, 2000, p. A1.

54. M.J. McCarthy, "Virtual Mortality: A New Workplace Quandry," *The Wall Street Journal,* October 21, 1999, p. B1.

55. T. Petzinger, "Edward O. Wilson: Human Nature, Dr. Wilson Believes, Has Changed Little in Many Millennia. And It Will Change Very Little in the Millennia Ahead," *The Wall Street Journal,* January 1, 2000, p. R16.

56. "Personal Internet Use on the Job Flourishes Despite Crackdowns," *The Wall Street Journal,* December 21, 1999, p. A1.

57. "Dropping Out: More College Students Leave School Early to Accept Job Offers," *The Wall Street Journal,* October 12, 1999, p. A1.

58. M.J. McCarthy, "Virtual Mortality: A New Workplace Quandry," *The Wall Street Journal,* October 21, 1999, p. B1.

59. R. Harborne, "Wisdom of the CEO: The Challenge to Business Leadership in the 21st Century," keynote presentation at the New England Business Administration Association International Conference, Southern Connecticut State University, April 28, 2000, Price Waterhouse Coopers.

60. R.M. Kanter, "Are You Ready to Lead the E-Cultural Revolution?" *Inc.,* February 2000, p. 43.

61. C. Hymowitz, "Remote Managers Find Ways to Narrow the Distance Gap," *The Wall Street Journal,* June 6, 1999, p. A1.

62. A.M. Townsend, S.M. DeMarrie, and A.R. Hendrickson, "Virtual Teams: Technology and the Workplace of the Future," *Academy of Management Executive* 12, No. 3 (1998), pp. 17–29.

63. R.M. Kanter, "Are You Ready to Lead the E-Cultural Revolution?" *Inc.,* February 2000, p. 43.

64. "Using the Internet for Training Workers Catches on Fast," *The Wall Street Journal,* May 2, 2000, p. A1.

65. T.E. Weber, "The New Dress Code for Corporate Training: Slippers and Pajamas?" *The Wall Street Journal,* January 31, 2000, p. B1.

66. "Online Recruiting," *The Wall Street Journal,* March 28, 2000, p. A1.

67. "Internet Job Recruiting It's Three Steps Forward and Two Steps Back," *The Wall Street Journal,* April 4, 2000, p. A1.

68. T.R. Zenger and C.R. Marshall, "Determinants of Incentive Intensity in Group-Based Rewards," *Academy of Management Journal* 43, No. 2 (2000), pp. 149–63.

69. G. Dessler, "How to Earn Your Employees' Commitment," *Academy of Management Executive* 13, No. 2 (1999), p. 58–67.

70. E. Lawler, High Involvement Management (San Francisco: Jossey-Bass, 1991), pp. 3–20.

71. T. Petzinger, "Peter Drucker: The 'Arch-Guru of Capitalism' Argues that We Need a New Economic Theory and a New Management Model," *The Wall Street Journal,* January 1, 2000, p. R34.

72. E. Lawler, High Involvement Management (San Francisco: Jossey-Bass, 1991), pp. 3–20.

73. "Just a Suggestion: Employers Solicit More Thoughts From Workers," *The Wall Street Journal,* January 9, 1999, p. A1.

74. Management Q & A, "Answering Your Questions on Motivating Tired Employees after Lunch and Handling Lab Staff Mergers," *Medical Laboratory Observer* 29, No. 2 (February 1997), pp. 20–21.

75. "The Suggestion Box Leads to the Jury Box," *The Wall Street Journal,* October 12, 1999, p. A1.

76. D. Shair, "An Economical Way to Track Employee Suggestions," *HR Magazine* 38, Iss. 8, August 1993, pp. 39–46.

77. T.R. Mitchell and A.E. Mickel, "The meaning of Money: An Individual-Difference Perspective," *Academy of Management Review* 24, No. 3 (1999), pp. 568–78.

78. "Microsoft Instituted a Series of New Employee Rewards," *The Wall Street Journal,* April 17, 2000, p. A1.

79. "Upward Pressure is Building at the Low End of the Pay Scale, Employers Say," *The Wall Street Journal,* February 22, 2000, p. A1.

80. F. Luthans and A.D. Stajkovic, "Reinforce For Performance: The Need to Go Beyond Pay and Even Rewards," *Academy of Management Executive* 13, No. 3 (1999), pp. 49–57.

81. S.L. Mueller and L.D. Clarke, "Political-Economic Context and Sensitivity to Equity: Differences Between the United States and the Transition Economies of Central and Eastern Europe," *Academy of Management Journal* 41, No. 3 (1998), pp. 319–29.

82. "Show Us the Money: Public Workers Profit from Their Own Ideas," *The Wall Street Journal,* March 25, 1997, p. A1.

83. J.R. Deckop, R. Mangel, and C.C. Cirka, "Getting More Than you Pay For: Organizational Citizenship Behavior and Pay-For-Performance Plans," *Academy of Management Journal* 42, No. 4 (1999), pp. 420–28.

84. V.D. Arnold and R.H. Krapels, "Motivation: A Reincarnation of Ideas," *Industrial Management* 38, No. 3 (May–June 1996), pp. 8–9.

85. Work Week, "A Special News Report about Life on the Job—And Trends Taking Shape There," *The Wall Street Journal,* August 26, 1997, p. B1.

86. G. Dessler, "How to Earn Your Employees' Commitment," *Academy of Management Executive* 13, No. 2 (1999), p. 58–67.

87. J.A. Gilbert and J.M. Ivancevich, "Valuing Diversity: A Tale of Two Organizations," *Academy of Management Executive* 14, No. 1 (2000), p. 93.

88. T. Petzinger, "Mihali Csikszentmihalyi: A 'Happiness' Expert Talks About Suburban Anxiety and the Search for Fulfillment," *The Wall Street Journal,* January 1, 2000, p. R51.

89. "Workers Perform Better when Companies Care," *The Wall Street Journal,* August 6, 1996, p. A1.

90. "The Checkoff," *The Wall Street Journal,* April 22, 1997, p. A1.

91. "The Checkoff," *The Wall Street Journal,* June 3, 1997, p. A1.

92. T. Tang, P. Tollison, and H. Whiteside, *Public Personnel Management* 22, No. 4, Winter 1993, pp. 579–90.

93. T. Petlinger, "So Long Supply and Demand," *The Wall Street Journal,* January 1, 2000, p. R31.

94. M. Uhl-Bien and G.B. Graen, "Individual Self-Management: Analysis of Professionals' Self-Managing Activities in Functional and Cross-Functional Work Teams," *Academy of Management Journal* 41, No. 3 (1998), pp. 340–350.

95. B.L. Kirkman and B. Rosen, "Beyond Self-Management: Antecedents and Consequences of Team Empowerment," *Academy of Management Journal* 42, No. 1 (1999), pp. 58–74.

96. *The Excellent Files,* 1997.

97. G.L. Stewart and M.R. Barrick, "Team Structure and Performance: Assessing the Mediating Role of Intrateam Process and the Moderating Role of Task Type," *Academy of Management Journal* 43, No. 2 (2000), pp. 135–48.

98. T. McEwen, "Communication Training in Corporate Settings: Lessons and Opportunities for the Academy," *Mid-American Journal of Business* 12, No. 1 (Spring 1997), pp. 49–58.

99. N. Grund, "From Sage to Artisan: The Many Roles of the Value-Driven Leader," *Academy of Management Executive* 11, No. 2 (February 1997), pp. 94–95.

CHAPTER 15

1. L. Secretan, "Integration, Not Balance," *Industry Week* 249, No. 11 (2000), p. 29.

2. H. Lancaster, "Managing Your Career, Managing Your Time In Real-World Chaos Takes Real Planning," *The Wall Street Journal,* August 19, 1997, p. B1.

3. R.D. Ramsey, "15 Time Wasters for Supervisors," *Supervision* 61, No. 6 (2000), p. 10.

4. Ibid.

5. "One of These Days," *The Wall Street Journal,* March 11, 1997, p. A1.

6. A. Garrett, "Buying Time to do the Things That Really Matter," *Management Today,* July 2000, p. 75.

7. D. Barry, C. Crampton and S. Carroll, "Navigating the Garbage Can: How Agendas Help Managers Cope with Job Realities," *Academy of Management Executive* 11, No. 2 (February 1997), pp. 26–42.

8. H. Lancaster, Managing Your Career, "Managing Your Time In Real-World Chaos Takes Real Planning," *The Wall Street Journal,* August 19, 1997, p. B1.

9. C. Hymowitz, "Advice on Organizing From the (Clean) Desks of Some Busy Workers," *The Wall Street Journal,* December 29, 1998, p. B1.

10. R. Quick, "A Makeover That Began at the Top," *The Wall Street Journal,* May 25, 2000, p. B1.

11. H. Lancaster, "Managing Your Career, Managing Your Time In Real-World Chaos Takes Real Planning," *The Wall Street Journal,* August 19, 1997, p. B1.

12. R. Quick, "A Makeover That Began at the Top," *The Wall Street Journal,* May 25, 2000, p. B1.

13. "The ABCs of Time Management," *Workforce* 79, No. 2 (2000), p. 30.

14. D. Barry, C. Crampton, and S. Carroll, "Navigating the Garbage Can: How Agendas Help Managers Cope with Job Realities," *Academy of Management Executive* 11, No. 2 (February 1997), pp. 26–42.

15. T. Pollock, "A Personal File of Stimulating Ideas, Little-Known Facts and Daily Problem Solvers," *Supervision* 61, No. 3 (2000), p. 13.

16. R.D. Ramsey, "15 Time Wasters for Supervisors," *Supervision* 61, No. 6 (2000), p. 10.

17. T. Pollock, "A Personal File of Stimulating Ideas, Little-Known Facts and Daily Problem Solvers," *Supervision* 61, No. 3 (2000), p. 13.

18. R.D. Ramsey, "15 Time Wasters for Supervisors," *Supervision* 61, No. 6 (2000), p. 10.

19. T. Pulliam, "Plan Your Work and Work Your Plan," *South Florida Business Journal* 20, No. 34 (2000), p. 47.

20. D. Barry, C. Crampton and S. Carroll, "Navigating the Garbage Can: How Agendas Help Managers Cope with Job Realities," *Academy of Management Executive* 11, No. 2 (February 1997), pp. 26–42.

21. S. Covey, "First Things First," *Success* 41, No. 3, April, 1994, pp. 8A–8D.

22. "If This is Tuesday...," *Inc.,* June 2000, p. 92.

23. T. Pollock, "A Personal File of Stimulating Ideas, Little-Known Facts and Daily Problem Solvers," *Supervision* 61, No. 3 (2000), p. 13.

24. S. Covey, "First Things First," *Success* 41, No. 3, April, 1994, pp. 8A–8D.

25. T. Pollock, "A Personal File of Stimulating Ideas, Little-Known Facts and Daily Problem Solvers," *Supervision* 61, No. 3 (2000), p. 13.

26. Ibid.

27. H. Lancaster, "Managing Your Career, Managing Your Time In Real-World Chaos Takes Real Planning," *The Wall Street Journal,* August 19, 1997, p. B1.

28. T. Pulliam, "Plan Your Work and Work Your Plan," *South Florida Business Journal* 20, No. 34 (2000), p. 47.

29. D. Barry, C. Crampton and S. Carroll, "Navigating the Garbage Can: How Agendas Help Managers Cope with Job Realities," *Academy of Management Executive* 11, No. 2 (February 1997), pp. 26–42.

30. "If This is Tuesday...," *Inc.,* June 2000, p. 92.

31. "How to Succeed in Business by Really Trying," *Journal of Accountancy* 190, No. 1 (2000), p. 12.

32. Lancaster, "Managing Your Career, Start Listening," *The Wall Street Journal,* p. B1.

33. "How to Succeed in Business by Really Trying," *Journal of Accountancy* 190, No. 1 (2000), p. 12.

34. C. Tejada, "Fickle Grads," *The Wall Street Journal,* June 16, 2000, p. A1.

35. A.R. Karr, "The Checkoff," *The Wall Street Journal,* April 18, 2000, p. A1.

36. "Mentors in the Workplace Can Boost Your Careers, But Few Employees Get On-the-Job Coaching, a Recent Survey Finds," *The Wall Street Journal,* May 7, 1996, p. A1.

37. "How to Succeed in Business by Really Trying," *Journal of Accountancy* 190, No. 1 (2000), p. 12.

38. Ibid.

39. H. Lancaster, "The Standard Resume Still Has a Role in Job Searches," *The Wall Street Journal,* February 3, 1998, p. B1.

40. *The Wall Street Journal,* August 11, 1997, p. A1.

41. "Briefs," *The Wall Street Journal,* October 10, 1996, p. A1.

42. H. Lancaster, "The Standard Resume Still Has a Role in Job Searches," *The Wall Street Journal,* February 3, 1998, p. B1.

43. Lancaster, "Managing Your Career, M.B.A. Degree," *The Wall Street Journal*, p. B1.

44. Ibid

45. F.M. Biddle, "The Checkoff," *The Wall Street Journal*, September 28, 1999, p. A1.

46. "How to Succeed in Business by Really Trying," *Journal of Accountancy* 190, Iss. 1 (2000), p. 12.

47. "Tee Time: African-American Students Learn Subtleties of Success," *The Wall Street Journal*, April 22, 1997, p. A1.

48. Lancaster, "Managing Your Career, M.B.A. Degree," *The Wall Street Journal*, p. B1.

49. "Never Satisfied," *The Wall Street Journal*, February 18, 2000, p. A1.

APPENDIX C

1. J. Pask, "It's On the Web, But is it Right?" *The Wall Street Journal*, November 4. 1999, p. 1.

Index